Imperial Incarceration

For nineteenth-century Britons, the rule of law stood at the heart of their constitutional culture, and guaranteed the right not to be imprisoned without trial. At the same time, in an expanding empire, the authorities made frequent resort to detention without trial to remove political leaders who stood in the way of imperial expansion. Such conduct raised difficult questions about Britain's commitment to the rule of law. Was it satisfied if the sovereign validated acts of naked power by legislative forms, or could imperial subjects claim the protection of Magna Carta and the common law tradition? In this pathbreaking book, Michael Lobban explores how these matters were debated from the liberal Cape, to the jurisdictional borderlands of West Africa, to the occupied territory of Egypt, and shows how and when the demands of power undermined the rule of law. This title is also available as Open Access on Cambridge Core.

Michael Lobban is Professor of Legal History at the London School of Economics and Political Science. He is the author of a number of notable works, including *White Man's Justice: South African Political Trials in the Black Consciousness Era* and *A History of the Philosophy of Law in the Common Law World*.

See the Studies in Legal History series website at
http://studiesinlegalhistory.org/

Studies In Legal History

EDITORS

Sarah Barringer Gordon, University of Pennsylvania
Lisa Ford, University of New South Wales
Michael Lobban, London School of Economics and Political Science
Reuel Schiller, University of California, Hastings College of the Law

Other books in the series:

Stefan Jurasinski and Lisi Oliver, *The Laws of Alfred: The Domboc and the Making of Anglo-Saxon Law*

Sascha Auerbach, *Armed with Sword and Scales: Law, Culture, and Local Courtrooms in London, 1860–1913*

Alejandro de La Fuente and Ariela J. Gross, *Becoming Free, Becoming Black: Race, Freedom, and the Law in Cuba, Virginia, and Louisiana*

Elizabeth Papp Kamali, *Felony and the Guilty Mind in Medieval England*

Jessica K. Lowe, *Murder in the Shenandoah: Making Law Sovereign in Revolutionary Virginia*

Michael A. Schoeppner, *Moral Contagion: Black Atlantic Sailors, Citizenship, and Diplomacy in Antebellum America*

Sam Erman, *Almost Citizens: Puerto Rico, the U.S. Constitution, and Empire*

Martha S. Jones, *Birthright Citizens: A History of Race and Rights in Antebellum America*

Julia Moses, *The First Modern Risk: Workplace Accidents and the Origins of European Social States*

Cynthia Nicoletti, *Secession on Trial: The Treason Prosecution of Jefferson Davis*

Edward James Kolla, *Sovereignty, International Law, and the French Revolution*

Assaf Likhovski, *Tax Law and Social Norms in Mandatory Palestine and Israel*

Robert W. Gordon, *Taming the Past: Essays on Law and History and History in Law*

Paul Garfinkel, *Criminal Law in Liberal and Fascist Italy*

Michelle A. McKinley, *Fractional Freedoms: Slavery, Intimacy, and Legal Mobilization in Colonial Lima, 1600–1700*

Karen M. Tani, *States of Dependency: Welfare, Rights, and American Governance, 1935–1972*

Stefan Jurasinski, *The Old English Penitentials and Anglo-Saxon Law*

Felice Batlan, *Women and Justice for the Poor: A History of Legal Aid, 1863–1945*

Sophia Z. Lee, *The Workplace Constitution from the New Deal to the New Right*

Mitra Sharafi, *Law and Identity in Colonial South Asia: Parsi Legal Culture, 1772–1947*

Michael A. Livingston, *The Fascists and the Jews of Italy: Mussolini's Race Laws, 1938–1943*

Imperial Incarceration

Detention without Trial in the Making of British Colonial Africa

MICHAEL LOBBAN

London School of Economics and Political Science

CAMBRIDGE
UNIVERSITY PRESS

University Printing House, Cambridge CB2 8BS, United Kingdom

One Liberty Plaza, 20th Floor, New York, NY 10006, USA

477 Williamstown Road, Port Melbourne, VIC 3207, Australia

314–321, 3rd Floor, Plot 3, Splendor Forum, Jasola District Centre, New Delhi – 110025, India

103 Penang Road, #05–06/07, Visioncrest Commercial, Singapore 238467

Cambridge University Press is part of the University of Cambridge.

It furthers the University's mission by disseminating knowledge in the pursuit of education, learning, and research at the highest international levels of excellence.

www.cambridge.org
Information on this title: www.cambridge.org/9781316519127
DOI: 10.1017/9781009004848

© Michael Lobban 2021

This work is in copyright. It is subject to statutory exceptions and to the provisions of relevant licensing agreements; with the exception of the Creative Commons version the link for which is provided below, no reproduction of any part of this work may take place without the written permission of Cambridge University Press.

An online version of this work is published at doi.org/10.1017/9781009004848 under a Creative Commons Open Access license CC-BY-NC-ND 4.0 which permits re-use, distribution and reproduction in any medium for non-commercial purposes providing appropriate credit to the original work is given. You may not distribute derivative works without permission. To view a copy of this license, visit https://creativecommons.org/licenses/by-nc-nd/4.0

All versions of this work may contain content reproduced under license from third parties.

Permission to reproduce this third-party content must be obtained from these third-parties directly.

When citing this work, please include a reference to the DOI 10.1017/9781009004848

First published 2021

A catalogue record for this publication is available from the British Library.

ISBN 978-1-316-51912-7 Hardback

Cambridge University Press has no responsibility for the persistence or accuracy of URLs for external or third-party internet websites referred to in this publication and does not guarantee that any content on such websites is, or will remain, accurate or appropriate.

Contents

List of Maps		*page* viii
Acknowledgements		ix
List of Abbreviations of Archival Sources		xi
1	Introduction	1
2	Martial Law and the Rule of Law in the Eastern Cape, 1830–1880	38
3	Zulu Political Prisoners, 1872–1897	80
4	Egypt and Sudan, 1882–1887	124
5	Detention without Trial in Sierra Leone and the Gold Coast, 1865–1890	159
6	Removing Rulers in the Niger Delta, 1887–1897	198
7	Consolidating Colonial Rule: Detentions in the Gold Coast and Sierra Leone, 1896–1901	238
8	Detention Comes to Court: African Appeals to the Courts in Whitehall and Westminster, 1895–1922	279
9	Martial Law in the Anglo-Boer War, 1899–1902	323
10	Martial Law, the Privy Council and the Zulu Rebellion of 1906	382
11	Conclusion	419
Index		440

Maps

1	The Eastern Cape, 1819–1866	*page* 40
2	Transkei, Pondoland and Griqualand East	48
3	The Gold Coast and Asante	164
4	The Oil Rivers	205
5	Sierra Leone: Colony and Protectorate	259

Acknowledgements

In researching and writing this book, I have benefited greatly from discussing the themes explored here with many different people. It was Michihiro Kaino who first started me down the path which has led here, by questioning me about nineteenth-century English ideas of the rule of law. My thinking on the subject has benefited immeasurably from many conversations about jurisprudence, history and the rule of law with Maks Del Mar. I have also much enjoyed the intellectual companionship in the past few years of the London Legal History group, including Steve Banks, David Foster, Catharine MacMillan, Charlotte Smith and Ian Williams. I have profited greatly from the insights and support of my colleagues at the London School of Economics, and their enthusiasm for the kind of interdisciplinary work done here. The thoughtful questions of my students have also helped sharpen the arguments of this book. I gratefully acknowledge the LSE's generous research funding, which has not only facilitated the research for this book, but also enabled it to reach a wider audience online. I also had the pleasure of spending part of the fall of 2018 as a visiting Bok Fellow at the University of Pennsylvania Law School, where Sally Gordon and Bill Ewald were marvellous hosts, and where I was able to explore some of the themes of this book with the excellent students there.

I am grateful for invitations to present parts of the work as lectures at the University of Lancaster (for the 2018 Iredell lecture) and the Cambridge Centre for English Legal History. Parts have also been presented at the conference on 'Legal History and Empires: Perspectives from the Colonised' held at the University of the West Indies, Cave Hill Campus, Barbados, in 2018 and as seminars to the

Max Planck Institute for European Legal History, to the London Legal History Seminar, to the History and Theory in Constitutional Development workshop of the University of Notre Dame in London, and to the Law and History Workshop at Tel Aviv University. Parts of the material discussed in Chapter 8 were delivered as a Current Legal Problems lecture at University College, London, in 2015, and published as 'Habeas Corpus, Imperial Rendition and the Rule of Law', *Current Legal Problems* (2015), pp. 27–84. I have also benefited greatly from the wider intellectual community of the American Society for Legal History, at whose annual conferences I have had many opportunities to discuss the development of this work. Many scholars have helped shape my thinking on the role of law in imperial history, both through their own work and through questions raised in conversation. Among those who have provided me with useful ideas, leads and suggestions in the last few years in this field are John Allison, Lauren Benton, Shaunnagh Dorsett, Lisa Ford, Patrick Graham, Trina Leah Hogg, Rande Kostal, Assaf Likhovski, John McLaren, Amanda Tyler, David Schorr, Tim Soriano and Inge Van Hulle. I am also grateful for the comments of the two anonymous reviewers who read this work for Cambridge University Press, and who helped to sharpen its argument. On a more practical level, I am grateful to Thembile Ndabene for the help given to me while I was working in the archives in Cape Town and to Anne Clarkson, for helping me tie up loose archival ends when the lockdown prevented further travel. A special word of thanks must go to Sally Gordon, who has been an exemplary editor of this book for the Studies in Legal History series, and a great editorial colleague (along with Holly Brewer and Reuel Schiller) for over a decade. I am also grateful to Cecelia Cancellaro, Rachel Blaifeder, Victoria Phillips and Ruth Boyes at Cambridge University Press, for making the publication process so smooth.

Closer to home, I am grateful to Frédérique Lachaud for her support, for her good company and for opening my eyes to a much wider vista of historical questions. I've also had the great pleasure over many summers – and more recently in 'virtual' form during the darker days of the Covid lockdown – of the companionship of my wider family, Caroline, Joe and Darragh, Joe and Ruth, and Sasha, Abbie and Ben. The book itself is dedicated to the memory of my nephew Daniel, whose company has been much missed by us all in the last decade.

Abbreviations of Archival Sources

The National Archives (United Kingdom), Kew

CAB 37	Cabinet Office: Cabinet Papers
CO 48	Colonial Office: Cape of Good Hope correspondence
CO 96	Colonial Office: Gold Coast correspondence
CO 167	Colonial Office: Mauritius correspondence
CO 179	Colonial Office: Natal correspondence
CO 267	Colonial Office: Sierra Leone correspondence
CO 273	Colonial Office: Straits Settlements correspondence
CO 417	Colonial Office: High Commission for South Africa correspondence
CO 427	Colonial Office: Zululand correspondence
CO 879	Colonial Office: Africa Confidential Print
CO 882	Colonial Office: Confidential Print Eastern
CO 885	Colonial Office: Law Officers' Opinions
DO 119	High Commissioner for South Africa correspondence
FO 2	Foreign Office: General Correspondence, Africa
FO 78	Foreign Office: General Correspondence, Ottoman Empire
FO 84	Foreign Office: Slave Trade Department correspondence
FO 141	Foreign Office: Egypt correspondence
FO 403	Foreign Office: Confidential Print Africa
FO 407	Foreign Office: Confidential Print Egypt and Sudan
FO 633	Cromer Papers
PRO 30	Miscellaneous private papers
T 1	Treasury Papers
TS 11	Treasury Solicitor Papers
TS 27	Treasury Solicitor Papers
WO 32	War Office: Registered Files

Western Cape Archives and Records Service (Cape Town)

WCA AG	Attorney General's files
WCA BK	British Kaffraria files
WCA CCP	Cape Colony Publications
WCA GH	Government House despatches
WCA LG	Lieutenant Governor of the Eastern Province memorials

I

Introduction

When A. V. Dicey declared in 1885 that 'England is a country governed, as is scarcely any other part of Europe, under the rule of law', he was expressing sentiments long shared by many of his compatriots.[1] For liberal public intellectuals of Dicey's generation, the constitution was pervaded by a unique spirit of legalism which was embedded in English constitutional culture.[2] It ensured that all powers exercised by government were given by the law and exercised in conformity with it and that all were equally answerable to the law. It also meant that no Englishman could be deprived of his liberty save for a breach of the law as determined by a court.[3] This principle, famously articulated in Magna Carta, was not simply an abstract right: it was practically secured by the great writ of liberty, habeas corpus, which gave the common law judges a power to free anyone imprisoned without cause. By the time that Dicey was writing, the imprisonment without trial of British political dissenters, or

---

[1] A. V. Dicey, *Introduction to the Study of the Law of the Constitution*, 5th ed. (London, MacMillan, 1897), p. 175. Cf. Francis Palgrave, *The Rise and Progress of the English Commonwealth* (London, John Murray, 1832), vol. 1, p. 281.
[2] See also Edward A. Freeman, *The Growth of the English Constitution from the Earliest Times* (London, MacMillan, 1872); and W. E. Hearn, *The Government of England: Its Structure and Development* (London, Longman, Green Reader and Dyer, 1867).
[3] Dicey, *Law of the Constitution*, pp. 179–195.

even their prosecution for such crimes as seditious libel or conspiracy, seemed to be a thing of the past.[4]

At the same time that this liberal view of political opposition took root at the metropolis, the number of people defined and held as 'political prisoners' in Britain's African empire increased sharply. The presence of large numbers of political prisoners here raised important questions about whether enemies of the state in the wider empire would enjoy the same protections offered by the rule of law as those in the metropolis. Those who celebrated the English conception of the rule of law did not consider it to be confined to domestic shores: rather, it also had a central place in British imperial thought. Part of the moral justification of empire was that it would bring the rule of law to 'backward' peoples, and free them from 'oriental despotism'.[5] As Lord Carnarvon put it in 1874, it was Britain's imperial duty to give 'our native fellow-subjects [...] struggling to emerge into civilisation' a system of wise laws, 'where the humblest may enjoy freedom from oppression and wrong equally with the greatest'.[6] This did not mean introducing English forms of government into all her possessions. Even that most impeccable liberal John Stuart Mill thought that '[d]espotism is a legitimate mode of government in dealing with barbarians, provided the end be their improvement',[7] and there was often much handwringing over when and whether particular communities could

---

[4] T. E. May, *The Constitutional History of England since the Accession of George III, 1760–1860*, 2nd ed., 2 vols. (London, Longman, Green, Longman, Roberts and Green, 1863), vol. 2, chs. 9 and 11.

[5] See Keally McBride, *Mr. Mothercountry: The Man Who Made the Rule of Law* (New York, Oxford University Press, 2016), pp. 22–23; and Thomas R. Metcalfe, *Ideologies of the Raj* (Cambridge, Cambridge University Press, 1995), pp. 37–39.

[6] Quoted in C. C. Eldridge, 'Sinews of Empire: Changing Perspectives', in C. C. Eldridge (ed.), *British Imperialism in the Nineteenth Century* (London, MacMillan, 1984), p. 185; and (partially) in Peter J. Cain, 'Character, "Ordered Liberty", and the Mission to Civilise: British Moral Justification of Empire, 1870–1914', *Journal of Imperial and Commonwealth History*, vol. 40:4 (2012), pp. 557–578 at p. 563.

[7] J. S. Mill, 'On Liberty', in *Collected Works*, vol. 18, ed. J. M. Robson (Toronto, University of Toronto Press, 1977), p. 224. Cf. J. F. Stephen, 'Foundations of the Government of India', *The Nineteenth Century*, vol. 14 (1883), pp. 541–568 at pp. 556–557. Historians have recently drawn attention to the contradictions for liberalism which empire entailed: see Uday Singh Mehta, *Liberalism and Empire: A Study in Nineteenth-Century British Liberal Thought* (Chicago, University of Chicago Press, 1999); and Jennifer Pitts, *A Turn to Empire: The Rise of Imperial Liberalism in Britain and France* (Princeton, Princeton University Press, 2005).

be considered ready for representative institutions. In many parts of the empire, imperial subjects were meant to be treated in the way that the metropolitan disfranchised were treated: denied a political voice, but subject to a rational, modern and equal system of laws.[8] Nor did it mean exporting the common law to all parts of the empire. Although settlers were said to carry the common law with them to new territories,[9] in conquered or ceded lands, such as Quebec or the Cape of Good Hope, existing legal regimes created by other European imperial powers were not replaced.[10] Within the empire, multiple forms of legal order might co-exist,[11] with different sets of rules applying to different peoples, as with the different regimes of 'personal law' for Hindus and Muslims in India which sat alongside codified versions of English law,[12] or the use of customary law in Africa alongside systems based on European jurisprudence.[13] It was thus not the details of English law which imperialists sought to export but rather its animating spirit,[14] at the heart of which was a commitment to 'the rudiments of procedural fairness', secured by a jurisdictional hierarchy with Westminster and

---

[8] For such a view, advocating a clear code of law, but administered by 'an enlightened and paternal despotism', see T. B. Macaulay's speech in *Parl. Debs.*, 3rd ser., vol. 19, col. 533 (10 July 1833).

[9] *Blankard* v. *Galdy* (1694) 2 Salk. 411; *Dutton* v. *Howell* (1694) Show. PC 24; *Anonymous* (1722) 2 P. Wms. 75. Only so much as was suitable to local conditions was so carried. See Mary S. Bilder, *The Transatlantic Constitution: Colonial Legal Culture and the Empire* (Cambridge, Harvard University Press, 2004), pp. 1–4; and Daniel J. Hulsebosch, 'The Ancient Constitution and the Expanding Empire: Sir Edward Coke's British Jurisprudence', *Law and History Review*, vol. 21 (2003), pp. 439–482.

[10] See Christian R. Burset, 'Why Didn't the Common Law Follow the Flag?', *Virginia Law Review*, vol. 105 (2019), pp. 483–542; and Hannah Weiss Muller, 'Bonds of Belonging: Subjecthood and the British Empire', *Journal of British Studies*, vol. 53 (2014), pp. 29–58.

[11] See Lauren Benton, *Law and Colonial Cultures: Legal Regimes in World History, 1400–1900* (Cambridge, Cambridge University Press, 2002).

[12] See D. A. Washbrook, 'Law, State and Agrarian Society in Colonial India', *Modern Asian Studies*, vol. 15:3 (1981), pp. 649–721; and Eric Stokes, *The English Utilitarians and India* (Oxford, Oxford University Press, 1959).

[13] See Martin Chanock, *Law, Custom and Social Order: The Colonial Experience in Malawi and Zambia* (Cambridge, Cambridge University Press, 1985); and Thomas Spear, 'Neo-traditionalism and the Limits of Invention in British Colonial Africa', *Journal of African History*, vol. 44:1 (2003), pp. 3–27.

[14] Metcalfe, *Ideologies of the Raj*, p. 39.

Whitehall at the top.[15] One of the principal benefits of being under this imperial jurisdiction was that, like their disfranchised counterparts in the metropolis, all those who became British subjects could claim the right to a writ of habeas corpus to be freed from unlawful imprisonment, or the right to sue any official at common law for invading their private rights.[16] In the eyes of its defenders, the common law constitution provided the tools to ensure that liberties could be secure throughout the empire.

Habeas Corpus and the Rule of Law

For jurists like Dicey, the most important legal tool to defend liberty was the writ of habeas corpus, which secured the release of anyone whose gaoler could not show the court a lawful reason for his detention.[17] Seventeenth-century legislation settled that no prisoner could be detained simply for reason of state or deported to evade the reach of the writ.[18] In 1861, the court of Queen's Bench confirmed that the writ had imperial reach, when the British and Foreign Anti-Slavery Society sought to prevent the extradition to the United States of a fugitive slave, John Anderson, who had killed a cotton planter while escaping from Missouri. After an application for a habeas corpus on his behalf had been rejected by the Queen's Bench in Toronto (on the ground that murder was an extraditable offence

---

[15] Lauren Benton and Lisa Ford, *Rage for Order: The British Empire and the Origins of International Law, 1800–1850* (Cambridge, Harvard University Press, 2016), p. 17.

[16] *Mostyn v. Fabregas* (1774) 1 Cowp. 161, *Campbell v. Hall* (1774) 1 Cowp. 204. Colonial governors were also liable to criminal proceedings in London, though only in very exceptional cases were they held accountable, even for murders. Joseph Wall, who had been Governor of Goree, was executed in London in 1802, after a trial for the murder twenty years earlier of a sergeant at the garrison. *The Times*, 21 January 1802, p. 2; 29 January 1802, p. 3. Attempts to prosecute Governor Picton of Trinidad and Governor Eyre of Jamaica did not succeed: see (for Picton) Lauren Benton and Lisa Ford, 'Island Despotism: Trinidad, the British Imperial Constitution and Global Legal Order', *Journal of Imperial and Commonwealth History*, vol. 46:1 (2018), pp. 21–46 and (for Eyre) R. W. Kostal, *A Jurisprudence of Power: Victorian Empire and the Rule of Law* (Oxford, Oxford University Press, 2005).

[17] On the writ, see Paul D. Halliday, *Habeas Corpus: From England to Empire* (Cambridge: Belknap Press, 2010); and Amanda L. Tyler, *Habeas Corpus in Wartime: From the Tower of London to Guantanamo Bay* (New York: Oxford University Press, 2017).

[18] Star Chamber Act 1641, 16 Car. I c. 10; Habeas Corpus Act 1679, 31 Car. II, c. 2.

Introduction

under the Webster–Ashburton treaty with the United States),[19] a writ from the English court was directed to the sheriff of York County in Canada, confirming the power of the Queen's judges in London to supervise the actions of her officials throughout the empire.[20] Although legislation in the following year qualified this power – denying courts in England the right to issue the writ to any colony or dominion with a court which could do so itself[21] – it confirmed that the writ would be available, one way or another, throughout the empire.

The power of the writ to supervise imperial detentions without trial was demonstrated early in Victoria's reign, when an attempt was made to move political prisoners from one part of the empire to another. In 1837, popular rebellions in both Lower Canada and Upper Canada were suppressed after martial law was declared.[22] With order restored, an ordinance was passed in Lower Canada to empower the executive to transport the leaders of the rebellion to Bermuda and to punish them with death should they return without permission.[23] This ordinance was disallowed by the imperial government, after the Whig opposition pointed out that the detainees would be freed on a writ of habeas corpus as soon as they arrived in Bermuda, 'as the proceeding was obviously and notoriously illegal'.[24] In Upper Canada, where those considered most morally guilty were to be tried for treason, legislation was passed to

---

[19] *In the matter of John Anderson* (1860) in C. Robinson (ed.), *Reports of Cases Decided in the Court of Queen's Bench*, vol. 20 (Toronto, Henry Rowsell, 1861), p. 124.

[20] The Court of Common Pleas in Toronto later freed Anderson on a technicality (*The Times*, 19 February 1861, p. 7; 27 February 1861, p. 12), rendering the intervention of the Westminster court unnecessary. By then, the English Law Officers had given an opinion that he could not be extradited under the Webster–Ashburton treaty, since it could not be murder for a person to kill someone attempting to enslave them: William Forsyth, *Cases and Opinions on Constitutional Law* (London, Stevens and Haynes, 1869), p. 373, Opinion dated 28 March 1861.

[21] Habeas Corpus Act 1862, 25 & 26 Vic. c. 20.

[22] See Colin Read and Ronald J. Stagg (eds.), *The Rebellion of 1837 in Upper Canada: A Collection of Documents* (Montreal, McGill-Queen's University Press, 1985); and F. Murray Greenwood and Barry Wright (eds.), *Canadian State Trials*, vol. II (Toronto, Osgoode Society, 2002).

[23] See Jean-Marie Fecteau, '"This Ultimate Resource": Martial Law and State Repression in Lower Canada, 1837-8'; and Steven Watt, 'State Trial by Legislature: The Special Council of Lower Canada, 1838-41', in F. Murray Greenwood and Barry Wright (eds.), *Canadian State Trials*, vol. II (Toronto, Osgoode Society, 2002), pp. 207-247 and 248-278.

[24] *Parl. Debs.*, 3rd ser., vol. 44, col. 1084 (9 August 1838, Lord Lyndhurst); PP 1839 (2) XXXII. 1, No. 53, p. 58.

empower the Lieutenant-Governor to grant conditional pardons to a second rank of rebels without such trials, if they petitioned for a pardon after being charged with treason. Under this procedure, nine men were given pardons conditional on their being transported to the penal colony of Van Diemen's Land for periods varying between seven years and life.[25] When the men were transported, opposition MPs in London again invoked habeas corpus to secure their liberty.

On their arrival at Liverpool, en route to Van Diemen's Land, their case was taken up by the radical MP J. A. Roebuck, who applied for a writ of habeas corpus on the ground that they had been brought to England as 'State Prisoners' without having 'been legally accused of any crime'.[26] The prisoners' first habeas corpus application – to the Queen's Bench – failed, after Lord Denman ruled that the Canadian statute was valid and that 'transports from the colonies on commuted sentences had been habitually received in England in their passage to the penal settlements'.[27] However, doubts remained over whether they could be removed from England to Van Diemen's Land,[28] and a second habeas corpus application was lodged in the court of Exchequer. On this occasion, Lord Abinger held that their imprisonment was lawful, since even if the pardon was void – or the men had renounced it – they were to be regarded as lawfully in custody on a charge of treason. Crucially, however, he left open the question of whether such men, who were not 'convicts', could be removed from England under the 1824 Transportation Act.[29] If they could not, then it

[25] See Rainer Baehre, 'Trying the Rebels: Emergency Legislation and the Colonial Executive's Overall Legal Strategy in the Upper Canadian Rebellion', in F. Murray Greenwood and Barry Wright (eds.), *Canadian State Trials*, vol. II (Toronto, Osgoode Society, 2002), pp. 41–61; Paul Romney and Barry Wright, 'The Toronto Treason Trials, March–May 1838', in ibid., pp. 62–99; and Colin Reid, 'The Treason Trials of 1838 in Western Upper Canada', in ibid., pp. 100–29. See also PP 1837-8 (524) XXXIX. 833, pp. 11–12; PP 1839 (54) XXXIV 197.
[26] The National Archives (UK) TS 11/679. Affidavit of J. A. Roebuck, 28 December 1838. Unless otherwise stated, all archival materials henceforth cited are held at the National Archives. A list of classes is to be found in the Abbreviations of Archival Sources.
[27] Alfred A. Fry, *Report of the Case of the Canadian Prisoners with an Introduction of the Writ of Habeas Corpus* (London, A. Maxwell, 1839), p. 82. See also *The Canadian Prisoners' Case* (1839) 3 State Trials new ser., 963.
[28] See 'Case Respecting Certain Canadian Prisoners: Opinion of the Attorney General and Solicitor General, 24 January 1839', TS 11/679.
[29] 5 Geo. IV c. 84, s. 17. *In the Matter of Parker and Others (the Case of the Canadian Prisoners)* (1839) 5 M. & W. 32 at 50.

Introduction

was clear that they would have to be tried for treason in England, or released. It was this dilemma that eventually forced the government in July to pardon them.[30] Although both the government and the judiciary in this case were content to see the men remain in prison, the logic of the decision dictated that the men had to be freed or tried. This seemed to suggest that once the law was put into operation – in this case by the Whigs and Radicals – it would be self-operating, to ensure the principles of Magna Carta were upheld even in an imperial dispute.

At the same time, however, the level of protection offered by the writ was limited by the ability of the legislature to suspend its operation, or to create legal regimes permitting detention without trial. Although this was not done on the mainland after 1818, it was done routinely in Ireland as well as in the wider empire in the nineteenth century. In addition to suspensions of habeas corpus, Ireland also saw a number of Insurrection Acts and Coercion Acts between 1807 and 1833, which gave authorities the power to use emergency powers in proclaimed areas.[31] Further legislation passed between 1848 and 1871 authorised the detention without trial of those suspected of plotting rebellion against the government in Ireland.[32] For a jurist like Dicey, coercive legislation in Ireland presented a challenge:[33] how could such legislation be reconciled with his vision of the rule of law? At first glance, his comment that where 'acts of state assume the form of regular legislation, ... this fact of itself maintains in no small degree the real no less than the apparent supremacy of law'[34] seemed to indicate that in the end, he was prepared to endorse a formal view of rule *by* law, according to which anything done under the authority of a valid act of parliament was legitimate. Such a position would abandon the common lawyers' view that the rule *of* law required

---

[30] On the government's doubts regarding the issue of transportation, see PP 1840 [221] XXXI. 219 at p. 21, No. 23. See also Cassandra Pybus, 'Patriot Exiles in Van Diemen's Land', in F. Murray Greenwood and Barry Wright (eds.), *Canadian State Trials*, vol. II (Toronto, Osgoode Society, 2002), at pp. 190–192.

[31] 47 Geo. III (sess. 2), c. 13; 3 Geo. IV, c. 1; 3 & 4 Wm. IV, c. 4.

[32] 11 & 12 Vic. c. 35; 12 & 13 Vic. c. 2; 29 & 30 Vic. c. 1; 29 & 30 Vic. c. 119; 30 & 31 Vic. c. 1; 30 & 31 Vic. c. 25; 31 Vic. c. 7; 34 & 35 Vic. c. 25.

[33] Yet another coercion act – the Protection of Person and Property (Ireland) Act 1881, 44 & 45 Vict. c. 4 – was passed shortly before he composed his famous treatise.

[34] Dicey, *Law of the Constitution*, p. 227. For a recent reading of this passage, see Mark D. Walters, *A. V. Dicey and the Common Law Constitutional Tradition: A Legal Turn of Mind* (Cambridge, Cambridge University Press, 2020), pp. 279–285.

fidelity to a deeper set of substantive principles which had been developed by the courts over centuries.[35] It would suggest that, for Dicey, the principle of parliamentary sovereignty could trump the rule of law. In fact, his position was more complex.

Both Dicey and his contemporaries assumed that English constitutional practice was suffused by a culture committed to protecting the substantive values found in the common law tradition. According to this view, the same 'spirit' or 'habit' of legality which pervaded the decisions of courts adjudicating contests about the rights of individuals also pervaded wider constitutional practice. It was animated by 'a whole system of political morality, a whole code of precepts for the guidance of public men, which will not be found in any page of either the Statute or the Common Law', and which had evolved over time.[36] At the heart of this political morality was a notion of accountability. Although parliament was legally sovereign, it was practically constrained by the need to conform to the will of the political nation which it represented, which was politically sovereign. Ministers were not only answerable to the common law courts for any breaches of the law, but they were also accountable to parliament, 'the constitutional representatives of the public', for the way they exercised those powers which lay in their discretion.[37] In these areas, they were – as Dicey famously expounded – expected to follow settled constitutional conventions, which also ensured that the will of the political nation was observed.[38] In Dicey's mid-Victorian view, the will of the nation was animated by the spirit of the rule of law, and could act as a check against the potential tyranny of the rulers.[39]

---

[35] For the distinction, see the discussions in Paul P. Craig, 'Formal and Substantive Conceptions of the Rule of Law: An Analytical Framework', *Public Law* (1997), pp. 467–487; Brian Z. Tamanaha, *On the Rule of Law: History, Politics, Theory* (Cambridge, Cambridge University Press, 2004), chs. 7–8; Jeremy Waldron, 'The Concept and the Rule of Law', *Georgia Law Review*, 43:1 (2008), pp. 1–62; and Jeremy Waldron, 'The Rule of Law and the Importance of Procedure', in James Fleming (ed.), *Getting to the Rule of Law* (New York, NYU Press, 2011), pp. 3–32.

[36] Freeman, *The Growth of the English Constitution*, p. 109.

[37] Hearn, *The Government of England*, p. 99.

[38] See also Adam Sitze, *The Impossible Machine: A Genealogy of South Africa's Truth and Reconciliation Commission* (Ann Arbor, University of Michigan Press, 2013), pp. 60–61, 66.

[39] In the eighth (1915) edition, Dicey bemoaned the demise of this spirit, and the rise of party spirit, which he argued could not be associated with the authority of the nation. A. V. Dicey, *An Introduction to the Study of the Law of the Constitution*, 8th ed. (London, MacMillan and Co, 1915), p. xii.

Introduction

With this perspective, Dicey regarded parliament not as a potential instrument of tyranny, but as an institution which worked to complement the common law. This meant that he, and his Whig and Liberal contemporaries, did not feel that the rule of law was undermined if parliament on occasion felt the need to confer extraordinary powers on the executive: for such powers could be conferred only by 'formal and deliberate legislation',[40] and the legislature might be trusted to do so only when the rule of law was itself under threat. Although Irish Coercion Acts made Liberals uncomfortable, they thought such legislation could be justified, since they felt that in the context of the Land Wars of the early 1880s, the very preconditions for the existence of a rule of law did not exist in rural Ireland.[41] Those who saw the unrest as being driven by a small number of dangerous agitators felt (in Sir Charles Dilke's words) that 'by locking up a small number of the chiefs the rule of law might be restored'.[42] For Dicey, legislation such as the 1881 Act could be 'tolerated as a necessary evil' when used to deal with offences 'condemned by the human conscience'. At the same time, he argued that coercion had to be accompanied by reforms to remove grievances. Coercion had to be accompanied by 'just legislation, [to] remove the source of Irish opposition to the law'.[43] According to this view, emergency legislation depriving people of their liberty was justified if it was implemented by a legislature which was committed to the broader culture of the rule of law. In an imperial context, this was to assume that emergency legislation would be used only when it was clearly necessary, and would be justifiable in a common law idiom.

Martial Law

If jurists were concerned to explain and justify the use of legislated coercive powers in Ireland, they also sought to explain martial law powers in a way consistent with their substantive view of the rule of

---

[40] Dicey, *Law of the Constitution*, pp. 336–337.
[41] 'In Munster and Connaught the ordinary law is set aside. True freedom has ceased.... We do not refuse to put out a fire until we have ascertained where and how it originated.' *The Times*, 14 December 1880, p. 9.
[42] Dilke Memoirs, B[ritish] L[ibrary] Add. MS. 43935, f. 12.
[43] A. V. Dicey, *England's Case against Home Rule* (London, John Murray, 1886), pp. 115, 120.

law. Although not used on the mainland, martial law was widely used in the nineteenth-century empire. It was used to crush slave rebellions in Barbados in 1816 and again in Demerara in 1823.[44] It was used to suppress rebellions in Upper and Lower Canada in 1837–1838, and to crush the Kandy rebellion in Ceylon in 1848.[45] In the following year, martial law was also proclaimed in Cephalonia, where Britain acted as a 'protecting sovereign' by treaty.[46] It was used on five occasions in New Zealand in the 1860s, and again in 1882. Martial law was also regularly used at the frontiers of empire, as colonial settlers came into conflict with indigenous communities,[47] particularly – as shall be seen in what follows – in Africa. The nature of martial law was debated in London on numerous occasions in the nineteenth century after its use in parts of the empire, most heatedly in the 'Jamaica controversy' which followed the proclamation of martial law by Governor Edward Eyre in Jamaica in 1865.[48] These debates raised questions about whether and when the military had the right to punish or imprison civilians without the due process of an ordinary trial.

By the middle of the nineteenth century, it was a settled principle in international law that when an army occupied foreign territory in wartime, it would apply martial law.[49] According to the Duke of Wellington, this was 'neither more nor less than the will of the general

[44] See Richard Gott, *Britain's Empire: Resistance, Repression and Revolt* (London, Verso, 2011), pp. 208, 213; Emilia Viotti da Costa, *Crowns of Glory, Tears of Blood: The Demerara Slave Rebellion of 1823* (New York, Oxford University Press, 1994).
[45] See R. W. Kostal, 'A Jurisprudence of Power: Martial Law and the Ceylon Controversy of 1848–51', *Journal of Imperial and Commonwealth History*, vol. 28 (2000), pp. 1–34 at pp. 6–7. Martial law was also used in Ceylon in 1818 after a previous rebellion against British rule.
[46] On its status, see Benton and Ford, *Rage for Order*, pp. 102–112. The Lord High Commissioner of the Ionian Islands exercised a 'High Police Power' under the Constitution of 1817 which gave him the power to proclaim martial law, institute courts martial and order the removal of Ionian citizens from one island to another. See PP 1852 (567) XXXII. 323, No. 21, pp. 56ff.
[47] See e.g. the use of martial law against indigenous Australian subjects in 1840, in Robert Foster, Rick Hosking and Amanda Nettelbeck, *Fatal Collisions: The South Australian Frontier and the Violence of Memory* (Kent Town, Wakefield Press, 2001), pp. 13–28.
[48] Kostal, *A Jurisprudence of Power*; Priyamvada Gopal, *Insurgent Empire: Anticolonial Resistance and British Dissent* (London, Verso, 2019), pp. 83–126.
[49] As Francis Lieber put it in an unpublished work, 'The Martial Law of hostile occupation – *occupatio bellica* – is recognized by the Law of nations as a necessary element of the *jus belli*': Francis Lieber and G. Norman Lieber, *To Save the Country:*

who commands the army'. This was not, however, arbitrary rule, for as Wellington explained, the general commanding should lay down the rules and regulations according to which his will was to be carried out, which in his experience entailed using the local laws and local courts.[50] Forms of military law were also used in newly settled areas at the margins of empire before the establishment of a system of civilian courts, as in the early penal colony at Botany Bay.[51] But what was the role of martial law in territories under British rule with settled legal systems? In the aftermath of the Demerara rebellion, Sir James Mackintosh told the House of Commons that when 'the laws are silenced by the noise of arms, the rulers of the Armed Force must punish, as equitably as they can, those crimes which threaten their own safety and that of society'; however, 'as soon as the law can act every other mode of punishing supposed crimes is itself an enormous crime'.[52] The notion that martial law could be permitted only when the civilian courts could not sit had a long pedigree in English legal thought, and was reiterated by the Law Officers in 1838 when commenting on the powers of the Governor of Lower Canada to proclaim martial law.[53] In their view, the mere fact of proclamation conferred no new powers, so that ordinary law needed to be used when the courts could re-open.[54] This view was questioned by other lawyers, however, who argued that the crown did have a prerogative power to proclaim martial law, which was 'another law than that which you could get from parliament' and which overrode all other law.[55]

The division of opinion over martial law became much more overt in the debates over its use in Jamaica in 1865, when a rebellion in Morant Bay was brutally suppressed by the military. Martial law powers remained in place here for a month, even though the unrest had been quelled within days. During this time, 439 black Jamaicans

A Lost Treatise on Martial Law, ed. Will Smiley and John Fabian Witt (New Haven, Yale University Press, 2019) p. 87.
[50] *Parl. Debs.*, 3rd ser. cxv (1 April 1851), cols. 880–881.
[51] See, further, Lauren Benton, *A Search for Sovereignty. Law and Geography in European Empires, 1400–1900* (Cambridge, Cambridge University Press, 2010), ch. 4.
[52] *Parl. Debs.*, new ser., vol. 11, cols. 1046–1047 (1 June 1824).
[53] Opinion of Sir J. Campbell and Sir R. M. Rolfe, 16 January 1838, in Forsyth, *Cases and Opinions*, p. 198. For Sir Edward Coke's view, see John M. Collins, *Martial Law and English Laws, c. 1500–c. 1700* (Cambridge, Cambridge University Press, 2016), p. 155.
[54] In the seventeenth and eighteenth centuries, colonial governors had frequently closed courts in order to allow martial law to be proclaimed: see Collins, *Martial Law*, ch. 6.
[55] PP 1850 (106) XII. 35, p. 179, q. 5455 (Judge Advocate General Sir David Dundas).

were shot or executed after martial law trials. They included George Gordon, a mixed-race member of the Jamaican assembly, and strong critic of Eyre's, who had been moved from Kingston (which was not under martial law) to Morant Bay, to be tried by the military. Eyre's actions were defended by those who saw martial law as a lawful power. His greatest legal champion was W. F. Finlason, who argued that the crown had an inherent prerogative power to proclaim martial law in times of war and rebellion.[56] In his view, martial law entailed 'the *suspension* of the common law, and the application to the population of absolute, arbitrary, military power', and continued in force not simply until the actual insurrection had been suppressed, but until the complete restoration of peace.[57] In such situations, martial law courts could be set up to deal with offences 'arising out of the rebellion'. Their actions would not be susceptible to review by the common law courts, and the officers involved would have no need for subsequent indemnification.[58]

This view was challenged by the members of the Jamaica Committee which sought to prosecute both Eyre and the officers who had conducted Gordon's trial. It was also challenged by Chief Justice Cockburn, in the speech he gave to the grand jury in the (failed) case brought against the officers.[59] Their view was that there was no such thing as 'martial law' operating beyond the reach of the common law. Although it might be necessary for the crown and its agents to act outside the law in times of rebellion or war in order to preserve the state, such actions could be justified only by the necessity of the case, which was (in cases of dispute) to be decided by a jury.[60] Indemnity acts could be passed to protect those who acted in good faith during

---

[56] W. F. Finlason, *A Treatise on Martial Law* (London, Stevens and Sons, 1866), pp. 9–10. Cf. W. F. Finlason, *Commentaries upon Martial Law* (London, Stevens and Sons, 1867), pp. 88–90. Whether a war or rebellion existed was a matter of fact for the crown to determine, by an act of state. Finlason, *A Treatise on Martial Law*, pp. xxii, 14, 16.
[57] Finlason, *A Treatise on Martial Law*, pp. v–vi.
[58] Finlason, *A Treatise on Martial Law*, p. xvi.
[59] See Frederick Cockburn (ed.), *Charge of the Lord Chief Justice of England to the Grand Jury at the Central Criminal Court in the Case of The Queen against Nelson and Brand* (London: William Ridgway, 1867). Though the case stalled when the jury failed to find a true bill. For an analysis of Cockburn's address, see Kostal, *A Jurisprudence of Power*, ch. 6.
[60] Dicey, *Law of the Constitution*, p. 273.

martial law, but their aim was less to render illegal acts legal than to protect bona fide officials from vexatious lawsuits. Nor did martial law courts have any legal authority to inflict punishment: although it might be lawful to kill rebels while restoring peace, any execution inflicted by a martial law court was 'technically murder', which would require indemnification by the legislature after the conflict had ended.[61] According to this liberal view, actions done under martial law remained constantly subject to review according to the ordinary standards of the common law: unlawful actions committed by military officers under the guise of martial law would be punishable unless the officer could justify his action though a plea of necessity which would convince a common law jury. While legislative indemnities could be given, under the Diceyan view, such indemnities represented a parliamentary judgment that the illegal acts committed by the executive during the emergency were necessary. They were not intended to give protection for acts done out of malice or in bad faith.

Liberal jurists may have got the better of the argument about martial law during this episode, but they failed to translate their theory into practice by securing any convictions. Nor did the debates over martial law in Jamaica settle conclusively the status of martial law, which would remain contested (as shall be seen) into the next major imperial use of martial law in the Anglo-Boer War. Furthermore, while many jurists favoured Dicey's view that martial law was 'unknown to the law of England',[62] officials realised that martial law powers would continue to be used in the empire. The Colonial Office itself acknowledged that a proclamation of martial law initiated a distinct legal order when, in the aftermath of the Jamaica Rebellion, it issued a Circular Despatch with rules for the guidance of officials in the colonies who had to exercise extraordinary powers. While they were designed only to offer guidance, and had 'in no respect the force of law', Lord Carnarvon's regulations sought to implement lessons learned during the Jamaica crisis, and to prevent a repetition of the kind of brutality and lawlessness seen in Jamaica in 1865. The regulations dealt with the manner of proclaiming martial law when armed resistance had broken out which could not be

---

[61] Dicey, *Law of the Constitution*, p. 276. See also Forsyth, *Cases and Opinions*, pp. 559–560.
[62] Dicey, *Law of the Constitution*, p. 270.

dealt with by the civil authorities without military help. They also made provision for the Governor to give instructions to officers concerning 'the punishment of offenders belonging to the civil population' as well as 'the continuance, resumption, or suspension of the ordinary tribunals'. Although acknowledging that the primary object of martial law was 'not the punishment of offences, but the suppression of revolt', the regulations did provide for the military trial of offenders. They stipulated that unless military reasons did not admit of a trial, offenders should be punished only after a trial before a court-martial consisting three officers. The accused were to be given every reasonable facility for making their defence, and all evidence was to be sworn. Records were to be kept and transmitted to the office of the Judge Advocate-General in London. Furthermore, no sentence should be imposed beyond the period of martial law, and penal servitude was not to be imposed.[63]

These regulations effectively rejected the view found in a number of older authorities that martial law could be resorted to only when the ordinary courts could no longer function, and anticipated that martial law would continue to be proclaimed in the colonies without prior authorising legislation. However, they did not settle the legal status of martial law. The Jamaica controversy and its aftermath therefore left certain questions unresolved – notably whether the courts could test the necessity of military action in times when martial law had been proclaimed, and whether they could order the release of those held in custody by the military, either with or without a military trial. These questions would be revisited again on a number of occasions in the later nineteenth and early twentieth centuries, providing an acid test as to how far the liberal view of men like Cockburn and Dicey would prevail.

Legislating for Emergencies

If the liberals of the Jamaica Committee strove hard to ensure that a substantive vision of the rule of law would prevail throughout the empire, things often looked very different when seen far from the metropolis. It was not simply that many colonial officials openly flouted the rule of law, often acting wholly outside the law to

---

[63] For the regulations, see PP 1906 (Cd. 2905) LXXIX. 503, Appendix 1.

maintain control through simple violence[64] or convicting perceived troublemakers on flawed evidence and with little due process.[65] More significantly still, in many imperial contexts, law itself became the tool of conquest and oppression. The sovereign lawmaker in the empire did not speak for its subjects in the way Dicey felt the Westminster parliament spoke for the nation: here, the interests of the imperial sovereign in maintaining order were prone to trump any concerns for common law rights. This was a much more testing environment for the common law culture of the rule of law.

At the same time that imperial authorities stressed the need for colonial rule to be formally embedded in a rule of law, they were also prepared in many areas to grant emergency powers to administrators and to create 'states of exception', where the ordinary requirements of the rule of law were abandoned. Historians examining the prevalence of 'exceptional' states of rule within the empire have drawn on Carl Schmitt's theory of the state of exception.[66] In Schmitt's formulation, states of exception are those moments when a sovereign decision-maker must act outside the frame of ordinary law to restore the order which is necessary for the legal system to operate.[67] In such times, the ordinary legal regime – the

---

[64] See e.g. the response to the 'Kooka Outbreak' of 1872 in Punjab by the local Deputy Commissioner J. L. Cowan, in Mark Condos, *The Insecurity State: Punjab and the Making of Colonial Power in British India* (Cambridge, Cambridge University Press, 2017), pp. 103–139.

[65] See e.g. Richard Price, *Making Empire: Colonial Encounters and the Creation of Imperial Rule in Nineteenth-Century Africa* (Cambridge, Cambridge University Press 2008), pp. 316–334; and Elizabeth Kolsky, *Colonial Justice in British India: White Violence and the Rule of Law* (Cambridge, Cambridge University Press, 2010).

[66] See Nasser Hussain, *The Jurisprudence of Emergency: Colonialism and the Rule of Law* (Ann Arbor: University of Michigan Press, 2003), pp. 19–20; and Pramod K. Nayar, 'Introduction', in *The Trial of Bahadur Shah Zafar* (Hyderabad, Orient Longman, 2007), pp. lxvi–lxix.

[67] For Schmitt's works, see esp. *Political Theology: Four Chapters on the Concept of Sovereignty* (1922), trans. G. Schwab (Chicago, University of Chicago Press, 2005); *Constitutional Theory* (1928), trans. and ed. Jeffrey Seitzer (Durham, Duke University Press, 2008); and *The Guardian of the Constitution: Hans Kelsen and Carl Schmitt on the Limits of Constitutional Law*, trans. and ed. Lars Vinx (Cambridge, Cambridge University Press, 2015). For commentaries and discussions, see esp. David Dyzenhaus (ed.), *Law as Politics: Carl Schmitt's Critique of Liberalism* (Durham, Duke University Press, 1998); David Dyzenhaus, *Legality and Legitimacy: Carl Schmitt, Hans Kelsen and Hermann Heller in Weimar* (Oxford, Oxford University Press, 1997); Jens Meierhenrich and Oliver Simons (eds.), *The Oxford Handbook of Carl Schmitt* (Oxford, Oxford University Press, 2017); and Giorgio Agamben, *State of Exception*, trans. Kevin Attell (Chicago, University of

Rechtsstaat – is unable to cope. Order must be restored by the sovereign, and the sovereign (in Schmitt's famous formulation) is he who 'decides on the exception'.[68] Schmitt did not see the state of exception as a juridical void, for in his view the sovereign dictator took action to defend a juridical entity, the state, which he saw as a concrete manifestation of the political unity of the people which preceded ordinary law. According to his view, the sovereign dictator stepped in to preserve a higher juridical order which ordinary law was powerless to defend against its 'enemy'.[69] If such a theory sought to offer a juridical justification for states of emergency in nation states, it had clear limitations when applied in the imperial state: for within the empire, the political unity which was to be maintained was that imposed by the coloniser on peoples defined – at least during the emergency – as 'enemies'. Furthermore, in many areas, 'legal regime[s] of exception [...] existed in tandem with the colonial rule of law':[70] they operated not as exceptions in the Schmittian sense, but as part of the ordinary law imposed on subject people by an imperial ruler, whose authority rested less on the rule of law than on what R. W. Kostal has dubbed 'a jurisprudence of power', made possible by the English theory of legislative sovereignty.

As a number of historians have pointed out, within the empire, law was not simply the beneficent repository of rights and protections which metropolitan champions of the common law defended. Rather, it was a tool 'to conquer and control indigenous people by

---

Chicago Press, 2005). For overviews of the debates over the reception of Schmitt, see Peter C. Caldwell, 'Controversies over Carl Schmitt: A Review of Recent Literature', *Journal of Modern History*, vol. 77 (2005), pp. 357–387.

[68] Schmitt, *Political Theology*, p. 5. According to the Schmittian view, emergency threats can never be dealt with by ordinary law: for even if the constitution were to provide for the executive to supersede the ordinary rules in times of crisis, it would remain for the executive to decide as a matter of fact whether a situation of crisis existed for it to suspend the law.

[69] On the distinction between friend and enemy, see Carl Schmitt, *The Concept of the Political*, ed. and trans. George Schwab (Chicago, University of Chicago Press, 2007), pp. 25–37.

[70] Elizabeth Kolsky, 'The Colonial Rule of Law and the Legal Regime of Exception: Frontier "Fanaticism" and State Violence in British India', *American Historical Review*, vol. 120:4 (2015), pp. 1218–1246 at p. 1223. Cf. Mark Condos, 'License to Kill: The Murderous Outrages Act and the Rule of Law in Colonial India, 1867–1925', *Modern Asian Studies*, 50:2 (2015), pp. 1–39.

the coercive use of legal means'.[71] In the imperial context, rule *by* law was often more important than the rule *of* law. It could be used for what John Comaroff and Jean Comaroff have described as 'lawfare': imperialism's 'use of its own rules [...] to impose a sense of order upon its subordinates by means of violence rendered legible, legal and legitimate by its own sovereign word'.[72] If, in one register, law was a means to control violence and protect rights, in another register it was a tool for imposing rule and asserting sovereign power. In this context, due process rights could be marginalised by the exercise of imperial sovereign will. Such was the case when, in early 1858, the Mughal Emperor Bahadur Shah II, who had been adopted as the figurehead for the rebels in the 'Indian Mutiny' of 1857 and was still the theoretical sovereign power in India, was tried and convicted by a British Military Commission in the Red Fort in Delhi for murder, rebellion and treason, in a trial designed to present a narrative of the rebellion as a 'Mahommedan conspiracy' and to justify his removal from India. In this case, '[t]he rule of law [...] spoke with the voice of the conqueror, with all the right trappings of power.'[73]

---

[71] John L. Comaroff, 'Colonialism, Culture and the Law: A Foreword', *Law and Social Inquiry* (2001), pp. 305–314 at p. 306. See also Condos, *The Insecurity State*. For twentieth-century studies of colonial violence, see Taylor C. Sherman, *State Violence and Punishment in India* (Abingdon, Routledge, 2010); David Anderson, *Histories of the Hanged: Britain's Dirty War in Kenya and the End of Empire* (London, Weidenfeld & Nicolson, 2005); Caroline Elkins, *Britain's Gulag: The Brutal End of Empire in Kenya* (London, Jonathan Cape, 2005); Fabian Klose, *Human Rights in the Shadow of Colonial Violence: The Wars of Independence in Kenya and Algeria* (Philadelphia, University of Pennsylvania Press, 2013); and Brian Drohan, *Brutality in an Age of Human Rights: Activism and Counterinsurgency at the End of the British Empire* (Ithaca, Cornell University Press, 2017).

[72] J. L. Comaroff and J. Comaroff, 'Law and Disorder in the Postcolony: An Introduction', in J. L. Comaroff and J. Comaroff, *Law and Disorder in the Postcolony* (Chicago, University of Chicago Press, 2006), pp. 29–30.

[73] Anindita Mukhopadhyay, *Behind the Mask: The Cultural Definition of the Legal Subject in Colonial Bengal (1715–1911)* (Oxford, Oxford University Press, 2006), p. 26. For the trial, see Tom Lloyd, 'Bandits, Bureaucrats and Bahadur Shah Zafar: Articulating Sovereignty and Seeing the Modern State Effect on the Margins of Colonial India, c. 1757–1858', in Crispin Bates (ed.), *Mutiny at the Margins: New Perspectives on the Indian Uprising of 1857, vol. 1: Anticipations and Experiences in the Locality* (London, Sage Publications, 2013), pp. 1–24; Nayar, 'Introduction'; and Lucinda Downes Bell, 'The 1858 Trial of the Mughal Emperor Bahadur Shah II Zafar for "Crimes against the State"', University of Melbourne PhD thesis, 2004, p. 131. For the proceedings, see PP 1859 (sess. I) (162) XVIII. 111.

Diceyan arguments about the nature of martial law, or the legal and constitutional protections for individual liberty, were entirely redundant in parts of the empire like India, which had created statutory regimes for detention without trial and martial law early in the nineteenth century. In 1818, Bengal's Regulation No. III provided for the detention of state prisoners on the orders of the Governor in Council 'for reasons of State' and 'without any immediate view to ulterior proceedings of a judicial nature'.[74] This was not a temporary suspension of habeas corpus, which might spring back into life when the emergency had passed – as was the norm in the motherland – but was permanent legislation, which gradually extended over all India and was to remain in place until independence.[75] On occasion, detainees challenged the legality of their detention under this legislation, but without success. As Justice J. P. Norman of the High Court at Fort William put it in 1870, 'the principles which justify the temporary suspension of the Habeas Corpus Act in England justify the Indian Legislature in entrusting to the Governor General in Council an exceptional power'.[76] This was to acknowledge the power of the sovereign to determine what was necessary to preserve order, but without Dicey's common law cultural baggage.

Nor did India have to worry about the qualms pertaining to martial law which so agitated the Jamaica Committee. Legislation had been passed in India in 1804 empowering the Governor General in Council to proclaim martial law and set up courts martial for the 'immediate punishment' of persons owing allegiance to the British government who were taken while

[74] PP 1821 (59) XVIII. 107 at p. 7. Similar legislation was passed in the other Presidencies: Regulation II in Madras in 1819 (PP 1821 (158) XVIII. 195 at p. 69) and Regulation XXV in Bombay in 1827 (PP 1829 (201) XXIII. 195 at p. 299). It was subsequently extended to cover all India: see Act No. XXXIV of 1850 (An Act for the Better Custody of State Prisoners), PP 1852 (338) XXXVI. 37 at p. 46, State Prisoners Act 1858, cited in John Reynolds, *Empire, Emergency and International Law* (Cambridge, Cambridge University Press, 2017), p. 85.

[75] For instance, it was used to hold Nilmani Singh, the Zemindar of Pachete in the 1857 rebellion: see the warrant in PP 1857–1858 (2449) enc. 445 in No. 1, p. 187; for the background, see Ata Mallick, 'The Resurgence of a Marginalized Society: 1857 Rebellion and the Santal Psychology', *Proceedings of the Indian History Congress*, vol. 76 (2015), pp. 444–454.

[76] *In the Matter of Ameer Khan* [1870] 6 Bengal Law Reports 392, Hussain, *Jurisprudence of Emergency*, pp. 92–95. Imperial legislation in 1833 had empowered the Governor General to legislate for the safety and peace of India without the concurrence of his council: 3 & 4 Wm. IV, c. 85, s. 49.

committing any overt act of rebellion.[77] By virtue of its provisions, in May 1857, martial law was proclaimed across northern India in response to the outbreak of the 'Mutiny', suspending the operation of the criminal courts and providing for martial law courts. This was followed by a raft of further enactments which increased the power to try rebels summarily in military tribunals, without legal argument or appeal. Under these enactments, the Governor General in Council was empowered to authorise 'any person' to issue a commission to try any Indian accused of a crime against the state, or any other 'heinous crime'.[78] In December 1857, the Governor General, Lord Canning, reported to the East India Company in London that '[t]hese enormous powers have been largely exercised', having been entrusted not only to military officers, but also to 'civil officers and trustworthy persons not connected with Government, who under martial law properly so called would have no authority', but who could be used in areas of the country where there were 'no officers to spare for such purposes'.[79] Over 3,000 were executed as a result of trials before these commissions, many being strapped to the mouths of cannons and then blown to pieces.[80] The response of the authorities in India to the shock of the 'Mutiny' was to repress it brutally, abandoning any fidelity to the rule of law by the manner of the trials, and abandoning a sense of humanity in the methods of execution, which were calculated to desecrate the bodies of the condemned. The 'Mutiny' and its brutal repression has been seen as a turning point in attitudes towards governance in India;[81] and it has also been seen as influencing the way Governors in other colonies – such as Edward Eyre – reacted to the danger of insurrection.[82]

---

[77] Regulation X of 1804. For a critical view of the use of these provisions in 1817, see R. Spankie's note of 27 April 1818 in William Hough, *The Practice of Courts Martial and Other Military Courts* (London, Parbury, Allen & Co., 1834), pp. 345–350.

[78] The relevant acts were Acts No. VIII, XI, XIV and XVI of 1857, discussed in A. W. Brian Simpson, *Human Rights and the End of Empire: Britain and the Genesis of the European Convention* (Oxford, Oxford University Press, 2004), pp. 77–78. The acts granted no power to deal with 'natural born subjects born in Europe'.

[79] PP 1857–1858 (26) XLIV. Pt I.1, pp. 3–4.

[80] For the figures, see Downes Bell, 'The 1858 Trial of the Mughal Emperor Bahadur Shah II Zafar', p. 131.

[81] See Karuna Mantena, *Alibis of Empire: Henry Maine and the Ends of Liberal Imperialism* (Princeton, Princeton University Press, 2010).

[82] See Jill C. Bender, *The 1857 Indian Uprising and the British Empire* (Cambridge, Cambridge University Press, 2016).

However, India was atypical in having such extensive legislative powers: unlike many parts of the empire (and indeed the metropolis), Indian legislation gave its governors a permanent, standing authority to abandon the rule of law, and implement the jurisprudence of power by making the exception routine. Furthermore, Indian subjects were not equal before the law, with 'European British subjects' enjoying greater rights than Indians.[83] Whether other parts of the British empire would show a greater fidelity to a substantive view of the rule of law than was shown by these Indian practices remained open to debate.

Ad hominem Legislation

As shall be seen in this study, detention without trial and martial law were frequently used in British colonial Africa. For the most part, Africa did not see the kind of general legislation authorising the proclamation of martial law or the detention of opponents which was a feature of Indian rule. Although the second half of the twentieth century would see emergency powers codified through orders in council throughout the empire, in the era before the First World War martial law retained the ambiguous legal status which had been the subject of so much discussion after 1865. Nor was the Colonial Office keen on giving general powers to detain without trial in Africa. When the Gold Coast legislature passed an ordinance in 1889 to authorise the Governor to detain anyone as a 'political prisoner', it was disallowed, since it was felt that such power should not be conferred by general legislation.[84]

Instead, the preferred method in this part of the empire was to pass *ad hominem* legislation to authorise the detention of specific individuals. As with suspensions of habeas corpus, this kind of legislation had a pedigree dating back to the reign of William III.[85]

---

[83] For instance, section 81 of the Indian Code of Criminal Procedure of 1872 (Act X of 1872) gave only 'European British Subjects' a right to challenge unlawful detentions in the High Court. See, further, Kolsky, *Colonial Justice in British India*, ch. 2.

[84] CO 96/205/1270, discussing Gold Coast Ordinance No. 21 of 1889.

[85] An act of 1696 authorised the continued detention of five men who had been held under a habeas corpus suspension act (8 & 9 Wm. III, cc. 4–5; the legislation was renewed in 1 Anne c. 23, 1 Geo. 1, s. 2, c. and 1 Geo. II, s. 1 c. 4). The last of these died in custody in 1736: see Tyler, *Habeas Corpus in Wartime*, pp. 43–47; and John Bernardi, *A Short History of the Life of Major John Bernardi* (London, J. Newcomb, 1729).

Introduction

Such legislation had also been passed in Westminster more recently, with an act in 1816 to authorise the detention of Napoleon Bonaparte at St Helena. After his defeat at Waterloo, Napoleon had surrendered to the British navy, claiming to put himself under the protection of British law.[86] After briefly considering returning him to France, the British government spent much time pondering over whether they were permitted by international law to continue to hold him as a prisoner of war.[87] Eventually, it was decided to confine him at St Helena, a remote island in the South Atlantic, in order to avoid any embarrassing legal questions which might arise were he to be kept in England. When news of this plan became public, a press campaign was launched by the radical lawyer Capel Lofft, who argued that '*deportation*, or *transportation*, or *relegation*, cannot legally exist in *this* country, except where the *law* expressly *provides* it on trial and sentence'.[88] Fearing that a habeas corpus application might be brought, the government swiftly gave instructions that Napoleon should be dispatched immediately to St Helena, without being admitted to land on British shores.[89] Legislation was subsequently passed to remove any doubts about the lawfulness of his removal and detention, by deeming him to be a prisoner of war, and to indemnify those responsible for his incarceration hitherto from any possible legal liability for their actions.[90]

---

[86] Michael John Thornton, *Napoleon after Waterloo: England and the St. Helena Decision* (Stanford: Stanford University Press, 1968), p.28. For the legal issues surrounding his detention, see R. A. Melikan, 'Caging the Emperor: The Legal Basis for Detaining Napoleon Bonaparte', *Tijdschrift voor Rechtsgeschiedenis*, vol. 67 (1999), pp. 349–362; and Renaud Morieux, *The Society of Prisoners: Anglo-French Wars and Incarceration in the Eighteenth Century* (Oxford, Oxford University Press, 2019), pp. 358–368.

[87] On 2 August 1815, a convention was signed between representatives of the allied powers in Paris declaring that Napoleon was their prisoner, and that his custody was entrusted to the British government, which bound itself to fulfil its engagements under this treaty. *British and Foreign State Papers 1815–1816* (London, James Ridgway and Sons, 1838), p. 200.

[88] *Morning Chronicle*, 2 August 1815.

[89] Lord Melville, First Lord of the Admiralty added, 'We may possibly have to apply to Parliament for their sanction to what we are doing respecting Bonaparte and the safe custody of his person, but we must do our duty in the meantime', quoted in H. Hale Bellot, 'The Detention of Napoleon Buonaparte', *Law Quarterly Review*, vol. 39 (1923), pp. 170–192 at p. 184.

[90] See *Parl. Debs.*, vol. 32, col. 665 (19 February 1816); vol. 33, cols. 213ff. (12 March 1816) and 1012ff. (8 April 1816); 56 Geo. III cc. 22 and 23.

In the second half of the nineteenth century, *ad hominem* laws of the kind used against the former emperor became the favoured device in many parts of the empire to authorise the detention of rulers who obstructed imperial expansion and their removal to distant parts of the empire, such as the Seychelles. The first leader to be exiled to the Seychelles under special legislation made for the purpose was Abdullah, Sultan of Perak on the Malay Peninsula.[91] Abdullah's case illustrates a pattern of official conduct which would be echoed in Africa as the colonial authorities sought to remove troublesome local rulers there. Britain had recognised Abdullah's position as Sultan in the 1874 treaty of Pangkor, in return for an agreement to receive a British Resident on whose advice he was to act in 'all questions other than those touching the Malay religion and custom'.[92] Tensions soon grew between the Sultan and the new Resident, J. W. W. Birch, who began actively to assert what he saw as British rights under the treaty and set about reforming the collection of taxes and the administration of justice. Birch's enthusiasm for increasing British control was shared by the Governor, W. F. D. Jervois, who proposed that Perak should henceforth be governed by British officers acting in the Sultan's name.[93] Faced with the threat of deposition, Abdullah agreed to Jervois's proposal, which was implemented in October 1875.[94] However, two weeks after the proclamation was issued implementing it, Birch was murdered, while posting notices announcing it.

It was this event which would eventually lead to Abdullah's deposition and deportation, but only after a number of other steps had been taken to bring Birch's killers to account. In March 1876, several villagers were tried

---

[91] See Cheah Boon Kheng, 'Malay Politics and the Murder of J. W. W. Birch, British Resident in Perak, in 1875: The Humiliation and Revenge of the Maharaja Lela', *Journal of the Malaysian Branch of the Royal Asiatic Society*, vol. 71 (1998), pp. 74–105; and Cheah Boon Kheng, 'Letters from Exile: Correspondence of Sultan Abdullah of Perak from Seychelles and Mauritius, 1877–1891', *Journal of the Malaysian Branch of the Royal Asiatic Society*, vol 64 (1991), pp. 33–74.

[92] *Enquiry as to Complicity of Chiefs in the Perak Outrages* (Singapore, 1876), p. 3. Cf. Emily Sadka, *The Protected Malay States, 1874–1895* (Kuala Lumpur, University of Malaya Press, 1968), p. 79n.

[93] PP 1875 (c. 1320) LIII. 55, p. 85, enc. 1 in No 26; *Enquiry as to Complicity of Chiefs in the Perak Outrages*, p. 6; PP 1876 (c. 1505) LIV. 287, No. 49, p. 31 at pp. 35–36.

[94] PP 1876 (c. 1505), p. 47, enc. 10 in No. 49; p. 50, enc. 15 in No. 49; Sadka, *The Protected Malay States*, p. 90.

Introduction 23

for the murder in a Malay court.[95] One of the defendants was executed after admitting that he had stabbed Birch. This did not, however, end the matter, for he also indicated that he had acted under the orders of Maharaja Lela, one of the Perak Malay chiefs.[96] Jervois had long suspected this man of instigating the crime, and had also harboured suspicions against a number of other leaders for resisting the British troops sent to restore order after the murder. A number of them were consequently taken into custody in Singapore, where they were held pending the findings of a commission set up to inquire into their complicity in the 'Perak outrages'.[97] To authorise their detention while the inquiry proceeded, an ordinance modelled on Indian legislation was passed in Singapore.[98] Suspicion soon fell on Abdullah,[99] whom Jervois wanted to summon to Singapore to answer accusations against him.[100] Given concerns over whether 'the Sultan of a protected State' could be held under the ordinance,[101] Abdullah was requested to come voluntarily to exonerate himself.[102] Since his status as sovereign in Perak also meant that he could not be sent back there for trial, it was decided that his case would treated as a political one, with the executive council of the Straits Settlements sitting as a commission of inquiry into his actions.[103] A precedent for this mode of proceeding was found in the commission of inquiry held in India in 1873 into the conduct of the Gaekwar of Baroda.[104] Setting aside earlier doubts, a decision was taken to hold

---

[95] PP 1876 (c. 1512) LIV. 669, No. 26, pp. 32, 34; No. 50, p. 54. The court was appointed by Abdullah, but with British assessors appointed by Jervois.

[96] P. L. Burns and C. D Cowan, *Sir Frank Swettenham's Malayan Journals, 1874–1876* (Kuala Lumpur, Oxford University Press, 1975), p. 330; and PP 1876 (c. 1512), No. 50, p. 54; enc. 1 in No. 50, p. 55 at p. 60. See also Cheah Boon Kheng, 'Malay Politics and the Murder of J. W. W. Birch', p. 85.

[97] PP 1877 (c. 1709) LXI. 395, enc. 2 in No. 6.

[98] Ordinance No. IV of 1876, CO 882/3/11, p. 2, modelled on Bombay's Regulation 25 of 1827.

[99] PP 1877 (c. 1709), enc. 1 in No. 14, p. 14.   [100] PP 1877 (c. 1709), p. 90, No. 77.

[101] Paraphrase of telegram from the Governor, 13 August 1876. He added, 'it is doubtless necessary to try, & important to convict: but it is also very desirable to leave no door open to objections being afterwards raised on the ground that we have exceeded our powers'. Minute dated 20 August 1876, CO 273/84/10357.

[102] PP 1877 (c. 1709), enc. 2 in No. 77, p. 95.   [103] PP 1877 (c. 1709), No. 27, p. 51.

[104] Minute dated 16 October 1875, CO 273/84/12088. On the Gaekwar of Baroda's case, see M. P. Kamarkar, 'A Study of British Paramountcy: Baroda (1870–75)', *Proceedings of the Indian History Congress*, vol. 24 (1961), pp. 225–237; and I. F. S. Copland, 'The Baroda Crisis of 1873–77: A Study in Government Rivalry', *Modern Asian Studies*, vol. 2:2 (1968), pp. 97–123; Benton, *A Search for*

Abdullah under the Straits Settlements' State Prisoners Ordinance while the inquiry proceeded,[105] and to exile him somewhere in the empire, if the case against him was made out, with legal cover being provided 'by virtue of a special ordinance'.[106]

In the ensuing proceedings, Abdullah was accused of conspiracy to murder, but was not given any form of trial. The council decided not to recall witnesses examined by the commissioners so that Abdullah could cross-examine them, since this would simply draw out the proceedings. As Jervois saw it, even if the case turned out to be 'not proven', the Sultan 'would still of necessity have to be dealt with summarily'.[107] Since this was not a criminal trial, but a political inquiry, it would be sufficient if the British authorities satisfied their own consciences that the evidence was strong enough to justify his removal from Perak.[108] The council duly concluded that Abdullah was implicated in the murder, whereupon the Colonial Office decided that he (and a number of other chiefs) should be sent to the Seychelles. The Governor of Mauritius was asked to prepare the necessary legislation to authorise their detention, and was informed 'that they are political prisoners who need not be considered objectionable as ordinary criminals would be'.[109] Abdullah sailed for

---

Sovereignty, pp. 250–260; and C. L. Tupper, *Indian Political Practice: A Collection of the Decisions of the Government of India in Political Cases* (Calcutta, 1895; reprinted Delhi, 1974), vol. I, pp. 49–54.

[105] PP 1877 (c. 1709), No. 45, p. 67.

[106] Carnarvon minuted on 10 October 1876, 'I believe that the Seychelles may perhaps be the safest & best. India will involve trouble with the Indian Govt: Ceylon is perhaps too near: Robben Island needs the consent of the Cape Got: other places are objectionable as regards climate: but the Seychelles combine most considerations.' W. R. Malcolm noted on 14 October 1876 that, while Abdullah would not be in legal custody on the high seas, 'if he is placed on board a ship which goes direct to Mauritius this may be chanced'. CO 273/84/12088.

[107] PP 1877 (c. 1709), p. 70, No. 51.

[108] PP 1877 (c. 1709), p. 90 at p. 91, No. 77; p. 71, No. 53.

[109] Minute by R. G. W. Herbert, 22 December 1876, CO 273/85/15085; PP 1877 (c. 1709), p. 82, No. 73. At the end of the year, Maharaja Lela was sent back to Perak to stand trial, along with six others. Some officials in London were troubled by this. As R. H. Meade noted, 'It will never do to hang the tools when the legal Head of the State who gave the orders gets off with what is after all a nominal punishment' (Minute of 9 October 1876, CO 273/84/12088, cf. 23 December 1876, CO 273/85/15169). However, Jervois insisted on carrying out the sentences and the men were hanged on 20 January 1877.

Introduction

the Seychelles in July 1877, the first political prisoner to be sent there.[110]

Ad hominem detention laws would see their most extensive use in Africa, where the legislation passed to authorise Abdullah's detention was often invoked as a model.[111] The passage of such legislation – detention by legislative fiat – was by definition an assertion of formal sovereign power: detention by force of a sovereign decree, rather than by virtue of a court's decision. As such, it savoured more of Schmitt than Dicey. Nonetheless, the fact that, in each instance, colonial administrators were compelled to pass ordinances to legalise their incarceration – in order to remove the threat of habeas corpus – was itself significant, since it opened some space for wider rule of law arguments to come into play. Colonial administrators were subject to two possible constraints. The first was an 'internal', bureaucratic constraint. Since local legislation was liable to disallowance by the Home government, ministers and officials in Whitehall and Downing Street had to be persuaded of its necessity. These officials were in effect a surrogate for the supervising parliament which Dicey had so lauded: and how far they sought to ensure that the detention of political prisoners in times of emergency was justified might depend on the degree of their own personal commitment to the rule of law, and on the weight of wider political pressures exerted on them, for instance by parliamentarians, the press and pressure groups such as the Aborigines Protection Society. The second was the 'external' constraint which might be offered by legal challenges. Although there were many practical impediments in the way of detainees getting to court, some challenges were made to the lawfulness of *ad hominem* laws, raising the question whether such subordinate legislation was compatible with the rights given by Magna Carta or the principles of the common law. How far such considerations would act as a constraint is another question, and one which will be explored in this book.

---

[110] Smith to Knutsford, PP 1890–1 (378) LVII. 513, 11 June 1891, No. 70, p. 61. On his exile, see Robert Aldrich, *Banished Potentates: Dethroning and Exiling Indigenous Monarchs under British and French Colonial Rule 1815–1955* (Manchester, Manchester University Press, 2018), pp. 107–109.

[111] In fact, the legislation drafted for Abdullah was itself in turn partly inspired by legislation passed at the Cape of Good Hope in 1874, to allow the continued detention there of the Hlubi chief Langalibalele: Cape Act No. 3 of 1874, discussed in Chapter 3.

Emergency Law in East Africa

Although the kind of emergency laws found in India were not enacted in most of Britain's African empire, one area which did make legislative provision for detention without trial was East Africa. This was an area where Indian law had long exerted a strong influence, for when the British acquired extraterritorial jurisdiction in Zanzibar, they made the Indian legal codes the applicable law.[112] As British jurisdiction expanded in East Africa, so Indian law followed it. It was extended first to the protectorate of Witu, which was acquired in 1890 as part of the Heligoland settlement with Germany.[113] Indian law was then applied in July 1897 to the East Africa Protectorate, which had been proclaimed over the territory between Zanzibar and Uganda in 1896.[114] It was next extended in August 1902 to Uganda, where a protectorate had been proclaimed in 1894, following the demise of the Imperial British East Africa Company.[115]

Indian law was occasionally used in East Africa in the 1890s to deal with political prisoners. This can be seen from the treatment in 1894 of Fumo Omari, Sultan of Witu, who had long proved a thorn in the side of the British and was now suspected of preparing for a renewal of hostilities with them.[116] He was arrested in November by the administrator of Witu, and sent to Zanzibar. However, consul-general Arthur Hardinge considered that his detention as a political prisoner at Zanzibar was 'open to certain objections'.[117] Prime among these was that Fumo Omari was a British protected person under the terms of the Zanzibar Jurisdiction Order in Council of 1893. This meant that he could not be subject to the 'native tribunals' of Zanzibar, but was under

---

[112] *London Gazette*, 10 August 1866, p. 4451; 24 October 1884, p. 4572. Appeals were to be made to the High Court in Bombay. The use of Indian law was suitable, given the large number of Indian merchants trading in the area. See Fahad Bishara, *A Sea of Debt: Law and Economic Life in the Western Indian Ocean, 1780–1950* (Cambridge, Cambridge University Press, 2017).

[113] Thomas R. Metcalf, *Imperial Connections: India in the Indian Ocean Arena 1860–1920* (Berkeley, University of California Press, 2007), pp. 23–27; and *London Gazette*, 25 November 1890, p. 6460.

[114] *London Gazette*, 1 September 1896, p. 4931; 9 July 1897, p. 3768.

[115] *London Gazette*, 22 June 1894, p. 705; 15 August 1902, p. 5307.

[116] See the papers in PP 1893–94 (c. 7111) LXII. 529; PP 1893–94 (c. 7248) LXII. 549; *Parl. Debs.*, 4th ser., vol. 14, col. 240 (15 August 1893); FO 403/193, enc. 1 in No. 28, p. 33; FO 403/195, p. 107, No. 115.

[117] FO 403/196, enc. 3 in No. 204, p. 184.

Introduction

British jurisdiction.[118] Hardinge therefore recommended that he be sent back to Witu, to be tried under a special commission for a violation of s. 122 of the Indian Penal Code, which criminalised collecting arms with the intention of waging war against the government. Although Hardinge admitted that this way of proceeding 'may seem to imply an excessive regard for legal technicalities', he thought it was 'better to be over-scrupulous in such matters, than to run the risk of taking any steps which, in the presence of the various Orders in Council, could be criticised as arbitrary or irregular'.[119] Fumo Omari was tried at Kilalana in the Witu Protectorate in November 1894, and sentenced to transportation for life: which in his case meant remaining under house arrest in Zanzibar.[120]

Indian legislation was not the only tool which the British could use in East Africa in the early 1890s. Political prisoners were also detained and deported in Zanzibar under the powers of the Sultan. Zanzibar became a British protectorate in 1890 as part of the Heligoland settlement.[121] Although the Sultan was nominally an independent sovereign, the succession to his throne was subject to British approval, and the British were able to exert increasing control over him. An example of Britain's use of his powers to deal with her political enemies there can be seen from the deportation in 1896 of Hilal-bin-Amr. A favourite of the Sultan Said Hamad bin Thuwaini, Hilal had antagonised Hardinge by unsettling the previously cordial relations the British had with the Sultan, and generating unrest in parts of his domains, including the island of Pemba. Since Hilal was also the brother of one of the leaders of a rebellion in Muscat, Hardinge used the pretext of a potential investigation of his role in that rebellion to propose his deportation to Oman.[122] When the Sultan proved

---

[118] For the order, see FO 403/183, No. 153, p. 109. [119] FO 403/196, No. 204, p. 180.
[120] FO 403/196, No. 236, p. 211. He died there on 27 August 1896: FO 403/227, No. 173, p. 171. A similar procedure had been used for his follower Mahathi: FO 403/196, No. 68, p. 47. Similarly, when a Beluchi messenger from the rebel Mubarak-bin-Rachid was caught in Zanzibar carrying a letter asking for ammunition, he was tried, as a British protected person, under s. 122 of the Indian Penal Code (and acquitted). FO 403/225, No. 300, p. 294. For earlier debates about how to deal with him, see FO 403/225, No. 106, p. 98; No. 111, p. 100; No. 113, p. 102.
[121] E. Hertslet, *The Map of Africa by Treaty*, vol. 2 (London, HMSO, 1894), p. 763.
[122] FO 403/211, No. 59, p. 58. Hardinge was also concerned about the number of troops in the Sultan's household establishment, a military force which he wanted disbanded. FO 403/211, No. 104, p. 84; No. 146, p. 117; No. 176, p. 138; No. 181, p. 139.

reluctant to co-operate, Hardinge tried to persuade him to send Hilal away from Zanzibar on an indefinite mission either to Mecca or India. At the same time, however, he threatened to remove Hilal by force, if the Sultan did not send him away.[123] Realising that such a step would fatally undermine his prestige, the Sultan agreed to deport Hilal, though he continued to prevaricate until the very moment that Hilal was taken into custody in June.[124] Hilal was taken to Aden, where he was taken into custody by a Resident answerable to the India Office, becoming in effect the prisoner of the British.[125]

The Sultan's powers to detain and deport were also drawn on in 1896 during another crisis. On the death of Hamad, his cousin Said Khalid bin Barghash seized the palace and proclaimed himself successor. The British – who insisted that no Sultan could be appointed without their consent – had already decided on another successor – Said Hamoud – and were determined to remove Khalid. When he refused to budge, he was removed by force, with the help of a military ship sent from the Mediterranean. During the bombardment, the palace was destroyed, but Khalid managed to escape to the German consulate, where he sought refuge as a political prisoner.[126] Khalid later reached Dar-es-Salaam in German East Africa (after boarding a German vessel from the consular foreshore), and the diplomatic dispute between the two powers over his extradition eventually fizzled out. In the meantime, the British had to decide how to deal with his Arab supporters, who had been with him in the palace, and who had been arrested. The Foreign Office decided that they should be kept in detention until they had paid a fine, and then be

---

[123] FO 403/211, No. 198, p. 147; FO 403/225, No. 131 p. 118; FO 403/226, No. 97, p. 143; No. 246, p. 277.

[124] As Cave told Salisbury on 14 July 1896, 'The Sultan was at first vacillating, but when the crisis came, acted loyally and energetically.' FO 403/227, No. 48, p. 74. For his arrest, see FO 403/227, No. 42, p. 69.

[125] FO 403/226, No. 279, p. 322. The British could obtain legal authority to detain him there from the Government of India: see FO 403/225, No. 140, p. 150*. In December 1896, Hilal was moved to Mombasa, and in August 1898, he was allowed to return to Zanzibar, ostensibly by the Sultan, but practically by Hardinge. FO 403/228, No. 46, p. 75; No. 98, p. 119; No. 244, p 276; FO 403/262, No. 187, p. 230. Hardinge told Salisbury in October 1898, 'Hilal seems greatly aged and broken in health and spirits since his fall from power and deportation over two years ago': FO 403/263, No. 95, p. 138 at p. 139.

[126] FO 403/227, No. 169, p. 169; FO 403/228, No. 96, p. 116.

deported.[127] Hardinge suggested deporting them initially 'to some place in British East Africa, where they would live under Government supervision, but without any uncomfortable restraint', and then to allow them to settle in Arabia, if their conduct was satisfactory.[128] In fact, in May 1897, after the fines had been paid, six of the Zanzibar sheikhs were released, and seven from Oman were deported. A few propertyless 'Comoros and Swahilis' who had supported Khalid were punished by exile on the mainland.[129] Eventually in May 1898, the Sultan cancelled the banishment sentences of all but one of those who had supported Khalid,[130] and they were allowed to return.

Legislative provision for detention without trial in East Africa was introduced in 1897 in the Native Courts Regulations introduced by Hardinge.[131] Hardinge wanted to introduce to the East Africa Protectorate the kinds of powers found in India under Regulation No. III and exercised by the Sultan in Zanzibar. His draft included provisions to empower the commissioner to remove or intern any person who was 'disaffected' to the government or whose conduct was dangerous to peace and good order, and to proclaim martial law in any area for a renewable period of ten days.[132] The martial law provisions were removed from the final version, but the provisions relating to detention were retained. They were also extended to Zanzibar two years later, when the system of courts was reformed there,[133] and to Uganda in 1902.[134] A template was therefore created for legislative detentions in East Africa of the kind seen on the other side of the Indian Ocean. Nonetheless, it is significant to note that,

---

[127] FO 403/227, No. 214†, p. 228*; No. 220†, p. 230*. An attachment was imposed on the property to prevent any quick collusive sale: FO 403/227, enc. in No. 99, p. 121; FO 403/228, No. 99, p. 119 at p. 120.
[128] FO 403/228, No. 121, p. 140.
[129] FO 403/242, No. 114, p. 117. In the meantime, Khalid's mother and a large number of her followers were also banished. FO 403/241, No. 82, p. 105.
[130] FO 403/261, No. 121 p. 179.
[131] Native Courts Regulations, No. 15 of 1897. See FO 403/243, enc. in No. 33, p. 44 (§ 77). See also J. B. Ojwang, 'Kenya', in A. Harding and J. Hatchard (eds.), *Preventive Detention and Security Law: A Comparative Survey* (Dordrecht, Martinus Nijhoff, 1993), p. 106; and Simpson, *Human Rights and the End of Empire*, p. 76.
[132] FO 403/241, No. 120, p. 164, §§ 79, 83–84.
[133] FO 403/280, enc. in No. 118, p. 129. For the background, see FO 403/263, No. 79, p. 121.
[134] *London Gazette*, 15 August 1902, p. 5307 (§§ 25–26).

despite the existence of these powers, the authorities resorted to *ad hominem* laws even in this region to remove African potentates who stood in the way of imperial expansion.

This can be seen from the detention and deportation of Mwanga, the king of Buganda, who was deported to the Seychelles in 1901, along with Kabarega, the king of Bunyoro. These kings shared an experience which was common for many of the West African rulers we will encounter in this book, although their cases generated less debate in Whitehall and Westminster. Mwanga had inherited an unsettled kingdom in 1884, for his father's introduction of Islam and Christianity into Buganda had created a set of powerful rival religious factions in the kingdom, which competed for power.[135] Mwanga was himself driven out of the kingdom in 1888 by the Muslim faction, but soon recovered the throne with Christian support. Seeking to make his position secure in the midst of the continuing political turmoil, he signed a treaty in December 1890 with the Imperial British East Africa Company. Although the company's representative, Capt. F. D. Lugard, sought to settle the rifts between the various factions, relations between the Protestant and Catholic factions deteriorated into fighting by the beginning of 1892. In this conflict, Lugard was himself pitted against Mwanga, whose defeat at the Battle of Mengo was followed by a second treaty of protection with the company, in which he not only recognised its suzerainty, but also agreed to fly its flag in his capital.[136] As Lugard now noted in his diary, 'the British are acknowledged de facto rulers of the country'.[137] With the demise of the company, in May 1893 Mwanga signed a treaty in the following year with Sir Gerald Portal, the consul-general for East Africa, putting himself under the Queen's protection, and granting vaguely defined jurisdictional rights.[138] It was on the basis of this treaty that Britain declared a formal protectorate over 'Uganda' in June 1894.[139]

---

[135] See D. A. Low, *Fabrication of Empire: The British and the Uganda Kingdoms, 1890–1902* (Cambridge, Cambridge University Press, 2009), pp. 60–68.
[136] Treaty dated 30 March 1892, PP 1893–94 (c. 6847) LXII.335, enc. in No. 28, p. 25.
[137] Low, *Fabrication of Empire*, pp. 145–146. See also Mwanga's letter to the Queen: PP 1893–94 (c. 6847) enc. in No. 24, p. 23.
[138] PP 1894 (c. 7303) LVII. 641, enc. in No. 3, p. 18.
[139] *London Gazette*, 19 June 1894, p. 3509. The protectorate was over Buganda.

Introduction 31

Like many other African leaders encountering British imperial expansion, Mwanga was unhappy with his new situation. Having been stripped of much of his political authority, in July 1897 he secretly left the royal enclosure at Mengo, and headed for Buddu, an area where there were already rumblings of revolt.[140] Sensing that he was now plotting rebellion, the senior British officer in the area, Major Trevor Ternan, moved to depose Mwanga[141] and engage him in battle. After Mwanga had fled and surrendered to the German authorities, Ternan asked them to hold him 'until some arrangements as to his extradition or otherwise can be arrived at by the respective Governments in Europe'.[142] His confidence that this small rebellion had been quelled was soon undermined by two events. First, in September, three companies of Sudanese troops in the recently formed Uganda rifles rose in a mutiny. Then, in December, Mwanga escaped from his German confinement, and returned to battle in Buddu.[143] Mwanga was now told that, if he surrendered, he would not be imprisoned, but would be allowed to live on the coast.[144] The offer did not tempt the deposed king, who continued to fight, despite incurring a heavy defeat in Ankole at the beginning of March 1898.[145]

In fact, it would take another year for him to be captured.[146] Mwanga continued to hold out with his followers, joining in a guerrilla campaign against the British together with both the Sudanese mutineers and his old adversary Kabarega, king of Bunyoro. Kabarega, who had succeeded to his father's throne in 1869 and had rebuilt the strength of his kingdom, had come into conflict with the British after Lugard's arrival in the area in 1890. Keen to establish a foothold in the Upper Nile basin, the British launched an attack on him in 1893, which was followed in the next year by the construction of a series of forts in the area. Five years of war

---

[140] PP 1898 (c. 8718) LX. 395, No. 3, p. 4; Low, *Fabrication of Empire*, p. 198.
[141] PP 1898 (c. 8718), No. 4, p. 4.
[142] PP 1898 (c. 8718), No. 7, p. 8. He also requested the Germans to move hold Mwanga as far as possible from Uganda, preferably on the coast: PP 1898 (c. 8718), No. 15, p. 12; PP 1898 (c. 8941) LX. 459, enc. 1 in No. 3, p. 9.
[143] 1898 (c. 8941), No. 5, p. 8.
[144] 1898 (c. 8941), enc. 1 in No. 7, p. 16. He was told that he would be treated as the Muslim Prince Mbogo had been: Mbogo was exiled to the coast in 1893, along with Selim Bey, after the latter's trial by Capt. J. R. L. Macdonald for mutiny for threatening revolt: see FO 403/184, No. 52, p. 50 with encs.
[145] PP 1898 (c. 8718), No. 27, p. 45.   [146] FO 403/281, No. 119, p. 209.

ensued, in which the British sought to put in place a set of local rulers who would be compliant – without bringing Bunyoro into the protectorate – while Kabarega continued to conduct a guerrilla campaign against them. With Kabarega joining with the Sudanese mutineers and Mwanga's rebels, the British found themselves in 1899 fighting in three conflicts. However, the arrival of Indian reinforcements and Baganda co-operation secured a British victory. When Mwanga and Kabarega were captured together in April, the Foreign Secretary (and Prime Minister) Lord Salisbury noted that the 'two great causes of unrest' in the area had been removed, and the way cleared for the British to consolidate their rule in the area.[147]

These kings were now removed as conquered potentates, rather than being dealt with in any judicial process. Although Mwanga had signed a treaty which conferred extraterritorial jurisdiction on the British, there was never any suggestion of putting him on trial.[148] To begin with, there were potential legal impediments. 'The political position of the Protectorate is somewhat peculiar', Salisbury noted after Mwanga's capture, since Buganda was under the 'nominal dominion of its king'.[149] There were also political considerations which had long been in the forefront of British minds. When plans had been made in August 1897 to remove him, George Wilson had stressed the need to treat him with the 'consideration due to his position', given the 'influence appertaining to kingly rank in Uganda'.[150] As for Kabarega, there was no foundation for any jurisdiction to try him, since it was only after his capture that plans were made to assert British jurisdiction in Bunyoro, which had signed no treaty of protection.[151] After their capture, the two men were simply taken to Zanzibar in May 1899 and handed over to the consul-general.[152] They were then interned in Kismayu, for which legal authority was provided by the 1897 Native Courts Regulations. They would not stay there very long. At the start of 1900, the special commissioner for Uganda proposed that they be sent to the Seychelles. He considered it to be of the highest importance that they never return to

---

[147] FO 403/282, No. 1, p. 1.
[148] There were good reasons to doubt whether the British had any jurisdiction under the Africa Order in Council of 1889 to try him. No such doubts stood in the way of a consular trial of the Itsekiri chief Nana Olomu in 1894: see Chapter 6.
[149] FO 403/282, No. 1, p. 1.   [150] 1898 (c. 8941), enc. 1 in No. 7, p. 16 at p. 17.
[151] FO 403/282, enc. 2 in No. 40, p. 61.   [152] FO 403/282, No. 12, p. 9.

Introduction

Uganda, and he considered it unsafe for them to remain at Kismayu.[153] Arrangements were duly made with the Governor of the Seychelles to pass the necessary legislation to authorise their detention there. In the middle of September 1901, they were sent from Kismayu via Mombasa to the Seychelles.[154] Mwanga died there in 1903, while Kabarega died in 1923, while on his way back to his homeland. As their experience showed, when it came to dealing with deposed rulers, *ad hominem* laws proved of more use than general legislation for detention.

From 'Rule of Law' to 'Lawfare'

The following chapters explore the use of exceptional measures to detain and imprison political prisoners in Africa during the period of British colonial expansion, and examine how and how far colonial administrators followed the rule of law. The very concept of the rule of law was, as has been seen, an ambiguous one. It could be read as simply demanding the formal authorisation by legislation of any executive action. But it could also be seen as demanding that all legislation be interpreted in the light of a broader common law tradition which recognised substantive rights and liberties, and that all executive action be tested by reference to these common law rights. The law did not itself determine which of these approaches would be followed by officials: that was determined by the attitudes and practices of particular individuals, and reflected the constitutional culture in which they operated. How far rule *by* law was constrained by the rule *of* law in different parts of the African empire depended on context and culture.

The substantive view tended to prevail where a culture of legalism and a commitment to due process permeated political and administrative offices as well as juridical ones. This was likeliest to occur where those subjected to exceptional measures were regarded as being part of the political community, as was the case at the Cape of Good Hope. As shall be seen in later chapters, some of the most liberal attitudes towards due process and the rule of law are to be found in the opinions of lawyers and politicians in this colony. The Cape had

---

[153] FO 403/308, No. 126, p. 190.
[154] FO 403/310, No. 191, p. 274; FO 403/311, No. 33, p. 25.

a well-established legal system staffed by lawyers trained in English law and applying Roman-Dutch law. It also had a system of representative government after 1853 and responsible government after 1872. The Cape had a tradition of political liberalism, manifested in Ordinance 50 of 1828 which gave free persons of colour the same rights as whites and in the non-racial franchise, which gave propertied, male black Africans the vote.[155] This colony saw some of the strongest defenders of the common law position to be found in our period, when dealing with the detention of rebels. By contrast, where rebels were not seen as part of the same political entity, but were regarded more as Schmittian 'enemies', the culture of common law due process had much less purchase on administrators and judges. This was the case in Natal, where a small settler community sought to govern a much larger disfranchised African population through a system of indirect rule.[156] Here, both the government and the judiciary took much less liberal views of what the rule of law required, being much keener to assert control by exceptional means.

A study of detention without trial in Africa is also significant for what it reveals about the culture of the rule of law in the metropolis. Officials in London were constantly aware of expectations that their actions had to comply with the rule of law, and their consciences were often pricked by the demands of the common law tradition when dealing with African political prisoners. The degree to which they insisted on following due process was influenced not only by their own personal commitment to common law values, but also by the strength of other pressures on them, whether that of local officials calling for a tougher policy, or domestic opinion calling for fidelity to the common law tradition. This can be seen from policy in Egypt,

---

[155] Timothy Keegan, *Colonial South Africa and the Origins of the Racial Order* (London, Leicester University Press, 1996), pp. 103–105. As Keegan points out (p. 13), there was an ambiguity in this liberalism, for its 'rhetorical commitment to the legal formalities of equality and freedom was in sharp contrast to its fundamental compatibility with cultural imperialism, class domination and, ultimately, racial subjugation'.

[156] See T. V. McClendon, *White Chiefs, Black Lords: Shepstone and the Colonial State in Natal, South Africa, 1845–1878* (Rochester: University of Rochester Press, 2010); and Jeff Guy, *Theophilus Shepstone and the Forging of Natal: African Autonomy and Settler Colonialism in the Making of Traditional Authority* (Scottsville, University of KwaZulu-Natal Press, 2013).

Introduction

where the British had *de facto* control after intervening in 1882 to suppress the nationalist revolt led by Urabi Pasha. Under pressure from British public opinion, officials insisted that Urabi be given a trial by the Egyptian authorities in proceedings in which British ideas of the rule of law would be observed. Four years later, however, the British themselves detained and deported the Sudanese leader Al-Zubayr Rahma Mansur without any form of due process, holding him under an *ad hominem* ordinance in Gibraltar. The different treatment these men received was largely determined by the government's awareness of the different public perceptions of the character of these men: while Britain's Liberal government felt itself to be on weak ground when it came to the detention of a popular Egyptian nationalist leader, it felt no qualms in holding a reviled Sudanese slave trader who had no public support. Where public opinion showed little interest in the fate of particular detainees – and wider cultural expectations about Britain's commitment to the rule of law consequently had little purchase – metropolitan officials were prepared to allow the formal vision to get the upper hand, particularly when under pressure with urgent entreaties from men on the ground.

Nor did the common law tradition find its champions among the metropolitan judiciary. As shall be seen, only on the rarest of occasions were judges in London asked to rule on the lawfulness of *ad hominem* laws, or on powers exercised under martial law. In these cases, judges both on the Judicial Committee of the Privy Council – the highest imperial court, but largely staffed by English judges – and in the English High Court and Court of Appeal showed themselves to be executive-minded defenders of order in the empire, rather than defenders of the common law in the tradition of Sir Edward Coke. Judges like Lord Halsbury were prone to see imperial detainees as 'enemies' as much as some colonial administrators were, and to take a formal view of the rule of law which reflected this position. Instead of treating the rule of law as a set of substantive principles which could be used to protect the rights of detainees, officials and the judiciary used a formal vision of legalism to help fashion effective tools with which the empire could conduct a form of 'lawfare'.

One of the most effective tools was the *ad hominem* ordinance. This was most frequently used in West Africa, where the nature of imperial jurisdiction was much more uncertain and contested than in areas such as the Cape or Natal. Besides dealing with troublesome subjects who resided within British colonies, administrators in West Africa also dealt with those who were not subjects, but resided in areas where Britain claimed some extraterritorial jurisdiction in 'protected' areas, as well as those resident in territories outside areas of British protection.[157] *Ad hominem* laws were often used for the very reason that jurisdiction was uncertain. They could be used as simple assertions of sovereign power over leaders whose territory was to be conquered, but over which the British had no prior claims to jurisdiction (as occurred in Asante). They could equally be used in areas where a form of jurisdiction was asserted, but where its legitimacy was so uncertain that legislative validation was needed. Detention ordinances were often resorted to when there was uncertainty about a political opponent's status as a subject, as when the Law Officers doubted whether Africans in protectorates owed any allegiance to Her Majesty. It is therefore no coincidence that the use of *ad hominem* laws in West Africa diminished as imperial power came to be set on firmer jurisdictional foundations, after 1900.

As shall be seen, the reasons for which imperial authorities resorted to detention without trial varied widely. In areas on the edge of an expanding empire, it could be used to remove an enemy during a process of conquest. In areas such as Asante and Zululand, the colonial authorities detained and deported potentates over whom they had no jurisdiction, treating them in effect as if they had been rebels against a sovereign authority which was being asserted in the very process of conquest. Elsewhere, where there was no doubt over British jurisdiction, detention ordinances were passed to hold those who were considered politically dangerous, but who had committed no offence. This was to use law for the kinds of political purposes which were by then considered quite unacceptable at home. At the same time,

---

[157] To complicate matters further, the very conception of 'protectorates' was being rethought during the scramble for Africa, following the Berlin Conference of 1884–1885. See Inge Van Hulle, *Britain and International Law in West Africa: The Practice of Empire* (Oxford, Oxford University Press, 2020), ch. 3, esp. pp. 161–163.

Introduction

detention ordinances were also used for peacekeeping purposes where inter-African conflicts threatened to destabilise British interests,[158] or to hold those accused of serious crimes but where the legal process had failed to secure a conviction. On occasion, detention might even be used for beneficent purposes, as where administrators realised that far more severe punishments might be meted out by the ordinary criminal process than a short-term detention to allow time for 'cooling off'.

Detentions sometimes followed after some form of investigation had been instigated, as had been the case with Abdullah of Perak. In such cases, the colonial authorities did not want to exercise simple sovereign power: they wanted to use quasi-legal proceedings – informal investigations, 'customary' trials, even hearings in consular courts – both to impart lessons on the local community and to show their masters in London that they had established the need for detention by some form of legalistic process. 'Lawfare' might involve the use of a form of trial, even if it fell far short of what English criminal procedure called for. Yet it was not only the imperial authorities who could use legal language and legal forms to fight their battles. The language of a substantive rule of law was on occasion invoked by detainees or their supporters when challenging detentions, whether by seeking review in the courts, or by using political pressure to assert the rights of detainees. As shall be seen in what follows, the amount of success they might enjoy depended in part on how strong their local resources were, and how successful they were in gaining attention in the metropolis.

---

[158] See further Van Hulle, *Britain and International Law*, pp. 191ff. on the use of force to intervene in such disputes.

2

Martial Law and the Rule of Law in the Eastern Cape, 1830–1880

In 1814, the Cape Colony was ceded by the Dutch to the British. The territory extended as far as the Great Fish River to the east and the Koussie River to the north. This land was home to approximately 60,000 people, of whom 27,000 were white descendants of Dutch and Huguenot settlers, and 17,000 indigenous Khoi, or 'Hottentot' people. For much of the nineteenth century, the border of the Cape colony was unsettled, as a series of 'frontier wars' was fought between the colonists and the Xhosa, which would ultimately lead to the subjection of the Africans and their incorporation into the empire. Martial law was declared in the Eastern Cape during these wars in 1835, 1846, 1850 and 1877. These periods of war and rebellion saw many people being detained either as prisoners of war or as rebels, and many more imprisoned after briefs trials in martial law courts. The Cape frontier would give the Colonial Office its first African experience of imprisonment in times of emergency. The wars here would raise questions about the nature of martial law and its relationship with ordinary civilian law. They would also raise questions about how far any idea of the rule of law would act as a constraint on official policy.

The Cape Colony was a settler colony, with an established judicial system. The Roman-Dutch law brought by the original settlers was the law applied by a Supreme Court constituted under royal charter in 1827 to succeed an earlier court of justice in the Cape. The new court, which used a common law judicial and procedural framework, was open to those who had been advocates in the preceding court, and to those who had received a legal education in England, Ireland or Scotland. Since Roman-Dutch law offered a remedy analogous to habeas corpus – the interdict *de homine libero exhibendo* – its courts offered the same kind of tools available in the metropolis to check abuses of power; and the court came to be staffed by a number of judges keen to defend a liberal view of the rule of law. At the same time, however, the frontier was a place of jurisdictional confusion. It was often unclear whether the territory over which colonial officials sought to exert control had come under the jurisdiction of the Cape, or had been conquered by the crown (and so was subject to the crown's discretionary rule), or remained an independent polity. It will be seen in what follows that officials, both in the locality and in the metropolis, were constantly aware of the legal problems posed by their actions. Legal niceties were not allowed to stand in the way of conquest, for British colonial governors were prepared to tear up treaties when it suited them, and to assume control over new territories without having a clear idea of the legal basis for their action. However, when it came to the incarceration of enemies and rebels, questions of legality were apt to impinge, and to constrain.

Four Wars and Two Rebellions

In 1820, 4,000 British migrants were sent to settle the frontier district of Albany, from which the Xhosa had been expelled in 1812. In order to create a buffer zone beyond this district, Governor Charles Somerset made a verbal treaty in 1819 with the Rharhabe Xhosa chief Ngqika,[1] under which he agreed to keep his people out of the area between the Keiskamma and the Great Fish Rivers which was now declared to be 'neutral territory'.[2] In 1829, the year of Ngqika's death, another buffer

---

[1] He (and his people) were also known as Gaika by the Europeans.
[2] Timothy Keegan, *Colonial South Africa and the Origins of the Racial Order* (London: Leicester University Press, 1996), pp. 129–131. For broader histories of the events discussed below, see in addition John S. Galbraith, *Reluctant Empire: British Policy on the South African Frontier 1834–1854* (Berkeley and Los Angeles, University of California Press, 1963); Noel Mostert, *Frontiers: The Epic of South Africa's Creation and the Tragedy of the Xhosa People* (London, Jonathan Cape, 1992); Clifton C. Crais, *White Supremacy and Black Resistance in Pre-industrial South Africa* (Cambridge, Cambridge University Press, 1992); Elizabeth Elbourne, *Blood Ground: Colonialism, Missions and the Contest for Christianity in the Cape Colony and Britain, 1799–1853*

MAP 1 The Eastern Cape, 1819–1866

against the Xhosa was created when Governor Lowry Cole and his Commissioner General of the Eastern Districts, Andries Stockenström, established the new Kat River Settlement, in which they settled 3,000 free people of colour, made up of 'Hottentots' (Khoi people), as well as people of mixed Khoi–Dutch descent. This settlement was within the Cape Colony, bordering the neutral space which came to be called the 'Ceded Territory'.[3] To make room for the new settlement, Ngqika's followers – led by his eldest son Maqoma, acting as regent for his heir

---

(Montreal and Kingston, McGill-Queen's University Press, 2002); Richard Price, *Making Empire: Colonial Encounters and the Creation of Imperial Rule in Nineteenth-Century Africa* (Cambridge, Cambridge University Press, 2008); Alan Lester, *Imperial Networks: Creating Identities in Nineteenth-Century South Africa and Britain* (London, Routledge, 2001); J. B. Peires, *The House of Phalo: A History of the Xhosa People in the Days of Their Independence* (Johannesburg, Ravan Press, 1981); and J. B. Peires, *The Dead Will Arise: Nongqawuse and the Great Xhosa Cattle-Killing Movement of 1856–7* (Johannesburg, Ravan Press, 1989).

[3] Robert Ross, *The Borders of Race in Colonial South Africa: The Kat River Settlement, 1829–1856* (Cambridge, Cambridge University Press, 2013); and Tony Kirk, 'Progress and Decline in the Kat River Settlement', *Journal of African History*, vol. 14:3 (1973), pp. 411–428 at pp. 412–413.

Sandile – were expelled from these lands, to which they had been allowed to return to graze their cattle in the 1820s.[4]

The frontier continued to be unsettled. As a result of conflicts over land in the Ceded Territory, a new frontier war – the sixth in a series dating back to the 1790s – broke out after Maqoma invaded the colony with 12,000 men in December 1834. Governor Benjamin D'Urban sent Col. Harry Smith to quell the disturbances, and on 3 January 1835 proclaimed martial law in a number of districts in the Eastern Cape.[5] By May, the Xhosa had been repelled. On 10 May 1835, with victory assured, D'Urban (who had fallen under the influence of settlers who wanted further expansion in the area) declared that the eastern border of the Cape Colony would now be the Kei River.[6] The new territory between the Keiskamma and Kei Rivers, acquired by conquest, would be called Queen Adelaide Province. On 16 June 1835, martial law was proclaimed in this province. Abandoning an initial ambition to expel the Xhosa to make room for settlers, D'Urban proposed to sign treaties under which the Africans (including the Ngqika) would be received as subjects of the English crown, to live under English laws.[7] However, this policy was vetoed by the Secretary of State, Lord Glenelg, an evangelical whose views were more in line with humanitarians at the Cape, who stated that 'any extension of His Majesty's dominions by conquest or cession is diligently and anxiously to be avoided'.[8] A new series of treaties was accordingly negotiated, under which the British withdrew forts from the Ceded Territory (much of which was loaned 'in perpetuity' to the Africans) and renounced sovereignty over the Province of Queen Adelaide in February 1837. During this time, martial law remained in place for different periods in different places. It was lifted in the districts of Graaff-Reinet, George and Beaufort and part of the district of Uitenhage on 17 June 1835, but remained in place

---

[4] Mostert, *Frontiers*, pp. 612–625, and Eric A Walker, *A History of South Africa* (London, Longman, Green & Co., 1935), p. 189.
[5] PP 1835 (252) XXXIX. 531, enc. 4 in No. 42, p. 130. Martial law was proclaimed in Albany, Somerset, Uitenhage, Graaff-Reinet, George and Beaufort.
[6] PP 1836 (279) XXXIX. 277, enc. 12 (A) in No. 3, p. 41.
[7] PP 1836 (279), enc. 5 in No. 9, p. 95.
[8] PP 1836 (279), No. 5, p. 59 at p. 68; PP 1837 (503) XLIII. 319, No. 23, p. 54; W. M. Macmillan, *Bantu, Boer and Briton: The Making of the South African Native Problem*, revised ed. (Oxford, Oxford University Press, 1963), pp. 175–176; and Galbraith, *Reluctant Empire*, pp. 130–131.

in Port Elizabeth, Albany and Somerset until 9 July 1836. It remained in place in the new province until 18 August 1836.

Any sense of security which the Xhosa may have obtained from these treaties was undermined with the arrival of Sir Peregrine Maitland as Governor in March 1844. By this point, the restraining influence of humanitarian philanthropists at the Cape had diminished significantly. Maitland thought the treaties placed 'unnecessary restrictions on the colonial farmer'[9] – who wanted access to the Ceded Territory to graze sheep – and so imposed new ones on the Xhosa chiefs.[10] He was particularly keen to subdue the Ngqikas, who 'have not only been very perfidious neighbours [...] but have retrograded exceedingly in civilization'.[11] With this in mind, he decided to build a fort on the eastern bank of the Keiskamma river, outside the Ceded Territory. This was a highly provocative act, which the British later saw as a pretext for the war which followed.[12] A seventh frontier war – or the 'War of the Axe' – began on 1 April 1846, when Lieutenant-Governor John Hare, 'no longer able to contain the tide of bellicosity rising round him',[13] ordered an invasion of the Ceded Territory, in response to the violent rescue by the Xhosa of a prisoner being marched to Grahamstown to be tried for the theft of an axe. Hare's pre-emptive strike had not been properly prepared, and his forces were soon driven back by the Ngqikas, who streamed into the colony, and threatened to overcome the colonial forces.[14] In response, on 21 April 1846, Hare proclaimed martial law in the eastern districts, in order to assemble a force of burghers and Khoi to fight the Xhosa, and on the following day, Maitland proclaimed martial law 'in force throughout the whole Colony for all cases, and in all matters connected with the assembling, embodying, conducting, and supplying Her Majesty's forces'.[15]

Following the proclamation of martial law, the tide of the war began to turn in favour of the British. However, it soon fell into a stalemate,

---

[9] Maitland to Lord Stanley, 7 December 1844, CO 48/245 f. 54.
[10] Macmillan, *Bantu, Boer and Briton*, p. 282; and Galbraith, *Reluctant Empire*, p. 168. See CO 48/245 ff. 73ff. for a comparison of the terms of the treaties.
[11] Maitland to Lord Stanley, 7 December 1844, CO 48/245 f. 54.
[12] Mostert, *Frontiers*, p. 862; and Macmillan, *Bantu, Boer and Briton*, p. 287. See also PP 1851 (635) XIV. 1, pp. 313–314.
[13] Keegan, *Colonial South Africa*, p. 215.   [14] Mostert, *Frontiers*, pp. 875–878.
[15] PP 1847 (786) XXXVIII. 27, Nos. 8–11, pp. 121–123.

with the British unable to engage the Xhosa in battle, and both sides becoming increasingly exhausted. Faced with starvation of their cattle, the Xhosa eventually gave up the fight. On 26 October 1846, Maqoma surrendered to the government, followed by Sandile on 17 December.[16] On 13 January 1847, with order apparently restored, Maitland revoked martial law.[17] One week later, as he prepared to return home, he wrote to Grey (the new Secretary of State, appointed in 1846) that every chief in the area – save the T'Slambie chief Phato – had given in their arms, and registered as a British subject.[18] In fact, as his successor, Sir Henry Pottinger, perceived, Maitland's confidence was premature. Pottinger thought that if Phato were not brought to submission, other chiefs, notably Sandile, might again become restive.[19] The war was revived, with a (failed) expedition being sent out in April 1847 to locate Phato. A large body of troops was also sent out to apprehend Sandile, who was proclaimed a rebel in August.[20] A merciless campaign against him made Sandile ready to come to terms by October, and, after two months' imprisonment, he made a formal submission to another new Governor, Sir Harry Smith.

The colonial borders were now redrawn again. By a proclamation of 17 December 1847, all existing treaties with the Xhosa were abrogated, and the boundary of the Cape Colony was defined to include the former Ceded Territory, as well as other areas further north, to constitute an area now called the Division of Victoria.[21] Six days later, at King William's Town, Smith read this proclamation out to the assembled Xhosa chiefs, who now included Phato. Having watched them all touch his staff of peace to signal their future intentions, he made each chief kiss his boot and acknowledge him as paramount chief.[22] Smith then read a second proclamation, which declared the area between the Keiskamma and Kei Rivers to be vested in the Queen as

---

[16] Peires, *House of Phalo*, p. 151, and Johannes Meintjies, *Sandile: The Fall of the Xhosa Nation* (Cape Town, T. V. Bulpin, 1971), pp. 157–158.

[17] PP 1847–48 (912) XLIII. 1, enc. in No. 4 (G), p. 20.   [18] PP 1847–48 (912), No. 4, p. 8.

[19] PP 1847–48 (912), No. 10, p. 27; and Mostert, *Frontiers*, p. 916.

[20] Mostert, *Frontiers*, p. 921; Basil le Cordeur and Christopher Saunders, *The War of the Axe, 1847* (Johannesburg, Brenthurst Press, 1981), p. 119; Macmillan, *Bantu, Boer and Briton*, p. 298; and PP 1847–48 (912), enc. No. 6 in No. 33, p. 126.

[21] PP 1847–48 (969) XLIII. 157, enc. 1 in No. 6, p. 22.

[22] A. L. Harington, *Sir Harry Smith: Bungling Hero* (Cape Town, Tafelberg, 1980), p. 103; and PP 1847–48 (969), No. 7, p. 24.

a separate colony of 'British Kaffraria'. This territory would be held by the chiefs under such rules and regulations as the High Commissioner 'shall deem best calculated to promote the civilization, conversion to Christianity, and general enlightenment of the benighted human beings subject to her rule'.[23] It would not be part of the Cape Colony and would be under neither Roman-Dutch law nor English common law.

Peace lasted for only three years, before the eighth frontier war erupted. In 1850, a time of severe drought, Governor Smith became alarmed at the influence of a young prophet named Mlanjeni, who had set out to purify the country of bewitching materials which he claimed had caused all the ills of the Xhosa.[24] Sandile was summoned to a meeting to affirm his loyalty, and was deposed as chief when he failed to attend.[25] Sandile's response was to visit Mlanjeni, and then to order all those who wanted to join his cause to kill one head of cattle, in accordance with the prophet's instructions.[26] The Xhosa fighters were now doctored for war. In response, Smith issued proclamations to loyal inhabitants to enrol as volunteers.[27] On 16 December 1850, he proclaimed Sandile an outlaw, and called a meeting of the Ngqika chiefs, where the severity of his tone convinced many of the chiefs that there would now be war.[28] After the meeting, Smith sent troops into the Amatola Mountains to flush Sandile out of the country. However, this force was ambushed, and on Christmas Day, three military villages in Victoria were attacked and destroyed by Xhosa fighters. Smith was himself besieged in Fort Cox, unable to break out until 31 December. He now proclaimed martial law in the frontier districts, and directed all men between the ages of eighteen and fifty to enrol for military service. He also proclaimed 'all rebel Kafirs [to be] treacherous enemies'.[29] The rebellion and war which ensued would continue until 1853.

---

[23] PP 1847–48 (969), enc. 1 in No. 7, pp. 25–26.
[24] PP 1851 (1334) XXXVIII. 1, enc. 2 in No. 2, p. 15.
[25] He was replaced as chief by Charles Brownlee: PP 1851 (1334), No. 9, p. 38; PP 1851 (1334), enc. 5 in No. 9, p. 44.
[26] PP 1851 (1334), p. 105. Jeff Peires explains that it was the dun and yellow cattle – whose colour most resembled that of whites – who were to be killed first. Peires, *The Dead Will Arise*, p. 10.
[27] PP 1851 (1334), enc. 6 in No. 14, p. 62.
[28] PP 1851 (1334), encs. 3–4 in No. 15, p. 68; PP 1851 (635), p. 385.
[29] Proclamation dated 25 December 1850, PP 1851 (1334), enc. 4 in No. 16, p. 74. Martial law was proclaimed in Albany, Uitenhage, Somerset, Cradock, Graaff-Reinet, Victoria

The Ngqika rebels were soon joined by the 'Hottentot' settlers of Kat River.[30] In previous confrontations with the Xhosa, these settlers had joined the levies which had gone to battle. By 1850, their enthusiasm to assist the British had disappeared, largely because of the high-handed treatment they had hitherto received, being defrauded of promised payment and returning to devastated homes when war was over. At the end of December, the half-Xhosa, half-Khoi leader of the Blinkwater settlement at Kat River, Hermanus Matroos – who had himself fought for the British during the War of the Axe – launched his own attack at Fort Beaufort. He was joined by large numbers of discontented Khoi.[31] Although acting in concert with Sandile, the Kat River rebellion was perceived to be an assertion of 'Hottentot' identity against the British. It was, moreover, a rebellion against the Queen by a people whose subjecthood was undoubted.[32] On 11 January 1851 – six days after Smith had issued a proclamation calling for a war of expulsion against Matroos, the Ngqika and Seyolo[33] – Matroos launched an attack on Fort Beaufort. Although he was killed at the end of a seven-hour battle, the rebellion continued under the leadership of Willem Uithaalder, who took Fort Armstrong on 22 January, turning it into a rebel citadel. For a month, the rebels remained in that stronghold, until it was recaptured by the colonial forces, with the loss of 27 rebel lives, and with 160 prisoners being taken.[34] This turned the tide for the rebellion, which had been suppressed by March.

In the meantime, the war against Sandile continued. By the middle of 1852, the large majority of the Ngqikas had been driven across the Kei. Smith's replacement as Governor, Sir George Cathcart, now decided to take the war across that river to Sarhili, the Gcaleka chief, who was seen to be providing support for the Ngqika (whose

---

and Albert. There was not much enthusiasm among the Dutch-speaking population to join these forces: PP 1851 (1334), No. 10, pp. 125–126.

[30] The community here was made up of people of Khoi descent, as well as those of mixed Khoi–European heritage ('Bastaards') and mixed African descent, who forged an identity as 'Hottentots': see Keegan, *Colonial South Africa*, pp. 118–121; and Ross, *The Borders of Race*.

[31] Elbourne, *Blood Ground*, pp. 349–350.   [32] Mostert, *Frontiers*, p. 1082.

[33] Seyolo (or Siyolo) was the only Ndlambe chief to join the insurrection. PP 1851 (1334), enc. 6 in No. 17, p. 79.

[34] PP 1851 (1352) XXXVIII. 153, enc. 3 in No. 7, p. 23.

paramount chief he was).[35] On 12 August 1852, colonial troops reached Sarhili's deserted kraal, burning it and capturing 9,800 head of cattle.[36] Although Sandile, Maqoma and Seyolo all still remained at large, Cathcart was now confident that he had gained complete control over the former Ngqika territory west of the Kei, and that the rebellion had been successfully suppressed by the force of arms. By January 1853, he was prepared to offer Sarhili pardon and peace, since he was now convinced that he would no longer aid the Ngqika rebels.[37] He was also soon willing 'to extend the Royal pardon to the late rebels, now sufficiently humbled and subdued'. This was not simply a matter of mercy, but of control; for, in the Governor's view, 'the only way of putting an end to the Gaika rebellion, with a prospect of permanent security, is to pardon the Chief Sandilli', provided he made 'due submission' and 'held himself responsible for his people's conduct'.[38] Sandile duly made the submission demanded and was pardoned.[39] By contrast, Seyolo, who had surrendered on 9 October 1852, was tried by a martial law court at Grahamstown for rebellion and sedition. He was sentenced to death, though this was commuted by Cathcart to life imprisonment.[40]

The Xhosa chiefs had not been subdued by the eighth frontier war, and the amount of territory they had lost was not great. It would only be four years later, in the aftermath of the great cattle-killing movement in Xhosaland in 1856–1857, that the power of these chiefs would be undermined.[41] Another new Governor, Sir George Grey, had the ambition to increase control over the chiefs; and the cattle-killing delusion gave him the perfect opportunity to secure his aims. In an eleven-month period commencing in April 1856, the Xhosa slaughtered 400,000 of their cattle, after a young girl had prophesied that the dead would arise and drive out the Europeans, once the people had destroyed their cattle. The result was catastrophic for the Xhosa,

---

[35] PP 1852–53 (1635) LXVI. 395, No. 25, pp. 124–125.
[36] PP 1852–53 (1635), enc. in No 29, p. 144; No. 38 p. 167; cf. PP 1852–53 (1635), enc. in No. 29, p. 145.
[37] See PP 1852–53 (1635), No. 39, p. 174; No. 40, pp. 175–176; No. 49, p. 215; No. 51, pp. 218–221; No. 52, p. 229; and enc. 1 in No. 53, p. 231.
[38] PP 1852–53 (1635), No. 51, p. 218 at p. 226.
[39] PP 1852–53 (1635), No. 54, p. 232; and Galbraith, *Reluctant Empire*, p. 264.
[40] PP 1852–3 (1635), No. 44, p. 191 at pp. 193, 197.
[41] See Peires, *The Dead Will Arise*; and Price, *Making Empire*, pp. 267–334.

40,000 of whom died of starvation. It also gave the colonial authorities a pretext to move against several chiefs (including Phato, Mhala[42] and Maqoma) by contending that the killings were not the result of superstition but were part of 'a plot for involving the country in war, and for the entire expulsion of the European race from ... the Frontier districts'. Although Maqoma was acquitted in November 1857 of inciting the murder of an informer by a summary court, he was convicted of receiving stolen cattle, and sentenced to twenty years' imprisonment for it.[43]

The next – the ninth and last – frontier war, known as the 'war of Ngcayecibi', broke out in 1877. After the cattle-killing of 1857, the Gcalekas were driven across the Mbashe River, but were subsequently allowed to resettle west of that river. There, they were ruled by Sarhili in a state of semi-independence, with a British Resident present. However, their ancestral lands were now occupied by the Mfengu, a matter which caused considerable resentment among the Gcaleka, and it was a clash between these groups which led to war. Although Sarhili wanted a truce with the British, he was unable to restrain his more warlike followers from continuing to fight the Mfengu. In response, imperial troops aided by colonial volunteers and Mfengus destroyed Sarhili's kraal and drove the Gcalekas over the Mbashe. The Governor of the Cape, Sir Bartle Frere, now decided that there was no alternative but to annex Sarhili's country and to depose the chief.[44] Although it appeared by the middle of November that Sarhili's forces had been broken up and driven out of Galekaland,[45] the war soon entered a second phase, when the Ngqika within the colony joined in rebellion.[46] After several farms and shops had been burned, and

---

[42] Mhala had stayed out of the wars but was considered by the British to be one of the most dangerous chiefs in Kaffraria.

[43] 'Proceedings and Findings of the Court which sat at Fort Hare on the 17th November 1857', W[estern] C[ape] A[rchives] GGP 1/2/1/5:G4. Although he was acquitted of inciting the murder, High Commissioner Grey concluded that Maqoma was 'morally responsible' for the murder 'committed by persons acting under his orders'.

[44] CO 879/12/3, No. 91, p. 214, enclosing the proclamation of 5 October. All residents would thereby become British subjects: CO 879/12/3, enc. 2 in No. 149, p. 300.

[45] CO 879/12/3, No. 139, p. 293. A summary of events can be found in CO 879/12/8, No. 10, p. 8. 'Galekaland' refers to the territory between the Kei and Mbashe rivers.

[46] British Kaffraria had been incorporated into the Cape Colony in 1866 (as will be discussed later in this chapter).

MAP 2 Transkei, Pondoland and Griqualand East

armed bands attempted to block the road to the Transkei, on 31 December 1877 Frere proclaimed martial law in the districts of Stutterheim and Komgha.[47]

In dealing with this outbreak, a conflict soon emerged between Frere and his ministers at the Cape, which had enjoyed responsible government since 1872, over control of the campaign. The Cape Prime Minister, J. C. Molteno, felt that suppression of the Ngqika revolt should be left to colonial forces under ministerial control, while imperial troops should deal with the revolt in Transkei.[48] Frere, who considered it 'entirely unconstitutional and illegal' to have two independent military authorities under different command in the

[47] PP 1878 (c. 2000) LV. 735, No. 79, p. 112.   [48] PP 1878 (c. 2079) LVI. 1, pp. 184, 186.

same area, dismissed both the suggestion and the ministry.[49] With a new ministry in place under Sir Gordon Sprigg, martial law was lifted on 25 February 1878.[50] By this point, the Gcaleka had been defeated, while the Ngqika rebels had retreated to the Amatola mountains, where fighting would continue until May. On 20 May 1878, Sandile, who had taken refuge in the mountains, was surrounded by Mfengus, and died during the subsequent exchange of gunfire. Seyolo was already dead.

At the same time that the ninth frontier war was raging, the authorities in the Eastern Cape faced another revolt in Griqualand East, lying north of Pondoland. This territory – also known as 'Nomansland' – had been settled by 2,000 Griquas, who had migrated in 1861–1862 from their settlement at Philippolis.[51] They had been ceded land by African chiefs, whose rights over it had been reserved in a treaty between the British and the Mpondo ruler Faku in 1844. Although Governor Grey refused to assent to their relocation unless they came as British subjects, his successors had treated them as if they were independent.[52] In this new home, they were governed according to their own constitution and laws by a *Kaptyn* – Adam Kok – and in 1872 had built a new capital, Kokstad. By this time, the Cape authorities were taking a greater interest in the Griquas, given their concern to ensure stability in the Transkei borderlands. They were particularly worried about what would happen if the elderly Adam Kok were to die with no clear successor in place. A select committee on native affairs was appointed at the Cape, which not only reported that the Griquas had not made 'any progress whatever in civilization' since their move from Philippolis, but also expressed the view that a majority of the inhabitants were 'extremely anxious to be taken at once under British rule'.[53]

Without bothering to consult Adam Kok, the British decided to take greater control in the area. Arriving in Kokstad in October 1874,

---

[49] PP 1878 (c. 2079), pp. 191, 200–203, 214.
[50] PP 1878 (c. 2100) LVI. 255, No. 11, p. 17.
[51] For the background, see Robert Ross, *Adam Kok's Griquas: A Study in the Development of Stratification in South Africa* (Cambridge, Cambridge University Press, 1976), ch. 7.
[52] Minute of Attorney General Thomas Upington, 3 March 1879, CO 48/489/6159; CO 879/7/16, No. 53, p. 136.
[53] *Report of the Select Committee on Native Affairs* (Cape Town, 1874), CPP A.12-'73, pp. 111–113.

Governor Sir Henry Barkly announced that the government would henceforth be conducted under the instructions of a British Resident.[54] While nothing more formal was done to signal the commencement of British control, the British began to assume governmental functions, including exercising magisterial jurisdiction and appointing a commission to investigate land claims.[55] After Adam Kok's death in December 1875, tensions began to escalate between the British and the Griquas, who were increasingly resentful about their treatment by the high-handed Resident, Capt. Matthew Blyth. In 1876, the decision was taken to annex Griqualand East; but, although the necessary legislation was passed in 1877 and letters patent drawn up, the annexation was not implemented until 1879.[56]

The rebellion which erupted in April 1878 was a reaction to the stern treatment of the Griquas by Blyth. Among the leaders of the rebellion were Adam 'Muis' Kok (a nephew of Adam Kok), his brother Lodewyk and Smith Pommer, who had been one of the Kat River rebels in 1851. A few months before the revolt erupted, Lodewyk had returned from the diamond fields of Griqualand West (which had been annexed to the crown in 1872), and had taunted his fellow Griquas for being so supine in surrendering their country. There were reports of Adam Muis, Lodewyk and Adam Kok's widow visiting neighbouring African areas and inciting rebellion among the Basutos, Mpondos and others.[57] In February 1878, Lodewyk was arrested after an argument with a white trader in Kokstad, during which – the worse for drink – he had threatened to shoot the owner and all Englishmen. Blyth, fearing that a general rising might erupt at any moment, summoned the brothers, who were charged with sedition. After a two-day trial in the following week, Lodewyk was sentenced to six months'

---

[54] Ross, *Adam Kok's Griquas*, p. 127. For a description of the meeting, see CO 879/8/10, No. 5, p. 94.

[55] *Report of a Commission Appointed by His Excellency the Governor to Inquire into the Affairs of the Territory of Griqualand East* (Cape Town, 1876), CPP G.37-'76.

[56] Griqualand East Annexation Act, No. 38 of 1877. The Act was promulgated in 1879, when Griqualand East was incorporated into the Cape Colony.

[57] PP 1878–1879 (c. 2220) LII. 1, No. 41, p. 126. The (unprinted) enclosures to this despatch are in CO 48/486/11782. See also *Papers Relating to the Rebellion in Griqualand East* (Cape Town, 1878), CPP A.51-'78. For an excellent narrative of the events, see Brett Cohen, '"Something Like a Blowing Wind": African Conspiracy and Co-ordination of Resistance to Colonial Rule in South Africa, 1876–1882', PhD Dissertation, Michigan State University, 2000, pp. 203–23.

imprisonment. Adam Muis fled to Pondoland before his trial.[58] He was well received both by the Mpondo chief Mhlangazo[59] and by his paramount chief Mqikela, whose attitude towards the British had hardened since the Gcaleka outbreak, and who sensed an opportunity to strengthen his position by joining a Griqua revolt.

Muis was joined in Pondoland by more disaffected Griquas, including Smith Pommer, who had been seeking the help of the Hlangweni chief Sidoi. Muis was also relying on help from the Mpondo chiefs, particularly Mqikela, who had received a request from Blyth to return the fugitive.[60] Mqikela's plan was to send the Griquas out of his territory under an armed escort, ostensibly to hand them over to Blyth, but in reality to join in the attack.[61] On Thursday, 11 April 1878, Muis and Smith Pommer entered Griqualand East with a ninety-four-man Mpondo escort. After taking a white farmer prisoner and robbing his farm,[62] the combined Griqua and Mpondo forces, numbering some 200, headed for the Old Laager, about three miles outside Kokstad, to prepare their revolt.[63] They remained there until the following Sunday. In the meantime, Blyth sent numerous messengers to them, asking them to lay down their arms, and requesting the widow of Adam Kok, who was seen to be one of the leaders of the rebellion, to come out from the camp. After a series of prevarications, Blyth gave a half hour ultimatum, at the end of which he launched an attack, in which eighteen men, including Adam Muis, were killed. Most escaped into the Ingeli mountains, where some (including Smith Pommer) were killed, and many more captured.

Blyth attributed the Griqua rebellion to 'the spirit of restlessness and disaffection towards the Government' which was to be found

---

[58] See Blyth's account in CO 48/486/11782, f. 145.
[59] Mhlangazo was angry at the British for demanding that he hand over fugitives accused of committing a murder in Griqualand East: see the report of J. Oxley Oxland, *Blue Book on Native Affairs* (Cape Town, 1879) CPP G.33-'79, pp. 121–122, and PP 1878–1879 (c. 2308) LIII. 225, enc. 4 in No. 13, p. 54.
[60] Blyth to Secretary of Native Affairs, 23 April 1878, CO 48/486/11782, f. 72.
[61] Deposition of Coenrad Wardvogel, CO 48/486/11782, f. 221. See also CO 879/14/6, No. 128, p. 192 at p. 193. As one British official later observed, the regiment was to 'act as a feeler, and if even a partial success had attended the Griqua outbreak, the whole Pondo army would have been poured into East Griqualand'. Oxley Oxland, *Blue Book on Native Affairs*, CPP G.33-'79, p. 122.
[62] Blyth to Secretary of Native Affairs, 23 April 1878, CO 48/486/11782, f. 72.
[63] For their warlike aims, see CO 48/486/11782, ff. 98, 250–251.

throughout the region at the start of 1878.[64] He saw no reason for them to rebel, being blind to their resentment at being taken over and effectively dispossessed of their land. Officials in the Cape and London both blamed Mqikela for encouraging the rising.[65] Although Blyth was excoriated in the *Natal Witness*, the Colonial Office commended his conduct.[66] After the rebellion was crushed, 140 were taken into custody. Depositions were taken from these prisoners, with admissions elicited from one witness being used to cajole more information from another. Officials in London favoured lenient treatment of the prisoners – other than the ringleaders – not least because many of the followers had been induced to join by threats or deception, and had been captured without arms. With nowhere to hold them in Griqualand East, they were sent first to Durban and then to Cape Town, where they were held (after August) in the Amsterdam Battery.

Over a period of a half-century, the Cape Colony saw repeated wars and emergencies on its eastern frontier. As shall now be seen, 'exceptional' measures were used in these emergencies to deal with rebels and enemies, in areas where the nature of colonial jurisdiction was sometimes questionable. On the frontier, there had always been officials, like Sir Harry Smith, who were keen on asserting power without worrying too much about legal niceties; but the ability of such men to act wholly outside the law was constrained by political and legal voices, both at Cape Town and in London, which called for legal procedures to be observed. The scope for rule-of-law arguments to impinge on executive action was all the greater in the Cape, since it did not resort to *ad hominem* statutes to detain its own enemies.

The Reach of Martial Law

Martial law was proclaimed in the Eastern Cape during each of these crises. Such proclamations raised important questions about the status of martial law, particularly if civilian courts remained in operation.

---

[64] Blyth's affidavit, in *In re Willem Kok and Nathaniel Balie*, in Eben J. Buchanan, *Cases in the Supreme Court of the Cape of Good Hope during the Year 1879* (Cape Town, Juta, 1880), p. 45 [Juta Reports, 1879, p. 45] at 59.
[65] Report of Oxley Oxland, *Blue Book on Native Affairs*, CPP G. 33-'79, p. 122; minute of Arthur A. Pearson, CO 48/486/11782.
[66] See Minute of Arthur A. Pearson, CO 48/486/11782.

Although such questions were often raised by officials when martial law courts were used to try rebels, the most important discussion of martial law by a South African court before the Anglo-Boer war came in a case of 1851 which had nothing to do with civil liberties. *Standen v. Godfrey* examined whether the normal processes of debt recovery could be used during martial law, when the debtor might have been called up to defend the frontier and be unable to answer the case. The fact that both martial law and civil law were in operation at this time generated much irritation in the Eastern Cape. According to *The Colonist*, it put shopkeepers 'in the position of the earthen pot, surrounded by iron pots. On one side they have the Kaffirs; on the other, the law.'[67] The matter was referred to the Cape's Attorney General, William Porter – 'as progressive an official as the Cape produced'[68] – who thought that a proclamation of martial law did not supersede the jurisdiction of the civil courts, though it might justify the acts of the military authorities.[69] In Porter's view, if the civil courts were closed and all executions of judgments suspended, it might favour *mala fide* debtors, and undermine credit.

The question then went before Cape Supreme Court, where Porter argued that the civil courts should proceed as if there were no martial law until such point that the Governor put a stop to their judicature.[70] However, this view did not persuade the Chief Justice, Sir John Wylde,[71] who held that civil law was dislodged in times of war. In his view, 'under a simple, direct and absolute proclamation of martial

---

[67] *The Colonist*, 5 July 1851, reprinted in *De Zuid-Afrikaan*, 17 July 1851, p. 3. Quoting the Duke of Wellington's definition of martial law as the will of the commander, it criticised Sir Harry Smith for failing to set out the rules and regulations according to which his will was to be carried out.

[68] Keegan, *Colonial South Africa*, p. 158. See J. L. McCracken, *New Light at the Cape of Good Hope: William Porter, the Father of Cape Liberalism* (Belfast, Ulster Historical Foundation, 1993).

[69] *Natal Witness*, 25 April 1851, p. 6. He suggested that civilian courts allow execution of judgment only where it was just to do so.

[70] His view reflected the 1757 opinion of the law officers that a proclamation of martial law did not suspend the ordinary course of law 'any further than is absolutely necessary, to answer the then military service of the public'. George Chalmers, *Opinions of Eminent Lawyers on Various Points of English Jurisprudence, Chiefly Concerning the Colonies, Fisheries, and Commerce*, 2 vols. (London, Reed and Hunter, 1814), vol. 1, p. 267.

[71] For Wylde, see F. St Leger Searle, 'Sir John Wylde', *South African Law Journal*, vol. 50 (1933), pp. 284–297. He was the brother of Thomas Wilde, who was (as Lord Truro) Lord Chancellor in Palmerston's government between 1850 and 1852.

law, the civil judicature was stayed, as the two jurisdictions cannot work concurrently'. Echoing the Duke of Wellington's recent definition, he added that under martial law, judges no longer ministered under the Royal Charter, 'but upon the sufferance and under the will of the commander-in-chief', who had the power to prevent witnesses or jurors from attending court. Indeed, he went so far as to say that it was for the Governor alone to decide on whether the emergency warranted recourse to martial law, and the court would not question it.[72] Wylde's *dictum* would later be seized on by those who sought to oust the jurisdiction of civil courts to review the detention of suspects under martial law; but its prime aim was to shield debtors from unexpected executions while they were fighting on the frontier.

Legislators at the Cape remained aware that martial law was a legal anomaly, and that it was necessary to pass indemnity acts once civilian rule was restored. On each occasion, martial law was followed by an indemnity act.[73] However, the passage of such legislation was not regarded simply as a matter of routine. After martial law was lifted in the Cape in 1836, legislation was prepared to indemnify the Governor (and those under him) for acts done '*bona fide*, in furtherance and in the execution of the objects for which martial law was proclaimed'.[74] On hearing of this, Secretary of State Glenelg questioned whether the colonial legislature had the authority to indemnify a Governor who was responsible to the king, parliament 'and, in certain cases, to the Court of King's Bench at Westminster, but not to the colonial tribunals'. Glenelg also disapproved of indemnifying all *bona fide* acts, commenting that many acts of injustice and cruelty might have been done '*bona fide*' and that the legislation should have referred to 'all acts necessarily or properly done'.[75] Despite his qualms, the wording was not changed.

Indemnity legislation could also be controversial. The indemnity ordinance which passed in March 1847 was pushed through because

---

[72] *Standen v. Godfrey* (1851) 1 Searle 61 at 63. A similar view was taken in Natal, where a landowner from Pietermaritzburg sought an interdict to prevent the levying of a force of Zulus (under martial law proclaimed south of the Umkomaas River on 23 January) to support the troops on the Cape's frontier. D. D. Buchanan v. Theophilus Shepstone, *Natal Witness*, 21 March 1851, p. 3.

[73] *Statute Law of the Cape of Good Hope* (Cape Town, Saul Solomon & Co, 1862): Ordinance 10 of 1836, p. 406; Ordinance No. 4 of 1847, p. 822; and Ordinance No. 8 of 1853, p. 1041; and Military Operations Indemnity Act, No. 23 of 1878.

[74] PP 1837 (503), enc. 1 in No. 21, p. 52.   [75] PP 1837 (503), No. 22, p. 53 at p. 54.

of the fear that advantage would be taken of the 'approaching Circuit of one of the Judges of the Supreme Court to institute Suits on a variety of points against the authorities'.[76] The speed of its passage caused disquiet in the press, for there was much anger over the way that waggon-drivers had been severely disciplined by military commanders, who it was felt needed to be held to account. 'The deep indignation occasioned among all classes of society at the personal injuries inflicted on some of the burghers, by subordinates, and sanctioned by Sir PEREGRINE MAITLAND has not abated', wrote *De Zuid-Afrikaan* in March.[77] They had in mind the case of a waggon driver named John Crawford Smith, who had refused an order to cut some wood, and had been given twenty-five lashes as punishment, as a result of which the waggon drivers became much more obedient. In fact, the ordinance was drawn up so as not to indemnify those actions which were already the subject of litigation or prosecution in the courts.[78]

During the frontier wars of the 1830s and 1840s, the primary purpose of declaring martial law was to facilitate the assembling and use of troops to fight the war, rather than to detain or punish. D'Urban's proclamation of martial law in January 1835 was designed to 'embody the inhabitants' of the districts in question to aid His Majesty's forces in repelling the invaders, and applied 'in all matters connected with the assembling and conducting the forces of the colony'.[79] Smith used martial law powers in Grahamstown to raise troops, and to discipline them – particularly the 'Hottentots', who complained about being kept in the field after white farmers had been allowed to return home, and who were not paid for their service to the Government.[80] Similarly, in 1846, Maitland declared martial law to be in force throughout the colony for all matters connected with

---

[76] Pottinger to Grey, 16 June 1847, WCA GH 23/17, f. [108]

[77] *De Zuid-Afrikaan*, 23 March 1847, p. 3.

[78] *De Zuid-Afrikaan*, 23 March 1847, p. 3. The case of the waggon-driver Smith was taken up by a cleric, Dr Tancred, who raised subscriptions to initiate a prosecution of Lindsay, and an action for assault was eventually brought in Grahamstown on 29 March 1847. Harriet Ward, *Five Years in Kaffirland*, 2 vols (London, Henry Colburn, 1848), ii: 269–274.

[79] PP 1835 (252) enc. 4 in No. 42 p. 130.

[80] Mostert, *Frontiers*, p. 679. On one occasion, Smith sentenced disobedient troops to 300 lashes and their leader to three months' solitary confinement, telling them, 'Now you see what martial law is; you think you cannot be forced to do anything, but I say you shall serve as long as it pleases His Majesty': PP 1836 (538) VII.1, p. 710.

assembling and supplying the troops.[81] Like Smith, he thought these powers were needed to call out and arm the burgher force. He also thought that he had no power to issue the martial law proclamation he considered necessary to raise the troops until the war had actually begun.[82] By contrast, his successor, Pottinger, did not think it essential to have martial law to raise troops. After Maitland had revoked martial law in January 1847, Pottinger (who felt that the revocation was premature, given the continuing problems on the frontier) opted not to reimpose it (since this might excite 'groundless alarm' and encroach on people's civil rights) but instead issued a proclamation calling for volunteers to aid the regular forces.[83]

Martial Law in Conquered Territories

Besides being used to raise troops, martial law was also used for a number of other purposes, which raised important legal questions about its nature and relationship with civil law. To begin with, it was used to rule newly conquered territories. This could raise complicated constitutional questions, as can be seen from the debates over Queen Adelaide Province, where martial law was declared on 16 June 1835. Early in October 1835, the senior puisne judge at the Cape, William Menzies, pointed out that this territory had to be regarded as governed by the laws of the Cape and be subject to its Supreme Court, thanks to Governor D'Urban's proclamation of May, which extended the Cape's border to the Kei. This presented potentially serious obstacles in the way of applying the peace treaties signed by D'Urban in September, since their provisions often contradicted Cape law.[84] As an example, Menzies pointed out that once martial law was lifted, any white settler who killed an African violating the thirteenth article of the treaty – which stated that armed Africans crossing the Keiskamma without a pass could be

---

[81] PP 1847 (786), No. 9, p. 122. A broader martial law was proclaimed in the eastern districts: ibid., No. 8, p. 121.

[82] As he explained, 'My own apprehension is that, according to the principles of the English Government, a resort to such extreme measures is only justifiable when the country is suffering invasion, and its soil is in the occupation of an enemy': PP 1847 (786), No. 16, p. 140 at p. 143.

[83] PP 1847–48 (912), No. 10, p. 27; enc. 2 in No. 13, p. 41.

[84] This was especially so of provisions relating to the movement of persons and to the liability of chiefs for depredations. PP 1836 (279), enc. 5 in No. 9, p. 95.

shot – would be liable to be tried for murder. In his view, this problem could only be avoided if the new province were severed from the Colony and treated as a conquered territory and governed under royal prerogative power, until such time as a constitution were granted to it.[85]

When he signed the treaties, D'Urban's intention was to keep martial law in force in the new province 'for a considerable time to come', without applying the laws of the Cape there. As he saw it, martial law would be enforced according to the spirit of the treaties, and could be supplemented and eventually replaced by ordinances 'specially adapted to the condition of these people, still keeping in view the principles of the treaties'.[86] This aspiration was based on a confused understanding of constitutional law, assuming that the new province could at the same time be treated as part of the Cape Colony, but ruled by a distinct legal order. The matter was referred to Sir John Wylde CJ, who (after consulting the judges) confirmed that the jurisdiction of the Supreme Court extended into the Province of Queen Adelaide. He also pointed to Sir Matthew Hale's opinion that martial law was impermissible in times of peace.[87] The judges further pointed to the anomaly that although the Supreme Court had jurisdiction (and martial law was *ultra vires*), no system of circuit courts or magistrates had been created in the province. As a result of these consultations, D'Urban concluded that martial law had to be revoked on 18 August 1836, and the jurisdiction of the circuit courts extended for the time being. The lifting of martial law prompted Stockenström and Harry Smith to conclude that the territory could no longer be held, for, as Smith put it, 'the sooner we march out of the province the better, for how am I to eat up a Kaffir according to Blackstone?'[88] Although he had anticipated more time to reorient British policy in this area,

---

[85] Menzies also felt that 'it is impossible that all the laws which are necessary for the protection of and due administration of justice to the civilized inhabitants of this colony can be effectually or beneficially made applicable to the Kafirs in their present state'. 'Legal Notes on the Treaty with the Kafirs of the 17th September 1835', PP 1851 (424), p. 197 at p. 198; cf. Macmillan, *Bantu, Boer and Briton*, pp. 152–153.

[86] PP 1836 (279), No. 9, p. 86 at p. 89; PP 1837 (503), enc. 2 in No. 3, p. 5.

[87] D'Urban to Stockenström, 19 August 1836, WCA LG 56, f. 13; referring to Sir Matthew Hale, *History of the Pleas of The Crown*, 2 vols. (London, 1736), vol. 1, p.500; *History of the Common Law of England* (London, 1713), pp. 40–41. See also Galbraith, *Reluctant Empire*, p. 139.

[88] C. W. Hutton (ed.), *The Autobiography of the Late Sir Andries Stockenstrom, Bart.*, 2 vols. (Cape Town, Juta & Co, 1887), vol. 2, p. 45.

Lieutenant-Governor Stockenström now hurried to enter into new treaties with the African chiefs and to renounce the Province of Adelaide. In this instance, legal concerns had a direct impact on policy.

The question of how to rule this territory returned in 1846, when the British took control of 'British Kaffraria'. In order to avoid having a 'Kafir Government under British Protection', Earl Grey wanted to assert British sovereignty over the area. Grey thought that a 'system of military rule' was 'the only one fitted for the circumstances of this country'. He felt this could be introduced either by annexing the territory to the Cape, and passing an ordinance instituting martial law in this area, or by holding it as a 'separate territory acquired by H.M. by right of conquest, and in which therefore military authority alone would be recognised until H.M. by order in council should otherwise direct'.[89] However, the permanent under-secretary of state, James Stephen, advised against any claim to sovereignty, since he doubted 'the possibility of maintaining, in any part of the *Queen's Dominions*, such a system of Government as the exigencies of this case seem to demand'. He did not want Kaffraria to be made a separate colony, since 'it must have a separate legislature, and we must take the chance of their legislating wisely or unwisely'. Nor did he favour the idea that it become part of the Cape, but with a martial law regime:

Martial Law is but another name for the suspension of all law – for the arbitrary dominion of mere force. I cannot conceive any Colonial Legislature fitting such a yoke to the necks of their fellow-Colonists. The local newspapers would inveigh, with all their power, against it. The lawyers of the place would set themselves to prove that such legislation was invalid. The judges and the juries would agree with them. Unless the Governor were strong-willed enough to dismiss the judges, and silence the editors, any such law would be defeated as soon as made. If the Governor were strong-willed enough for this purpose, our own newspapers would hold him up as a monster of Colonial oppression [...] nor would there be wanting in the House of Commons the usual amount of successful invective against the tyranny of the Colonial Office and its ministers abroad.[90]

Stephen's objections persuaded the Secretary of State, whose instructions to the new Governor, Pottinger, explained that the

---

[89] Undated note by Grey, CO 48/264, f. 387.
[90] Memorandum from James Stephen to Lord Grey, 28 September 1846, CO 48/264, f. 410.

territory should not be annexed either as a new colony or as a part of the Cape Colony, since this would require the introduction either of the English common law or the laws of the Cape, neither of which would be suitable. He rather wanted the tribes 'to acknowledge the Queen as the protector of their nation, and to receive a British officer as the commander in chief of all their national forces'.[91] According to this plan, 'British Kaffraria' would be a kind of protectorate, for which the Cape Governor would be responsible, in the capacity of a High Commissioner.[92]

The plan for British Kaffraria was therefore to rule through the chiefs, but under regulations set by the High Commissioner's representative. In practice, this was a system of martial law.[93] Commissioners would be appointed to reside near the chiefs, to guide them. European traders would have the status of 'camp followers', subject to martial law for petty offences; and subject to the Cape colony's extraterritorial jurisdiction for more serious ones.[94] In March 1849, Attorney General Porter wrote an opinion on the legal status of this new colony. In his view, it was a conquered country held by military occupation, awaiting the issue by the crown of the formal instructions which would turn it into a colony. There was no time limit for this transitory state. In Porter's view, this kind of regime suited the people of the country. 'The "word" of the great chief sent from the colony is the law the Kafirs look to, and the only law they understand,' he argued, 'With them the Governor is the Government.'[95]

Although Letters Patent were issued by the crown in 1850, authorising the Governor of the Cape to set up an executive council and judicial system for the new territories, they were not published for another decade.[96] Only after 1860 were steps taken to introduce a regular system of judicature in this area, which was finally incorporated into the Cape in 1866. In the intervening period, the

---

[91] PP 1847–48 (912), No. 1, at p. 3.
[92] For Pottinger's plan, see PP 1847–48 (912), enc. 1 in No. 19, p. 73.
[93] Macmillan, *Bantu, Boer and Briton*, p. 301.   [94] PP 1847–48 (969), No. 3, p. 26.
[95] CO 879/1/1, enc. 2 in No. 3, p. 10 at p. 20.
[96] *British Kaffraria: The People's Blue Book Containing the True and Full Account of the Political Commotion in British Kaffraria* (King William's Town, S. E. Bowles, 1863), pp. 12–14; and Peires, *The Dead Will Arise*, p. 283. See also Grey's explanation to Labouchere for the delay in his despatch of 8 December 1857, CO 48/385/1269, f. 138.

territory was ruled under martial law; though as increasing numbers of settlers were introduced into the new colony, magistrates were appointed who dealt with some civil disputes and crimes, and a special criminal court was created in 1857 to deal with serious crimes.[97] British Kaffraria in effect operated in a kind of constitutional void, with the system of martial law imposed on this conquered territory not being subject to supervision either by the Cape courts or the highest court in the empire, the Privy Council.

Even here, however, the legal conscience of Cape officials could act as a limited restraint on executive action. After the Xhosa chiefs, Phato and Mhala, had been tried in the aftermath of the cattle killings in 1858, their cases were sent to William Porter for his opinion, before Grey confirmed the sentences. The men had been tried under the same summary procedure which had been used against Maqoma.[98] Both were convicted for receiving stolen cattle, while Mhala was also convicted of devising war against the Queen. Porter had severe reservations about both cases. He was troubled by the fact that, in Phato's case, a second trial had been ordered by chief commissioner Maclean after evidence was introduced at the first trial which showed that he had not known that the cattle were stolen.[99] Although Grey responded that in the unsettled state of Kaffraria, Africans could not 'claim every technical advantage which would be awarded to a British subject in a regularly constituted Court',[100] he sentenced Phato only to five years' transportation to Cape Town, where he would be allowed to remain 'comfortably taken care of' in the hospital. Porter was also critical of the proceedings against Mhala, pointing out that the

---

[97] For a study of its administration see Denver A. Webb, 'More Than Just a Public Execution: Martial Law, Crime and the Nature of Colonial Power in British Kaffraria', *South African Historical Journal*, vol. 65:2 (2013), pp. 293–316.

[98] According to the Attorney General of British Kaffraria, Henry Barrington, it was expedient in these cases 'to omit the forms usual among the civilized people of Europe in criminal cases ... and to proceed in the simplest and most natural manner'. Memorandum 30 April 1857, WCA BK 14. The trials were presided over by special magistrates, sitting with military officers.

[99] As Porter explained, 'the expediency of maintaining inviolated [sic] the independence of Courts Martial, trying Kafirs, and of proving to Kafirs that these Courts are really independent, is very great, and many repetitions of what has taken place in this case would go far to turn Courts Martial into a farce'. Memorandum dated 17 March 1858, WCA GH 8/34, f. 1003. See also Peires, *The Dead Will Arise*, p. 231.

[100] WCA GH 8/34, ff. 1038–1039.

evidence would not have been sufficient to persuade a Cape jury to convict.[101] Porter's own view of the evidence was that 'fanaticism had more to do with the suicidal movement' of the cattle killing than conspiracy. He also thought that the treason charges brought against Mhala – under the British Treason Felony Act of 1848 – could not be sustained, since (even if the Act applied in Kaffraria, which he doubted) it was nowhere alleged that he was a subject owing allegiance to the crown. Although Porter conceded that, in the current conditions, the removal 'of such a wily and influential chief' might have been necessary for 'the welfare of all classes in Kafirland', he added that 'I would prefer to rest his detention in this Colony upon considerations of this sort, than upon a conviction under an inapplicable statute, supported by what strikes me as somewhat defective evidence.'[102] In response, Mhala's sentence was reduced from transportation for life to five years' imprisonment, with a provision for its remission 'if it should subsequently be thought that the Attorney-General is right and I am wrong'.[103] These trials had been intended to prove that the great cattle-killing had been a plot hatched by the Xhosa chiefs, a manipulation of law and its forms as a form of lawfare against those who stood in the way of imperial expansion. While the conscience of the Cape's Attorney General did not secure these chiefs their liberty, it was enough to draw something of the sting of Grey's lawfare.

Martial Law Trials

Martial law was not generally used in the earlier wars in the Cape against non-subject Africans to detain them or try them as rebels. Thus, when revoking martial law in January 1847, Maitland informed Grey that the 'few Kafir prisoners of war detained in the colony have been passed over the Keiskamma and dismissed'.[104] Pottinger also regarded those who were taken in arms during the campaign against Sandile as 'prisoners of war' to be disarmed and released.[105] However, from the 1850s, martial law courts were used on a number of occasions to try

---

[101] WCA GH 8/36, Opinion dated 4 November 1858, f. 337.
[102] WCA GH 8/36, Opinion dated 6 November 1858, f. 379.
[103] Quoted in Peires, *The Dead will Arise*, p. 236.
[104] PP 1847–48 (912), No. 4, p. 8 at p. 10.
[105] PP 1847–48 (912), No. 37, p. 137 at p. 141.

rebel subjects. This raised the question of the status of martial law courts when civilian courts were open, and of the validity of the sentences of these courts once martial law was lifted.

In the aftermath of the Kat River rebellion, when Governor Smith determined to try the captured rebels, he consulted his Attorney General on which tribunal to use.[106] Porter thought it best to use martial law courts, since it would be 'unusual' to send rebels to a civilian tribunal 'in the midst of actual hostilities and during the existence of martial law'. He was also aware that Justice William Musgrave – the judge who was due to take the next circuit – had qualms about holding a civil court when martial law remained in place. In addition, Porter pointed out that in September 1848, in Bloemfontein, Smith had himself ordered the execution under martial law of the burgher Thomas Dreyer, after Andries Pretorius's Boer Rebellion at Boomplaats.[107] Since Dreyer might have been given a civilian trial under the Cape's extraterritorial jurisdiction,[108] he argued that for the British now to give 'Hottentots' the kind of trial they had denied Boers would only cause resentment. Smith agreed with this advice, which would have the advantage of imposing speedy punishment.[109] The Colonial Office took a more cautious approach. Mindful of the recent parliamentary debates over martial law in Ceylon, Secretary of State Grey pointed out that the sentences of martial law tribunals had no validity unless sanctioned by legislation. While it was the practice to pass indemnity acts to protect soldiers who had inflicted punishments in times of emergency, they did not validate continuing sentences of transportation or imprisonment. For such purposes, an ordinance would be needed to confer powers on martial law courts to try and punish offenders.[110]

---

[106] Smith's initial intention was to try the more prominent rebel leaders in a civilian tribunal, in part because he did not feel he could spare the officers needed for the military tribunals. PP 1851 (424), No. 1, p. 1 at p. 3; PP 1852 (1428), enc. in No. 6, p. 36 at p. 37.
[107] PP 1849 (1059) XXXVI. 433, No. 14, p. 57. For the battle, see Tim Couzens, *Battles of South Africa* (Claremont, David Philip, 2004).
[108] 6 & 7 William IV c. 57 (1836), which gave the Cape extraterritorial jurisdiction over British subjects south of the 25th degree of southern latitude.
[109] 31 March 1851, PP 1852 (1428), enc. in No. 6, pp. 36–37; PP 1851 (424), No. 3, p. 11 at pp. 12–13.
[110] CO 879/1/8, No. 1, p. 1.

In the meantime, local white settler opinion began to call for a judicial commission of inquiry into the rebellion and for the judges to try the rebels.[111] This was not out of sympathy for the rebels, since the settlers were of the view that the government's stance towards them had been too lenient. One newspaper was horrified that Smith had given many of the rebels passes allowing them to return home, and recruited others into the military: it argued that the ringleaders should have been summarily executed, and the rest put to labour on public works.[112] Those who urged a judicial commission felt that martial law trials entailed 'nothing less than the throwing open a wide door for the escape of delinquents'.[113] However, the Executive Council of the Cape rejected the proposal to have civilian trials before men who were also being asked to investigate the rebellion. It took the view that there was not very much difference between civilian trials and trials in military courts, save that the former had juries and were constituted according to the Charter of Justice.[114]

Martial law trials consequently proceeded, albeit without the empowering ordinance Grey had in mind. Fifty-four prisoners were tried by a martial law court, which sat between 18 March and 30 April 1851. Of these, forty-seven were sentenced to death, three were sentenced to terms of transportation, and the rest acquitted. With one exception, Smith reported, the men were all 'persons of the lowest class ... the tools of more intelligent men whom I have failed to arrest'. The one exception, captured at Fort Beaufort when Hermanus Matroos was killed, was the son of Andries Botha, the Field Cornet of Buxton, who had in the past assisted the British in fighting the Xhosa, and who had himself sought to dissuade the Khoi youth from rebelling.[115] Andries Botha was himself also arrested, for the colonial authorities were convinced that he had plotted the rebel outbreak with

---

[111] *Graham's Town Journal*, 22 March 1851, p. 3.
[112] *Cape Frontier Times*, 8 April 1851, reprinted in *De Zuid Afrikaan*, 17 April 1851, p. 6.
[113] *Graham's Town Journal*, 3 May 1851, p. 2.
[114] PP 1852 (1428), enc. in No. 6, at p. 38. The Attorney General himself favoured sending brigands who had taken advantage of the revolt to commit robberies and murders for trial by martial law courts, rather than holding them for civilian trials, but the military were not keen to try them: Attorney General to Clerk of the Peace, Albany, 3 May, 12 June 1851, WCA AG 2051, ff. 58, 94.
[115] PP 1852 (1428), No. 10, p. 72.

Sandile. He was sent to Cape Town, where he was tried and convicted for treason in 'the first of South Africa's show trials'.[116]

Reviewing the sentences of the martial law prisoners, the Executive Council decided that the death penalty should not be carried out in any of the cases referred to them. Although the council was satisfied that the men were British subjects guilty of levying war against the Queen, and that neither the trials nor the sentences were unlawful, it was considered impolitic to execute them, given that so many other captured rebels had been dismissed with passes, with many subsequently being enrolled by the military to fight the Xhosa. In terms of personal criminality, no distinction could be drawn between those who had been tried and those who had not: it therefore seemed quite random to impose the death penalty on these men. Given the delay which had elapsed, there was also concern that executions would serve not to check insurrection, but to further discontent. In the view of the council, the death penalty should be reserved for three classes of rebels: the ringleaders, those who had been particularly bloodthirsty or malicious, and those who had deserted in the field from the military.[117]

After the council recommended that sentences of life imprisonment with hard labour be imposed, Smith asked the Attorney General whether he had the power to impose such a penalty. Porter replied that colonial legal opinion was divided on the question of martial law. Some felt that the Governor's proclamation instigated it *de jure*, and that it was within the executive's power to establish martial law with no additional legislative sanction. Others, including himself, felt that an act of indemnity would be needed to justify any act (including imprisonment) which had no other legal sanction bar the Governor's proclamation. He added that difficulties would arise if the prisoners were moved out of the area in which martial law had been proclaimed, since courts in those areas might not recognise its validity. Although members of the council realised that it would be necessary to pass legislation to give legal cover to sentences which for practical reasons needed to be served in the Western Cape, they were in no rush to pass it. They well understood how unlikely it was that any attempt would be

---

[116] Ross, *Borders of Race*, p. 277; *Trial of Andries Botha* (Cape Town, Saul Solomon & Co., 1852). His death sentence was commuted to life imprisonment, and he was released in 1855.

[117] PP 1852 (1428), enc. 3 in No. 10, p. 74.

Martial Law in the Eastern Cape, 1830–1880

made to challenge the imprisonment of those convicted under martial law, given both the leniency with which they had been treated and the fact they could be tried again for treason if released.[118] Eventually legislation was passed in November to legalise the continued detention of those who had been tried by the martial law courts, and to validate any future sentences by these courts.[119] The Kat River prisoners did not remain long in gaol. By 1858, none of the 123 convicted rebels and their widows who applied for the restoration of their land were still in gaol.[120] However, they were not the only ones to be tried in martial law courts: among those tried in this way at Grahamstown was Seyolo, who was charged with rebellion and sedition and for waging war against the Queen. He was sentenced to death, but this was commuted by Cathcart to life imprisonment.[121]

The question of trying rebels by martial law courts was raised again in the ninth frontier war. Martial law was proclaimed at the end of 1877 only when the Ngqika – who lived under the crown's jurisdiction in the Cape – joined in rebellion. Governor Frere did not want to proclaim martial law, since he 'did not contemplate suspension of ordinary law courts for ordinary offences'.[122] Indeed, he suggested that a special session of the High Court might be arranged for the trial of offences against the state.[123] However, the Cape's ministry preferred a declaration of martial law following the precedents of previous frontier wars, and they were advised by Attorney General Andries Stockenström that, if time was of the essence, then drumhead courts-martial should be used, with an Indemnity Act to follow.[124] Although Frere soon conceded that martial law would have to be

---

[118] 8 May 1851, PP 1852 (1428), enc. 3 in No. 10, pp. 78 ff.

[119] *De Zuid-Afrikaan*, 17 November 1851, p. 3. Ordinance No. 4 of 1851, in *Statute Law of the Cape of Good Hope* (Cape Town, 1862) p. 915

[120] Ross, *Borders of Race*, p. 277. Military courts-martial continued to try cases against Khoi who had joined the military levies or were in the Cape Mounted Rifles, who were accused of spreading disaffection. Corporal Caspar Sneyman, of the Kat River Levy was sentenced to seven years' transportation for spreading false reports: *De Zuid-Afrikaan*, 29 November 1851, p. 3.

[121] PP 1852–53 (1635), No. 44, p. 191 at pp. 193, 197.

[122] PP 1878 (c. 2079), enc. in No. 86, p. 220. He initially proposed instead a proclamation authorising the military to assist the police: PP 1878 (c. 2079), p. 218.

[123] PP 1878 (c. 2079), enc. in No. 86, p. 222 at p. 223.

[124] PP 1878 (c. 2079), enc. in No. 86, p. 221.

proclaimed,[125] he thought that rebels could be given fair trials in well-constituted martial courts. The model he had in mind was that of the tribunals set up in India after the Mutiny of 1857.[126] On 1 January 1878, he appointed five special commissioners to conduct the trial of rebels taken in the field, with one commissioner accompanying every military column. The commissioners were to have the powers of a circuit court, and could impose the death sentence (subject to confirmation by the government). They were to be instructed to ensure 'that all the essentials of a fair trial are secured', with specific charges and clearly stated evidence.[127] Frere's aim was to make hearings under martial law approximate as closely as possible to the legalism of a civilian trial.

When he saw these provisions, Prime Minister Molteno protested that the 'cumbrous machinery' it created would 'entirely frustrate the object which we had in view in proclaiming martial law'. In his view, all rebels taken in arms should be tried by drumhead courts-martial and shot without delay, while those who laid down their arms should be sentenced to death after summary trials by the commissioners, these sentences being subject to the Governor's approval.[128] However, Frere was concerned to avoid the kinds of trials which had caused so much controversy in Jamaica, and condemned drumhead courts as being little better than lynch law.[129] Molteno modified his views after his Attorney General clarified his advice, having studied Cockburn CJ's change in the Jamaican case of Nelson and Brand.[130] The purpose of drumhead trials, Stockenström now explained, was simply to allow

[125] PP 1878 (c. 2000), No. 79, p. 112. Frere felt that the colony's law regarding public order was 'extremely defective', not least because of the constant resort to martial law at times of unrest: the major defect was that the only legislation permitting disarmament was an 1837 Ordinance which applied only to 'foreigners' entering the colony: since the Ngqikas were British subjects, they might lawfully resist attempts to disarm them.
[126] PP 1878 (c. 2079), No. 1, p. 1. Frere had an excessively rosy view of the Indian commissioners (who had been appointed under statute): see Rudrangshu Mukherjee, 'The Kanpur Massacres in India in the Revolt of 1857: Reply', *Past and Present*, No. 142 (1994), pp. 180–181; and Chapter 1.
[127] PP 1878 (c. 2079), enc. in No. 86, pp. 219–220.
[128] PP 1878 (c. 2079), enc. in No. 86, p. 221.
[129] CO 879/12/8, enc. 12 in No. 120, p. 263; PP 1878 (c. 2079), enc. in No. 86, p. 221 at p. 222.
[130] CO 879/13/1, No. 6, p. 15. See also PP 1878 (c. 2144) LVI. 373, enc. 2 in No. 69, p. 125.

officers in the field to distinguish between captured rebels – who could justifiably be killed on the field of battle – and 'other enemies', who could not. If men were removed from the battlefield for trial by the commissioners, their execution after such trial would be illegal and would require an indemnity, which might be hard to obtain if they could have been tried in ordinary courts.[131] For his part, Frere was unconvinced by Stockenström's view of the powers of drumhead courts-martial,[132] and was sceptical that the Cape assembly would refuse an indemnity, given that his initial suggestion of using the High Court had been rejected by his ministers, and that a tribunal with a legalistic format had been put in place.[133] The Secretary of State, Sir Michael Hicks Beach (who had already sent Frere copies of the 1867 Circular Dispatches to help guide him),[134] similarly assumed that, if the trials were to be by special commissioners conducting fair hearings, there would be no difficulty in obtaining an Indemnity Act.[135] Officials in London also frowned on Molteno's desire 'for vigorous measures ... in the form of entrusting excited young officers & civilians to administer Lynch law'.[136]

In the event, martial law did not remain in place for very long after the dismissal of the ministry at the start of February. Soon after assuming office, the new Attorney General, Thomas Upington, reviewed the topic.[137] In his view, martial law 'strictly comes within the scope of military jurisdiction', and only 'courts martial properly constituted' could be seen as the kind of 'clearly legal tribunals' which could impose punishments under it. It was therefore necessary to withdraw the powers which had been conferred on the civilian special commissioners. At the same time, he noted that, if the special

---

[131] Stockenström also now thought that sentences pronounced by Frere's proposed special commissioners could be challenged by habeas corpus applications. PP 1878 (c. 2079), enc. 1 in No. 86, pp. 222, 223.
[132] CO 879/13/2, enc. 5 in No. 33, p. 48 at p. 49.
[133] PP 1878 (c. 2079), enc. in No. 86, p. 222–223. He also doubted the practicality of attempting to distinguish between rebels and enemies in the field.
[134] PP 1878 (c. 2079), No. 13, p. 21. Given that the Cape was now a colony with responsible government, officials doubted whether the circulars applied: CO 48/485/1442.
[135] CO 879/13/1, No. 50, p. 78.
[136] Minute dated 13 February 1878, CO 48/485/1783, f. 42.
[137] CO 879/13/2, enc. 3 in No. 33, p. 47 at p. 48; and PP 1878 (c. 2079), enc. 1 in No. 86, p. 225.

commissioners' powers were revoked, martial law would become a dead letter, since the prisoners had by now all been lodged in ordinary prisons awaiting trial by them. In this situation, there was no reason not to try them now in ordinary courts. On 25 February 1878, the appointment of the five special commissioners was duly cancelled and martial law lifted.[138] In all, fifty-two people had been tried by the commissioners, of whom thirty-six had been convicted. The longest sentence was one of twenty-one years' imprisonment with hard labour for aiding and abetting murder. Twenty-one others had been convicted of sedition, two of whom had been sentenced to ten years' imprisonment with hard labour.[139]

Officials in London were pleased that martial law had been 'practically a dead letter while it lasted'.[140] However, they wanted to establish which was the correct view of martial law – Stockenström's, Upington's or Frere's – a matter which was also debated both in the Cape parliament and in the Westminster parliament.[141] Edward Fairfield, barrister and clerk in the Colonial Office, felt that Upington's views were sound. Pointing out that the 1867 instructions contemplated that martial law should be administered only by the military, he was concerned that five civilian commissioners had been appointed. He was also concerned that they had imposed sentences of transportation beyond the colony, which even the most regular tribunal had no power to enforce. Assistant under-secretary of state W. R. Malcolm was also troubled by Stockenström's idea that the commander in the field could sift rebels from alien enemies and then kill them in cold blood, which seemed to confuse a right to kill in the heat of battle with a right to execute after the battle was over.[142] It was decided to ask the Law Officers for their opinion on which was the better view of martial law. They were also asked about the effect on any sentences of the ending of martial law, and whether an indemnity act would be needed.[143] The

---

[138] PP 1878 (c. 2100), No. 11, p. 17.   [139] CO 48/486/14675; WCA AG 97, ff. 208 et seq.
[140] Minute by Edward Fairfield, 10 April 1878, CO 48/485/4039.
[141] PP 1878 (c. 2144) LVI.373, No. 69, p. 117; *Parl. Debs.*, third ser., vol. 241, col. 126 (24 June 1878).
[142] As he put it, 'A preliminary sifting of the prisoners such as is suggested at once shows that no such over powering necessity exists, & that the slaughter is not for self preservation but for some quasi-judicial or deterrent object – in other words it would be a massacre.' Minute dated 11 April 1878, CO 48/485/4039.
[143] CO 879/13/5, No. 16, p. 12.

opinion given by the Law Officers John Holker and Hardinge Giffard on 23 July 1878 echoed Cockburn's position: acts done 'under the authority of so-called martial law' were justifiable only if necessary for the preservation of the state. They could not be given legal sanction by drumhead courts 'nor any other such tribunal'. The instructions given to the commissioners had been improper, since they were 'directed to do acts unnecessary for the restoration of order and having operation intended to continue after order was restored'. The Law Officers advised that as soon as the danger had passed and the necessity for martial law had eased, all those gaoled under it would be entitled to immediate release. An act of indemnity would also be necessary where illegal acts had been committed.[144] Hicks Beach duly advised the Governor to pass an indemnity act.[145]

The indemnity act which was passed indemnified the Governor and commanders of the forces and all acting under them for acts done *bona fide* 'in the prosecution and carrying out of the aforesaid military operations against the aforesaid enemies or rebels'.[146] The legislation said nothing, however, about the sentences of those imprisoned by the commissioners. When the Colonial Office questioned this in November 1878, Attorney General Upington admitted that the legislation might not render the continued incarceration of the prisoners valid after the end of martial law, and recommended passing a short act to legalise this. In his view, it would be out of the question 'to release the convicts who have all been guilty of the open acts of treason in which they were captured red-handed', and he felt that commuting the sentences would have a disastrous effect on 'the Kafir mind' which would see it as a sign of weakness.[147] The necessary legislation was duly passed.[148]

This episode provided the fullest discussion of martial law between the Jamaica controversy and the Anglo-Boer war. On this occasion, different views on what kind of approach to take were taken by the ministry, the Governor, and the metropolitan authorities: on this occasion, it was the common law view, stressed by the Law Officers in London, which prevailed over both the Governor's attempt at

---

[144] Law Officers' Opinion, 23 July 1878, CO 879/13/5, No. 179, p. 301.
[145] CO 879/13/5, No. 204, p. 341.
[146] The Military Operations Indemnity Act, No. 23 of 1878.
[147] Upington to Colonial Secretary, 3 January 1879, CO 48/489/2716.
[148] Martial Law Prisoners Detention Act, No. 21 of 1879.

a hybrid form of legalism and the ministry's desire to use unconstrained martial law power.

Detention without Trial

The general policy adopted during the frontier wars was to try rebels in martial law courts and to come to terms with enemies after having subdued them. Throughout this period, outside of times of martial law, a number of African leaders were also detained, though without the kind of *ad hominem* legislation which would later become common. For instance, after Ngqika had secured his position as the chief of the Rharhabe clans of the Xhosa with Somerset's help in the battle of Grahamstown in 1819, his main opponent Makhanda (also known as Nxele) was removed to Robben Island.[149] Over thirty years later, when Mlanjeni began to alarm the authorities with his prophecies, he was regarded as exerting a similar influence over the people as Nxele had, and plans were made to deal similarly with him.[150] 'If you catch this Mahomet let him be right well secured', Governor Smith wrote to his administrator in British Kaffraria, 'and he shall very speedily find himself in Robben Island.'[151]

Colonial administrators were aware that legal cover could be supplied easily enough. This is evident from Sir George Grey's response to an inquiry from Lord Canning, Governor-General of India, whether the last Mughal emperor of India, Bahadur Shah Zafar, could be banished to the Cape after his trial by a military commission in the wake of the 1857 'Indian Mutiny'. Responding to Canning's concern that special legislation would be needed to authorise it, Grey responded that, if Zafar arrived in South Africa, and 'this difficulty presents itself, then, as the Proclamation of the High Commissioner in British Kaffraria has the force of law, I shall issue the necessary Proclamation, and then place him in King William's

---

[149] See Julia C. Wells, *The Return of Makhanda – Exploring the Legend* (Scottsville, University of KwaZulu-Natal Press, 2012).
[150] Peires, *The Dead Will Arise*, pp. 1–2; Crais, *White Supremacy and Black Resistance*, p. 175.
[151] PP 1851 (1334), enc. 2 in No. 2, p. 15: as Peires points out (*The Dead Will Arise*, p. 8), he may have had in mind the lunatic colony in that place.

Town.'[152] For its own dissidents, however, the Cape authorities had other tools available. Another leader who ended his days on Robben Island was Maqoma. Within two years of his release from imprisonment in 1869, the authorities were troubled by his attempts to recover his old lands, which might 'give an immense deal of trouble to the Government'.[153] Since he was regarded as a prisoner still on parole, it was easy enough for the government to return him to Robben Island.

The Gcaleka chief, Hintsa, suffered an even worse fate at British hands. During the sixth frontier war, British forces had crossed the Kei into his territory, suspecting him of encouraging the Ngqika warriors and of harbouring stolen cattle for them. At the end of the war, when Hintsa sought to make peace with D'Urban, the Governor demanded an immediate payment of 25,000 head of cattle, with a further 25,000 to be delivered a year later. He also wanted Hintsa to punish those who had killed two British subjects and to deliver two hostages as security.[154] When Hintsa failed to produce the killers, D'Urban declared that 'I have a full and just right to consider and treat him as a prisoner of war, and send him to Cape Town.'[155] However, he opted instead to allow Hintsa to remain where he was, on condition that he assist the troops in locating the killers and collect the cattle. While riding out with Smith and George Southey and a corps of guides to collect the cattle, Hintsa made an attempt to escape. Both Smith and Southey gave chase, which ended in the chief being shot in the head. According to Smith, the chief had been warned that he would be shot if he tried to escape, and he was killed by Southey when he refused to surrender and raised an assegai.[156] Other reports indicated that Hintsa was hit several times before the fatal shot, and had cried out for mercy before he was killed; and that Southey had cut off one of his ears as

---

[152] Grey was equally confident that the Cape assembly would pass a law 'giving the same effect to the sentence passed upon the King of Delhi, as it would have had if it had been passed by the Supreme Court of this Colony'. Grey to Labouchere, 11 November 1857, CO 48/384, f. 279. In the end, Zafar was exiled to Rangoon.

[153] Barkly to Kimberley, 2 December 1871, WCA GH 23/31, p. [346]. His incarceration on Robben Island was authorised by Act 25 of 1857; see also Price, *Making Empire*, p. 353. For the background, see Timothy J. Stapleton, 'Reluctant Slaughter: Rethinking Maqoma's Role in the Xhosa Cattle-Killing (1853–1857)', *International Journal of African Historical Studies*, vol. 26:2 (1993), pp. 345–369.

[154] PP 1836 (279), enc. 7 (2) in No 3, p. 33 at p. 35.

[155] PP 1836 (279), enc. 12 (C) in No. 3, p. 42.

[156] Smith to D'Urban, 18 May 1835, PP 1836 (279), enc. 18 in No. 3, p. 48 at p. 49.

a trophy.[157] The killing was followed by an outcry, and, in July 1836, D'Urban ordered a military court of inquiry to investigate the circumstances of Hintsa's death.[158] Hintsa's fate continued to weigh on the mind of his son, Sarhili: it was one of the reasons why he refused to respond when Frere summoned him after the outbreak of the war of Ngcayecibi.[159]

The legal basis for holding enemy chiefs was often unclear, given the jurisdictional ambiguities in these territories. During the seventh frontier war, the Ngqika chief Sandile was held without trial for two months in 1847. He surrendered in October, after being given guarantees respecting his 'personal life', and agreed to go to Grahamstown, under the impression that he would be able to air his grievances and negotiate terms with the British.[160] He soon discovered that Pottinger regarded him simply as a prisoner. Pottinger had made plans as early as June for Sandile to 'be placed in confinement as a state prisoner, pending the pleasure of Her Majesty's Government'.[161] Two months later, he had proclaimed Sandile to be a rebel who had 'set at nought the paramount power which he had acknowledged', even though he was an African chief living in an area not under British rule.[162] The legal basis of his detention was unclear: martial law was not in operation in the Eastern Cape, and if he was to be regarded as a rebel, rather than as a prisoner of war, he should have been charged or freed.[163] But given that there was no likelihood that a habeas corpus application would be brought on his behalf, such legal niceties did not trouble the men on the ground. After two months' incarceration, he was finally released by Pottinger's successor as Governor, Sir Harry Smith, in a manner calculated to humiliate the chief. When Sandile was brought before the new Governor, he was (in his own words)

---

[157] Lester, *Imperial Networks*, pp. 124ff.
[158] *Proceedings of the Court of Inquiry on the Fate of the Caffer Chief Hintza* (Cape Town, 1837).
[159] CO 879/12/3, No. 74, p. 172.
[160] Le Cordeur and Saunders, *The War of the Axe*, pp. 217, 220–224, 234; Mostert, *Frontiers*, p. 927.
[161] PP 1847–48 (912), enc. 1 in No. 26, p. 88. [162] PP 1847–48 (912), No. 6, p. 126.
[163] When Pottinger contemplated reimposing it in mid 1847, it was not to authorise the detention of state prisoners, but to raise troops. Le Cordeur and Saunders, *The War of the Axe*, p. 130.

'dictatorial in the extreme'.[164] On asking Sandile who was his paramount chief – and being told it was Sarhili – Smith shouted in response, 'I am your paramount chief, and the kaffirs are my dogs!'[165] As a sign of his submission to his new overlord, Sandile was made to kiss the Governor's foot, and he was told that he was to surrender all his arms, or he would again be hunted down.

If Pottinger and Smith were untroubled by the legal basis on which they held an enemy chief, the matter was debated more in 1877 during the ninth war, when the Cape authorities contemplated holding Sarhili as a state prisoner. After destroying his kraal and driving his followers over the Mbashe River, they pondered whether they could try him for murder or rebellion; but they remained unsure whether he was to be regarded as an independent chief or as in some sense 'under' the British government, which had permitted him to return to Galekaland, albeit without becoming a subject.[166] In addition, as Attorney General Stockenström pointed out, there were 'grave technical difficulties' in the way of trying him for any acts committed outside the colony, though he felt that the government would be justified both in depriving him of the land to which he had been allowed to return and in incarcerating him.[167] Lord Carnarvon agreed that it would be impossible to try the chief, but thought that he could be held as a state prisoner when captured.[168] The point became moot when, with the onset of rains, Commandant Griffith gave up his pursuit of the chief.[169]

The legality of holding men whose status as rebel subjects or enemy aliens was unclear was more directly addressed at the end of the Griqua rebellion in 1878, when 140 prisoners were captured in Kokstad and removed to Cape Town. Neither of these places was under martial law, and no warrant was issued for their detention. Instead, Attorney General Upington was asked to take charge of them, and when they were sent to the Amsterdam Battery, verbal orders were given to the gaoler by the Colonial Secretary, J. Gordon Sprigg, to hold them. From

---

[164] PP 1847–48 (969), No. 6, p. 21.
[165] Mostert, *Frontiers*, p. 932; Harington, *Sir Harry Smith*, p. 101; Peires, *The Dead Will Arise*, pp. 5–6.
[166] CO 879/12/3, No. 149, p. 297 at p. 298.
[167] Opinion of A. Stockenström, 19 October 1877, CO 879/12/3, enc. 3 in No. 135, p. 282.
[168] CO 879/12/3, No. 144, p. 295.   [169] CO 879/12/3, enc. 1 in No. 157, p. 314.

the moment of their arrival at the Cape in June, their case was taken up by the Cape politicians Saul Solomon and Andries Stockenström. At the end of February, they had obtained a writ *de homine libero exhibendo* on behalf of two detainees, Willem Kok and Nathanial Balie, in a test case seeking their liberation. Making a verbal return to the court, Upington stated that they had been arrested as prisoners of war, and produced an affidavit from the Undersecretary for Native Affairs, which stated that the release of a large number of prisoners taken in war would damage the prospects of peace.[170] The status of the rebels was central to the case: if they were British subjects, they could not be held as prisoners of war but had to be tried. At the first hearing, Upington claimed there was a state of war with the nation of 'Adam Kok's Griquas', who were not British subjects, since the Griqualand East Annexation Act had not yet been implemented, and since their Raad had never agreed to the cession and had resisted British authority.[171]

In considering how to treat the Griquas, the court bore in mind a recent case which had raised similar questions, which had been tried by Chief Justice Henry de Villiers. This was the case of Nehemiah Moshoeshoe (son of the paramount chief Moshoeshoe), who had been charged with sedition for acts committed in Griqualand East. In 1865, the Griquas had driven Nehemiah out of Matatiele, an area in the north of Nomansland where he had settled in 1859, and an area which he was determined to recover. In September 1876, his followers clashed with the British Resident, Capt. Blyth, in Matatiele in a very minor skirmish.[172] Those who resisted authority were captured, and a court of inquiry was held by the resident magistrate. Nehemiah was found to be the instigator of a rebellion and was arrested for trial. After some hesitation about where he should be tried,[173] he was eventually tried on charges of sedition, riot and assault before the Chief Justice in King William's Town – 'clear evidence being forthcoming that he is

---

[170] *In re Willem Kok and Nathaniel Balie*, in Eben J. Buchanan, *Cases in the Supreme Court of the Cape of Good Hope during the Year 1879* (Cape Town, Juta, 1880), p. 45 [Juta Reports, 1879, p. 45] at pp. 49–50.
[171] *Cape Times*, 1 March 1879, p. 3.
[172] PP 1877 (c. 1748), No. 119, p. 148; No. 126, p. 155.
[173] See PP 1877 (c. 1748), No. 150, p. 186; enc. 1 in No. 172, p. 225; PP 1877 (c. 1776), No. 11, p. 6; enc. in No. 43, p. 55.

a British subject'.[174] Although the offences were committed outside the colony, the Cape court was able to try the case on the assumption that he was British, by virtue of its extraterritorial jurisdiction. In the event, Nehemiah was acquitted by the jury, which found that – even if he was a British subject – Blyth had no authority as chief magistrate in this area.[175]

The relevance of this case for the Griqua prisoners was this: if Nehemiah was treated as a subject who could be tried for sedition, why should the Griqua prisoners not also be treated as subjects and put on trial? Stockenström pointed to a wealth of evidence which showed that the British had regarded them as such. This included Sir George Grey's letter of 1861 that he would not assent to the Griquas moving to Nomansland as an independent people, but would only permit them to come as British subjects.[176] It was also evident from the affidavits given to the court that the Griquas had been treated as rebels, rather than as enemies. Indeed, Upington himself had thought that they were British subjects when they took up arms, but did not want to prosecute them as such, since he had no conclusive documentary evidence of their status. Since he considered that their discharge from custody in the event of the failure of any prosecution against them would be disastrous, he opted to hold them as prisoners of war.[177] Upington did not seem concerned by the fact that a state of war no longer existed, which might justify their continued incarceration: as he explained in October, in another context, 'It has been the custom in this Colony, rightly or wrongly, to detain without legislative enactment, after cessation of hostilities, prisoners of war whose release would be dangerous to the public safety.'[178]

---

[174] PP 1877 (c. 1776), enc. in No. 96, p. 133. The indictment is in *Natal Witness*, 1 May 1877, p. 3.
[175] *Cape Times*, 9 May 1877, p. 3. The result was welcomed in many sections of the press: see *Leselinyana La Lesotho*, 1 June 1877, p. 10; *Natal Witness*, 11 May 1877, p. 3.
[176] *Report of the Select Committee on Native Affairs* (Cape Town, 1874), CPP A.12-'73, p. 143. However, as Fairfield pointed out, 'a High Commissioner cannot naturalise aliens by his own authority': it required legislation or annexation. Minute 25 April 1879, CO 48/489/6159.
[177] Minute of Attorney General Thomas Upington, 3 March 1879, CO 48/489/6159.
[178] CO 879/16/5, enc. 3 in No.257, pp. 540–541, referring to the detention of the Zulu king Cetshwayo, discussed in Chapter 3.

From the beginning, it was clear that the application for the writ would be dropped if the detainees were guaranteed an early trial. Upington at first refused to give any undertakings on this point without an admission by the detainees of their subjecthood, but later indicated that he would be able to prove their status and so was prepared to go to trial. With this in prospect, the court was prepared to remand them to prison awaiting trial, while still allowing them the option to renew their application for a discharge. It was at this point that Upington backtracked, and obtained a postponement to bring affidavits to show that they were indeed prisoners of war. However, when the affidavits arrived, the most significant of them – Matthew Blyth's – showed conclusively that he had treated them as subjects all along. When the court reconvened in the middle of May, the Attorney General accordingly proposed that they be tried. He was now prepared to consent that they be released, albeit in order to be re-arrested; but Stockenström, who had agreed to a trial provided it was speedily brought, insisted that judgment should be given in the case before them, since he had received an undertaking from the crown that this would be a test case for all the men captured.[179]

Giving judgment, Chief Justice de Villiers noted that, if the men were prisoners of war – which was the crown's original claim – then the court could not interfere. However, he was unconvinced that they were such prisoners. For more than fifteen years, the British had exercised *de facto* jurisdiction over Griqualand East, and ever since Adam Kok's death it had been 'treated in all respects as a dependency of this colony'.[180] Nor was de Villiers convinced that the skirmishes with the Griquas – which had been described in the affidavits as a 'rebellion' – amounted to a state of war. Even if there had been one, it was admitted that it had ended. This (the Chief Justice noted) must have happened on the day the Griquas were defeated, which was before the detainees were arrested. De Villiers's analysis of the events from the affidavits showed that Blyth – in seeking to charge Lodewyk Kok and Adam Muis with offences – had purported to exercise the kind of jurisdiction over the Griquas which could be exercised only over British subjects. If they were not such subjects, they were perfectly within their rights to resist. On the other hand, if they were subjects,

---

[179] *Cape Times*, 16 May 1879, p. 3.   [180] *In re Willem Kok and Nathaniel Balie*, p. 61.

then the return to the writ which stated that they were prisoners of war was false. Turning to the court's power, the Chief Justice emphasised 'the bounden duty of the Court to protect personal liberty whenever it is illegally infringed upon'.[181] De Villiers's judgment was a ringing endorsement of the rule of law; and it was one which this liberal judge would refer back to on numerous subsequent occasions. In making his judgment, de Villiers addressed the argument that the country was in such an unsettled state, and the detainees men of such a dangerous character, that the court should not exercise a power which 'under ordinary circumstances might be usefully and properly exercised'. It was an argument he found unappealing. In a phrase much quoted thereafter, he declared,

> The disturbed state of the country ought not in my opinion to influence the Court, for its first and most sacred duty is to administer justice to those who seek it, and not to preserve the peace of the country. If a different argument were to prevail, it might happen that injustice to individual natives has disturbed and unsettled the whole tribe, and the Court would be prevented from removing the very cause which produced the disturbance ... The Civil Courts have but one duty to perform, and that is to administer the laws of the country without fear, favour or prejudice, independently of the consequences which may ensue.[182]

In the same judgment, he held that 'the rights of personal liberty, which persons within this colony enjoy, are substantially the same, since the abolition of slavery, as those which are possessed in Great Britain'.[183] For good measure, he added that, although there were times when martial law might be proclaimed, it could be justified only by necessity, and was exercised by the military at their peril, without any assistance from civil courts.

After de Villiers had ordered the detainees' release, they were re-arrested, with a view to putting them on trial.[184] The case attracted attention in London. In July, W. H. James raised their case in the Commons, and in the press, asking why they were now to be tried as

---

[181] *In re Willem Kok and Nathaniel Balie*, p. 64.
[182] *In re Willem Kok and Nathaniel Balie*, p. 66. See Albie Sachs, *Justice in South Africa* (Berkeley and Los Angeles, University of California Press, 1973), p. 245; Stephen Ellmann, *In a Time of Trouble: Law and Liberty in South Africa's State of Emergency* (Oxford, Oxford University Press, 1990), p. 210.
[183] *In re Willem Kok and Nathaniel Balie*, p. 64. [184] *Cape Times*, 16 July 1879, p. 3.

rebels, having been taken first to Cape Town as prisoners of war.[185] The Kokstad magistrate Charles Brownlee examined the detainees who had been sent back, releasing many on bail (varying from £5 to £100) and freeing others, and sent affidavits from the prisoners to show that they had been well treated.[186] Brownlee reported that the situation had calmed since the conviction of Lodewyk Kok for sedition (for a second time) in July.[187] In the end, a handful of the Griqua rebels were tried.[188]

Conclusion

During fifty years of frontier wars and rebellions, the authorities in the Cape Colony resorted to extra-legal detention without trial only on the rarest of occasions, as when Sandile was held without any charges for two months in 1847. On the frontier, captured enemies were more likely to be treated as prisoners of war, and released at the end of the conflict. The kinds of *ad hominem* detention laws which would frequently be used in much of the empire from the late 1870s were not passed at the Cape to deal with troublesome enemies of empire on the edges of its jurisdiction. This is not to say that other forms of 'lawfare' were not used: the trials in British Kaffraria of Maqoma, Mhala and Phato in 1857–1858 by a special tribunal established under the martial law regime in that possession allowed the imperial state to abandon the procedures and protections found in an ordinary trial, in order to remove the Xhosa chiefs to Robben Island and effectively destroy their power. The legal and constitutional right of the High Commissioner to act in this way here might have been questionable, but there was no forum in which this right could be

---

[185] *Parl. Debs.*, third ser., vol. 248, col. 969 (22 July 1879), col. 1297 (25 July 1879); *The Times*, 29 July 1879, p. 8.

[186] CO 879/16/5, enc. 3 in No. 256, p. 516. He reported that 'those who have land have returned to their farms and are cultivating them, others are in service, some are loafing about the canteens in Kokstadt, and several have been imprisoned for drunkenness and disorderly conduct'. PP 1880 (c. 2482), enc 1 (1) in No. 135, pp. 358–359. See also *Cape Times*, 30 July 1879, p. 3.

[187] CO 879/16/5, enc. 3 in No. 256, p. 516; *Natal Witness*, 31 July 1879, p. 2. Lodewyk had not been one of the Cape detainees, having been already imprisoned.

[188] See Samuel James Halford, *The Griquas of Griqualand* (Cape Town, Juta, 1949), p. 173; I. B. Sutton, 'The End of Coloured Independence: The Case of the Griqualand East Rebellion of 1878', *Transafrican Journal of History*, vol. 8:1/2 (1979), pp. 181–200, at p. 195; and *Cape Times*, 30 July 1879, p. 3.

Martial Law in the Eastern Cape, 1830–1880

questioned, even if the chiefs had had the means to do so.[189] However, even here, questions were raised by the Cape's Attorney General about how compatible the procedures used were with constitutional principles of the rule of law, which led to lesser punishments being imposed than had initially been contemplated. Moreover, when the Cape authorities did attempt to hold detainees without any form of legal cover, seeking to exploit the ambiguity between prisoner of war status and that of political prisoners, in the case of the Griqua rebels, their power to do so was robustly rejected by the Cape Supreme Court.

By contrast, the Cape did resort to martial law courts to try rebels on a number of occasions. Martial law remained unprovided for at the Cape by the kinds of statutes found in India, and so its use raised the same legal questions as were debated after the Jamaica rebellion. In this location, a view of martial law came to prevail which reflected the common lawyers' position, which sought to subject it to the rule of law. As shown by the debates of 1878, local political demands for swift exemplary action by use of martial tribunals could be checked within the colony by the legal and constitutional objections raised both by legal officials at the Cape and by imperial officers articulating a Diceyan view of martial law. At the same time, colonial officials accepted that the passage of indemnity acts could not be taken for granted, and that the actions to be indemnified needed to be evaluated for their necessity. The fact that this was so reflected both the political culture at the Cape – where a liberal judiciary and liberal politicians could always raise questions about executive action – and the watchfulness of ministers and officials in London.

---

[189] For the questions raised, see Price, *Making Empire*, pp. 333–334, n. 21.

3

Zulu Political Prisoners, 1872–1897

During the frontier wars, the Cape Colony used martial law trials to sentence and imprison rebels against its authority, but it did not resort to *ad hominem* legislation for this purpose. When such legislation was passed at the Cape, in 1874 and 1880, its purpose was to authorise the detention of prisoners sent from elsewhere in southern Africa. The first was Langalibalele, the Hlubi chief who was tried for rebellion against the authorities in Natal in an ad hoc 'customary' court in Pietermaritzburg; the second was the Zulu king Cetshwayo, who was taken prisoner by imperial forces at the end of the Anglo-Zulu war in 1879. In both of these cases, detention was used as a form of 'lawfare', a means of subduing potential African resistance to imperial rule.

The political and legal contexts in which these detentions took place contrasted strongly with the Cape. White settlement of Natal began only in 1824, and only in 1843 did Natal became a British colony, peopled by British settlers. These settlers were heavily outnumbered by an African population, to whom (under legislation introduced in 1849, which was amended in 1875) a distinct system of 'native' customary law applied, and who were denied the political rights given to whites.[1]

---

[1] Ordinance No. 3 of 1849; Law No. 26 of 1875. For the background to the 1849 measure, see PP 1850 (1292) XXXVIII. 501 sub-encs. 1–8 to enc. 7 in No. 9, pp. 38–48. For the restriction of political rights, see Law No. 11 of 1865.

Under the Secretary of Native Affairs, Theophilus Shepstone, a form of indirect rule was introduced, through a hierarchy of chiefs he patronised.[2] Consequently, in Natal, 'Europeans inhabited a separate privileged world legally removed from the majority of the population.'[3] The system of government introduced in Natal – and the political culture underpinning it – was thus significantly less liberal than that found at the Cape. Its illiberal nature was clearly exposed in the authorities' reaction to Langalibalele's apparent defiance, when he was tried under a hybrid form of customary law in which the Governor presided as supreme chief, and various measures were enacted to break up his tribe, after the colonial forces had taken brutal revenge against his people. In his trial, a form of law – quite unknown to metropolitan lawyers' idea of the rule of law – was used to exert colonial power over this chief.

Whereas Langalibalele's imprisonment was the work of colonial officials, Cetshwayo's was part of an imperial project. In the aftermath of the crisis in Natal, Lord Carnarvon at the Colonial Office turned his mind to the creation of a confederation in South Africa which would include the colonies and Boer Republics. For proponents of confederation, including Sir Bartle Frere (High Commissioner for South Africa) and Theophilus Shepstone (administrator of the newly annexed Transvaal), the project was threatened by the risk of African kingdoms uniting against them; a risk which could only be countered by extending British power over them. The Zulu kingdom was perceived to be one of the main threats, and so an ultimatum was issued in December 1878 to the Zulu king Cetshwayo to dismantle the military organisation on which his kingdom was built. In setting impossible demands, the bellicose British paved the way for the Anglo-Zulu war of 1879.[4] When the ultimatum expired, British soldiers invaded from Natal. The war ended with the capture of the king and his imprisonment at the Cape, with his

---

[2] Thomas V. McClendon, *White Chiefs, Black Lords: Shepstone and the Colonial State in Natal, South Africa, 1845–1878* (Rochester, University of Rochester Press, 2010).
[3] Norman Etherington, Patrick Harries and Bernard K. Mbenga, 'From Colonial Hegemonies to Imperial Conquest, 1840–1880', in Carolyn Hamilton, Bernard K. Mbenga and Robert Ross (eds.), *The Cambridge History of South Africa, Vol. I: From Early Times to 1885* (Cambridge, Cambridge University Press, 2009), p. 365.
[4] See Richard L. Cope, *Ploughshare of War: The Origins of the Anglo-Zulu War of 1879* (Pietermaritzburg, University of Natal Press, 1999).

incarceration under an *ad hominem* statute being an exertion of British sovereign power over this defeated king.

The treatment of Langalibalele and Cetshwayo bore the hallmarks of the use of exceptional powers to cement imperial rule. At the same time, the use of these powers did not remain unquestioned. Although Natal lacked the kind of liberal political culture found at the Cape, it did have one prominent family – that of Bishop J. W. Colenso – who took up these cases, both in local courts and on the imperial political stage. Officials in London, under pressure from a public opinion whose interest had been aroused by Colenso's campaigning, were also uncomfortable at the denial of due process, particularly to Langalibalele. The cases of these leaders attracted much attention in the metropolis, where the imperial authorities sought to put pressure on the colonial ones to ensure that the rule of law was observed. How effective that pressure would be depended in part on political needs within the colonies: as shall be seen, Langalibalele did not benefit from any pangs of conscience felt in London, though Cetshwayo was able to use his own political position to secure his freedom. At the same time, the experience of these detentions in the late 1870s helped shape the authorities' reaction to the next major conflict in the region: when Cetshwayo's son Dinuzulu was arrested in 1888, the authorities strove to stage a form of trial which would not attract the same kinds of criticisms as had been levelled at Langalibalele's. Like Napoleon, Dinuzulu would be exiled to St. Helena; but only after a trial and procedure which satisfied the Privy Council of its legality.

The Trial and Detention of Langalibalele

The clash which took place at Bushman's River Pass in the Drakensberg mountains in 1873, as Langalibalele led his followers out of the colony, may have been a minor skirmish, but it triggered a violent backlash, for this was the first time that white soldiers had been killed by Africans in Natal.[5] Langalibalele's amaHlubi people – numbering

---

[5] For histories, see McClendon, *White Chiefs, Black Lords*; Norman Herd, *The Bent Pine* (Johannesburg, Ravan Press, 1976); W. R. Guest, *Langalibalele: The Crisis in*

some 7,000 – had settled in Natal in 1848.[6] Their migration from Zululand was a result of its complex politics in the era of king Shaka and his successors. Once the dominant chiefdom in the region, the Hlubi's power had diminished, and when Langalibalele was installed as chief in 1836 or 1837, it was as a tributary of the Zulu monarch. This was a highly volatile political world, with rulers frequently being assassinated by their rivals. Although Langalibalele managed to navigate these difficult political waters well, by the late 1840s he fell foul of the Zulu king Mpande. Seeking refuge in Natal, the Hlubi initially settled on land on the Klip River, but after one year were removed to land near Champagne Castle. This unpopulated land was chosen for them by the British so that they would provide a buffer against bushmen raids. Land was also allocated to 5,000 Putini people, who were seen as vassals of the Hlubi.

Langalibalele was a co-operative ruler, who was prepared to supply warriors when called upon by the colonial authorities. One such episode would have a strong impact on his later views of colonial authority. In 1858, he contributed to a force sent against the Sithole leader Matshana, who was suspected of killing a man accused of witchcraft. After Matshana failed to answer a summons, John Shepstone (brother of the Secretary of Native Affairs, Theophilus) attempted to lure the chief into a trap, by persuading his followers to leave their weapons behind, and then using his own armed troops to seize Matshana. The plan did not succeed, for Matshana escaped, after twenty-five of his men had been shot dead, and Shepstone himself had been severely injured by an assegai.[7] The episode left a lasting distrust of the authorities in the minds of many Africans.

It was not until the early 1870s that Langalibalele's relations with the authorities began to deteriorate, in particular over the imposition of a marriage tax in 1869 and the requirement that Africans had to register their firearms.[8] Although Langalibalele's followers were not

---

Natal 1873–1875 (Durban, University of Natal, 1976); John Wright and Andrew Manson, *The Hlubi Chiefdom in Zululand-Natal: A History* (Ladysmith, Ladysmith Historical Society, 1983); and Jeff Guy, *The Heretic: A Study of the Life of John William Colenso, 1814–1883* (Scottsville, University of Natal Press, 1983).

[6] Wright and Manson, *The Hlubi Chiefdom*, ch. 3.

[7] Herd, *The Bent Pine*, ch. 7; CO 879/9/1, enc. 5 in No. 3, p. 232.

[8] See McClendon, *White Chiefs, Black Lords*, pp. 86–95; Wright and Manson, *The Hlubi Chiefdom*, p. 48; Guest, *Langalibalele*, pp. 34–35; PP 1874 (c. 1025) XLV. 415, No. 45, p. 69; PP 1875 (c. 1141) LII. 455, p. 21; PP 1875 (c. 1119) LIII. 229, pp. 26ff.

the only ones who failed to register their guns, he was singled out in particular for compliance. In March 1873, he was summoned to see the Resident Magistrate, John Macfarlane, in Estcourt. However, he failed to come, claiming to be too unwell to be able to travel.[9] Regarding this as defiance, Macfarlane referred the matter to Theophilus Shepstone in Pietermaritzburg. Over the next six months, Langalibalele would be summoned three times to see Shepstone, and would fail to comply on all three occasions. Langalibalele's reluctance to travel was the product not (as he claimed) of ill-health, but of fear. For only two chiefs had been summoned in this way in recent memory – Sidoi and Matshana – and both ended with their tribes being 'eaten up'.[10]

After the second summons in May – when he was warned that the Hlubi 'would cease to be a tribe' if he did not respond[11] – the pressure on Langalibalele relented, as Shepstone went to Zululand for the installation of Cetshwayo as king. In the meantime, Langalibalele was rumoured to have made contact with Molapo, son of the Basuto king Moshoeshoe, and Adam Kok, the ruler of Griqualand East, to ask them to shelter him in case of need. In an effort to lower the temperature, he also sent men to pay his overdue tax, and expressed his willingness to meet Macfarlane in Estcourt. Macfarlane was in no mood to compromise, however: he wanted the Hlubi's escape routes to Basutoland blocked, and for Langalibalele to be deposed and imprisoned.[12] The third and final summons was sent at the beginning of October, after Shepstone's return. In his message, Shepstone told Langalibalele that the 'Supreme Chief' – the Lieutenant-Governor, Sir Benjamin Pine – was astonished to hear 'that you had asked the Basuto Chiefs to receive your cattle under their protection, while you resisted an order of the Natal Government, which you expected would be made and enforced', and instructed him to come to Pietermaritzburg within fourteen days of receiving the message.[13] Shepstone sent two Africans – Umyembe and Mahoiza – to convey his message. They later claimed to have been humiliated when they got to the chief's kraal, by being

---

[9] PP 1875 (c. 1141), p. 21.
[10] See further Thomas McClendon, 'You Are What You Eat Up: Deposing Chiefs in Early Colonial Natal, 1857–58', *Journal of African History*, vol. 47:2 (2006), pp. 259–279.
[11] PP 1875 (c. 1025), p. 54.   [12] Wright and Manson, *The Hlubi Chiefdom*, pp. 55–57.
[13] PP 1874 (c. 1025), p. 65.

forced to strip naked, so that they could be searched for hidden weapons.[14] They reported that Langalibalele refused to obey the summons, recalling his own brother's murder when answering a summons from the Zulu king Dingane. He was, however, willing to pay a fine, and sent a messenger to Pietermaritzburg with a bag of gold as an instalment.[15] When the messenger got to the capital, the money was rejected, but the messenger was kept overnight, to allow the Natal authorities to prepare an expedition against Langalibalele without his receiving advance notice of it.

By now, Shepstone had decided to remove the Hlubi from their present location and to resettle them as labourers on white farms.[16] On 27 October 1873, the decision was taken to arrest Langalibalele. Pine decided to lead a military expedition against the chief, who was given an ultimatum of 3 November to surrender.[17] Meanwhile, the Hlubi lands were cordoned off by troops to prevent them migrating to Basutoland, and the remaining inhabitants were told to surrender or be treated as rebels. The military expedition turned out to be disastrous. Pine's plan had been for two sets of troops to meet at Bushman's River Pass at the top of the escarpment, where they would cut off the Hlubi. Because of poor maps, Captain Albert Allison's troops never reached the pass, while Major Anthony Durnford's were delayed by bad weather. By the time Durnford reached the pass, Langalibalele was already in Basutoland. When Durnford attempted to persuade the 200 Hlubi at the top of the pass to return, tensions mounted. With the thirty-seven-strong volunteer force heavily outnumbered and under instructions from Pine not to fire the first shot, the colonial forces withdrew.[18] As they descended the pass, they were fired on, with three men being killed. The official reaction to this clash was fierce. Pine proclaimed martial law in the locations occupied by the Hlubi and Putini tribes. Langalibalele and his people were declared to be rebels, and proclamations were issued breaking up both the Hlubi tribe and

---

[14] PP 1874 (c. 1025), p. 57.   [15] PP 1875 (c. 1141), p. 29.
[16] PP. 1874 (c. 1025), enc. 2 in No. 35, p. 33.
[17] PP 1874 (c. 1025), No. 6, p. 6; Proclamation, 2 November 1873, ibid., enc. 3 in No 35, p. 35.
[18] PP 1874 (c. 1025), No. 11, p. 9.

the Putini tribe, and confiscating their lands.[19] Violent retribution followed, with as many as 200 being killed by the end of the month.

Capture and Trial

The leaders Langalibalele hoped would shelter him assisted the colonial forces in effecting his capture, and at the end of December, he was marched in chains into Pietermaritzburg.[20] Martial law had been revoked on 22 November 1873, and the decision was taken to try prisoners 'under native law or under the common law, as circumstances require'.[21] Langalibalele was put on trial on 16 January 1874, just over a fortnight after his capture. He was to be tried under native law in a court presided over by Pine, in his capacity of Supreme Chief, accompanied by members of the Executive Council, as well as a number of nominated chiefs.[22] This was hardly an unbiased panel, including as it did both Pine and Theophilus Shepstone, who had already proclaimed Langalibalele a rebel, and D. Erskine, the Colonial Secretary, whose son was one the three men killed at the Bushman's River Pass. Furthermore, any appeal from its decision would go to the Executive Council, whose members were part of the panel.

The charges were an amalgam of notions vaguely drawn from English and African law. 'Langalibalele and the Hlubi tribe' were charged firstly with seditiously conspiring to leave the colony, 'well knowing that so to do was a defiant contravention of the law under which they live, and rebellion against the authority of the Supreme Chief'. This charge was premised on the assumption that any attempt to leave the territory of the Supreme Chief was regarded as rebellion under African customary law. Secondly, they were charged with killing the Queen's subjects in carrying out this design. Thirdly, Langalibalele was charged with encouraging his people to procure firearms, with the intention of resisting the authority of the Supreme Chief. Put together, in Pine's view, these charges amounted to 'high treason – for rebellion against the authority of Her Majesty the Queen'.

[19] PP 1874 (c. 1025), encs. in No. 1, pp. 13–14; No. 36, p. 36.
[20] Herd, *The Bent Pine*, pp. 42ff.; Wright and Manson, *The Hlubi Chiefdom*, pp. 69ff.
[21] PP 1874 (c. 1025), No. 12, p. 14; Proclamation, PP 1874 (c. 1025), p. 15.
[22] For a detailed account, see Herd, *The Bent Pine*, chs. 4–6.

The Lieutenant-Governor's powers relating to native law derived from an ordinance of 1849.[23] It conferred on him all the authority enjoyed under African customary law by the Supreme Chief, but did not specify exactly what his powers were. In fact, customary law was not monolithic. According to one manual drawn up for colonists, criminal matters were for the chief, but customary law was not bloodthirsty. Penal sanctions for most criminal cases – including murder – consisted of fines, with all the property of the accused being taken in the most serious cases.[24] These manuals did not dwell on crimes like rebellion – perhaps because it was evident enough from the sanguinary history of the Zulu nation that in such cases the response would be bloodthirsty. However, they did discuss the fact that it was common for Africans to seek refuge with another chief. 'When a Kafir wishes to leave his own chief and join another', the Tambookie agent wrote in 1856, 'he can only do so by flying at night in the most stealthy manner, if he has any live stock; for should his intention become known, he would most certainly be "eaten up"' – which meant the complete confiscation of his property.[25] At the same time, such compendia explained that the custom was for a chief to receive and protect any refugee who came to him – a custom which 'has greatly kept in check any arbitrary and oppressive conduct which the chiefs might have felt disposed to exercise towards their people'. If the refugee had committed a wrong, such as taking his neighbour's cattle with him, the receiving chief would return the cattle; but the refugee himself was protected.[26] The 'customary' law which Pine purported to exercise was thus rather indeterminate. Instead of acknowledging this, he began the hearing against Langalibalele by asserting that 'under their own law, if strictly administered, the prisoner would not be alive now'. He went on to declare that he would temper native law with Christian mercy, for Christians did not 'like to put men to death', at least without 'a fair and impartial trial'.[27]

---

[23] Ordinance No. 3 of 1849, which repealed so much of an Ordinance of 1845 (introducing Roman-Dutch law into Natal) which had supplanted African customary law.
[24] Col. C. B. Maclean, *A Compendium of Kafir Laws and Customs* (Cape Town, Saul Solomon & Co., 1866), pp. 23, 32, 35–40, 58–59.
[25] Quoted in Maclean, *Compendium*, p. 73.
[26] Maclean, *Compendium*, p. 116. Cf. Colenso's citation in PP 1875 (c. 1141), p. 2.
[27] PP 1874 (c. 1025), pp. 48–49.

In fact, the trial was highly irregular. As soon as the charges had been read out, Langalibalele was asked to plead. According to some reports, the chief (speaking in Zulu) denied committing murder or burglary, which suggested that he did not understand the charges.[28] He admitted going over the Drakensberg mountains with his people, and accepted that he had treated the Supreme Chief's messengers with disrespect, albeit out of fear. However, he denied asking his followers to procure weapons. He also laid the blame for the killings at Bushman's River Pass on his headman, Mabuhle, who was present at the spot. Once he had spoken, Pine observed that the chief's fear of the government's potential treachery was itself an 'aggravation of the insult' and then called on the chiefs present to express their views on his plea. Each of these men condemned Langalibalele. According to one of them, Mafingo, he was in the position of a dog, 'which if it bit its master, would be killed with little consideration'. The session ended with Pine reminding Langalibalele of the principle of collective responsibility in customary law which made the chief responsible for the acts of his tribe. Since the court regarded Langalibalele's statement as a guilty plea, evidence against him was heard only on the second day, 'for the purpose of placing on record the extent of the prisoner's crime'.[29] It was not until the third day that Pine agreed to allow a lawyer to appear for Langalibalele, though his lawyer – Harry Escombe – declined to proceed after being told that he could only make arguments in extenuation of Langalibalele's guilt. On the fourth day, Pine announced that the members of the Executive Council – who had been present so far 'to look on and assist with their advice' – would not appear on the following day, 'because, not forming a part of the Court, they cannot take part in judgment'.[30]

Pine handed down his judgment, convicting Langalibalele on all charges, on the sixth day. The judgment was grounded neither on any specific principles of African customary law nor on the criminal law of Natal, but rested on a mingling of Pine's assumptions about customary law with his perception of what English ideas relating to

---

[28] Herd, *The Bent Pine*, p. 52.   [29] PP 1874 (c. 1025), pp. 51, 53.
[30] PP 1874 (c. 1025), p. 68.

public order would require.[31] Thus, he noted that Langalibalele's defiance of magisterial authority, while not serious enough 'to warrant the use of forcible coercion according to our laws and custom', was 'perfectly clear and significant according to native law and custom', and was 'dangerous as an example to other natives and to the peace of the Colony'.[32] Similarly, while the colonial government had never treated the mere removal of a tribe as treason and rebellion, even though it was so regarded in native law, his attempts to take his cattle out of the colony under an armed escort manifested 'a determination to resist the Government with force and arms'. Turning to the clash at Bushman's River Pass, which had occurred in Langalibalele's absence, Pine declared that, since Mabuhle was his most trusted *induna*, who rejoined and remained with him after the killings, Langalibalele was to be taken to have identified himself with the murders and to be responsible for them. Langalibalele's apparent *ex post facto* complicity in the killings played a central part in Pine's determination, though it was an inference which was open to challenge. Indeed, during a second trial which began before the judgment was given, in which Langalibalele's seven sons and three *indunas* were tried, evidence was presented that Langalibalele had given special instructions to Mabuhle not to shoot first in any clash.[33] Although Pine stated that Langalibalele was liable to the death penalty, he sentenced him to banishment or life transportation, after taking into account extenuating circumstances.[34] This was a sentence unrecognised by African customary law and not authorised by colonial law.

Bishop Colenso's Appeals

As Bishop Colenso observed the trial, he became increasingly aware of flaws in the case against Langalibalele. For the bishop, the treatment of the chief raised vital matters of principle, which he felt morally compelled to take up, even though it would alienate him from the

---

[31] Compare this with his explanation to Carnarvon that the proclamation breaking up the tribe 'was drawn up by Mr Harding the late Chief Justice and myself with the English law books before us defining the circumstances under which persons were guilty of aiding and abetting treasonable practices': CO 179/115/815.
[32] PP 1874 (c. 1025), p. 74.   [33] PP 1875 (c. 1119), p. 14.   [34] PP 1874 (c. 1025), p. 75.

majority of his white Natal congregation, and lead to the end of his close friendship with Shepstone. With Colenso's aid, Langalibalele first lodged an appeal to the Executive Council, under the 1849 ordinance. His petition challenged Pine's power to constitute the court which tried the chief, and argued that only a colonial court had the jurisdiction to deal with offences (such as the killings at Bushman's River Pass) which occurred outside the colonial borders. The petition claimed that the proceedings had been conducted in an irregular manner, and also asked for new evidence to be taken into account, notably that presented at the trial of his sons. Finally, it was argued that the sentence was *ultra vires* under the 1849 Ordinance, which gave the Supreme Chief only the power to depose.[35]

Since this was a political body a number of whose members had participated in the trial, it could have come as no surprise that the Executive Council rejected all the arguments in the petition.[36] In its view, the fact that serious crimes had hitherto been tried in the colonial courts did not oust the Supreme Chief's native jurisdiction, particularly in cases involving offences with which the colonial courts could not deal, such as the removal of a tribe. In making its pronouncements on the nature of native law, the Executive Council both rejected and drew on the Cape compendium of native law cited by Colenso, as suited its arguments.[37] It held that a Supreme Chief, who had a power of life and death, also had the power to banish. Nor was the absence of legal representation a ground for objection, since native law knew no such thing as a professional lawyer. As for the fact that Pine had already expressed a view on the chief's guilt before the trial, '[p]rejudice in the mind of a judge does not render a judgment invalid.'[38] With all of Langalibalele's arguments rejected and the conviction confirmed, the public in attendance burst into applause.

Having failed to persuade Pine of the illegality of his initial decision, Colenso made a second attempt to challenge the sentence against the chief, by applying to the Supreme Court for an interdict to prevent his

---

[35] See PP 1875 (c. 1141), pp. 137ff.; *Natal Witness*, 26 June 1874, p. 3; 14 July 1874, pp. 2–3.

[36] *Natal Witness*, 17 July 1874, p. 6. Colenso also printed the judgment with his own answers: PP 1875 (c. 1141), pp. 149ff.

[37] See minute by E. Fairfield, dated 5 September 1874, CO 179/115/10411.

[38] *Natal Witness*, 17 July 1874, p. 6.

removal.[39] Colenso's efforts failed again, when the court rejected the argument that there was no power to deport anyone from the colony save under imperial legislation regulating the removal of prisoners, by instead holding that native chiefs had the power to transport inferior chiefs to any place they wished. Acting Chief Justice Sir Henry Connor added for good measure that the court would never issue an interdict against the Governor.[40] Colenso was exasperated by the result, particularly when he discovered that Pine already knew that London felt his powers were constrained by the Colonial Prisoners Removal Act of 1869.[41] With the application to forbid his removal having been dismissed, Langalibalele and his son were put on a steamer on 3 August 1874 and sent to the Cape, where legislation had been passed in July at Pine's request to authorise their detention, just as if they had been sentenced by the Supreme Court of that colony.[42]

In fact, Pine had asked the Cape government to hold Langalibalele on Robben Island after his conviction even before his trial had begun.[43] His request for legislation shows that the Lieutenant-Governor was aware that, even if he had the power to banish the chief, there was no legal authority to imprison him at the Cape without the kind of legislation passed to detain Napoleon at St Helena. The bill proved controversial in the Cape, where it was strongly opposed by Saul Solomon and John X. Merriman, but its passage gave legal authority of the most formal kind for his incarceration.[44] Pine thus appeared to have succeeded in his use of 'lawfare' – using an improvised form of 'native law', endorsed by the Supreme Court of Natal, and then secured by *ad hominem* legislation – to subdue this troublesome chief, and give a signal to the African population of Natal of the power of the colonial state. It now remained to be seen how the Colonial Office would react.

---

[39] *Natal Witness*, 17 July 1874, p. 7; PP 1875 (c. 1141), p. 163.

[40] *Natal Witness*, 17 July 1874, p. 7. A native of Dublin, Connor practised as a barrister there from 1841 to 1854, before commencing a judicial career in the Gold Coast and Natal: see Steven D. Girvin, 'The Architects of the Mixed Legal System', in Reinhard Zimmermann and Daniel Visser (eds.), *Southern Cross: Civil Law and Common Law in South Africa* (Oxford, Clarendon Press, 1996), pp. 110–111.

[41] 22 & 23 Vict. c. 10.   [42] Cape Act No. 3 of 1874.   [43] PP 1874 (c. 1025), No. 39, p. 38.

[44] Herd, *The Bent Pine*, p. 83; Phyllis Lewsen, *John X. Merriman: Paradoxical South African Statesman* (New Haven, Yale University Press, 1982), pp. 44ff.

Reactions in London

While settler opinion in Natal stood strongly behind Pine, Colenso strove to ensure that the public conscience in the motherland would be pricked. By the time Langalibalele's trial was in progress, organisations such as the Anti-Slavery Society, the Peace Society and the Aborigines Protection Society were already publicising the recent 'Atrocities in Natal' in the press, and putting pressure on the government for a full investigation, on the lines of the Jamaica inquiry.[45] Colenso wrote his own account, *Langalibalele and the Amahlubi Tribe*, which was presented to parliament in January 1875.[46] Public opinion in England was also informed by the publication of a series of Blue Books containing the correspondence between London and Natal. Commenting on this material at the end of 1874, the lawyer John Westlake described the trial of the chief as a 'farce'.[47] For Thomas Gibson Bowles, the case raised the question of whether men who were appointed to administer the law were to be allowed to place themselves above the law.[48] There was consequently strong pressure on the metropolitan authorities to ensure that the rule of law was observed in their colony.

The Colonial Office also began to take a closer interest in the case after February 1874, when the Earl of Carnarvon returned to the post he had held during the Jamaica crisis, after the fall of the Liberal government. Both Carnarvon and his officials were troubled by the trial and sentence.[49] One of these officials, the barrister Edward Fairfield, was particularly sceptical about the applicability of native law in this case, commenting that 'it is only by the fiction of considering

---

[45] *Glasgow Herald*, 22 January 1874, p. 2; PP 1874 (c. 1025), No. 22, p. 22; No. 44, p. 42.

[46] This was written in answer to *The Kafir Revolt in Natal in the Year 1873, Being an Account of the Revolt of the Ama-Hlubi Tribe under the Chief Langalibalele, and the Measures Taken to Vindicate the Authority of the Government, Together with the Official Record of the Trial of the Chief and Some of His Sons and Indunas* (Pietermaritzburg, Keith & Co., 1874).

[47] John Westlake, 'The Kafir Revolt of 1873', *Fortnightly Review*, vol. 22 (December 1874), pp. 701–713 at p. 707.

[48] T. G. Bowles, 'The Case of Langalibalele', *Macmillan's Magazine*, vol. 31 (1875), pp. 331–339 at pp. 331, 339.

[49] PP 1874 (c. 1025), No. 47, p. 78; No. 50, p. 79; PP 1875 (c. 1121) LIII. 295, No. 5, p. 4; enc. 1 in No. 5, p. 8.

Sir B. Pine a Native "whose ignorance and habits unfit him for civilized life" that a crime against him is thought within Native Law at all'.[50] He also doubted that Pine had an inherent power as Supreme Chief to impose penalties unknown to native law.[51] Officials were also concerned about the passage of the Cape Act to legalise Langalibalele's detention, which appeared to by-pass the provisions of the Colonial Prisoners Removal Act. William Malcolm thought that the Cape act was *ultra vires*, in recognising and punishing an offence committed outside the colony, and should be disallowed. The view in Downing Street was that Langalibalele's punishment should be commuted and he should be allowed to resettle in the colony.[52]

In seeking a solution to the problem of Langalibalele's detention which would satisfy metropolitan demands for the rule of law to be observed without antagonising opinion in the colonies, Carnarvon consulted Colenso and Shepstone, both of whom had come to London to lobby for their view. A despatch was then drafted which set out the Secretary of State's own view of the case. It was clear that Carnarvon did not see Langalibalele's conduct as constituting any kind of rebellion. As he saw it, neither Langalibalele's recalcitrance in complying with the new marriage regulations nor his failure get to his people to register their arms were serious matters; though his refusal to appear when summoned was an offence to which the government was bound to respond. At the same time, he accepted that the chief's failure to appear had been driven by fear and that the crisis might not have occurred if matters had been handled differently. Instead, if greater pains had been taken to 'sift the rumours' then 'a truer conception of his attitude towards the Government would have been formed'. Unlike Pine, Carnarvon did not see Langalibalele's flight as an act of treason. He was also critical of the trial, which he felt should have been conducted under the ordinary law. Although he accepted that Langlibalele deserved punishment for failing to appear when summoned, he thought the sentence should be reduced.[53]

[50] Minute dated 5 September 1874, CO 179/115/10411.
[51] Minute dated 7 September 1874, CO 179/115/10414; see also Note by W. R. Malcolm (assistant under-secretary of state), 7 September 1874, CO 179/115/10411.
[52] Minutes by Fairfield and Malcolm, 7 September 1874, CO 179/115/10414.
[53] Draft despatch, November 1874, CO 879/7/6.

While Carnarvon was pondering his options, the Law Officers gave their opinions on two matters. First, they reported that the Cape Act authorising his detention was not void for being repugnant to the Colonial Prisoners Removal Act: although the Natal court had no power to deport Langalibalele, he was in legal custody in the Cape by virtue of their legislation.[54] Secondly, they agreed with Carnarvon that the best way to deal with him would be to offer him a pardon on condition that he remained in the Cape, even though it would be legally impossible to enforce the condition.[55] Since the sentence of the Natal court was void, the crown had no power to commute it into a sentence of banishment in the Cape; and since he was in prison 'only by reason of fictitious sentence for some imaginary crime' declared by the Cape legislature, the crown had no power to impose a penalty beyond that provided for by the Cape's lawmakers. This advice having been given, Colenso was called to the Colonial Office and told that Langalibalele would be allowed to leave Robben Island, but would not be permitted to return to Natal. Instead, a location would be provided for him in the Cape, where his followers could join him.[56] Two days later, a despatch based on the November draft was sent to Pine, who was to be recalled. After giving a detailed review of the proceedings, almost in the manner of a court of appeal, Carnarvon concluded that 'the guarantees which every English Court of Law desires for its own sake and in the ends of justice to secure' had not been accorded to Langalibalele. Nonetheless, since he merited some punishment for his disobedience, he was to be moved to a location in the Cape, with strict instructions not to re-enter Natal.[57]

Colenso returned to the Cape, expecting to be able to tell the chief the news of his imminent release. However, by the time he reached Cape Town, the Cape government had decided not to release Langalibalele, since they felt it would be impossible to control him if he were released from Robben Island.[58] They also informed the Colonial Office that, if the Act authorising Langalibalele's detention were disallowed, they would have no option but to return him to Natal. This response disappointed Carnarvon, who wanted the matter settled without a major debate in parliament; but he remained

[54] Opinion dated 12 November 1874, CO 885/12.
[55] Opinion dated 27 November 1874, CO 885/12.   [56] Guy, *The Heretic*, p. 228.
[57] PP 1875 (c. 1121), No. 26, p. 86.
[58] PP 1875 (c. 1158) LIII. 401, No. 1, p. 1 with enclosures.

conscious of the need to respect the autonomy of ministers in a responsible government. He advised the Cape government to pass legislation which would allow them to remove Langalibalele from Robben Island while still restricting his movements outside the location to which he would be settled. In the meantime, he delayed disallowing the Act.[59]

The matter came before the House of Lords in April 1875, in a debate which pitched past and present secretaries of state against each other. In the debate, it was the members of the Conservative government who sought to defend an imperial vision of the rule of law, while the recently ousted Liberal leaders defended the rights of the responsible government at the Cape to deal with this question. The Liberals took the view that the Colonial Office should defer to local knowledge and not seek to overturn the views of the Cape assembly and the Natal Supreme Court.[60] As Grey saw it, colonial Governors had to be allowed to act in a vigorous way if 'the obedience of an almost barbarous people many times out-numbering the White population was to be preserved'.[61] Kimberley also thought that his successor in office had no power to order the Cape to move the chief. Carnarvon, however, vigorously defended his policy, condemning the trial and sentence and observing that the so-called 'rebellion' only merited the name of a 'disturbance, which a few policemen would have effectually dealt with'. He felt the Cape legislation could not stand, since it implemented an illegal sentence on a man entitled to all the rights of a British subject. Indeed, it was the duty of the imperial authorities to condemn injustices committed in any part of the empire.[62] Lord Chancellor Cairns agreed: 'England exercises too wide a sway, has too large an Empire, and interests much too high at stake, to allow or tolerate that which is an absolute and thorough injustice to be perpetrated with impunity in any part of her dominions.'[63]

Such fine words masked the fact that the government's policy was not to liberate Langalibalele, but to move him to another location. Pine's successor, Sir Garnet Wolseley, was determined that Langalibalele should not return to Natal, since it would 'unsettle the minds' of the

---

[59] PP 1875 (c. 1158), No. 2, p. 5. [60] *Manchester Guardian*, 14 April 1875, p. 5.
[61] *Parl. Debs.*, 3rd ser. vol. 223, col. 671 (12 April 1875).
[62] *Parl. Debs.*, 3rd ser. vol. 223, cols. 683, 688 (12 April 1875).
[63] *Parl. Debs.*, 3rd ser. vol. 223, col. 699 (12 April 1875).

Africans, and increase the influence of a chief with reputed supernatural powers who had defied the government. In his view, if the Cape could not accommodate him, he should be sent somewhere distant like St Helena. Wolseley was also worried about the impact of public opinion in England on the Secretary of State, and warned him not to be taken in by 'sensational narratives'.[64] In the meantime, the Cape parliament began to debate legislation to permit the further detention of the chief. The bill proved controversial, and generated strong opposition, but eventually passed at the beginning of June. It repealed Act No. 3 authorising Langalibalele's detention, and made provision for a location to be defined where Langalibalele, his son and his followers could live under regulations restricting them to the location. The legislation presumed that Langalibalele was to be held for the period of his sentence – a life term – but it gave power to the Governor, acting on advice from the Executive Council, to release him.[65] Land was chosen at Uitvlugt, on the Cape Flats, where he was moved in August.[66]

As the Colonial Office perceived, Langalibalele's removal and detention involved the use of exceptional powers by a Governor determined to make a very public example of those who defied his authority. His use of 'lawfare' raised serious questions in London about how such uses of power could be reconciled with metropolitan understandings of the rule of law. In the end, however, the chief's detention was made legally bullet-proof not by the claims of the Governor to act in his capacity of a supreme African chief, but by *ad hominem* legislation at the Cape. However concerned they may have been about due process not having been followed in Langalibalele's case, the Colonial Office was more swayed by the hawkish Wolseley's insistence that the chief be kept out of Natal, and by the practical impossibility of coming to any other legal arrangement which would suffice. Put into a constitutionally legitimate form by statute, Carnarvon was prepared for political reasons to accept Langalibalele's exceptional treatment. In 1880, the Colonial Office, with Kimberley back at the helm, made inquiries as to whether he could be released,[67] but Natal's Legislative Council remained

---

[64] PP 1875 (c. 1342–1), No. 25, p. 27.   [65] PP 1875 (c. 1342–1), enc. 1 in No. 30, p. 33.
[66] As Malcolm minuted on 23 June 1875, 'if the bill now in progress at the Cape becomes Law the difficulty of settling the Kafir chief will be met': CO 179/117/7028.
[67] CO 879/17/19, pp. 5, 9; CO 48/494/10200. His son Malambule was sent back to Natal in August 1878, on medical advice: CO 48/494/1480.

strongly opposed to his release.[68] He was not to return to Natal until 1887, when he was restricted to an area near Pietermaritzburg.

Cetshwayo's Capture and Detention

One reason for Langalibalele's continued detention in the Cape was that, by the early 1880s, the Zulu king Cetshwayo was also being held there, and there were fears that, if Langalibalele were freed, Cetshwayo's family would 'intrigue for his release'.[69] Cetshwayo had been captured on 31 August 1879 at the end of the Anglo-Zulu War, and was removed to Cape Town, where he arrived on 15 September.[70] The Zulu king had been captured as a prisoner of war, but it was soon evident that his continued detention was essential for British imperial policy, which required his deposition from the throne, and the division of his country into separate chieftainships.[71] Like Napoleon, this was a ruler who needed to be kept away from his kingdom.

With the decision having been taken to hold Cetshwayo as a state prisoner at the Cape, there was some discussion over whether special legislation was needed to authorise his detention.[72] According to the Cape's Attorney-General, Thomas Upington, the king could be held as an alien enemy without such legislation, since he was at war with the empire of which the Cape was a part.[73] Invoking Vattel, he argued that the liberation of prisoners was one of the articles of peace, and that prisoners could be held until a formal peace had been concluded.[74]

---

[68] PP 1880 (c. 2695) LI. 449, No. 24, p. 54; PP 1881 (c. 2950) LXVII. 301, enc. 2 in No. 3, p. 4. See also PP 1880 (c. 2695), enc. 2 in No. 33, p. 74. By 1883, the Executive Council was no longer opposed to his return, at least under certain conditions, but the Legislative Council remained opposed: CO 879/20/5, pp. 7, 26.

[69] CO 879/18/5, p. 133.

[70] On Cetshwayo, see further Jeff Guy, *The Destruction of the Zulu Kingdom: The Civil War in Zululand, 1879–1884* (Pietermaritzburg, University of Natal Press, 1994 [1979]); and C. T. Binns, *The Last Zulu King: The Life and Death of Cetshwayo* (Longmans, London, 1963).

[71] CO 879/16/5, sub-enc. 2 in No. 10, p. 28; enc. in No. 70, p. 135.

[72] This was the recommendation of Wolseley: PP 1880 (c. 2695), enc. 2 in No. 6, p. 4.

[73] CO 879/16/5, enc. 13 in No. 116, p. 281.

[74] PP 1880 (c. 2695), enc. 3 in No. 7, p. 7. Upington did, however, ask for a warrant be issued to authorise the detention, fearing that without one an application for such

However, the Law Officers in London, who had in mind the Napoleonic precedent, advised that legislation would be necessary to authorise his continued detention after the *status belli* had ended.[75] Secretary of State Sir Michael Hicks Beach duly asked the Cape government to introduce legislation as soon as possible, which should also include indemnity provisions. In the meantime, Cetshwayo was to be held in military custody.[76]

It was not only the Zulu king whom Wolseley wanted detained at the Cape. After having defeated Cetshwayo, he had resumed the campaign against the Pedi chief Sekhukhune, another of the African leaders who was perceived to stand in the way of imperial interests after the British annexation of the Transvaal in 1877. The campaign against Sekhukhune was interrupted by the Anglo-Zulu war, but in December 1879, Wolseley (who had returned to South Africa as commander-in-chief) defeated the Pedi and brought their leader to Pretoria. Just as Wolseley wanted Cetshwayo far away from Zululand, so he wanted Sekhukhune far away from Transvaal.[77] The Colonial Office concurred with this plan, and saw financial benefits in detaining both leaders on the same farm as Langalibalele.[78] Legislation was accordingly passed in Natal to allow Sekhukhune to be moved through that colony on the way to the Cape, without any risk of a habeas corpus application being brought to free him there.[79] In the event, this legislation was not needed for Sekhukhune, who remained in Pretoria until he was freed under the terms of the Pretoria Convention of 3 August 1881, at the end of the war which re-established the

---

a writ might succeed. CO 879/16/5, enc. 13 in No. 115, p. 281; enc. 7 in No. 140, p. 332. Secretary of State Hicks Beach expressed some concern at the issue of a warrant which gave it a 'quasi-civil character', rather than moving Cetshwayo simply under military auspices: CO 48/491/15570.

[75] Law Officers' opinion, 20 October 1879, CO 885/12, No. 210.

[76] CO 879/16/5, No. 178, p. 381. For Hicks Beach's awareness of the difference between military and civil custody, see also CO 879/16/5, No. 283, p. 581.

[77] PP 1880 (c. 2695), enc. 3 in No. 10, p. 9.   [78] PP 1880 (c. 2695), No. 15, p. 17.

[79] *Natal Witness*, 29 January 1880, p. 3; Act No. 20 passed in March 1880. Although amended to allow only the detention of anyone convicted of a crime, or being deported 'with the object of being brought to trial, or being prisoners of war, or otherwise legally deported', it also declared the colonial courts incompetent to inquire into the circumstances under which such person was detained or apprehended.

South African Republic, under British suzerainty.[80] It remained on the books, however, and would be drawn on in future.

Throughout the first half of 1880, Cetshwayo was kept as a military prisoner of war in the castle at Cape Town, pending legislation to allow his civilian detention. No legal challenge was made to his detention, though the ex-king did write letters both to Frere and to the Queen asking to be sent back to Zululand as a private person.[81] While neither the High Commissioner nor the Colonial Office would countenance this,[82] they felt that he should be allowed greater personal freedom than was permitted to Langalibalele, given that he had not resisted British authority, but had been an enemy.[83] Legislation was introduced in the Cape House of Assembly in June to permit the government to continue to keep Cetshwayo and Sekhukhune as prisoners of war.[84] Officials in London at first worried that the bill contained no indemnity clause, which caused concern since Cetshwayo's 'military' detention hitherto might not have been lawful, and '[t]here are some partisans in England who will prosecute [Frere] if they get a chance.'[85] The bill was consequently amended to include an indemnity provision.

According to the act which passed, Cetshwayo and Sekhukhune would be detained 'during the pleasure of the Governor'. This left it unclear whether the decision to free them would lie in the hands of the imperial authorities or in those of the Cape's responsible government.[86] In Langalibalele's case, the Cape's legislation had

---

[80] See Peter Delius, *The Land Belongs to Us: The Pedi Polity, the Boers and the British in Nineteenth-Century Transvaal* (Berkeley, University of California Press, 1984), p. 251.

[81] PP 1880 (c. 2695), enc. in No. 18, p. 31; enc. 2 in No. 20, p. 48.

[82] At the Colonial Office, Herbert noted that 'we have entered into engagements with the Zulu Chiefs, wholly inconsistent with the return of Ketchwayo to Zululand': Minute 10 June 1880, CO 48/494/8342.

[83] PP 1880 (c. 2695), No. 25, pp. 55–56; No. 36, p. 76. [84] PP 1880 (c. 2695), No. 29, p. 57.

[85] Minute dated 11 June 1880, CO 48/494/8621.

[86] When the bill was debated in Cape Town, Saul Solomon objected to the wording and argued that it should be made clear that they were held during Her Majesty's pleasure; but his opponents argued that he wanted to leave the power to release Cetshwayo in London's hands, so that the Aborigines Protection Society could pressure the government there to order his release. PP 1880 (c. 2695), enc. 2 in No. 29, p. 58.

empowered the Governor to release 'with the advice of the Executive Council'; but this phrase was omitted in the bill relating to Cetshwayo, which suggested that the Governor could act without ministerial advice, on the direction of the crown.[87] From London's point of view, while the Cape was to host Cetshwayo, he was to remain an imperial prisoner. The act was duly passed in July, with the proviso that it would take effect only on a date named by the Governor in a proclamation. In the meantime, he remained a military prisoner of war.[88] The Colonial Office now began to pressure the Cape authorities to move Cetshwayo to a civilian location where he might have greater liberty.[89] Arrangements were made for Cetshwayo and his followers to be located on a farm at Oude Molen which would adjoin the land on which Langalibalele was located, and, after the requisite proclamation had been issued, he was moved there at the beginning of February 1881.[90]

Like Langalibalele, Cetshwayo had the strong support of Bishop Colenso. In November 1880, he visited Cetshwayo, and suggested that he petition the crown to be allowed to present his case in England.[91] The following March, Cetshwayo requested permission to lay his case before the Queen and the British parliament.[92] Secretary of State Kimberley's response was not encouraging. Since it was impossible to undo the settlement reached in Zululand, Cetshwayo could not hope to be 'released from the detention which paramount considerations of policy render unavoidable'.[93] Soon

---

[87] Officials at the Colonial Office, who had spotted this, were sure that the ministers did not wish to leave the power in London's hands, 'and are not aware of the trap which this bad drafting is laying for themselves'. Minute 14 July 1880, CO 48/494/10200.

[88] Act No. 6 of 1880, in PP 1881 (c. 2950), enc. 1 in No. 10, p. 25. It was implemented by proclamation in the *Government Gazette* on 25 January 1881: PP 1881 (c. 2950), No. 10, p. 26.

[89] PP 1881 (c. 2740) LXVI. 1, No. 25, p. 30; PP 1881 (c. 2950), No. 1, p. 1.

[90] Robinson to Kimberley, 1 February 1881, PP 1881 (c. 2950), No. 6, p. 18. For the regulations imposed on him at Oude Molen, see PP 1881 (c. 2950), enc. 9 in No. 8, p. 23.

[91] Guy, *Destruction of the Zulu Kingdom*, p. 126.

[92] PP 1881 (c. 2950), enc. 2 in No. 42, pp. 129, 138. See also PP 1881 (c. 2866) LXVII. 67, enc. 2 in No. 95, p. 185.

[93] PP 1881 (c. 2950), No. 69, p. 189 at p. 190.

after this news reached Cetshwayo, Deputy Governor Smyth visited the ex-king, and found him 'in a very depressed condition', contemplating suicide.[94] Cetshwayo continued to plead his case, asking the Governor, Sir Hercules Robinson, '[b]y what law of nations am I kept here without even a chance of seeing the people that have talked so untruthfully against me[?]'[95] His entreaties eventually pricked the consciences of both Kimberley and Gladstone, who were uneasy about the Zulu war, and who were under increasing pressure from growing Liberal sympathy in England for the ex-king. In September, Robinson was informed that the government was willing to entertain Cetshwayo's request to visit England.[96] Cetshwayo began to plan his visit for March 1882, writing letters to the Queen and the Prince of Wales.[97]

However, there remained some legal complications to be resolved before he left. According to the legal advice received at the Cape, once he was released, Cetshwayo could not be detained there again without fresh legislation.[98] The Law Officers in London confirmed this, but noted that Cetshwayo could still be regarded as being a prisoner of war, both during his visit to England and thereafter. To signal his continuing status as such, they suggested putting him back into imperial military custody at the castle in the Cape, prior to his trip to England.[99] Kimberley gave the necessary instructions, and also asked Robinson about the possibility of passing a second act at the Cape to provide for his detention on his return.[100] When the Cape government responded that they would not support a second act,[101] Cetshwayo was told that it might become necessary after his trip to England to send him elsewhere, such as Mauritius.[102] Cetshwayo's travels were delayed further when the new Governor of Natal, Sir Henry Bulwer, asked for the trip to be postponed, since the visit was being used 'for purposes of agitation in Zululand'.[103]

---

[94] PP 1882 (c. 3247) XLVII. 1, No. 1, p. 1.   [95] PP 1882 (c. 3247), enc. in No. 6, p. 5.
[96] PP 1882 (c. 3247), No. 4, p. 3; Guy, *Destruction of the Zulu Kingdom*, p. 130.
[97] Letters dated 27 December 1881, PP 1882 (c. 3247), encs. in No. 21, p. 15.
[98] Opinion of A. W. Cole, January 1882, PP 1882 (c. 3247), enc. 2 in No. 24, p. 17.
[99] Opinion dated March 1882, CO 885/12, No. 274.
[100] Kimberley also wanted to secure assurances from the ex-king that he would obey all instructions given to him when he left the Cape. PP 1882 (c. 3247), No. 31, p. 22.
[101] Robinson to Kimberley, 3 May 1882, PP 1882 (c. 3247), No. 56, p. 47.
[102] PP 1882 (c. 3247), No. 57, p. 47; No. 83, p. 78.
[103] PP 1882 (c. 3247), 10 May 1882, No. 59, p. 50; No. 90, p. 86.

Once it became evident to the Colonial Office that this was not the case, Kimberley felt that the trip had to proceed, since it might make the long-term settlement of Zululand more difficult if the promise to the king were not kept.[104] In July, Cetshwayo duly sailed from Cape Town with three chiefs, bound for London.

If the British authorities had been keen to ensure that Cetshwayo would still be regarded as a prisoner of war when he left South Africa, they hardly treated him as one when he arrived in England. He was lodged in a house in Kensington, and given tours of Woolwich Arsenal and the London Docks – to impress him with Britain's military power – and was also taken to parliament and to meet the Queen.[105] Cetshwayo's visit attracted much attention in the British press, which found the Zulu king to be a very different figure from the savage uncivilised warrior he was portrayed to be during the war.[106] Nor did the Colonial Office see the purpose of the visit as simply giving an eminent African detainee the opportunity to ask for mercy. By the summer of 1882, it was clear that the settlement which Wolseley had imposed on Zululand after defeating Cetshwayo was not working.[107] In dividing Zululand into thirteen small chieftainships, Wolseley, and his adviser John Shepstone, believed that they had set up a system where each chief would guard his independence from the others, and maintain a balance among various Zulu factions. In practice, it had the reverse effect, since neither the territories defined nor the chiefs appointed reflected the preceding structures of Zulu politics and society. In September 1881, as he contemplated allowing Cetshwayo to visit London, Kimberley had noted that 'we neither control the affairs of Zululand, nor are we free from responsibilities for them'. Had the British either annexed Zululand, or left Cetshwayo on the

---

[104] PP 1882 (c. 3270) XLVII. 101, No. 5, p. 19; PP 1883 (c. 3466) XLIX. 49, No. 49, p. 81.
[105] Guy, *Destruction of the Zulu Kingdom*, p. 152.
[106] See Catherine E. Anderson, 'A Zulu King in Victorian London: Race, Royalty and Imperialist Aesthetics in Late Nineteenth-Century Britain', *Visual Resources*, vol. 24:3 (2008), pp. 299–319.
[107] Under the plan thirteen independent chiefs were to rule Zululand, which would not be annexed to the British crown, though a British Resident would be appointed. See Guy, *Destruction of the Zulu Kingdom*, pp. 69–78.

throne, their policy would have been coherent.[108] As it was, the system under which great power was given to the appointed chiefs – particularly John Dunn and Zibhebhu – greatly antagonised the Usuthu chiefs who had lost out in the settlement and who remained loyal to their king, threatening civil war. The Colonial Office realised that Zululand would remain unsettled without a recognised paramount authority, and that unless the British themselves assumed that authority – which they did not want to do – the only alternative was the restoration of Cetshwayo. At the same time, they felt duty bound to assign separate lands to those chiefs they had dealt with who were not willing to be ruled by Cetshwayo.[109] Consequently, when Kimberley met Cetshwayo shortly after his arrival, and was asked by the ex-king what he had done wrong, the Secretary of State said that it was no use to talk of the past.[110] He saw the meeting as an opportunity for the British government to lay down terms for the future administration of Zululand, and Cetshwayo's part in it. Kimberley's proposal was that he would be allowed to return to Zululand, but that 'a portion of the country' would not be under his control, but would be 'reserved for other purposes'. Additionally, he would have to accept a British Resident.[111] Although Cetshwayo was unhappy at the partition of his country – and at continuing British support for the perfidious chiefs – he agreed to the terms of his restoration.

It was decided that Cetshwayo should return to Oude Molen pending the completion of arrangements for his restoration. However, on this occasion, he was not to be regarded as a prisoner, and the only restrictions imposed on him would be the ones he had agreed to observe when coming to England. There was consequently no need to pass another act at the Cape, and the local government were happy to host him in the interim.[112] At the beginning of September, Cetshwayo sailed back for Cape Town. He remained there while the

---

[108] CO 179/138/15682, f. 175, 6 September 1881, quoted in Guy, *Destruction of the Zulu Kingdom*, p. 131.
[109] PP 1883 (c. 3466), No. 114, p. 216.   [110] PP 1883 (c. 3466), enc. 1 in No. 61, pp. 105ff.
[111] PP 1883 (c. 3466), enc. 1 in No. 61, p. 107.
[112] PP 1883 (c. 3466), No. 68, p. 115; No. 76, p. 132.

Colonial Office and the Natal authorities figured out the details of the arrangement. In the event, the plans for Zululand were far from settled when Cetshwayo returned to the Cape, and he would take no part in shaping them. The settlement agreed between Kimberley and Sir Henry Bulwer was that Zululand would be partitioned into three parts, only one part of which would be under the king's control. Land to the north of his territory was allocated to Zibhebhu, chief of the Mandlakazi, and land to the south became a 'Zulu Native Reserve', where those chiefs wishing to escape the king's chiefs could settle.[113] Cetshwayo was very dissatisfied with the amount of territory which was reserved, but had no choice but to accept the partition of his kingdom.[114] In January 1883, the king sailed back towards Zululand.

In the case of the Zulu king, his detention at the Cape was a continuing part of Britain's war of conquest in Zululand, conducted by means of law. Although he had been defeated on the battlefield, he remained a danger to British plans for the area, and so had to be kept incarcerated. The British had no jurisdiction to hold Cetshwayo. As the war with the Zulus had ended, he could no longer legitimately be regarded as a prisoner of war. Nor was he a subject, who had committed any kind of offence against the crown: he was the ruler of a neighbouring kingdom, which at the end of the war the British opted not to annex. Aware of the support that he enjoyed – and the risk that his friends might seek a habeas corpus application – legal cover was given to his detention by means of a statute. If this suggested that London was no less averse to using exceptional measures to detain African leaders when they felt it necessary than administrators in the colonies, it was also the case that the tools of 'lawfare' were not always fit for purpose. The detained Cetshwayo himself was able to put pressure on the British, who soon found that they needed him more as a figure of authority in Zululand than as a prisoner at the Cape.

The examples of Langalibalele and Cetshwayo showed that while 'exceptional' measures could be used to detain political opponents, there were costs involved in using them. Such measures could serve as much to discredit imperial rule as to bolster it. The lesson was learned

---

[113] Guy, *Destruction of the Zulu Kingdom*, pp. 160–161.
[114] PP 1883 (c. 3466), No. 138, pp. 240ff.

in Natal, for in the next major conflict, involving Cetshwayo's son Dinuzulu, the imperial authorities were insistent that the rule of law would be seen to have been followed.

Dinuzulu's Trial and Exile

Dinuzulu's 'Rebellion'

Cetshwayo's return to his home did not turn out to be a happy one. By 1883, relations between Cetshwayo's Usuthu branch of the royal house and Zibhebhu's Mandlakazi branch had descended into a civil war which had been brewing since the middle of 1881. In July, Zibhebhu attacked the king's capital at Ulundi, slaughtering hundreds.[115] Cetshwayo himself was injured, but escaped. He died in February 1884 at Eshowe, where he had lived for four months under the protection of the Resident Commissioner. The conflict between the Usuthu and the Mandlakazi continued after Cetshwayo's death. Soon after his father's death, Dinuzulu allied with the Boers, who offered him support in exchange for the promise of land in which they could create a new self-governing republic. In June, the Usuthu and Boers attacked the Mandlakazi and inflicted a crushing defeat on Zibhebhu, who sought refuge in the Zulu Native Reserve. Given the young king's promises of land for the Boers, this victory hardly strengthened his power, for it prompted the British to set limits to Boer expansion. In 1887, having agreed a boundary with the New Republic, Zululand was annexed as a British colony, whose Governor (also the Governor of Natal) was to be Supreme Chief.

The new colonial government was not slow to assert its authority over Dinuzulu, who was summoned (along with his uncle Ndabuko) to appear before Governor Sir Arthur Havelock, who accused him of disloyalty and misconduct, in again communicating with the New Republic. While accepting Dinuzulu's denial of any treasonable intent,[116] Havelock chided him for presenting himself as the

---

[115] Guy, *Destruction of the Zulu Kingdom*, pp. 200–204.
[116] PP 1887 (c. 5331), No. 37, p. 57 at p. 58. It had been planned to charge them with treason-felony if they did not appear when summoned: PP 1887 (c. 5331), No. 33, p. 50.

successor to the Zulu kings,[117] telling him that the Queen who had conquered Cetshwayo was now the ruler of Zululand. The House of Shaka was dead: 'It is like water spilt on the ground.'[118] At the same time, Havelock was happy to allow the anti-Usuthu chiefs Zibhebhu and Sokwetshata to return to the lands they had previously occupied in northern Zululand and on the coast, in order (as Theophilus Shepstone put it) to 'throw the balance of Zulu power into the hands of the Government'.[119]

If Havelock expected that Zibhebhu's return would create a stable balance of power in the area, it was a massive miscalculation. Given their memories of the slaughter of Ulundi, the Usuthu were hardly likely to wish to live peacefully alongside the Mandlakazi. To make matters worse, much of the land in the area was occupied by Usuthu, who were brutally driven off it by Zibhebhu.[120] Many of them sought refuge with Dinuzulu at Ivuna, in the Ndwandwe district. The refugees' movements alarmed the authorities, who feared that Dinuzulu was preparing a force to attack Zibhebhu, which (the young king was told) would be considered as an attack on the government. Although Havelock came to realise that Dinuzulu's behaviour might be due to 'fear and suspicion [of Zibhebhu] and to defensive rather than aggressive intention',[121] the Resident Commissioner, Melmoth Osborn, felt that the main obstacle to British rule in Zululand was the fact that Dinuzulu 'would not settle down as a subject of the Queen and live under the law'. As he saw it, the return of Zibhebhu simply gave Dinuzulu a pretext for discontent. Nothing short of 'severe measures' would suffice to put a stop to his intrigues.[122]

Viewed from this perspective, Dinuzulu's defensive move to Ceza on the border with the New Republic in May 1888 was interpreted as

---

[117] PP 1887 (c. 5331), enc. 1 in No. 30, p. 44 at p. 45.
[118] PP 1887 (c. 5331), enc. 2 in No. 37, p. 64. See also Guy, *Destruction of the Zulu Kingdom*, p. 237.
[119] PP 1887 (c. 5331), No. 9, p. 23; enc. 4 in No. 9, pp. 27–29.
[120] PP 1887 (c. 5522) LXXV. 533, enc. 2 in No. 6, p. 15. Furthermore, officials set a boundary for Zibhebhu's territory which allocated much more land to him than his tribe had previously occupied. PP 1888 (c. 5522), No. 6, p. 11. See further John Laband, 'British Boundary Adjustments and the uSuthu–Mandlakazi Conflict in Zululand, 1879–1904', *South African Historical Journal*, vol. 30:1 (1994), pp. 33–60 at pp. 46–48.
[121] PP 1887 (c. 5331), No. 53, p. 84.   [122] PP 1888 (c. 5522), enc. 1 in No. 16, p. 27 at p. 28.

aggressive 'open defiance of Government'.[123] After reports were received that Dinuzulu had been involved in cattle stealing, Osborn was instructed to send a force to arrest him and bring him to Eshowe to face charges for that offence.[124] However, the attempt to apprehend him ended in a clash in which two soldiers and over 100 Usuthu were killed. The colonial police and troops retreated without making their arrest.[125] Young Usuthu warriors then went on the rampage, killing two white storekeepers. The authorities were further alarmed when Shingana, another of Dinuzulu's uncles (who had been thought to be loyal), went over to Dinuzulu's side, taking 250 followers into the mountains at Hlophekhulu.[126] The conflict escalated when, on 12 June 1888, Zibhebhu's men attacked the kraal of chief Msutshwana – who had aligned himself with Dinuzulu – and killed the chief, in revenge for an attack by his son on some of Zibhebhu's followers.[127] The murder was brutal and it elicited a fierce response from the Usuthu. On 23 June, they attacked Ndunu Hill, killing 250 of Zibhebhu's men, including nine of his brothers.[128] The colonial authorities reacted to the Usuthu victory with some alarm,[129] which only increased at the end of the month when Usuthu on the Lower Mfolosi led by Somkhele launched an attack on Sokwetshata, which appeared to show that the coastal chiefs were openly joining what was now seen as Dinuzulu's rebellion.[130] In fact, the unrest was soon quelled. At the beginning of July, the colonial forces launched an attack on Shingana, who had taken his followers to the mountains at Hlophekhulu, with a view to intercepting him before he could join Dinuzulu at Ceza.[131] After six hours of fighting (and seven fatalities on the colonial side), Shingana – for whom a warrant had been issued – escaped. The colonial forces then turned their sights on Ceza itself. With the troops on his tail, and a warrant against him on

---

[123] The phrase is Osborn's, quoted PP 1888 (c. 5522), No. 24, p. 42 at p. 43.
[124] PP 1888 (c. 5522), No. 27, p. 45. He was to be charged under Law 10 of 1876.
[125] PP 1888 (c. 5522), enc. 2 in No. 38, p. 62.   [126] PP 1888 (c. 5522), No. 43 with enc., p. 66.
[127] See the evidence in *Reg v. Usibebu Ka Mapita* in PP 1890 (c. 5892) LII. 421, sub-enc. 2 in enc. 9 in No. 190, p. 352; PP 1888 (c. 5522), enc. in No. 72, p. 117; Jeff Guy, *The View across the River: Harriette Colenso and the Zulu Struggle against Imperialism* (Charlottesville, University of Virginia Press), p. 227.
[128] J. P. C. Laband, 'The Battle of Ivuna (or Ndunu Hill)', *Natalia*, vol. 10 (1980), pp. 16–22.
[129] PP 1888 (c. 5522), enc. 2 in No. 52, p. 90.   [130] PP 1888 (c. 5522), enc. in No. 67, p. 109.
[131] PP 1888 (c. 5522), p. 57, No. 36; No. 66, p. 103; enc. 4 in No. 66, p. 107.

charges of murder, cattle-stealing and public violence, Dinuzulu headed for the Transvaal. What had looked to the British like a rebellion had clearly been crushed by the end of July.

Dinuzulu's Arrest and Rendition

With peace restored, the colonial authorities determined to put the rebels on trial. Preliminary investigations began when Ndabuko surrendered in September 1888.[132] However, Dinuzulu remained at large until the day when the first of the trials of seventeen men for their part in the rebellion began on 15 November at Eshowe. After he had fled to the South African Republic, Governor Havelock wanted to request Dinuzulu's extradition,[133] but the Colonial Office (fully aware that a political offender would not be extradited) was content to see him interned in the Republic at a distance from the border.[134] Dinuzulu eventually returned to Pietermaritzburg in November, thanks to the influence of Harriette Colenso, the daughter of the bishop, who advised him to surrender to the authorities, even though it would mean facing a charge similar to that faced by Langalibalele.[135] Harriette – known to the Zulus as 'Udhlwedhlwe', the 'walking stick' and support of her father – would remain a tireless champion of the Zulu king, seeking to keep his case ever present in the eyes of the British public, even as she became an outcast in white Natalian society.

Having escaped from the Republic's police force, Dinuzulu made his way to the Colenso home at Bishopstowe, from where he sent a message to the Governor. A force of policemen was sent to arrest him on a charge for murder, for which a warrant had been issued in Zululand. Since Zululand was a neighbouring colony, the Secretary of Native Affairs, Henrique Shepstone, also issued a provisional warrant

---

[132] PP 1890 (c. 5892), No 19, p. 28; No. 44, p. 76.
[133] PP 1890 (c. 5892), enc. 1 in No. 5, p. 10; CO 879/30/2, No. 7, with encs. p. 15.
[134] Minute by R. H. Meade, 12 September 1888, CO 427/2/18234; PP 1888 (c. 5522), No. 63, p. 101; CO 879/30/2, No. 15, p. 31; CO 879/30/2, No. 55, p. 90; PP 1890 (c. 5892), No. 47, p. 78; CO 879/30/2, p. 53 (No. 40); PP 1890 (c. 5892), No. 7, p. 11. See also Fairfield Minute, 11 September 1888, CO 427/2/18234.
[135] PP 1890 (c. 5892), enc. 2 in No. 3, p. 5; PP 1890 (c. 5892), enc. 1 in No. 3, p. 3. See also Guy, View across the River, ch. 17.

under the 1881 Fugitive Offenders Act; but as Dinuzulu was willing to come voluntarily, the warrant was not executed.[136] Since the relevant paperwork had not yet arrived from Zululand, Shepstone asked him to sign a paper consenting to be sent to Eshowe without going through the formalities of the 1881 Act. Dinuzulu, however, declined to agree, insisting that he had not come to Pietermaritzburg in order to be sent to Zululand for trial for murder.[137] He also took legal steps to prevent his removal. On the basis of an *ex parte* application on 17 November, the Natal Supreme Court granted a fifteen-day interdict to prevent his removal, on the ground that the provisions of the 1881 Act had not been complied with.[138] Instead of releasing Dinuzulu, however, the Governor issued another warrant under Law 20 of 1880, the legislation which had been passed to facilitate the passage of Sekhukhune through Natal, but which had never been used. This was designed to trump the restrictions of the Fugitive Offenders Act.

When the case returned to the Supreme Court on 20 November, the court set aside the interdict, rejecting the argument of Dinuzulu's lawyer (G. A. de Roquefeuil Labistour) that Law 20 had no application in a case like this and that the provisions of the 1881 Act had to be complied with. While admitting that this kind of case was not contemplated by those who passed Law 20, Chief Justice Connor – who had upheld Governor Pine's sentence against Langalibalele – construed the statute in such a way as to allow Dinuzulu to fall within its provisions.[139] Connor was clearly disturbed by the prospect that Dinuzulu might escape his projected trial. During argument, he opined that '[i]t would he absurd to say that Dinuzulu having come here cannot be touched in any way', and speculated that he might even be tried for his offence in Natal under the common law.[140] In the wake of this decision, Havelock lost no time in moving Dinuzulu to Eshowe and commencing preliminary proceedings against him, which led to his being committed for trial on charges of treason, rebellion and public violence, though not for murder, the charge for

---

[136] PP 1890 (c. 5892), No. 70, p. 107; No. 76, p. 112. See also Guy, *View across the River*, p. 260.
[137] PP 1890 (c. 5892), p. 135.
[138] See his petition to the Privy Council in PP 1890 (c. 5892), p. 139.
[139] *In re Dinizulu* (1888) *Natal Law Reports*, new ser. Vol. IX, p. 257 at p. 259.
[140] *In re Dinizulu* (1888) *Natal Law Reports*, new ser. Vol. IX, p. 257 at p. 258.

which he had originally been held.[141] However, Dinuzulu's lawyers immediately gave notice of their intention to appeal against Connor's decision to the Judicial Committee of the Privy Council, and Harry Escombe (who was in London on a pre-arranged trip) prepared the paperwork for this.[142] The point of this appeal was not simply to challenge the legality of his rendition: it was also intended to discredit the proceedings in Natal and Zululand, and to pave the way for a wider inquiry into the causes of the disturbances in 1888.[143]

On 22 January 1889, the Judicial Committee granted Dinuzulu leave to appeal.[144] On the same day, the Law Officers responded to the Colonial Office's queries about the legality of Dinuzulu's arrest and the effect any reversal by the Privy Council of the Natal's Supreme Court's judgment would have on a trial of Dinuzulu in Zululand. While they considered that Dinuzulu was not within the class of people covered by the Law of 1880 (and so might have a cause of action against those who had deported him illegally from Natal), the Law Officers advised that an adverse decision by the Privy Council would not affect the competency of the Zululand court to try him. At the same time, they thought that the Judicial Committee might refuse to intervene, on the grounds that a lawful warrant might have been issued at the time under section 35 of the Fugitive Offenders Act, and that the deportation had now taken place.[145] Before receiving this advice, officials in London had contemplated sending Dinuzulu back to Natal, in order to comply with the requirements of the Fugitive Offenders Act.[146] When it was pointed out that Dinuzulu's lawyers would resist any attempt to remove him to Natal, Havelock asked whether he should be removed by *'force majeure* and

---

[141] PP 1890 (c. 5892), No. 76, p. 112; No 107, p. 155.
[142] PP 1890 (c. 5892), No. 86, p. 122; No. 90, p. 126.
[143] Guy, *View across the River*, pp. 276–277.
[144] *The Times*, 23 January 1889, p. 3. The Order in Council approving the report of the Judicial Committee is in CO 879/30/5, enc. in No. 6, p. 5.
[145] Law Officers' opinion, 23 January 1889, CO 885/13. Bramston was himself of the same view, taking *R. v. Sattler* (1858) Dearsly and Bell's Crown Cases Reserved 525 at pp. 546–547 as his authority: CO 427/4/4557.
[146] CO 879/30/2, No. 143, p. 198; Nos. 150, 151, p. 207. Indeed, before the Privy Council hearing, Bramston informed members of the judicial committee that this would be his advice to the Secretary of State, so that 'possibly they would hear no more of the matter': CO 427/3/1773.

surreptitiously'.[147] The Law Officers' reassurance allowed such exceptional contingency plans to be abandoned.[148]

This left the question of whether Dinuzulu's trial could proceed before the Privy Council had come to a final decision on his appeal. Although the judicial committee had not made any order suspending any proceedings against Dinuzulu (which had been requested), Lord Chancellor Halsbury was reported to have said that anyone who proceeded to try Dinuzulu, in light of the leave given, would be guilty of 'a very grave dereliction of duty', since the offence was a capital one.[149] However, both the Governor and his crown prosecutor wanted the trial to proceed without waiting for the decision of the Privy Council, fearing that Dinuzulu would resume his activities if he were released on bail.[150] Havelock was so concerned by this prospect that he proposed passing an ordinance for Dinuzulu's detention and deportation. By contrast, neither ministers nor their officials were troubled by Halsbury's words[151] – since no capital sentence could be executed until it had been reviewed in London[152] – and so the Colonial Office authorised the trial to proceed.[153]

The Trials of the Rebels

It was clear from the moment that the rebellion was suppressed that the authorities wished to hold the rebels to account in 'ordinary' trials, for they were conscious of the criticisms which had been made of Langalibalele's trial, where judicial and political offices had been mixed together. To avoid having the men tried in a court presided

---

[147] CO 879/30/5, No. 2, p. 1. As a result of an editorial error by Fairfield, a reference to this despatch was inadvertently printed in a Blue Book (PP 1890 (c. 5892), No. 127, p. 191), leading to a question in the Commons: *Parl. Debs.*, 3rd ser., vol. 344, col. 1573 (22 May 1890); see also CO 427/10/9488.

[148] CO 879/30/5, No. 5, p. 5.

[149] *The Standard*, 3 March 1889, p. 2. See also the letter from Charles Hancock (a supporter and correspondent of Harriette Colenso's, who strove to keep the Eshowe trials before the British public) in *Daily News*, 4 March 1889, p. 6. See also his letters in *Daily News*, 9 February 1889, p. 3; 11 April 1889, p. 2.

[150] CO 879/30/5, No. 8, p. 8.

[151] As Bramston noted, 'The Lord Chancellor's obiter dictum would I feel sure not be repeated after argument': CO 427/4/4557.

[152] *Parl. Debs.*, 3rd ser, vol. 333, col. 1288 (8 March 1889).   [153] CO 879/30/5, No. 9, p. 8.

over by Osborn – who as chief magistrate was the designated person under the applicable law in Zululand – Natal's Attorney General Sir Michael Gallwey proposed appointing Justice Walter Wragg, senior puisne judge of the Supreme Court of Natal, together with two magistrates from Natal to hear the cases.[154] The Colonial Office was also keen for this to be seen as a regular trial. For the Secretary of State, Knutsford, African confidence in the system had to be earned by showing it to be impartial and independent.[155] Mindful of the fact that Langalibalele's case had ended in 'a gross miscarriage of justice principally through the Court accepting false evidence without testing it', the Colonial Office was also keen to ensure that the rebels would be defended by counsel.[156] It was also agreed that all the evidence should be transmitted to London, and that no sentence should be carried out until it had been reviewed by Her Majesty's Government at home.

The decision was taken to set up a special commission, under the Governor of Zululand's existing power to appoint magistrates, to try only offences connected with the rebellion.[157] The court was appointed by proclamation on 16 October 1888; at the same time that Gallwey was appointed Attorney General for Zululand.[158] The proclamation's wording (about which London was not consulted) was not felicitous. As Dinuzulu's lawyers pointed out, it denied witnesses the right to refuse to answer questions which might incriminate them, and its preamble seemed to presume guilt.[159] Despite these flaws, the Colonial Office was confident that the court would investigate the central question of guilt. Nine indictments were prepared against seventeen men. Dinuzulu and Ndabuko faced charges of treason, rebellion and public violence. The acts of treason they were charged with included a clash on 26 April 1888, when police sent to arrest four men and collect a cattle fine were resisted; Dinuzulu's withdrawal to Ceza in May; the clash on 2 June, when two soldiers were killed; the attack on Zibhebhu on 23 June; and the collision with the police and

[154] PP 1890 (c. 5892), No. 24, p. 32.   [155] PP 1890 (c. 5892), No. 31, p. 43.
[156] Minutes by Fairfield and Herbert, 27–28 September 1888, CO 427/2/19214. See further Guy, *View across the River*, pp. 241–242, 246.
[157] For a discussion of the kind of tribunal to establish, see Minutes dated 2 October 1888, CO 427/2/19214.
[158] PP 1890 (c. 5982), No. 61, p. 90.
[159] Minute by Fairfield, CO 427/4/6639, 5 March 1889; PP 1890 (c. 5892), enc. 1 in No. 134, p. 197.

troops at Hlophekhulu in July. The coastal chiefs also faced charges connected with the attack on Sokotshana on 30 June.[160]

The lawyers assembled by Harriette Colenso for the defence intended to call into question the policy of the colonial authorities, in order to lay the blame for the unrest on the maladministration of government. They intended to engage in their own kind of 'lawfare'. Aware that it would take time to assemble the necessary documentation and witnesses to prepare the defence, they protested both about the speed of the proceedings and about the fact that they were taking place at Eshowe, where the authorities were able to exert official influence. When the court refused a request from Ndabuko's lawyer, W. Y. Campbell, for a postponement, he withdrew from the case, claiming that the proceedings would be 'a farce as far as the ends of justice were concerned'.[161] Faced with a barrage of criticism from Dinuzulu's supporters, the Colonial Office agreed that a postponement was needed to ensure that there could be no question of the inquiry not having been fair.[162] Justice Wragg duly granted a seven-week adjournment, though he had to be persuaded to withdraw a resignation tendered in protest at the Secretary of State's interference in a trial which had already begun.[163]

While seeking to ensure that Dinuzulu would enjoy the kind of regular legal procedures denied to Langalibalele, some officials in London were uncomfortable with the very policy of dealing with the disturbances through these political trials. Even before court had been constituted, Edward Fairfield proposed setting up a hybrid tribunal which would not only investigate all the charges made against the Usuthu leaders (and sentence them for any criminal offences) but also make good the promise which had been held out to Dinuzulu and Ndabuko to investigate their complaints. Fairfield worried that if the trials went ahead first, the leaders might be sentenced to death and hanged, only for a later inquiry to find them to 'have been more sinned

---

[160] For the details of these events, see Guy, *View across the River*, pp. 209–236. See the indictments against Ndabuko and Somhlolo in PP 1890 (c. 5892), enc. 2 in No. 59, p. 86. See also 'The Zululand Trials. By a Reporter', [George Burgess] in Bodleian Library, MSS. Brit. Emp. s. 22/G12.

[161] PP 1890 (c. 5892), enc. 1 in No. 108, p. 157; enc. 1 in No. 77, p. 113.

[162] Fairfield minute 26 December 1888, CO 427/3/24979; Knutsford to Havelock, 3 December 1888, CO 879/30/2, No. 90, p. 127.

[163] CO 879/30/2, Nos. 93–94, pp. 138–139; No. 101, p. 146; CO 427/3/24049.

against than sinning'.[164] This proposal went nowhere, but he again voiced his unease about the trials after the defence had been given more time to prepare. He now suggested that the crown should accept guilty pleas from the chiefs on the lesser charges of public violence, which would be acted on only after a broader political inquiry had been held. In his view, a political tribunal, which could consider whether they had a good moral defence, would be able to consider 'the only real question – which is what, as a matter of political expediency, ought to be done with Dinuzulu and the other leaders in the next few years'.[165] Fairfield's suggestions – which were not far from what Escombe wanted[166] – were not taken up by Knutsford;[167] and his liberal views on how to deal with the Usuthu were criticised by his colleague Bramston, who attributed the problems in Zululand to the underhand work of 'the Colenso faction', and who was quite happy to see Dinuzulu and Ndabuko hanged. Between these two views was that of Knutsford, who thought the likeliest outcome was that Dinuzulu and Ndabuko would have to be 'interned somewhere in Natal'.[168]

Commencing on 14 March 1889, Dinuzulu's trial was the fifth of the trials, following those of Somhlolo,[169] Somkhele, Ndabuko and Shingana.[170] In his defence, which took the court through the history of Zululand, Escombe sought to show that Dinuzulu had no hostile intent against the crown which could be construed as treason, and that 'the fight was against [Zibhebhu] and not against the Queen'.[171]

---

[164] Minute dated 26 September 1888, CO 427/2/19214. To show that this would accord with Zulu ideas of justice, Fairfield had (perhaps mischievously) referred his colleagues to a 'Memorandum on Native Affairs' drawn up by Shepstone in 1874 (to justify the hybrid procedure used in Langalibalele's case): CO 879/7/8.
[165] Fairfield minute, 7 December 1888, CO 427/3/24094; PP 1890 (c. 5892), No. 69, p. 105.
[166] Escombe wanted an inquiry after the men had given security for good behaviour and been pardoned: PP 1890 (c. 5892), No. 78, p. 118.
[167] PP 1890 (c. 5892), No. 71, p. 109; cf. Knutsford's minute 10 December, CO 427/3/24094.
[168] Minutes, 15 March 1889, CO 427/4/5164.
[169] Lacking legal representation, Somhlolo tried to explain his actions, only to find himself dealt with by prosecutor and judge 'as an accused person in France is dealt with by the *juge d'instruction*', eliciting such information as they felt would convict not only him, but also the other chiefs yet to be tried. 'The Zululand Trials. By a Reporter' [George Burgess] in Bodleian Library, MSS. Brit. Emp. s. 22/G12, ts p. 5.
[170] Guy, *View across the River*, pp. 268–270.
[171] Speech of Escombe, in Bodleian Library, MSS. Brit. Emp. s. 22/G12, ts p. 134.

Zulu Political Prisoners, 1872–1897

However, Dinuzulu was convicted, the court finding that he had endeavoured 'to regain that power to which annexation by Her Majesty had put an end', with the intention of overthrowing 'the existing form of Government in Zululand'.[172] Since there was no jury to address, there was no summing up of the evidence. Consequently, as George Burgess (who observed the trials) pointed out, the judges shed little light on whether the disturbances were due to treason (as alleged by the crown) or to official mismanagement (as claimed by the defence). As he put it, '[t]he trials were conducted throughout as if the decision was a foregone conclusion.'[173] On 27 April, the sentences against the three main chiefs were handed down: Ndabuko was given fifteen years, Shingana twelve years and Dinuzulu ten.

After the trial ended, Dinuzulu's lawyers lodged protests with the Colonial Office, itemising the flaws in the trials, which were said to be so unfair as to amount to a denial of justice.[174] They also returned to the Privy Council. The record of the Natal Supreme Court's proceedings had arrived in London in April 1889, but – with the expense of the case falling heavily on Miss Colenso's limited means – the appellants had yet to deposit the £300 security for costs required for the case could be heard. They were advised that as long as the conviction of Dinuzulu stood, the Privy Council would think the appeal would have no practical effect, since his irregular removal to Zululand would not invalidate the conviction. The only way forward was to seek leave to appeal against the conviction, asking the court at the same time to waive the security for costs in the case already before it pertaining to Dinuzulu's removal, so that all the issues at stake could be discussed together.[175] The combined cases came before the Privy Council at the end of July, where Lord Chancellor Halsbury displayed a robust lack of sympathy for the arguments put for the Zulu leader. Refusing leave to appeal from the decision of the Special Commission, Halsbury rejected the argument that the Governor of Zululand had no authority to create the Special Commission by

---

[172] Harry Escombe and Frank Campbell Dumat, *A Remonstrance on Behalf of the Zulu Chiefs* (Pietermaritzburg, 1889), p. 1. This pamphlet was based on their defence.

[173] 'The Zululand Trials. By a Reporter' [George Burgess] in Bodleian Library, MSS. Brit. Emp. s. 22/G12, ts p. 3.

[174] CO 879/30/5, enc. 1 in No. 82, p. 122; enc. in No. 84, p. 160.

[175] Memorandum and Opinion, MSS. Brit. Emp. s. 22/G12.

proclamation.[176] Nor did he feel it necessary to consider whether there had been any violation of procedural rights (such as failure to follow the necessary forms of an indictment). As Halsbury explained, leave to appeal could only be given where there was 'some real foundation for the suggestion that the ordinary principles of justice have not been observed', and not to satisfy merely technical objections.[177] In his view, nothing could be more destructive of the administration of criminal justice than the idea that appeals could be brought to London on merely technical points.[178] The court also refused to waive the need for security for costs in the appeal against the Natal Supreme Court's decision. This was a crushing blow for Dinuzulu's supporters, who had hoped that a positive outcome from the Privy Council might open the way for a broader inquiry; though, as Harriette Colenso told her brother, 'We here have never had much faith in Lord Halsbury.'[179] The appeal against Dinuzulu's unlawful removal was finally dropped in March 1890.[180]

Dinuzulu's Removal

Although it would take months for the evidence to arrive and be sifted prior to a formal decision being made on whether to confirm the sentences, less than a week after the end of his trial, Havelock recommended that Dinuzulu and his uncles be removed from Zululand if their sentences were confirmed. Since he doubted that the Cape or Natal would pass the legislation necessary for their detention there, he suggested St Helena as a suitable place for exile.[181] Knutsford was not keen on the site of Napoleon's incarceration – since 'we should never hear the last of it either here or in France'[182] – and suggested the Seychelles; but Havelock pointed out that the climate there would be unsuitable for the Zulu chiefs. The legal minds at the Colonial Office

---

[176] *The Times*, 31 July 1889, p. 3.
[177] He followed the Privy Council's decision in *The Queen v. Joykissen Mookerjee* (1862) 9 Moore Indian Appeals 172.
[178] Judgment of the Privy Council, 30 July 1889, PP 1889 (c. 5892), enc. 2 in No. 182, p. 335.
[179] Quoted in Guy, *View across the River*, p. 302.   [180] PP 1890 (c. 6070), No. 8, p. 23.
[181] CO 879/30/5, No. 46, p. 65; Minute by Fairfield, 11 July 1889, CO 427/5/12417. Cf. PP 1890 (c. 5892), No. 162, p. 248.
[182] CO 427/5/9017, minute dated 3 May 1889.

now began to chew over the best instrument to be used to remove them. They concluded that the prisoners fell within the provisions of the 1884 Colonial Prisoners Removal Act, in part because there was no prison in Zululand suitable for these long-term prisoners. No special legislation would be needed therefore to send the men to the Seychelles or St Helena or another African possession. Once again, in contrast with the cases of Langalibalele and his father, Dinuzulu would be dealt with by regular legal procedures.

Dinuzulu's supporters, who were aware that London would review the evidence, and who hoped that this might entail a larger inquiry, continued to press their case, supported by the Aborigines Protection Society.[183] His lawyers also sent extensive commentaries on the trials and the broader wrongs suffered by the Usuthu.[184] Reading this material in July, Fairfield commented that 'really it is all "much-a-do about nothing"' since 'no formidable or humiliating form of imprisonment is contemplated as regards the Chiefs'. At the same time, he added that it 'might save worry to explain this privately to the members [of parliament] who are having their feelings harrowed by Messrs Escombe & Dumat'.[185] In the end the Colonial Office decided there would be no further inquiry.[186] By November, the notes of evidence from the special commission had all arrived in London, and had been printed. There was much debate in official circles whether to publish this material as a 'Trial Blue Book', but, given the extent of the material, the cost of printing it and the disputes over which budget was to bear the cost, it was decided simply to deposit copies in the libraries of the Houses of Parliament.[187]

Having reviewed the evidence, Knutsford decided not to remit any part of the sentences of Dinuzulu and his uncles,[188] though the sentences against the other chiefs were reduced.[189] In preparing the

---

[183] See PP 1890 (c. 5892), No. 143, p. 208; No. 180, p. 333.
[184] PP 1890 (c. 5892), No. 170, p. 256; No. 172, p. 294. Questions were also raised in parliament: *Parl. Debs.*, 3rd ser. vol. 337, col. 9 (17 June 1889).
[185] Minute dated 19 July 1889, CO 427/5/13106.
[186] Fairfield to Bramston, 27 January 1890, CO 427/10/1991.
[187] CO 879/30/5, p. 23n. See further CO 427/4/5997, *Parl. Debs.*, 3rd ser. vol. 341, col. 303 (14 February 1890).
[188] PP 1890 (c. 5893), No. 2, p. 6.
[189] PP 1890 (c. 6070), No. 2, p. 17; No. 4, p. 19; PP 1890 (c. 5893), No. 4, p. 8; No. 5, p. 8. Wragg wrote a report on the trials while in London, which was drawn on by the

paperwork to remove them to St Helena, the Colonial Office remained anxious lest legal proceedings be undertaken by Harriette Colenso to challenge their removal. Plans were initially made to embark the men at Port Durnford, in Zululand, to avoid what Herbert called the 'very great risk of complications if we sent the prisoners through Natal'. Even though the Colonial Office was confident of their legal powers, they feared Escombe might cause trouble by attempting to bring a habeas corpus application, while 'Miss Colenso may demand interviews with them & counsel them to attempt escape.'[190] However, given the real risk that the men might be drowned in any hazardous embarkation attempt here, it was decided to send them via Durban. The chiefs themselves were not told until 19 January 1890 that they were to be deported, eight and a half months after Havelock had begun to plan for it. On 3 February they were taken from Eshowe gaol to Durban in both secrecy and haste.[191]

After Dinuzulu's exile, Harriette Colenso worked hard to keep his case before the public eye, remaining in England between 1890 and 1893, giving speeches, writing articles and putting pressure on the Colonial Office. Dinuzulu's case was also debated on a number of occasions in parliament, but on each occasion the Undersecretary of State, Baron Henry De Worms, batted away complaints by asserting that Dinuzulu had been found guilty by a properly constituted court.[192] With the return of the Liberals to power in August 1892, policy towards the Zulus began to change. The following May, Osborn retired, and was replaced by Sir Marshal Clarke, who was asked to report on the condition of Zululand and particularly to consider the position of Dinuzulu. In Secretary of State Ripon's view, it was appropriate to adopt 'a policy of clemency and oblivion' when a country had quieted down after an insurrection. Ripon was equally clear that Dinuzulu was no ordinary criminal, for, as he put it, 'the question... is not one of releasing a convicted prisoner from jail, but of

Colonial Office: Minute dated 30 July 1889, CO 427/6/15002; PP 1890 (c. 6070), No. 1, p. 1.
[190] Minute dated 3 December 1889: CO 427/6/23331; CO 879/32/4, No. 2, p. 4.
[191] For the preparations, see CO 427/8/3639. See further Guy, *View across the River*, pp. 334–335.
[192] *Parl. Debs.*, 3rd ser., vol. 348, cols. 789, 801–802 (12 August 1890), on which see Guy, *View across the River*, pp. 318–321; *Parl. Debs.*, 3rd ser., vol. 355, cols. 950, 954 (10 July 1891); *Parl. Debs.*, 4th ser., vol. 2, cols. 1259–1260 (18 March 1892).

allowing an exile to return, under proper conditions, to his country'.[193] In January 1893, Clarke recommended that Dinuzulu be allowed to return; and that he should be appointed as an *induna*, or salaried government adviser.[194] Governor Walter Hely-Hutchinson of Natal was happy for him to return on these terms. In his view, if the chief were detained at St Helena until his imprisonment expired, he would not be as 'amenable to reason' on his return as he would be if he were liberated as an act of grace. By the end of July, Ripon had decided that he would implement Clarke's recommendation,[195] though insisting that all be kept secret until all the arrangements had been put in place.

In the event, the return of Dinuzulu was postponed for another three years, thanks to the politics of Natal. Natal, which had gained responsible government in 1893, had long looked to the African territories on its borders both to supply more land for white settlement and as a location from which to draw African labour and to which to relocate surplus African population. White opinion in Natal was not pleased by the incorporation of part of Zululand into the South African Republic in 1887, nor by the incorporation of Pondoland into the Cape in 1894, both of which seemed to diminish the colony's potential hinterland. In 1894, the two questions of Dinuzulu's return and the incorporation of Zululand into Natal became inextricably linked as it became clear that a promise that Zululand might eventually be incorporated into Natal would help remove opposition to the chiefs' return.[196] Within the Natal Government, two positions had emerged. On the one side, Harry Escombe, now Attorney General, argued for Dinuzulu's immediate return, with Zululand being incorporated into Natal after his return. On the other, Prime Minister Sir John Robinson wanted Zululand to be incorporated before Dinuzulu's return, and thought that Zululand needed a couple of years to settle down before incorporation.[197]

[193] CO 879/41/4, No. 1, p. 1 at p. 2.
[194] CO 879/41/4, enc. in No. 3, p. 9. This suggestion was not far from the proposal made in print by Miss Colenso in March: but she remained unaware of the new policy which was being developed in strict secrecy. See H. E. Colenso, *The Present Position among the Zulus, 1893, with Some Suggestions for the Future* (London, Burt and Sons, 1893).
[195] This was reported to the Cabinet on 26 July 1894: CO 879/42/3.
[196] CO 879/41/4, No. 11, p. 17; No. 27, p. 31.
[197] CO 879/41/4, No. 16, p. 20; 3 May 1894, CO 879/41/4, No. 14, p. 19; No. 18, p. 21.

When Hely-Hutchinson saw that Robinson would not actively dissent from his proposal to repatriate the chiefs, plans were made for their imminent return. However, these plans were kept secret from the ministry in Natal, even as the Governor of St Helena was sent a document which would inform Dinuzulu of the conditions of his return.[198] As these secret plans were being made to return Dinuzulu in February, Harry Escombe dropped a bombshell, telling the Governor that Harriette Colenso (who was planning to visit Dinuzulu in St Helena) had told him that she was strongly in favour of the incorporation of Zululand into Natal before Dinuzulu returned, and that she had sent a telegram to the Aborigines Protection Society to this effect. He added that she would proceed from St Helena to London to argue this case.[199] Having received this information, London telegraphed St Helena to cancel Dinuzulu's return. This was an extraordinary intervention on Harriette Colenso's part, for it prevented the liberation of the men whose case she had fought for nearly five years. It also paved the way for the annexation of Zululand by Natal, whose effect could only be to weaken the traditional chiefs she had spent her life supporting.[200] In fact, as Jeff Guy has demonstrated, it was Escombe who persuaded her – at a time when she was in the dark as to the government's real plans – that the incorporation of Zululand into Natal was a necessary preliminary to Dinuzulu's return.[201] Escombe – soon to be Natal's Prime Minister – was more interested in incorporation than in Dinuzulu's fate, and may have perceived that London's desire to return the king might force an issue on which the Colonial Office appeared to be dragging its heels. With the two issues now inextricably bound together, and with Ripon determined not to be bullied into agreeing to immediate incorporation, Dinuzulu's return was postponed.[202] It would not be until the end of

---

[198] CO 879/41/4, No. 41, p. 40.   [199] CO 879/41/4, No. 44, p. 42.

[200] She had wanted Clarke to remain Resident Commissioner under a reformed, non-Shepstonian system, but, when it became clear that Zululand might be annexed to Natal, Clarke made it clear that he would not accept what would be demotion to a colonial position outside the imperial service: CO 879/41/4, No. 93, p. 69.

[201] Guy, *View across the River*, pp. 375–376. See also [H. E. Colenso], *Zululand, the Exiled Chiefs, Natal, and the Colonial Office: 1893–5* (London [1895]), pp. 9, 12–13.

[202] CO 879/41/4, No. 123, p. 93; and Guy, *View across the River*, p. 394.

1897, after the passing of the Zululand Annexation Act, that Dinuzulu and his uncles returned.[203]

With memories of Langalibalele's case still fresh in official minds, the authorities sought to deal with Dinuzulu not through extraordinary legislation empowering his detention, but in mounting a political trial in which the accused would be given the benefit of more regular legal procedures. The aim was still to remove a troublesome opponent, but the means were different. In Dinuzulu's case, an 'ordinary' trial was to be used to brand him (and the other chiefs) a rebel, and to construct an official narrative of events in 1888. By allowing the defendants the full benefit of counsel, who were able to challenge the proceedings of the court up to the Privy Council, the imperial authorities sought to give a legitimacy to the process which went beyond the legislative fiat used elsewhere. There were many flaws in this process. As George Burgess pointed out, serious questions remained about the fairness of the trials these chiefs received. Equally, the Judicial Committee of the Privy Council was – not for the last time – less than punctilious in ensuring that legal procedures had been properly followed. Nonetheless, the form of trial Dinuzulu was given was much more in accordance with metropolitan common lawyers' ideas of what the rule of law required than the treatment given to Langalibalele and Cetshwayo. It was the political response to those detentions which shaped the kind of treatment Dinuzulu would get, just as it was politics which would determine how and when he would be released.

Conclusion

Langalibalele, Cetshwayo and Dinuzulu were all political leaders whom the colonial authorities wished to subdue and control, for fear that they could rally support against colonial rule. However, the instruments used against them varied and developed over time, as pressure increased on the local authorities to follow a form which would satisfy the demands of the rule of law. Each of these leaders

---

[203] Dinuzulu would again be tried and convicted for treason in 1908 in the aftermath of Bambatha's rebellion: see Shula Marks, *Reluctant Rebellion: The 1906–1908 Disturbances in Natal* (Oxford, Clarendon Press, 1970).

was treated in his own way as a rebel, though whether they could properly be seen as such was questionable. Langalibalele's act of 'rebellion' was to lead his people out of the colony to seek fresh pastures, the very thing he had done twenty-five years earlier when entering the colony. This was no crime under the common law of Natal, and Governor Pine's response to try him under what he understood to be native law in a tribunal of his own making was an attempt to give his decision to exile the chief a veneer of legality. Although it satisfied some – including Natal's Supreme Court – it fell short of Carnarvon's understanding of what the rule of law required, informed as it was by the recent Jamaica debates. But practical politics put limits on the Colonial Office's commitment to the principles of Magna Carta. If Langalibalele's detention in the Cape was formally validated by legislation, it was because the Secretary of State persuaded himself that the chief needed punishment for refusing to obey a summons, and because the authorities in Natal and the Cape considered his continued imprisonment to be politically necessary. The substantive principles of the rule of law had to give way to expediency.

Langalibalele was joined for a time by Cetshwayo. Cetshwayo was not a rebel, but a defeated enemy, whose country had been conquered, but he was held at the Cape under similar *ad hominem* legislation as that under which Langalibalele was held. Although a precedent for such a detention could be found in the statute which authorised Napoleon's detention in St Helena, the motivations for incarcerating the Zulu king were very different. In his case, there was no international convention requesting Britain to keep him prisoner, nor was there a list of crimes which the Zulu king might have committed to justify imprisonment, as had been so widely discussed in the case of Napoleon. Instead, he needed to be removed because his presence might interfere with the post-conquest arrangement which had been made for a territory effectively under British control, albeit not yet annexed. In other words, he needed to be prevented from becoming a rebel against that settlement. In dealing with this leader, the colonial authorities sought to satisfy themselves at every stage that they had lawful authority to detain him – either under a (stretched) interpretation of military rights over prisoners of war or under local legislation. In the event, of course,

Cetshwayo proved to be too important to be left at the Cape, and it was the British need to resettle Zululand which trumped the legislation.

The treatment of Dinuzulu suggests that, when dealing with this part of the empire, the colonial authorities became increasingly concerned to follow the rule of law. How far Dinuzulu was a rebel could be questioned: his conflict with Zibhebhu was part of a continuing Zulu civil war (stoked by British maladministration), rather than a campaign against the brand new imperial power. But as a subject of the British colony of Zululand who had led warlike forces in the colony, he was – as his lawyers admitted – amenable to its laws. In dealing with the young king, the colonial authorities did not want another Langalibalele, and wanted to be seen to follow the ordinary rules of law as closely as they could. This was of course a political trial of political prisoners, and questions could be raised about how far either the trial court or the Privy Council protected rights they might have expected under the rule of law. Nonetheless, it is clear that, with a leader as politically important as Dinuzulu, the authorities both in Pietermaritzburg and in London realised that a proper legal trial had to be conducted.

The Colonial Office's increasing concern that the rule of law be observed in these cases was in no small part due to the fact that these men enjoyed the support of people like the Colensos, who had the means both to organise legal challenges, in Natal and in London, and to rally support from other groups in the metropolis. The legal challenges themselves often failed, as judges both in Pietermaritzburg and in Whitehall showed themselves less enthusiastic for a Diceyan vision of the rule of law than the plaintiffs might have desired. Nonetheless, the constant stream of articles in the metropolitan press and questions in parliament kept the issue firmly in the minds of officials, who would need to justify their actions in this court of public opinion.

4

Egypt and Sudan, 1882–1887

Imperial officials showed a greater concern to follow due process the more they came under pressure from domestic public opinion guided by well-connected supporters of detainees, and the greater the opportunities were for the detainees to issue challenges through legal channels. This was all the more so where there were no countervailing pressures from settler communities, such as existed in South Africa. The more pressure was exerted by public opinion, the more ministers and officials felt the need to demonstrate Britain's fidelity to the common law tradition, and to avoid detention without trial. At the same time, not all detainees attracted the same level of attention and support, and, in the absence of political pressure to ensure that due process was followed, these same ministers and officials were content if the formal demands of law were met with the passage of *ad hominem* detention laws. These contrasting approaches can be traced in British policy in Egypt after Britain's occupation of the country in 1882, in the different treatment accorded to the Egyptian nationalist leader Ahmed Urabi Pasha and the Sudanese leader Al-Zubayr Rahma Mansur.

Though Egypt would not formally become a protectorate until 1914, Britain's military occupation of Egypt in 1882 has long been seen as a turning point in the history of imperial expansion in Africa.[1] It

---

[1] As Robinson and Gallagher put it, 'When the British entered Egypt on their own, the Scramble began': Ronald Robinson and John Gallagher, *Africa and the Victorians: The Official Mind of Imperialism*, 2nd ed. (London, MacMillan, 1981), p. 465. For discussions of this episode, see further Robert T. Harrison, *Gladstone's Imperialism in*

was triggered by an Arab nationalist revolt led by Urabi Pasha, which was perceived to threaten British financial and imperial interests. After the revolt had been crushed, Urabi was tried by an Egyptian court, and exiled to the British colony of Ceylon. In this case, with the eyes of domestic public opinion firmly on the case, the British government strove to ensure that Urabi would obtain a fair trial, which would satisfy the demands of British justice. Moreover, his exile to Ceylon would be a voluntary one, with no legislative restrictions imposed on him. Three years later, at a time when the British were attempting to suppress the Mahdist revolt in Sudan, Zubayr was detained in Alexandria, and removed to Gibraltar, suspected of being a supporter of the Mahdi. Unlike Urabi, Zubayr attracted little support in Britain, since he was regarded as a notorious slave trader. As a result, the military authorities were free to insist on his continued incarceration, even as both the Colonial Office and the Foreign Office found it increasingly embarrassing. With few public voices coming to Zubayr's support, the formality of *ad hominem* legislation was considered sufficient to validate his detention and deportation.

The Exile of Ahmed Urabi Pasha

The Nationalist Revolt and the British Invasion of Egypt

The nationalist movement headed by Ahmed Urabi arose in response to the efforts of Britain and France after 1876 to impose controls in Egypt, designed to protect the interests of European bondholders.[2] The

---

Egypt: Techniques of Domination (Westport, Greenwood Press, 1995); P. J. Cain and A. G. Hopkins, *British Imperialism, 1688–1914* (London, Longman 1993), pp. 362–368; A. G. Hopkins, 'The Victorians and Africa: A Reconsideration of the Occupation of Egypt, 1882', *Journal of African History*, vol. 27:2 (1986), pp. 363–391; A. Schölch, *Egypt for the Egyptians! The Socio-political Crisis in Egypt, 1878–1882* (London, Ithaca Press, 1981); John S. Galbraith and Afaf Lutfi al-Sayyid-Marsot, 'The British Occupation of Egypt. Another View', *International Journal of Middle East Studies*, vol. 9:4 (1978), pp. 471–488; D. M. Reid, 'The Urabi Revolution and the British Conquest, 1879–1882', in M. W. Daly (ed.), *The Cambridge History of Egypt* (Cambridge, Cambridge University Press, 1998), pp. 217–238; and William Mulligan, 'Decisions for Empire: Revisiting the 1882 Occupation of Egypt', *English Historical Review*, vol. 135 (2020), pp. 94–126.

[2] See Richard A. Atkins, 'The Origins of the Anglo-French Condominium in Egypt, 1875–1876', *The Historian*, vol. 36 (1974), pp. 264–282; Harrison, *Gladstone's Imperialism in Egypt*; Elizabeth F. Thompson, *Justice Interrupted: The Struggle for*

army became the focal point of nationalist aspirations, and in 1881, Urabi, the leader of the Young Officers Society, came to prominence in the bloodless 'September Revolution', in which he marched on the Khedival palace, demanding a return to the constitutionalist policies which Khedive Ismail had introduced in 1879 in response to popular pressure, before his deposition (at the behest of the Powers) and replacement by his son Tewfik.[3] Three months of peace followed, during which the constitutionalist Sherif Pasha agreed to return to office and the Chamber of Notables was recalled.[4] Although the British were anxious about the developments in Cairo, they did not want to intervene unless Egypt descended into anarchy.[5] It was only when it became apparent that the developments in which Urabi played a central role might threaten British financial and strategic interests that the decision was taken to intervene, with the prime aim of removing this troublesome nationalist.

When the Chamber of Notables met at the end of December, it began to draft a constitution, which would make the government accountable to the assembly and give it control of revenues not set aside for the foreign debt.[6] This development alarmed both the Financial Controllers appointed by Britain and France and the new hawkish French leader, Léon Gambetta. In a bid to strengthen Tewfik's hand, a 'joint note' was issued by the French and British on 6 January 1882, in which they resolved to guard 'against all cause of complication, internal or external, which might menace the order of things established in Egypt'.[7] Instead of having a calming effect, however, it caused a sensation in Egypt, and strengthened the hands of the nationalists.[8] On 5 February, the Khedive was compelled to appoint a nationalist ministry, which passed the Organic law. Urabi now became Minister for War. During the first half of 1882, tensions mounted between the ministry and the Khedive, with Urabi's role being an increasing cause for concern for the foreign powers. The ministry's

---

Constitutional Government in the Middle East (Cambridge, Harvard University Press, 2013).

[3] PP 1882 (c. 3161) LXXXII. 9, enc. 1 in No. 2, p. 3. The Chamber of Notables, first set up in 1866, had been recalled by Khedive Ismail in 1879.

[4] PP 1882 (c. 3161) No. 76, p. 49.   [5] PP 1882 (c. 3161), No. 122, p. 72 at p. 73.

[6] Galbraith and Marsot, 'The British Occupation of Egypt', pp. 473–474.

[7] PP 1882 (c. 3230), No. 24, p. 21; PP 1882 (c. 3230), enc. 2 in No. 42, p. 34 at p. 35.

[8] Galbraith and Marsot, 'The British Occupation of Egypt', p. 475.

prosecution of the 'Circassian plotters' against Urabi's life in April and its convocation (without the Khedive's assent) of the Chamber of Notables in May were taken as signs that the country was falling increasingly under the army's control.[9] In response, France and Britain decided to send a joint fleet, ostensibly for the protection of their subjects, but also to strengthen the Khedive. The British Consul-General Edward Malet was instructed to advise the Khedive to take advantage of the fleet's arrival to form a new ministry. He also called for 'the temporary retirement from Egypt' of Urabi.[10] However, Tewfik's attempt, backed by the two Powers, to force the ministry's resignation failed when it became clear that neither the army nor the people would accept their being replaced.[11] Rather than weakening Urabi, the arrival of the warships, without any backing in the form of troops, had only served to strengthen his position.

Increasingly concerned by these developments, the European Powers called a conference in June in Constantinople to settle 'the conditions on which coercive measures should be adopted if such measures were to become indispensable'.[12] As Gladstone's principal private secretary, Edward Hamilton, now saw it, Britain was 'in rather a plight in Egypt'. Urabi, 'whose banishment we demanded as a *sine qua non*' not only remained in Egypt, but was 'the de facto government'. To recognise his position 'would be eating our own words', while refusing to do so 'means an Egyptian war while the points of difference in the terms we demand & the Egyptians profess are to all intents & purposes *nil*'.[13] But by July, even Gladstone thought that Britain might have to intervene to 'put Arabi down' if 'neither the Sultan, nor Conference, nor France will act – and if the Khedive, really or ostensibly, settles his affairs with Arabi'.[14] A number of events accelerated British intervention.

---

[9] See Galbraith and Marsot, 'The British Occupation of Egypt', p. 477; PP 1882 (c. 3249) LXXXII. 213, No. 161, p. 115; No. 126, p. 100; No. 138, p. 104; No. 143, p. 106; No. 145, p. 107; No. 163, p. 117; 11 May 1882, No. 167, p. 118; No. 173, p. 120. See also PP 1882 (c. 3249) LXXXII. 213, No. 162, p. 116.

[10] PP 1882 (c. 3249), No. 211, p. 140; PP 1882 (c. 3251) LXXXII. 367, No. 30, p. 15; No. 76, p. 34.

[11] PP 1882 (c. 3251), No. 65, p. 28; No. 101, p. 43; No. 117, p. 49.

[12] PP 1882 (c. 3251), enc. in No. 139, p. 56; Mulligan, 'Decisions for Empire', p. 17.

[13] Diary of E. W. Hamilton, 25 June 1882, BL Add. MS. 48632, f. 74v.

[14] Gladstone to Granville, 1 July 1882, BL Add. MS 89317/7/347.

On 11 June 1882, riots erupted in Alexandria. They began with an altercation between an Arab donkey boy and his Maltese passenger, which soon developed into a fight between different communities, ending with more than fifty people dead.[15] The authorities were slow to respond, for the military commanders in Alexandria, in particular Col. Suleiman Sami, refused to act without formal orders to do so, and Urabi – who had authority to give the order but was in Cairo – did not hear of the events until late in the afternoon.[16] Once the command had been given, order was restored quickly. On the following day, Urabi guaranteed the maintenance of public order by the troops, and undertook implicitly to obey all orders given by the Khedive.[17] In spite of this, these events further increased British suspicion of Urabi. Although the commander of the British fleet, Sir Beauchamp Seymour, initially described them as a 'serious nonpolitical disturbance',[18] Malet soon reported that it was 'generally believed' that the riots 'were got up by the military'.[19] The riots also had a strong effect in changing the parliamentary mood in London towards intervention.[20]

The construction of fortifications at Alexandria, which posed a potential threat to Seymour's ships, was another cause of concern for the British. Work on these fortifications ceased after the British protested to the Sultan about them at the beginning of June.[21] However, one month later, London learned of plans to resume work on the fortifications and sent instructions to Seymour to prevent this, by force if necessary.[22] Work on the fortifications stopped after another protest from the British;[23] and on 6 July Seymour warned the military commandant of Alexandria that, if it resumed, the works in the course of construction would be fired on. Three days later, on

---

[15] See M. E. Chamberlain, 'The Alexandria Massacre of 11 June 1882 and the British Occupation of Egypt', *Middle Eastern Studies*, vol. 13:1 (1977), pp. 14–39.
[16] Chamberlain, 'The Alexandria Massacre', p. 24.
[17] PP 1882 (c. 3295) LXXXII. 455, No. 114, p. 44.
[18] FO 78/3470, quoted in Chamberlain, 'The Alexandria Massacre', p. 18.
[19] Malet to Granville, 12 June 1882, BL Add. MS 89317/7/381, f. 110.
[20] Mulligan, 'Decisions for Empire', p. 15.
[21] PP 1882 (c. 3295), enc. in No. 11, p. 4; No. 36, p. 13; No. 54, p. 22; No. 125, p. 49.
[22] C. L. Seymour, 'The Bombardment of Alexandria: A Note', *English Historical Review*, vol. 87 (1972), p. 790; PP 1882 (c. 3391), No. 92, p. 69. The Khedive was to be informed of this: PP 1882 (c. 3391), No. 110, p. 76.
[23] PP 1882 (c. 3391), No. 122, p. 81; No. 151, p. 93.

Egypt and Sudan, 1882–1887

seeing that guns were being mounted, he decided to give the Egyptian military twenty-four hours not simply to stop the work, but to surrender the forts.[24] Seymour's action in effect forced the British government's hand at a time when its ally France had decided not to take any military action unless fired on, and at a moment when London was aware that the earthworks in Alexandria posed no threat.[25]

Seymour's ultimatum was rejected at a meeting of the Egyptian Cabinet presided over by the Khedive. He was told that the Egyptians would retaliate if he bombarded the forts. The Khedive himself was playing a double game, privately urging the British to bombard the city, while publicly holding that it would be dishonourable to remove defensive guns.[26] On 11 July, the bombardment began. When an Egyptian flag of truce was raised on the second day, Seymour regarded it simply as a ruse to buy time to evacuate Egyptian troops.[27] The Khedive now sought refuge on a British ship in Alexandria and summoned Urabi, intending to arrest him if he came, and declare him an outlaw if he did not.[28] On hearing of this, the Egyptian Council decided to ignore his orders, and gave Urabi power to defend the country. With Urabi defying the Khedive, the British pressed for him to be declared a rebel, both by the Khedive and by the Sultan.[29] If Seymour's show of force had been intended to induce Urabi to capitulate, it had failed; and with the Suez canal perceived to be in danger, an expeditionary force was sent under Sir Garnet Wolseley to suppress what was now regarded as a military revolt. As Sir Julian Pauncefote of the Foreign Office saw it, 'a military despotism' had ruled Egypt since May, which had 'sedulously fostered a fanatical feeling against foreigners', caused the 'catastrophe' of the Alexandria riots, and subverted the constitution and 'completely paralyzed' the Khedive's authority.[30]

---

[24] Secretary to Admiralty to Tenterden, 9 July 1882, PP 1882 (c. 3391), No. 182, p. 105; Seymour, 'The Bombardment of Alexandria', p. 794.
[25] Galbraith and Marsot, 'The British Occupation of Egypt', p. 485.
[26] A. M. Broadley, *How We Defended Arabi and His Friends*, 2nd ed. (London, Chapman and Hall, 1884), pp. 124–125n; and Galbraith and Marsot, 'The British Occupation of Egypt', p. 486.
[27] PP 1882 (c. 3391), enc. in No. 400, p. 203; No. 255, p. 139.
[28] PP 1882 (c. 3391), No. 277, p. 147.
[29] PP 1882 (c. 3391), No. 535, p. 271; No. 409, p. 205; No. 521, p. 263.
[30] FO 881/4741, No. 1D, p. 6B (13 July 1882).

Britain's invasion of Egypt in August 1882 – which represented a radical *volte-face* for Gladstone's foreign policy – was ostensibly driven by the need to suppress a rebellion and restore the rule of the Khedive, whose authority had been defied. In reality, it was driven by the need to protect Britain's own strategic and financial interests, which would ensure that British involvement did not end with the defeat of Urabi on 13 September.[31] Indeed, the very designation of Urabi as a rebel was contentious, since his main act of rebellion was to resist the military aggression of a foreign power, initially with the support of the Khedive. However, given the contentious nature of British intervention, it was vital to portray Urabi as a rebel who had to be punished by the authority against whom he had rebelled.

Urabi's Arrest and the Preparations for His Trial

The legal nature of Britain's role in assisting the Sultan in suppressing the 'rebellion' remained ambiguous. Although they wished to act under the authority of a proclamation from the Sultan, the British did not want to see any Turkish troops in Egypt.[32] By the time the proclamation was issued, the British military action which it ostensibly authorised had already begun.[33] Moreover, a proposed military convention setting out the arrangements for the intervention remained unsigned – and Ottoman troops unsent – when Wolseley's victory at Tel-el-Kebir rendered it redundant.[34] The idea that British troops were assisting the Ottomans at their request was also belied by words in the

---

[31] See Hopkins, 'The Victorians and Africa'.
[32] As Hamilton noted in his diary, 'the Turk when once admitted into Egypt will be difficult to turn out, and we may find ourselves in the long run driven to fight the Egyptians plus Turks': Entry 7 July 1882, BL Add. MS 48632, f. 81v. Malet told Granville that the Egyptian government did not want to see Turkish troops in the country, 'because they are convinced that in reality Constantinople makes common cause with Araby'. BL Add. MS 89317/7/381, 12 September 1882, f. 183.
[33] For the Proclamation, see *The Times*, 7 September 1882, p. 5; PP 1882 (c. 3401) LXXXIII. 391, No. 150, p. 67; No. 122, p. 59; No. 132, p. 61, Gladstone to Granville, 10 August 1882, BL Add. MS 89317/7/347, f. 126. For the prior negotiations, see PP 1882 (c. 3391), No. 460, p. 228; No. 519, p. 262; No. 542, p. 277; No. 478, p. 240; No. 502, p. 255; No. 522, p. 265; No. 620, p. 312; No. 623, p. 315.
[34] PP 1882 (c. 3391), No. 523, p. 265; No. 549, p. 283; No. 583, p. 297; No. 608, p. 307; PP 1882 (c. 3401), No. 151, p. 69.

proclamation which spoke (to London's irritation) of Urabi's having 'provoked the armed intervention of foreign powers'.

Britain was keen, from the outset, to be seen to follow principles of legality in the actions it took. This was evident in the War Office's decision to treat the insurgents 'according to the recognised rules of civilized warfare, including the exchange of prisoners'.[35] It was also seen in the Foreign Office's insistence that they should be handed over only if the Khedive agreed that none would be executed without British consent,[36] and in Gladstone's view that the British should 'specify something about equitable trial according to civilized usage'.[37] The Foreign Office thought that only those who were implicated in the murder of Europeans or who had taken part in the burning of Alexandria or been guilty of abusing the flag of truce should be executed.[38] However, it remained a matter of debate whether the same rule should apply in the case of Urabi himself. Within a week of his capture, Gladstone expressed the view *'pure & simple* that (unless there is doubt about the facts) he should be hanged', on account of 'his most traitorous correspondence with the Sultan: traitorous not only against the Khedive but *against the liberties* of Egypt'.[39] Gladstone also reassured the hawkish Queen that the British would not 'interpose a negation' should the Khedive choose to execute him for rebellion.[40] By contrast, Lord Chancellor Selborne argued that Britain should prevent a capital sentence being passed on Urabi, 'unless he should be proved to have been guilty of any such atrocious offences as massacres or incendiarism, in addition to his political delinquency'.[41] At the same time, much of the British press argued against sanguinary

---

[35] PP 1882 (c. 3391), No. 641, p. 322.
[36] PP 1882 (c. 3401), No. 73, p. 36. Tewfik's ministers protested that this would infringe his prerogative of mercy: see FO 407/23, No. 163, p. 68.
[37] Gladstone to Granville, 7 September 1882, BL Add. MS 89317/7/347.
[38] FO 407/23, No. 75, p. 34.
[39] Gladstone to Granville, 7, 22 September 1882, BL Add. MS 89317/7/347. See also the entry in Hamilton's diary, 23 September 1882, BL Add. MS 48632, f. 135v.
[40] Gladstone to Granville, 7 September 1882, BL Add. MS 89317/7/347. See also John S. Galbraith, 'The trial of Arabi Pasha', *The Journal of Imperial and Commonwealth History*, vol. 7:3 (1979), p. 276; and Agatha Ramm, *The Political Correspondence of Mr. Gladstone and Lord Granville, 1786–1886*, 2 vols. (Oxford, Clarendon Press, 1962), vol. I, p. 428.
[41] Selborne to Granville, 25 September 1882, 12 October 1882, BL Add. MS 89317/7/362.

reprisals against Urabi, taking the view that Britain should agree to his execution only 'if the massacres of July and the burning of Alexandria are clearly traced to him'.[42]

When the Khedive's government agreed to try the prisoners in a public court with proper defence counsel,[43] London – which remained keen to monitor the proceedings closely[44] – insisted that a British officer observe the proceedings, to ensure that they were conducted 'in accordance with our views of established justice'.[45] Without an observer present, it would be impossible to determine whether any capital sentences should be vetoed.[46] Sir Charles Wilson, former military consul at Anatolia, was appointed to watch the proceedings.[47] The Foreign Office was particularly keen to ensure Urabi was seen to have a fair trial, since he had a number of supporters in Britain who were keeping his case before the press. They included the well-connected Wilfrid Scawen Blunt, who had attempted to act as an intermediary between the British authorities and Urabi in the months before the bombardment of Alexandria.[48] Alarmed by an article in *The Times* suggesting that Urabi might be shot after a court martial, Blunt hired two lawyers, A. Meyrick Broadley and Mark Napier, to defend him. Although British officials in Egypt did not welcome Blunt's interference, one of the conditions on which they handed over prisoners was that no improper restrictions were to be put on their defence.[49] This proposal alarmed the Egyptians, who feared that if all the political prisoners – amounting to 120 – were allowed counsel, the trials would not only be protracted, but would also turn into a political show.[50] Indeed, the

---

[42] *Pall Mall Gazette*, 25 September 1882, p. 12. See also *Pall Mall Gazette*, 21 September 1882, p. 12.
[43] FO 407/23, No. 153, p. 66.
[44] Papers seized on his arrest were also transmitted to London 'for our inspection', and returned in time for the trial: FO 407/23, No. 204, p. 84, 6 October 1882, FO 407/24, No. 43, p. 23. They proved of little interest: Memorandum by J. W. Redhouse, 4 October 1882, FO 78/3618; and Broadley, *How We Defended Arabi*, pp. 71ff.
[45] Ramm, *Political Correspondence*, vol. I, pp. 431–432 (the phrase of Selborne).
[46] FO 407/23, No. 299, p. 156; Note by Sir J. Pauncefote, FO 78/3618.
[47] FO 407/24, enc. 3 in No. 134, p. 66.
[48] For Blunt's role, see Priyamvada Gopal, *Insurgent Empire: Anticolonial Resistance and British Dissent* (London, Verso, 2019), ch. 3.
[49] Note by J. Pauncefote, FO 78/3618; FO 407/24, No. 71, p. 36.
[50] British officials were more sympathetic to Egyptian concerns about the presence of foreign counsel: Malet to Granville, 16 October 1882, FO 407/24, No. 101, p. 40. Malet felt Britain's insistence on allowing counsel would be misunderstood in Egypt,

Egypt and Sudan, 1882–1887 133

Khedive was so concerned at his authority being undermined that he suggested that the main culprits should be tried by a British court martial, with the Egyptian government prosecuting.[51]

Selborne was asked his views on how to respond to these concerns. He ruled out the idea that Urabi should be tried by the British. As he explained, no ordinary British court could have jurisdiction in this case, while his execution by a British court martial not for any violation of the laws of war, but for rebellion, would be 'an outrage upon any principle of humanity and civilization'. Although he acknowledged the theoretical possibility that Urabi could be exiled by the kind of legislation passed for Napoleon – and recently used against Cetshwayo – it was not an option he (or anyone else in government) took seriously.[52] To assuage the Khedive's fears, he suggested that counsel should conform to certain rules, avoiding 'arguments or evidence, as to political motives or reasons, in justification of the offences imputed to the prisoners'.[53] Proposals based on Selborne's views were relayed to the Khedive, and foreign counsel were admitted on these terms.[54]

Rules of procedure for the hearings were drawn up between Broadley and the prosecutor, Octave Borelli, a Frenchman who was legal adviser to the ministry of the interior.[55] Under their arrangement, Broadley would play a major role in the preliminary proceedings – so that the construction of the case would not simply be in the hands of the prosecutor – while the court martial would then decide on the written case presented to it.[56] In the weeks that followed, there were many arguments over whether these rules were being followed, and whether the court could modify them.[57] British officials regarded these

where it would be 'considered as a sign that we, in fact, befriend him and mistrust the Khedive': Malet to Granville, 1/ October 1882, Add. MS 89317/7/381, f. 227.
[51] Malet to Granville, 16 October 1882, FO 407/24, No. 99, p. 47.
[52] Comments by Selborne on Edward Hertslet's Memorandum on 'precedents for the disposal of Arabi Pasha', 21 November 1882 21, BL Add. MS. 89317/7/362. See also Pauncefote's Note: 'Arabi Trial', FO 78/3618.
[53] Selborne to Granville, 16 October 1882, FO 78/3618.
[54] FO 407/24, No. 124, p. 59; No. 95, p. 44.
[55] FO 407/24, No. 145, p. 74; No. 196, p. 100. They were published in *The Times*, 7 November 1882, p. 10.
[56] See Broadley, *How We Defended Arabi*, pp. 43–49.
[57] FO 407/25, p. 102, enc. 1 in No. 173; Broadley, *How We Defended Arabi*, pp. 197–199.

rules as merely a private agreement among the lawyers, and were untroubled by any alleged departure from them.[58] At the same time, they did not always remain entirely neutral, but could intervene if the fairness of the proceedings was called in question. For instance, when the Préfet de Police of Cairo told the court that it was no use searching the homes of the prisoners unless he could also put pressure on their servants and imprison them, Wilson 'replied that no ill-treatment of servants for the purpose of extracting information from them could be allowed'.[59]

Urabi's Trial

Urabi faced four charges: abusing the flag of truce on the day of the bombardment of Alexandria by withdrawing troops and looting the town while it was flying; inciting Egyptians to arm against the government; continuing the war after peace had been concluded; and inciting people to civil war, and committing acts of 'destruction, massacre and pillage'.[60] Since the first charge had no basis under Ottoman law, while the others were a combination of offences under its military and ordinary codes,[61] questions were raised in parliament as to their exact basis, to ensure that Urabi would be properly tried according to recognised rules.[62] Political pressure at home would continue to focus the government's attention on the need for due process. When MPs challenged the provision that no arguments 'as to political motives' were to be allowed, the undersecretary of state, Dilke, had to respond that 'we inserted this Rule when we had in view ordinary crime' and that it did not apply to political crime, where such evidence could be admitted.[63]

At the end of October, Broadley proposed that an inquiry should be made to distinguish between purely political offenders – who in his

---

[58] FO 407/26, No. 7, p. 3; No. 69, p. 34. Pauncefote note: 'Arabi Trial', FO 78/3618. See also FO 407/25, No. 18, p. 5.
[59] FO 407/25, enc. in No. 122, p. 67; No. 141, p. 79.   [60] FO 407/24, No. 159, p. 77.
[61] FO 407/25, No. 96, p. 41; and Broadley, *How We Defended Arabi*, p. 51. For the codes, see FO 78/3618.
[62] *Parl. Debs.*, 3rd ser., vol. 274, cols. 1184 (10 November 1882), 1195–1196 (10 November 1882).
[63] PP 1882 (c. 3407) LXXXIII. 477, No. 2, p. 9 at p. 10; *Parl. Debs.*, 3rd ser., vol. 274, col. 1303 (13 November 1882).

view included Urabi – and those accused of ordinary crimes. In his view, the ordinary criminals should be put on trial, and the political ones exiled or pardoned. He declared that 'Arabi's only wish is to leave Egypt.'[64] He also made his case on a wider stage, telling *The Times* that there had not 'been any rebellion in its legal sense', since the Sultan had from first to last approved of Urabi's action.[65] Pressure on the authorities was increased by the publication of a letter from Urabi, denying that he was a rebel, and claiming to have acted under the Sultan's authority when fighting a Khedive who had given up the country to foreigners, in breach of Islamic law.[66] In the face of such pressure, by the middle of November, the British cabinet came round to the view that it would be best if Urabi were exiled. Gladstone was particularly exasperated when he received a telegram from Malet telling him that the original *acte d'accusation* against Urabi had been cancelled and that it was possible that new articles might be added to the final one. 'Is it not in fact an infraction of all our ideas of justice?', he asked. In his view, the time had come to urge the Egyptian Government to adopt a summary method 'of getting quit of the whole proceedings for the trial of Arabi, as they are themselves apparently making them such that they will stink in the nostrils of all men'.[67]

A meeting was convened in Westminster with ministers from the Foreign Office and military departments, where a decision was taken that the proceedings had to be brought to a close. It was resolved that the Marquess of Dufferin, who had been sent to Cairo at the end of October to deal with the aftermath of the invasion, should 'try to get a solution out there', which would take the form of the Khedive declaring that there was insufficient evidence to proceed against

---

[64] FO 407/24, No. 254, p. 122; enc. 1 in No. 255. See also *The Times*, 2 November 1882, p. 9. For British reactions, see Minute by Selborne, 3 November 1882, BL Add. MS 89317/7/362 and Malet to Granville, 7 November 1882, BL Add. MS 89317/7/381, f. 273.

[65] *The Times*, 21 November 1882, p. 8 (letter dated 10 November). See also the affidavit of John Ninet, in *The Times*, 20 November 1882, p. 4; and FO 407/25, No. 53, p. 18.

[66] *The Times*, 14 November 1882, p. 8, discussed in *Parl. Debs.*, 3rd ser., vol. 274, col. 1551 (16 November 1882).

[67] Gladstone to Granville, 15 November 1882, BL Add. MS 89317/7/347, FO 407/25, no. 105, p. 43. Selborne also thought any shifting of charges would 'produce the worst possible impression': Selborne to Granville, 14 November 1882, BL Add. MS 89317/7/362.

Urabi for his crimes, but that he would be handed over to the British 'for the undoubted fact of rebellion'.[68] Dilke later noted in his diary that 'If [Dufferin] decides (as he will be privately told to decide), that there is no proof of common crimes, then by arrangement between the Khedive & us we are to put him away safely in Burmah, Barbadoes, Bermuda, Ascension, – or some other place than St. Helena, wh wd be ridiculous.'[69] Dufferin agreed that the trial had 'got into a nasty mess', and that the best way forward would be for Urabi only to face charges of rebellion, and for any sentence to be commuted to banishment.[70] He discussed the matter with the Minister of the Interior, who wanted a few more days to see whether there might be sufficient evidence to connect Urabi with the Alexandra riots. The evidence he had in mind was that of Suleiman Sami, who had been arrested in Crete and returned to Egypt, and who claimed that he had been commissioned by Urabi to have the Khedive shot. Dufferin reported that if the evidence (which was tainted) was not sufficient, the Khedive would follow his recommendation for Urabi to be deported.[71] This begged the question of how this was to be done. Dufferin disagreed with Gladstone's view that Urabi should simply be exiled by the Sultan,[72] since that would allow him to come to London and be 'feted by his partizans'.[73] In his view, Urabi's exile would have to be penal. Since he could not be transported without a trial and sentence,[74] this could be best effected if he entered a guilty plea.

On 22 November, Dufferin received the five-volume case of the prosecution against Urabi and passed it on to Wilson, to advise whether the capital counts were sustained by the evidence. Three days later, Wilson reported that the evidence was not sufficient for an

---

[68] Granville to Gladstone, 15 November 1882, BL Add. MS 89317/7/347. See also FO 407/25, No. 127, p. 75.
[69] Diary of Sir Charles Dilke, BL Add. MS 43925, 15 November 1882.
[70] Dufferin to Granville, 13 November 1882, BL Add. MS 89317/7/387.
[71] FO 407/25, No. 130, p. 75; No. 137, p. 77.
[72] Gladstone doubted 'whether *we* can or ought to take the custody of him': Note by Gladstone, 15 November 1882, BL Add. MS 89317/7/347.
[73] FO 407/25, No. 130, p. 75.
[74] Dufferin had earlier argued in favour of sending Urabi, with his consent, to a place on British territory, since 'We should not then be responsible for his custody.' Among the places discussed by ministers were the Cape, Bermuda and Fiji: Dufferin to Granville, 21 November 1882, FO 407/332, No. 86, p. 69; Gladstone note, 22 November 1882, BL Add. MS 89317/7/347; FO 407/25, No. 177, p. 105.

English court martial to convict Urabi.[75] Wilson's brief initial report was measured, but in another despatch at the end of the year he spelled out in greater detail the weakness of the case against Urabi. In his view, the prosecution seemed to be based on the theory that the Alexandria riots could not have occurred unless Urabi had ordered them, and that this was sufficient evidence to prove that he did so. In fact, he concluded that the evidence for the prosecution could itself have provided a sound case for the defence. The only direct evidence against Urabi came from Suleiman Sami, who claimed that Urabi had ordered him to burn Alexandria and kill the Khedive; but Wilson was very suspicious of this evidence, which had first been presented to the commission at an extraordinary sitting which he had not been informed of. Suleiman Sami was himself so deeply implicated in the burning and looting of Alexandria that the British observer thought it natural that he would attempt to shift the blame.[76] Wilson also noted that there were some 'doubtful points about the legality of the court', which might have been raised by the defence. For instance, evidence had been given against Urabi both by a member of the commission and by the man selected to be president of the court martial (Mohammed Reouf Pasha).

Dufferin concluded that, with such a weak prosecution case, it would not be possible to establish Urabi's guilt 'in a way to satisfy the public conscience'.[77] It was clear that he could not be convicted of any ordinary crime, for which the British would permit an execution. Dufferin was also concerned that, were the trial to continue, it would become a *cause célèbre* in which Urabi would be portrayed as a patriotic martyr. Aware that Urabi's lawyers were keen to effect a compromise,[78] he now sought to persuade the Egyptian government that its chances of making out its case on the principal charges were 'very slight', and that any further prolongation of the trial would frustrate the very end they were seeking to achieve, that of Urabi's 'destruction'. After some hesitation, the Khedive's ministers agreed to accept a guilty plea from Urabi and his fellow accused to the charge of

---

[75] Wilson to Dufferin, 25 November 1882, FO 78/3618.
[76] Wilson to Dufferin, 30 December 1882, FO 78/3618.
[77] Dufferin to Granville, 4 December 1882, FO 78/3618.
[78] Broadley perceived that Urabi's slow response to the riots was a weak point in his defence: Dufferin to Granville, 27 November 1882, BL Add. MS 89317/7/387.

rebellion. The death penalty for this offence would be commuted to perpetual exile, with the prisoners giving a solemn undertaking to 'repair of their own free will' to whatever place designated by the Egyptian and British governments.[79] If they returned to Egypt, the death sentence would be implemented without more ado. On 3 December, Urabi entered a guilty plea, and had his death sentence commuted on giving the solemn undertaking. Over the next days, the other six rebel leaders who had been charged were similarly disposed of by the court.[80]

Through this manoeuvre, the authorities obtained an admission from Urabi that he had been a rebel, something which he had persistently denied. For the British, this was a charge which hardly required proof,[81] but one which needed more lenient punishment. Shortly after the sentence had been passed, the cabinet agreed (against the advice of the Viceroy of India) to send Urabi to Ceylon.[82] However, this was to be a voluntary exile. Consequently, when Dufferin told Broadley in December 'that the exile into which the capital penalty has been commuted was in its nature of a penal character',[83] he was mistaken. The limit of the penalty imposed on the rebel leaders was their exile from Egypt, degradation and loss of property. As Pauncefote pointed out, the colonial authorities in Ceylon would have no greater legal power over them than over any other resident.[84] The Governor of Ceylon, Sir James Longden, was told that the exiles – who had given their word not to leave the island without the sanction of the crown – 'are not to be considered in the custody of your Government'.[85]

Longden wanted to be given the power to exclude them from parts of the island from which they might intrigue with other Muslims in Ceylon or in India, and to deport them if they entered into any such intrigues.[86] Although some officials thought it might be 'prudent to announce' that anyone who broke his parole 'would probably be sent

---

[79] Dufferin to Granville, 4 December 1882, FO 78/3618. They would be executed if they returned to Egypt: FO 407/26, No. 1, p. 1.
[80] FO 407/26, Nos. 14–15, p. 5; Bland to Dufferin, 4 December 1882, FO 78/3618.
[81] FO 407/26, No. 69, p. 34 at p. 35.
[82] Dilke's Diary, BL Add. MS 43925, 5 December 1882, f. 38. For later discussions, see FO 407/26, No. 60, p. 32; No. 77, p. 40.
[83] Dufferin to Granville, 18 December 1882, FO 78/4267.
[84] Note dated 29 December 1882, FO 78/4267.
[85] Draft despatch, 21 December 1882, FO 78/4267.
[86] Longden to Derby, 21 January 1883, FO 78/4267.

to the Seychelles',[87] no legislation to permit this was drafted, and the men were simply told to inform the Inspector General of Police if they wished to reside outside Colombo. Legally, the men remained in Ceylon solely on the basis of their own solemn undertakings.[88] Although the men were put under surveillance, the Governor was given no instructions to prevent Urabi leaving Ceylon, beyond telegraphing the Colonial Office.[89]

The question of whether to put his exile on a legal footing was raised again in November 1883, when news of the defeat of Hicks's troops by the Mahdi prompted Longden to suggest legislation to allow the authorities forcibly to detain Urabi in case he was tempted by the idea of 'giving us the slip'.[90] However, officials in London saw both political and legal difficulties in the way. Rather than pass legislation immediately, they asked the Ceylonese authorities to keep a close watch on the exiles and to report any signs that they intended not to observe the terms of their parole.[91] If Urabi and the others attempted to leave the island, they were to be prevented by force, whereupon an ordinance should be passed retrospectively to legalise the proceedings.[92] In the event, the exiles showed no signs of wishing to escape, and all settled in comfortable bungalows in Colombo. In December 1883, the Inspector General of Police could report that the exiles were mild-mannered and polite, and kept orderly households, though Urabi did complain about having to report all his movements.[93]

The Aftermath of Urabi's Trial

In the aftermath of the conflict, over 1,600 people were held on criminal charges connected with the disturbances, in addition to those whose offences were regarded as political. After the sentences on Urabi and the five others charged with him had been pronounced, a Khedival decree was issued, which exiled thirty-nine others for

---

[87] R. G. W. Herbert to Foreign Office, 20 February 1883, FO 78/4267.
[88] *Parl. Debs.*, 3rd ser., vol. 276, cols. 305–306 (19 February 1883).
[89] *Parl. Debs.*, 3rd ser., vol. 276, col. 706 (23 February 1883).
[90] J. R. Longden to Meade, 23 November 1883, FO 78/4267.
[91] Draft telegram from Pauncefote to the Colonial Office, 29 November 1883, FO 78/4267.
[92] Colonial Office to Foreign Office, 4 December 1883, FO 78/4267.
[93] Mr G. W. R. Campbell to Sir John Douglas, 3 December 1883, FO 78/4268.

various periods, and put twelve under house arrest and thirty-two under surveillance.[94] At the beginning of 1883, an amnesty decree was issued by the Khedive for those suspected of political crimes,[95] though trials of those implicated in acts of violence, and of those against whom proceedings had commenced, continued.[96] These legal proceedings continued to be followed closely in Britain. Urabi's lawyers, who were now defending others (including Suleiman Sami and Said Khandeel, Alexandria's prefect of police), protested that the authorities were now departing from the model insisted on by the British for Urabi. They also claimed to have evidence which implicated both Omar Lufti Pasha, the civil commander of Alexandria at the time of the riots, and the Khedive himself in the massacres which ensued.[97] These explosive accusations – which would exonerate Urabi – were raised in parliament in May 1883 by Lord Randolph Churchill, and repeated in June, after Suleiman's hasty execution.[98] At the end of that month, Churchill submitted a lengthy dossier to the government setting out his accusations against the Khedive, which were widely reported in the press.[99]

The matter was referred to Selborne. Having reviewed the material, he concluded that it was impossible 'to treat these papers as of the slightest importance', and that Churchill's aim had been simply 'to throw discredit upon the whole policy pursued by the British Government in Egypt, to insult and vilify the Khedive, and to vindicate Arabi and the (so-called) "national party"'.[100] Although Selborne felt that no public notice should be taken of the matter, this was hardly feasible, given the attention the affair had attracted. A despatch was drafted to be sent to Malet (enclosing the papers submitted by Churchill), containing the government's comments on the accusations.

---

[94] PP 1883 (c. 3528) LXXXIII. 489, No. 11, p. 33.   [95] PP 1883 (c. 3528), No. 34, p. 53.
[96] By the end of April, 1,595 cases had been examined, 1,139 were released or bailed for acts of minor pillaging, 26 were sentenced to death, and 124 to periods of imprisonment or penal servitude. PP 1883 (c. 3632) LXXXIV. 201, No. 5, p. 4 (with enclosures).
[97] Letters from Mark Napier and Richard Eve, *The Times*, 11 June 1883, pp. 5, 12.
[98] *Parl. Debs.*, 3rd ser., vol. 279, col. 561 (11 May 1883); vol. 280, cols. 35 (8 June 1883), 229 (11 June 1883). See the discussion of these events in Chamberlain, 'The Alexandria Massacre', pp. 27–31.
[99] PP 1884 (c. 3851) LXXXVIII. 263.
[100] Letter from Selborne, 5 July 1883, FO 78/3617.

'The whole case', the government proclaimed in this despatch, 'rests on surmise, suspicion, and hearsay, on unsupported statements made by unnamed persons or by those whose hatred of the Khedive has been created or embittered by the measures taken against them during the rebellion', and offered no prima facie evidence of any case to be answered.[101] Churchill's claims were dismissed, and would not help Urabi return to Egypt. Although a number of petitions were made from the exiles to return home, which were refused by the Egyptian authorities, it would not be until October 1901 that Urabi would return to Egypt.

In Ceylon, the once-powerful Egyptian nationalist leader in effect suffered the same fate that many other African leaders would in the era of Britain's imperial expansion: exile from his homeland, stripped of all political power. Unlike them, however, he was not exiled as a result of an *ad hominem* statute, giving the formal stamp of legality to incarceration by the British. Instead, the British – who had invaded Urabi's country, defeated him, and had long planned his removal from Egypt – ensured that a process would be used, which would allow them to be seen as champions of the rule of law, restraining a potentially arbitrary oriental government, while securing the outcome they wanted. In Urabi's case, if the end was the same, the means were different: rather than using an exceptional measure of sovereign power to exile this leader, they used the language of the rule of law which was designed to present a narrative of Urabi as a rebel, which could justify the British occupation of Egypt, and to present the invading power as a disinterested ally committed to constitutional conduct. Their need to do this was in turn driven by politics. When it ordered the invasion of Egypt in 1882, the Liberal government appeared to engage in a policy at odds with the vision proclaimed so radically in Gladstone's recent Midlothian campaign.[102] With the eyes of Britons so closely following events in this new theatre of war, and at a time when the policy of coercion in Ireland needed justification, it was imperative for the government to be seen to observe the rule of law in its overseas engagements. Nor was this insignificant for Urabi: for

---

[101] PP 1884 (c. 3851), p. 1.
[102] W. E. Gladstone, 'Aggression in Egypt and Freedom in the East', *Nineteenth Century*, 2 (August 1877), 149–166.

while the British were able to secure their goal of removing Urabi, he was spared the much more bloodthirsty penalty his Egyptian enemies had initially wanted.

The Detention of Al-Zubayr Rahma Mansur

It soon appeared that one consequence of the invasion of Egypt was that Britain would be entangled in the Sudan, for the British intervention coincided with the Mahdist uprising in Sudan, which had been under Egyptian administration since 1819. Having publicly proclaimed himself to be the Mahdi, Mohammed Ahmad ordered his followers to join him in a holy war of liberation. During the Urabi crisis, it was left to the governors in the Sudanese provinces to deal with the revolt, but, by 1883, the Khedive's government was ready to take action to crush it. Col. William Hicks was given full powers as commander in chief, and set off in September with 8,000 troops to recapture El Obeid, which had been taken by the rebels. The expedition turned out to be a disaster: on 3–4 November, the Mahdist forces destroyed Hicks's army, and killed its commander, before expanding throughout Sudan and gaining control of the vital communication route between Berber on the Nile and Suakin on the coast.

Hicks's defeat made it apparent that Sudan could not be held without the kind of military intervention which Britain wanted to avoid. The British proconsul in Egypt, Sir Evelyn Baring, therefore advised that a British officer should be sent to withdraw the garrisons from all but the eastern provinces of Sudan.[103] The officer chosen to carry out this policy was that 'half-cracked fatalist'[104] Col. Charles Gordon,[105] whose famous exploits in the east had earned him the epithet of 'Chinese Gordon'. The mission would end with Gordon's decapitation by Mahdists after a 317-day siege of Khartoum at the end of January 1885. Six weeks later, Zubayr, whom Gordon had once regarded as an enemy, but had come to see as a potential ally, was detained in Alexandria, suspected of supporting the Mahdists. Unlike

---

[103] PP 1884 (c. 3844) LXXXVIII. 1, No. 170, p. 143.
[104] The expression is E. W. Hamilton's: diary entry (23 January 1884), quoted in Richard Shannon, *Gladstone: God and Politics* (London, Continuum, 2007), p. 351.
[105] Anthony Nutting, *Gordon: Martyr and Misfit* (London, Constable & Co., 1966), p. 223.

Urabi, he was not put on trial, but was whisked away to Gibraltar, to be kept under special legislation. Lacking the kind of political support enjoyed by the Egyptian leader, his appeals to be accorded British justice fell on deaf ears, thanks to his notoriety as a slave trader.

Zubayr, Gordon and British Intervention in Sudan

The name of Al-Zubayr Rahma Mansur had been familiar to Gordon since the late 1870s, when the Englishman had been the Khedive's Governor-General of Sudan. From the mid 1860s, Zubayr had built a slave-trading commercial empire in Bahr el-Ghazal, which he ran like an independent kingdom. After having fought and killed the Governor of Bahr el-Ghazal, Zubayr was appointed Governor of the province of the White Nile, since this was the only way for the Khedive to secure his claims to the area.[106] This did not satisfy Zubayr's ambitions, and, in November 1874, he routed the forces of the Sultan of Darfur, and seized his capital. Although he offered Darfur to the Khedive, the Egyptian authorities were alarmed at the prospect of his growing power, and he was ordered to return to Bahr el-Ghazal. In response, Zubayr went to Cairo in 1875 to present his grievances; but on his arrival he was put under house arrest by the Khedive, who regarded him as too powerful an adversary to be allowed to return to Sudan. In fact, he would not return to Sudan until 1900, despite numerous attempts to secure permission to do so by bribes and appeals to the government.

By the time Gordon was appointed Governor-General in May 1877, Zubayr's affairs were in the hands of his son Suleiman, who had ambitions to re-establish his family's power. Gordon sought to rein Suleiman in, and in September 1877 ordered him to return to Bahr el-Ghazal. He also began to suspect Zubayr of plotting a rebellion to be led by his son.[107] Gordon therefore insisted that Zubayr should continue to be detained in Cairo, just at the time when he was

---

[106] See R. S. O'Fahey, 'Al-Zubayr's Early Career', *Sudanic Africa*, vol. 16 (2005), pp. 53–68; and Fiona Shaw, 'The Story of Zebehr Pasha, as Told by Himself', *Contemporary Review*, vol. 52 (November 1887), pp. 658–662.

[107] 'Condensed Translation from a Lithographed Arabic Pamphlet' [by Charles Gordon], 6 December 1879, FO 78/4914. Zubayr denied this: Shaw, 'The Story of Zebehr Pasha', p. 675.

attempting to secure his liberation by offering the government an annual payment of £25,000.[108] To add insult to injury, Zubayr's property was also now confiscated. However, the threat posed by his family continued. After having launched an attack on a government station, killing its garrison of 200, Suleiman was captured early in 1879 by the Italian soldier-explorer Romolo Gessi, who had been sent by Gordon to deal with him. To prevent his escape, Suleiman was ordered to be shot, in defiance of Gordon's wishes; while Zubayr himself was condemned to death in Khartoum in absentia, for his alleged complicity in this revolt.[109] However, when Gordon quit his post in Sudan in December 1879, Zubayr remained in Cairo, still attempting to use his influence to secure his release.

Having previously considered Zubayr as dangerous, once the Mahdist revolt had broken out, the Egyptian government began to see the benefit of enlisting his support against the rebels. Reports began to circulate that he was to accompany Valentine Baker – Baker Pasha – in command of Bedouin forces against the Mahdi, with the promise of the reward of the government of Kordofan and Darfur.[110] However, the idea that the largest slave trader in Sudan should be given such a role raised strong protests in Britain, particularly from the Anti-Slavery Society.[111] When Gordon was asked for his views on the matter, while en route from England to Egypt, he responded by asking for Zubayr to be moved to Cyprus, so as not to be able to interfere with his mission.[112] Gordon also sent a memorandum to Baring, stating his view that the best policy for Sudan was to restore the country to the 'different petty Sultans' who had ruled it at the time of its conquest by Mehemet Ali, adding that, if Zubayr was not kept away from Sudan, 'he would in no time eat up all the petty Sultans and consolidate a vast State, as his ambition is boundless'.[113]

Once he had arrived in Cairo, however, Gordon began to modify his views, and requested a meeting with Zubayr. The meeting was

---

[108] Nutting, *Gordon*, p. 169. [109] Nutting, *Gordon*, p. 172.
[110] *The Times*, 1 December 1883, p. 5; 6 December 1883, pp. 5, 7.
[111] FO 78/4194; *The Times*, 10 December 1883, p. 12.
[112] Gordon to Granville, 22 January 1884, FO 78/4194. Granville saw there were no legal powers to detain him at Cyprus: FO 407/60, No. 155, p. 75; No. 172, p. 88. Baring responded that it had now been decided not to send him to Sudan, and that it was not necessary to deport him: FO 407/60, No. 171, p. 88.
[113] FO 407/60, No. 222, p. 117.

a difficult one, for there were old scores to be settled. At the end of it, British officials in Cairo concluded that, if Gordon and Zubayr went together to Sudan, they would not both return alive. They considered it best to keep Zubayr in Cairo, and to tell him that his future treatment would depend both on his conduct and on the fate of Gordon.[114] At the same time, Gordon himself became increasingly convinced of Zubayr's usefulness. By the time he reached Khartoum, he had concluded that the only way to avoid anarchy after the British withdrawal was to appoint Zubayr ruler of the Sudan, on his undertaking not to enter Darfur, Bahr el-Ghazal or Equatoria. The arrangement he had in mind was analogous to that in Afghanistan, where the British gave moral support to the Emir: it would keep 'a large proportion of Arab-speaking lands nominally under our control' and strengthen 'our hold on Egypt'.[115]

Though Baring worried that Gordon's impulsiveness was threatening to draw Britain into intervention rather than evacuation, he agreed that some provision had to be made for Sudan's future stability. He also agreed that Zubayr's prolonged residence in Cairo had modified his character, and was content for him to be appointed ruler of Sudan, albeit without any promise of moral support from the British.[116] By early March, both Gordon and Baring had become increasingly insistent on the need to send Zubayr to Sudan as a potential bulwark against the Mahdi.[117] However, the Foreign Secretary, Granville, felt that British public opinion would not tolerate the appointment of a notorious slave trader to such a position, and was concerned that Zubayr might ally with the Mahdi.[118] He pointed to the very objections which Gordon had articulated when on his way to

---

[114] PP 1884 (c. 3969) LXXXVIII. 393, enc. in No. 33, p. 38; FO 407/60, enc. 1 in No. 454, p. 222; PP 1884 (c. 3969), No. 33, p. 38; FO 407/76, enc. in No. 387, p. 172.
[115] FO 407/60, enc. 1 in No. 440, p. 198 (redacted in PP 1884 (c. 3969), enc. 1 in No. 114, p. 71).
[116] FO 407/60, No. 442, p. 200 (redacted in PP 1884 (c. 3969), No. 115, p. 71); PP 1884 (c. 3969), No. 169, p. 114; and Earl of Cromer, *Modern Egypt*, 2 vols. (London, MacMillan & Co., 1908), pp. 488-493.
[117] PP 1884 (c. 3969), enc. 4 in No. 202, p. 136; enc. 5 in No. 202, pp. 136-137; FO 407/60, No. 633, p. 308 (redacted in PP 1884 (c. 3969), No. 222, p. 146).
[118] PP 1884 (c. 3969), No. 137, p. 95; No. 177, p. 120. However, he hinted in private that, if pushed, the cabinet would probably follow what Baring, Gordon and Egyptian Prime Minister Nubar Pasha thought. FO 633/7, No. 33, p. 20, in Cromer, *Modern Egypt*, vol. 1, p. 498.

Egypt, and asked how this policy would advance the British aims of ending the slave trade and evacuating Sudan.[119] Baring despaired at the Foreign Secretary's response, and arranged for Gordon to send a telegram which would make things clear.[120] In this telegram, Gordon said that he saw no way to evacuation save with Zubayr's co-operation. He added that the Mahdi and Zubayr would never combine, since the former had the power of a Pope, the latter the power of a Sultan. He also dismissed concerns about the slave trade, indicating that the 1877 treaty outlawing it was a dead letter.[121] Meanwhile, Zubayr – whose animosity towards Gordon was diminished by the general's support in his attempts to restore his finances – told the British that he was willing to go to Khartoum, on condition that they made good his financial losses.[122]

In the meantime, Gordon's plans for Zubayr to be appointed Governor reached the British press,[123] eliciting further protests both from the Anti-Slavery Society and from Members of Parliament.[124] By the time the cabinet met, it was also clear that the Commons would not agree to Zubayr being used.[125] Granville duly telegraphed Baring that Zubayr could not be used and that troops which had been requested would not be sent to Berber.[126] On the same day, Baring forwarded a telegram to London which he had received from Gordon, saying that, if he heard no more, he would 'hold on to Khartoum and await Zebehr and British diversion at Berber'.[127] Shortly thereafter, the telegraph wire was cut, and Granville's message would never reach Gordon. The government's ultimate decision not to use Zubayr was based on its calculation that the Mahdi, if left to himself, lacked the organisational and military capacity to be a threat, but that he could pose a serious threat to Egypt with Zubayr's help.[128] This was a severe miscalculation.

---

[119] PP 1884 (c. 3969), No. 210, p. 140.   [120] Cromer, *Modern Egypt*, vol. 1, p. 508.
[121] PP 1884 (c. 3969), enc. in No. 221, p. 145.
[122] FO 407/63, No. 124, p. 100; enc. in PP 1884 (c. 3969), No. 184, p. 122.
[123] *The Times*, 10 March 1894, p. 5.
[124] PP 1884 (c. 3969), No. 224, p. 147, in *The Times*, 12 March 1884, p. 4; *Parl. Debs.*, 3rd ser., vol. 285, cols. 668 (6 March 1884), 1061, 1069 (10 March 1884). The effect of this intervention, and the merits of not using Zubayr, continued to be a subject of disagreement long after: see Chas. H. Allen, 'Edmund Sturge and Zebehr Pasha', *The Anti-Slavery Reporter*, vol. 21:1 (1901), pp. 19–21.
[125] Cromer, *Modern Egypt*, vol. 1, p. 522.   [126] PP 1884 (c. 3969), No. 236, p. 158.
[127] PP 1884 (c. 3969), No. 234, p. 158.   [128] PP 1884 (c. 3970) LXXXIX. 1, No. 2, p. 1.

In May, the Mahdi captured Berber, and the siege of Khartoum began. This was to end in Gordon's death, when the British forces – misled by Gordon's reassurances that he had the ability to hold out for months – arrived too late to save him.

Gordon's Death and the Arrest of Zubayr

At the end of January, with the British forces still five days away, the Mahdi attacked Khartoum and Gordon got the martyrdom that he had so long craved. It was in the aftermath of this rout that the British decided to detain Zubayr. The trigger for this was his proposal to the Khedive that he should go on a mission with two officials and two *ulemas* to ascertain the Mahdi's intentions.[129] When Baring asked General Wolseley for his opinion on this, the commander responded that '[i]t would be madness to allow Zebehr to do as he proposes, as his tribe has done more than any other to bring about the present state of things in Soudan.'[130] Wolseley wanted Zubayr and other 'friends and correspondents of the Mahdi' to be detained 'in the interests of this army if the autumn campaign is to succeed'. Baring knew of no evidence to convict them ('although presumption of their guilt is strong'),[131] and thought it unwise to commence legal proceedings. He outlined two options. The first was 'to act without legal warrant on the ground of military necessity'. This was potentially problematic since Cairo could not be said to be within the sphere of military operations. The second was to persuade the Egyptian government to pass a law after the arrest of Zubayr and others, retrospectively legalising their detention and deportation. In Baring's view, such a law should not be passed in advance, since that would alert them to the danger.[132] Although Baring had previously urged Zubayr's employment, he now began to believe reports that Zubayr was in communication with the Mahdi, and feared that much harm could be done if Zubayr escaped and joined him. His view was that if Zubayr 'is

---

[129] FO 407/64, enc. in No. 350, p. 234.   [130] FO 407/64, No. 361, p. 244.
[131] There had been some reports in the second half of 1884 of communications passing between Zubayr and the Mahdi, but little concrete evidence: see FO 407/62, No. 251, p. 155; No. 443, p. 269; FO 407/63, No. 229, p. 203 with encs.
[132] Baring to Granville, 7 March 1885, FO 78/7194.

not for us he will be entirely against us', and that he should now be prevented from doing harm.[133]

On 14 March, Zubayr was arrested on the streets of Alexandria and put on board the *Isis*. He asked to be allowed to go to his house and change clothes, but permission was refused. Twelve hours later, he was joined on board by his sons and agent, who had (he later claimed) been arrested 'bare footed and undressed'. The ship sailed out of Alexandria on the next day, initially for Malta.[134] While on board, Zubayr discussed the situation in Egypt with the ship's captain, Ernest Rice, professing his loyalty, and expressing the view that Egypt would never be safe if the British did not recapture Khartoum. He also complained about his arrest, and about the fact that, unlike Urabi, he was not put on trial. Rice reported to Lord John Hay (the commander-in-chief) that he had been 'careful not to allow Zebehr to consider himself a prisoner in the strict sense of the word, but as a person whom, for political reasons, it is better should be absent from Egypt, for the present'.[135] News of Zubayr's arrest was widely reported in the press, with some reports suggesting that he had been in close communication with the Mahdi, and had even plotted Gordon's killing, in revenge for his son's death.[136] However, Gladstone confirmed in parliament that the government had no intelligence to that effect; and no precise information about any communications between Zubayr and the Mahdi was ever to reach the Foreign Office or Colonial Office.[137]

Arrangements for Zubayr's detention were hurriedly made. On 25 March, the Foreign Office requested the Colonial Office to make the necessary legal provisions for the detention in Gibraltar of Zubayr and his relatives, who were being held for 'reasons of State'.[138] The Governor of Gibraltar, Sir John Adye, was instructed to enact an ordinance 'to take effect at once without publishing Draft'.[139] The ordinance was passed on 27 March, and published on the arrival of

---

[133] Baring to Granville, 12 March 1885, FO 78/7194.
[134] *The Times*, 26 March 1885, p. 6. [135] FO 407/65, enc. 1 in No. 108, pp. 66–67.
[136] *Manchester Guardian*, 1 April 1887, p. 7, *The Times*, 2 April 1885, p. 6. See also *The Observer*, 15 March 1885, p. 5, *New York Times*, 15 March 1885, p. 2.
[137] *Parl. Debs.*, 3rd ser., vol. 296, col. 1307 (10 April 1885).
[138] FO 407/64, No. 440, p. 307. The detainees were Zubayr, his sons Mahomed Fadl and Ali Faik, his foster son Tasin Kamel, and his agent Abdallah.
[139] Derby to Governor of Gibraltar, 25 March 1885, FO 78/4194.

the men in Gibraltar, three days later. Drafted in a hurry in Gibraltar, it was not modelled on any precedent. Its two clauses authorised the Governor to order the arrest and detention during Her Majesty's pleasure of the named 'Egyptian subjects'. It did not explicitly prevent any writ of habeas corpus being issued, though officials in London assumed that the ordinance would be an answer to any such application.[140] When sent to London for confirmation, officials were less concerned by the prospect of a challenge on Zubayr's behalf than by the possibility that the Sultan would be offended by its reference to 'Egyptian subjects'.[141] Adye arranged for them to be lodged in his cottage, Europa House, which was isolated and at a distance from the town. Zubayr expressed himself content with the arrangements made for his comfort – though he complained of the cold – but asked if his secretary and stepson might be allowed to return to Egypt, to look after his family. Although the Governor had no objection, Wolseley thought that it would be seen as a sign of weakness to allow them back.[142] At the end of May, Baring told the Colonial Office that it would still be some months before the effect of the evacuation policy on Sudan and Egypt would be clear, and that in the meantime Zubayr should be kept in Gibraltar.[143]

Zubayr in Detention at Gibraltar

Unlike Urabi, who had led a military insurrection, there was no concrete evidence that Zubayr had committed any hostile acts against either Egypt or the British. It was therefore not possible either to try him in Egypt, or offer the apparently magnanimous sanctuary publicly offered to Urabi. At the same time, since he was an unpopular slave trader with little public or legal support, the British did not have to worry about the political consequences of keeping him in detention. Furthermore, whereas the arrest of Urabi had sealed the defeat of his

---

[140] The Colonial Office telegraphed Adye, 'If shown to be invalid, telegraph for instructions': 4 April 1885, FO 78/4194.
[141] Draft reference, 6 April 1885, FO 78/4194. Although the Law Officers did not think the wording was perfect, they considered it inadvisable to amend an Ordinance which had already been published. The ordinance itself was published in PP 1884–1885 (156) LIII. 481; see also *The Times*, 30 April 1885, p. 6.
[142] Baring to Granville, 18 April 1885, FO 78/4914.
[143] Baring to CO, 31 May 1885, FO 78/4194.

movement, the Sudanese border remained unsettled, with the Mahdi entrenched in power. Under these circumstances, the military felt that Zubayr had to be kept under their control.

Two days after his detention, *The Times*'s correspondent in Cairo wrote '[i]t is at least singular that the English authorities, who refused to try Arabi, a prisoner of war, should arrest and deport Zebehr without formal inquiry.'[144] However, the government was not worried about such legal niceties. When questioned about the arrest in parliament, Granville told the Conservative peer Viscount Bury that the British had acted out of military necessity, while the Attorney General, Sir Henry James, told John Gorst that Zubayr was detained under a special ordinance which the Governor of Gibraltar had legal authority to issue.[145] The question was raised again in parliament in April 1886 by Thomas Lister, Lord Ribblesdale, who had been assigned to guard Zubayr for three months in Gibraltar and who had come to admire him as a result of their conversations there.[146] Ribblesdale condemned the arbitrary nature of Zubayr's detention, and challenged the Foreign Secretary to produce any precedent for the detention of the subject of a 'civilized nation' without any preliminary investigation, let alone a trial.[147] He was supported by Lord Fitzgerald, the Irish lord of appeal (and Liberal Unionist). Fitzgerald argued both that Zubayr's detention was unlawful unless justified by military necessity (which was not evident) and that the Gibraltarian authorities did not have the power to issue ordinances which were contrary to the law of England.[148] These points did not move the Foreign Secretary, Lord Rosebery. Admitting that there were no constitutional arguments which could be put for detaining Zubayr, he stated that the government was 'dealing with an extraordinary and

---

[144] *The Times*, 16 March 1885, p. 5. For further (mixed) press reactions, see *The Times*, 17 March 1885, p. 5; *Pall Mall Gazette*, 16 March 1885, p. 5; 17 March 1885, p. 4.

[145] *Parl. Debs.*, 3rd ser., vol. 295, col. 1429 (17 March 1885); vol. 296, col. 986 (30 March 1885). See further questions in *Parl. Debs.*, 3rd ser., vol. 296, col. 1100 (31 March 1885), col. 1629 (14 April 1885); vol. 297, col. 23 (17 April 1885). Both Bury and Gorst joined Salisbury's short-lived Conservative government in June, but did not take up Zubayr's cause while in office.

[146] Thomas Lister Ribblesdale, *Impressions and Memories* (London, Cassell & Company, Ltd., 1927), 139; and Lord Ribblesdale, 'Conversations with Zobeir Pasha at Gibraltar', *The Nineteenth Century*, vol. LXIII (1908), pp. 936–948.

[147] *Parl. Debs.*, 3rd ser., vol. 304, col. 706 (5 April 1886).

[148] *Parl. Debs.*, 3rd ser., vol. 304, col. 714 (5 April 1886).

exceptional state of things'. His detention was a question of military necessity, arising out of Britain's occupation of a country which was neither a protectorate nor subject to British sovereignty.[149] Nor did Ribblesdale's intervention attract wide sympathy in the press. *The Times*, which thought that Ribblesdale 'has been captivated by his captive', thought it idle to consider too closely the constitutional and legal principles involved in the detention of this slave trader accused of communication with the tribes fighting British troops.[150]

Although Fitzgerald's arguments might have formed the basis for a full legal challenge, no steps were taken to challenge Zubayr's detention in court. Instead, Zubayr wrote a number of letters to the Foreign Office, protesting against the injustice of his detention, and asking to be allowed to explain himself in London.[151] Rather than taking a confrontational line, he wrote in the idiom of a loyal supplicant. When his letters went unanswered, he protested 'This is not the British justice I have known.'[152] His case was taken up in London by an Indian Muslim, Abdul Rassool, who wrote a series of letters to the Colonial Office asking to be allowed to visit Zubayr in Gibraltar.[153] At the end of August 1885, the Foreign Office received a letter from a firm of solicitors, saying that they had been instructed by a 'friend and relation' of Zubayr to take up his defence, and requesting to know both whether he was being held in military or civilian custody at Gibraltar and how they could communicate with him.[154] The letter was passed on to the Law Officers, who advised that these lawyers were not entitled either to communicate with Zubayr or to receive any further information.[155] This stalling tactic had the desired effect of

---

[149] *Parl. Debs.*, 3rd ser., vol. 304, cols. 715–716 (5 April 1886). The *Pall Mall Gazette* reported Ribblesdale's speech, but not the reply: 6 April 1886, p. 11. See also the response to Henry Labouchere's later questioning the detention: *Parl. Debs.*, 3rd ser., vol. 312, col. 1782 (29 March 1887).
[150] *The Times*, 7 April 1886, p. 9. Contrast the positive tone of the *Pall Mall Gazette*, 6 April 1886, p. 3.
[151] Letter from Zubayr, 30 March 1885, FO 78/4194.
[152] Letter from Zubayr, 20 August 1885, FO 78/4195.
[153] British officials became so suspicious of this obscure individual that he was surreptitiously hired by the librarian of the India Office (without ministerial sanction) 'to keep an eye on him'; but they found nothing of any interest. Sir Owen Burne to Currie, September 1886, FO 78/4195.
[154] Gadsden and Treherne to Foreign Office, 31 August 1885, FO 78/4195.
[155] Foreign Office to Gadsden and Treherne, 25 September 1885, FO 78/4195.

stifling any further legal attempts to question Zubayr's detention. The Foreign Office continued to pass on Rassool's letters, considering them 'quite worth reading as giving the impression of an oriental on the present state of English policy'. Rassool himself became more strident in his criticism of the British, pointing to the injustice of the fact that Urabi, who had been tried and banished as a rebel, was allowed to move freely in Ceylon, whereas Zubayr was confined in one place, though he had never been convicted of the smallest crime;[156] but his criticisms had no effect on policy.

Zubayr also got to know two other Britons while in Gibraltar, who would argue his cause. One was the Governor, Sir John Adye, who came to regard him as a man of 'considerable ability', whose views about Sudan made much sense.[157] The other was the journalist Flora Shaw (later Lady Lugard), who visited Zubayr once a week over a four-month period during his detention. At the end of June 1887, she published a short article on 'Zebehr Pasha at Gibraltar' in the *Pall Mall Gazette*, in which he was quoted as saying 'your Government took me and made me a prisoner, and when I asked why, they would give me no reason'.[158] In spite of the support of such friendly figures, however, Zubayr continued to draw the hostility of such powerful groups as the Anti-Slavery Society, who kept in the public mind the image of a slave trader who was 'ruthless, with a heart of iron'.[159]

The Long Road to Release

British policy towards both Egypt and Sudan would remain ambiguous for the next two years. Although Wolseley argued that it was 'almost imperative on us to destroy the Mahdi's power at Khartoum',[160] the Liberal government had no wish to hold Khartoum, and decided in

---

[156] Abdul Rassool to Zubayr, 15 September 1885, FO 78/4195.
[157] General Sir John Adye, *Recollections of a Military Life* (London, MacMillan and Co., 1895), p. 374
[158] *Pall Mall Gazette*, 28 June 1887, pp. 1–2. Later in the year, she published a sympathetic account of his life in 'The Story of Zebehr Pasha, as Told by Himself', *Contemporary Review*, vol. 52 (1887), pp. 333–349, 568–585, 658–682.
[159] See e.g. the report of his release in *The Anti-Slavery Reporter*, vol. 7:4 (1887), pp. 140–141.
[160] PP 1885–1885 (c. 4392) LXXXIX. 201, No. 52, p. 35.

May 1885 that troops should be withdrawn from Sudan.[161] Soon after, the government was replaced by Salisbury's seven-month Conservative ministry, which also wanted to 'withdraw with honour'. To effect this policy, Salisbury sent Sir Henry Drummond Wolff as an emissary to Constantinople, to negotiate an eventual evacuation by the British not only from Sudan, but from Egypt as well. At Constantinople, Wolff negotiated a preliminary convention under which two commissioners – Wolff himself and Muktar Pasha for the Porte – would report on how to create the conditions allowing the withdrawal of British troops to take place. One of the matters to be considered was what to do with Zubayr.

The civilian authorities had already turned their minds to this question. With Wolseley's military operations having concluded, Baring felt that Zubayr could be released, since the reason for his detention had been to prevent him from hampering these very operations.[162] The acting Consul General in Cairo, Edwin Egerton, similarly favoured Zubayr's release, provided some place were found 'in which to employ him'. The Egyptian government – which did not consider Zubayr to have been imprisoned on their account – also wanted him to be released.[163] This prompted Salisbury on 23 September to consult the military on the conditions for his release.[164] However, the generals began to get cold feet, and raised objections to Zubayr's return, which had the support of the War Office. Hearing these views, Egerton rowed back, recommending delay and arguing that it would be better to keep Zubayr in Gibraltar either until the frontier had been settled or until some plan had been developed to send him cheaply to some part of Sudan where he might be left without harm.[165] The delay in liberating Zubayr exasperated Salisbury. 'The continued detention of Zebehr Pasha is a cause of expense and embarrassment', he told Wolff, 'and Her Majesty's Government would be glad both on grounds of humanity and policy

---

[161] *Parl. Debs.*, 3rd ser., vol. 298, col. 152 (11 May 1885). See further M. P. Hornik, 'The Mission of Sir Henry Drummond-Wolff to Constantinople, 1885–1887', *English Historical Review*, vol. 55 (1940), pp. 598–623, at pp. 601–602.
[162] Baring letter, 14 September 1885, FO 78/4195.
[163] FO 407/66, Nos. 211–212, p. 121.   [164] FO 407/66, No. 223, p. 128.
[165] FO 407/67, Nos. 2–3, p. 1.

if an arrangement could be devised which would admit of his liberation without danger to Egyptian or British interests.'[166]

By the middle of December 1885, Wolff had come to the view that Zubayr could be safely brought back, at least if he swore an oath on the Koran to remain peaceful.[167] At the beginning of January, General Stephenson also told Wolff that he would agree to Zubayr's release if he swore an oath of loyalty and retired 'to his tribe between Berber and Khartoum', leaving his wives and family in Cairo as hostages.[168] In their discussions as to how to pacify Sudan, Wolff and the Ottoman Commissioner Muktar Pasha also raised the possibility of employing Zubayr for this purpose.[169] In an intervention which did not please Zubayr, Abdul Rassool, who was now in Cairo, also went to see Baring to urge that Zubayr be sent to Sudan to restore order, with his sons (and Rassool himself) being kept hostages as security in Cairo.[170] However, when Salisbury asked Wolseley for his opinion on using Zubayr, the response was firm opposition.[171] The military (and their political masters of both stripes) continued to oppose any proposal to use Zubayr in the pacification of Sudan.[172]

Zubayr's release also depended on the agreement of a number of different government departments, which had different views of the problem. The matter was of interest to the Colonial Office, which was responsible for Gibraltar, whose Governor was concerned about the effect of detention on Zubayr's mental health.[173] It was also a matter of concern for the Treasury, which baulked at the £1,800 spent annually

---

[166] Salisbury to Wolff, 4 November 1885, FO 78/4195.
[167] FO 407/76, No. 384, p. 166. Wolff had earlier thought it best to postpone the question of Zubayr's release until the Ottoman Commissioner, Muktar Pasha, had arrived in Cairo, so that he could obtain securities for good behaviour from Zubayr: FO 407/76, No. 329, p. 139.
[168] FO 407/68, No. 5, p. 2. Lt. Edward Stuart-Wortley had earlier told Wolff that 'no harm could result' from sending Zubayr back to Sudan and setting him up as a ruler in Khartoum, although, in his view, Zubayr should not be allowed to return to Cairo: FO 407/76, enc. 3 in No. 384, p. 168.
[169] FO 407/77, No. 34, p. 19; cf. No. 22, p. 9.
[170] Baring note, 8 January 1886, FO 78/4195; Zubayr to Abdul Rassool, 26 December 1886, FO 78/4196.
[171] FO 407/77, No. 42, p. 22; FO 407/68, No. 30, p. 23.
[172] FO 407/77, No. 98, p. 78; War Office to Foreign Office, 18 February 1886, FO 78/4195.
[173] Sir John Adye to Col. Stanley, 30 November 1885, FO 78/4195.

Egypt and Sudan, 1882–1887 155

to maintain Zubayr,[174] and became increasingly insistent on the need either to transfer him to the custody of the Egyptian government, or to free him.[175] Despite this pressure, the Foreign Office – which was responsible for Egyptian policy – insisted that they could not go against the views of the military, who thought that Zubayr could not be freed until Sudan had been fully pacified.[176] The stalemate continued to the end of 1886, when the Foreign Office again sounded out the military on the matter of Zubayr's release. Again the answer was negative. As Stephenson saw it, Sudanese affairs had reached a critical moment – the 'dervish movement is thoroughly broken'. With negotiations about to commence regarding the frontier, it was considered too risky to allow him to return.[177] Once again, Zubayr was held hostage to events on the border.

In the following months, when Wolff was negotiating the date of a projected British withdrawal from Egypt, the question of what to do with Zubayr was regularly revisited. In March 1887, Sir John Adye, now retired as Governor of Gibraltar, argued that Zubayr posed no threat and might well use his influence in favour of the British if released. He doubted whether there had been any serious reason for detaining him in the first place, and thought that, under the changed military circumstances in Sudan, there was no reason to keep him.[178] This intervention had the effect of nudging the Foreign Office to make yet another attempt to induce the military to give ground. On this occasion, they received promising news from Baring: with the military preparing to withdraw troops from Aswan, the generals were now of the view that Zubayr's influence over the black troops

---

[174] Treasury to Foreign Office, 27 November 1885, FO 78/4195. The War Office claimed that (like Cetshwayo), Zubayr should be regarded as a military prisoner only until the detention ordinance had been passed for his detention. However, the Foreign Office insisted the item remain in the army estimates, since neither Gibraltar nor Egypt should be expected to pay: Note from Financial Secretary's Department, War Office, 26 August 1885, FO 78/4195, see also Foreign Office to Treasury, 11 September 1885, FO 78/4195.

[175] FO 407/77, No. 128, p. 98. The Treasury again raised the question of Zubayr's release after the government agreed in June 1886 that his wife, a tutor for his children and three servants could be sent to Gibraltar, increasing the costs still further: see FO 407/68, No. 222, p. 163; FO 407/69, No. 155*, p. 111*; No. 165, p. 138.

[176] FO 407/68, No. 82, p. 45; FO 407/77, No. 145, p. 106.

[177] FO 407/69, No. 183, p. 145; No. 185, p. 146; FO 407/70, No. 7, p. 4.

[178] Adye to Foreign Office, 10 March 1887, FO 78/4196.

had waned and that he would pose no further danger.[179] Although Wolseley, who had returned to England in 1885, again raised objections, the cabinet overruled them.[180] At the end of April, Salisbury requested Baring to inform the Egyptian government of the decision to release Zubayr, and to ascertain their wishes as to the date of his arrival.[181] The Egyptian government was content for him to return, though it required him to make a formal pledge to observe certain conditions.[182]

Although all seemed set for Zubayr's release, its timing proved problematic, for it coincided with a delicate moment in Wolff's negotiations with the Porte. By the middle of May 1887, a convention had been drafted which stipulated that the British would withdraw their troops from Egypt within three years of its signing, unless their continued presence proved to be necessary as a result of internal or external dangers.[183] However, rather than accelerating Zubayr's release, these negotiations only served to delay it further. British officials were concerned about potentially adverse political effects in Egypt if the announcement of Zubayr's release, or his arrival in Cairo, coincided with the announcement of the convention, and Britain's planned withdrawal under it.[184] Salisbury agreed that it was therefore best to delay his release until the convention had been ratified.[185] In the event, the convention was never ratified by the Powers, and Wolff left Constantinople in July, with the long anticipated withdrawal of British troops postponed *sine die*. Consequently, it was only the collapse of Wolff's project that finally opened the way for Zubayr's return, and Salisbury issued instructions to this effect on 19 July, the day his emissary left Constantinople.[186] Zubayr arrived in Cairo on 28 September 1887. He agreed to the conditions imposed, which included the abandonment of his financial

---

[179] Baring to Salisbury, 28 March 1887, FO 78/4196.
[180] Wolseley suggested that Zubayr be sent to Cyprus. War Office to Foreign Office, 20 April 1887, FO 78/4196.
[181] Salisbury to Baring, 29 April 1887, FO 78/4196.
[182] PP 1888 (c. 5316) CX. 325, No. 84, p. 56.
[183] PP 1887 (c. 5050) XCII. 481, enc. in No. 84, p. 48 at p. 49.
[184] FO 407/70, No. 180, p. 143; No. 181, p. 143.
[185] Foreign Office to War Office, 24 May 1887, FO 78/4196.
[186] FO 407/71, No. 10, p. 8.

claims against the Egyptian government in exchange for a monthly allowance.[187] The *Pall Mall Gazette* congratulated the government on its decision to release Zubayr, describing his detention as 'high-handed and thoroughly un-English'.[188] His release raised the question of whether it would now be an appropriate time to release Urabi, but the government quickly put paid to any such hopes.[189] Discussing this issue, the *Pall Mall Gazette* published an article based on interviews with Zubayr – perhaps by Flora Shaw – which showed that, in 1882, he had rejected Urabi's overtures to join the rebellion, and had backed the Khedive.[190]

As observers in Britain realised, the treatment of Zubayr contrasted sharply with that given to Urabi. His detention in Gibraltar was rendered lawful by simple legislative fiat: an exercise of sheer power dressed up in legal garb. As officials in Cairo realised, there was no evidence that Zubayr had done anything wrong, which might justify any kind of legal proceedings against him. In any event, the British had no claim to jurisdiction over him: this was not even the kind of case – found elsewhere in Africa – of jurisdictional ambiguity, where a detention ordinance was resorted to in order to deal with an offender who fell between jurisdictional cracks. Nor did the Egyptian government show any interest in levelling the kinds of accusations against Zubayr which had been made against Urabi. Instead, having been seized in Cairo by an 'act of state' executed by the British military, Zubayr was detained to satisfy military demands to remove someone whose presence might disrupt their campaign to pacify Sudan. While this was in effect an act of imperial military power, it had to be given legal cover, with an ordinance designed to comply with the constitutional requirement that no one be held without legal authority. Such a measure was necessary, given both the questions raised by those like Lords Ribblesdale and Fitzgerald about the basis of his detention and the possibility that his detention might

---

[187] Despite the agreement at the time of his release, Zubayr continued to seek to recover his property in Cairo, hiring an English lawyer in 1893 to pursue his claims: *Morning Post*, 9 December 1893, p. 5. Although the matter was raised in parliament, the British government now considered that it had nothing to do with them. *Parl. Debs.*, 4th ser., vol. 11, col. 1632 (1 May 1893).

[188] 'The Release of Zebehr Pasha', *Pall Mall Gazette*, 19 August 1887.

[189] *Parl. Debs.*, 3rd ser., vol. 319, col. 1099 (19 August 1887).

[190] 'Two Views of Arabi Pasha', *Pall Mall Gazette*, 24 August 1887, p. 2.

be challenged by a habeas corpus application. However, given his reputation as a slave trader, few in Britain worried about Zubayr. In his case, the most formal kind of law served to satisfy most metropolitan consciences; and the legality of the ordinance under which he was held was never challenged in court.

The notion of the rule of law, which public intellectuals at home saw as permeating their constitutional culture, was, as has been seen, an ambiguous one, even in the hands of its most vocal legal champion, A. V. Dicey. As he had explained, the demands of the rule of law might be met even by legislation removing rights of due process: for anything permitted by valid legislation was by its nature lawful. Zubayr was detained on perhaps the weakest of legislative foundations – an ordinance issued by a colonial governor under crown powers.[191] This form of legislation by-passed the constitutional guarantees Dicey found in a parliament, which he considered as a kind of national jury to evaluate the needs of an emergency. But these guarantees in turn depended on the moral pressure exerted by a wider political community, which expected ancient rights to be observed; and where that community was untroubled by such legislation, a purely formal rule of law could be used as cover for the exercise of sovereign power for political ends. To that degree, the nature of the 'rule of law' applied – whether it was more 'substantive' or more 'formal' – depended on how the problem was perceived in the wider political culture. The kind of rule of law which liberal nationalist leaders were expected to enjoy was not the same as that accorded to unappetising slave traders.

---

[191] These powers would later be questioned by another detainee from Egypt, Zaghlul Pasha: see Chapter 8.

5

Detention without Trial in Sierra Leone and the Gold Coast, 1865–1890

Zubayr's detention did not follow any kind of preliminary assessment of whether he had been guilty of any kind of offence, as in the cases of Abdullah of Perak or Langalibalele, and neither was he a defeated enemy, like Cetshwayo. His was a preventative detention, of a potential troublemaker. He was not, however, the first African political prisoner to be detained by virtue of an ordinance passed simply to hold him. In the four years before his detention, ten ordinances were passed in Sierra Leone and the Gold Coast to allow political prisoners there to be held without trial. In the following sixteen years, thirty-eight more such ordinances would be passed in these colonies.[1] Further ordinances were also passed in Gambia and (after 1886) the colony of Lagos. It was in West Africa that the Colonial Office pioneered the use of *ad hominem* ordinances to detain people who had committed no offence, for political reasons. This chapter will explore the origins of the policy of passing ordinances to detain political prisoners, and the different purposes for which they were used in the 1880s.

The British Presence in West Africa

The use of such ordinances developed at a time when British policy in West Africa was undergoing significant transition. In 1865, when

---

[1] This does not count the ordinances passed in Sierra Leone for the reception of those already detained in the Gold Coast and vice versa.

a select committee of the House of Commons recommended a gradual withdrawal from West Africa,[2] there was only a small British presence in the region. Britain's most important colony – and one which the committee wished to retain – was Sierra Leone. It had become a crown colony in 1808, when the British government assumed control of the peninsula from the abolitionist Sierra Leone Company. In 1861, part of the Koya chiefdom – British Quiah – and some territory at the mouth of the Sherbro River was ceded to the British, but the colony remained very limited in extent.[3] At the same time, numerous treaties were made with local rulers.[4] Such treaties were often entered into to suppress the slave trade within the territory of the ruler, and to open it to British traders; and they also often stipulated that disputes between the ruler and any other chief in his dominions were to be referred to the Governor to determine.[5]

Although the chiefs received a stipend in return from the British government, the treaties did not create protectorates, nor did the local chiefs consider that a protectorate existed.[6] However, in many of the treaties, sovereign rights were ceded over land within a quarter of a mile of a river. The British also sought to exert a degree of extraterritorial jurisdiction over the hinterland.[7] An Order in Council was issued in 1850 (under the provisions of the 1843 Foreign Jurisdiction Act)[8] providing for extraterritorial jurisdiction over

---

[2] PP 1865 (412) V. 1, iii.
[3] Christopher Fyfe, *A History of Sierra Leone* (Oxford, Oxford University Press, 1962), pp. 310–12. See further Bronwen Everill, *Abolition and Empire in Sierra Leone and Liberia* (Basingstoke, Palgrave Macmillan, 2013).
[4] In 1865, eighty-two treaties entered into by the Sierra Leone Government were still in force, of which fifty-seven were treaties of amity and commerce. See CO 879/35/1 for a 'Collection of Treaties with Native Chiefs &c on the West Coast of Africa'.
[5] See Inge Van Hulle, *Britain and International Law in West Africa: The Practice of Empire* (Oxford, Oxford University Press, 2020), ch. 2; and Richard Huzzey, *Freedom Burning: Anti-slavery and Empire in Victorian Britain* (Ithaca and London, Cornell University Press, 2012), pp. 141–147.
[6] Evidence of Col. Ord to the select committee, PP 1865 (412), q. 518, p. 26; and see his 1865 Report, PP 1865 (412), p. 349.
[7] See W. Ross Johnston, *Sovereignty and Protection: A Study of British Jurisdictional Imperialism in the Late Nineteenth Century* (Durham, Duke University Press, 1973); and Inge Van Hulle, 'British Protection, Extraterritoriality and Protectorates in West Africa, 1807–80', in Lauren Benton, Adam Clulow and Bain Attwood (eds.), *Protection and Empire: A Global History* (Cambridge, Cambridge University Press, 2018), pp. 194–210.
[8] 6 & 7 Vic. c. 94.

crimes recognised in English law which had been committed in areas outside the colony whose rulers had entered into treaties conferring such power.[9] The order and treaties were intended only to confer jurisdiction over British subjects, liberated Africans and others living in the colony who had committed crimes in the hinterland. However, in 1871, the West Africa Settlements Act conferred extraterritorial jurisdiction over anyone who was not the subject of a civilised power, who had committed offences within twenty miles of the boundary of a British settlement or 'adjacent protectorates' against any British subject or person living within these areas, and who had been apprehended in these areas.[10]

The colonial settlements at the Gold Coast were also very small.[11] Originally forts owned by the Royal African Company, they had come into government hands in 1821 when the successor African Company was dissolved. Formally under Sierra Leone, the four forts at Dixcove, Cape Coast, Anomabo and Accra were in practice left to a committee of merchants to run until the crown resumed control in 1843. In this year, Britain set up separate governments both for the Gold Coast settlements and for Gambia (in effect Bathurst), which were now formally separated from Sierra Leone. The precise extent of British territory on the Gold Coast was undefined, though it was often taken to be the land within a cannon-shot from the forts.[12] Beyond that territory, officials by the 1860s spoke of a 'protectorate', without being entirely clear as to its nature. The expression 'Natives under British protection' – referring to the Fanti – had been used in an 1817 treaty with the Asante, but nothing

---

[9] PP 1854–55 (383) XXXVII. 375, No. 7, p. 34. It was implemented in 1853 after the necessary treaties had been signed. The 1861 Sierra Leone Offences Act (24 & 25 Vict. c. 31) made the colony's laws applicable to all British subjects in the hinterland, while making no claim to any sovereign rights over this land.

[10] 34 & 35 Vict. c. 8. In drafting this legislation, the Colonial Office accepted the rule that one country could not exercise jurisdiction over the subjects of another, but limited its application to the subjects of 'civilized powers'. See Johnston, *Sovereignty and Protection*, pp. 72–74.

[11] See David Kimble, *A Political History of Ghana, 1850–1928* (Oxford, Oxford University Press, 1963); and Rebecca Shumway, 'Palavers and Treaty Making in the British Acquisition of the Gold Coast Colony (West Africa)', in Saliha Belmessous (ed.), *Empire by Treaty: Negotiating European Expansion, 1600–1900* (Oxford, Oxford University Press, 2014), pp. 161–183.

[12] PP 1865 (412), p. 41, q. 883. See also Kimble, *A Political History of Ghana*, pp. 209–210.

was said about the nature of the protection given.[13] A further step in the development of British 'protection' over the coastal rulers came in 1844, when a number of Fanti rulers signed a Bond, which acknowledged the exercise of British 'power and jurisdiction' in places adjacent to the forts and settlements. It stipulated that murders, robberies 'and other crimes' would be tried by the Queen's officers and the chiefs of the district, 'moulding the customs of the country to the general principles of British law'.[14] An Order in Council issued in the same year under the 1843 Foreign Jurisdiction Act also gave colonial courts the power to try crimes committed in 'places adjacent to Her Majesty's forts and settlements'. In this case, the jurisdiction was aimed to cover Africans living in the hinterland of the forts, for the Order in Council stipulated that judges should observe such local customs as were compatible with the principles of English law.[15]

In April 1852, a 'legislative assembly of native chiefs upon the Gold Coast', presided over by the Governor, was set up by agreement, and instituted a poll tax on the 'population enjoying the protection of the British Government'. It was agreed that a proclamation on the basis of these resolutions would be implemented by the Governor, and would be 'binding upon the whole of the native population being under the protection of the British Government'.[16] Nonetheless, if there was a 'protectorate' over the Fanti, it was not clearly defined by treaty or ordinance, but was merely implied from instruments such as the Bond and the Poll-Tax Ordinance. Officials testifying to the 1865 committee saw the commitments implied by protection as being

---

[13] 'Treaty with Ashantee. Peace and Commerce', Art IV, in Edward Hertslet, *A Complete Collection of the Treaties and Conventions and Reciprocal Regulations at Present Subsisting between Great Britain and Foreign Powers*, vol. XII (London, Butterworths, 1871) [henceforth Hertslet, *Commercial Treaties*], p. 1.

[14] Declaration of Fantee Chiefs: Hertslet, *Commercial Treaties*, vol. XII, p. 30. See also J. B. Danquah, 'The Historical Significance of the Bond of 1844', *Transactions of the Historical Society of Ghana*, vol. 3 (1957), pp. 3–29. The declaration was aimed at the suppression of the practice of human sacrifice, on which see Ivor Wilks, *Asante in the Nineteenth Century: The Structure and Evolution of a Political Order* (Cambridge, Cambridge University Press, 1975), pp. 591–592.

[15] PP 1854–55 (383), No. 5, p. 81. At that point, only Sierra Leone had a Supreme Court (as required by the 1843 Act).

[16] PP 1865 (412), p. 420. The tax proved hard to collect and by 1861 had ceased to be paid. See Kimble, *A Political History of Ghana*, ch. 4.

very vague.[17] Nor were these commitments regarded as desirable by the British at this point. As the draft report of the select committee put it, 'The protectorate of tribes about our forts on the Gold Coast assumes an indefinite and unintelligible responsibility on our part, uncompensated by any adequate advantage to the tribes'.[18] This was not something which the British then wanted to expand. With a view to retrenchment, in the aftermath of the select committee, a single 'Government of our West African Settlements' based at Freetown was set up, covering not only Sierra Leone, the Gold Coast and Gambia, but also Lagos, which had been ceded to Britain in 1861.

In the event, the policy of retrenchment proved impossible to execute. It was rethought after the Asante invaded the 'protectorate' in 1873, claiming that they had sovereign rights over Elmina, which the British had acquired by treaty from the Dutch in 1872.[19] In the ensuing war, the Asante were crushed, and their capital Kumasi destroyed. In the subsequent treaty of Fomena, Britain's right to Elmina was confirmed, and a heavy indemnity of 50,000 ounces of gold was imposed on the Asante.[20] Although the Colonial Office did not at this stage want to annex Asante, it wanted to define its position on the Gold Coast more clearly. In July 1874, Letters Patent were therefore issued which again separated the Gold Coast and Lagos from Sierra Leone, and created a separate Gold Coast Colony, with its own Legislative and Executive Councils.[21] This was followed by an Order in Council which gave the Legislative Council powers under the 1843 Foreign Jurisdiction Act to legislate in respect of the adjacent territories.[22] A proclamation was prepared to define these legislative

---

[17] In his 1865 report, Col. Ord suggested that the Fantis understood 'protection' in terms of Great Britain's duty to protect them militarily from the Asante: this was not specified in the treaties and Ord suggested that any such duty implied by the payment of tax was removed by its non-payment: PP 1865 (412), Appx. No. 1, p. 356. See also the evidence of T. F. Elliott, PP 1865 (412), q. 125, p. 7; Sir Benjamin Pine, PP 1865 (412), q. 2988ff., p. 127. See also Shumway, 'Palavers and Treaty Making', pp. 166–169.

[18] PP 1865 (412), p. xiv, quoted in Kimble, *A Political History of Ghana*, p. 207.

[19] Michael Crowder, *West Africa under Colonial Rule* (London, Hutchinson, 1968), p. 146.

[20] See *Parl. Debs.*, 3rd ser., vol. 218, col. 1592 (24 May 1874).

[21] PP 1875 (1140) LII. 325, Appx. No 1, p. 97.

[22] PP 1875 (1139) LII. 277, enc. in No. 1, p. 1.

MAP 3 The Gold Coast and Asante

powers as well as the extent of the protectorate, something which officials in London felt would have the effect of turning it virtually into a colony.[23] In fact, the proclamation itself was never issued, though a Supreme Court Ordinance was passed in 1876, which introduced English law to the Gold Coast as it stood in July 1874.[24] This was designed to cover not only the British settlements on the coast, but also the territory inland to the Prah. Two years later, a Native Jurisdiction Ordinance was passed, which defined and limited the powers of chiefs in the protected areas, in effect putting them under the power of the Governor and his council. Any chief who refused to recognise the authority of the crown would lose his power.[25]

---

[23] PP 1875 (c. 1139), enc. in No. 2, p. 5; Minute by E. Fairfield, 6 November 1874, CO 96/112, quoted in Robert B. Seidman, 'A Note on the Construction of the Gold Coast Reception Statute', *Journal of African Law*, vol. 13 (1969), pp. 45–51 at p. 46.
[24] Gold Coast Supreme Court Ordinance, 1876, ss. 17, 85.
[25] See Francis Agbodeka, *African Politics and British Policy in the Gold Coast, 1868–1900: A Study in the Forms and Force of Protest* (London, Longman, 1971), pp. 113–116; and Native Jurisdiction Ordinance No. 8 of 1878; cf. The Gold Coast Native Jurisdiction Ordinance, No. 5 of 1883. See G. E. Metcalfe, *Great Britain and Ghana: Documents of Ghana History, 1807–1957* (Edinburgh, University of Ghana, 1964), pp. 390–393.

The precise relationship between colony and protectorate – and even their geographic areas – remained undefined, however, until 1891, when the Protected Territories were annexed to the Gold Coast Colony.[26]

Britain's change of policy in the Gold Coast was in part a response to the perceived threat of Asante. However, in the aftermath of the 1873–1874 war, that kingdom suffered a period of instability. The kingdom, at whose head stood the Asantehene, was made up of a number of constituent kingdoms or states. These included the 'metropolitan' Amantoo states, whose kings participated in the election of the Asantehene and his placing on the golden stool, and the 'provincial' Amansin states. From the mid 1870s, a number of kings from these states began to rebel or secede, many seeking refuge within the protectorate.[27] While the British were happy to see the break-up of the powerful Asante state, until the end of the 1880s, the Colonial Office wished to avoid direct intervention (even when local officials were calling for it), and sought rather to maintain peace as far as possible with this neighbouring state.

Detention without Legal Authority

In an era in which British colonial possessions in West Africa were small, the authorities faced potential threats to their stability from Africans resident outside the colony, over whom British jurisdiction was often questionable. The question of how to deal with them – and how far the demands of legalism had to be complied with – was one which increasingly came to concern the Colonial Office in London. Before 1881, a number of chiefs were detained in the region without legal authority. For instance, in 1853 Cally Mahdoo, the chief of Madina in the Sierra Leone hinterland, was briefly detained in Freetown. As part of Britain's policy to suppress the slave trade, Cally Mahdoo was required, under a treaty signed with Bey Sherbro in 1852, to prevent slaves being traded in his area.[28] However, he proved to be 'refractory', and seemed rather to be encouraging slave trading. When he refused to hand over two liberated Africans who had

---

[26] Kimble, *A Political History of Ghana*, pp. 313–315.
[27] See Agbodeka, *African Politics and British Policy in the Gold Coast*, ch. 4.
[28] CO 879/35/1, No. 49, p. 152.

brought a man they had enslaved to Madina, Governor Kennedy lost patience and ordered him to come to Freetown, the order being backed by a threat to burn his town.[29] He was not kept long. As Commander Reed (who brought him to Freetown) put it, 'Cally Mahdoo has been properly humbled, and will, no doubt, in future, respect British power and British justice.'[30] In fact, there was no legal basis for this brief detention. As a report from the Queen's Advocate in Freetown showed, in this case the British had no jurisdiction over the Africans accused of slave dealing, let alone the Chief of Madina himself.[31] However, this did not bother the *Illustrated London News*, which reported that he had been 'brought as a hostage for the men demanded'[32] – in effect mimicking a common practice of hostage-taking in the region.

Thomas S. Caulker, chief of the Plaintain Islands, had a similar experience in 1859. One of the numerous descendants of Thomas Corker who became rival chiefs in the Sherbro region,[33] he had entered a number of treaties with the British.[34] Caulker came to the attention of the colonial authorities when in early 1859 he claimed land in Sherbro and 'created great disturbance and jealousy among the Native Chiefs',[35] as well as clashing with the French commodore in the region. It was in this context that Commodore Wise, commander of the *Vesuvius*, intervened and brought him to Sierra Leone, where he promised not to engage in any more wars to obtain territory in the Sherbro country. The Acting Governor allowed Caulker to return to the Plaintain Islands, on condition that he sign a peace treaty, promising not to meddle in any lands beyond his own.[36] The British looked no more closely into the legal basis of Caulker's removal than they did into that of Cally Mahdoo.[37] Nor was the government interpreter, T. G. Lawson, much concerned with the legal basis of his

---

[29] PP 1852–53 (1680) LXV. 291, No. 12, p. 23, with enclosures.
[30] PP 1852–53 (1680), enc. 5 in No. 12, p. 27. [31] PP 1852–53 (1680), enc. in No. 13, p. 28.
[32] *Illustrated London News*, 14 May 1853.
[33] See Imodale Caulker-Burnet, *The Caulkers of Sierra Leone: The Story of a Ruling Family and Their Times* (Bloomington, Xlibris, 2010).
[34] CO 879/35/1, No. 39, p. 129; No. 54, p. 159.
[35] Acting Governor Fitzjames to the Duke of Newcastle, 11 August 1859, CO 267/264/9145.
[36] CO 879/35/1, Nos. 58–59, p. 168.
[37] Caulker's treaty with the British omitted the frequently used clause referring disputes between warring factions to the Governor, and allowing other chiefs to join with him in punishing any who refused to comply with his decision.

actions when he brought two other chiefs from British Sherbro to Sierra Leone in 1870 and 'placed [them] under my care as hostages'.[38]

The first important political detention on the Gold Coast was that of John Aggery, king of Cape Coast, in 1867.[39] Aggery's election as king of Cape Coast in January 1865 was ratified by Governor Richard Pine, though the new king did not swear any oath of allegiance to the British crown. Irritated by the way the British exercised their jurisdiction over Africans, Aggery began to exert his own jurisdiction at Cape Coast in ways that antagonised the Governor. When Pine protested that his actions violated the compact between the Queen and the 'tribes under her protection', Aggery reminded him of his 'right as King to rule over my country'.[40] Tensions continued to rise, particularly after a riot occurred in September between the townspeople and troops from the West Indian regiments, which resulted in two civilian deaths, and which Aggery described to the Secretary of State as 'a general attack upon the natives generally'.[41] Eventually, on 6 December 1866, Aggery wrote an angry letter to the Administrator of the Gold Coast, Edward Conran, in which he protested against the insults he had received as king. He also alluded to the 'fearful acts ... when my people were butchered by your soldiers', and stated his presumption that 'your object is to endeavour all in your power to incite me and my people to enact more of those fearful things that took place in Jamaica' – an allusion to the recent events in Morant Bay.[42] This was the last straw for Conran, who 'made a prisoner of this arrogant man' on 8 December, and shipped him to Sierra Leone, at the same time deposing him as king and closing his courts.[43]

Once Aggery had arrived in Sierra Leone, officials began to consider legal questions in a way not done in the preceding cases. Governor-in-Chief Samuel Blackall's legal adviser thought that Aggery could be tried for sedition (under the jurisdiction derived from the Foreign Jurisdiction Act), but worried that the ex-king would be able to

---

[38] CO 879/4/3, enc. 2 in No. 107, p. 124.
[39] See John K. Osei-Tutu, 'Contesting British Sovereignty in Cape Coast, Ghana: Insights from King John Aggery's Correspondences 1865–72', *Transactions of the Historical Society of Ghana*, vol. 7 n.s. (2003), pp. 231–251; and Kimble, *A Political History of Ghana*, ch. 5.
[40] PP 1867 (198) XLIX. 287, encs. 4–5 in No. 1, pp. 5–7.
[41] PP 1867 (198), enc. in No. 9, p. 44.   [42] PP 1867 (198), enc. 1 in No. 23, p. 72.
[43] PP 1867 (198), enc. 1 in No. 23, p. 73.

return to Cape Coast after his sentence had expired and cause more trouble. He suggested that it might be more prudent to exile him.[44] In London, the Secretary of State, Carnarvon – then dealing with controversy raised by the use of martial law in Jamaica – asked his officials a number of questions pertaining to the legality of Aggery's detention. The advice he received was that there had been no legal authority to deport him from the Gold Coast.[45] Nor was it possible to try him at Sierra Leone, since the Gold Coast, which had obtained its own Supreme Court in 1853, was no longer under the jurisdiction of Freetown. Although the legal adviser at the Colonial Office, H. T. Holland, considered the possibility that Aggery might be charged with sedition at the Gold Coast – since 'we have in fact treated the native Chiefs within the Protectorate in some cases as if they were British subjects & imprisoned them'[46] – Carnarvon concluded that there remained doubts both about 'how he can be tried at the G. Coast' and about the possible outcome of any such trial.

Although things looked unpromising from the government's point of view, Carnarvon had no doubt that there had to be 'an end to the absurdity of a native "king" in the town of C[ape] C[oast]'. He proposed that 'Aggery's deposition should be effected by the broad & undisguised exercise of the Supreme Power which created him "King"', through a formal proclamation.[47] This was duly done, and Aggery was banished to Bulama Island where he remained until 1869, when he was allowed to return to Cape Coast on renouncing any claims to kingly power. In this case, the Colonial Office remained aware that it was acting outside any lawful authority, but it did so on grounds of policy. Nor were these events unknown in England, for papers relating to the case were printed by the House of Commons in 1867. Furthermore, the British press was untroubled by Aggery's detention, *The Times* quoting Governor Blackall's view that British presence on the Gold Coast had not yet 'done much towards civilizing

---

[44] PP 1867 (198), enc. 2 in No. 23, p. 73.
[45] Conran did not appear to have acted under powers derived from the Foreign Jurisdiction Act; but even if he had, he had not complied with its provisions. Minutes by T. H. Elliott and H. T. Holland, 8 and 11 February 1867, CO 96/72, ff. 249, 251.
[46] Minute by Holland, 11 February 1867, CO 96/72, f. 251. Cf. PP 1865 (412), p. 315, q. 8140.
[47] CO 96/72, f. 255, minute dated 12 February 1867.

the natives' and that 'nothing but a firm enforcement of British law over those chiefs' could prevent 'a return to the abominations of slavery and torture, in which they appear to rejoice'.[48]

Six years later, another African king challenging British authority on the Gold Coast, Kobina Edjen of Elmina, was detained without any authorising legal instruments, and with only minimal advice on precedents. Although he was 'on the best terms with the Government' after the cession of Elmina to the British,[49] things changed towards the end of November 1872, when a new Administrator, Col. R. W. Harley, arrived with a much more high-handed approach towards the Africans. This could be seen, for instance, in his detention in Elmina of two feuding kings from Sekondi, who had to be released in early March after Governor Hennessy reprimanded him for acting without first seeking legal advice.[50] In the same month, Harley summoned Kobina Edjen and his chiefs to the palaver hall of Elmina Castle to take an oath of allegiance to the Queen, since he suspected the king of having entered into an alliance with the Asante king, who was planning to back his claims to Elmina with an invasion (which led to the war of 1873–1874).[51] Having already been antagonised by Harley on other matters, the king became angry when asked to take the oath, and declared, 'I am not afraid of your power. You may hang me if you like. I will not sign any paper. Myself and some of the people of Elmina have taken fetish oath to oppose the English Government coming to Elmina, and we have not broken that oath yet.'[52] No sooner had he finished than he was told that he and two other chiefs were now prisoners, and would be taken to Cape Coast Castle. Harley told the Secretary of State, Kimberley, that this arrest had 'helped to checkmate the Ashantee movements and plans', and had forestalled a general rising on the coast.[53] The men were removed to Freetown towards the end of April before any instructions had been received from London. No legal instrument was prepared to authorise this, though

---

[48] *The Times*, 4 July 1867, p. 10 (quoting PP 1867 (198), No. 23 at p. 72).
[49] See CO 879/4/1, enc. in No. 75, p. 82; No. 183, p. 299; PP 1874 (890) XLVI. 1, No. 126, p. 221.
[50] Hennessy to Harley, 8 February 1873, CO 879/4/1, No. 186, p. 308.
[51] CO 879/4/1, No. 237, p. 422.   [52] CO 879/4/1, enc. in No. 237 at p. 428.
[53] CO 879/4/1, No. 270, p. 499.

the government interpreter, T. G. Lawson (who was instructed to take Kobina Edjen to Freetown) prepared a memorandum for the Governor in Chief containing a number of precedents, including those of Cally Mahdoo, Thomas S. Caulker and Aggery.[54] Although Kimberley initially refused to authorise the removal – on the grounds that 'so extreme a measure' should not be resorted to without clear proof of an emergency – he later sanctioned it after receiving a further despatch.[55] In this case, the pressure for detention came from a zealous local administrator, but London was content in the end to take his word for its necessity, and asked for no further legal authority than his list of precedents.[56]

Into the late 1870s, detentions without legal authority continued both in the Gold Coast and in Sierra Leone. For instance, in 1880, the Sierra Leone government made plans to detain Lahai Bundoo and Bocary Bombolie, who were involved in disturbances in the Quiah district which threatened British interests. W. W. Streeter, the administrator in chief, laid a trap for Lahai Bundoo, summoning him to Songo Town to discuss peace, with plans to remove him to Freetown by coercion '*if necessary*'; but Lahai Bundoo did not fall for it.[57] However, Bocary Bombolie – a man who had been imprisoned in 1857 for slave dealing, and whose continued slaving activity had previously led the Governor to threaten to detain him – was taken into custody.[58] Reading Streeter's comment that he did 'not propose to release him until quiet has been thoroughly restored', Augustus Hemming (one of the more senior clerks in the African and Mediterranean Department at the Colonial Office) minuted that this was 'Roughish justice but I suppose inevitable while we stay in these countries'.[59] In the end, a peace treaty was brokered in September 1880 between Lahai Bundoo and Gbannah Sehrey to end this Quiah war,

---

[54] PP 1874 (890), enc. 2 in No. 51, p. 85.
[55] CO 879/4/1, No. 284, p. 524; CO 879/4/3, No. 18, p. 24.
[56] In 1877, Governor Freeling received a petition requesting that Kobina Edjen and his two chiefs be allowed to return, but the conditions imposed by the Governor – that he could return only as a private individual – were declined. Précis: Quabina Edjen's deportation: CO 96/167/17382.
[57] W. W. Streeter to W. Budge, 23 May 1880, CO 267/340/8793.
[58] Lawson to Streeter, 3 July 1880, CO 267/341/11080.
[59] Streeter to Kimberley, 3 July 1880, Minute by A. Hemming, 23 July 1880, CO 267/341/11080.

Detention in West Africa, 1865–1890 171

and Bocary Bombolie was released.[60] However, his warman Doombuyah, who had been detained in January for raiding British territory and abducting twenty-three people, remained in custody.

Regularising Detentions

Driven by the Secretary of State, Kimberley, after 1881 the Colonial Office began to insist that detentions in West Africa be put on a legal footing, through the passing of ordinances which would need to be approved in London. The impetus for change came from concerns over the treatment of a number of men both in the Gold Coast and in Sierra Leone. One of the most prominent was Asafu Agyei, who had been detained first in 1877, and then again in 1880, as a result of his plotting against Asante. He was the ruler of Juaben, the most powerful of the Amantoo states, and had been in conflict with the Asantehene since General Wolseley's march on Kumasi in 1874.[61] Although the British initially supported this secessionist ruler as a counter-weight to Asante, matters were complicated when Juaben fell back under Asante control in 1875, forcing Asafu Agyei and his followers to flee into the British protected area. Asafu Agyei's attempts to launch military attacks on Asante from here now became an embarrassment for the British.[62] The authorities at the Gold Coast were also worried by the support Asafu Agyei enjoyed from King Tackie of Accra. After Asafu Agyei ignored a warning that he would be expelled if he did not desist from his activities,[63] he was summoned by Governor Freeling and informed that he was now a state prisoner and a 'hostage for the good behaviour of his people'. Six of his chiefs and his daughter (the Queen) were also

---

[60] Streeter to Kimberley, 16 September 1880, CO 267/341/15411; Streeter to Kimberley, 18 September 1880, CO 267/341/15742.
[61] On the context, see Wilks, *Asante in the Nineteenth Century*, pp. 511–512; Kimble, *A Political History of Ghana*, pp. 270–279; Agbodeka, *African Politics and British Policy in the Gold Coast*, pp. 78–84; and R. Addo-Fening, 'The Background to the Deportation of King Asafo Agyei and the Foundation of New Dwaben', *Transactions of the Historical Society of Ghana*, vol. 14:2 (1973), pp. 213–228.
[62] Freeling to Carnarvon, 2 January 1877, CO 96/120/1313, f. 5.
[63] Governor Freeling to Carnarvon, 18 July 1877, CO 96/121/9758, f. 348.

detained.[64] Having first been sent to Elmina, Asafu Agyei was deported to Lagos, where he was held until October 1879.[65]

On his return from Lagos, Asafu Agyei resumed his intrigues with Tackie. By now, he had also fallen out with his daughter, Queen Afracoomah, both over who had the right to the stool of Juabin and over whether to continue to plot against Asante. Tackie, who had by now been formally deprived of most of his powers by the British, offered to settle the dispute between them – though he was clearly in favour of Asafu Agyei's claims – and attempted to compel the Queen to submit by force. This led Governor H. T. Ussher to intervene by arresting both men. They were subsequently examined by the Council (along with other witnesses), which came to the unanimous conclusion that they were guilty of treasonable practices against the protectorate, and that Asafu Agyei should be sent back to Lagos, and Tackie to Elmina.[66] When the matter was referred to the Colonial Office, Hemming considered the permanent deportation of Asafu Agyei to Lagos to be a 'proper step'. Although he thought it possible to try Tackie in the Supreme Court – since he was 'to a certain extent a British subject' – he considered it unlikely that a jury would convict him, and thought it better 'to dispense with the ordinary forms of law & deal with him out of hand' by deporting him to Sierra Leone. However, the Secretary of State, Kimberley, responded that Tackie should be sent to Sierra Leone only 'if it can *be legally done*'.[67] Given his doubts, Kimberley suggested legislation to authorise the detention or deportation both of Asafu Agyei and of Tackie, and the Gold Coast Ordinance No. 1 of 1881 was duly passed to effect this.[68] He also informed the authorities in Sierra Leone that an ordinance would be

---

[64] Governor Freeling to Carnarvon, 10 August 1877, CO 96/121/10857, f. 429; Freeling to Carnarvon 23 August 1877, CO 96/121/11622, f. 518; Addo-Fening, 'The Background to the Deportation of King Asafo Agyei', p. 221. A large amount of arms and ammunition was recovered: Freeling to Carnarvon, 13 September 1877, CO 96/122/12609, f. 29.

[65] Addo-Fening, 'The Background to the Deportation of King Asafo Agyei', pp. 223–224. Although Freeling also considered sending Tackie to Lagos, he decided to give him one last chance, to avoid any instability which might follow from removing him from his stool. Freeling to Carnarvon 14 August 1877, CO 96/121/11380, f. 452.

[66] CO 96/132/769, ff. 248ff., Minutes of Proceedings of Executive Council.

[67] Kimberley minute, 23 January 1881, CO 96/132/769, f. 182.

[68] Kimberley minute 3 February 1881, CO 96/132/769; Rowe to Kimberley, 17 May 1881, CO 96/134/10415.

needed there, and sent the Mauritian ordinance authorising Abdullah of Perak's detention as an example. In the event, this ordinance was not needed, for Tackie continued to be held at Elmina until his release in 1883.[69] By contrast, Asafu Agyei was not released, despite petitions from the Juabin chiefs, since Governor Rowe considered him 'a difficult man to manage', who was best kept well away from the Juabins.[70]

Around the same time, the Colonial Office came to be concerned about the fate of a number of political prisoners being held in Freetown, either on the government's initiative or at the request of an African chief.[71] Towards the end of 1875, one 'of the ringleaders of a band of marauders' by the name of Vangang, who had attacked British subjects in June in British Sherbro, was placed in Freetown gaol after being handed over by chiefs he had subsequently attacked.[72] Governor Rowe's plan to release him in April 1880 was shelved when Vangang was hospitalised because of ill health.[73] Another detainee was William T. G. Caulker, who in 1878 challenged the authority of his kinsman chief George Caulker in the Cockborroh district, in defiance of an agreement of 1870 which had settled the succession to various territories held by the Caulker family.[74] When George heard that William was at a Mission Station in Shenge, he had him put in the stocks, and (according to T. G. Lawson) would have had him put to death. Fearing that this might lead to a wider conflagration, Governor Rowe sent Lt. A. W. Bright Smith to intervene, who told the chief that 'that he had much better deliver the prisoner to me to bring to Freetown for His Excellency to judge'.[75] William was then taken to Freetown, and

---

[69] Rowe to Earl of Derby, 9 March 1883, CO 96/149/6186.
[70] Minute by Samuel Rowe, 31 August 1882, CO 96/141/14566, f. 37. Asafu Agyei died in exile in Lagos in 1886: Addo-Fening, 'The Background to the Deportation of King Asafo Agyei', p. 225.
[71] See esp. Trina Leah Hogg, 'From Bandits to Political Prisoners: Deportation and Detention on the Sierra Leone Frontier', in Nathan Riley Carpenter and Benjamin N. Lawrence (eds.), *Africans in Exile: Mobility, Law and Identity* (Bloomington, Indiana University Press, 2018), pp. 54–68.
[72] Havelock to Kimberley, 15 September 1881, CO 267/345/17577; PP 1875 (c. 1343) LII. 779, encs. 1 and 2 in No. 21, pp. 42–43. Hogg identifies Vangang as the first political prisoner to be detained.
[73] Havelock to Kimberley, 15 September 1881, CO 267/345/17577.
[74] For the settlement (confirmed by treaty), see CO 879/35/1, No. 74, p. 191.
[75] Reports of Arthur W. Bright Smith (11 October 1878), J. B. Elliott (2 October 1878) and T. G. Lawson (9 May 1881) in CO 267/344/9812. See also PP 1887 (c. 5236) LX. 263, No. 102, p. 127.

placed in the gaol. Although Rowe intended to investigate the matter fully, pressure of other business meant that he had not got round to it by the time of his appointment as Governor of the Gold Coast in January 1881. These were not the only men detained in Freetown without proper legal authority. Sharkah Bollontoh and Mustapha, whose plunder of a canoe in 1877 threatened to lead to a tribal war, were ordered to be detained in March 1880 at the request of the chiefs.[76] Another man accused of being the 'prime mover and perpetrator' of plundering against British traders was Beah Jack, who was also detained in 1880 after being handed over by another chief.[77]

In the spring of 1881, officials at the Colonial Office became aware of these apparently forgotten detainees. In April, a letter from W. T. G. Caulker reached Kimberley, asking for his detention to be looked into.[78] When a number of other prisoners petitioned for their release in May,[79] Francis Pinkett, the administrator in chief in Freetown, wrote to London explaining the circumstances in which they had been detained, and expressed his doubts about the wisdom of releasing them. However, officials in London were troubled that men like Caulker remained in prison without having their cases investigated.[80] The matter was referred to Governor Havelock, who handed Vangang over to Chief Lahai Serifoo (holding him responsible for his good conduct)[81] and released Caulker on a solemn promise not to leave Freetown until he was given permission to do so.[82] As for Sharkah Bollontoh and Mustapha, Havelock conceded that their imprisonment was illegal, but he feared their release might lead to a petty war.[83] To put matters on a legal footing, he drafted an ordinance to empower the detention of any 'persons dangerous to the peace or good order of the settlement'. However, London refused to sanction so general an ordinance.[84] In the meantime, pressure on the Colonial Office mounted when the Liberal MP Charles Hopwood

---

[76] A. Havelock to Kimberley 29 July 1881, CO 267/344/14804.
[77] See Hogg, 'From Bandits to Political Prisoners', p. 61, Havelock to Kimberley, 27 August 1881, CO 267/345/16535.
[78] CO 267/344/9812. [79] CO 267/344/10442.
[80] CO 267/344/9812, minute dated 9 June 1881.
[81] Havelock to Kimberley, 15 September 1881, CO 267/345/17577.
[82] Havelock to Kimberley, 28 July 1881, CO 267/344/14794.
[83] Havelock to Kimberley, 29 July 1881, CO 267/344/14804.
[84] Draft despatch to Havelock, CO 267/345/16535.

raised their cases in parliament, prompting the undersecretary of state, Leonard Courtney, to admit that 'they are State prisoners, detained without any clear warrant of law', but adding that he expected them to be released soon.[85]

Sharkah Bollontoh and Mustapha were released in August 1881 (when the Governor in Chief found a way of settling the dispute arising from the original plunder).[86] Doombuyah and Beah Jack were not. 'Doombuyah seems to have made a raid on British territory', Edward Wingfield (assistant undersecretary of state) noted, 'and may therefore be regarded as somewhat in the nature of a prisoner of war.' Although he felt that Beah Jack might be freed (since 'it is not stated whether Beah Jack's acts of plunder and outrage were committed on British Territory'), Kimberley thought he needed to be kept in detention, since the chiefs were unable to control him, and 'the interests of our settlements require that disorder should not exist on our borders'. He therefore asked Havelock to pass an ordinance to legalise the detention of Doombuyah and Beah Jack retrospectively, and to authorise their deportation to Lagos (where they might be allowed more freedoms than they could enjoy in Freetown gaol).[87] As requested, the Gold Coast also passed an ordinance to allow their detention in Lagos.[88] With this legislation, the Colonial Office sought to give a legal stamp to the detention and deportation of men who were perceived to be troublemakers from beyond the borders of the colony.[89]

In light of Kimberley's new policy that special ordinances had to be passed 'when it is necessary for political reasons to remove & detain a chief in custody against whom there is no legal case',[90] officials also began to examine other cases. After Hopwood had raised the matter privately,[91] they realised that the legality of the king of Elmina's

---

[85] *Parl. Debs.*, 3rd ser, vol. 45, col. 726 (23 August 1881).
[86] A. E. Havelock to Kimberley, 25 August 1881, CO 267/345/16534.
[87] Minutes dated 20–21 September 1881, and draft despatch dated 28 September: CO 267/345/16535 (enclosing a copy of the Mauritius ordinance No. 9 of 1877); Havelock to Kimberley, 27 October 1881: CO 267/345/20055; Ordinance No. 8 of 1881.
[88] Ordinance No. 5 of 1882: Political Prisoners Detention (Doombuyah and Beah Jack).
[89] Doombuyah never returned to Sierra Leone, and died in the Colonial Hospital in Lagos in March 1891. CO 267/389/9856.
[90] Minute by R. Meade, 26 August 1882, CO 96/141/15042.
[91] Précis: Quabina Edjen's deportation: CO 96/167/17382.

detention in Freetown had not 'occurred to any one until now'; and an ordinance was passed in due course to authorise it.[92] The new policy of passing ordinances was driven by the Secretary of State himself, who, like Carnarvon, was concerned with the legality of these detentions. Unlike Carnarvon in 1867, Kimberley had a recent precedent which could provide a model for a legal means of detention: the ordinance for the removal and detention of Abdullah of Perak. Troublesome West African chiefs did not attract the kind of public support which the Zulu leaders or Urabi had enjoyed in metropolitan circles. Nonetheless, the kind of awkward questions posed by parliamentarians like Hopwood did beg questions about whether the British imperial authorities could detain troublemakers without any legal authority. The answer given by the Colonial Office was to provide a formal cover for these detentions, in the form of *ad hominem* ordinances. This formal compliance with the rule of law was something that Kimberley – who had, after all, defended the Cape's right to detain Langalibalele by special legislation – was comfortable with. At the same time, his policy was driven not only by the need for legal forms to be observed: he was also concerned about the fate of men who were detained without any form of investigation of their cases. Even when men were held without any kind of trial, the Colonial Office wanted to ensure that the cases of detainees would be reviewed, both by the Secretary of State, when deciding to allow or disallow detention ordinances, and by the local Governor with periodic review.

'Peacekeeping' Detentions in Sierra Leone

Once the first detention ordinances had been passed, others followed thick and fast. Within the next ten years, Sierra Leone passed another fifteen ordinances authorising the detention or deportation of African chiefs. In this colony, the authorities were primarily interested in maintaining the peace, such that British interests would not be

---

[92] Gold Coast Ordinance No. 14 of 1883, Political Prisoner Detention (Quabina Edjen), was passed after Ordinance No. 10 of 1882: Political Prisoner Detention (Quabina Edjen) was disallowed on account of its faulty drafting (CO 96/144/21415). Although Kobina Edjen petitioned to be allowed to return to the Gold Coast in 1885 (CO 96/167/17382), he would not be released until 1895: PP 1896 (c. 7944–10) LVII. 331, p. 30.

unsettled. They consequently sought to intervene when wars between different African factions disrupted the country behind the colony, and when areas regarded as within British protection were attacked.[93] In this area, where British jurisdiction over Africans beyond the frontiers of the colony was uncertain, detention ordinances provided a means to assert authority.

A number of ordinances were passed to allow the detention of particular individuals who were perceived to be troublemakers. They included Buyah Sammah, the local chief at Kitchum (near Mambolo) on the Great Scarcies river (an area within British jurisdiction). He was accused both of extorting from European traders rent which should have been paid to the Mambolo chiefs and of transferring his allegiance to a neighbouring ruler under French influence. On hearing of this, Havelock proceeded to the spot with armed police, deposed him and ordered him to repay the extorted money. Havelock's action was clearly designed to remind the locals of British authority in the area, as well as shoring up the authority of Mambolo over Kitchum. As a further security for good order, he brought Buyah Sammah to Freetown and lodged him in the debtor's prison, passing an ordinance to legalise his detention in May 1882.[94] By the time London came to approve of the ordinance, he had been released.[95] In August, another ordinance was passed to legalise the capture and detention of Lahsurru.[96] He was arrested as a result of disturbances on the Jong River (in Sherbro) in May 1882, when Acting Commandant W. M. Laborde, who had gone to attend the coronation of the Sycammah king of the Jong Country, encountered a hostile reception, which resulted in his being assaulted, and his boat being captured and plundered.[97] Havelock duly proceeded to the spot to demand an explanation and restoration of the items taken. After

---

[93] It should be noted that the British had tried and executed those accused of murdering British subjects within twenty miles of the frontier. For instance, John Caulker, Kinigbo and Vermah were tried and executed in 1876 for the murder of a police constable in an attack at Sherbro: CO 879/9/6, No. 38, p. 50; PP 1876 (c. 1402) LII. 403, No. 53, p. 62; No. 60, p. 65.
[94] Havelock to Kimberley, 25 May 1882, CO 267/348/10609, CO 267/348/10610.
[95] Hemming minute, 22 June 1882, CO 267/348/11006.
[96] Havelock to Kimberley, 24 August 1882, CO 267/349/16647, enclosing report on Ordinance No. 14 of 1882.
[97] See PP 1883 (c. 3597) XLVIII. 317, p. 3 and PP 1882 (c. 3420) XLVI. 551.

shots had been exchanged, Havelock set fire to the huts of those concerned in the outbreak and then detained Lahsurru, who was thought to be behind all the trouble.[98] Perhaps as a result of the inquiries by Charles Hopwood, the papers relating to this affair were published; though there was not much concern over the fact that Lahsurru had been detained without charge.[99] However, he would not be released until the end of 1888.[100]

The policy of detaining troublesome chiefs was taken one step further by Francis Pinkett, who took over as Administrator while Havelock was in London. Pinkett was worried about lawlessness in Sherbro, which was affecting trade. He was particularly concerned at the activities of Chief Gpow, whose men had seized a boat bringing the monthly pay for the policemen stationed at Barmany, at the edge of the area under British protection. Hearing of this, Pinkett took a steamer with fifty-five policemen to open up the Boom and Kittam rivers by destroying Gpow's defences.[101] Pinkett failed to capture Gpow, but in June he arrested Bey Yormah, Tongofoorah and Gangarah, Gpow's chief men. This action did not impress the Secretary of State, the Earl of Derby, when he was asked to approve an ordinance to authorise their detention. Since Tongofoorah was accused of leading the attack on the pay-boat within British territory, Derby felt he should be charged in an ordinary court for robbery rather than being held as a political prisoner. As for the other two, there was 'scarcely sufficient evidence' to justify their detention. Derby was prepared to defer to Pinkett's view of the necessity of detaining them in the short term, but wanted Havelock to reconsider it on his return.[102] By the time of Havelock's return, Gangarah had died in Freetown gaol, but Bey Yormah and another detainee, Langobah, were freed, while Tongofoorah was charged in a civilian court.[103]

---

[98] See PP 1882 (c. 3420), p. 4; PP 1883 (c. 3597), No. 9 at p. 16.

[99] *The Times* wrote 'Lahsurru doubtless has earned his term of imprisonment by turbulence and disorder.' 18 December 1882, p. 9. However, 'A West African merchant' retorted that Lahi-Sarrihoo (as his name was properly spelled) was a 'loyal native West African' whose detention was 'only another instance of that want of tact and knowledge by British officials which lies at the root of nearly all our troubles in that country'. *The Times*, 26 December 1882, p. 8 (also in PP 1883 (c. 3597), Appx. 2, p. 31).

[100] CO 267/372/24677.   [101] PP 1883 (c. 3765) XLVIII. 349, No. 1, p. 1.

[102] PP 1883 (c. 3765), No. 15, p. 40.

[103] John Joseph Crooks, *A History of the Colony of Sierra Leone* (Dublin, Browne and Nolan, 1903), p. 265.

Besides using ordinances to deal with individual troublemakers, the British also detained numerous warrior chiefs during the persistent Yoni wars in the late 1880s. At this time, the Yonis were seeking to expand their trade routes, which led them to conflicts with the Mende people. In November 1885, they raided and plundered Songo Town – which was within British jurisdiction – killing a number of Africans and taking others into slavery.[104] Seven of the raiders were captured. Initial plans to prosecute foundered on doubts over whether the evidence gathered against them would secure a conviction. Instead a first ordinance was passed to detain them 'until it be possible to make some farther arrangement of the difficulties between the Yonnie and Bompeh-Sherbro and Mendi tribes than has yet been effected',[105] and further ordinances followed to allow their deportation to Gambia.[106] The relative indifference of the British to jurisdictional niceties is shown by the fact that the men detained under the ordinance included a man not involved in the raid, Bye Jabbee, who was unsettling affairs in areas outside British jurisdiction, and whose detention was requested by a local chief enjoying British support, Bocarry Governor. He was not brought to Freetown until the day before the Council met, when his name was added to the ordinance just before it passed.

In 1887 the conflict flared up again with a Yoni attack in February on another town, Macourie, notionally within British jurisdiction.[107] The attack was led by Koliama, who was captured by the Mendes, handed over to Madam Yoko, chief of Senehu, and then passed on to the British. Administrator J. S. Hay thought that he should be detained and deported (like the earlier Yoni detainees) if there was not enough evidence to convict.[108] The Secretary of State, H. T. Holland, duly authorised an ordinance on the model of that passed one year earlier, though he added in a subsequent despatch that this process should be used only in cases of urgent necessity, and that Governor Rowe should

---

[104] For the history of these conflicts, see Fyfe, *A History of Sierra Leone*, pp. 448–484.
[105] Governor Rowe to Colonial Office, 17 June 1886, CO 267/363/12500. Ordinance No. 1 of 1886 authorised the detention of Sesi, Sey Yammo, Yamba, Angumanah Barfeh alias Blackey, Will Mormoh Sankoh and Bye Jabbee.
[106] Ordinance No. 17 of 1886 (Sierra Leone) and Ordinance No. 1 of 1887 (Gambia).
[107] PP 1887 (c. 5236), No. 47, p. 66. [108] PP 1887 (c. 5236), No. 77, p. 92 with enclosure.

review it on his return.[109] More Yoni raids followed in November. On this occasion, the British felt that a severe lesson should be given for what was seen as a serious violation of the 'British Protectorate'.[110] An expeditionary force was sent under Col. Sir Francis De Winton, which was intended to capture the war chiefs – especially Kondor, Congor and Kallowah – who were regarded as the instigators of the raids on British territory,[111] and to demonstrate British power by destroying the Yoni war towns. De Winter also sought to recoup some of the cost of the campaign by fining chiefs who had supported or given protection to the Yonis.[112] One of these was Bey Simmareh of Massimerah,[113] who was taken as a prisoner to Freetown, after he failed to keep his promise to find the wanted men.[114] He was released only when the Colonial Office overruled Rowe's wish to continue his detention.[115]

Most of the leaders were subsequently captured and sent to Freetown as prisoners of war.[116] There, the Yoni prisoners were divided into various classes. Those put in the first class were to be deported to Lagos:[117] besides Congor and Kallowah, they also

[109] PP 1887 (c. 5236), Nos. 63–64, pp. 80–81. Ordinance No. 5 of 1887, 'An Ordinance to legalise the capture, detention and confinement of Koliama', passed on 15 April 1887. Officials on the ground also proposed detaining another chief, Commander, who was accused by Madam Yoko of instigating the Yoni attack: however, Holland felt that he should only be given a warning: PP 1887 (c. 5236), Nos. 57–58, p. 76.
[110] PP 1888 (c. 5358) LXXV. 669, No. 6, p. 2.
[111] PP 1888 (c. 5358), No. 22 at p. 20; PP 1887 (c. 5236), No. 47, p. 66, enc. 1 in No. 47, p. 68; CO 879/27/2, enc. 3 in No. 103A, p. 99.
[112] CO 879/27/2, No. 78, p. 83. De Winter spoke of Kondor, Congor, Kallowah, Yamba Fakla and Selah and Rabbin Bundu as the main leaders: CO 879/27/2, enc. 3 in No. 103A, p. 99.
[113] For earlier suspicions against this chief, see CO 879/27/2, No. 74, p. 77.
[114] CO 879/27/2, enc. 5 in No. 103A at pp. 104–105. Rowe and De Winter had hoped that Bey Simmareh would be able to hand over the Yoni leaders, and his failure to do so increased the fine imposed on him.
[115] CO 879/27/6, No. 41, p. 55.
[116] They included Congor, Kallowah, Pa Mela, Yamba Fakla and Selah, as well as Alimamy Conteh, the uncle of Koliama, who had helped Congor gather war men. PP 1888 (c. 5358) No. 59, p. 73. For the capture of Kallowah, see PP 1888 (c. 5358), No. 60, p. 74.
[117] Ordinance No. 13 of 1888: Political Prisoners, CO 267/372/23716. Hay advised against sending the men to Gambia, where other Yoni leaders had already been deported.

included Koliama (who had already been detained under an earlier ordinance).[118] The rest, having been in prison for nine months, were thought to have been taught the necessary lesson, and so could be released. Besides authorising the deportation of the Yoni prisoners, the ordinance also covered the deportation of the Mende chief, Commander, who had been investigated earlier in the year for assisting the Yoni raiders.[119] In these cases, there was no discussion of putting the men on trial. The question of whether to try Yoni warriors was, however, raised and dismissed in November 1889, when the British captured Pa Mahung.[120] Although the Queen's Advocate felt that he had satisfactory evidence to prosecute him, he concluded that 'a conviction for murder could not be expected having regard to the fact that the prisoner was engaged in what, to native minds, is called "war"'. In his view, there was no reason why he should be treated differently from the other Yoni ringleaders, 'who are now political prisoners'.[121] An ordinance was duly passed to authorise his detention.[122] Kondor – the one remaining Yoni leader at large – was also later captured, and an ordinance was passed in 1890 to authorise his detention and deportation.[123] At this point, some of the Yoni prisoners in Gambia petitioned for their release, claiming that they had not known they had violated any British laws when engaged in their warfare. However, the petition fell on deaf ears, not least because their deportation was so recent. Assistant undersecretary of state Robert Meade minuted, 'They will be none the worse for a little imprisonment.'[124]

The Yoni warriors were not the only fighting chiefs to find themselves detained and exiled. The Largo chief Makaia, who in 1887 launched attacks in the Sulima District on towns held by

---

[118] The others in this class were Yamba Fakla and Selah, and Alimany Conteh. The last named was released on the ground that he had been promised a pardon if he brought in the 'robber chiefs', which he had done. CO 879/29/5, No. 1, p. 1; PP 1888 (c. 5358), enc. 5 in No. 58, p. 66.
[119] Despite earlier suspicions, he was not detained until December 1887. PP 1888 (c. 5358), enc. 5 in No. 58, p. 66.
[120] Officer commanding detachment at Robari to Administrator of Gold Coast colony, 4 December 1889, CO 267/382/10052.
[121] CO 267/382/10052. [122] He died in Freetown gaol in January 1891: CO 267/388/3162.
[123] Ordinance No. 2 of 1890, CO 267/381/3393.
[124] Minute, 19 March 1890, CO 267/381/5118.

Bocarry Governor's allies, was captured in 1889 and deported along with his ally Gpabor.[125] Bocarry Governor himself had by then been exiled, when the British concluded that his presence in Sulima was not conducive to peace. Efforts were at first made to persuade him to come voluntarily to Freetown, which he eventually did in February 1888.[126] However, by November, the Colonial Office had concluded that his removal (along with his supporter George Bapoo) was necessary for the restoration of peace in the Sulima district. 'It may be a somewhat high handed measure to seize & deport these men', Hemming minuted, 'but, as it appears to be impossible to persuade the W[ar] O[ffice] to undertake a punitive expedition, there seems to be no other or better way of pacifying the country.'[127] Since it was felt that they could not be kept under such surveillance in Sierra Leone as would prevent their communicating with their allies at Sulima, ordinances were passed to allow their removal to Gambia.[128]

Although some of these warriors might have been tried in the ordinary courts for offences committed within British jurisdiction, for the most part they seem to have been regarded as prisoners of war, whose continued detention (by ordinance) was considered necessary after the end of any hostilities. However, in other cases, detention by ordinance was used to overturn an inconvenient trial outcome. One example of this was Ordinance No. 9 of 1888, dealing with Momodou Canoobah, Richard Canraybah Caulker and others. It arose from the trial of William T. G. Caulker, who had previously been detained for his part in earlier Caulker wars. Although a peace had been brokered between the warring Caulkers after William's release from detention in 1881,[129] the conflict boiled over again very violently in May 1887, when William, with the support of his uncle Momodou

---

[125] Ordinances Nos. 6 and 9 of 1889.
[126] PP 1887 (c. 5236), enc. in No. 132, p. 172; CO 879/27/2, No. 71, p. 74, enc. in No. 78, p. 84; CO 879/27/6, No. 13, p. 24.
[127] Minute, 25 November 1888, CO 267/37123020; PP 1889 (c. 5740) LVI. 853, No. 7, p. 10; CO 879/29/5, No. 8, p. 11.
[128] PP 1889 (c. 5740), No. 45, p. 53. Given that the coastal chiefs had threatened to kill Bocarry Governor if he returned to the Gallinas, his removal might have been beneficial for his own safety. Fyfe, *A History of Sierra Leone*, p. 480. Bocarry Governor returned to the Kissy Asylum in Sierra Leone in 1891, having been diagnosed as insane: CO 267/388/8679.
[129] Report of Chief Justice to Rowe, 7 May 1888, CO 267/371/15336.

Canoobah and cousin Richard, launched an attack on Shaingay, with the aim of deposing chief Thomas Neale Caulker.[130] When reminded by the Deputy Governor Hay that he had agreed to keep the peace, William justified the insurrection on the grounds of the despotic acts of Thomas.[131] The Inspector-General of Police, Capt. Halkett, was sent with a force to quell the disturbances, which had taken place in an area notionally under British jurisdiction.[132] Thirteen of the leaders, including William, were apprehended and brought to Freetown, with a view to putting them on trial for murder.

A trial duly followed in January 1888 of eight of the war leaders, including William Caulker, for the murder of Gbannah Sengeh, one of the victims of the attack who had later died in Freetown.[133] After a protracted and expensive trial, three of the accused were convicted: Lahai (who was proven to be one of the war party sent to seize Thomas), William Caulker and Richard Caulker. The two Caulkers were not proven to have been at Shaingay, but the jury – who had been asked to find a special verdict – found that they should, as reasonable men, have known that sending the warboys there would lead to loss of life.[134] The jury's recommendation of mercy was rejected by the Executive Council,[135] and all three were executed.[136] These events troubled Charles Hopwood, who wrote to the Colonial Office expressing concern that the men had been tried for what were acts of war. When the question was referred back to the Chief Justice, Quayle Jones, he disputed the proposition that they were acts of war – 'for both Bompeh and Shaingay are as much British territory as Freetown itself'[137] – but also expressed his doubts about the utility of protracted court proceedings in such cases. Although the men were

---

[130] PP 1887 (c. 5236), No. 97, p. 125.
[131] PP 1887 (c. 5236), encs. 1–2 in No. 102 at pp. 134–135.
[132] As Hay noted, the jurisdiction had 'never as yet been actively exercised'. PP 1887 (c. 5236), No. 97, p. 125.
[133] PP 1887 (c. 5236), enc. in No. 107, p. 139.
[134] Report of Chief Justice to Rowe, 7 May 1888, CO 267/371/15336.
[135] Maltby to Knutsford, 15 October 1888, CO 267/371/21627. According to Chief Justice W. H. Quayle Jones, the jury's recommendation 'simply amounted to this, that it was the custom of the country to break the law in this way when it suited them'. Chief Justice to Rowe, 9 July 1888, CO 267/371/15336.
[136] Both the Secretary of State and his officials privately noted that it would have been sufficient to execute William: CO 267/371/15336.
[137] Chief Justice to Rowe, 9 July 1888, CO 267/371/15336.

legally guilty of murder, he thought that criminal trials following the rules of English law were no more suitable in such cases than they would have been in the middle ages 'when the Great Feudal Lords had fights amongst themselves and death ensued'. In his view, rather than using the ordinary rule of law in such cases – which had ended here in executions – they could better be dealt with in a more summary way by 'the Governor in Council being authorized to deport or incarcerate the promoters of such raids'. Secretary of State Knutsford's scribbled response was: 'Certainly it would be more summary but ? more expedient or fair.'[138]

While the Colonial Office insisted that the ordinary course of the law had to be followed in the case of the three convicted men, the others did not get the benefit of their acquittal. They were not released, ostensibly because there were other charges still outstanding against them. However, further legal proceedings against them were abandoned, and instead an ordinance was drafted to provide for their detention and deportation. The Queen's Advocate justified this on the grounds that there was sufficient evidence adduced at the trial to implicate them in the raids. By the time it passed, the men had been detained without charge for a further four months, and so the ordinance also indemnified officials for their detention.[139] Four men were deported to Gambia under the ordinance, though three others, who were considered to have no influence, were released.[140] Not all the leaders of the Shaingay raids had been captured, however. Mormoh Darwah, described by Halkett as the chief warrior,[141] had remained at large at the time of the trial. He was captured only in March 1890, and an ordinance was subsequently passed to deport him. Given the volume of evidence against him, Hemming 'thought the better plan would have been to try this ruffian for what he did in 1887, & hang him'; but, as Wingfield replied, 'The Colonial Govt probably dreaded a repetition of the Caulker trial.'[142]

---

[138] Chief Justice to Rowe, 30 May 1888, CO 267/371/15336.
[139] Maltby to Knutsford, 19 October 1888, CO 267/371/22034.
[140] The four were Momodou Canoobah, Richard Canraybah Caulker, Beah-Hai and Morannah. Maltby to Knutsford, 19 October 1888, CO 267/371/22037.
[141] Halkett to Private Secretary, 8 July 1887, PP 1887 (c. 5236), enc. in No. 107, p. 144. He stated (at p. 143) that 'Darwah and Lahai ordered one captive after another for execution.'
[142] According to the report of the Queen's Advocate, James A. McCarthy, 23 May 1891, 'Had he been caught then [in 1887] and placed on his trial, I have no doubt but that he would have been convicted of wilful murder and hanged.' CO 267/389/11791.

By 1890, the authorities in Sierra Leone had fallen into the routine of passing ordinances for the detention and deportation of political prisoners. However, it could still take time for detentions to be regularised. In May 1888, Bangang – described as 'a Mendi freelance' engaged in slave hunting expeditions 'far beyond the recognised limits of our jurisdiction' – was captured and lodged in prison in Freetown.[143] However, the authorities forgot to take any steps to regularise his detention, and it was only in May 1890, when preparing Pa Mahung's ordinance, that this oversight was noticed, and the detention regularised.[144] Moreover, ordinances could be passed to imprison those who posed no real threat. One such was Santiggy Karay, who was accused of plotting to attack Macama, an area within British protection. He had collected a war party and had been ready to disturb the peace, but had been prevented from so doing.[145] Preparing the 1891 ordinance under which he was detained, the Queen's Advocate, James A. McCarthy, admitted that the evidence against him was 'not very serious' but that 'the moral effect of his detention and imprisonment on Native Chiefs and headmen will be most salutary'. The proposed ordinance troubled London. Meade noted: 'The system of locking up people as political prisoners is convenient but may easily be most oppressive and should be reserved for exceptional cases.'[146] It was allowed only on the understanding that he would be released 'in a month or so'.[147]

Political Detentions in the Gold Coast

Whereas detentions in Sierra Leone were primarily used to maintain peace in the hinterland, in the Gold Coast and Lagos, they were related for the most part to the defence of British interests in areas over which they sought to exert their influence.[148] In a number of cases, the British

---

[143] CO 879/25/4, No. 23, p. 20; CO 879/27/6, No. 30, p. 47.
[144] Bangang was detained in Freetown gaol until January 1893, when he was moved to the Isles de Los. He was finally released in September 1894: Cardew to Ripon, 14 September 1894, CO 267/412/17457.
[145] Legislative Council Minute, 21 May 1891: CO 267/389/12396.   [146] CO 267/389/12396.
[147] He was released in September: Crooks to Knutsford, 7 September 1891, CO 367/390/19190.
[148] Some were also detained for peacekeeping purposes, such as Quacoe Mensah detained under Ordinance 15 of 1884 (for whom see CO 96/161/56, Minute

were concerned about possible attempts by Africans to switch their allegiance to another European power. It was this fear which lay behind the 1883 Katanu Political Prisoners Detention Order, which related to events in an area which would ultimately fall under French rule during the scramble for Africa, but which had signed a treaty of protection with the British in 1879.[149] In 1883, a deputation from Katanu visited Lieutenant Governor W. Brandford Griffith at Lagos, asking for the British to show that the area was still under their protection. They were concerned that King Tofa of Porto Novo (which was under French influence) was attempting to appoint a king at Ekpe (whose appointment was in the king of Katanu's hands). They also revealed that he was being assisted by plotters within Katanu.[150] Griffith duly went to Katanu with sixty Houssas, to make a very public demonstration of British power and support for the local king. Although the king felt that the conspirators should be punished for their treasonable practices, he had done nothing about it himself, and it was the British who arrested eleven men. In the investigation which followed on Griffith's ship, one of them, Savi Brah, was found to have been the main intermediary with Porto Novo, and to have enlisted people to support that king.[151] Griffith concluded that strong measures were necessary: 'I considered that the best way to terrorise the men who had not been caught, and to teach a lesson to the people there generally, was to deport ten of the men I had in custody to the Gold Coast.'[152] He detained these men and moved them to Elmina without consulting London. On learning of it, the Colonial Office reminded him that an ordinance was needed, which should be time-limited to two years to allow their case to be reconsidered in due course.[153] In this case, the colonial authorities acted in response to a local request, but intervened largely in order to protect their position in an area where tensions with the French were mounting.

Another detainee who threatened British interests and flirted with another European power was Geraldo de Lima.[154] Born Adzoviehlo

---

2 January 1885) and Chief Kwabina Okyere of Wankyi detained under Ordinance 18 of 1888 (for whom see the enclosures in CO 879/28/1, No. 10, pp. 66ff.).
[149] Treaty of 24 September 1879, CO 879/35/1, No. 23, p. 327.
[150] CO 879/21/11, enc. 1 in No. 2, p. 2. [151] CO 879/21/11, enc. in No. 6 at p. 13.
[152] CO 879/21/11, enc. in No. 6 at p. 8. [153] CO 879/21/11, No. 19, p. 19.
[154] See D. E. K. Amenumey, 'Geraldo de Lima: A Reappraisal', *Transactions of the Historical Society of Ghana*, vol. 9 (1968), pp. 65–78.

Detention in West Africa, 1865–1890

Atiogbe, he had been the domestic slave of a Brazilian slave dealer, Cosar Cerquira Geraldo de Lima, whose name and business he took over on the latter's death. Over the next twenty years, he sought to secure his position as a middle-man in the palm-oil trade on the Ewe coast, east of the Volta, and to frustrate British attempts to expand into this trade. This led to a number of conflicts. His first clash with the British came in 1865, when, having been driven out of Ada, he joined with the rival Anlo in a retaliatory war, in which the British supported the Ada. Although the Anlo were defeated, Geraldo evaded capture. In 1871, when he was suspected of encouraging Asante attacks and fomenting disorder along the Volta, another attempt was made to capture him.[155] However, Geraldo remained out of reach, across the lagoon, from where he was able to continue his trade, and to evade the customs duties imposed by the British after they extended their jurisdiction into Anlo in 1874. Matters came to a head in 1884, when a conflict broke out between Chief Tenge of Anyako (where Geraldo resided) and the Keta chiefs who had come to an agreement with the king of Anlo to open up the route to Krepi. Geraldo, who was keen to protect his own economic interests, was only too happy to come to Tenge's support. Convinced that Geraldo was behind the blockade of Keta, the British now once more offered a reward for his capture. He was finally arrested in January 1885 and sent to Accra to stand trial for inciting the Anlo to rebel.[156]

However, it soon became clear that it would be difficult to secure a conviction, since witnesses could not be found who would be willing to testify against him.[157] 'I fear that as far as criminal prosecution is concerned, it is hopeless to obtain further evidence', Governor Young noted in March, 'but there is an abundance of evidence, I think, to warrant his detention as a political prisoner; and I think that we had better pass an enabling Ordinance without further delay.'[158] In fact, the evidence he referred to related mainly to his activities over a twenty-year

---

[155] See the stipulation in the peace treaty brokered between the Ado and Anlo: CO 879/35/1, No. 15, p. 320 at p. 321.
[156] An unsuccessful attempt was made to rescue him en route, in which two Houssas were killed: CO 879/21/9, No. 82, p. 191.
[157] CO 879/22/15, No. 55, p. 102.   [158] Minute dated 12 March 1885, CO 96/166/12306.

period as a thorn in the British side.[159] Unlike previous Gold Coast ordinances, this one was not intended to legalise an existing illegal detention, but to authorise the continued detention and deportation of a prisoner whose trial had been abandoned. Accepting that Geraldo was a dangerous intriguer, officials in London concurred with Griffith's view that he should be sent to St Helena. The Colonial Office thought the case to be analogous to that of Abdullah of Perak, and held that, although the Gold Coast had no jurisdiction over Geraldo outside the Colony, the Secretary of State could order his removal as an act of state.[160] In the event, St Helena was unable to accommodate the request and Geraldo remained in detention at Elmina.[161]

The British also used detention ordinances repeatedly as a tool of policy relating to Asante affairs. The fact that this was a matter of *Realpolitik* can be seen from the detention of Yaw Awua in 1884. An Asante who had settled at Cape Coast, he was, along with the elder John Owusu Ansa, a supporter of the restoration of the deposed Asantehene Kofi Kakari.[162] The colonial authorities in Accra opposed his restoration, fearing that Kakari would seek to reconquer the territories whose secession had weakened the Asante kingdom. When it was discovered that Yaw Awua had delivered a message from Ansa to the Asante king of Bekwai claiming British support for Kakari, the decision was taken to detain him. Although all of Yaw Awua's activities had taken place outside the protectorate, and hence beyond any British jurisdiction, the Executive Council thought that he should be punished for conveying the false message.[163] The Colonial Office confirmed the ordinance, but wondered why action had not been taken against Ansa, rather than Yaw Awua, 'who appears to have acted merely as his tool'.[164] It was

---

[159] Enclosure in Quayle Jones to Griffith, 6 June 1885, CO 96/166/12306. Of the recent activities, what caused most concern was his plotting 'to hand over the mainland behind the lagoon to the Germans'. There were also claims that he had killed a Houssa engaged in an anti-smuggling operation in 1880 or 1881.
[160] Despatch of 28 July 1885, CO 96/166/12306.
[161] A request to be released was refused in 1891, since Griffith still suspected him of intriguing; and he was released only in 1893. Griffith to Knutsford, 15 April 1891: CO 96/216/10014.
[162] Wilks, *Asante in the Nineteenth Century*, pp. 631, 713–715.
[163] CO 879/21/9, No. 22, p. 80.
[164] London also made it clear that this kind of legislation was to be used 'sparingly', and that there should be a time limit on it, so that the detainee would not be forgotten. CO 879/21/9, No. 26, p. 82.

only then that the Executive Council proceeded to investigate Ansa's complicity, summoning Yaw Awua out of detention for an examination as to the exact nature of the message conveyed to Bekwai, and Ansa's role in it. On the basis of this examination, the Council concluded that the best way to prevent any further intrigues from the coast unsettling Asante was for both men to be deported, to St Helena if possible.[165] However, before any decision was taken, both Kofi Kakari and the incumbent king of Asante (Kwaku Dua) died. This made the colonial government rethink its approach entirely. While Ansa was still regarded as an inveterate intriguer, it was now thought wise to wait and see what view he would now take of affairs in Asante. As the Governor put it, 'He might possibly prove useful to the Government.'[166] In fact, Ansa himself died at Cape Coast in November, and, with his death, the need to keep Yaw Awua in detention appeared to have evaporated. He was duly released in December 1884, but asked to give his word of honour that he would engage in no further intrigue.[167] His detention in 1884 was an act of pure political expediency, as part of an effort to influence politics in Asante.

Yaw Awua was detained once more in 1888, this time at the request of Prempeh, who had become the king of Asante in March 1888, and who wanted the British to drive away all Asante living on the coast who were meddling in his polity.[168] He was arrested on 10 June. An ordinance was hurriedly passed after his arrest and removal to Elmina Castle, whereupon a messenger was sent to Asante with the news, which Griffith was confident would 'do much towards strengthening the hands of the newly elected King of that country at the outset of his reign'.[169] Recommending the confirmation of the ordinance, Hemming at the Colonial Office observed that Yaw Awua had broken his promise to intrigue no more '& deserves his fate'.[170] The ordinance authorised his detention for a year, but Yaw Awua was not released when it expired. Indeed, it was only in the following year, when the Governor asked for a return of political prisoners, that the

---

[165] CO 879/21/9, No. 64, p. 160. [166] CO 879/21/9, No. 66, p. 175.
[167] CO 879/21/9, No. 77, p. 186. [168] CO 879/28/1, No. 29, p. 223.
[169] Griffith to Knutsford, 11 June 1888, CO 96/192/14004. In 1894 (when addressing the younger John Owusu Ansa), Griffith observed 'Do you remember a man by the name of Yow Awuah? He was as happy as possible at Cape Coast one morning, and two hours later I had had him locked up in Elmina Gaol as a political prisoner.' PP 1896 (c. 7918) LVIII. 707, No. 19 at p. 31.
[170] Minute 17 July 1888, CO 96/192/14004.

authorities noticed that he was still being detained, without any legal authority. An ordinance was now passed to regularise his detention, without any time limit being imposed, in order to give the government more leeway to decide when he should be released. Yaw Awua remained in custody until 1893, when British relations with Prempeh turned sour, and he returned to Kumasi in 1896 after the British occupation. The man who had once been a pariah to the British now found them much friendlier: after assisting them in the war against Queen Yaa Asantewaa, he was given the stool of one of the rebel kings deported in 1901.[171]

Officials sometimes struggled with the legal basis of their actions when dealing with exiled Asantes. This can be seen from the 1887 case of Bo Amponsam, king of the Adansis. The Adansis were refugee dissidents from Asante, who had settled in Denkera (within the protectorate) and were now using it as a base to conduct very violent raids into Asante. Bo Amponsam was arrested after complaints about the raids were received from the king of Bekwai, and after evidence had been gathered that he had incited to murder and accepted bribes.[172] As a consequence, he and two others were charged under the Foreign Enlistment Act 1870. On 20 July, Justice Smith – the brother-in-law of the men's lawyer – ordered that they be released from Elmina Castle on bail.[173] They were immediately re-arrested as political prisoners, whereupon their lawyer announced his intention to apply for a writ of habeas corpus. In order to forestall this application, an ordinance was hurriedly passed to legalise their detention.[174] This way of proceeding raised eyebrows in London. Pointing out the Colonial Office's dislike of such special legislation 'unless absolutely necessary', R. H. Meade questioned why men who were to be tried on criminal charges had been detained in this way: 'Surely it is a queer proceeding to lock up in their political capacity prisoners

---

[171] Wilks, *Asante in the Nineteenth Century*, p. 714; PP 1902 (Cd. 938) LXVI. 753, enc. in No. 12, p. 29.

[172] For the background, see CO 879/25/6, No. 33, p. 42; enc. in No. 34 at p. 45; enc. 1 in No. 69, p. 102; enc. 2 in No. 69 at p. 106; enc. 3 in No. 69, p. 107; enc. 1 in No. 71, p. 121.

[173] While frustrated at this turn of events, the authorities admitted (after some scrutiny) that the judge had the power to bail them: Acting Advocate General to Colonial Secretary, 7 October 1887: CO 96/183/22495.

[174] Ordinance No. 8 of 1887; White to Holland, 7 October 1887, CO 96/183/22495.

admitted to bail on a criminal charge?'[175] By the autumn, the Gold Coast government had abandoned its attempt to prosecute these men, for legal reasons: they were not convinced that the defendants were British subjects and that the offences were committed within British territory. In the view of Acting Advocate-General Griffith, it was unwise to risk a failed prosecution, particularly where the offences were 'really of a political nature and may be most appropriately punished by a special Ordinance', such as the one under which they were already being detained.[176] London agreed with this legal analysis. Since it was now no longer a question of a special ordinance being used to deprive prisoners of a right to bail given by a judge – given the apparent absence of jurisdiction – Edward Fairfield noted that the 'proceedings against them must be regarded as at an end, and their detention is to be judged by the same class of considerations, as other cases of political detention in West Africa'.[177]

Having been deprived of his stool, Bo Amponsam was released in the following spring. However, when the government discovered that he was attempting to resume his authority, he was re-arrested and taken back to Elmina Castle. Considering him a man not to be trusted, Griffith decided to keep him as a political prisoner until such time as another king of Denkera had been elected, at which point his political base would evaporate.[178] A further detention order was prepared, which London approved as 'inevitable'. Although this ordinance authorised his detention for just one year, he remained in Elmira Castle, like Yaw Awua, without any legal basis for his incarceration. This came to Governor Griffith's notice in July 1890 – more than a year after he should have been released – but he decided not to call the Legislative Council together until its next planned meeting in September, when it passed another ordinance to legalize the detention. Although London was unimpressed by Griffith's

---

[175] Minute, 14 September 1887, CO 96/182/18290.
[176] Acting Advocate General's Report, 24 August 1887, CO 96/183/22574.
[177] CO 96/183/22574: regarding the question of jurisdiction, he noted that a 'similar difficulty to that which has been experienced in this case arose in Cyprus in 1881, and it was met by passing an Order in Council containing a brief code of neutrality law'.
[178] Griffith to Knutsford, 27 June 1888, CO 96/192/15257.

cavalier 'method of dealing with inconvenient politicians',[179] the ordinance was approved. Bo Amponsam remained in Elmina Castle, where he died in November 1890.

Another group of Asante exiles who were detained after using the protectorate as a base from which to launch attacks in Asante were the followers of Kwasi Mensa, from Inkwanta, who were captured in February 1890. After the passing of an ordinance in April 1890 to authorise the detention of some of them,[180] a second one had to be hurriedly passed in July to allow the detention of others, whose intended prosecution had stalled (when the witnesses disappeared), and whose supporters had applied for a habeas corpus.[181] These prisoners remained incarcerated until 1891, when they were released, in part in response to pressure exerted by the Aborigines Protection Society, which had learned that the ordinance had been passed to frustrate a habeas corpus application. Although London felt the conduct of the local officials was 'very unsatisfactory',[182] Hemming thought it best 'to let the matter drop unless the Society again refers to it'.[183]

Besides dealing with raids on Asante, the British also used detention ordinances to maintain order within the protectorate when the ordinary forms of law failed. This can be seen from British intervention in the war between the king of Krepi and the rebellious Taviefe people, who had defied Krepi rule since 1870. After the king of Krepi reported an attack in April 1888, Assistant Inspector Dalrymple was sent (with a detachment of fifty Houssas) to make the Taviefes obey their king and to arrest the Taviefe ringleaders responsible for the deaths in an earlier attack they had made on Chavi, with a view to putting them on trial.[184] On 30 April, Dalrymple met the Taviefe chief, Bella Kwabla (also known as Bella Kwabina), who appeared ready to co-operate. However, after the arrests had been made, Dalrymple was

---

[179] Griffith to Knutsford, 24 October 1890, and note by R. H. Meade, CO 96/212/23462.
[180] Griffith to Knutsford, 24 October 1890, CO 96/212/22737, relating to Ordinance No 4: Srahah Political Prisoners' Detention Ordinance.
[181] Hodgson to Knutsford, 15 July 1891, CO 96/217/16758.
[182] CO 96/212/22738: Ordinance No. 5 of 1890: Denkera Political Prisoners Detention Order.
[183] Minute, 23 August 1891, CO 96/217/16758.
[184] CO 879/28/1, encs. 13 and 14 in No. 18, p. 153; enc. 15 in No. 18, p. 154.

shot dead in an ambush thought to have been orchestrated by Bella Kwabla.[185] The British now sought those responsible for Dalrymple's death, as well as the Chavi killings. Another force under Assistant Inspector Akers was sent out, which defeated the Taviefe in June, after a campaign which took a great toll on them.[186] At the end of August, Bella Kwabla and two others were sent for trial in Accra on charges relating to the death of Dalrymple and the Chavi killings. However, the jury acquitted the defendants in the first trial, which related to the murder of Dalrymple, when they concluded (against the judge's instructions) that Taviefe was beyond the court's jurisdiction. The Queen's Advocate then dropped the second case, since it was evident that there would be another acquittal, even though he felt that there was both the evidence and jurisdiction for a conviction.[187] With the colonial authorities determined that the chief should not return, an ordinance was passed for the men's indefinite detention.[188] Only when calm had been restored to Taviefe were they released, in August 1890.[189]

In many of the cases involving chiefs and kings from the protectorate, the possibility of proceedings under the ordinary law was contemplated.[190] Detention as a political prisoner was used as an alternative, which avoided the risk of acquittals and allowed the option of discretionary removal. Governor Griffith was also content to detain prisoners without lawful authority, while pondering how to proceed. For instance, no ordinance was passed to authorise the detention in Elmina Castle of Essal Cudjoe and Quabina Insiaku in October 1889, after they had been arrested, on the authority of a letter from a District Commissioner, for attempting to create disturbances in Eastern Wassa (in a dispute over a stool). Griffith was not prepared to

---

[185] CO 879/28/1, enc. 17 in No. 18 at p. 157. On the background, see CO 879/28/1, No. 11, p. 80.
[186] CO 879/28/1, No. 28, p. 222. Not only did the Taviefe lose 167 fighting men, but a great many of their people had also died from starvation and exposure. 'This is terrible retribution', Griffith wrote to Knutsford, 'but there was no avoiding the struggle for supremacy': CO 879/28/1, No. 32 at p. 246.
[187] CO 879/28/1, No. 55, p. 345.
[188] Tawiewe Political Prisoners Detention Ordinance, No. 22 of 1888: CO 96/194/20203.
[189] CO 879/31/11, No. 94, p. 90.
[190] For instance, Brennan recommended that Kwabina Okyere be arrested in Accra for taking up arms against the government: CO 879/28/1, enc. 22 in No. 24, p. 204.

let them go until they had entered into sureties for very large sums.[191] His officials assumed that they would be able in due course to rely on a Political Offenders Ordinance intended to confer a general power of detention, which was then passing through the legislature. In the meantime, Griffith did not want to treat them as political prisoners, and told London that it was not necessary to pass an ordinance, since it was unlikely that the proceedings would be 'challenged in any manner'.[192] Griffith's cavalier attitude to detentions troubled officials in London. They were especially troubled by the Political Offenders Ordinance, which was designed to 'afford a much more convenient and regular form of exercising the paramount power of the Crown'. Officials here doubted the wisdom of granting a general power to detain. As Meade put it, 'The more trouble it gives passing in each case the special ordinance, the better. No Colonial Govt & least perhaps of all the Gold Coast colonies are fit to be trusted with general Powers to this tremendous effect.'[193] The ordinance was duly disallowed.

In July 1890, the Deputy Sheriff was instructed to draw up a list of political prisoners then being detained in Elmina Castle. He returned a list of twenty-six prisoners, which included men deported from Sierra Leone as well as Gold Coast detainees.[194] When the list reached the Colonial Office in December, Meade felt that the number being held was 'not creditable', and argued that at least some should be released after a review. Authorising the continued detention both of Yaw Awua and of Bo Amponsam, the Colonial Office began to insist on regular reports.[195] In response, Governor Griffith acknowledged that detaining people as political prisoners was 'in itself objectionable' and should be used only 'in rare instances', but argued that 'the good of the greatest number may necessitate such treatment on occasion arising when dealing with natives over whom from their position in the interior the Government cannot continually exercise other than the

---

[191] Griffith to Knutsford, 24 October 1890, CO 96/212/23462. As officials in London noted, this was of doubtful legality, since they had been detained only on the basis of a confidential letter.
[192] Griffith to Knutsford, 3 February 1891, CO 96/215/4624.
[193] Minute dated 25 January 1890, CO 96/205/1270.
[194] CO 96/212/23462. The list omitted Geraldo de Lima.
[195] Wingfield minute, 1 December 1890, CO 96/212/22740.

Detention in West Africa, 1865–1890

control of moral force'.[196] He now began to make periodic visits to Elmina Castle, and, by May 1891, the number of political prisoners detained had been reduced to thirteen. However, the policy of detaining troublesome Africans continued.[197]

Conclusion

In West Africa, the use of *ad hominem* legislation to authorise detention became the standard way to deal with 'political prisoners' after 1880. If, in this context, the due process expected by a substantive vision of the rule of law was routinely replaced by a regime of exceptional measures, it was nonetheless significant that the Colonial Office insisted in 1881 that detentions be put on a legal basis, after more than a decade in which the British authorities in West Africa had routinely detained political prisoners without trial. The need for such legislation was in part a response to pressure from parliamentarians such as Charles Hopwood, who were raising awkward questions about detentions in West Africa at a time when British policy towards detention without trial in Ireland was proving controversial.[198] The imperial solution to this problem – *ad hominem* laws taking away the power to seek a writ of habeas corpus – gave legal cover to the authorities, rather than protection to the detainees. At the same time, the need to put detentions on some kind of legal footing was also motivated by the discomfort of officials in London at the widespread use of detention of political prisoners in West Africa without any apparent kind of control. Under the new system, colonial officials had to provide some justification for detention ordinances before the Colonial Office was prepared to approve them; and officials in London also began to call for regular returns of detainees, so that they would not be lost in the system, as had been the case all too often hitherto. These may have been very thin forms of protection for the detainees, but they might act as some form of restraint of local officials.

In this area, the resort to detention without trial was often the result of jurisdictional uncertainty or ambiguity. In many cases, it was

---

[196] Griffith to Knutsford, 3 February 1891, CO 96/215/4624.
[197] See the Yow Donko Detention Ordinance No. 1 of 1891, CO 96/216/11523.
[198] See Stephen Gwynn and Gertrude M. Tuckwell, *The Life of the Rt. Hon. Sir Charles W. Dilke*, vol. 1 (New York, MacMillan, 1917), p. 370.

a perception that the British lacked a formal jurisdiction over areas considered within their political sphere of influence, and over which they felt compelled to keep the peace, that led them to use ordinances which would cut through the complexity by an assertion of sovereign power over the troublemaker. At the same time, both the colonial authorities and their imperial masters often found such instruments to be convenient, to deal with people who were within British jurisdiction. Such ordinances could be used when the authorities lost confidence in the ordinary processes of law – or found that they could not achieve their aims by using them – and also when they simply wished to detain political opponents against whom no charges could be formulated. Such ordinances were also used for a variety of purposes – from peacekeeping and the punishment of crimes, to political brokering and the suppression of dissent.

Far away from London, and largely out of the public eye, the imperial authorities were far less constrained in their use of exceptional powers in this part of Africa than they would be elsewhere. If the Colonial Office gave itself the power to scrutinise detention, in practice the degree of scrutiny given to these detentions was minimal. Furthermore, Africans detained here had few opportunities to mount legal challenges to their detention, so that the validity of the ordinances was never called in question. Nor did they enjoy significant support from opinion-formers or people of influence in the metropolis. There were occasional efforts to bring cases to the attention of bodies such as the Aborigines Protection Society and friendly MPs,[199] but it was not easy to translate this into effective action. For instance, when the members of the jury who had acquitted Bella Kwabla read in the minutes of the Legislative Council that their decision had been against the evidence, they wrote a long memorial in protest to the Secretary of State – copied to the Aborigines Protection Society – explaining that the men had been 'justly acquitted ... *in accordance with the evidence given in the case*'.[200] They followed this with a protest at the Governor's 'trampling' upon their right to acquit by assuming 'the uncontrolled and dangerous

---

[199] In June 1886, the Aborigines Protection Society received a petition from the chiefs of Elmina sent to the Secretary of State: Bodleian Library, MSS Brit. Emp. s 22/G17, f. 9.

[200] Bodleian Library MSS Brit. Emp. s 22/G17, f. 12, p. 50.

power of deporting and imprisoning the said prisoners for the same charge for which they had been tried'.[201] The matter was subsequently raised by James Picton in parliament in May 1889, but the undersecretary of state, Baron De Worms, batted it away by saying that their detention was 'in the interest of the public peace, and because a renewal of disturbance is apprehended were they to be sent back at the present time'.[202] With public opinion scandalised by the violent death of Dalrymple, it was not easy to protest against the detention of Africans suspected of plotting it.

[201] Memorial dated 21 August 1889, CO 96/204/19567.
[202] *Parl. Debs.*, 3rd ser., vol. 335, col. 1126, 1136 (3 May 1889).

6

Removing Rulers in the Niger Delta, 1887–1897

By the mid 1880s, Britain had joined the 'scramble for Africa'. The European powers were now not simply seeking to open up trade with African rulers, but to make exclusive territorial claims. With a framework established at the Berlin Conference for how imperial powers could claim territory on the West African coast, each of them hurried to assert their rights in particular areas.[1] In contrast to her European neighbours, Britain did not wish to annex large swaths of new territory as colonies, both because of the potential expense involved and because of the legal problems presented by making British subjects of people who still practised slavery. However, in the context of intense territorial competition between the European powers, the traditional English conception of protectorates came under pressure. In an era when both diplomats and international lawyers were increasingly viewing African polities as lacking the capacity to be actors on the international stage, the British notion that protectorates were at base relationships founded on treaty obligations gradually gave way to the view held by the other European powers that

---

[1] On the Berlin conference and the scramble, see Ronald Robinson and John Gallagher, *Africa and the Victorians: The Official Mind of Imperialism*, 2nd ed. (London, MacMillan, 1981); S. Crowe, *The Berlin West African Conference 1884–1885* (London, Longmans Green & Co., 1942); and S. Förster, W. Mommsen and R. Robinson (eds.), *Bismarck, Europe and Africa: The Berlin Africa Conference 1884–1885 and the Onset of Partition* (Oxford, Oxford University Press, 1988).

protection was a form of imperial control.[2] At the same time, the traditional British distinction between colonies and protectorates was not effaced, so the exact position of those living under British protection would remain ambiguous.

In the decade after the Berlin conference, as Britain's interest in the region of the Oil Rivers in the Niger delta increased, so the imperial authorities encountered a number of rulers who stood in the way of their economic ambitions. These rulers signed treaties with the British – and so came under their 'sphere of influence' – but sought to maintain a level of control in their regions which the new imperial power could not accept. Between 1887 and 1897, Britain removed three rulers in this area, the detention of each of whom would – at least eventually – be formally regularized by an *ad hominem* ordinance. In this region, the responsible department in Whitehall dealing with the detentions was not the Colonial Office, but the Foreign Office, since treaties of protection came within the remit of foreign policy rather than colonial administration. Officials here were less punctilious about the legal basis of detention than their counterparts at the Colonial Office; for they could leave it to the colonial authorities to pass the necessary legislation when detainees were removed to a colony. At the same time, they sought to lay foundations for the detentions they ordered by holding quasi-legal inquiries of the sort generally eschewed in the Gold Coast and Sierra Leone. Although these inquiries always fell far short of the due process requirements of the rule of law, they were intended to justify the actions taken against these rulers both to domestic audiences and to African ones. As shall be seen, the nature of the inquiry used also changed over time, as the particular rulers provided for were increasingly regarded as subject to British power rather than being independent rulers.

---

[2] On the development of a notion of *territorium nullius* which denied that African rulers could hold territorial sovereignty, although they had the capacity to alienate their property rights, see Andrew Fitzmaurice, *Sovereignty, Property and Empire, 1500–2000* (Cambridge, Cambridge University Press, 2014), ch. 9. See further Antony Angie, *Imperialism, Sovereignty and the Making of International Law* (Cambridge, Cambridge University Press, 2005); Jennifer Pitts, *Boundaries of the International: Law and Empire* (Cambridge, Harvard University Press, 2018); and W. Ross Johnston, *Sovereignty and Protection: A Study of British Jurisdictional Imperialism in the Late Nineteenth Century* (Durham, Duke University Press, 1973).

The British Presence in the Oil Rivers

In contrast to the Gold Coast and Sierra Leone, there were no formal colonial settlements on the Bights of Benin and Biafra, though the British had long traded along this coast.[3] British official presence in the region was limited to consular representation. In 1849, John Beecroft was appointed consul, tasked with promoting legitimate trade and preventing the 'frequent misunderstandings' which arose between coastal chiefs and British merchants.[4] As part of this mission, he encouraged the creation of informal courts of equity to resolve commercial disputes.[5] Regarded as a 'quasi-protectorate' during the 1850s, with its own permanent consul, Lagos was formally ceded to the crown in 1861.[6] Courts of equity were also set up further down the coast in the Niger River Delta by the consul responsible for the Bight of Biafra. The British obtained more formal powers in 1872, when an Order in Council gave the consul jurisdiction

---

[3] See Martin Lynn, *Commerce and Economic Change in West Africa: The Palm Oil Trade in the Nineteenth Century* (New York, Cambridge University Press, 1997); Robin Law (ed.), *From Slave Trade to 'Legitimate' Commerce: The Commercial Transition in Nineteenth-Century West Africa* (New York, Cambridge University Press, 1995); Michael Crowder, *West Africa under Colonial Rule* (London, Hutchinson, 1968); K. O. Dike, *Trade and Politics in the Niger Delta, 1830–1885* (Oxford, Oxford University Press, 1956); G. I. Jones, *The Trading States of the Oil Rivers: A Study of Political Development in Eastern Nigeria* (London, Oxford University Press, 1963); G. I. Jones, *From Slaves to Palm Oil: Slave Trade and Palm Oil Trade in the Bight of Biafra* (Cambridge, African Studies Centre, 1989); J. D. Hargreaves, *Prelude to the Partition of West Africa* (London, Macmillan, 1963); J. D. Hargreaves, *West Africa Partitioned* (Madison, University of Wisconsin Press, 1974); and W. D. McIntyre, *The Imperial Frontier in the Tropics, 1865–75* (New York, St. Martins Press, 1967).

[4] See Martin Lynn, 'Britain's West African Policy and the Island of Fernando Po, 1821–43', *The Journal of Imperial and Commonwealth History*, vol. 18:2 (1990), pp. 191–207; and K. O. Dike, 'John Beecroft, 1790–1854: Her Britannic Majesty's Consul to the Bights of Benin and Biafra, 1849–1854', *Journal of the Historical Society of Nigeria*, vol. 1:1 (1956), pp. 5–14.

[5] Martyn Lynn, 'Law and Imperial Expansion: The Niger Delta Courts of Equity, c. 1850–85', *The Journal of Imperial and Commonwealth History*, vol. 23:1 (1995), pp. 54–76. Beecroft also intervened in local polities periodically, playing a part in unseating both King Kosoko of Lagos and King Pepple of Bonny: Robert Smith, 'The Lagos Consulate, 1851–1861: An Outline', *Journal of African History*, vol. 15:3 (1974), pp. 313–416 at pp. 397–399; and Toyin Falola and Matthew M. Heaton, *A History of Nigeria* (Cambridge, Cambridge University Press, 2008), p. 97.

[6] See PP 1862 (2982) LXI. 339.

in the Oil Rivers area over British subjects, those enjoying British protection and foreigners who consented to it.[7] It also gave him power to reorganise the courts of equity, which were to be regarded henceforth effectively as consular courts. The extraterritorial jurisdiction thus regulated was assumed to come from African sufferance rather than treaty, though the Oil Rivers area over which it extended was not at this stage regarded as a protectorate or in any way under British sovereignty.[8]

At the beginning of the 1870s, the consular district extended from the border of the Lagos colony to Carisco Bay, south of the Cameroons. Although the level of active British involvement remained small, by the early 1880s British officials were increasingly worried by the interest shown by other European powers in the area. The British consul, Edward Hewett, was particularly concerned about French ambitions in the Cameroons – whose chiefs had petitioned for an 'English government' in 1879 – and argued in favour of placing the whole region 'under British rule', whether as a colony or protectorate or under a chartered company.[9] This idea elicited different reactions from different departments. While the Colonial Office opposed any plan which would increase the government's responsibilities in West Africa,[10] the Foreign Office felt that, if the Cameroons' 'formal offer of cession' were turned down, the French would step in. The policy agreed at the end of 1883 was that the request of the rulers of the Cameroons for some form of British administration should be accepted. This would not take the form of a colony,[11] but rather there should be British sovereignty over a half-mile-wide strip of the coastline, and 'protection should be extended' inland as far as was necessary to fulfil the treaty engagements with the rulers.'[12] A treaty of protection was duly drafted.[13] As for the Lower Niger and Oil Rivers area, the Foreign Office wanted nothing more than an extended consular jurisdiction over crime and trade disputes, effected by treaties with

---

[7] *London Gazette*, 27 February 1872, p. 762.
[8] Johnston, *Sovereignty and Protection*, pp. 66–69. [9] FO 403/18, No. 1, p. 1; No. 9, p. 20.
[10] FO 403/18, No. 22, p. 28. [11] Meade to Pauncefote, 5 January 1884, FO 84/1681, f. 1.
[12] Note 21 November 1883, FO 84/1655, f. 309. [13] Draft treaty, FO 84/1681, f. 17.

local chiefs 'acknowledging a nominal Protectorate of England, and binding them not to cede any land to any other Government'.[14]

In order to execute this policy, in May 1884, Hewett was sent first to conclude treaties with chiefs in the Niger and Oil Rivers areas,[15] before moving on to the Cameroons. The printed treaties Hewett took followed a standard form. They extended the Queen's 'gracious favour and protection' to the signatory kings, who promised not to enter into any agreements with foreign powers without British assent and to allow free trade. They stipulated that the kings were to act on the consul's advice on matters of justice, good government and commerce.[16] The treaties also gave consular officials extraterritorial jurisdiction over British subjects and 'foreign subjects enjoying British protection', and provided that the consular authorities would settle any disputes (such as between the signatory kings and British or foreign traders).[17] At the same time that Hewett was signing treaties, the chief agent of the National Africa Company, David McIntosh (who was himself appointed a Vice-Consul on the Niger), also began to sign treaties with African rulers, which went further, in that the chiefs ceded 'the whole of their territories' to the company, as well as promising not to trade with foreign powers without the company's approval.[18] Hewett's plan to go on to the Cameroons and bring them under British protection failed, however, when he was beaten in the race to offer their rulers a treaty by the German Consul-General.[19]

---

[14] Memorandum by T. V. Lister, 24 October 1883, FO 84/1655, f. 25; FO 403/19, No. 6, p. 7.

[15] PP 1884–85 (c. 4279) LV. 1, No. 22, p. 16.

[16] For the standard form, see FO 403/31, enc. 1 in No. 88, p. 58.

[17] These treaties were followed by a new Order in Council in 1885 regulating extraterritorial jurisdiction: *London Gazette*, 10 April 1885, p. 1617. For various drafts, see FO 84/1659.

[18] John E. Flint, *Sir George Goldie and the Making of Nigeria* (London, Oxford University Press, 1960), p. 60. When Hewett signed treaties with these rulers, they were subject to the trading terms agreed by the rulers with the company: see Hertslet, *Commercial Treaties*, vol. 17, p. 158. For a list of the treaties and their form, see PP 1899 (c. 9372) LXIII. 417, pp. 17–35.

[19] Sir William M. N. Geary, *Nigeria under British Rule* (Routledge, London, 2013), pp. 93–95.

Hewett's mission began shortly after the conclusion of the Berlin Conference, whose General Act set out the formalities to be observed by the powers in respect of new occupations on the African coast.[20] The act required the signatories to notify the other powers if they assumed a protectorate.[21] It was with a view to complying with this requirement that an announcement was made on 5 June 1885, in the *London Gazette*, that the territories in the Niger districts between the Lagos colony and the western bank of the Rio del Rey were 'placed under the Protection of Her Majesty the Queen' by virtue of 'certain Treaties' concluded over the previous year and 'by other lawful means'.[22] The notification did not purport to make any new claims, but merely to confirm an already existing situation. At the same time, plans were made to 'enable Great Britain to carry out the duty imposed on her by the Berlin Conference to enforce the freedom of navigation on the Niger', through an amended West African Order in Council and by granting a charter to the company – which would in 1886 become the Royal Niger Company.[23] While Britain wanted to secure its interests in this region, it was not interested in incurring expenses; Britain was therefore happy to allow the Royal Niger Company to take on much of the financial responsibility. Under the charter, the company obtained broad powers to govern those areas in the Lower Niger region in which it had signed treaties, which it continued to exert until 1899.

Although Britain proclaimed a protectorate in 1885, it was not until 1891 that steps were taken to increase effective control in the area. In 1890, the government sent a special commissioner, Major Claude MacDonald, to the region to consider its future administration. Having recommended a 'strong Consular administration' with an executive with power to maintain order and 'assist in opening up the country',[24] MacDonald was appointed the first Consul-General. He was given instructions to amend the treaties which had been signed

---

[20] For a discussion, see Johnston, *Sovereignty and Protection*, ch. 7.
[21] Article 34: PP 1884–85 (c. 4361) LV. 133, p. 312.
[22] Joseph C. Anene, *Southern Nigeria in Transition, 1885–1906: Theory and Practice in a Colonial Protectorate* (Cambridge, Cambridge University Press, 1966), p. 67.
[23] See Pauncefote to Granville, 10 March 1885, FO 84/1879, f. 67; see further Flint, *Sir George Goldie*, pp. 74–87.
[24] Instructions to MacDonald, 17 January 1889, FO 84/1940, f. 1 at f. 5; Anene, *Southern Nigeria in Transition*, pp. 121, 130–131.

with the local chiefs 'in order to consolidate the Protectorate and strengthen the foundation on which it rests', and to sign further treaties to bring all the territories under a uniform system of administration. He was also instructed to pave the way for direct British rule by developing legitimate trade, promoting civilization, inducing the Africans to relinquish their 'barbarous customs, and by gradually abolishing slavery'.[25]

Jaja of Opobo

In the years which followed the Berlin Conference, as Britain sought to increase her influence in this area, she came into conflict with three leaders who had signed Hewett's treaties. Their obstruction to the opening of their territory to British trade, and ultimately British rule, would lead to their deposition and removal from their territory. The first to be removed was Jaja, king of Opobo.[26] Jaja, born about 1821, had progressed from being a domestic slave within the house of the king of Bonny to becoming a prosperous trader and ruler of Opobo. Jaja established himself in Opobo after going to war with the king of Bonny. Having brokered a peace treaty between Jaja and Bonny, the British entered into a treaty with Jaja in 1873, which acknowledged his status as king. Since the British wanted to keep European traders out of the area (given the high cost of protecting them), the treaty also stipulated that no European trading establishments would be permitted in Opobo and that the Opobo River would be closed to traders above a certain point.[27]

In the early 1880s, Jaja's relations with the British began to deteriorate. When in 1881 he claimed sovereignty over the Qua Eboe river and its people, Consul Hewett warned him off, stating that they

---

[25] Salisbury to MacDonald, 18 April 1891, FO 84/2110 f. 14 at ff. 15–16. See also MacDonald's Report on the Administration of the Niger Coast Protectorate, 16 August 1894, FO 403/200, enc. 1 in No. 123, pp. 199ff.

[26] For Jaja's history, see Sylvanus Cookey, *King Ja Ja of the Niger Delta: His Life and Times, 1821–1891* (New York, NOK, 1974); and E. J. Alagoa, *Jaja of Opobo: The Slave Who Became a King* (London, Longman, 1970). See further Paul MacDonald, *Networks of Domination: The Social Foundations of Peripheral Conquest in International Politics* (Oxford, Oxford University Press, 2014), pp. 170–175.

[27] PP 1888 (c. 5365) LXXIV. 149, No. 2, p. 3; No. 8, p. 14.

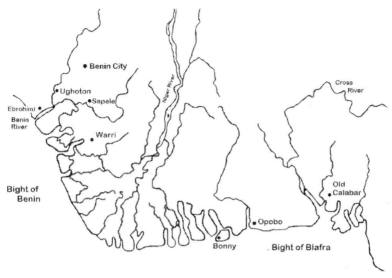

MAP 4 The Oil Rivers

were under British protection.[28] Disagreements over Qua Eboe continued to the end of 1884, when Jaja signed the standard-form treaty which Hewett had brought to Africa.[29] In fact, it took time to persuade Jaja to agree. In July, Hewett was only able to induce him to sign a preliminary treaty – containing the first two clauses of the main treaty – since he 'found with Ja Ja that it would take too much time to explain and *argue* out all the clauses'.[30] At the same time, he reassured Jaja that he would still govern the country if he signed the treaty, since 'the Queen does not want to take your country or your markets'.[31] When eventually he did sign the treaty, Jaja struck out Article VI, which would have allowed for free trade in every part of his territories.[32]

In the meantime, a conflict was also brewing between Jaja and British merchants, who wanted to cut their costs by dropping the commissions paid to African traders. To secure this, they formed a cartel; but Jaja

---

[28] PP 1888 (c. 5365), No. 4, p. 4, enc. 4 in No. 4, p. 8. In fact, no treaty of protection had been signed with the people of Qua Eboe: FO 403/86, No. 8, p. 12.
[29] By the time Hewitt got to Jaja, he had already sent thirty-seven concluded treaties to London. FO 403/33, No. 28, p. 23.
[30] Hewett to Granville, 30 July 1884, FO 84/1660, f. 178.
[31] PP 1888 (c. 5365), enc. in No. 13, p. 29; FO 403/31, No. 88, p. 57.
[32] PP 1888 (c. 5365), No. 12, p. 27.

induced one firm, Miller, Brother and Co. of Glasgow, to withdraw from the cartel in return for a large share of the trade.[33] The remaining firms sought to undermine Jaja's position as a middleman by opening up the markets of the interior themselves, which they considered they had a right to do by virtue of Hewett's treaties. Since Jaja considered that the treaty he had signed did not require him to yield his markets to Europeans trading on 'my river',[34] he maintained his control by turning back the white agents of the cartel members, and flogging their African ones. Faced with his obstruction, the cartel thought that the only way to make Jaja understand his duties under the treaty was 'to send a man-of-war here to settle the dispute for us'.[35] This was a view shared by the newly arrived Vice-Consul, Harry Johnston, who felt that the most effective way to support commerce in the area would be 'the humiliation or banishment of Jaja'.[36] The Foreign Office also considered that Jaja's behaviour might 'make the exercise of the British Protectorate difficult unless he is sharply dealt with'. They kept the Admiralty fully informed of developments, in case military assistance was needed.[37]

In March 1886, having called Jaja and the merchants together to a palaver on board the *Watchful*, Hewett concluded that the merchants had a right to go up the river, since the British government had declared that 'they will allow no monopolies in trade in their countries'. He also found that Jaja had violated the 1873 treaty by enforcing commission payments, and imposed a fine for this alleged breach, which Jaja paid under protest.[38] Although the Foreign Office supported Hewitt's actions, it concluded that he had erred in fining the king under the terms of the 1873 treaty, since that treaty had authorised Jaja to deny British traders the access to the interior markets which Hewett insisted they should have.[39] The view of the Foreign Office was that Jaja had rendered the 1873 treaty nugatory by his acts, and that it had been superseded by the

---

[33] PP 1888 (c. 5365), enc. 3 in No. 18, p. 31.
[34] PP 1888 (c. 5365), No. 13, p. 28; No. 16, p. 30; enc. 5 in No. 18, p. 33.
[35] PP 1888 (c. 5365), enc. 6 in No. 18, p. 33.   [36] FO 403/86, No. 7, p. 11.
[37] FO 403/86, No. 9, p. 13. Admiral Hunt-Grubbe was ready to remove Jaja to Ascension in case of need, though he felt that the king should first hear Hewett's advice: enc. 1 in No. 11, p. 14.
[38] PP 1888 (c. 5365), enc. in No. 24, p. 41; No. 21, p. 35; No. 22, p. 36.
[39] Hewett had told the palaver that Europeans had the right to go upriver by virtue of the Berlin agreement; though he did not make this point in the record of the decision or his report to the Foreign Office. FO 403/86, enc. in No. 13, p. 17 at p. 18.

1884 Protectorate Treaty.[40] On 16 June 1886, Foreign Secretary Rosebery duly informed Jaja that the 1873 treaty had been superseded, and told him that the Queen's aim in assuming the 'Protectorate of territories on the Gulf of Guinea', was '[t]he promotion of the welfare of the natives ... by insuring the peaceful development of trade'. No chief would be allowed to obstruct this policy to benefit himself.[41] This was to ignore the particular provisions of Jaja's treaty, and in early 1887, Jaja reminded Rosebery's successor at the Foreign Office, Salisbury, of the promise that the Queen did not want to take his country or his markets.[42] He also sent his sons and some chiefs to London to put his case directly to the Foreign Office.

A new dispute flared up in the middle of 1887 over access to the market at Ohambele, the main Ibo market. When traders from the cartel sent steamers upstream, they found the locals in terror of speaking to them, having been threatened by Jaja.[43] Jaja had also deposed the local king and replaced him with one friendly to himself, Ekike Notsho.[44] In response, the Acting Consul, Johnston, was sent to Opobo in July, where he called a palaver with the merchants and Jaja. At the meeting Jaja admitted that – 'in spite of the Berlin Conference, the Protectorate Treaty, and divers admonitions from Foreign Secretaries and Consuls' (as Johnston put it)[45] – he had made the people of the interior take solemn oaths – 'chop ju-ju' – that they would deal only with him: effectively excluding the British traders. Johnston informed the king that he would consider the matter closed if he agreed to punish any of his subjects who obstructed trade, and if he sent chiefs with Johnston into the interior to lift the oath.[46] Otherwise a gunboat would be sent. Although Jaja agreed to the conditions at a second palaver some days later, he protested that his agreement had been exacted under

---

[40] FO 403/86, No. 20, p. 24; PP 1888 (c. 5365), No. 25, p. 42.
[41] PP 1888 (c. 5365), No. 25, p. 42. Although the Foreign Office realised that the fine should have been remitted (as void), Jaja was told that it would be held over for a year, subject to his behaving well.
[42] PP 1888 (c. 5365) No. 27, p. 43; No. 33, p. 47.
[43] FO 403/73, No. 81, p. 57; enc. 1 in No. 109, p. 85.
[44] FO 403/73, No. 99 with enclosures, p. 78.
[45] PP 1888 (c. 5365), enc. 2 in No. 52, p. 65 at p. 66.   [46] PP 1888 (c. 5365), No. 39, p. 50.

compulsion, and stated that he wanted to let the matter rest until his envoys had returned from London.[47]

The day after the second palaver, Johnston went to Ohambele with three of Jaja's chiefs. Although Jaja's men were not entirely cooperative, the ju-ju was broken, and the Eboe agreed to enter a treaty.[48] However, when he returned some days later, Johnston was informed by Ekike Notsho – who claimed to speak for the Eboe – that the treaty would not be signed, and that the whites would not be allowed to trade rubber or palm oil. The whole question of free trade now seemed to Johnston to rest on the outcome of the dispute over Ohambele, since 'from Benin to Old Calabar, all the native Chiefs are watching with interest the long struggle between the traders and the Trader-King of Opobo'.[49] He now prohibited any trade between Jaja and British subjects.[50]

Johnston's belief in the need for tough action was echoed by Hewett, who was in London on a period of leave. He told Salisbury that 'this upstart of a King' needed to be 'dealt with in a severe and exemplary manner', by being deposed and deported to St Helena or Ascension.[51] However, Salisbury was more cautious, seeking more information about exactly which promises Jaja had broken.[52] He was also reminded by Jaja's envoys, who had arrived in London, that Jaja's rights over trade (recognised in 1873) had been purposely preserved in 1884, and that he would not have signed Hewett's treaty had Article VI not been struck out.[53] Reviewing the case, Salisbury concluded that Jaja appeared to be *de facto* suzerain of Ohambele, so that it was perfectly within his power to prohibit European trade. He saw no infringement of the treaty of 1873 which would justify intervention, and considered that Rosebery's letter of June 1886 had no authority. In

---

[47] 1888 (c. 5365), enc. 5 in No. 46, p. 61; No. 46, p. 59. He was advised by A. H. Turnbull, the agent of Miller, Brother & Co., to sign under protest and to complain to the Foreign Office: FO 403/73, enc. in No. 156, p. 118.

[48] PP 1888 (c. 5365), No. 45, p. 55.   [49] PP 1888 (c. 5365), No. 59, p. 70.

[50] PP 1888 (c. 5365), enc. 1 in No. 59, p. 72. He also threatened the agent of Miller, Brother & Co. that if he continued to trade, he would himself be deported. Johnston's actions led to protests from the company. See FO 403/73, No. 103, p. 80; No. 112, p. 87; No. 123, p. 98; FO 403/86, enc. 4 in No. 80, p. 71; enc. in No. 73, p. 62 at p. 65; encs. in No. 103, p. 84.

[51] FO 403/73, No. 106, p. 82.   [52] FO 403/73, No. 106, p. 83 at p. 84.

[53] FO 403/86, No. 26, p. 29.

his view, there was no cause of war against Jaja 'according to any sort of rules of international right'.[54] Salisbury came to the conclusion that an investigation was needed into the exact nature of Jaja's rights, both under the treaty of 1873 and with respect to Ohambele. If he had imposed an illegal blockade, then he could be punished; if not, there would have to be negotiations about the future.[55] Consequently, when Jaja's envoys, accompanied by a representative from Miller, Brother and Co., had a meeting with Sir James Fergusson, the undersecretary of state, on 13 September, they were informed that an investigation would take place, conducted by a naval delegation.[56]

London's caution was overtaken by events on the ground. When Johnston attempted to go upriver at the start of September, to help establish trading stations, he found the Azumena creek blocked by hostile Africans who appeared to be acting on Jaja's orders.[57] Fearing what Jaja's future plans might be if his envoys did not succeed,[58] Johnston sent a telegram to London asking permission to remove Jaja to the Gold Coast.[59] A mix-up seemed to give him the answer he wanted. Ten minutes before his telegram arrived at the Foreign Office, a telegram was sent to him, approving his action with regard to Jaja.[60] This telegram referred to earlier correspondence from Johnston, but he read it as a response to the telegram he had just sent, giving him the green light to detain Jaja. He now proceeded to execute his plan. He summoned Jaja to a meeting on 19 September, reassuring the king that everything would be done in a friendly and temperate spirit, without the use of force.[61] However, when Jaja came to the meeting, he was told that he would be taken to Accra for an inquiry into the charges against him. If he was found guilty, he would be exiled, if not he would be restored to his position. Jaja was also told that if he did not come voluntarily, this would be taken as an admission of guilt, and any resistance offered would be mercilessly crushed.[62] Jaja had no option but to accept, and within the hour, he was

---

[54] FO 403/73, No. 118, p. 91.   [55] FO 403/73, No. 131, p. 102.
[56] PP 1888 (c. 5365), No. 53, p. 68.   [57] PP 1888 (c. 5365), No. 63, p. 78.
[58] As he wrote to Captain Hand, 'He may either sell his country to France ... Or he may sack the factories, kill the white men, and retire into the inaccessible interior with his plunder': FO 403/86, enc. 7 in No. 112, p. 96 at p. 97.
[59] PP 1888 (c. 5365), No. 43, p. 54.   [60] FO 403/86, No. 37, p. 37.
[61] FO 403/86, enc. 3 in No. 124, p. 104; PP 1888 (c. 5365), No. 67, p. 80.
[62] PP 1888 (c. 5365), enc. 1 in No. 67, p. 83.

on his way to Accra. Johnston then proclaimed free trade, and ordered the arrest of Ekike Notsho.

The Foreign Office was alarmed at this turn of events. It could not disown the actions of its consul, but neither could it go back on the promise of an investigation, which Salisbury now began to regret. The prospect of having to pass an ordinance to authorise Jaja's detention also worried Salisbury, who noted, 'Do not let us have another Zebehr'.[63] The authorities initially hoped that Jaja could be persuaded to remain in Accra voluntarily, but Governor White was compelled within two days to introduce the required ordinance since Jaja had broken his 'parole' by 'listening to ill-advised counsel' (the lawyer Edward Bannerman), and by 'telegraphing to friends in England with a view to obtaining his release'.[64] Provision was also made to hold his envoys, whom Johnston wanted to be detained on their return either as hostages (in the case of his sons) to secure Jaja's good behaviour, or (in the case of the chiefs Cookey Gam and Shu Peterside) to keep their followers in Opobo quiet.[65]

Meanwhile plans were made for the investigation which had been promised. In order to ensure that it would be perceived to be impartial, Rear-Admiral Walter Hunt-Grubbe, Commander-in-chief on the Cape of Good Hope and West Coast of Africa station, was appointed to conduct it.[66] To allow Jaja to attend (and be represented by Bannerman), Hunt-Grubbe decided to hold the inquiry at Accra, rather than Opobo.[67] According to his instructions from the Foreign Office, which appeared to accept Jaja's view of the 1884 treaty, Hunt-Grubbe was to examine whether Jaja had merely exercised his right to control trade within his own jurisdiction, or whether he had barred 'the trade to the inland districts beyond his own jurisdiction, such as Ohombela is alleged to be'. Hunt-Grubbe would be 'at liberty to inflict whatever punishment he may deem right' if Jaja had blocked the highway; but if he had only restricted trade within his own areas, there would be negotiations to obtain favourable terms for British traders.[68]

---

[63] FO 403/86, No. 50, at p. 49.
[64] FO 403/73, enc. 2 in No. 238E, p. 189; enc. 4 in No. 238C, p. 190A (Opobo Political Prisoners Detention Ordinance No. 16 of 1887). See also White to Holland, 5 October 1887, CO 96/183/22136.
[65] Johnston to White, 3 October 1887, CO 96/183/22136. He had sent a telegram to White on 18 September, asking him to detain the envoys: CO 96/183/18885.
[66] PP 1888 (c. 5635), enc. in No. 60, p. 74.   [67] FO 403/86, No. 137, p. 114.
[68] Foreign Office to Admiralty, 27 September 1887, PP 1888 (c. 5635), No. 51, p. 63.

In the event, Hunt-Grubbe approached the inquiry with a broader brush. When the investigation began on 29 November, he set out three questions to be investigated. First, had Jaja barred trade to places beyond his jurisdiction, such as Ohambele was said to be? Second, had he at any time blocked the highway? Third, had he 'loyally endeavoured' to carry out the 1884 treaty?[69] Jaja denied blocking the creek, breaking the treaty of 1884, or making 'ju-ju' since that date. He also pointed out that the treaty had said nothing about opening new markets to the Europeans.[70] The main evidence against him came from Johnston, who was hardly an independent witness. Besides blaming him for the event on the Azumena creek,[71] Johnston complained that Jaja had breached Article V of the treaty, under which he agreed to act on the advice of the consular representative, by sending a deputation to London without first communicating with him. The Rear-Admiral clearly found the evidence against Jaja more comprehensible than that in his favour, for he later reported 'I found it quite impossible to take minutes as is usual at a Court of Inquiry, the vernacular of the natives being so peculiar.'[72] He gave his decision on 1 December. Jaja's central argument, that he had preserved rights under the 1884 treaty which the British were seeking to infringe, was not addressed in Hunt-Grubbe's finding, though he did accept that it had not been proven that Jaja had barred the trade to Ohambele. As for the obstruction on the Azumena creek, Hunt-Grubbe found that Jaja's men were present, and 'though they took no active part in obstructing the Consul, they were the reverse of friendly'. This was sufficient in his view to prove the second charge. As for the third, the charge of failing loyally to carry out the provisions of the treaty was proven not only by Jaja's reluctance to break the 'ju-ju', but also by his sending a mission to England without Johnston's knowledge or sanction. The real grounds of the decision were to be found in Hunt-Grubbe's concluding remark: 'Opobo requires rest to enable proper and free trade to be developed. Your presence in the river would be fatal to peace and progress.' Hunt-Grubbe's recommended that Jaja be exiled for at least five years, with the king being allowed to choose between Ascension, St Helena, the Cape Colony or the West Indies.[73]

[69] FO 403/74, enc. in No. 1, p. 2. [70] FO 403/74, enc. 3 in No. 6, p. 7.
[71] FO 403/74, enc. 6 in No. 6, p. 9. [72] FO 403/74, enc. 7 in No. 6, p. 11.
[73] FO 403/74, enc. in No. 1, p. 2.

It did not take long for Miller, Brother and Co. to complain about the nature of the proceedings,[74] nor for the matter to be raised by the Irish Nationalist MP William Redmond in parliament.[75] Under sustained pressure from MPs, the government agreed to publish a Blue Book, though there were concerns over how much material to include in it. Looking through Hunt-Grubbe's précis of evidence, the Foreign Office's legal adviser, W. E. Davidson, noted that the only point established by independent evidence at the hearing was that the king had made 'ju-ju' since 1884. It was clear to Davidson that the proceedings fell far short of the standards expected of English criminal law, and that there would be plenty for hostile critics to attack if it were published.[76] On his advice, the précis of evidence was left out of the Blue Book. The published version did, however, contain one potential hostage to fortune, which was spotted by the Foreign Office's lawyers: a careful reading of the telegrams published in it would reveal that Johnston had detained and removed Jaja on a misapprehension that he had authority to do so. The fact that he had no authority would mean that Jaja's rendition from Opobo to Accra had been illegal, which might open the way for legal proceedings on his behalf. On advice from the Law Officers that the transit of a detainee between colonies could be regarded as an act of state[77] – removing his right of action – but only if it was properly ratified, the Foreign Office formally notified Johnston on 7 April 1888 that it was ratifying his actions in removing Jaja.[78] In this way, the Foreign Office sought to ensure that its treatment of Jaja was, at least formally, legally watertight.

In May 1888, Jaja sailed for St Vincent, where an ordinance was passed to authorise his detention. When Jaja's health began to deteriorate, Salisbury worried that his death in exile 'would be very extreme embarrassment. It would induce a close inquiry into the circumstances of his deportation which cannot be defended according to European notions of good faith.'[79] Eventually, the Foreign Office decided to move him to Barbados, but when his health continued to decline there, the decision was taken that he should be

---

[74] FO 403/74, No. 4, p. 4; No. 19, p. 21; No. 28, p. 26.
[75] *Parl. Debs.*, 3rd ser., vol. 323, col. 24 (2 March 1888).   [76] FO 403/74, No. 78, p. 65.
[77] FO 403/74, No. 62, p. 50, referring to *Buron* v. *Denman* (1848) 2 Ex. 166.
[78] FO 403/74, Nos. 73–74, p. 61.
[79] Salisbury minute 17 June 1889, FO 84/1940, quoted in Cookey, *King Ja Ja*, p. 154.

sent home. But Jaja never made it: sent first to Tenerife, to await MacDonald's arrival, he died on the island in July 1891.

Jaja was the first of a number of rulers in the Niger delta who would be deposed and removed by the British as they asserted their authority in the region in the aftermath of the Berlin Conference. At a turning point in the imperial project, the changing notion of protectorates placed Jaja in an uncomfortably ambiguous position, halfway between sovereign and subject. Jaja regarded himself as an independent sovereign, whose relationship with Britain was defined by a treaty which preserved his rights over trade in areas which included Ohambele. By contrast, his adversaries – including Johnston and Hunt-Grubbe – regarded the king as bound to act on the advice of the British consul, and disregarded the reservation of his rights. In the view of the consular officials, Britain's right to trade derived from the broader agreement at Berlin, of which Jaja was not a part. In principle, the dispute between Jaja and the British over his right to control trade was a question of international law, for Jaja was not a subject and had violated no domestic law. In the end, the British came up with a Napoleonic solution to the problem of how to deal with him – exile by *ad hominem* legislation. However, to justify this, they conducted a non-judicial investigation into his conduct, as they had with Abdullah of Perak. In Abdullah's case, the justification for this was that the Sultan was suspected of criminal conduct for which he could not otherwise be prosecuted; but in Jaja's, his offence was simply that he had obstructed British trade ambitions. Here, the rule of law gave way to *Realpolitik* and to the economic interest of British merchants. If Jaja had the better of the legal arguments, they counted for little in the eyes of British officials who justified their actions in terms of economic advantage, and who were able to impose their will thanks to their military power. As had happened elsewhere in West Africa, the local officials were able to drive the policy, so that the Foreign Office was ultimately prepared to put aside such legal doubts as they had. With relatively weak support in England, Jaja was unable to make his voice heard. In this context, the legal instruments used to authorise the king's removal were formalities, which gave the stamp of legality to economic self-interest.

Nana Olomu

In 1896, nine years after Jaja's removal to the Gold Coast, another ruler from the Niger delta, Nana Olomu, was removed to Christiansborg Castle, where he was detained under an ordinance passed for the purpose. However, the legal route taken by the British in Nana's case was markedly different from that taken in Jaja's. By this stage, earlier British ideas that the jurisdiction of the protecting power over Africans depended on the express terms of a treaty had given way to the view that 'the existence of a protectorate in an uncivilised country imports the right to assume whatever jurisdiction over all persons may be needed for its effectual exercise'.[80] At a time when the protectorate had been established in the Oil Rivers with a structure of administration and governance, Nana would be treated much more like a recalcitrant subject than an autonomous ruler, in the end facing trial in a consular court. In his case, a more elaborate version of 'lawfare' was used to remove another obstructive ruler.

Nana was the most powerful Itsekiri chief.[81] The Itsekiri were middlemen in the trade in palm oil, buying oil from the Urhobo further inland, and selling it to European merchants. Much of the Itsekiri population had migrated in the middle of the nineteenth century from Warri to the lower Benin River, where two branches, or Houses, established themselves on opposite banks of the river.[82] Nana's father Olomu, who by the 1860s was the wealthiest trader on the river, was a member of the house of the Ologbotsere (on the north bank). Following the pattern of richer Itsekiri, he established his own village at Ebrohimi on the Benin River, from where he was able to establish his supremacy over trade on the river, monopolising it through his large fleet of war canoes. In 1879, Olomu was elected Governor of the River, a position which had been created on the initiative of Consul Beecroft, after a succession crisis in the middle of

---

[80] Law Officers' Opinion (relating to the Gold Coast), 14 February 1895, CO 885/14, No. 78.
[81] See Obaro Ikime, *Merchant Prince of the Niger Delta: The Rise and Fall of Nana Olomu, Last Governor of the Benin River* (London, Heinemann, 1968); and Anene, *Southern Nigeria in Transition*, pp. 149–161.
[82] See P. C. Lloyd, 'The Itsekiri in the Nineteenth Century: An Outline Social History', *Journal of African History*, vol. 4:2 (1963), pp. 207–231; and A. F. C. Ryder, *Benin and the Europeans, 1485–1897* (London, Longmans 1969), pp. 243ff.

Removing Rulers in the Niger Delta, 1887–1897

the century left the Itsekiri crown in abeyance.[83] The task of the Governor was to maintain peaceful trade on the river, and – at least in the eyes of the Itsekiri – to protect their trading interests.

When Olomu died in 1883, control of his trade passed to his son Nana. One year later, Consul Hewett asked the Itsekiri elders to elect a new Governor of the River, and Nana was chosen. In the same year, he signed Hewett's protection treaty, though, like Jaja, he did not agree to the clause opening up the river to free trade.[84] In 1885, he was presented with a staff of office 'sent by Her Majesty's Government, under whose protection Nana and his people had placed themselves', so that the other chiefs present could acknowledge their allegiance to him and 'know that the power of Her Majesty's Government supports you in your authority'.[85] The actions of the Foreign Office in purporting to confer authority on Nana were in part explained by potential jurisdictional conflicts it had in this area with other elements of the British imperial state, namely the Royal Niger Company and the Colonial Office: in particular, it wanted to ensure that Nana's authority to make treaties on behalf of other chiefs was recognised, since this would override any protection treaties they might have made with the Royal Niger Company.[86] At the same time, the Foreign Office's jurisdiction over Nana was put in question by the proclamation made in February 1886 by Governor W. Brandford Griffith under which the north bank of the Benin River – where Ebrohimi lay – was to be added to the colony of Lagos.[87] As for Nana, he did not himself think that he owed his position to any British appointment.

---

[83] Lloyd, 'The Itsekiri in the Nineteenth Century', p. 216, citing Beecroft to Palmerston, 19 April 1851, FO 84/858, f. 162 at f. 191ff.

[84] Nana and Chanomi signed the treaty, but added the words 'except as regards Articles VI and VII which are to be left for negotiation on a future occasion'. Hewett to Granville, 30 July 1884, FO 84/1660, f. 178.

[85] Presenting it, Vice-Consul Blair added, 'I look to you as the executive power through which the decrees of Her Majesty's Consular Court are to be exercised and enforced': FO 84/2109, f. 105v.; FO 2/64, f. 360.

[86] Hewett to Granville, 25 August 1884, FO 84/1660, f. 204. MacDonald concluded that Nana had not made out his claim to jurisdiction over Goolah and Borutu, and that they had made valid treaties with the company: FO 84/2109, f. 110v.

[87] Nana was not informed about this and 'considered himself under consular jurisdiction and not as belonging to the Colony of Lagos'. FO 84/2109, ff. 105–106.

From the British point of view, Nana's position as Governor became redundant in 1891 with the establishment of the Oil Rivers Protectorate. When MacDonald toured the rivers in the summer to explain the operation of the new system, Nana signed a declaration consenting to the new customs duties to be imposed; though he also took the opportunity to make an impassioned complaint about the way he had been treated by Acting Consul George Annesley, when he purported to depose him from the position of Governor in 1890. The British were now keen to open up trade in the interior and to by-pass middlemen such as Nana, who (as MacDonald put it) was 'already sufficiently powerful, and threatens to become a second Ja-Ja'.[88] Despite complaints of Nana's obstruction of trade,[89] the new Vice-Consul for the Benin River, Capt. H. L. Gallwey, remained optimistic that, once law and order had been put on a sound footing, white traders would have direct access to the markets of the Urhobo. He even assured the Urhobo, who were constantly at war with the Itsekiri and complained about only being able to deal with Nana, 'that trade was free now' and that anyone obstructing it 'would be severely punished'.[90] However, Nana continued to exert his authority over the African trade and to restrict access to these markets. This prompted Gallwey in June 1892 to accuse him of 'playing a very dangerous game' and to threaten gun boats.[91] In April 1894, MacDonald again warned Nana not to interfere with freedom of trade, telling him that 'the Government of the Queen is established here, you are no longer chief of the Jakri [Itsekiri] people'.[92]

When MacDonald went on leave in the summer of 1894, his replacement, Ralph Moor, began to take some more decisive steps to deal with this obstructive chief.[93] After hearing that Nana's people were 'generally terrorizing the locality',[94] he went to the Benin River and summoned Nana to discuss some matters of 'vital importance'. When Nana sent an excuse for not attending, Moor wrote back that he

---

[88] FO 403/171, No. 61, p. 39 at p. 42; cf. Nana to Salisbury, 14 December 1890, FO 2/64, f. 364.
[89] For example, Hewett to Nana, 24 February 1887, FO 2/64, f. 362.
[90] FO 403/171, enc. 1 in No. 118, pp. 81–82.
[91] Gallwey to Nana, 21 June 1892, FO 2/64, f. 366.
[92] MacDonald to Nana, 5 April 1894, FO 2/64, f. 373.
[93] Anene, *Southern Nigeria in Transition*, pp. 154–155.   [94] FO 403/200, No. 124, p. 240.

wanted to discuss both Nana's interference with the trade and the fact that his headman Ologuy had seized several Urhobo. Nana was given fourteen days to return the captives and to replace Ologuy. He was warned that if he did not comply, the Ethiope river would be closed to his people.[95] In his reply, Nana denied any desire to interfere with the Urhobo traders, and explained that the men taken captive were being held as security for a debt of the Eku Urhobos.[96] This did not satisfy Moor. In his view, in seizing Urhobo slaves as security for his debt, Nana had taken the law into his own hands, when he should have referred the matter to the consular court. Moor told Nana to hand over the captives to this court, and to produce Ologuy to give evidence. Until this was done, the Ethiope river would be closed to his people.[97] Having heard that Nana was threatening to attack two friendly chiefs, Dore and Dudu, he further arranged for the *Alecto* to be sent to the river.[98]

Summoning him to another meeting in August, Moor promised Nana that he would not be molested in any way if he attended, but warned that, if matters were not settled in a friendly manner, 'other measures must be taken'.[99] However, Nana remained convinced that he would suffer the same fate as Jaja if he went. He therefore sent a representative to this meeting, where the other Itsekiri chiefs entered a new treaty which included the free trade provisions. Nana was now informed that his people were forbidden to use any waterways in the Benin or Warri districts, and was ordered to remove a gate which he had placed on the creek leading to Ebrohimi, in violation of government orders that all waterways in the district were to be free for all traders.[100] Although Moor gave him one last chance to come and sign the same treaty as the other chiefs, Nana remained convinced that the consul's aims were not peaceful. 'Please try your best and leave me, alone, Consul General', he wrote, 'I afraided the wars, of Government, no blackmens fitted to do anything against the Government, except the Lord God.'[101] By then, the *Alecto* had

[95] Moor to Nana, 25 June 1894, FO 2/64, f. 378.
[96] Nana to Moor, 25 June 1894, FO 2/64, f. 380.
[97] Moor to Nana, 20 July 1894, FO 2/64, f. 382.
[98] FO 403/200, No. 124, p. 240.
[99] Moor to Nana, 31 July 1894, FO 2/64, f. 388.
[100] Moor to Nana, 2 August 1894, FO 2/64, f. 392.
[101] Nana to Moor, 4 August 1894, FO 2/64, f. 393.

already destroyed the barrier which Moor had objected to. During this operation, there was an exchange of gunfire with the Africans, which in Moor's view 'materially changed' matters: and he now ordered a blockade of Ebrohimi, to force Nana's submission.[102]

Moor also set about disciplining those chiefs who supported Nana. After an Idzo chief – whose followers had attacked a neighbouring village – failed to respond to a summons from Moor (claiming he had referred the matter to Nana), Moor ordered the *Alecto* to burn down his village, 'exercising a form of *lex talionis* as punishment'. This was intended to convey the message that those who ignored British orders, on the assumption that Nana's was the only government, would face serious consequences.[103] Nana's response was to hoist a white flag at the mouth of the creek leading to Ebrohemi and to place a notice there stating that he wanted peace. However, he still refused to meet Moor. Furthermore, his people still appeared to be attacking other villages and canoes. Moor now concluded that it was useless to continue to negotiate, and that a second gunboat would be needed.[104]

The crisis deepened when, on the morning of 24 August, an armoured steam-cutter, which had been sent up the Brohemie creek to reconnoitre for obstacles in the way of an attack on the town, was fired on, killing two men and severely injuring three.[105] Five days later, a large force was sent to open up a route to take the town by land. Faced with a very difficult terrain and unexpectedly strong defences erected by Nana, the decision was taken to blockade and shell the town in order to force Nana's surrender.[106] When Nana sent messages seeking peace, he was told that the British would only accept his unconditional surrender, whereupon his life would be spared.[107] Ebrohemi was finally captured on 25 September, but during the attack on the town Nana and many of his followers escaped.[108] On the same day, Moor issued a proclamation declaring Nana an outlaw until such time as he surrendered to stand trial for

---

[102] Moor to Foreign Office, 6 August 1894, FO 403/200, p. 240.
[103] FO 403/200, No. 125, p. 242.
[104] FO 403/200, No. 130, p. 250C; FO 403/200, enc. 3 in No. 143*, p. 270.
[105] FO 403/200, No. 143, p. 264.   [106] FO 403/200, No. 143, p. 264 at p. 267.
[107] FO 403/200, enc. in No. 161, p. 286; enc. 2 in No. 172*, p. 300.
[108] FO 403/200, No. 177, p. 302.

Removing Rulers in the Niger Delta, 1887–1897

levying war against the government of the Oil Rivers Protectorate. All his property was declared forfeited to the government.[109]

Besides putting pressure on friendly chiefs to secure Nana's capture,[110] Moor contacted the Governor of Lagos, Sir Gilbert Carter, for assistance, should he go to Lagos.[111] However, the colonial Governor was more concerned with ensuring that legal formalities were complied with than the acting Consul-General. Carter told Moor that Nana could only be arrested – under the provisions of the Fugitive Offenders Act 1881 – if an appropriate warrant were issued.[112] Indeed, when Nana surrendered voluntarily to Carter on 30 October, the Governor, who was aware that he had no legal authority to detain the chief, told him that he would be left at liberty as long as he made no attempt to escape.[113] He planned to hand over Nana to MacDonald, on his way back to the Oil Rivers Protectorate, provided that an appropriate warrant was issued. However, when MacDonald presented the warrant (which he had been forced to obtain by a detour to Forcados), Carter – perhaps influenced by the extensive discussions of the case which had taken place in Lagos – raised a further objection. He now asserted that, being on the right bank of the Benin River, Ebrohimi was within the colony of Lagos. This meant not only that Nana could not be handed over, but that he might even have a cause of action against the protectorate government.[114] In the end, the dispute over jurisdiction – which was settled by a search through official correspondence in MacDonald's favour – became moot when Nana agreed to return voluntarily to the protectorate.[115]

In contrast to the naval investigation which looked into Jaja's conduct, Nana was to be put on trial. However, the trial turned out to be far from a model of the rule of law. Nana requested a trial at Lagos, where he had already consulted lawyers, but MacDonald opposed this, since he distrusted the verdicts of the mixed juries of

---

[109] FO 403/200, inc. 4 in No. 177, p. 310.
[110] FO 403/200, No. 215, p. 351; No. 216, p. 351 at p. 353.
[111] FO 403/200, enc. 2 in No. 201, p. 345.
[112] He also pointed out that there were no powers for the government of Lagos to seize any of his assets held there. FO 403/200, enc. 4 in No. 201, p. 346.
[113] FO 403/200, enc. 1 in No. 210, p. 344.   [114] FO 403/200, No. 216, p. 351.
[115] FO 403/200, No. 216, p. 351; enc. in No. 218, p. 355.

Europeans and Africans found there.[116] Instead, the trial, which began on 30 November, took place in the consular court at Old Calabar, under the provisions of the Africa Order in Council of 1893.[117] It was presided over by MacDonald himself – a career soldier with no legal training, and sitting without assessors – in a court which heard no legal argument, and in which neither side was represented by lawyers. Nana was to be held to account both for his armed resistance to the British military and for his political resistance to the opening up of the creeks to free trade. The first charge against him was that he had levied war against Her Majesty's Government, and endeavoured with arms 'to avoid carrying out the terms' of the treaty entered into in July 1884 (which under section 16 of the Order in Council was to have effect as part of the law to be enforced). The second charge accused him of acting in opposition to British Consular officers in the execution of their duties, and in not taking their advice in matters relating to peace, order and good government 'and the general progress of civilization'. A third count charged him with breaches of the peace, and a fourth with incitement to breach of the peace.

The legal basis of these charges was not very clear, for the charge sheet only made three marginal references to legal provisions. Next to the charge of levying war, reference was made to section 48 of the Order in Council, which stipulated that 'any British subject' who levied war or joined in rebellion 'against any King, Chief, tribe or power' without Her Majesty's authority was liable to be imprisoned for two years, with or without a £1,000 fine; the conviction also rendering the offender liable to deportation. Given that Nana was charged with levying war against the British Government – rather than any other local power – it was not quite clear why this section was relevant, particularly since the Order in Council explicitly provided that anything which constituted treason, felony or misdemeanour in England was also a punishable offence in the protectorate. In either event, the question was begged whether Nana was a 'subject' who could be amenable to such a charge. Furthermore, the charges

---

[116] FO 403/200, No. 216, p. 351.
[117] Passed under the 1890 Foreign Jurisdiction Act, this extended the Africa Order in Council of 1889: see Francis E. Hodges, *Consular Jurisdiction in Her Majesty's Protectorate of the Niger Coast* (London, Stevens & Sons, 1895). The Foreign Office authorised the creation of consular courts for various districts in the protectorate in July 1891: FO 403/171, No. 38, p. 26.

relating to breaches of the peace made reference to section 102 of the Order rather than to any English offence. However, this section was not concerned with offences, but with the punishment of deportation. It stated that a person convicted of any offence could be required to give security for future good behaviour, and could – in default of such security – be deported. It also provided that anyone suspected of being about to commit a breach of the peace might be ordered to give security, or (in default thereof) be deported. The fact that it was mentioned in the margin of the charge sheet, in relation to the accusation of breaches of the peace, suggests a very hurried reading of the Order in Council by someone whose grasp of legal technicalities was very limited.[118]

Seven witnesses testified against Nana: the Consular Agent R. F. Locke, Moor and five African witnesses. Much of the evidence of the white administrators described the events since March, during which time Nana had stopped trade and seized slaves, and defied orders to attend meetings. Drawing heavily on correspondence seized from Nana's canoe, Moor painted a picture of a chief who owed his position to British patronage, and who persistently defied demands to allow free trade.[119] Nana's accusers considered that he was bound by his treaty obligations to allow free trade: and indeed, the copy of his treaty, authenticated by MacDonald on the day that the trial commenced, included Article VI which guaranteed it.[120] Although Nana had struck out this provision, unlike Jaja he did not at his hearing challenge the right of the British under the treaty to open up the area for free trade. Indeed, he did not ask Moor any questions at the trial, and when it came to making his defence, he denied obstructing trade.[121]

Nana also had to answer the charges of violence. Moor testified that Nana's adherents had burned villages and captured people, and raided canoes belonging to the Itsekiri chiefs Dore and Dudu. He claimed that

---

[118] As for the second charge, relating to his failure to carry out the treaty provisions, Nana might have been charged under section 49, which made it an offence wilfully or knowingly to act in contravention of any treaty as defined in the order; but the charge sheet made no such specification.
[119] *Regina versus Nanna Alluma*, FO 403/215, enc. in No. 71*, pp. 46B–46C.
[120] Exhibit 'A', FO 2/64, f. 346.
[121] *Regina versus Nanna Alluma*, FO 403/215, enc. in No. 71*, pp. 46K–46L.

Nana had conducted regular slave-raids, so that, at the time of his defeat, he had 5,000 slaves. As further evidence of his violence, Moor described the decapitated bodies found in the creeks near Ebrohimi after the capture of the town. Evidence was also given, by Nana's own messengers, of his brutal execution of two men in his town, one for an alleged murder and the other for adultery. Much of this evidence did not relate to specific charges against Nana, who was charged neither with slave-raiding nor with murder, but related to the broader accusation that he had terrorised the country. He denied slave-raiding, claiming that it was customary to take people as security for a trust or debt. He also denied any knowledge of the decapitations.[122] According to Nana's account, the disturbances which occurred in the middle of 1894 derived from a long-standing feud between his father and Dore's father, and had nothing to do with the British, with whom he claimed to have no quarrel.

There was no denying that he had assembled a considerable arsenal of weapons and fought the British after the *Alecto* had arrived. However, Nana sought to portray himself as a man who was constantly keen to make peace – witnessed by his hoisting a white flag – but was too frightened to submit to Moor. He claimed to have given orders that white men were not to be fired on, and that even when Ebrohimi was attacked, any firing was to be over the heads of the white soldiers, to frighten them off. As for the fatal exchange with the cutter, he claimed that the Africans had been fired on first, and that they had only seen that there were white men on the ship after the shots had been exchanged. Nana's defence strategy was clearly one designed not to challenge British authority, but to accept the premises of colonial authority and deny culpability. Nana did not have the benefit of a lawyer, either to present his case or to cross-examine the witnesses for the prosecution. Nor did he call any witnesses of his own: his defence consisted solely of a statement made to the court.

On 6 December, Sir Claude MacDonald gave the finding of the court. This was not a reasoned judgment, for MacDonald neither explained the nature and meaning of the charges, nor did he go through any of the evidence to establish whether the charges were made out in detail. Instead, he merely listed the four counts against

---

[122] *Regina versus Nanna Alluma*, FO 403/215, enc. in No. 71*, p. 46L.

Nana and convicted him on all four. Taking into consideration the fact that Nana had not been 'on all occasions a free agent in the action taken', the Consul-General sentenced him to deportation for life from the Benin district 'to such part of the Niger Coast Protectorate as may be from time to time directed by the Court'.[123] At the same time, he confirmed Moor's proclamation under which his property was declared forfeited. MacDonald reported to the Foreign Office on 13 December that Nana had been deported to the Upper Cross River.[124]

When the papers from the trial arrived at the Foreign Office, officials puzzled over the provisions of the Africa Order in Council, as applied to Nana's case. The main charge against him, so it appeared, was under section 48 of the Order, which made provision for a sentence of imprisonment and/or a fine. However, officials in Whitehall doubted whether MacDonald had any power to deport the chief, unless – following the provisions of section 102 – he had first been required to give security for good behaviour, and had then failed to comply. It was admitted that this was a debatable point, but the legal adviser at the Foreign Office took the view that, were the matter to go to the Privy Council, it might be held that there was no power to deport, in the way that MacDonald had. However, he thought the best advice was to 'let things slide' and take no notice of the official despatch. London would wait until the matter was raised, if ever. In the meantime, it was also agreed that it was unnecessary to put Nana's trial in print, since, by the middle of 1895, 'it is not now probable that questions will be asked.'[125]

In June 1896, still in detention at Old Calabar, Nana petitioned the Governor of Lagos to be allowed to live there. Consul-General Moor was not sympathetic to the application. He thought that Nana's punishment had served as a good example to others in the protectorate, and the good would be undone if he were allowed to live in Lagos, which would soon be easily accessible from Benin. Moor wanted him to be removed to the Gold Coast, 'where there is proper accommodation for looking after natives in his position'. In Moor's

---

[123] *Regina versus Nanna Alluma*, FO 403/215, enc. in No. 71*, p. 46N.
[124] Nana's conviction was followed by the trial of seven of his associates on similar charges, six of whom were convicted. *Regina versus Nanna Alluma*, FO 403/215, enc. in No. 71*, p. 46P.
[125] Minute by William Edward Davidson, dated 18 June 1895, FO 2/64, f. 292.

view, it would be a good thing to let 'the semi-civilized Chiefs' of the coastal region know that they would be removed from the protectorate altogether if they took up arms against the government.[126] The Foreign Office duly asked the Colonial Office whether it would authorise this.[127] The instructions were given, and the relevant ordinance passed at the Gold Coast.[128] The fact that this was all done by legislative fiat – rather than by following the procedures provided for under the Colonial Prisoners Removal Act and the Foreign Jurisdiction Act – might suggest that officials remained aware of the slender legal basis on which Nana's removal to Old Calabar rested.

As an African potentate seeking to protect his position as a middleman in trade from British encroachments, Nana Olomu's position was much like that of Jaja. Unlike the king of Opobo, however, he was treated as subject to British jurisdiction and tried in a consular court. If Nana was regarded as sufficiently sovereign to sign a treaty of protection, his sovereignty was not sufficient to make British officials feel that – like Abdullah – he could not be put on trial. By the time that Nana was tried, the very idea of a protectorate was changing. The traditional legal view that a protecting power had extraterritorial jurisdiction only over its own subjects and outsiders who also enjoyed its protection[129] had given way – at least in post-Berlin Africa – to a view (incorporated in the Africa Order in Council) that jurisdiction was also acquired over anyone residing within the protected area, if the consent of the ruler or community could be implied.[130] In Nana's case, the Foreign Office's officials simply assumed that the wider protectorate – which had been extended and renamed the Niger Coast Protectorate in 1893 – had jurisdiction over him, which did not derive from his own consent, whether express or implied. It was a contentious interpretation of the law, and one which would not be followed four years later by the Colonial Office and the Law Officers in London, when considering the case of Bai Bureh in Sierra Leone. If there

---

[126] FO 403/234, No. 16, p. 27 at p. 28. Officials in London noted that 'Moor's reasons are strong against the Chief's going to Lagos': FO 2/101, f. 124v.
[127] FO 403/234, No. 29, p. 42.
[128] FO 403/234, No. 50, p. 61; No. 58, p. 65; Gold Coast Ordinance 10 of 1896.
[129] Johnstone, *Sovereignty and Protection*, pp. 66–68.
[130] For the provision of the 1889 Order in Council, see Hodges, *Consular Jurisdiction*, p. 93. See further W. E. Hall, *A Treatise on the Foreign Powers and Jurisdiction of the British Crown* (Oxford, Clarendon Press, 1894), p. 213.

were questions to be raised about the basis of the jurisdiction in Nana's case, there were also further questions to be raised about the form of the trial, the nature of the charges against him, and the sentence imposed. This was not the rule of law in action; it was a form of lawfare, designed to impress both on Nana and on his followers that they were now subject to British jurisdiction; and one which, in the end, needed the same kind of formal authentication by ordinance as had been used against Jaja.

Ovonramwen

The third important ruler to be removed in this region was the Oba of Benin, Ovonramwen. The kingdom of Benin, over which he ruled, had been the dominant political authority in the region in the middle of the nineteenth century, before internal divisions and growing British influence on the coast began to weaken its authority.[131] For most of this period, the British showed little interest in exploring Benin, even though they had a well-established trade on the lower reaches of the Benin river. '[N]othing can be said in favour of Benin', Richard Burton (then consul at Fernando Po) wrote in 1863 after visiting the city, 'the place has a fume of blood, it stinks of death.'[132] No British official would return for nearly three decades. However, once the scramble for Africa got under way, interest grew in opening up trade routes to Benin City. In May 1885, Vice-Consul David Blair was sent with one of Hewett's treaties, but he fell ill *en route* and died before he could get there.[133] Three years later, Harry Johnston reported that, with the recent accession of Ovonramwen as the new Oba, Benin City 'appears to be more open to European influence than formerly'.[134]

---

[131] See Ryder, *Benin and the Europeans*, ch. 7; Philip A. Igbafe, 'The Fall of Benin: A Reassessment', *Journal of African History*, vol. 11:3 (1970), pp. 385–400; P. A. Igbafe, *Benin under British Administration: The Impact of Colonial Rule on an African Kingdom 1897–1938* (London, Humanities Press, 1979); and Robert Home, *City of Blood Revisited: A New Look at the Benin Expedition of 1897* (London, Rex Collings, 1982).

[132] Richard Burton, 'My Wanderings in West Africa', *Fraser's Magazine*, vol. 67 (March 1863), pp. 273–289 at p. 287.

[133] Ryder, *Benin and the Europeans*, p. 167; FO 403/71, No. 61, p. 70.

[134] H. H. Johnstone, 'A Report on the British Protectorate of the Oil Rivers', FO 84/1882, f. 136. Sir Percy Anderson reported on 10 September 1888 that Ovonramwen had told Johnston that he would forcibly resist any attempt to incorporate his territory into the Lagos colony: FO 403/76, No. 182, p. 216 at p. 217.

However, nothing more was done until 1890, when an unsuccessful attempt was made by Consul Annesley to get Ovonramwen to sign a treaty. It was not until March 1892, when Gallwey visited the city, that a treaty was obtained. On this occasion, the king proved reluctant to commit himself, but conceded after Gallwey threatened to leave, and not to return 'as a friend'. The king, in full ceremonial dress for the occasion, agreed to the standard form treaty, though he did not himself touch the pen which made the cross on his behalf.[135]

Although MacDonald told the Foreign Office in May 1892 that 'trade, commerce and civilization' in the area were paralysed by the fetish government, he had high hopes of opening up 'this rich and most important' territory.[136] Gallwey also thought that the treaty would be the foundation of a new order of things. In his view, two things stood in the way. The first was the power of the fetish priests, which needed to be broken before trade would be fully open. The second problem was that Ovonramwen exerted a tight control on trade in the Benin country, imposing taxes, forbidding trade in many products and frequently stopping trade for reasons which were hard to fathom.[137] In the event, little progress was made in opening up the area. Although the British had 'hopes that the lesson given to Chief Nana in Benin River would lead to the King of Benin city receiving a Representative',[138] efforts to open up communication with Benin met with little success. When Vice-Consul Copland-Crawford was sent in August 1895 to open up the district for trade, Ovonramwen sent a messenger saying he could not receive any white visitors during this time of traditional customary celebrations.[139] The king also continued his old practices in matters of trade by placing a 'ju-ju' on the most profitable items – imposing a death penalty for trading in them – and also closing his markets until he was paid presents. In Moor's view, Ovonramwen was acting flagrantly in breach of the treaty, and the first opportunity should be taken to open up the country, 'if necessary, by force'.[140] The Oba had good reason to fear British bellicosity. The previous November, he had sent messengers to the consulate to ask why Nana's towns had been destroyed only to be told that it was because Nana had disobeyed the orders of the Queen

---

[135] FO 403/171, enc. 1 in No. 164, p. 112; enc. 2 in No. 164, p. 114.
[136] FO 403/171, No. 164, p. 111.   [137] FO 403/187, enc. 1 in No. 6, at pp. 12–13.
[138] FO 403/234, No. 141, p. 151.   [139] FO 403/216, enc. in No. 108, p. 228.
[140] FO 403/216, No. 108, p. 227 at p. 228.

and not respected his treaty.[141] Mistrustful of the men on the ground, the Oba told Copland-Crawford that he wanted to send messengers to London, an attitude which MacDonald felt could only be attributed to the influence of 'educated natives' from Lagos or elsewhere.[142] Nonetheless, MacDonald urged caution before bellicose action was resorted to. He suggested that patient efforts should be made to open up communication with the king over the coming dry winter months; only if this failed should an expedition be sent in the following dry season.[143]

However, when MacDonald left West Africa in February 1896 to become minister to China, he was succeeded by men of a more bellicose frame of mind. When Ovonramwen stopped all trade with the Itsekiri in April 1896,[144] the new Consul General Moor concluded that the policy of peace had failed, and that preparations should be made for an expedition to remove the king.[145] When Moor went on leave to England, his acting replacement as Consul General, James R. Phillips, also recommended deposing the king, who was still blocking trade. In November, he requested permission to launch an expedition the following February to unstool the king, and set up a new native council in its place.[146] Having consistently taken a much more cautious approach to this matter,[147] the Foreign Office concluded (after consulting the Colonial Office and the War Office) that the necessary troops could not be spared. Phillips was duly instructed by telegram on 8 January 1897 to postpone the proposed expedition for a year.[148]

By then, Phillips was dead. Without first consulting his masters in London, he set off from Sapele on 2 January with 9 Europeans and 220 African carriers on a mission to Benin City to negotiate with the king.

---

[141] FO 403/216, No. 130, p. 243. [142] FO 403/216, No. 130, p. 243.
[143] His view was shared by the Foreign Office: FO 403/216, No. 151, p. 252.
[144] See Moor to Hill, 6 June 1896, FO 2/101, f. 117, quoted in Ryder, *Benin and the Europeans*, p. 281. For details, see FO 403/234, No. 139, p. 145 at pp. 146–147; FO 403/248, enc. in No. 7, p. 7.
[145] Moor to Foreign Office, 14 June 1896, FO 2/101, f. 143.
[146] FO 403/234, No. 139, p. 145. Moor concurred with this plan: No. 144, p. 151.
[147] FO 403/234, No. 33*, p. 43. Hill minuted, 'our men should keep their heads & not burst into "punitive expeditions" on every pretext. The King of Benin may have to be dealt with but it should be set about with care & with a sufficient force & at our own time': FO 2/101, f. 149v.
[148] FO 403/248, Nos. 13–14, p. 13.

On being given notice of this intended peaceful visit, Ovonramwen replied that he could not meet Phillips for at least a month, since he was engaged in customary ceremonies. Even then, he would only be prepared to meet Phillips and one Itsekiri chief, since he 'had heard of the white men going all over the country and taking the Chiefs prisoner'.[149] The party spent the night Ughoton, where the friendly Itsekiri chief Dore – Nana's nemesis – warned Phillips that it would 'be certain death to go'. Phillips decided nonetheless to proceed, although he sent back the drum and fife band of the Niger Coast Protectorate Force, which had originally accompanied the party, since their military uniforms might alarm the king of Benin. On 4 January, the party was ambushed and all the whites save 2 were killed, along with 124 Africans.[150] Reports were later received from the Principal Medical Officer that the decapitated bodies of some of the Europeans were later found in Benin City, but this information was suppressed to avoid distress to their relatives.[151]

This ambush – which attracted considerable media attention in Britain[152] – changed policy. The decision was taken to send an expeditionary force as soon as it could be mustered, to rescue any possibly surviving members of Phillips's party, to capture Benin city, and to punish the king for this outrage.[153] In Gallwey's view, 'the punishment to be inflicted' for the outrage 'cannot be too severe'. It would also have the effect of removing an obstacle to British expansion, for 'the destruction of Benin city, the removal and punishment of the King, the punishment of the fetish priests, the opening up of the country, &c, will prove a wonderful impetus to trade in this part of the Protectorate'.[154] The expeditionary

---

[149] FO 403/248, enc. 1 in No. 126, p. 89.
[150] FO 403/248, No. 125, p. 87. The two survivors were District Commissioner Ralph Locke and Captain Alan Boisragon. On the events, see Alan Maxwell Boisragon, *The Benin Massacre* (London, Methuen & Co., 1897).
[151] Moor to Foreign Office, 18 March 1897, FO 2/121 f. 257, with enclosures.
[152] As the *Manchester Guardian* explained (12 January 1897, p. 7), '[m]ost of the captives were well known in official and club circles in London.' For the coverage of the events in the British press, see Annie E. Coombes, *Reinventing Africa: Museums, Material Culture and Popular Imagination in Late Victorian and Edwardian England* (New Haven, Yale University Press, 1994), pp. 11–22.
[153] FO 403/248, No. 54, p. 29; No. 92*, p. 44A. See also Moor's interview, *The Times*, 16 January 1897, p. 5.
[154] FO 403/248, No. 133, p. 96 at pp. 98, 99.

force advanced rapidly, reaching Benin City on 18 February. It took much of the day to capture the city, at a cost (to the British forces) of nine lives. By the time it was taken, the king and all the inhabitants had fled, leaving only a mass of sacrificial corpses.[155] From a mile and a half out, the forces encountered the disembowelled bodies of people freshly sacrificed to prevent the conquest of the town. Having entered Benin, Moor (who had left England as soon as news of the attack reached him) described 'the horror of this most terrible city', with the stench of decomposing bodies in open pits and altars covered with streams of dried blood. In one of the pits, under a pile of bodies, they found a servant of one of the traders who had been in Phillips's party. 'All about the houses and streets are dead natives, some crucified and sacrificed on trees, others on stage erections, some on the ground, some in pits', wrote Felix N. Roth, a surgeon accompanying the party, 'by God! may I never see such sights again!'[156] Moor concluded that it was 'imperative that a most severe lesson be given the Kings, Chiefs, and Ju Ju men of all surrounding countries, that white men cannot be killed with impunity, and that human sacrifices, with the oppression of the weak and poor, must cease'.[157]

Moor's men destroyed the sacrificial altars and began burning the chiefs' compounds. He determined to level the city entirely, to forestall any future rebuilding on this site. He also seized a large number of bronze castings, and ivory and wood carvings from the city, some of which were sold to help pay the expenses of the expedition, and many more of which would find their way into the British Museum.[158] On the third day, four messengers arrived from the king, asking for a palaver. Moor gave a non-committal answer but left a way open for the chiefs to come in. He had already planned to settle matters 'by native palaver, country custom being very strict in demanding an eye for an eye and a tooth for a tooth'.[159] At the end of March, by which time eighteen of the principal chiefs had come in, Moor

---

[155] H. Ling Roth, *Great Benin: Its Customs, Art and Horrors* (London, Routledge 1968 [1903]), Appendices, xii.
[156] Roth, *Great Benin*, Appendices, viii, x. [157] FO 403/248, No. 154, p. 141 at p. 144.
[158] See Coombes, *Reinventing Africa*, ch. 1; and Mary Lou Ratté, *Imperial Looting and The case of Benin*, University of Massachusetts MA thesis, 1972.
[159] FO 403/248, No. 154, p. 141 at p. 144.

elaborated on his plan. He would hold a court under native custom to try the men responsible for the massacre. The aim was to demonstrate to the local people that the king and the chiefs could not perpetrate such acts with impunity. This would help undermine the authority of the king and the chiefs in the eyes of the people, allowing their place to be taken by a native council under government supervision.[160]

By early June, thirty chiefs had sworn 'submission to the rule of the white man' in the traditional manner.[161] '[H]aving become sick of his unaccustomed roaming bush life', the king himself returned to Benin City on 5 August, accompanied by some 800 followers. In full royal dress and before a crowd of 1,000, he made his submission to the Acting Political Resident, Captain E. P. S. Roupell in the traditional manner – putting his forehead on the ground – and was informed that he had been deposed.[162] Moor now proceeded to Benin City, where he assembled the king and seventy chiefs for a palaver on 1 September. It was held in the court house of the consular court, which had been set up at Benin under the Africa Order in Council in July.[163] Those present included Moor, Roupell and Captain Carter (the officer commanding the troops), nine members of the newly established native council, and sixty other chiefs, besides the king. 'I am not going to talk this palaver in the white man's fashion, but I am going to talk it in the native fashion', Moor began, 'and we are going to settle by your own custom and law.' He also made it clear that the Africans were not on trial for having taken up arms. 'The white man has no palaver with King and Chiefs because they fought for their country and lost', he told them, 'Every man that fights for his country is right.' Instead, the aim was to find out who was responsible for the murders and to deal with them according to native law.[164]

---

[160] FO 403/248, No. 198, p. 204. [161] FO 403/249, No. 122, p. 143 at p. 144.
[162] Roth, *Great Benin*, Appendices, xiii–xiv.
[163] FO 403/249, No. 30 p. 23, referring to Moor's despatch of 8 June 1897 (FO 2/122, f. 54). In this Moor said a court needed to be established in Benin City as many Africans were coming there from Lagos 'and the protected provinces' and had 'to be dealt with as either British subjects or British protected *subjects* under the Order'. The Foreign Office wrote that the expression to be used was 'British-protected persons', not 'British-protected subjects'.
[164] FO 403/250, enc. 1 in. No. 203, p. 198. See also the report of the trial in Roth, *Great Benin*, Appendices, xii–xviii.

Rather than taking the form of a trial, in which particular defendants were charged with particular offences, and in which prosecution and defence would be conducted by lawyers, this palaver took the form of an inquiry into who had instigated the massacre, and what part the king played in it. On the first day, evidence was given by three 'boys' – men in the retinues of Obahawaie and Obassieki. They identified six chiefs as having been present when the white men were killed, and who gave orders to kill them: Obaiuwana, Obahawaie, Usu, Ugiagbe, Obadesagbo and Ologbosheri. Only four of these men were in court, for Obadesagbo had died before the trial began, while Ologbosheri was still at large. At the end of the first day, the four men were taken into custody. Moor told them that if they were able to show that it was not their palaver, he would let them go; but otherwise, they would be dealt with by native law. By the time the court reconvened, Obaiuwana had killed himself by cutting his throat.

The first of the chiefs to speak was Obahawaie. He recounted that, ever since the war against Nana, it had been feared that the whites would make war on Benin. He blamed the massacre on bellicose chiefs rather than the king, who was described as a somewhat reclusive figure. According to Obahawaie, when the king was told that the whites were bringing war, he told his chiefs not to fight them, but to allow them to come. However, the chiefs, led by Ologbosheri and Iyasheri, rejected this and gave the orders to fight. When Obahawaie questioned them – having heard the whites were unarmed – he was himself threatened with death unless he joined the attack. Usu told a similar story of attempting to persuade the more bellicose chiefs not to kill the whites, as the king had forbidden it. Other witnesses related how Ologbosheri had said that it would be folly not to kill the white men, since they would themselves be killed if this were not done. The evidence of these chiefs clearly placed responsibility for the ambush on Ologbosheri and Iyasheri (who had also killed himself after his arrest).[165] At the end of the hearing, Ovonramwen himself spoke. He claimed to be a friend to the white man, and that he had urged his chiefs 'not to fight the white man, even if he brought war'.[166]

---

[165] FO 403/250, No. 203, p. 195, referring to him as Iguobasoyemi.
[166] FO 403/250, enc. 1 in. No. 203, p. 203.

By the end of these hearings, Moor came to a number of conclusions which he reported to the Foreign Office. After the fall of Nana, the king and chiefs of Benin had expected their country to be taken over, and had determined to resist. They had stationed people on the road from Ughoton to watch any attempt by the British to approach. Once they had learned of Phillips's approach, a force of 1,000 warriors was assembled 'for the purpose of repelling any attempt to take the country by force'.[167] He accepted that the king himself did not want to fight the whites, but was overruled by a majority of the chiefs. Moor realised that the Africans might have suspected that the unarmed party of whites had weapons, but also considered that the attackers might have been motivated in part by a desire for plunder. Giving his judgment to the court, Moor began by invoking native law and custom, which held (he asserted) that, if a king was killed, a king must die, and if a chief was killed, a chief must die. In this case, both Phillips – 'the King of the white men' – and his deputy had died. Although this seemed to suggest that Ovonramwen and his second man, Chief Aro, should die, Moor qualified it by adding that he accepted 'there is some doubt as to your action in killing the white men'. In his judgment, the king and all his chiefs could not be seen as murderers, since they thought that the whites had come to make war on them, and thought they were fighting for their country, something Moor regarded as an honourable thing. However, since those chiefs who took part in the ambush could see that the whites were unarmed, they had to be condemned as murderers. While Ugiagbe was spared, since he was only a 'small boy' who did what he was ordered, Obahawaie and Usu were sentenced to death, and were shot the following morning. Moor also announced that Ologbosheri would suffer the same penalty, and that until he was brought in, he would hold the lives of five chiefs as hostages for his crime.[168]

The trial reflected an odd form of hybrid legalism. Sitting in the room of the consular court, the Consul General arrogated to himself the right to try by what he took to be native law, and to order an

---

[167] FO 403/250, No. 203, p. 195 at p. 196.
[168] Ologbosheri was captured in June 1899, and was tried in Benin City in another 'native court', presided over by Moor. The judgment, given by the chiefs, was that 'Ologbosheri was not sent to kill white men, and we therefore decide that according to native law his life is forfeited.' PP 1899 (c. 9529) LXIII. 395 at p. 22.

execution by British troops. If this showed echoes of Langalibalele's experience, Moor could not claim the right to native jurisdiction which Governor Pine had as the statutory 'supreme chief'. This was another trial without lawyers, and one in which no formal charges were laid, even if it was clear that the men were accused of participating in murder. In contrast to Nana's case, there was no notion that this chief, who had signed the same treaty as Nana – albeit without striking out any clauses – was liable to prosecution under protectorate law for violating the terms of the treaty, and resisting with arms. Indeed, Moor saw this as something honourable. At this stage, it was clear that he did not wish to treat Ovonramwen in the same way that Nana had been treated.

Three days after the executions, another meeting was held in the consular court with the king and the native council and chiefs. Ovonramwen had little to say, telling Moor, 'I have only come to beg you.' In fact, the purpose of this meeting was not to try the Oba, but to inform him of the new political dispensation in what had been his kingdom. Moor told the assembled chiefs that Ovonramwen was no longer king: 'There is only one King in the country, and that is [the] white man.'[169] After explaining the new administrative structure, he informed Ovonramwen that he would henceforth be chief of Benin City, with the same rank as other chiefs. During the time that would be required to allocate villages to Ovonramwen to support his chiefdom, he was to accompany Moor to other places in the protectorate, to see how they were governed. Rather than being exiled, he would be educated in how to be a good chief, and one who was a friend to the white man. Ovonramwen agreed to this, and was told to return two days later at 9 am. At the same time, he was warned that if he made any attempt to leave the city, he would be captured and hanged.

Ovonramwen did not appear at the appointed time on the morning when he was due to return. When people were sent to fetch him, he ran away, only to return when persuaded by his followers. Later in the day, when a group of soldiers was sent to his house to collect him, he again ran away to a nearby village, where he was later found hiding in a bush

[169] FO 403/250, enc. 1 in No. 203 at p. 205.

hut.[170] By now, Moor had lost patience. 'You are now in the position of a prisoner', he told the Oba, 'and you will be treated as any other prisoner.' Though he had not been given any trial, he was given a sentence of exile: 'from this day, and for the rest of your life, you have done with your people and with your country'.[171] On 13 September, Ovonramwen was moved to Ughoton, where he was transferred to a vessel to take him to Old Calabar. Only two of his eighty wives were permitted to accompany him, and two followed later. When Moor's report reached the Foreign Office, Sir Clement Hill, head of the African department, commented that he had acted 'with great care and judgment' and proposed that his conduct be cordially approved. Hill, a man who had spent thirty years at the Foreign Office and who had no background in law, was untroubled by the lax nature of the proceedings. 'I do not suppose that any one will raise questions in the future about it', he told Salisbury, 'unless it is some rabid Aborigines protectionist.'[172]

Ovonramwen remained in exile until his death at the beginning of 1914. It was not until May 1911, however, that any ordinance was passed to legalise his removal from Benin. After living quietly in exile in Old Calabar, in February 1911 Ovonramwen petitioned the Governor of Southern Nigeria, Sir Walter Egerton, to be allowed to return to his home. When permission was refused, the ex-king threatened to bring proceedings in the Supreme Court. The ordinance was duly passed, as Attorney General A. R. Pennington explained, '[i]n order to guard against any eventuality', though 'there is no intention of using this power if Overami remains quietly at Calabar'.[173] The measure attracted the attention of the radical Liberal MP Sir William Byles in the House of Commons. Byles criticised the fact that, in what was meant to be an empire of freedom, a Governor was being given 'the power to do anything he pleases', and that the writ of habeas corpus was being denied to his 'victims'.[174] The Secretary of State (Harcourt) replied rather

---

[170] See Ryder, *Benin and the Europeans*, p. 294.
[171] FO 403/250, enc. 2 in No. 203, p. 208 at p. 209.
[172] Minute dated 18 October 1897, FO 2/123, f. 74. The approval was duly sent: FO 403/250, No. 306, p. 313.
[173] Report of A. R. Pennington, 8 May 1911, CO 520/103/18451, reporting on the Overami Detention and Deportation Ordinance, No. 11 of 1911.
[174] *Parl. Debs.*, 5th ser., vol. 28 (20 July 1911), col. 1315.

airily that he thought that the ordinance was unnecessary, but had only been passed 'to clear up a technical doubt, because I believe the ex-king has suddenly taken, under legal advice, some technical point as to past action'.[175]

Another ruler whose actions obstructed British trade in the area, Ovonramwen's treatment differed both from Jaja's and from Nana's. Although he had signed Hewett's treaty, and although a consular court had been set up in Benin City, he and his chiefs were not tried under consular jurisdiction for the deaths of the Europeans. Instead, Moor conducted a hearing under what he perceived to be native law – although, unlike Governor Pine of Natal, he had no clear sense of the source of his power to apply that law, or any guide to what that law might have been. In this informal 'trial' of murder, Moor acquitted Ovonramwen, but then imposed a political penalty – his deposition and dethronement – which was unrelated to any charges. The further penalty of exile which was imposed after the king had tried to run away was equally unfounded in any law or possible legal justification.

Conclusion

In many ways, Jaja, Nana and Ovonramwen had very similar experiences at the hands of the British. Each was a king or chief who had signed one of Hewett's protection treaties, and each had sought to protect his markets by resisting British encroachments. It was for this resistance to British expansion that these rulers were deposed and deported. In each case, an *ad hominem* ordinance was used to authorise their detention, though in each case the ordinance was passed at different stages in the process. In the case of Jaja, who had the support in London of the merchant house of Miller, Brother & Co., legal cover was provided as soon as there was any suggestion that a legal challenge might be brought. In Nana's case, an ordinance was passed only when the decision was taken to move him from the Niger Coast Protectorate to the Gold Coast, whereas Ovonramwen was kept at Calabar for fourteen years before the ordinance was passed, as a kind of insurance, to legalise his deportation. In their cases, the authorities were clearly confident that there was no risk of habeas

---

[175] *Parl. Debs.*, 5th ser., vol. 28 (20 July 1911), col. 1347.

corpus proceedings being brought while they remained in the protectorate, for these men had few supporters in London to take up their case. It was only when this fear became real in Ovonramwen's case that the authorities reacted.

In each case, their fate was determined not by the rule of law, but by the exercise of power, formally endorsed by ordinances. From the point of the three rulers, they had committed no offence against British jurisdiction, but had simply resisted British claims to open up trade in their areas. They were defending their rights against aggressive encroachment by an external power. Jaja was the most articulate defender of this position: as a ruler who had both signed a treaty with the British reserving his rights, and who had not come into armed conflict with British forces, he presented legal arguments which the British struggled to answer. In an era of changing Western perceptions of protectorates, his claim to be an independent ruler still had some political purchase, at least at the Foreign Office, which was initially inclined to treat this more as a matter of international law than as a matter of local discipline, and engage with his arguments. It was this which explains the form of inquiry which was held to investigate his alleged breaches of his treaty obligations. However, in this case, the interest in engaging with Jaja's legalism soon gave way to pressure from local officials and traders, who simply wanted this troublesome chief removed. As in Abdullah's case, the inquiry served as a political justification to enact the kind of legislation used against Napoleon, as a means to assert sovereignty and jurisdiction over a ruler who stood in the way of British interests.

With the Niger Coast Protectorate having been established, the Foreign Office appears to have been more confident in its power to deal summarily with Nana, who (unlike Jaja) had actively resisted the British military in an area where they now claimed jurisdiction. Nana was neither treated as an independent ruler, nor did he assert his rights as one, in the manner of Jaja. Where Jaja had drawn specific attention to what he had – and what he had not – agreed in the 1884 treaty, Nana's reservation of his rights was simply ignored. However, Nana was not simply removed by ordinance, in the way that political prisoners in the Gold Coast and Sierra Leone were simply removed. Instead, in the protectorate, officials elected to use a form of consular trial to portray Nana as a rebel against British authority. This was to give a signal to other local rulers that troublesome chiefs who were resisting an authority they now had to obey would be duly punished. If this was a form of lawfare, it hardly complied with metropolitan ideas of the rule of law, given the flaws both in the charges against Nana and in the procedures used at the hearing. However, consular officials were not worried about ensuring that the spirit of the common law was followed: they wanted to use law to convey other messages about British power, and they faced very few restraints from their political masters in the Foreign Office in doing so. In the case of Ovonramwen and his chiefs, protectorate officials once more asserted their jurisdiction to conduct a criminal hearing – physically in the consular court – again in order to give signals about the nature of British power. In this case, the form of 'lawfare' used was quite different from that used in Nana's case, with Ralph Moor purporting to apply against the chiefs a native law which he had no authority to administer. This was yet a further step away from English conceptions of the rule of law. Once the trial was over, and the two chiefs executed, Moor clearly felt he had sent all the 'legal' signals which were needed: so that, when Ovonramwen was exiled, it was by simple administrative fiat, with no law at all being applied.

7

Consolidating Colonial Rule: Detentions in the Gold Coast and Sierra Leone, 1896–1901

1896 and 1897 were significant years in the consolidation of British rule both in the Gold Coast and in Sierra Leone. In 1896, Asante, which had for so long been a troublesome African neighbour to the British colony and protectorate at the Gold Coast, was conquered by a military expedition which deposed and deported the Asantehene, Kwaku Dua III, more commonly known as Prempeh. In the same year, a protectorate was proclaimed over the territories adjacent to the colony of Sierra Leone, which the French and British had agreed to be within the latter's sphere of influence. Britain's attempt to raise revenue for its new administration in Sierra Leone prompted a rebellion – the 'Hut Tax war' – which also ended in the detention and deportation of a number of local leaders, the most prominent of whom was Bai Bureh.

In contrast to the expansion of British rule in the Niger delta, which took place under the direction of the Foreign Office, in these areas it was the Colonial Office which took political responsibility. British policy in the Oil Rivers region was informed by a changing view of the relationship between the imperial state and the rulers of protected polities, with officials increasingly considering protectorates as in some way subject to imperial power. It was because of such views that officials in those areas felt free to try men like Nana Olomu or Ovonramwen in ways which were of questionable legality, but which seemed to those officials to justify their detention or deportation. By contrast, in the areas further up the coast, where the Colonial Office was master, there was less evidence of this kind of shadowy *mi-souveraineté*.

Consolidating Colonial Rule, 1896–1901

Instead, in these areas there was a stark contrast between the approach taken in Asante, where the British had not yet established any kind of jurisdictional foothold, and in Sierra Leone, where an Order in Council implementing the Foreign Jurisdiction Act had been passed, and a new system of administration set up.

As shall be seen, in Asante, the deposition and detention of Prempeh, largely orchestrated and driven by the local Governor, was treated in the manner of an act of state, arising out of war. Legal concerns played very little part in the events leading to his detention, even though the Governor made sure – for his own political reasons – that Prempeh's closest adviser would be subjected to an ordinary trial for an ordinary crime. By contrast, in Sierra Leone, where the British had already established their authority by the time of the revolt, officials were highly law-minded, striving to find adequate legal means to deal with the rebels. In the end, it was their realisation that they lacked the full jurisdiction they wanted that led them to detain Bai Bureh, rather than to try him.

The Deposition of Prempeh of Asante

Prempeh, the king of Asante, whose long exile in the Seychelles would not end until 1924, became the best known of all the West African deportees.[1] Formally installed on the Golden Stool of Asante in June 1894 as King Kwaku Dua III, having been elected to that

---

[1] William Tordoff, 'The Exile and Repatriation of Nana Prempeh I of Ashanti (1896–1924)', *Transactions of the Historical Society of Ghana*, vol. 4 (1960), pp. 33–58; William Tordoff, *Ashanti under the Prempehs, 1888–1935* (Oxford, Oxford University Press, 1965); Adu Boahen, 'Prempeh I in exile' in Toyin Falola (ed.), *Africa in the Twentieth Century: The Adu Boahen Reader* (Trenton, Africa World Press, 2004), pp. 355–370; Adu Boahen, 'A Nation in Exile: The Asante on the Seychelles Islands, 1900–24', in Enid Schildkrout (ed.), *The Golden Stool. Studies of the Asante Centre and Periphery* (Washington: American Museum of Natural History, 1987), pp. 146–160, Joseph K. Adjaye, 'Agyeman Prempe I and British Colonization of Asante: A Reassessment', *International Journal of African Historical Studies*, vol. 22:2 (1989), pp. 223–249; Ivor Wilks, *Asante in the Nineteenth Century: The Structure and Evolution of a Political Order* (Cambridge, Cambridge University Press, 1975); and Thomas Lewin, *Asante before the British: The Prempean Years, 1875–1900* (Lawrence, Regents Press of Kansas, 1978). See also A. Adu Boahen, Emmanuel Akyeampong, Nancy Lawler, T. C. McCaskie and Ivor Wilks (eds.), *"The History of Ashanti Kings and the Whole Country Itself" and Other Writings, by Otumfuo, Nana Agyeman Prempeh I* (Oxford, Oxford University

position six years earlier, he was deposed by the British in January 1896, and detained in Elmina Castle, along with twelve others. One year later, the detainees were transferred to Freetown, and in August 1900, they were moved to the Seychelles, where they would soon be joined by a tranche of new political prisoners exiled after the revolt led by Yaa Asantewaa. His detention and removal was part of a policy to consolidate British control over Asante.

The Kingdom of Asante, which seemed slowly to be falling to pieces after the war of 1873–1874, began to revive under Prempeh, an independent-minded ruler who showed little interest in being taken under British protection. When Governor Griffith of the Gold Coast sent a commissioner to Kumasi with a draft treaty in 1891 – without first asking London – Prempeh rejected it, declaring that 'Ashanti is an independent kingdom.'[2] Instead, he sought to bring together the various Asante states which had seceded in the previous years, a policy which bore fruit when he was formally enstooled as Asantehene with the support of the Amantoo states.[3] Equally worryingly for the British, Prempeh also wanted to open up a trade route to the sea without passing through land under their influence.[4] When Prempeh took military action to effect this in the summer of 1893, Britain offered treaties of protection to rulers in these areas, and warned Prempeh that they would retaliate if he attacked them.[5] Although this threat was enough to make Prempeh back down,[6] British officers on the ground considered that it might be necessary to take the whole of Asante into the protectorate. Acting Governor F. M. Hodgson also advised a policy 'to hasten the annexation of Ashanti', and proposed in November that an ultimatum backed by the threat of force be issued to Prempeh.[7]

Press, 2003); and R. S. S. Baden-Powell, *Downfall of Prempeh: A Diary of Life with the Native Levy in Ashanti, 1895–96* (London, Methuen & Co., 1900).

[2] PP 1896 (c. 7917) LVIII. 455, enc. 1 in No. 16, p. 70.

[3] Francis Agbodeka, *African Politics and British Policy in the Gold Coast, 1868–1900: A Study in the Forms and Force of Protest* (London, Longman, 1971), pp. 153–158. Britain did not recognise his status, claiming that the kings of Kokofu and Mampon were not present, and so continued to refer to him as the king of Kumasi: PP 1896 (c. 7918) LVIII. 707, No. 25, p. 41 at p. 42.

[4] Agbodeka, *African Politics and British Policy*, pp. 161–166.

[5] PP 1896 (c. 7917), Nos. 26–27, p. 82.

[6] PP 1896 (c. 7917), No. 33, p. 96; No. 34, p. 99; No. 36, p. 100.

[7] PP 1896 (c. 7917), No. 42, p. 101; No. 44, p. 120; enc. 1 in No. 44, p. 122.

However, the Secretary of State, Lord Ripon, would not countenance a policy which required the backing of troops. Instead, he suggested a 'via media', whereby Prempeh would be asked to receive a British 'agent', who would settle disputes between the different tribes and promote the development of trade, without interfering in domestic matters.[8] A proposal to this effect was made in February 1894,[9] but over the summer it became increasingly clear that the authorities in Kumasi had no desire to submit to British protection, although they did not rule out the kind of relationship which existed between the British crown and the Emir of Afghanistan.[10] Instead of sending the Governor an answer, the Asante planned to send an embassy, led by Prempeh's Prime Minister, the younger John Owusu Ansa and his brother Albert, to present their case in London. Griffith, who felt that it would be a waste of time to deal with the Ansas, thought that strong measures should be taken 'to compel the obedience of Ashanti to Imperial control'.[11] When Prempeh's representatives arrived in Accra in December, he told them that the Queen would never receive a mission from a ruler accused of human sacrifice[12] – an allusion to press reports (denied by the Asante) that 400 people had been sacrificed at Prempeh's enstooling.[13] However, his attempt formally to forbid them from going to England failed:[14] and when Griffith sent messengers to Kumasi in January to demand Prempeh's response to the proposal for a Resident, they were told that his response was in the hands of his ambassadors, who would deliver it to the Queen.[15]

Griffith continued to advocate a policy of taking complete control of Asante 'by promptly dealing a crushing blow to that country'.[16] Like Hodgson, he was aware that a pretext for intervention could be found in the Asante's breaches of the treaty of Fomena of 1874: in particular,

---

[8] PP 1896 (c. 7917), No. 53, p. 147.
[9] PP 1896 (c. 7917), enc. 2 in No. 67, p. 167; enc. in No. 77, p. 179.
[10] Wilks, *Asante in the Nineteenth Century*, p. 640. On 5 October 1884, Prince Albert Owusu Ansa wrote to Griffith that it was essential that Britain formally acknowledge Asante as independent and enter a similar understanding to that with Afghanistan: PP 1896 (c. 7917), enc. 1 in No. 97, p. 211.
[11] PP 1896 (c. 7917). No. 100, p. 214. His view was shared by other officials on the ground: encs. 3 and 4 in No. 100, pp. 222, 223.
[12] PP 1896 (c. 7917), No. 108, p. 235; No. 110, p. 237.
[13] PP 1896 (c. 7917), No. 94, p. 206.   [14] PP 1896 (c. 7918), enc. 5 in No. 4, p. 15.
[15] PP 1896 (c. 7918), No. 7, p. 20.   [16] PP 1896 (c. 7918), No. 12, p. 22.

the fact that only 1,000 ounces of 50,000 due as an indemnity under that treaty had been paid.[17] Furthermore, although the Colonial Office remained reluctant to commit itself to a military solution, it began to prepare for this eventuality. Instructions were given to the new Governor of the Gold Coast, William Maxwell, that, if the king continued to refuse to come to a peaceful settlement (accepting a British Resident), he was to remind him of his breaches of the treaty, which could be followed by an ultimatum, backed by force.[18] On 23 September 1895, the ultimatum was sent, with a deadline for the reply set for the end of October.[19] In the meantime, the Asante envoys in London found neither the Colonial Office nor the Foreign Office receptive to their requests for meetings.[20] They did, however, enter into an agreement with a British entrepreneur, George Reckless, to grant a concession for the development of Asante to a new chartered company, on the model of the British South Africa Company. Since the concession provided for the establishment of a Resident Agent and courts, the envoys thought that all Britain's reasonable demands for the development of the country had been met. However, the Colonial Office declined to recognise any concession made by them.[21]

When the deadline passed, preparations were made for a military expedition to be sent, even though Britain's policy aims remained at best hazy. As the Secretary of State Joseph Chamberlain explained, had Prempeh simply accepted the terms of the ultimatum, London would have been satisfied with the establishment of a Resident. However, once it became necessary to send a military force, it would no longer be possible to allow Prempeh to remain in his position. Instead, some sort of new administration would have to be set up. Although Chamberlain

---

[17] PP 1896 (c. 7918), enc. 1 in No. 4, p. 6.   [18] PP 1896 (c. 7918), No. 25, p. 41.
[19] PP 1896 (c. 7918), No. 62, p. 99; enc. 1 in No 77, p. 105. See also CO 879/43/1, No. 46, p. 62 at pp. 65, 67 (redacted in PP 1896 (c. 7918), No. 45, p. 83).
[20] They sought the assistance of H. C. Richards MP, who presented the Colonial Office with a memorandum from them. PP 1896 (c. 7918), No. 52, p. 92. London's response was that they were going to deal directly with the king in Kumasi, and that, if the embassy wished to be of use to him, they ought to return. The government regarded Prempeh as only the head of a tribe, with no standing to send ambassadors: PP 1896 (c. 7917), No. 110, p. 237.
[21] PP 1896 (c. 7918), No. 79, p. 107; No. 95, p. 116. The concession is in PP 1896 (c. 7918), enc. in No. 82, p. 109. See also Wilks, *Asante in the Nineteenth Century*, p. 107; and Lewin, *Asante before the British*, p. 191.

Consolidating Colonial Rule, 1896–1901   243

left it to the Governor to submit proposals on its shape,[22] he also told his officials in late December that 'Ashanti should be practically annexed to the Colony with provisions ensuring a certain amount of independent control to the different chiefs.'[23] At the same time, both he and his officials realised that any annexation might raise difficult questions about how to deal with the continuing existence of slavery in Asante. When Maxwell had sent his ultimatum to Prempeh, he had instructed his messengers to reassure the king, if he raised the question of slavery, that the Resident would 'not interfere with the institutions of the country';[24] but this kind of policy would become impossible if Asante were annexed into the colony, since it would become subject to the Gold Coast's Ordinance No. 2 of 1874, which forbad slavery. Given that this ordinance had not been applied in other Asante areas which had come peacefully into the protectorate, Augustus Hemming thought that 'we should not press for it immediately, as it would probably upset the whole domestic system of the country.' Seeking guidance on this, Chamberlain telegrammed Maxwell on 13 January asking both whether Asante should be annexed to the protectorate and whether it should be exempt from the slavery ordinance.[25] On 19 January (by which time he had arrived in Kumasi), Maxwell sent an ambiguous reply:

Referring to your telegram of 13th January recommend[ing] British Protectorate, Ashanti. If Prempeh detained as prisoner, it will be necessary to limit jurisdiction Supreme Court so that Chiefs and others may not be summoned to Cape Coast Castle. Have no doubt that I can satisfy Chiefs about operation of Ordinance No. 2 of 1874, which is practically little put in execution in remote districts recently acquired.[26]

One source of ambiguity in this telegram was the fact that the word used in the cipher code meant both 'recommend' and 'recommending', so that officials in London were unsure whether he was advising taking Asante into the protectorate, or thought that it was London's policy.[27]

---

[22] PP 1896 (c. 7918), No. 90, p. 113; cf. PP 1896 (c. 7918), No. 87, p. 112 (redacting a passage relating to the ultimate need to make treaty provisions against slave raiding: CO 879/43/1, No. 119, p. 111). See also PP 1896 (c. 7918), No. 115, p. 127 at p. 128.
[23] CO 96/262/22687.   [24] CO 879/43/1, enc. 2 in No. 86, p. 97 at p. 98; No. 119, p. 111.
[25] Minute 26 December 1895, CO 96/262/22687; CO 879/44/7, No. 16, p. 10.
[26] CO 879/44/7, No. 27, p. 17.
[27] Minute by R. Antrobus, 20 January 1896, CO 96/270/1421, f. 85.

Even at this late moment, neither London nor Accra had any clear idea what the future relationship between Asante and the Gold Coast would be.

Nor did the British have a consistent set of demands to put to Prempeh. When Prempeh answered Maxwell's demands in early November by referring to his envoys in London, the Colonial Office saw this as 'simple defiance' and as a rejection of the ultimatum. It confirmed Chamberlain in his view that a military expedition had to be sent, to secure complete British control in Asante, imposed by force if need be.[28] At the same time, however, negotiations continued in London with the agent of the envoys, the barrister Thomas Sutherst, who reported that they were ready for a British Resident to be installed at Kumasi. Preparations for the military expedition continued, in part because the Colonial Office did not trust the envoys' authority. At this point, a new demand was added by the British, requiring the king to pay the costs incurred in preparing the expedition. Through Sutherst, the envoys accepted the British demands, and also agreed to pay the full 1874 indemnity, albeit with the payment spread over time.[29] In light of these concessions – and given the risk that Prempeh might 'be driven to fight thinking that we mean in any case to attack him' – Chamberlain wanted the king reassured that the 'expedition will be a peaceable one if he submits & accepts terms of ultimatum'.[30]

If the Secretary of State was veering to the view that Prempeh might already have conceded all that was needed, his Governor in Accra was not. When two of Prempeh's envoys, Kwame Boatin and Kwaku Foku, returned to Cape Coast in the middle of December, they were given a message for Prempeh from Maxwell that he would have to recognise the independence of tribes seeking British protection, pay the cost of the expedition, give land for a fort, and supply hostages as security for fulfilment of the treaty conditions.[31] By the end of the year, Maxwell and Chamberlain had agreed that Prempeh would not be deposed if he

[28] Minute by Augustus Hemming, 13 November 1895, CO 96/262/20074; PP 1896 (c. 7918), No. 97, p. 116; No. 104, p. 120; No. 135, p. 141; No. 114, p. 126; No. 115, p. 127.
[29] PP 1896 (c. 7918), No. 101, p. 117; No. 102, p. 118; No. 103, p. 120; No. 107, p. 121. Although Sutherst at first queried the expenses of preparing an expedition, his later communication signalled a 'complete acceptance' of British terms.
[30] Minutes by Chamberlain and Meade, 24 November 1895, CO 96/262/20868.
[31] CO 879/44/7, No. 22, p. 11.

made a full submission at Kumasi and paid the cost of the expedition;[32] but, if the Asante resisted, the British would be free to seize the Golden Stool – which Chamberlain assumed would increase the prestige of the British government in African eyes – and make Prempeh's rival Yaw Twereboanna king of Kumasi.[33] When the expeditionary force set off for Kumasi in January, it took a draft treaty containing the terms set out to Boatin and Kwaku Foku.[34] With the expedition en route, the Asante desperately sought to make concessions, sending messengers offering the required hostages, and agreeing to all demands, save that of paying the (unaffordable) costs of the expedition. However, Maxwell insisted that the terms of the treaty would have to be dictated at Kumasi, once he had arrived.

The Arrest of Prempeh

When the imperial troops arrived in Kumasi on Friday 17 January 1896, accompanied by the sound of bugles and drums, there was no resistance by the Africans, who welcomed them with tomtoms. Maxwell had made plans to seize and detain 'the palace party' (including Prempeh and his parents) in case they did not comply with the government's full demands, which included an immediate payment of 50,000 ounces of gold towards the war indemnity. Faced with Maxwell's demands, Prempeh offered to pay an instalment (since he could not pay it all), and to make a private submission.[35] Maxwell stuck to his terms. He considered Prempeh insolent, and thought that the Asantehene assumed that the British could be bought off with a small payment. In fact, Prempeh was prepared to concede, even if he was not permitted to save face. When a deadline set for his submission expired on the Monday, Prempeh made the necessary public concession, grasping Maxwell's feet 'in the attitude of a suppliant'.[36] However, since he still offered only 680 ounces of gold, he was immediately detained along with thirteen other chiefs then present, and moved to Cape Coast. The decision to detain Prempeh had been Maxwell's alone; but once it had

---

[32] CO 879/44/7, No. 72, p. 45. [33] CO 879/44/3, No. 53, p. 22.
[34] CO 879/44/7, No. 64, p. 35 and enclosures. [35] CO 879/44/7, No. 98, p. 70.
[36] CO 879/44/7, No. 83, p. 49 at p. 50. Wilks, *Asante in the Nineteenth Century*, p. 657.

been reported in the press as 'an unqualified success',[37] it was impossible for the Colonial Office to reverse.

Maxwell immediately informed London of the detentions, and of the fact that he had sent instructions for an ordinance to be passed legalising them, and suggested that Prempeh and his chiefs be deported to Sierra Leone.[38] Officials in the Colonial Office were troubled by the policy which was being made on the ground. As Chamberlain wired to Maxwell, 'Deportation or detention as political prisoners not contemplated by ultimatum.'[39] He and his officials were also troubled by the fact that the Governor was demanding an indemnity the king could not pay. As Chamberlain put it, '"la plus belle fille ne peut donner que ce qu'elle a" & if he has no money he cannot pay.'[40] His officials realised that the detention would be hard to justify in parliament if its only purpose was 'to extort more money'. They were prepared to see the detainees taken to Cape Coast Castle in military custody in the short term, but wanted more information. 'The question how long Prempeh & Co are to be kept at Cape Coast must first be considered before we can authorize an ordinance detaining them as political prisoners', Meade minuted, 'The shorter the detention the better.'[41] The same official later commented, 'I fear it will not be easy to justify getting rid of Prempeh – however desirable.'[42]

Maxwell explained his approach in two despatches, one written on the day of the detentions and one a week later. In his view, taking the king prisoner was the only way to demonstrate that Britain's paramount influence had been established in Asante. To have accepted the mere assurances from a 'frightened but unpunished savage' would have rendered the expedition abortive and emboldened the Asante.[43] The decision to detain was taken both 'as a measure of punishment in

---

[37] *Manchester Guardian*, 21 January 1896, p. 8. The report stated, 'King Prempeh is neither an imposing nor an attractive monarch. In fact he is little better than a drunken sentimentalist.' See also *Manchester Guardian*, 23 January 1896, p. 8; and *The Times*, 23 January 1896, p. 5; 29 February 1896, p. 15.
[38] CO 879/44/7, No. 28, p. 17; No. 30, p. 18.
[39] Chamberlain to Maxwell, 22 January 1896, CO 879/44/7, No. 37, p. 20.
[40] Chamberlain minute, 21 January 1896, CO 96/262/1470 f. 89. Bramston reminded Chamberlain of his telegram of 31 December, telling Maxwell that, if the king hesitated to pay expenses, new terms could be imposed: CO 879/44/3, No. 100, p. 46.
[41] Minute, 21 January 1896, CO 96/262/1486.
[42] Meade minute, 9 February 1896, CO 96/270/2933, f. 67.
[43] CO 879/44/7, No. 83, p. 49 at p. 50.

Consolidating Colonial Rule, 1896–1901   247

default of payment of a reasonable sum on account of the expenses of the expedition and as the only possible means of securing that complete and efficient British control at Kumasi which has been declared by Her Majesty's Government to be indispensable.' In Maxwell's view, there could be no settlement of affairs in Asante unless these political prisoners were 'deprived of all power to interfere with the gradual establishment of a better state of things by being kept for some years in a place where they can do no mischief'.[44] In a private letter to John Bramston (assistant undersecretary of state), he added that the instructions he had been given in the despatch of 22 November, which allowed him to dictate terms if force were required, had left him considerable latitude.[45] More significantly, Maxwell revealed how he was influenced by his earlier colonial experiences. Before his appointment to the Gold Coast in 1895, he had spent most of his career in the Straits Settlements (where his father was chief justice). While a deputy commissioner, Maxwell was decorated for his part in the expedition against the killers of J. W. W. Birch, the British Resident at Perak, which resulted in the deportation of Sultan Abdullah. Looking back on this, he told Bramston that British attempts to bring civilisation and law and order to the Malay states had been impeded by 'underhand opposition' on the part of Rajas and chiefs; and that British success in the peninsula after 1876 had been rendered effectual by their removal. 'With this experience', he wrote, 'I know that the removal of the elements of mischief is expedient and indeed absolutely necessary.'[46] Given his explanations, the Secretary of State approved his actions, and expressed his appreciation of the prompt and decisive action taken.[47]

Prempeh had been detained and removed before any ordinance had been drawn up, but Maxwell felt justified in holding him as a prisoner of war, having issued a declaration under section 189 of the Army Act in December.[48] However, he was advised by his Attorney General,

---

[44] CO 879/44/7, No. 98, p. 70 at pp. 72, 75.
[45] Maxwell to Bramston, 29 January 1896, CO 96/270/4814, referring to PP 1896 (c. 7918), No. 115, p. 127.
[46] Maxwell to Bramston, 29 January 1896, CO 96/270/4814.
[47] CO 879/44/7, No. 105, p. 87.
[48] CO 879/44/7, No. 83, p. 49 at p. 51. In October 1896, a Colonial Defence Order in Council was issued which empowered Governors in certain named colonies to issue proclamations subjecting all people in the colony to the Army Act. However, the only African colony in which this applied was Sierra Leone: CO 323/1594/3.

William Geary, that, since Prempeh's position as a prisoner of war was doubtful and since the Army Act provision (which was designed for camp followers) did not apply to him, it would be wise 'ex majore cautela to pass the usual Ordinance'.[49] The ordinance was duly passed by the Legislative Council on 23 January, and assented to by the Governor eleven days later. It retrospectively legalised all acts done in connection with the arrest and detention of Prempeh and his supporters, and authorised their further detention or deportation.[50] A second ordinance had to be passed by the legislative council on 28 January, since Maxwell had omitted to send down all the names of those political prisoners being detained: this second ordinance legalised the detention of six Asante, in addition to the seven whose detention was already provided for.[51]

The Trial of John Owusu Ansa

One reason why the British sent their military force to Kumasi rather than accepting the king's concessions was the continued uncertainty over the status of the envoys led by John Owusu Ansa. Ansa himself arrived back on the Gold Coast on 27 December, eleven days after the other envoys. When he met the Governor, Maxwell demanded to see his credentials as the king's representative, only to discover that Prempeh had not authenticated them himself, but that the mark had been made at Cape Coast by Ansa and the king's linguist, Kwaku Foku, and the seal later added in London.[52] On discovering this, Maxwell refused to have anything further to do with Ansa, and referred the matter to the Attorney General.[53] The apparent flaw in Ansa's credentials was reported to the Colonial Office, which released Maxwell's telegram to the press, with the warning that the government would not recognise any concessions purportedly granted by Ansa.[54]

[49] CO 879/44/7, enc. 3 in No. 112, p. 90. [50] CO 879/44/7, No. 112, p. 89.
[51] CO 879/44/7, No. 113, p. 91.
[52] CO 879/44/3, no. 92, p. 38; CO 879/44/7, No. 45, p. 23.
[53] CO 879/44/7, No. 46, p. 29. The enclosed report confirmed that he could be prosecuted in the colony for forgery and possibly for fraud and false pretences.
[54] *The Times*, 31 December 1895, p. 3; and *Daily Telegraph*, 31 December 1895 ('The Sham Ambassadors: Forged Credentials').

John and Albert Owusu Ansa were among those arrested by Maxwell at Kumasi on 20 January. Rather than being detained, they were sent back to the coast to stand trial in the colony for forging the king's credentials.[55] Although Bramston regarded these arrests as a mistake,[56] Maxwell replied that their prosecution had been requested by the Asante war chiefs, who 'demanded punishment of Ansahs for being [the] cause of [the] present difficulties'.[57] One month later, Maxwell visited the detainees at Elmina Castle. Perhaps sensing the chance of securing their own release, they now sought to put the blame on Ansa. At the meeting, Asafu Boachi, one of the war chiefs who had accused the Ansas when Maxwell was at Kumasi, spoke for the king. He said that the Asante had wanted to agree to the British terms, but that John had refused to agree to this. He added that Ansa had not been appointed ambassador, his trip to England had been disapproved, and he had no authority to grant concessions. Prempeh himself then spoke: 'I have had no hand in the whole thing', he announced: 'Ansah deceived me. I never authorised him to go to England, and I want to beg the Governor to have this case decided for me.'[58] While these words did not secure the prisoners' release, they certainly fortified the determination of the authorities in Accra to press on with the prosecution.

The prosecution was designed to portray the Ansas as private adventurers, who wanted to make personal profits by selling concessions in the king's name.[59] The authorities in the Gold Coast had long thought that Ansa was living a life of luxury, paid for by a deluded king who thought that his envoy could do anything for him. They now sought to uncover any other material which might

---

[55] CO 879/44/7, No. 83, p. 49.
[56] Minute, 21 January 1896, CO 96/262/1486. Antrobus also doubted 'whether it was worth while to prosecute him, unless Mr Maxwell has done it to keep him from making mischief in Ashanti': 24 January 1896, CO 96/263/1696.
[57] CO 879/44/7, No. 52, p. 33. Under these circumstances, the Colonial Office had to concede, but was still sceptical: Bramston minute, 24 January 1896, CO 96/270/1831.
[58] CO 879/44/7, enc. 2 in No. 229, pp. 211, 216.
[59] Bramston came to think that both Sutherst and Ansa were anxious to prevent Prempeh's overthrow because they needed him to confirm their concessions, which made him observe, 'What a lot of rogues!' 19 March 1896, CO 96/270/5916.

incriminate John, including potential bigamy charges.[60] Although the brothers were to be tried for an ordinary crime, the Gold Coast authorities were very aware of their political importance, and Acting Governor Hodgson asked for permission to detain them as political prisoners 'in the interests of pacification of Ashanti' in case of their acquittal. Chamberlain's reply was there were no sufficient grounds for detaining them as such, but that they should not be allowed to proceed to Asante.[61] If this was a sign that the Colonial Office did not feel that it was appropriate to redetain after an acquittal (at least in this case), the legal basis for preventing their return to Kumasi was unclear.

The trial began with the Ansas challenging the court's jurisdiction: as they were the ambassadors of a foreign state, they claimed not to be subject to arrest by the colonial authorities. The crown's lawyer answered this by arguing that international law applied only to civilised states and not to barbarous ones; and adding that, even if this were not the case, only ambassadors recognised as such by the host state could claim such protection. The Ansas also argued that their arrest and rendition to Cape Coast was unlawful, both because Kumasi was beyond the Gold Coast's jurisdiction and because there had been no warrant to authorise it. The trial proceeded after the court had decided to reserve any questions as to the jurisdiction, to be determined in the event of a conviction. The crown called Kwaku Foku and Boatin as witnesses. Contradicting what Ansa had said on his return, they denied having seen the document until they visited Sutherst's home in London.[62] However, they did testify that they had been sent to England by the king, and that Prempeh had conferred full power on Ansa to use his discretion. The brothers were duly acquitted by the jury. Fearing another acquittal, the Attorney General decided not to proceed with a second set of charges, after the judge made it clear that he agreed with the verdict. Reflecting on the case, Geary told Acting Governor Hodgson that the verdict 'in a certain way tells

---

[60] CO 879/44/7, No. 123, p. 120; CO 879/44/7, No. 110, p. 88. London was not keen on these investigations: Minute by Bramston, 18 March 1896, CO 96/270/5918.
[61] CO 879/44/7, No. 174, p. 159; No. 180, p. 160.
[62] This might have cast doubt on the prosecution's allegation that the offence had been committed in the Gold Coast.

Consolidating Colonial Rule, 1896–1901

in favour of the dethronement of King Prempeh, as it shows that he preferred to elect to send the Ansahs to England on the chance of obtaining better terms than to accept the ultimatum by direct communication with the Governor'.[63] This was in effect to concede that Ansa was indeed acting as the representative of the king. Maxwell, however, continued to insist that the acquittal constituted a miscarriage of justice.[64]

Having been forbidden to return to Asante, the Ansas returned to England in September, to seek compensation for their troubles.[65] The following spring, Sutherst presented a petition to the Colonial Office on their behalf, complaining that they had been marched from Kumasi to Cape Coast Castle as common criminals, while their property was taken and their homes destroyed.[66] Having already been told by Maxwell that the Ansas had only been given authority to act as translators and that they had been seeking personal gain,[67] the Colonial Office batted away the petition, on the ground that there had at least been a case to answer.[68] The Ansas did not leave it at that. In a further letter, they reiterated that they had been arrested without warrant in an independent country over which the British had no jurisdiction, and had been charged with some offences (such as stealing from Prempeh) which could not be cognisable in Her Majesty's Courts. Moreover, they asked, 'does Her Majesty's Government maintain that in these days the property of any person charged with a criminal offence, and who is duly tried and acquitted, is liable to confiscation?'[69] At Chamberlain's request, more information was sought relating to the alleged destruction of Ansa's property, but Maxwell denied that any of it had been confiscated or destroyed by the government.[70] Unable to return to Asante, the Ansas remained in England, still seeking to recover their lost assets, and taking libel proceedings against various newspapers for comments made when publishing Maxwell's telegram calling in question the authenticity of

---

[63] CO 879/44/7, enc. in No. 199, p. 173 at p. 176.
[64] Maxwell to Colonial Office, 13 October 1896, CO 879/44/7, No. 216, p. 194.
[65] CO 879/44/7, No. 215, p. 191; *Manchester Guardian*, 30 October 1896, p. 7.
[66] CO 879/49/1, No. 21, p. 25, and enclosed petition.   [67] CO 879/44/7, No. 216, p. 194.
[68] CO 879/49/1, No. 22, p. 28.   [69] CO 879/49/1, No. 27, p. 30.
[70] CO 879/49/1, No. 28, p. 33; No. 34, p. 36.

their credentials.[71] The attempts stalled when a bankruptcy petition was brought against John in 1898.[72]

Prempeh's Exile

Prempeh remained imprisoned in Elmina Castle while Maxwell was setting up a new system of administration in Kumasi.[73] The British now began to worry about the cost of the military expedition, which had turned out to be far more expensive than had been anticipated when it was decided to make Prempeh pay for it.[74] In the view of R. H. Meade at the Colonial Office, 'as this is really an expedition largely undertaken in the interests of trade development, it is only fair that the Gold Coast should pay.'[75] Chamberlain agreed that the colony could pay by instalments, but he still wanted to see whether the famed Asante treasures might be located, to help pay for the expedition.[76] Although little treasure had been found when Prempeh's house was searched at the time of his arrest,[77] officials remained convinced that there was hidden treasure which had yet to be located, and District Commissioner Hendrick Vroom was sent to Elmina Castle to discuss the outstanding indemnity with Prempeh. When Vroom held out the possibility of a pardon if money were found, Prempeh – who had been allowed to consult Boatin and Kwaku Foku on this matter – sought more concrete assurances that a further payment would secure his release. By now, however, Maxwell had begun to doubt whether any hidden treasure would be located, and suspected that Prempeh's plan was to raise the necessary money by compelling contributions in Asante. Since this would be possible only if the British allowed him

---

[71] *Ansah* v. *Johnstone*, in *The Times*, 23 April 1898 p. 5; 26 April 1898, p. 5; 27 April 1898, p. 11.

[72] *The Times*, 19 October 1898, p. 13; and *Manchester Guardian*, 2 November 1898, p. 3. He had already been sued successfully for arrears of rent for the property he had taken for the embassy: *Plowden* v. *Ansah* in *The Times*, 8 December 1896, p. 15.

[73] CO 879/44/7, No. 114, p. 93.   [74] Minute, 16 January 1896, CO 96/262/1191.

[75] Minute, 26 January 1896, CO 96/270/1614.   [76] CO 879/44/7, No. 88, p. 61.

[77] The items found were either sent to London, where some were kept back for an exhibition at the Imperial Institute with the rest disposed of by auction, or auctioned to soldiers for souvenirs of their expedition: CO 879/44/7, No. 95, p. 64; No. 102, p. 86.

to restore his authority there, it was a plan which was out of the question.[78]

Prempeh remained incarcerated. When Acting Governor Hodgson visited Elmina Castle in July, he 'begged earnestly' to be allowed to return to his country, blaming his troubles on the Ansas. Realising that a return to Asante was impossible, Hodgson suggested that he be deported to Sierra Leone, where he might live under greater freedom. This plan had the advantage that it would help quieten Asante, where there were still expectations of his return.[79] His enthusiasm to deport Prempeh was bolstered by his discovery that Kwaku Foku and Boatin were levying a £5 fee on all Asante traders coming to Cape Coast, to build up a fund to pay lawyers to secure the king's release. Hodgson promptly ordered that they be brought to Accra, and told London that he wanted them to be placed with the other political prisoners, and better still be deported.[80] It was evident that Prempeh was in touch with supporters in Kumasi, and that he had plans to get legal help. By the end of August, a petition had been drawn up for Prempeh by lawyers instructed by Kwaku Foku and Boatin, once more accepting the British terms and offering to arrange for the payment of the indemnity.[81] After discussing the matter with Maxwell, when on leave in London, Chamberlain came to the view that Prempeh should be removed to Sierra Leone (along with the other prisoners), and that Kwaku Foku and Boatin should be detained and removed with them, and instructions were sent for the necessary ordinances to be passed.[82] A measure was accordingly passed in Sierra Leone, which conferred on the Governor the power not only to detain these 'political prisoners', but to commit any of them to Freetown Gaol by warrant, in case they attempted to escape or were guilty of any disobedient or insubordinate

---

[78] CO 879/44/7, No. 150, p. 140. [79] CO 879/44/7, No. 205, p. 182.
[80] CO 879/44/7, No. 209, p. 183. When it was discovered that boxes of gold were being collected in Kumasi for Prempeh, Hodgson wanted them to be seized: CO 879/44/7, enc. 2 in No. 210, p. 185.
[81] CO 879/44/7, No. 211, p. 186, with enclosed petition from Prempeh. In this petition, Prempeh stated that he had sent the Ansas to London as envoys. Maxwell sent a long refutation of material in the petition: CO 879/44/7, No. 229, p. 207.
[82] CO 879/44/7, No. 217, p. 196. An Ordinance (No. 12 of 1896) was duly passed at the Gold Coast to authorise their detention on 24 November: CO 879/49/1, enc. 1 in No. 2, p. 2.

conduct.[83] This provision was out of the ordinary, but was explained by the fact that the authorities feared that it might be difficult to obtain a conviction from a Freetown jury in case any charges had to be brought.

Prempeh was told at the end of November that he and the others were to be removed. The news was conveyed by the Acting Chief Justice, Francis Smith, who was told to stress that they were being moved in order to allow them greater liberty. Prempeh was clearly disconcerted by the news, and told Smith that they would prefer to remain under greater confinement in Elmina. He again offered to obey all the commands of the Resident if allowed to return to Kumasi.[84] It was to no avail. On 31 December, Kwaku Foku and Boatin were put on board the SS Bakana at Accra, and the following day, the rest were added at Elmina. Maxwell's instructions were that the detainees were to be allowed 'comparative freedom', and that accommodation and an allowance were to be provided, at the expense of the Gold Coast.[85] The whole party which arrived in Freetown on 5 January was made up of forty-four people, a number which increased when shortly after arrival another son was born to Prempeh.[86]

In the meantime, Prempeh's cause was taken up in the House of Commons by the Irish Nationalist Michael Davitt. He asked why Prempeh had been deposed, after he had been reassured by the British that, if he did not resist and accepted the British terms, matters would be settled amicably. Chamberlain's response drew attention to reports that Prempeh had been seeking the help of Samory – 'a powerful chief who has been slave-raiding in the Hinterland' – to resist the British.[87] Chamberlain's invocation of the threat of Samory was somewhat disingenuous. Although there had been concerns about the ambitions of this Muslim chief towards the end of 1895 – when some had called for action against Prempeh to forestall any danger of Samory's intervention[88] – the Colonial Office had not thought that there was any risk of Prempeh obtaining Samory's

---

[83] CO 879/49/1, No. 10, p. 7.   [84] CO 879/49/1, enc. in No. 3, p. 4.
[85] CO 879/49/1, enc. 1 in No. 13, p. 10. For their 'relative freedom' there, see Tordoff, 'The Exile and Repatriation of Nana Prempeh I', p. 35.
[86] CO 879/49/1, enc. 1 in No. 19, p. 21.
[87] *Parl. Debs.*, 4th ser., vol. 45, cols. 678–679 (28 January 1897).
[88] For example, *Manchester Guardian*, 25 September 1895, p. 7.

help.[89] However, by the middle of 1897, there was concern that the Kumasi chiefs appointed by Maxwell to administer local affairs were beginning to intrigue with Samory. Furthermore, in June, Vroom reported that he strongly suspected the existence of a secret understanding between Samory and Prempeh's supporters.[90] Maxwell worried that these chiefs were beginning to meddle in political matters, and contemplated not only depriving them of their powers, but removing them to the coast as political prisoners as well.[91] Vroom's report also made the Governor rethink the question of how to deal with Prempeh. Seeing that his followers in Kumasi remained disaffected, Maxwell worried that their place of banishment in Sierra Leone was not sufficiently distant from Asante to be safe, particularly since people at the coast were unsettling the minds of the Asante with reports that his release was imminent. In August, he visited Kumasi, telling the chiefs at a public meeting that Prempeh was not returning, and that, if the hope of his return continued to 'unsettle' people, he would have to be removed farther away. The meeting turned out to be a fractious one, when the chiefs asked for Prempeh's return:

OPOKU MENSAH: I beg the Governor to let Prempeh come back. It was his father who advised him badly and caused all the mischief.
GOVERNOR: Let those who desire to see Prempeh back here pay the sum of £200,000, which I demanded of him.
OPOKU MENSAH: I cannot afford to pay the money.
GOVERNOR: Prempeh was not sent away because his father advised him badly, but because he did not pay the money which he said he would pay.
OPOKU MENSAH: The Queen of England is rich.
GOVERNOR: It is a waste of time to talk further of this matter.[92]

Although he subsequently recommended that they be removed to the Seychelles,[93] the impetus to remove them fell away when Asante settled. Prempeh petitioned to be allowed home once more in May 1898, again promising to pay the money claimed in instalments, and to abide by whatever conditions the British government imposed. Governor Hodgson told Chamberlain that, since Asante was not yet at

---

[89] CO 879/43/1, enc. 2 in No. 86, p. 97 at p. 98 (redacted in PP 1896 (c. 7918), enc. 2 in No. 77, p. 106). See also CO 96/262/21444. Contrast Wilks, *Asante in the Nineteenth Century*, pp. 654–655.
[90] CO 879/49/1, enc. in No. 36, p. 39 at p. 43.   [91] CO 879/49/1, No. 36, p. 39.
[92] CO 879/49/1, enc. in No. 44, p. 47 at p. 49.   [93] CO 879/49/1, No. 44, p. 46.

rest, it was 'most inopportune to consider the question of granting pardon to these political offenders'.[94] In the middle of the following year, Hodgson told the detainees while on a visit to Freetown that they were not being held because of their failure to pay money owed – since Britain could now raise as much money as it wished in Asante – but because their presence would hinder the peaceful reorganisation of the country.[95]

It was only after another revolt had broken out in Asante in 1900 that the decision was taken to move the prisoners to the Seychelles.[96] In February 1900, Chamberlain approved a proposal that the Asante should be taxed, in the form of interest charged on the outstanding war debts of 1874 and 1896.[97] The trigger for the revolt was a provocative speech made by Governor Hodgson on 28 March, when he went to Kumasi to announce the new annual levy of 16,000 ounces of gold. Hodgson wanted to impress on the Asante that Queen Victoria was now their ruler, and that neither Prempeh nor Yaw Twereboanna would ever rule Asante. He also wanted to locate the Golden Stool of Asante, which had been hidden after Prempeh's deposition. The Governor was aware of the political importance of the stool, and regretted that the British had not secured it in 1896, since it provided a rallying point for malcontents against British rule.[98] 'Why am I not sitting on the Golden Stool at this moment?', the Governor asked the chiefs, 'I am the representative of the paramount power; why have you relegated me to this chair?'[99] After receiving evidence as to the possible location of the stool, Hodgson sent a detachment to find it. Instead of locating the stool, they were faced with armed resistance.[100] The combination of an attempt to secure this most venerated Asante artefact with the imposition of a new tax provoked the last armed

---

[94] CO 879/49/1, No. 53, p. 57.
[95] Tordoff, 'The Exile and Repatriation of Nana Prempeh I', p. 36.
[96] CO 879/62/8, No. 314, p. 97. On 30 July, the Administrator of the Seychelles authorised to legislate to permit their detention and on 3 August the ordinance was passed: CO 879/62/8, No. 328, p. 101; No. 337A, p. 104.
[97] CO 879/62/10, No. 6, p. 14.
[98] As he later explained, as long as the Golden Stool remained 'in the hands of the Ashantis, so long does the power of the king – whether the king exists or not – remain with them'. PP 1901 (Cd. 501) XLVIII. 443, No. 79, p. 110 at p. 113.
[99] PP 1901 (Cd. 501), enc. 1 in No. 32, p. 16.
[100] PP 1901 (Cd. 501), No. 3, p. 1; No. 32, p. 10.

revolt against British rule, led by Queen Yaa Asantewaa.[101] By December, the rebel leaders, including the Queen, had been captured. A further ordinance was passed in 1901 to authorise the deportation of fifteen Asante rebels, to join Prempeh in the Seychelles.[102]

Like the rulers in the Oil Rivers region, Prempeh stood in the way of British imperial interests. Unlike them, he had entered into no treaty with the British, and had not offered any military resistance to them; nor could he be claimed to be in any respect subject to British jurisdiction. His offence was his refusal to surrender effective control of his country to the imperial power. The drive to subdue Asante was driven by colonial officials on the ground, who found the fig leaf of a *casus belli* to launch an expedition against him, and it was Governor Maxwell who took the decision – on the hoof – to detain Prempeh. Influenced by his memory of Abdullah's treatment, Maxwell's decision to remove Prempeh had nothing to do with any offence he had committed, but was occasioned by his view that it was politically necessary to remove the king, and thereby give a signal to the Asante about the nature of British paramount power. What started as warfare – with Prempeh at first regarded as a prisoner of war by Maxwell – turned to lawfare after an ordinance was hurriedly passed to validate his continued detention. In this process, action which could not be justified under the international law of war was justified by imperial law, which in the process made its own jurisdictional claims over Asante. While officials in London realised that such action might be hard to justify, political expediency drowned out any rule of law concerns.

At the same time, detention was not the only form of 'lawfare' used in respect of Asante. For at the same time that his king was held

---

[101] See A. Adu Boahen, *Yaa Asantewaa and the Asante–British War of 1900–1* (James Currey, Oxford, 2003); and Agbodeka, *African Politics and British Policy*, pp. 170–180.

[102] See CO 879/67/3, No. 38, p. 65, reporting on the causes of the rebellion, and how rebels were to be dealt with. The Deputy Governor was instructed to draw up an ordinance to authorise the detention and deportation of forty-seven rebels, who were initially to be held at Elmina Castle. On 25 April 1901, Ordinance No. 4 of 1901 (the Ashanti Political Prisoners Detention and Deportation Ordinance) was passed. Fifteen ringleaders were deported to the Seychelles, while thirty-one were held at Elmina. In September, an ordinance was passed, Ordinance 12 of 1901, to authorise the detention of another rebel, Kwame Boakye. See CO 879/67/3 enc. 2 in No. 38, p. 89; enc. 1 in No. 52, p. 110; No. 54, p. 116; enc. 1 in No. 84, p. 169.

without trial, John Owusu Ansa was tried at the Gold Coast for the ordinary crime of forgery. Maxwell's dual strategy of detention and prosecution may have appeared contradictory: not only did the king's detention without trial acknowledge that he had committed no offence recognised by law, but the prosecution of his envoy as a self-interested impostor might have implied that the king himself was a victim of deception, rather than an obstructive enemy. Yet Maxwell was not concerned to ensure logical consistency in his actions; whereas the detention of the king served a particular political purpose in West Africa, the prosecution of Ansa may rather have been designed to send a signal to anyone in London, who might have had commercial dealings with the king's envoy.

Sierra Leone's Hut Tax War and the Detention of Bai Bureh

Whereas Asante came under British rule as a result of military operations, imperial authority arrived in the hinterland of Sierra Leone as a result of foreign policy and proclamation. In January 1895, France and Britain agreed to settle the boundary between the territories under their respective influence adjacent to Sierra Leone.[103] The following August, an Order in Council, issued under the 1890 Foreign Jurisdiction Act, conferred jurisdiction over territories adjoining the colony, and empowered the Sierra Leone Legislative Council to legislate for them. At the end of August 1896, a protectorate was proclaimed over the territory lying on the British side of the line, and ordinances were passed to introduce a new system of administration in these areas.[104] The protectorate was divided into five districts, each of which had a European District Commissioner who was given jurisdiction over more serious offences involving Africans (for which he sat with assessors) and over all cases which did not involve them (unless the offence was capital, in which case it had to go to the Supreme Court). This new administration had to be paid for, as did the Frontier Police set up by an ordinance in 1890 to keep the peace in an area already referred to as the 'protectorate'. Governor Frederick Cardew,

---

[103] Christopher Fyfe, *A History of Sierra Leone* (Oxford, Oxford University Press, 1962), p. 524.
[104] Fyfe, *A History of Sierra Leone*, p. 541.

Consolidating Colonial Rule, 1896–1901

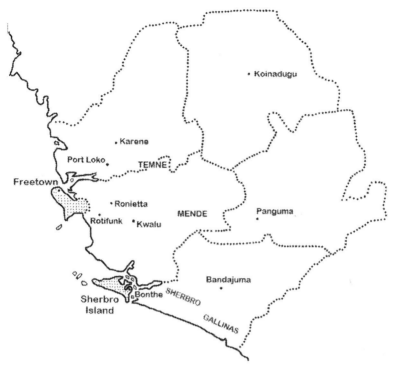

MAP 5 Sierra Leone: Colony and Protectorate

appointed in 1894, thought that the protectorate itself should pay, and so provision was made in the Protectorate Ordinance for the levying of a house tax, as well as the imposition of store and spirit licences. The chiefs were to be responsible for raising the tax, which was to be collected from the beginning of 1898 in three of the five districts – Karene, Ronietta and Bandajuma.

Cardew's project for a house tax not only raised eyebrows at the Colonial Office,[105] but also led to protests in Sierra Leone. When the new system was explained to the chiefs in October 1896,[106] they were alarmed both by the financial demands and by the British claims to jurisdiction. Many chiefs had never signed treaties of protection, and so did not understand the basis for British claims of authority; and many feared that the claim to tax their homes indicated a claim to the

---

[105] Fyfe, *A History of Sierra Leone*, p. 550.   [106] PP 1899 (c. 9391) LX. 183, p. 566.

very property itself. The Freetown press condemned the 'hut-tax' and traders protested against it.[107] In February 1897, a group of Mende chiefs led by Gbanna Lewis and Francis Fawundu came to Freetown to petition against the Protectorate Ordinance; and in the middle of the year, a group of Temne chiefs also came to petition against it.[108] However, Cardew was determined to press ahead with its collection.

The Hut Tax Revolt

Captain W. S. Sharpe, the District Commissioner in Karene, began to collect the tax on 5 February at Port Loko, the most populous place in the district. Being unable to persuade either the Krio traders or the African chiefs to pay, he first detained the local regent, Bokari Bamp, and then arrested the Krios who were refusing to pay. Sharpe's interpretation of his powers under the Protectorate Ordinance was a generous one: since he had power to distrain property in case of a refusal to pay the tax, and to impose a fine if no property could be found, he felt justified in taking a short cut, simply arresting and detaining non-paying Krios on the assumption that no property would be recovered. Once the tax had been paid, they were released.[109] Having been released after his overnight stay in detention, Bokari Bamp was re-arrested and tried with four others for refusing to pay the tax and inciting others to defy the law. The men were sentenced to periods of imprisonment of between twelve and eighteen months after a very summary trial, and on a questionable reading of the ordinance.[110] This show of authority was specifically designed to bring in the tax: for, as Sharpe noted, he intended to ask for Bokari Bamp to be released once the country was quiet and the tax paid.[111]

When Bokari Bamp was first detained, large numbers of what Sharpe was informed were 'Bai Bureh's war-boys' came to Port Loko from Kasse to effect a rescue.[112] Sharpe had already heard rumours

---

[107] PP 1899 (c. 9391), pp. 569 ff.   [108] Fyfe, *A History of Sierra Leone*, pp. 555–556.
[109] PP 1899 (c. 9391) pp. 205–212.
[110] PP 1899 (c. 9391), p. 212. Sharpe's account is in CO 879/55/1, enc. 3 in No. 25, p. 26.
[111] CO 879/55/1, enc. 3 in No. 25, p. 26 at p. 29. W. H. Mercer at the Colonial Office minuted, 'Mr. Sharpe seems to have managed matters very smoothly at Port Loko and a word of commendation might be given to him': CO 267/437/6315.
[112] PP 1899 (c. 9391), p. 208.

Consolidating Colonial Rule, 1896–1901 261

that Bai Bureh was collecting arms to resist the government;[113] and he considered this chief to be the main obstacle to the collection of the tax. 'Bai Bureh' was the title held by Kebalai, as chief of Kasse. A war chief and slave raider of Loko descent, Kebalai had been elected to this position in the late 1880s. He had been active in the war of succession in the Moria country which had continued for twenty years from the early 1860s, without ever coming into conflict with the British. It was only after 1890, when Britain took a more interventionist stance, with a view to bring peace in this area, that he came to their attention. British attitudes to Bai Bureh were ambivalent. On occasion, they found him useful, as in 1892 when he supplied troops for their Tambi expedition against Karimu.[114] At other times, when his warlike policies threatened to interfere with British interests, they had attempted to arrest him, though without success.[115]

Convinced that the people were in awe of Bai Bureh, Sharpe thought that it would be impossible to collect the tax successfully unless steps were taken 'to effect his immediate capture' if (as Sharpe assumed) he refused to pay it when summoned to do so.[116] Cardew agreed that he had to be arrested and deposed. 'He is a great drunkard and a worthless character', he told Chamberlain, 'and it is only by a combination of recklessness and good luck that he has succeeded in giving trouble for such a long time.'[117] He certainly appeared to be defying the tax. According to Sharpe, a letter sent from Port Loko informing him of a visit to collect the tax was returned with a verbal message 'that the first time I set foot in his town I should be a dead man'.[118] In response,

---

[113] District Commissioner to Colonial Secretary, 12 February 1898, CO 879/55/1, enc. 3 in No. 25, p. 26 at p. 27.
[114] Fyfe, *A History of Sierra Leone*, pp. 501–503.
[115] He escaped after being arrested in 1890 (for failing to abide by a peace brokered by the British in a war he had joined against Karimu of Samaia); while in May 1894, another attempt to arrest him (for assisting in raids against territory under French control) failed, and the matter was settled by the imposition of a fine. See 'Bai Bureh's antecedents', CO 267/445/4692; and Fyfe, *A History of Sierra Leone*, pp. 501–503, 522.
[116] CO 879/55/1, enc. 3 in No. 25, p. 26 at p. 28.
[117] CO 879/55/1, No. 25, p. 22 at p. 23.
[118] PP 1899 (c. 9391), p. 214. In his subsequent report on these events, Sir David Chalmers found that the original letter had never reached Bai Bureh, but that Sharpe's messenger had been sent back by the chief's war-boys, who would let no one pass: PP 1899 (c. 9388) LX. 1, p. 36.

a party was sent out to Romani to arrest Bai Bureh. Arriving on 18 February, they did not find the chief, but found the town full of war-boys. When Sharpe drew blood by hitting one of them on the head, the crowd began to jeer and pelt the police, who decided to withdraw. They were then pursued by the jeering war-boys, and, finding themselves surrounded, fired on the crowd to disperse them.[119] Several Africans were killed in this volley, and the war-boys returned fire, though without effecting any casualties. With this exchange, the 'Hut-Tax War' began. Sharpe now felt that a large force needed to be sent to disarm the Africans and take Bai Bureh, dead or alive. As the conflict escalated, Chamberlain minuted 'I am afraid this Hut Tax in its present form was a mistake. But we must wait for peace to reconsider it.'[120]

On 2 March 1898, martial law was proclaimed in the Karene District.[121] Troops started to disarm the people, and repelled attacks, inflicting large casualties on the Africans. With the fire power of the British forces so much greater than that of the Temne, by 9 March Cardew could report that the rebellion was 'very nearly quelled'.[122] However, the experienced warrior Bai Bureh had built extensive stockades to provide cover for his soldiers, who were able to prolong the conflict by using disciplined guerrilla tactics.[123] London's response was to authorise the Governor first to raise more Frontier Police, and then to raise troops for a West African Regiment to suppress the revolt.[124] The troops were able slowly to destroy the stockades and weaken resistance, albeit while suffering some casualties. The most high-profile casualty of the conflict was Rev. William Humphrey of the Church Missionary Society, who was killed at the end of March by insurgents who also mutilated his body.[125] By the time news of this event had reached Cardew, Bai Bureh was seeking peace.[126] He told an intermediary that he had never been asked to pay the hut-tax and had never intended to make war on the government: he had only turned to resistance when the British sent Captain Sharpe 'to take off his head'.

---

[119] See Chalmers' summary of events in PP 1899 (c. 9388), pp. 35–40, and the reports by Sharpe and Tarbet, PP 1899 (c. 9391), pp. 606–607 and 608–609.
[120] Minute dated 19 March: CO 267/437/6218.
[121] CO 879/55/1, enc. 3 in No. 26, p. 33.   [122] CO 879/55/1, No. 22, p. 21.
[123] Fyfe, *A History of Sierra Leone*, p. 565.
[124] Minute dated 22 March 1898, CO 267/437/6473; CO 879/55/1, No. 36, p. 46.
[125] CO 879/55/1, No. 71, p. 74.   [126] CO 879/55/1, No. 44, p. 56.

Consolidating Colonial Rule, 1896–1901

Aware that his forces could never be a match for the British, he intimated that he would seek protection from the French if things continued as they were.[127] He also denied any involvement in Humphrey's death, claiming he was not responsible for the war-boys who did it. However, the Governor would not countenance any peace which did not entail the surrender of Bai Bureh and the punishment of Humphrey's killers.[128]

By the middle of May, the rebellion in Karene had been largely suppressed.[129] Although a number of the ringleaders were detained, Bai Bureh himself remained uncaptured. In June, another attempt was made to broker a peace, but Cardew rejected it,[130] since he still wanted Bai Bureh's unconditional surrender. At the beginning of October, Bai Bureh again sought to make peace, this time communicating via Freetown Muslims with the special commissioner who had been sent out in July to investigate the causes of the outbreak, Sir David Chalmers.[131] Chalmers – who wanted to pacify the country as quickly as possible – suggested that the reward offered for Bai Bureh's capture be withdrawn, and that the demand for an 'unconditional' surrender be dropped.[132] However, his intervention did not go down well with the Governor, who had let it be known that Bai Bureh's life would be spared if he surrendered.[133] Bai Bureh was finally taken into custody on 11 November.[134]

Just as the back of the Temne revolt was being broken, a new uprising erupted on 27 April in the Mende, Sherbro and Gallinas countries. The Mende rising was sudden, co-ordinated and violent. The rebels were bound by a secret oath – the 'one word Poro' – to rise up together, and attack both Europeans and Krio. Missions were attacked and the inhabitants slaughtered, and factories burned down. Any 'alien' who was found was butchered. Reports came in of events such as those at the American mission at Rotifunk, where the missionaries were caught attempting to escape, stripped naked, and marched back to Rotifunk, where they were hacked to death, after one

---

[127] CO 879/55/1, enc. 4 in No. 71, p. 77.   [128] CO 879/55/1, No. 71, p. 74.
[129] CO 879/55/1, enc. in No. 139, p. 194.   [130] CO 879/55/1, No. 122, p. 156.
[131] CO 879/55/1, No. 182, p. 264.   [132] CO 879/55/1, enc. 1 in No. 188, p. 273.
[133] Minute, 4 November 1895, CO 267/440/23781.
[134] For the circumstances of his capture, see Christopher Fyfe, *A Short History of Sierra Leone*, new ed. (London, Longman, 1979 [1962]), p. 121.

of the women had been raped.[135] Refugees began to flee to Freetown for protection. Unlike the Temne rebellion, this one seemed to have no obvious leader, though there was suspicion that it must have been co-ordinated by the chiefs. The rebellion may also have been encouraged by rumours of Bai Bureh's successes in resisting the British. Cardew was slow to react, and it was only at the start of May that warships were sent to intervene and to remove refugees.[136] The British also responded by sending two columns of troops, which managed to quell the rebellion by the beginning of July.[137]

The Legal Response

The Governor and the Colonial Office were already planning their legal response to the Temne rising when the Mende revolt occurred. From the beginning, the plan was to put the rebels on trial. Cardew proposed to enact an ordinance for the 'trial of insurgent bands for capital punishment by [a] Special Commission', thereby avoiding the need to use the ordinary courts.[138] He explained the need for a special commission by drawing attention to two different 'classes' of killings, neither of which could be successfully prosecuted in existing courts. The murder of Rev. Humphrey fell into the first class: he was a European victim, whose killers could only be tried in the colony. The second class comprised the killings of 'Soribonkeh [a] loyal chief, and two natives alleged to have been killed by order of Bai Bureh', whose killers could be tried at a District Commissioner's court including a native chief.[139] In neither case did Cardew feel he would obtain a conviction. As to the first, it was clear to the colonial authorities that the civilian population of Freetown was opposed to direct taxation and sympathetic to the Temne rebels, and so would not convict. As to the second, it was equally unlikely that an African chief would agree to a conviction.

---

[135] CO 879/55/1, No. 100, p. 112 at p. 113.
[136] See Fyfe, *A History of Sierra Leone*, pp. 570–577.
[137] See PP 1899 (c. 9391), pp. 633–640.
[138] CO 879/55/1, No. 48, p. 60. Chamberlain responded cautiously, stating that the death penalty should be imposed only in cases of murder: CO 879/55/1, No. 52, p. 66.
[139] CO 879/55/1, No. 53, p. 66.

Chamberlain agreed that punishments should be inflicted in every case for murder or outrage. At the same time, he was far from sure that a special commission would be able to differentiate between acts of murder and acts of war.[140] While awaiting further information on the proposed special commission, he sent instructions that murder charges should be brought only in cases where the killings would have been treated as murder in peacetime, and not where they had occurred in the context of rioting. Rebel chiefs who could not be charged with 'ordinary' murder should be tried for instigating disturbances, 'unless you consider the case would be better met by passing special detention Ordinances, for which there are many precedents'. As for the ordinary rioters, and chiefs not implicated in any killings, there should be an amnesty. Indeed, Chamberlain wanted to grant a general amnesty as soon as the rebellion had been suppressed, since he was 'strongly inclined to believe that we brought it on ourselves by injudicious legislation & especially by not making our intentions clear to the natives'.[141]

On 13 April, four days after this telegram was sent, Cardew's despatch containing the draft ordinance to set up the special commission arrived in London.[142] The draft ordinance did not include any provision as to the legal qualifications either of the president or of the members of the proposed commission – though the Attorney General advised that 'at least the President should be a duly qualified barrister' – and left it to the president to make rules regulating procedure. The commission was to have the power to inflict the death penalty, which could be imposed after a majority verdict (with the president having the casting vote). Clauses were included both to prevent any of its decisions being questioned by habeas corpus and to indemnify anyone acting under its orders from any potential liability.[143] On seeing the draft, officials were concerned by the proposal that judges appointed on an ad hoc basis should have the power of life and death. Chamberlain's private secretary, H. F. Wilson, suggested enacting alternative legislation, based on the model of a New Zealand statute passed in 1869 to deal with Maori resistance. This measure had allowed

---

[140] As he noted, 'what is murder in warfare? The line is rather difficult to draw': minutes of 27 April 1898, CO 267/438/9094.
[141] CO 879/55/1, No. 57, p. 68; Minutes of 27 April 1898, CO 267/438/9094.
[142] CO 879/55/1, No. 60, p. 69.   [143] The text of the draft is in CO 267/437/9748.

barristers of seven years' standing to be appointed temporary judges of the Supreme Court to try certain offences within proclaimed areas, and had made provision for juries to be available where expedient.[144] Wilson felt that some provision needed to be made for the possibility of a jury trial, and that the pool from which commissioners might be drawn needed to be better defined. Bertram Cox agreed that the New Zealand model should be sent to Freetown, though he was convinced by Cardew that the ordinary provisions relating to trial by jury in the colony should not be used, since public opinion in Freetown was so hostile to the tax.

These discussions took place at a point when the Temne revolt seemed to be under control and news of the Mende one had yet to reach London. In the aftermath of the second outbreak, Cardew's policy changed. It was evident that, in the Mende revolt, very many 'ordinary' murders had been committed; and, since a large number of the victims were Krios, there was now little danger of Freetown juries not convicting. However, rather than leaving everything to the Supreme Court (whose civil business would grind to a halt if overloaded with this criminal business), he advised appointing a special commissioner to try murder cases on the spot.[145] Cardew explained that the two risings needed to be dealt with distinctly. He was willing to offer an amnesty in Karene, once the rebellion there had been completely suppressed and Bai Bureh captured. In his view, the Temne had conducted the war 'on fairly humane principles', and had generally refrained from killing non-combatants. By contrast, the Mende rebellion had been marked by 'savage barbarism and cruelty', with the rebels killing almost all the Europeans and Krios who fell into their hands. In his view, no amnesty should be offered to the Mende until all those concerned in any murders had been convicted. To re-establish order, it was imperative to act quickly and firmly.[146]

Officials in London debated how to put this into effect. Wilson once more urged a variant of the New Zealand example, suggesting the appointment of a deputy judge to try cases with assessors. Cox did not feel that such emergency legislation was needed. Noting that the

---

[144] Disturbed Districts Act 1869 (32 & 33 Vict. c. 20); Minute by Wilson 12 May 1898, CO 267/437/9748.
[145] CO 879/55/1, No. 96, p. 107.   [146] CO 879/55/1, No. 120, p. 150.

Consolidating Colonial Rule, 1896–1901

colony had recently passed a Jury Amendment Ordinance (1897), which authorised non-jury trials (with assessors) in non-capital cases,[147] he suggested that this ordinance could simply be amended by removing the words limiting its operation to non-capital cases, to allow a juryless court to hear murder cases. Officials now favoured the appointment of a deputy judge under existing legislation, who could hear cases on the spot once legislation had been passed to empower Supreme Court judges to sit at any place in the protectorate.[148] Instructions to this effect were accordingly sent to Cardew.[149] A procedure was thus put in place to try those accused of outrages during the Hut Tax rebellion, but one which would still follow the procedures of the Supreme Court, rather than an 'emergency' tribunal staffed by non-lawyers, as originally proposed by the Governor. In August, G. A. Bonner, a barrister on the English Midland circuit, was appointed deputy judge to deal with cases outside Freetown, after London had rejected Cardew's recommendation of the former Attorney General of Sierra Leone, Sir Nevill Geary.[150] At the same time Sir David Chalmers was sent out as a royal commissioner to inquire into the causes of the insurrection and into the state of Sierra Leone. Although legislation was passed to give this commissioner special powers to summon witnesses, it was clear that he would have no part in the judicial proceedings.[151]

In the meantime, an ordinance was also passed 'to empower the Governor to apprehend and detain such persons as he shall suspect of conspiring against Her Majesty's Government'.[152] By the time this measure had been assented to at the end of May, a number of

---

[147] The ordinance, which allowed the Attorney General to opt for a non-jury trial, had been passed in response to the acquittal of a number of men who had organised the destruction of a rival church: Fyfe, *A History of Sierra Leone*, p. 580.

[148] Minutes, 1–2 July 1898, CO 267/439/14555.

[149] CO 879/55/1, No. 123, p. 163. The Supreme Court (Further Amendment) Ordinance 1898 (No. 2) was subsequently passed.

[150] CO 879/55/1, No. 109, p. 142; No. 133, p. 180; No. 136, p. 192; No. 137, p. 192. Regarding Geary, Edward Wingfield minuted 'neither his law nor his common sense is such as to fit him for responsible judicial duties': CO 267/437/9748.

[151] Ordinance No. 21 of 1898, the Special Commission Inquiry Ordinance: CO 879/55/1, enc. 1 in No. 149, p. 211. This was modelled on the Dominica Ordinance No. 1 of 1893 (CO 879/55/1, No. 112, p. 146).

[152] The Insurgents' Temporary Detention Ordinance, No. 14 of 1898, in CO 879/55/1, enc. 1 in No. 119, p. 149.

insurgents who had been captured by the military were being held in Freetown, as well as a few chiefs whose headmen had been prominent in the rebellion. The ordinance was to remain in force only during the course of the rebellion, and Attorney General Smyly indicated in his report that its purpose was to allow the authorities to gather evidence against the detainees pending their trial.[153] In the view of officials, once a tribunal was in place to try the rebels, detention under the ordinance would no longer be needed.[154] London had no qualms about sanctioning this ordinance, for Chamberlain had already suggested detention as one option to use against the rebellious chiefs. There had been protests at a public meeting in Freetown on 19 May against extending this measure to the colony – which seemed to cast doubt on the loyalty of the Krios – but the Sierra Leone government was clear that it had to be applied in the colony, for the simple reason that this was where the captured rebels had been taken.

Bonner began to hear cases in October at Kwalu, Bonthe and Bandajuma. At the end of September, sixteen were sentenced to death at Kwalu.[155] The Colonial Office was content to see these men executed. As W. H. Mercer noted, 'They are all cases of murder of specified persons and no question of law as to the amenability of the prisoners seems to have been involved.' The executions also had a good effect in pacifying the country.[156] After twenty-one further death sentences had been imposed at Bonthe, Cardew proclaimed a free pardon for those who had taken part in the rising, though this did not (to London's relief) extend to the convicted killers.[157] At Bandajuma, 107 were tried for murder: 65 were convicted, 35 of whom were given a commuted sentence.[158] Having finished here, Bonner returned to Bonthe to try more prisoners. In the end, he tried 180 prisoners, of whom 67 were acquitted and 112 capitally convicted.[159] Bonner tried to recommend to mercy as often as possible, but found his assessors in a more hawkish mood. In the end, sixty-six death sentences were confirmed by the Executive Council. It was evident that both the

---

[153] CO 879/55/1, enc. 2 in No. 119, p. 149.   [154] Note by Wilson in CO 267/439/14542.
[155] CO 879/55/1, No. 190, p. 287. One of these sentences was later commuted to life imprisonment.
[156] Minute, 25 November 1898, CO 267/441/26076.
[157] CO 879/55/1, No. 192, p. 289; No. 207, p. 298.   [158] CO 879/55/1, No. 206, p. 298.
[159] One escaped. CO 879/55/1, enc. in No. 226, p. 317; CO 879/58/8, No. 23, p. 42.

Colonial Office and the Governor wanted the Mende rebels prosecuted under the ordinary criminal law for uncontrovertible offences. Cardew had instructed District Commissioners not to commit cases in which the evidence was doubtful, or where the perpetrators were war-boys or slaves acting under the orders of headmen. As a result (as he pointed out), the number of those tried bore a small proportion to the number killed in the insurrection.[160]

Bai Bureh's Capture

Bai Bureh was captured while these trials were proceeding. Officials in London, who bore in mind Chamberlain's distinction between cases of murder and cases of levying war, and who recalled Cardew's promise to spare his life if Bai Bureh surrendered, were keen not to see him capitally charged.[161] Cardew's proposal that he be tried by Deputy Judge Bonner with assessors at Karene for treason or treason-felony, but with no question of the death penalty being imposed,[162] did not resolve their concerns. Edward Fairfield thought it would be prudent to ask the Law Officers whether Bai Bureh could be considered a British subject for the purposes of the treason laws, since it would be 'very awkward' if Bonner were to take the view at trial that he was not, or if Bai Bureh were to challenge any conviction in the Privy Council.[163] Cardew was accordingly instructed to suspend all action against Bai Bureh until the Law Officers had responded. The question referred to them by the Colonial Office made no assumption that Sierra Leone had become a territory of the crown by virtue of being proclaimed a protectorate or that its inhabitants were subject to the crown's jurisdiction – though these were the very assumptions which lay behind the Foreign Office's approach to troublesome protected rulers in the Niger Delta. The Law Officers, Richard Webster and Robert Finlay, were asked to consider the position of an African chief residing

---

[160] O 879/55/1, No. 226, p. 316.
[161] Minute by Mercer, 14 November 1898, CO 267/441/25645.
[162] CO 879/55/1, No. 196, p. 291. Ernest J. Watts, who had defended the accused in the murder trials, offered to defend Bai Bureh should he be prosecuted: Watts to Chamberlain, 6 December 1898, CO 267/444/27654. No member of the Freetown bar was prepared to act, since the fees paid were so low: CO 267/447/21435.
[163] Minute 16 November 1898, CO 267/441/25785.

in a protectorate in which British subjects had been given the right to trade and travel through treaties with the chiefs, and in which British jurisdiction had been exercised 'entirely by usage and sufferance of the chiefs and people themselves'. They were also instructed that, in Sierra Leone, English law as it stood in 1880 was introduced into the colony in 1889 (insofar as local conditions allowed), which meant that English treason laws were in force there. Jurisdiction had also been extended over the protectorate under the Foreign Jurisdiction Act (and it was under this jurisdiction that the murder trials had been held).

The Law Officers reported on 25 November that Bai Bureh could not be tried for treason, since the protectorate could not be considered to be part of the Queen's dominions, and Bai Bureh was not a British subject.[164] While it was settled that someone who was not a subject could be tried for treason committed within the Queen's dominions (under the doctrine of local allegiance), and that a subject could be tried for treason committed outside the crown's dominions, they considered Bai Bureh to fall into neither category.[165] They advised, however, that Bai Bureh might be prosecuted either for murder (if there was evidence against him on that charge), or under the general article 67 of the 1897 Protectorate Ordinance, which allowed an unlimited penalty for disobeying instructions.[166] They also recommended passing an ordinance to criminalise levying war or offering armed resistance against the protectorate government. This advice in effect

---

[164] In 1855, an earlier set of law officers had given an opinion that natives of the Ionian Republic – who lived under British protection – could not be regarded as subjects who might be liable for treasonable acts committed in aiding the enemy during the Crimean War: Opinion dated 10 May 1855, CO 885/3/1 No. 57, p. 62.

[165] CO 879/55/1, No. 202, p. 294. They distinguished the case of Dr Leander Jameson, who was tried in 1896 under the Foreign Enlistment Act of 1870, which criminalised preparing military expeditions against a friendly state from within British dominions, for his acts in preparing the Jameson Raid on the South African Republic from the Barolong area of Bechuanaland. In that case (they explained), it was held that 'a Protectorate was part of Her Majesty's dominions for the purposes of the Foreign Enlistment Act' rather than treason. In fact, British Bechuanaland (in which the activity had taken place) had been annexed to the Cape Colony, and was distinct from the Bechuanaland Protectorate which lay north of the Molopo River. See *The Times*, 25 July 1896, p. 14 and *The Queen* v. *Jameson* [1896] 2 QB 425.

[166] Article 67 of Ordinance 11 of 1897 (the Protectorate Ordinance) enacted that 'any Chief who shall be ordered by the Governor either directly or by a deputy or messenger to do or refrain from doing any public act or acts and shall either defy or neglect promptly to obey such order shall be guilty of an offence.'

scuppered the plans to put Bai Bureh on trial. Since there had been no suggestion hitherto that he was directly implicated in any murder, Wingfield ruled this option out. He preferred 'to deal with Bai Bureh as a political prisoner and pass an ordinance authorizing his detention as has been done before with other refractory Chiefs', rather than prosecuting him under the Protectorate Ordinance.[167] Chamberlain was inclined to be more lenient. Given that the protectorate was only newly established, he thought it was natural that there should be discontent which might break out into insurrection. Since Bai Bureh was clearly a man of influence, 'it could be better to use him if possible than to lock him up', perhaps imposing a fine and giving him a warning about his future conduct.[168]

Faced with the three choices, Cardew opted to detain Bai Bureh as a political prisoner.[169] An ordinance was passed in December authorising his detention and deportation, and indemnifying those involved in his capture and detention from any legal action.[170] The report of the Attorney General on this legislation did not explain why it was necessary to detain Bai Bureh, beyond saying that he had been engaged in acts of rebellion against the government. Two months after the ordinance had been passed, Cardew sent London a memorandum on 'Bai Bureh's antecedents', which described his activities over a decade, but said little about his actions during the Hut Tax war, beyond the comment that he 'was leading and directing the insurgents'. Reading this document, Selborne noted, 'This record does not seem to me to be what can reasonably be called a bad one in a native chief'.[171] Chalmers also took a much more lenient view of Bai Bureh's actions than did the Governor. In his report on the crucial event which sparked Bai Bureh's resistance – the attempt to arrest him – Chalmers concluded that the chief had not given the defiant response attributed to him by Captain Sharpe, and that *'the arrest of Bai Bureh which was*

---

[167] Minute, 26 November 1898, CO 267/443/26666.
[168] Minute, 27 November 1898, CO 267/443/26666.
[169] CO 879/55/1, No. 206, p. 298; No. 211, p. 300; No. 219, p. 309.
[170] Ordinance No. 39 of 1898, 'The Political Prisoner's (Bai Bureh) Ordinance, 1898, CO 879/58/8, enc. 1 in No. 14, p. 10. He was initially held in Karene, but moved to Freetown in February after one of his guards tried to help him escape. Fyfe, *A History of Sierra Leone*, p. 594.
[171] Cardew to Chamberlain, 10 February 1899, CO 267/445/4692. This was written in response to a request from London: CO 879/58/8, No. 3, p. 4.

intended, and the attempt to effect which led to the collision, was aggression pure and simple on the part of the authorities.'[172] Nonetheless, when the acting Governor, Major Matthew Nathan, reviewed his detention in April, he did not recommend his release: Bai Bureh was 'one of the most successful of the insurgent chiefs' and it was in the interest of peace 'that it should be known that such defiance receives severe punishment'.[173]

By April 1898, a number of other chiefs had also been detained under special ordinances. They included a number of Temne rebels who had been convicted in the District Commissioner's court for levying war, but whose convictions were regarded as void, in light of the Law Officers' advice.[174] They also included Nyagwa, the chief of Panguma.[175] Although Panguma was not one of the areas in which the hut tax was to be paid, the Acting District Commissioner in the area, J. E. C. Blakeney, reported in April that Nyagwa was suspected of making preparations for war to 'drive the white man out of his country'.[176] After demanding that he surrender all his arms, Blakeney arrested him in early May.[177] Hostilities now broke out in this area, and attempts were made to rescue Nyagwa.[178] Nyagwa was charged with conspiracy to levy war and sentenced by Blakeney to banishment for fourteen years under the Protectorate Ordinance of 1897.[179] Then, in July, he was moved from Panguma to Freetown, where he was

---

[172] PP 1899 (c. 9388), p. 38 (emphasis in original).
[173] CO 879/58/8, No. 36, p. 82 at p. 83.
[174] They included Bai Bureh's ally Alimami Lahai, Bai Kura Hari and Bai Forki: CO 879/58/8, enc. in No. 36 at pp. 87–88. Ordinance No. 8 of 1899, Political Prisoners' Ordinance (No. 3) 1899, CO 879/58/8, enc. 1 in No. 35, p. 81. As Antrobus put it, 'The ordinance is in the usual terms: it was necessary to provide for the detention of these persons': CO 267/446/10148.
[175] He was well known to the Sierra Leone government, having briefly sheltered Makaia during the Yoni disturbances of 1889, before handing him over. He had also co-operated with the British on a number of other occasions: Fyfe, *A History of Sierra Leone*, pp. 518–521; CO 879/58/8, enc. in No. 36, p. 84.
[176] CO 879/55/1, enc. in No. 61, p. 70 at p. 71.
[177] CO 879/55/1, enc. 3 in No. 87, p. 87; enc. in No. 36, pp. 84–85; Blakeney remained convinced that Nyagwa had supplied most of the men and materiel for the fighting in Bandajuma: See CO 879/55/1, No. 129, p. 168; No. 95, p. 105 at p. 107.
[178] CO 879/55/1, enc. in No. 154, p. 216 at p. 217.
[179] Section 68 of Ordinance 11 of 1897 (the Protectorate Ordinance) enacted that 'any person who resists or with others conspires to resist the execution of any process of law or to overawe by force or show thereof any public officer in the exercise of his duty shall be guilty of an offence.'

detained under the Insurgents' Temporary Detention Ordinance of 1898. Although it was intended to prosecute him for murder, no charge was brought, and at the end of February 1899, his continued detention (or deportation) was provided for in the Political Prisoners' Ordinance of 1899.[180]

The government also used special ordinances to detain Mende leaders. The most prominent of these was Gbanna Lewis, Bai Sherbro of Yoni,[181] who was thought to be behind the resistance to the hut tax. He was one of the chiefs who had gone to Freetown in 1897 to protest against the Protectorate Ordinance; and he had subsequently organised a Poro to boycott European trade (a practice which was soon banned by an ordinance). He was also thought to be behind the 'one word Poro' which led to the Mende uprising. He was arrested on 7 May 1898, and 'treated as a suspect' (as Chalmers put it in his report), although there seemed to be no evidence against him.[182] The ordinance under which he was detained (No. 3 of 1899) also provided for the detention of Bimba Kelli, another one of the Mende chiefs who protested in Freetown in February 1897. He had been arrested in June 1898, and had been twice tried and acquitted for murder. He was re-arrested at the request of the District Commissioner at Bonthe, who considered that his continued presence in the Imperri country would be dangerous.[183] The Colonial Office approved this ordinance, but reiterated its view that 'political prisoners should not be detained longer than is absolutely necessary' and that there should be reports on them every six months.[184]

Continuing the Detentions

On 17 January 1898, a general amnesty was proclaimed, which exempted only those in custody and awaiting trial, and those involved in the killing of Humphrey and two African chiefs.[185] With the war over, and an amnesty proclaimed for rebels, the question was begged whether the detainees should be released. The Colonial Office

---

[180] Ordinance No. 3 of 1899, which also provided for the detention of Gbanna Lewis (Bai Sherbro) and Bimba Kelli. CO 879/58/8, enc. 1 in No. 29, p. 46.
[181] For his background, see Fyfe, *A History of Sierra Leone*, p. 556.
[182] PP 1899 (c. 9388), p. 49.   [183] CO 879/58/8, enc. in No. 36, at pp. 87–88.
[184] Minute by Antrobus, CO 267/445/7124.   [185] CO 879/58/8, enc. in No. 20, p. 41.

was particularly concerned about the treatment of Bai Bureh, since both Chamberlain and Chalmers took a more benevolent view of his actions than did Cardew. In March, press reports reached London that Bai Bureh had refused to eat the prison food, and was asking for different treatment from that usually accorded to prisoners.[186] Responding to them, Cardew explained that he was being kept separately from other prisoners and given a special diet. At the same time, he proposed deporting Bai Bureh to Gambia or the Gold Coast.[187] This proposal did not go down well in London. While Mercer accepted that there was in effect nowhere to keep Bai Bureh in Freetown apart from the prison, he thought that this hardly necessitated his deportation. His hope was that the incoming Acting Governor, Nathan, would 'be able to secure him as what he was formerly, an ally'. Wingfield also hoped he could be released before long, and Chamberlain refused to countenance his deportation until he had decided on the recommendations in Chalmers's report.[188]

In April, Nathan reviewed the cases of all seven chiefs still confined in Freetown gaol. Although he opposed Bai Bureh's release, he recommended freeing both Bai Kura Hari and Nyagwa. While he considered the former not to be a chief of any particular importance, he noted that the latter had done good service for the government on previous occasions. In addition, Nathan thought that the suspicions against Nyagwa which had led to his arrest (before the rebellion broke out in his area) were exaggerated, and he worried that the Panguma district was 'disorganised' by this important chief's absence. As for the other four, he recommended their continued detention. Nathan thought that there was evidence that Gbanna Lewis had been 'largely responsible' for the Mende uprising; but in any case, since he had long been a disruptive influence, it would pose too great a risk to the peaceful trade of Sherbro to release him. Although Alimami Lahai was much less important, he was a chief whose influence, like Bai Bureh's, rested largely on his reputation as a warrior, and 'we do not wish to give scope to his talents in that direction.' Bai Forki and Bimba Kelli were also to remain in detention because their influence might be

---

[186] *Morning Post*, 7 March 1899, p. 7.   [187] CO 879/58/8, No. 26, p. 45; No. 27, p. 46.
[188] Minutes, 9 March 1899, CO 267/445/5870; Cardew was instructed on the next day to take no steps in respect of deportation until Chamberlain had considered the report. CO 879/58/8, No. 28, p. 46.

Consolidating Colonial Rule, 1896–1901

used to bad effect.[189] Although Nathan felt that all of these men had been detained under ordinances as a result of the Law Officers' opinion that they could not be tried for treason or treason-felony, his reasons for keeping them incarcerated had more to do with his concern about their future influence than their past conduct. His recommendation to London was that Bai Bureh, Bai Sherbro of Yoni and Bai Forki should be banished to the Gold Coast, and that Alimami Lahai and Bimba Kelli should be kept in Freetown prison 'for a year or two'. Although officials in London were minded to follow these recommendations, the Colonial Office was markedly less hawkish than officials in West Africa: Edward Wingfield expressed a hope that they could all be released before long, while Chamberlain minuted, 'I am sorry that Major Nathan does not see his way to recommend the restoration of Bai Bureh who has rather enlisted my sympathy.'[190]

The hawkish approach of the West African officials was soon manifested in overturning the decision to release Nyagwa and reinstate him as Paramount Chief. When the matter was referred to Cardew (on leave in London), he saw no reason for any leniency towards this chief, whom he regarded not only as 'a notorious drunkard, and a savage and cruel ruler', but also as 'a powerful factor in the rising'.[191] In the meantime, Nathan had received a further report on Nyagwa from Captain Birch, the District Commissioner in Panguma, which argued that releasing this chief would be taken as a sign of weakness by the Africans, who had got the idea that the British never punished, but merely detained people for a short time and then released them.[192] In light of this report, Nathan changed his recommendation, and now urged that Nyagwa be deported, along with Bai Bureh and Gbanna Lewis.[193] Chamberlain's reaction summed up the reaction of the Colonial Office: 'I very much regret the decision, but in view of this strong report I have no choice.'[194] Their deportation to the Gold Coast was duly authorised, and at the end of July (by which point the Gold Coast had passed the necessary legislation to receive them), Nyagwa, Bai Bureh and Gbanna Lewis left Freetown for the Gold Coast. Bai Bureh remained in the Gold Coast until 1905, when he was allowed to return

[189] CO 879/58/8, No. 36, pp. 82–83. [190] Minute of 16 May 1899, CO 267/446/10395.
[191] CO 879/58/8, No. 40, p. 89. [192] CO 879/58/8, enc. 1 in No. 44, p. 91.
[193] CO 879/58/8, No. 44, p. 91.
[194] Minute, 28 June 1898, CO 267/446/15653. See also CO 879/58/8, No. 46, p. 93.

to Sierra Leone and reinstated as chief. The other two men did not live to see their homelands again, Nyagwa dying at the Gold Coast in 1906, and Gbanna Lewis six years later.[195]

Although, like Prempeh, Bai Bureh was eventually detained by virtue of an ordinance, the approach taken in his case contrasted strongly with that taken in that of the Asantehene. Bai Bureh was not the ruler of a kingdom who stood in the way of British expansion, but a rebel against a new British system of administration. When dealing with rebels against the new protectorate, the Colonial Office was determined to proceed by ordinary legal means, and sought to avoid reliance on 'exceptional' methods, such as the creation of an ad hoc tribunal. It was as a result of their concern that the legal steps they were taking would be watertight that officials asked the Law Officers whether Africans in the protectorate could be regarded as subjects, liable to charges of treason; and it was only in response to the Law Officers' advice that they could not be so regarded that the decision was taken to detain Bai Bureh by ordinance.

The decision not to attempt to prosecute Bai Bureh under the Protectorate Ordinance also raises a contrast with the treatment of Nana Olomu. In Nana's case, the colonial authorities were none too worried about the precise nature of the charges brought against him on the basis of the Africa Order in Council of 1893, and nor were officials at the Foreign Office concerned with looking too closely at whether this instrument would bear the gravity of the charges against him. By contrast, in Bai Bureh's case, where officials were aware that he could be charged under the Protectorate Ordinance, they came to the rapid conclusion that, as Wingfield put it, 'it is scarcely adequate to treat such action as that of Bai Bureh as merely disobedience to lawful orders or resistance to process of law.'[196] Both he and his political masters preferred to detain Bai Bureh via an ordinance rather than to try him on charges which would not signal the gravity of his alleged offence. In taking this approach, officials in London may have wanted to avoid

---

[195] Fyfe, *A History of Sierra Leone*, pp. 594–595.
[196] Minute dated 26 November 1898, CO 267/443/26666. He noted this even though he was aware that the ordinance set no limits to terms of imprisonment, and may also have been aware of the provision (Article 77 of Ordinance 11 of 1897) which allowed District Commissioners to banish anyone from their district in the interests of 'security, peace or order'.

being seen to stretch the new legal system; equally, they may have wanted to retain a level of flexibility in dealing with Bai Bureh, whom Chamberlain wanted to be released as early as was possible. If the end result for Bai Bureh was the same kind of ordinance as that which detained Prempeh, the officials who endorsed it clearly felt that the demands of due process needed to be taken more into account in a territory where they were seeking to build a new legal system than in locations of conquest.

Conclusion

The contrast between these cases suggests that the more territories were perceived to be under imperial control, the more aware the Colonial Office became of the need to use ordinary forms of law to deal with political offenders. Nor was it long before Asante, whose constitutional position remained initially ambiguous after Prempeh's fall, came to be more formally under imperial control. Asante was not annexed in 1896, though a British Resident remained in Kumasi, exercising criminal and civil jurisdiction. In 1899, the Gold Coast's Chief Justice, Brandon Griffith, argued that it should be regarded as part of the colony (along with the other protected areas south of the Prah).[197] The Law Officers in London disagreed with his view of the law, holding that the Gold Coast's legislature did not have any jurisdiction over Asante.[198] The Colonial Office now wanted an Order in Council, in order to put the crown's jurisdiction in Asante on a firm footing, and gave instruction for an Asante Protectorate Order in Council to be issued. However, Asante was annexed after the war of 1900, by imperial Order in Council of 26 September 1901, which declared that it had been conquered. Asante now became a colony, separate from the Gold Coast, whose Governor was empowered to exercise all the legislative and judicial powers of the crown in Asante. Another Order in Council (of the same date), issued under the Foreign Jurisdiction Act 1890, provided for the government

---

[197] Griffith Memorandum, 9 August 1899, CO 879/62/10, enc. 5 in No. 4, p. 8; cf. David Kimble, *A Political History of Ghana, 1850–1928* (Oxford, Oxford University Press, 1963), p. 316.

[198] Chamberlain to Hodgson, 19 February 1900, CO 879/62/10, enc. 5 in No. 7, p. 15; cf. Kimble, *A Political History of Ghana*, p. 316.

of the 'Northern Territories', African polities north of Asante with which the British had signed treaties. Although accorded the status of a Protectorate, the structure of government here was very similar to that of Asante.[199] Asante and the territories north of it were now formally within the British imperial sphere, as was Sierra Leone.

With the defeat of Yaa Asantewaa's Asante warriors and the suppression of the Hut Tax revolt in Sierra Leone, *ad hominem* ordinances to detain and deport political prisoners in these areas fell into disuse, after a twenty-year period in which on average more than one had been passed every year. They had been important tools of control at a time when the extent of British jurisdiction over these enemies was unclear, and when there was strong resistance to British encroachment. However, in the new dispensation in the decade that followed, tailor-made ordinances to remove particular opponents fell out of use, even if West Africa would continue to see the deposition and removal of chiefs under general ordinances which gave great discretion to the executive.[200]

---

[199] Kimble, *A Political History of Ghana*, pp. 324–325.

[200] See esp. the Nigerian Deposed Chiefs Removal Ordinance, No. 59 of 1917: see Tunde Oduwobi, 'Deposed Rulers under the Colonial Regime in Nigeria: The Careers of Akarigbo Oyebajo and Awujale Adenuga', *Cahiers d'études africaines*, vol. 171 (2003), pp. 553–571; Bonny Ibhawoh, *Imperialism and Human Rights: Colonial Discourses of Rights and Liberties in African History* (Albany, State University of New York Press, 2007), pp. 67–68; and Bonny Ibhawoh, *Imperial Justice: Africans in Empire's Court* (Oxford, Oxford University Press, 2013), ch. 5, discussing the case of Eshugbayi Eleko, removed from Lagos in 1925, resulting in a challenge in the Privy Council: *Eshugbayi Eleko v. the Officer Administering the Government of Nigeria and Another* [1931] AC 662.

8

Detention Comes to Court: African Appeals to the Courts in Whitehall and Westminster, 1895–1922

Although the detention of African leaders had become routine since the early 1880s, particularly in West Africa, and its legality had occupied much of the time of officials in the Colonial Office, the question of the lawfulness of *ad hominem* ordinances did not come before the courts in the imperial metropolis until the last years of the century. Given the practical and financial problems faced by African detainees in bringing their cases to courts in London, it was only on very rare occasions that judges there were asked to consider the lawfulness of detentions made under local ordinances. On the few occasions when such cases did reach the metropolis – either at the Privy Council or at the Supreme Court of Judicature – judges had to confront the question of how far these detentions fitted with the rule of law so beloved of the common law system. Those who challenged detention ordinances made the claim that they violated fundamental principles inherent in the common law, confirmed by Magna Carta and subsequent statutes, which limited the power of colonial governors or administrators to order their detention either under local ordinances or by virtue of crown prerogative powers. In making these challenges, they drew on a rich, substantive vision of the common law, which was to be found not only in such constitutional texts as Dicey's *Law of the Constitution*, but also in the Whig histories which did so much to define Victorian Englishmen's understanding of their constitution. Those who defended the detentions looked to a more formal vision, seeking to establish the legality of the detention by a process of legislative affiliation.

The cases to be considered in this chapter did not come from West Africa, where political detentions had come to be routine after 1880. Although, as has been seen, there were occasional attempts to challenge detentions in the Gold Coast – and local lawyers, such as Edward Bannerman, willing to give advice – detainees in this part of Africa lacked the means and the support to get their cases to London. This was less true in South Africa, where detainees like Langalibalele, Cetshwayo and Dinuzulu had been able to draw on the help of supporters like the Colensos to make political cases for their liberation in London. The first cases to make legal claims for liberation here also came from South Africa. In the first of these, Sigcau's, the litigation reached the Privy Council as a result of the detainee's successful appeal to the Cape Supreme Court, which the Cape government wished to overturn in the highest imperial court. In the second, Sekgoma Letsholathibe's, the chief was able to litigate in London thanks to the help of a local supporter, and the fact that he had access to the necessary financial resources. In the third case to be considered – the post-war case of the Egyptian nationalist leader Saad Zaghlul Pasha – the detainee was the leader with the highest public profile to be detained in Africa since Urabi, and his network of support ran far wider than that enjoyed by the southern African.

The legal position which emerged from these cases was one which ultimately endorsed the formal vision of the rule of law, rather than the broad substantive vision invoked by the detainees. Rather than looking from the point of view of the liberties of the detainees, the courts concentrated on whether the powers exercised derived from a valid legislative source; and in exploring how far absolute powers could be delegated to local officials, the highest courts were to take an expansive view, to the detriment of African liberties. In upholding the executive's power to legislate for detention, judges often made assumptions about the political necessity for these powers, trusting to the executive to use such drastic *ad hominem* laws only in case of emergency. In fact, as shall be seen, these powers were rather used for convenience, by officials who had plans to release the detainees in question, at the very moment that they strove to defend their powers in court.

Sigcau, Sir Henry de Villiers and the Privy Council

The first significant case to raise these matters was *Sprigg v. Sigcau*, heard by the Privy Council in 1896. The case concerned the detention without trial of the paramount chief of the Mpondo. Although a treaty with the Mpondo had existed since 1844, Pondoland had never been annexed, in part because both the Cape Colony and Natal wanted to acquire it. However, British imperial interest in the area was renewed after 1890, as it became increasingly unstable, thanks to a conflict between Sigcau and his former prime minister, Mhlangaso. In this context, in exchange for British support, Sigcau agreed first to accept a British resident in his territory, and then in 1894 to a full cession to the British Crown. Under the terms of the cession, Sigcau was to remain nominally paramount chief, and was to receive a stipend, but his territory would be administered by the Cape government.[1]

Shortly before the cession, Sigcau had made one last push against Mhlangaso, who was driven to an area called Isiseli. As part of the settlement brokered by the British, Mhlangaso was to be removed from the territory, and the inhabitants of Isiseli were to submit to Sigcau and pay a fine to him of 200 cattle. However, it proved harder to settle these long-standing conflicts than the Cape government had hoped. Only 125 cattle were tendered, which Sigcau refused to accept. Keen to assert his authority, he demanded that the Isiseli people present themselves before him as a body, and that their leader, Patekili, should attend in person. Sigcau's high-handed treatment of the deputations sent from Isiseli served only to prolong the tensions the British wanted to assuage. Sigcau's attitude towards the colonial authorities also caused concern. Having agreed to explain the new system of tax registration to his people, Sigcau instead took the opportunity to attack the government because they had not ensured that the promises regarding the Isiseli were carried out to the letter, inducing his people to think that they did not need to register until the matter was settled. When the Registration Officers came to register his

---

[1] On the background, see esp. William Bramwell, 'Loyalties and the Politics of Incorporation in South Africa: The Case of Pondoland, *c.* 1870–1913', unpublished Ph.D. Dissertation, University of Warwick, 2015. See further William Beinart, *The Political Economy of Pondoland, 1860–1930* (Cambridge, Cambridge University Press, 1982).

own homestead, he was accused of insulting them. He was also accused of having a defiant attitude towards the chief magistrate, after attending a meeting accompanied by insolent followers carrying assegais. In addition to these particular acts, he was also accused of obstructing the administration of justice, in attempting to exercise his former chiefly jurisdiction. Nothing in Sigcau's conduct could be described as seditious or rebellious: but his reluctance to accept the realities of his new position made him an inconvenient thorn in the side of the colonial administration.

On 11 June 1895, Sir Hercules Robinson, the Governor of the Cape, accordingly issued a proclamation stating that Sigcau's presence in East Pondoland was a danger to public safety and good order, and authorising his detention.[2] On 18 June, he surrendered himself and was taken to Kokstad (in Griqualand East, into which East Pondoland had been merged). Four days later, the Governor-in-Council appointed a three-man commission to investigate Sigcau's conduct since the annexation of his territory.[3] The inquiry, which took place in Kokstad in the first two weeks of July, was not a judicial one: no criminal charges were made, and the commission did not observe judicial rules of evidence. The commissioners examined various accusations against Sigcau, but their conclusions were hardly damning. While they reported that his behaviour had 'been in many respects obstructive to the satisfactory magisterial administration of Pondoland' and likely to induce his followers to be unco-operative with the colonial authorities, they found 'that in each instance, excepting the case of the Patekili fine and the submission of the Isiseli people and registration, where obstructive conduct was brought home to Sigcau and complained of to him, he withdrew obstruction'.[4] At the same time, they found that the attitude and conduct of the people as a whole had been praiseworthy, and that this was something for which 'the chief

---

[2] Proclamation 231 of 1895.
[3] They were the chief magistrate of Griqualand East (W. E. M. Stanford), the assistant chief magistrate of Tembuland and Transkei (J. H. Scott) and the Cape Town chief of police (H. A. Jenner).
[4] 'Report of the Commissioners appointed to inquire into the acts and behaviour of the Pondo Chief Sigcau since the annexation of East Pondoland' (in the Privy Council papers for Case No. 12 of 1896: *Sir John Gordon Sprigg* v. *Sigcau*: British Library: PP 1316), p. 7.

should receive some credit'.[5] Although he had on numerous occasions sent letters to magistrates seeking to influence them, the commissioners felt that they did not constitute serious attempts to interfere with the magistrates, and they thought it natural that his followers would appeal to him in such cases. The commissioners also noted that he had surrendered himself to the authorities and had co-operated with the inquiry.[6]

Despite these findings, Sigcau was informed on 13 July that he could not return to Pondoland. He was given the choice either to stay 'closely guarded' in unspecified territories nearby or be removed to the Cape Colony, where he would be allowed greater freedom. In response, Sigcau asked what crime he had committed, whether the proposed exile would be for life, and which territories he might be sent to. Having received no reply, on 29 July he petitioned the Cape Supreme Court for his release. At the hearing on the following day, counsel for the Cape government argued that the Governor had used his powers under the Cape's 1894 Pondoland Annexation Act, which stated that the territory 'shall be subject to such laws, statutes, and ordinances as have already been proclaimed by the High Commissioner, and such as, after annexation to the Colony, the Governor shall from time to time by proclamation declare to be in force in such Territories'.[7] In its view, the Cape parliament had effectively delegated legislative powers to the Governor, insofar as the Transkeian territories which included Pondoland were concerned. The government's lawyers also pointed to the laws enacted to detain Langalibalele and Cetshwayo, to show that there were precedents of men held without charge under *ad hominem* laws. Sigcau's lawyers countered that there were constitutional limits on the power of the Cape parliament to issue such laws. According to Constitution Ordinance and Royal Instructions, the Governor could not assent to any legislation repugnant to the law of England or her treaty obligations, but had to reserve it for the signification of royal assent in London.[8] Since it was

---

[5] 'Report of the Commissioners', p. 7.   [6] 'Report of the Commissioners', p. 15.
[7] Pondoland Annexation Act, No. 5 of 1894. The governor's powers in the territories were also governed by similar legislation relating to Tembuland (Act No. 3 of 1885) and Griqualand East (Act No. 38 of 1877).
[8] They cited *Cameron* v. *Kyte* (1835) 3 Knapp 332 for the proposition that the powers of a colonial governor were limited by his instructions.

clearly repugnant to the law of England to pass a law which authorised the imprisonment of an individual on the order of the Governor, the legislation under which he had acted was argued to be void.

In a judgment which gave an eloquent 'substantive' defence of the rule of law, the Cape court ordered Sigcau's discharge. The liberal Chief Justice, Sir Henry de Villiers CJ, was clearly troubled by the fact that Sigcau was punished by a proclamation which made no specific charges against him, even though a criminal code had been introduced in Pondoland, which defined offences – including offences against the administration of justice and the gathering of taxes – for which he could have been charged. While sympathetic to the constitutional arguments made on behalf of Sigcau, de Villiers did not consider it necessary to settle the question of whether a Cape statute assented to by the Governor in defiance of his instructions would be void.[9] Instead, he looked to whether the power in question had been delegated under the Annexation Act. As de Villiers saw it, while the Act authorised the Governor to legislate for Pondoland, it did not confer on him any judicial or quasi-judicial powers.[10] In the absence of clear language to that effect – and in light of the fact that a criminal code had been introduced into Pondoland – there was nothing to show that 'the Legislature intended to confer on the governor the power, in time of peace, of exercising arbitrary executive functions under the guise of legislative functions'. Invoking definitions given by Grotius, Blackstone and Austin, he noted that '[t]he term "laws" is wholly inapplicable to decrees directed against individuals.'[11] De Villiers spelled out the consequences of a finding for the crown:

The exercise of such a power would deprive the subject of the right to be tried only by a constituted Court of law according to the forms provided by the law for specified offences only against the law, and it would debar him also of the

---

[9] *Sigcau v. The Queen* (1895) 12 SCR 256 at 265. A fuller version of his judgment is to be found in the records of the Privy Council appeal, Case No. 12 of 1896: *Sir John Gordon Sprigg v. Sigcau*; BL, PP 1316. He noted in passing that the Cape parliament had never yet legislated for the detention of an individual without trial, observing that Langalibalele had been tried in Natal and that Cetshwayo had been a prisoner of war. De Villiers, 'Reasons for judgment', BL, PP 1316, p. 22.

[10] De Villiers, 'Reasons for judgment', BL, PP 1316, p. 23; see also *Sigcau v. The Queen* (1895) 12 SCR 256 at 267.

[11] De Villiers, 'Reasons for judgment', BL, PP 1316, p. 24.

right of appeal, in the last resort, to the Privy Council. If it was legal to sentence Sigcau to perpetual exile for his alleged 'obstructive' conduct, it would have been equally legal to sentence him to death, and the sentence could have been carried out before the meeting of Parliament. He is a native, but he claims to be and is a British subject, and there are many Englishmen and others resident in the territories who are not natives and who, if the Respondent's contention be correct, would be liable to be deprived of their lives and property as well as their liberty otherwise than by the law of the land.'[12]

De Villiers was also sceptical about the crown's claims that there would be disorder in Pondoland if Sigcau were released, reiterating the comment he had made in Willem Kok's case that a court's 'first and most sacred duty is to administer justice to those who seek it and not to preserve the peace of the country'.[13] In any event, he added that, '[i]t must tend to enlist the natives on the side of the laws if they know that the Courts of law are as ready and willing to protect their legal rights as they are to punish them for offences against the law.'[14]

The Cape government sought special leave to appeal to the Privy Council, arguing that the decision 'detrimentally interfered with' the administration of the territories in question, whose population 'is mainly composed of barbarous aboriginal tribes specially requiring firm administration'.[15] Although the House of Lords had held in 1890 that there could be no appeal from a habeas corpus decision to free a prisoner,[16] the Privy Council – confirming that a different approach would be taken in colonial appeals[17] – granted leave to appeal, on condition that the crown paid the costs. Leave having been granted in December 1895,[18] the case was argued in the following July, with judgment being given in February 1897. The

---

[12] De Villiers, 'Reasons for judgment', BL, PP 1316, p. 25.
[13] De Villiers, 'Reasons for judgment', BL, PP 1316, p. 27, quoting from his judgment in *In re Willem Kok and Nathaniel Balie* (1879) in Eben J. Buchanan, *Cases in the Supreme Court of the Cape of Good Hope during the Year 1879* (Cape Town, Juta, 1880), p. 45 at p. 66 [Juta Reports, 1879, p. 45].
[14] De Villiers, 'Reasons for judgment', BL, PP 1316, p. 27. Cf. 'The Liberty of the Subject', *Cape Law Journal*, vol. 12 (1895), pp. 193–196 and 'The Law of Personal Liberty in the Cape', *Cape Law Journal*, vol. 13 (1896), pp. 252–255.
[15] Petition to Her Majesty in Council for leave to appeal, 27 August 1895, 'Record of Proceedings', p. 33.
[16] *Cox v. Hakes* (1890) 15 App. Cas. 506.
[17] *Attorney General of Hong Kong v. Kwok-a-Sing* (1873) LR 5 PC 179.
[18] *The Times*, 9 December 1895, p. 13.

judgment, dismissing the Cape government's appeal, was delivered by Lord Watson. Discussing the proclamation, Watson held that it purported to exercise powers 'which are beyond the competency of any authority except an irresponsible sovereign, or a supreme and unfettered legislature, or some person or body to whom their functions have been lawfully delegated'. If the Governor had such powers, the court 'would be compelled, however unwillingly, to respect his proclamation', but if he did not, 'then his dictatorial edict was simply an invasion of the individual rights and liberty of a British subject'.[19]

Watson went on to express his satisfaction that no attempt had been made to trace the Governor's power to enact the proclamation from any authority derived from the Queen, 'because autocratic legislation of that kind in a Colony having a settled system of criminal law and criminal tribunals would be little calculated to enhance the repute of British justice'.[20] Looking more closely at the Pondoland Annexation Act, Watson held that it did not give the Governor the power to make any new laws, such as one detaining Sigcau. As he put it, '[t]here is not a word in the Act to suggest that it was intended to make the governor a dictator, or even to clothe him with the full legislative powers of the Cape Parliament.' It allowed him only to introduce into the territory general laws which already existed in other parts of the colony. The scheme of the legislation was 'to delay the enactment of many salutary laws elsewhere prevailing throughout the Colony until the native inhabitants of the newly annexed territories had so far advanced in civilization and in social progress as to make the gradual introduction of these laws advisable'. That being so, the Governor had acted *ultra vires* in purporting to enact new legislation to detain Sigcau.[21] The case was widely reported in England,[22] and the Judicial Committee's decision was interpreted by many as a reaffirmation of the rule of law.[23]

---

[19] *Sprigg* v. *Sigcau* [1897] AC 238 at 246.   [20] *Sprigg* v. *Sigcau* [1897] AC 238 at 247.
[21] *Sprigg* v. *Sigcau* [1897] AC 238 at 247.
[22] 'An Illegal Proclamation', *The Standard*, 27 February 1897, p. 3; and *Morning Post*, 27 February 1897, p. 4. *The Spectator* noted that Watson 'spoke very strongly as to the illegality committed' (6 March 1897, p. 322).
[23] In December 1901, the Law Officers invoked this case as a contemporary illustration of Blackstone's comment that the law was 'benignly and liberally construed for the benefit of the subject': CO 885/15, quoting W. Blackstone, *Commentaries on the Laws of England*, 4 vols. (Oxford, Clarendon Press, 1765–1769), vol. 1, p. 134.

Watson's words also provided ammunition for those who sought to argue that colonial legislators did not have the power to pass 'autocratic' detention legislation which would by-pass an established system of civil and criminal procedure.[24] However, Watson's point that the proclamation would have been valid if it had derived from a lawfully delegated sovereign power did confirm that properly drawn legislation could confer draconian powers.

By the time that the Privy Council's judgment had been handed down, the Cape's Prime Minister Sir Gordon Sprigg no longer saw Sigcau as a threat,[25] and the government paid him £1,000 to settle a claim for false imprisonment.[26] The Cape ministry was less content, however, to leave the law as laid down by the Judicial Committee. After the decision, it introduced legislation 'to declare the powers of the Governor with reference to the Proclamation of Laws' in the Transkeian territories. This empowered the Governor by proclamation to authorise the summary arrest and detention of any person he considered dangerous to public peace for up to three months, and validated all proclamations purportedly issued hitherto under the Annexation Acts. In deference to the Judicial Committee's decision, the proclamation relating to Sigcau was the sole one exempted.[27] The proposal attracted strong parliamentary opposition from John X. Merriman and J. W. Sauer (who pointed out that Sigcau's release had not endangered the public peace),[28] but passed both houses.

In light of the decision in *Sprigg* v. *Sigcau*, the legislation was reserved by Governor Sir Alfred Milner for confirmation by the Secretary of State for the Colonies, Joseph Chamberlain, since it raised important questions of policy. Admitting that the measure was 'at variance with the principles which have been recognised in England for the protection of the liberty of the subject', the Cape government drew attention to the 'exceptional circumstances' which made it

---

[24] Montague Lush, arguing the case of Sekgoma Letsholathibe (discussed below), told the Court of Appeal that it would be 'congenial to our love, as a nation, of liberty and justice to act on the eloquent words of Lord Watson': CO 879/103/3, p. 236.
[25] *The Times*, 21 December 1896, p. 5.
[26] *Manchester Guardian*, 12 January 1899; and *Truth*, vol. 40 (12 January 1899), p. 141.
[27] Act 29 of 1879 (the text of which is in CO 879/51/5, Appendix, enc. in No. 1, p. 93).
[28] Quoted in David Welsh, 'The State President's Powers under the Bantu Administration Act', *Acta Juridica*, vol. 81 (1968), pp. 81–100 at p. 85.

necessary in the colonies: in the Transkeian territories, 'a handful of whites have settled down in the midst of an overwhelming mass of Kaffirs, who are but slowly emerging from barbarism ... and the power of the Chiefs, although gradually waning, is still a fact which has to be reckoned with.'[29] Milner recommended that the measure be assented to, explaining that '[t]here is a great difference – there is no use in blinking it – between British ideas as to the treatment of native races and Colonial ideas.'[30] The Law Officers also reported that there were no legal or constitutional objections to the measure which would make it improper for the Queen to assent to it: 'The necessity for the suspension of the Habeas Corpus Act, and for empowering the Governor to legislate, is a matter of which the Cape Parliament must judge.'[31] In contrast to de Villiers's approach, which raised a question over whether the Cape legislature could delegate a power to implement legislation violating the principles of English law, officials in England simply presumed such a power existed. For them, what de Villiers had seen as a constitutional question was viewed as a political question, which was best left in the hands of colonial responsible governments.

Sigcau's case was the first challenge to the lawfulness of *ad hominem* detention legislation. The chief's successful application reaffirmed that African subjects were accorded the same legal rights, associated with Magna Carta and the ancient constitution, of which Englishmen were so proud, even as they were denied those political rights which an increasingly large proportion of Englishmen were beginning to enjoy. At the same time, Lord Watson's judgment left room for those rights to be removed, provided that it could be shown that the powers exercised by the colonial legislature or Governor were validly delegated from the sovereign source. Starting with the Cape ministry itself, colonial authorities learned to be careful in drawing up legislation to empower detention. In turn, the courts would be asked whether such laws should be broadly or narrowly construed; and, as shall be seen in the cases of Sekgoma and Zaghlul, courts in London, animated by similar fears to those articulated by the Cape ministry, soon opted for the narrower, formal view.

---

[29] Minute, 30 June 1897, CO 879/51/5, Appendix, enc. in No. 1, p. 93.
[30] CO 879/51/5, Appendix, No. 1, p. 92.   [31] CO 879/51/5, Appendix, No. 3, at p. 96.

Sekgoma Letsholathibe

Whereas Sigcau's case came to the Privy Council in London, thanks to an appeal lodged and paid for by the Cape government, the second African case to reach the metropolis was brought by a detainee with the funding and support to bring his case directly before the English common law courts. The case was brought on behalf of Sekgoma Letsholathibe, the Tawana chief of the ruling tribe of Ngamiland, in the north-west of the Bechuanaland Protectorate.[32] Unlike Sigcau, whose territory had been annexed and become part of the Cape Colony, Sekgoma's homeland was in the constitutionally ambiguous position of some of the West African territories already encountered.

The British had declared a protectorate over Bechuanaland in January 1885, having in May 1884 entered into treaties with the chiefs of the Batlapins and Barolongs which conferred considerable powers – including the power to tax and pass laws – on the British.[33] These tribes had long sought protection, and the protectorate was proclaimed to prevent incursions from Boers from the South African Republic seeking land in these areas. In September 1885, the area of Bechuanaland south of the Molopo River was proclaimed to be part of British territory ('British Bechuanaland'), while the area to the north was to remain 'under Her Majesty's protection' (the 'Bechuanaland Protectorate').[34] British intervention in the protectorate was at first minimal, but in May 1891 a further Order in Council was issued, under the 1890 Foreign Jurisdiction Act.[35] This Order in Council made no reference to any particular treaties with African chiefs, but defined the area of the protectorate to extend to the Chobe and Zambezi Rivers. It conferred on the High Commissioner all powers which the Queen had 'within the limits of this Order'. It also empowered him to appoint administrators and magistrates and to

---

[32] On the Tawana, see A. Sillery, *The Bechuanaland Protectorate* (Oxford, Oxford University Press, 1952), ch. 14.

[33] The newly proclaimed protectorate, however, extended over a larger area than was occupied by these tribes. The Order in Council of 27 January 1885 is reproduced in PP 1885 (c. 4432) LVII. 359, enc. 1 in No. 1, p. 1. See W. Ross Johnston, *Sovereignty and Protection: A Study of British Jurisdictional Imperialism in the Late Nineteenth Century* (Durham, Duke University Press, 1973), pp. 150ff.

[34] Sillery, *The Bechuanaland Protectorate*, p. 58; and Johnston, *Sovereignty and Protection*, pp. 151ff.

[35] PP 1905 (130) LV. 7 at p. 6.

provide 'for the peace, order and good governance' of the protectorate by proclamation. The protectorate was thus in the same ambiguous position as a number of other African protectorates: although not annexed as a colony, British claims went beyond merely claiming a right to jurisdiction over British subjects by virtue of a treaty concession – the traditional view of a protectorate – to something which was closer to the general legislative and adjudicative powers of a sovereign, which was more in line with the continental view.

The Detention of Sekgoma

Sekgoma was the son of Chief Letsholathibe. On his death in 1874, Letsholathibe was succeeded by his son Moremi, who died in 1891 leaving a nine-year-old son, Mathiba. In 1895, Sekgoma became acting chief of the tribe with the support of the British, who told him that they would both recognise his authority over his country 'and will guarantee you in the possession of it'.[36] However, in 1905, his right to be chief was challenged by the supporters of Mathiba.[37] The immediate cause of the dispute was said to be Sekgoma's alleged ill-treatment of his wife, whom he accused of infidelity, though deeper political rivalries lay behind this apparently domestic quarrel.[38] In December 1905, his opponents petitioned for Sekgoma's removal, claiming that he had only been regent for Mathiba. The Resident Commissioner for Bechuanaland, Ralph Williams, was initially untroubled by this quarrel, but matters escalated after Sekgoma visited the colony in February on personal

---

[36] CO 879/53/6, enc. 2 in No. 137, p. 178.

[37] See J. M. Chirenje, 'Chief Sekgoma Letholathibe II: Rebel or 20th Century Tswana Nationalist?', *Botswana Notes and Records*, vol. 3 (1971), pp. 64–69; A. Sillery, 'Comments on Two Articles', *Botswana Notes and Records*, vol. 8 (1976), pp. 292–295; and J. M. Chirenje, 'Military and Political Aspects of Map-Making in Ngamiland: A Rejoinder to Anthony Sillery's Comment', *Botswana Notes and Records*, vol. 9 (1977), pp. 157–159. See also A. J. G. M. Sanders, 'Sekgoma Letsholathebe's Detention and the Betrayal of a Protectorate', *Comparative and International Law Journal of South Africa*, vol. 23 (1990), pp. 348–360.

[38] Sekgoma's wife was the niece of Chief Khama, while her alleged lover was the son of Dithapo, who was the prime petitioner against his rule. Sekgoma had quarrelled with Khama in 1900, and thought that he had been plotting his removal ever since: see F. B. Winter to Selborne, 29 April 1910: CO 417/483/20273, f. 40.

business.³⁹ In his absence, some members of his tribe sent for Mathiba to return and assume the chieftainship, whereupon Sekgoma's followers called him back to the tribe's capital, Tsau. Williams now began to fear a conflict, which might endanger white interests.⁴⁰ On his advice, the High Commissioner, Lord Selborne, decided that both Sekgoma and Mathiba should be kept away from their tribal homeland (the Batawana Reserve) pending an investigation into their respective claims. Sekgoma was met at Mafeking by two Bechuanaland policemen, and escorted into the protectorate. On 20 April 1906, a warrant was issued in Serowe (in the protectorate) to detain them both.

Two months later, an inquiry conducted by Williams in Tsau determined that Mathiba was the rightful chief.⁴¹ Mathiba was duly released and instructed to return to Tsau, while Sekgoma remained in detention in Gaberones, protesting at being deposed without a trial.⁴² As officials would soon discover, the legal basis for his detention was far from firm. Segkoma had been arrested under a simple warrant in Selborne's name, purportedly under the Expulsion of Filibusters Proclamation of 30 June 1891, which had been passed with the aim of removing disruptive Transvaal Boers from the protectorate. Selborne's advisers doubted whether Sekgoma could be properly dealt with under this legislation, and plans were made to replace it with a proclamation to authorise both Sekgoma's detention and his deportation. Influenced by his predecessor Lord Kitchener's proposal in 1901 to exile the troublesome Bakwena chief Sebele, Selborne wanted to remove Sekgoma from South Africa, preferably to the Seychelles.⁴³ To facilitate this, he repealed the 1891 proclamation and issued a new one on 14 September, which authorised him to order anyone he considered dangerous to the peace, order and good governance to leave the protectorate, and legalised the detention of anyone held within its provisions.⁴⁴

---

[39] He wanted to commence divorce proceedings and consult a doctor about suspected cancer. CO 879/91/1, enc. 1 in No. 26, p. 44; enc. in No 37, p. 64; enc. 1 in No. 50, p. 76.
[40] CO 879/91/1, enc. 3 in No. 50, p. 77.
[41] CO 879/91/1, enc. 1 in No. 139, p. 216; and Sir Ralph Williams, *How I Became a Governor* (London, John Murray, 1913), ch. 22.
[42] CO 879/91/1, enc. 1 in No. 147, p. 232.
[43] CO 879/91/1, No. 186, p. 340; for Sebele, see CO 879/69/2, No. 260, p. 373.
[44] CO 879/91/1, enc. in No. 188, p. 341.

In order to avoid sending Sekgoma through the Cape, whose court had freed Sigcau, plans were made to remove him via Southern Rhodesia and Beira.[45] However, these plans foundered on the opposition of the Secretary of State, for just as Chamberlain had vetoed Sebele's deportation to the Seychelles, so Elgin vetoed Sekgoma's. Elgin pointed to 'the obvious objections to the penal transportation of a man who has committed no offence and is subject to no condemnation, and whose power to disturb the public peace may prove to be of a transient character'.[46] Nor was he prepared to consent to Sekgoma's detention for any longer than was necessary for Mathiba 'to establish his position completely'.[47] Elgin also pointed out the legal flaws in Selborne's new proclamation: since it was worded in such a way as to apply only to those who had already been told to leave but had not yet done so, it did not apply to Sekgoma.[48] Given these flaws, Sekgoma's detention could only be seen as an act of state, without legal warrant, which meant that further legislation, including indemnity provisions, would have to be passed.[49] London accordingly sent a new proclamation – 'founded on the experience of other similar cases' – to authorise the detention specifically of Sekgoma,[50] which was issued by Selborne on 5 December 1906.

Two weeks before the new proclamation was issued, Sekgoma applied to the High Court in Kimberley to obtain his release, having served a summons on the new Resident Commissioner of Bechuanaland, Col. F. W. Panzera, as he passed through the town. Aware that the warrant under which Sekgoma had been detained was invalid, Panzera realised that it was 'necessary, *pro forma*, to quote some authority', and so he simply responded that Sekgoma was being held under a warrant issued by the High Commissioner on 2 April.[51] News of this action reached the Colonial Office too late to give any direct instructions on how to defend the action, but a telegram was sent

---

[45] CO 879/91/1, No. 194, p. 349 at p. 350.   [46] CO 879/91/1, No. 212, p. 364 at p. 365.
[47] CO 879/91/1, No. 205, p. 361.
[48] The legal advice Elgin received added that the proclamation permitted only the detention of such persons for three months from September 14: DO 119/778/3335/06.
[49] CO 879/91/1, No. 205, p. 361; No. 212, p. 364.
[50] CO 879/91/1 No. 212, p. 364 at p. 365.
[51] CO 879/91/1, enc. 6 in No. 236, p. 412.

signalling Elgin's approval of the conduct of his officials in respect of Sekgoma's detention. The careful wording was designed formally to ratify his detention as an act of state, and hence (if necessary) to put it beyond the court's jurisdiction, but without doing so overtly, given that the proceedings had already commenced.[52] This precaution turned out to be unnecessary, for Lange J accepted the crown's argument that this court in the Cape Colony had no jurisdiction to determine a case between a resident of the Bechuanaland Protectorate and its government. Since Sekgoma's own affidavit stated that he had only been arrested after he had entered the protectorate, Lange advised Sekgoma to appeal to the High Commissioner, and if necessary to the Privy Council.[53]

Over the next three years, Sekgoma remained in detention in a house in Gaberones, while the colonial authorities debated what was to be done with him. In March 1907, Sekgoma said he was willing to give up his claims to be chief, if he were allowed to move with his followers to another area, such as Barotseland.[54] Although Panzera was willing to entertain this proposal, Selborne rejected it, fearing that Sekgoma might return to Tsau, which might lead to bloodshed.[55] Mindful that it was both expensive and 'distasteful' to keep Sekgoma a prisoner, Selborne suggested in January 1908 that he might be allowed to live (under a proclamation) elsewhere in southern Africa, such as Nyasaland.[56] However, this proposal was again vetoed by Elgin, who opposed any removal which was not entirely voluntary, and who reminded Selborne that the chief was to be detained only until Mathiba was fully established.[57] This was not, however, an imminent prospect, for, as Panzera put it, Mathiba was 'more imbued with the characteristics of a lady missionary than those of a ruler'.[58]

In March 1908, the acting magistrate at Tsau, Lt. H. D. Hannay, detained four of Sekgoma's followers, having intercepted a letter

---

[52] See the minutes of Cox and Graham on this in CO 417/425/43031, f. 601, seeking to apply the rule in *Buron* v. *Denman* (1848) 2 Ex. 166.
[53] *Sekgome Letsholathebe* v. *Panzera* (1906) 10 Griqualand High Court Reports 90.
[54] CO 879/95/4, enc. 1 in No. 95, p. 139.
[55] Elgin agreed, though he wanted the question revisited 'a year or so hence'. CO 879/95/4, No. 95, p. 138; No. 100, p. 143; No. 119, p. 192.
[56] CO 879/98/1, No. 14, p. 20. The cost of keeping him at Gaberones was £756 per annum, whereas he could be given an annuity (as other chiefs had been) of £300.
[57] CO 879/98/1, No. 30, p. 57.   [58] CO 879/98/1, enc. 3 in No. 101, p. 179.

purportedly from Sekgoma, ordering them to go to Portuguese territory, where he would join them.[59] This led officials once again to contemplate removing Sekgoma, whose continued presence in Bechuanaland was now considered to be disruptive.[60] At the same time, Sekgoma promised that, if he were released, he would report weekly to the Resident Commissioner at Mafeking and would not enter the protectorate without permission.[61] Panzera was keen to take up this offer, and move the chief to the Cape or Basutoland, but Selborne was not prepared to trust to Sekgoma's good will, and repeated his earlier proposal to deport him to the Seychelles via Beira.[62] Once again, he was rebuffed, for the new Secretary of State, the Earl of Crewe, was reluctant to bring a bill before parliament to allow his transportation over the seas, and thought it likely in its absence that Sekgoma's legal advisers would bring a writ of habeas corpus.[63] In Crewe's opinion, he would simply have to be held on parole elsewhere in South Africa, whatever the risks of his escape. As a result of these discussions, Sekgoma was offered a farm in the Barberton District of Transvaal.[64]

Although initially keen on accepting this offer, Sekgoma suddenly changed his mind at the beginning of March 1909, telling Acting Resident Commissioner Barry May that 'I wish to have my case tried before the Courts in England or else to be killed.'[65] What prompted his change of mind was the settlement of a dispute over his property, which freed funds to allow his case to be taken to London. When it came to dealing with Segkoma's rights to property, the authorities showed themselves to be much more legally punctilious than they were in dealing with his liberty. After his detention, the authorities had valued Sekgoma's assets in Ngamiland at 240 cattle, 176 sheep and goats, a handful of other

[59] CO 879/98/1, in enc. 1 in No. 66, p. 115. They were removed from the Twana Reserve to Quagganaai, using powers under Proclamation No. 15 of 1907, where they were detained until June 1909: CO 879/98/1, No. 98, p. 169, with enclosures; CO 879/102/1, enc. 1 in No. 171, p. 234.
[60] CO 879/98/1, enc. 1. in No. 52, p. 83.
[61] CO 879/98/1, in enc. 1 in No. 101, p. 178; enc. 1 in No. 68, p. 126.
[62] CO 879/98/1, enc. 1 in No. 101; enc. 2 in No. 101, p. 179; No. 102, p. 183.
[63] CO 879/98/1, No. 129, p. 217.   [64] CO 879/102/1, No. 47, p. 74.
[65] CO 879/102/1, in enc. 2 in No. 78, p. 109.

animals and £88 in cash.⁶⁶ They at first considered appointing a *curator bonis* to manage this property while Sekgoma was in detention, but found that the Resident Commissioner's court had no power to do so. Plans to legislate to allow the appointment of a *curator bonis* for a detainee then stalled when Elgin objected that such powers were suitable only for managing the property of convicted prisoners.⁶⁷ They became redundant when at the beginning of 1908 Sekgoma gave a power of attorney to Charles Riley, a man of mixed race, who had lived in the protectorate for twenty-six years and who would be Sekgoma's dogged champion over the next four years. Riley also took up Sekgoma's claims to a much larger number of cattle in Ngamiland, and signalled his intention to commence proceedings for this property in the Assistant Commissioner's Court in Francistown. The prospect of these proceedings alarmed the authorities, given that it might require the presence in court both of Sekgoma and of many witnesses from distant Tsau.⁶⁸ A proclamation was therefore passed to empower a special commissioner's court to hear any disputes concerning Sekgoma's property at Tsau.⁶⁹ At these hearings, Sekgoma's agent laid claim to over 8,500 head of cattle, title to many of which depended on his right as chief. In the end, he was awarded only 1,260 head of cattle claimed,⁷⁰ to add to the 637 cattle which Riley had already recovered in the Acting Commissioner's court. If the award was less than Sekgoma had anticipated, it nevertheless provided valuable assets which could be used to fund his challenges to his continued detention.

With funds available, Riley proposed to go to London, along with the editor of the *Mafeking Mail*, G. N. H. Whales, to put the matter of Sekgoma's incarceration before the British public.⁷¹ Meanwhile, negotiations over a possible relocation continued. By now, May had come to the view that the two Tawana factions would never be reconciled, and that Selborne's attempt to confer all power on

---

⁶⁶ CO 879/95/4, enc. 5 in No. 44, p. 74. At the same time, there were claims of some £848 against him.
⁶⁷ CO 879/95/4, enc. 6 in No. 44, p. 75; No. 58, p. 87; No. 60, p. 88; No. 111, p. 153.
⁶⁸ CO 879/98/1, No. 22, p. 42; enc. 1 in No. 39, p. 66.
⁶⁹ Proclamation 20 of 1908: CO 879/98/1, enc. in No. 46, p. 77; No. 47, p. 78.
⁷⁰ CO 879/102/1, enc. in No. 42, p. 64.   ⁷¹ CO 879/102/1, enc. 1 in No. 70.

Mathiba had prevented the kind of tribal secession which was natural in Tswana society. He therefore proposed allowing Sekgoma and his followers to settle elsewhere in the region.[72] May met Riley in Mafeking, and discussed the possibility of relocating Sekgoma and his followers on land to the north of the Molopo River, but found Riley unwilling to enter into any commitments until he had returned from England. Selborne suggested, uncharitably, that Riley and Whales, who were on the verge of bankruptcy, simply wanted to travel at the chief's expense; more charitably, May suggested that Riley did not think he could advise Sekgoma to accept the offer of land on the inhospitable Molopo until he had exhausted all other options.[73] On 7 April, Riley and Whales sailed to London, along with Sekgoma's secretary, Kebalepile, to put their case before the British public.

Meanwhile, officials in London were confident that they had put themselves in a strong position if any question were raised in parliament. As Lambert minuted, having made two offers – of land in the Transvaal for Sekgoma himself, or territory near the Molopo where he could take his followers – the government could 'say that he is alone responsible for our having to keep him in detention at Gaberones to prevent his setting part of the Protectorate a blaze, and the sooner Messrs Riley & Whales are made to understand that they are wasting S's money in vain the better for Sekgoma'.[74] With the Colonial Office digging in its heels, at the beginning of September, Riley instructed solicitors to commence proceedings against Selborne – then in London – both for damages for false imprisonment and for a writ of habeas corpus. By the time the documents were ready to serve on the High Commissioner, however, he was on a ship bound for South Africa.[75] In his absence, the decision was taken to commence proceedings against the Earl of Crewe.

The Litigation in the King's Bench Division and the Court of Appeal

Sekgoma's application for a habeas corpus was filed in October 1909. In his answering affidavit, Crewe stated that Bechuanaland was

---

[72] CO 879/102/1, enc. 1 in No. 81. [73] CO 879/102/1, No. 84, p. 120; enc. in No. 95, p. 133.
[74] Minute by Lambert, 6 May 1909, CO 417/466/15267, f. 58.
[75] F. B. Winter to Crewe, 6 September 1909, T1/11299.

a foreign country, where the crown had jurisdiction by virtue of the Foreign Jurisdiction Act; that Sekgoma was lawfully detained by virtue of the proclamation of December 1906; and that his detention was an act of state which could not be questioned by the court. He also submitted that he did not himself have custody of Sekgoma and that in any event no writ of habeas corpus could run into this foreign territory. Against this, Sekgoma's lawyers took the view that Sigcau's case had established that a proclamation such as this was 'absolutely illegal', and that the African chief had a right to a habeas.[76]

In the Divisional Court, the judges saw two obstacles in the way of Sekgoma's application. The first obstacle related to the court's power to issue the writ. Chief Justice Lord Alverstone agreed that, if the protectorate were a foreign country, then the court would have no jurisdiction. However, in view of the fact that no court had yet determined 'the exact position of these Protectorates', and given that Sekgoma had been described as a British subject in Panzera's original affidavit in Kimberley, he was prepared to assume that Bechuanaland was a British dominion. Nonetheless, Alverstone held that Sekgoma was still debarred from seeking the writ in London: since, in his view, there were courts in the protectorate – set up under the Proclamation of 11 February 1896 – which could issue the writ, his application was barred by the 1862 Habeas Corpus Act, which enacted that no English court could issue the writ to a colony or 'foreign dominion' whose courts had the power to issue it. Instead of seeking his remedy in Westminster, Sekgoma should have gone to the Assistant Commissioner's court in Bechuanaland, and appealed from there to the Privy Council.[77] The second obstacle related to the choice of the Earl of Crewe as defendant. On this issue, the court held that the Secretary of State had neither custody of Sekgoma nor control of his gaoler. Since his only power was to advise the crown, he was not a suitable recipient of the writ.[78] This was, in fact, a rather artificial view to take: not only had Lord Crewe monitored all the negotiations with Sekgoma's representatives, but he was also the man who took the final decisions. Indeed, when preparing for the case in September, the

---

[76] This was Montague Lush's view, as expressed in the Court of Appeal: CO 879/103/3, p. 72.
[77] 'Proceedings', CO 879/103/3, pp. 66–67.   [78] 'Proceedings', CO 879/103/3, pp. 63–69.

Colonial Office itself took the view that Crewe was the appropriate defendant.[79]

This court did not pronounce a judgment on the substantive question of the validity of the proclamation, though it was evident that the judges were sympathetic to Sekgoma's position on this point. Had the procedural points not got in the way, Alverstone indicated, the court would have granted the writ, since he felt that the question of the *vires* of the proclamation could not be settled merely on affidavits, but might require a special case.[80] He added that a proclamation providing for the detention of a particular individual was 'a very serious step indeed', which could be justified only by showing 'paramount authority recognised as being lawful'. In his view, such a provision would be impossible in any part of the British dominions where there was constitutional government, and could exist only in such places where no laws had been laid down by the crown and where no local law could deal with the matter.[81] Justice Darling, in his concurring judgment, added that the proclamation could not be seen as an act of state, but was a legal instrument whose validity could be questioned by the court. 'I am very much inclined to think', he concluded, that the proclamation 'does exceed the powers conferred upon the High Commissioner.'[82]

As Riley headed back to South Africa, optimistic of ultimate success, officials in London made preparations for the appeal, seeking a determination that would show that Sekgoma had no remedy in any imperial court. They were particularly keen to challenge the argument that Sekgoma was entitled to the rights of a subject. When asked about Panzera's affidavit describing him as a subject, Selborne replied that it had been drafted with 'imperfect legal knowledge', and connoted only that the chief was born within the limits of the area proclaimed a protectorate in 1885.[83] Legal advice was obtained from the India Office that no decision had ever been taken on the status of residents in the protected states, and notice was also taken of a Law Officers' opinion that they were not British subjects.[84] Evidence was

---

[79] As on official put it, 'the detention is clearly being continued with his authority'. Minute, 14 September 1909, T 1/11299.
[80] 'Proceedings', CO 879/103/3, pp. 38, 63.   [81] 'Proceedings', CO 879/103/3, p. 65.
[82] 'Proceedings', CO 879/103/3, p. 69.
[83] Selborne to Colonial Office, 5 January 1910, CO 417/481/642, f. 55.
[84] A. J. Hare to Cox, 4 January 1910, CO 417/481/642, f. 52.

marshalled from treaties of protection and Orders in Council to establish that Africans in protected states were not British subjects.[85] Officials also looked for precedents in case law. For Bertram Cox, 'Our real sheet anchor is Staples v R if we can only get our counsel to read the shorthand notes.'[86]

Cox's reference was to an unreported case which went to the Privy Council in 1899, in which a British settler challenged his conviction for theft by the High Court of Matabeleland, which had no jury. Staples claimed that as a British subject, he had carried the rights of Magna Carta with him, and that these rights had been violated by the Matabeleland Order in Council which had been issued under the Foreign Jurisdiction Act. No formal decision had been handed down in this case, but the Colonial Office obtained a memorandum on the grounds of Privy Council's report, advising the Queen to reject the appeal. This memorandum – probably drafted by Lord Halsbury – related that Matabaleland was a foreign country, much like the Indian princely states which remained for important purposes foreign states whose subjects were not British. In places such as this, by virtue of the Foreign Jurisdiction Act, the crown had 'absolute power to say what law should be applied, as if it was by absolute conquest'. Although section 12 of the Act limited this absolute power by disallowing any orders 'repugnant to the provisions of any Act of Parliament extending to Her Majesty's subjects in that country', this did not refer to acts such as Magna Carta but only to legislation which 'applied in some special way to British subjects in the foreign country in question'. In the view of the committee, '[i]t would be a most unreasonable limit on the Crown's power of introducing laws fitting to the circumstances of its subjects in a foreign country if it were made impossible to modify any Act of Parliament which prior to the Order in Council might be invoked as applicable to a British subject.'[87]

---

[85] They pointed to Protection treaties, such as that with Zanzibar, which distinguished between British subjects and subjects of the Sultan: minute by Cox, 8 January 1910, CO 417/481/642; cf. E. Hertslet, *The Map of Africa by Treaty*, vol. 2 (London, HMSO, 1894), p. 769.

[86] Minute from Cox, 9 January 1910, CO 417/481/642, f. 51.

[87] *The Queen* v. *Staples*: Report of Proceedings before the Judicial Committee of the Privy Council 27 January 1899 and Memorandum of Reasons for the decision of the committee, CO 879/103/2, p. 3; last passage quoted by Farwell LJ, *Ex parte Sekgome*, p. 615.

Unlike the lower court, the Court of Appeal directly addressed the substantive issue of the validity of the proclamation, for it disagreed with the Divisional Court on the two procedural points. On the jurisdictional point, Sekgoma's counsel, Montague Lush, carefully demonstrated that the Bechuanaland courts did not have the superior court power to issue the writ.[88] On the point as to whether the Secretary of State was the right defendant, it was clear that the judges did not wish this point to get in the way of their determining the larger question.[89] The central question for the court to consider was hence that of the validity of the proclamation. At issue were the powers of the High Commissioner under the Order in Council of 1891. The crown's argument was that the king had absolute power in ceded or conquered territories, which (thanks to the Foreign Jurisdiction Act) Bechuanaland was deemed to be,[90] and that these powers could be delegated. Sekgoma's lawyers questioned this by arguing that the crown's powers were constitutionally limited. In so arguing, Lush invoked Lord Mansfield's dictum in *Campbell* v. *Hall*, that 'a country conquered by the British arms becomes a dominion of the King in the right of his Crown' and hence subject to parliament. While the king alone had the power to introduce new laws in such places, 'this legislation being subordinate [...] to his own authority in Parliament, he cannot make any new change contrary to fundamental principles'.[91] Furthermore, any rights the king had as a conqueror were given up when he set up a constitution and laws for the conquered or ceded land, as had been done when the system of courts was set up in Bechuanaland under the 1896 proclamation. Lush also challenged the idea that Bechuanaland was a 'foreign' territory to which the writ could not run. Since the crown had set up a system of government in Bechuanaland, it enjoyed *dominium* to all intents and purposes, which meant that the chief was entitled to the rights of Britons, including habeas corpus.

---

[88] *Ex parte Sekgome*, p. 591.
[89] CO 879/103/3, pp. 100–101; *Ex parte Sekgome*, p. 592 (Vaughan Williams LJ); p. 606 (Farwell LJ); p. 618 (Kennedy LJ, who disagreed, thinking Selborne should have been the defendant).
[90] CO 879/103/3, p. 143.
[91] *Campbell* v. *Hall* (1774) 1 Cowper 204 at 208–209. Cf. Joseph Chitty, *A Treatise on the Law of the Prerogatives of the Crown* (London, Joseph Butterworth & Son, 1820), p. 29.

Lush further argued that the powers conferred on the High Commissioner under the Order in Council were not arbitrary. To begin with, a crown whose own powers were constitutionally limited could not confer greater powers on its delegates than it enjoyed itself. Furthermore, under section 12 of the Foreign Jurisdiction Act, the crown had no power to issue an Order in Council repugnant to the Star Chamber Act of 1641, which Lush considered to fall within the Act's definition of legislation 'extending to the subjects of the Crown in that country'. As to the Bechuanaland Order in Council itself, section 2 stipulated that the High Commissioner could take only such actions as were 'lawful', which Lush contended meant lawful according to wider constitutional principles, which in turn placed a limit on his power to provide for peace, order and good government. While Lush did not deny that parliament had the power to legislate in an arbitrary way – as Lord Watson had conceded in Sigcau's case – he argued that a close examination of the instruments would reveal that this was not the case here.[92]

In answer, Sidney Rowlatt argued that the king was a constitutional monarch only in those dominions where constitutional government had been set up.[93] To dislodge Lord Mansfield's point that the crown's own power was limited by fundamental law, he argued that the rule from *Campbell v. Hall* had been clarified and modified by the Colonial Laws Validity Act of 1865, which was itself echoed in section 12 of the Foreign Jurisdiction Act. Invoking *R. v. Staples*, he argued that by virtue of this legislation, the crown's legislative capacity in the colonies was bound only by imperial legislation 'extending to the colony' or 'Her Majesty's subjects' in the jurisdiction in question. The crown's legislative powers in these areas were as extensive as those which had been conferred on colonial assemblies. To show the extent of these powers, he invoked *Phillips v. Eyre*,[94] where the Exchequer Chamber had recognised the power of the Jamaican legislature to pass an indemnity act after the Morant Bay rebellion, which qualified the feted 'fundamental laws'. Countering Lush's argument that the High Commissioner's powers to legislate for

---

[92] 'Proceedings', CO 879/103/3, p. 92 (in the Court of Appeal), p. 35 (in the Divisional Court).
[93] 'Proceedings', CO 879/103/3, p. 41 (in the Divisional Court).
[94] *Phillips v. Eyre* (1869) LR 4 QB 225; (1870) LR 6 QB 1.

peace, order and good government were limited, he also cited the 1885 Privy Council decision in *Riel* v. *the Queen*, in which Lord Halsbury held that similar words in the British North America Act conferred 'the utmost discretion' on the Canadian legislature, and empowered it (and similar legislatures) to pass laws which authorised 'the widest departure from criminal procedure as it is known and practised in this country'.[95]

All three of the judges in the Court of Appeal agreed in dismissing Segkoma's application. The clearest judgment was given by Lord Justice Farwell. He began by noting that the 'solution of the present case' was to be found in the fact that the despotic powers claimed by the crown in Bechuanaland derived not from the royal prerogative, but from the legislature, through the 1890 Act.[96] Turning to the question of whether these powers were limited by any 'fundamental law', Farwell drew on Willes J's comment in *Phillips* v. *Eyre* that this expression could connote either repugnancy to an imperial statute which applied to the colony or repugnancy 'to some principle of natural justice, the violation of which would induce the Court to decline giving effect even to the law of a foreign sovereign State'.[97] Answering Lush's argument that legislation directed against an individual was against natural justice, he cited Willes's view that the question of whether particular steps had to be taken to ensure the safety of the state was a political question for the legislator, not a judicial one. Farwell accepted Rowlatt's argument that the Colonial Laws Validity Act (and consequently the Foreign Jurisdiction Act) had in effect taken the place of Lord Mansfield's principle.[98] While he agreed that certain imperial acts could not be repealed by an Order in Council – such as the Slave Trade Act of 1843, which declared that it applied to 'British subjects wheresoever residing' – he held that the Star Chamber Act did not so apply. His reasons for taking this line were entirely political: 'The truth is that in countries inhabited by native tribes who largely outnumber the white population such acts, although bulwarks of liberty in the United Kingdom, might, if applied there, well prove the death warrant of the whites.' Principles which were

---

[95] *Riel* v. *the Queen* (1885) 10 App. Cas. 675 at 678.
[96] *Ex parte Sekgome*, pp. 611–612.
[97] *Phillips* v. *Eyre* (1870) LR 6 QB 1 at 20.   [98] 'Proceedings', CO 879/103/3, p. 174.

admirable when applied in 'an ancient well-ordered State' would be 'ruinous when applied to semi-savage tribes'.[99] On the further question of the extent of the High Commissioner's power to issue proclamations under the Order in Council, Farwell accepted Rowlatt's broad conception of these powers. For Farwell, the Foreign Jurisdiction Act was the crucial empowering legislation, for in his view, without such empowering legislation, the crown could not of itself authorise the acts complained of.

In his judgment, Farwell accepted Lush's contention that Sekgoma was a British subject, since the 1890 Act appeared to confer jurisdiction only over Her Majesty's subjects resident in foreign countries. By contrast, neither Vaughan Williams LJ nor Kennedy LJ regarded Sekgoma as a subject. While disagreeing with the position taken in W. E. Hall's treatise on the *Foreign Powers and Jurisdiction of the British Crown* that the Foreign Jurisdiction Act applied only to subjects,[100] Vaughan Williams thought that, if it did not apply, then the detention of Sekgoma could still be seen as an act of state, beyond the remit of the courts.[101] In Kennedy's view, even if Hall's interpretation of the act was correct, the crown still had a separate prerogative power to issue the Order in Council in any 'barbarous and unsettled territory' under British protection.[102] Unlike Farwell, Kennedy was thus prepared to accept that the crown had unlimited prerogative powers in some contexts. Notwithstanding their doubts about the reach of the Act, both these judges also derived the High Commissioner's powers from parliamentary authorisation. Vaughan Williams LJ admitted that his greatest doubts in the case derived from the fact that what was in effect a proclamation of the outlawry of an individual had been issued without any regard to earlier laws dealing with dangerous persons. Nonetheless, he accepted that the High Commissioner had the full legal discretion to issue such a proclamation under section 4 of the Order in Council.[103]

---

[99] *Ex parte Sekgome*, pp. 614–616.
[100] W. E. Hall, *A Treatise on the Foreign Powers and Jurisdiction of the British Crown* (Oxford, Clarendon Press, 1894), p. 221.
[101] *Ex parte Sekgome*, p. 596.
[102] *Ex parte Sekgome* p. 626, citing Hall, *A Treatise on the Foreign Powers*, pp. 224–225.
[103] *Ex parte Sekgome*, p. 604.

The Colonial Office was acutely aware of the importance of the case. As Lambert told Cox a week before the judgment was handed down, 'the Sekgome case involves the very basis of our administration in this & all Protectorates & we cannot afford to lose it, whether we look to the danger of tribal war among the Batawana, or the legal difficulties in every country administered under the Foreign Jurisdiction Act.'[104] They were well rewarded for the wait. In coming to its conclusion, the court did far more than justify the detention of Sekgome, who might have been portrayed simply as a foreign ruler held by virtue of an act of state. The decision recognised an open-ended legislative power for the crown in the protectorates, uncontrolled by broader common law principles. Taking a very formalistic view of the rule of law, the Court of Appeal traced the kind of sovereign powers which Lord Watson had said in Sigcau's case would be needed to authorise the kind of legislation under which Sekgome was detained from the Foreign Jurisdiction Act. This was a very slender base for such large power. The Foreign Jurisdiction Act had been drafted to deal with the extraterritorial jurisdiction of the crown over its subjects resident in foreign territories, and not to define its constitutional position in protectorates where it now sought to establish systems of government which local rulers were bound to obey. There was nothing in the words of the act to suggest that it was meant to apply to non-subjects, nor did it appear to confer general legislative powers over such people to the crown.

In deciding on the ambit of the crown's powers here, the judges relied on *R. v. Staples*, a case which was concerned with the much narrower question of whether an individual British subject carried all his common law rights into a foreign country in which the crown had extraterritorial jurisdiction. The judges' expansive interpretation of the act echoed the increasingly expansive view taken of protectorates at that moment. The words of the Order in Council were also broadly interpreted, with the judges taking the view that the limitation of the High Commissioner's powers to do such things as were 'lawful' was qualified only by section 12 of the 1890 Act. Similarly, the very broad discretionary powers conferred by the Order in Council on the High Commissioner were regarded as the equivalent of the legislative

---

[104] Lambert to Cox, 19 April 1910, CO 417/482/11600, f. 157.

powers of the parliament of Canada. This contrasted strongly with the approach taken by Chief Justice de Villiers in interpreting the ambit of delegated powers in Sigcau's case. De Villiers's distinction between legislative and judicial powers was not remarked upon by the judges in this case. Lush did try to invoke Lord Watson's judgment in support of his view that the High Commissioner could not be seen to have the despotic powers of an absolute sovereign, but with little effect. As Farwell LJ observed during argument, '[t]he actual decision was only on the construction of the Pondoland Annexation Act, and the reasons given were rather contrary to the general ideas.'[105]

Aftermath

The Court of Appeal's decision was informed in part by a sense of the imminent danger to the handful of white traders in Ngamiland were Sekgoma to be accorded the rights of an Englishman. Yet it was clear by then that the Colonial Office no longer regarded the chief as any kind of threat. At the same time that court proceedings were in progress, Riley was continuing to negotiate a settlement. He returned to Mafeking after the habeas hearings in the King's Bench Division, and consulted Sekgoma. Riley now advised the chief to accept any reasonable offer, but, as a back-up, he proposed further litigation, including an appeal from the adverse decision and an action of false imprisonment against Selborne.[106] In March 1910, Segkoma asked for a reserve on the Molopo River (as already proposed by the government) as well as an annuity of £150 and a *solatium* of £5,000 in settlement of all his claims against the government.[107] However, the government remained reluctant to release Sekgoma until it was sure that his troublesome followers would leave Ngamiland. They also baulked at the demand for £5,000, which Selborne regarded as a ruse by the 'unscrupulous and penniless adventurers' who had supported Sekgoma to extract more money.[108] Panzera agreed, telling High Commissioner Herbert Gladstone, '[t]he belief that a half breed like Mr Riley could force the hand of the Government would be a serious

---

[105] 'Proceedings', CO 879/103/3, p. 183.   [106] CO 879/104/2, No. 28, p. 27.
[107] CO 879/104/2, enc. in No. 53; No. 28, p. 48.
[108] CO 879/104/2, No. 52, p. 44 at p. 46; enc. 2 in No. 58, p. 53.

blow to our prestige and dignity.'[109] In the end, the government agreed to pay a settlement of £2,000 and released Sekgoma in March 1911. The question of where to resettle Sekgoma continued to be debated over the next three years, with matters being complicated when the authorities found they had underestimated the size of his following. At the time of his death in January 1914,[110] plans were already being made for his followers to return to the Batawana Reserve, which could be divided between his followers and Mathiba's.[111]

Saad Zaghlul Pasha

Sekgoma's case determined that colonial authorities could make use of general delegated powers to legislate for the peace, order and good government of a territory to pass *ad hominem* laws to detain particular individuals indefinitely without trial. The Court of Appeal did not attempt to interpret such legislation narrowly, in order to make it consistent with the wider principles of the common law, but held that, where a formal line of valid authority could be traced from statute to proclamation, the rule of law had been complied with. It would take another decade before judges in London had to consider the lawfulness of a detention ordinance involving another African, where the legislation had been passed not under statutory powers, but by virtue of the prerogative. The litigation in question arose from the other end of Africa, and involved a much-higher-profile detainee, the Egyptian nationalist leader Saad Zaghlul Pasha. As in Sekgoma's case, the question of whether to continue the detainee's detention remained a political one which was more contested than the court perceived; and, as in Sekgoma's case, the court's reading of the law proved very friendly to the executive.

Zaghlul's Campaign for Egyptian Independence

Although the British had exercised *de facto* control since 1882, Egypt remained *de jure* a part of the Ottoman empire until the beginning of

---

[109] Panzera to Gladstone, 24 February 1911, T 1/11299.   [110] CO 879/114/5, No. 8, p. 5.
[111] CO 879/114/5, No. 11, p. 7. See further CO 879/113/1, No. 14, p. 24; No. 21, p. 40; No. 26, p. 48; No. 33, p. 59; No. 39, p. 64; No. 46, p. 70 (and all enclosures therein).

the First World War. In December 1914, Egypt was declared a British protectorate, one month after the Ottomans had joined the war and martial law had been proclaimed. Remembering many promises made since 1882 that Britain had no ambitions to annex Egypt, Egyptian politicians assumed that the protectorate would be temporary only. By 1918, there were also high expectations that President Woodrow Wilson's declaration that the nations under Ottoman rule should be given the opportunity of autonomous development would be acted on to secure Egyptian independence. In the same week that the armistice was signed, a delegation – or *Wafd* – visited the British High Commissioner in Cairo, Sir Reginald Wingate, to put the nationalist claim. It was led by Saad Zaghlul Pasha. Zaghlul was a man of long political experience. Born in July 1858, he had been a journalist, a judge and a government minister, acting first as Education Minister and then as Minister of Justice. Having resigned the post in 1912, he was elected to the Legislative Assembly in the following year, becoming its vice-president.[112] Zaghlul's request in 1918 to be allowed to go to London to put forward the case for Egyptian independence was rejected by the Foreign Office, which considered Egypt far from ready for self-government.[113] In response, Zaghlul and his newly formed political party, *al-Wafd al-Misri* organised a mass campaign in favour of independence.[114]

Zaghlul proved to be a thorn in the side of the British administration, which soon took steps against what was considered

---

[112] See C. W. R. Long, *British Pro-Consuls in Egypt, 1914–1929: The Challenge of Nationalism* (Abingdon, RoutledgeCurzon, 2005), pp. 177–181; Afaf Lutfi Sayyid-Marsot, *Egypt's Liberal Experiment, 1922–36* (Berkeley, University of California Press, 1977), ch. 2; and James Whidden, 'The Generation of 1919', in Arthur Goldschmidt, Amy J. Johnson and Barak A. Salmoni (eds.), *Re-envisioning Egypt 1919–1952* (Cairo and New York, American University in Cairo Press, 2005), pp. 19–45. See also 'Outline of Saad Pasha Zaghlul's career as a nationalist leader, more particularly since the Proclamation of the British Protectorate over Egypt on December 18, 1914', TS 27/17a.

[113] FO 407/183, No. 142, p. 213; No. 144, p. 214; No. 146, p. 215. See also M. Daly, 'The British Occupation, 1882–1922', in M. W. Daly (ed.), *The Cambridge History of Egypt: Volume 2: Modern Egypt, from 1517 to the End of the Twentieth Century* (Cambridge, Cambridge University Press, 1998), pp. 239–251.

[114] On this party, see Marius Deeb, *Party Politics in Egypt: The Wafd and Its Rivals* (London, Ithaca Press, 1979); and Janice J. Terry, *The Wafd 1919–1952: Cornerstone of Egyptian Political Power* (London, Third World Centre for Research and Publishing, 1982).

to be his campaign of intimidation. After he had presented a petition designed to pressure the Sultan,[115] the Foreign Office authorised his removal (under martial law powers) to Malta, where Egyptian political prisoners were already being detained under wartime legislation along with enemy aliens and prisoners of war.[116] The deportation of Zaghlul and three others on 9 March 1919 proved to be a political miscalculation, for it was followed by riots and demonstrations in Egypt, which served only to add strength to the nationalist movement. General Sir Edmund Allenby, who was sent to Egypt as Special High Commissioner in March with instructions to put the government on a 'secure and equitable basis', realised that concessions would have to be made to the nationalists.[117] Zaghlul was freed from detention, and proceeded immediately to Paris, where he intended to put Egypt's case to the post-war peace conference. Although he was denied the opportunity to do this, Zaghlul remained in Paris, keeping the case of Egypt in the public mind, by lobbying politicians and giving press interviews.

The 'Revolution of 1919' which followed the deportations forced the British government to rethink its policy.[118] In May, the decision was taken to send a special mission to Egypt, headed by Lord Milner, to inquire into the disturbances and report on 'the form of the Constitution which, under the Protectorate, will be best calculated to promote its peace and prosperity'.[119] When the Mission finally arrived in December, it received a hostile reception from the nationalist movement, which had called for a boycott. In this climate, Milner realised that he needed to engage with Zaghlul's *Wafd* party, which had gained a complete 'ascendancy over the Egyptian public'. Although Zaghlul could not be persuaded to meet the Mission in

---

[115] FO 407/184, enc. in No. 74, p. 62.
[116] Malta's Ordinance XX of 1914 gave the governor additional powers to secure public safety during the war. For wartime internment, see Matthew Stibbe, *Civilian Internment during the First World War: A European and Global History, 1914–1920* (London, Palgrave MacMillan, 2019); and Stefan Manz and Panikos Panayi, *Enemies in the Empire: Civilian Internment in the British Empire during the First World War* (Oxford, Oxford University Press, 2020).
[117] Peter Mansfield and Nicolas Pelham, *A History of the Middle East*, 5th ed. (Harmondsworth, Penguin, 2019), p. 199.
[118] See Long, *British Pro-Consuls in Egypt*, pp. 105–119.
[119] FO 407/184, No. 304, p. 255 at p. 256.

Egypt, he and seven other *Wafd* representatives went to London in June 1920 to negotiate with Milner.[120] These negotiations resulted in a memorandum, which came to be known as the Milner–Zaghlul Agreement. It envisaged a treaty being signed in which Great Britain would recognise the independence of Egypt as a constitutional monarchy, and in which Egypt would allow a British military force to remain in the country and officials to be appointed to protect foreign interests.

The 'agreement' was incomplete, for the parties remained at odds over a number of important questions, including the nature of the British military presence in Egypt. Although Zaghlul wanted to re-open some questions, Milner saw no purpose in any further discussions, since the 'agreement' was no more than a basis for future negotiations.[121] However, after Milner's report was published in February 1921, the British government proposed further consultations with an official delegation to be named by the Sultan. This delegation was to be made up of conservative nationalists, including Adli Yakan Pasha, who had acted as an intermediary with Zaghlul in the previous year, and who would become Prime Minister in March. Adli wanted to include Zaghlul in the delegation, and entered into negotiations with the *Wafd* leader to secure this. However, Zaghlul demanded too high a price for his participation: not only did he insist on the lifting of martial law and an assurance regarding the end of the protectorate, but he also wanted to lead a *Wafd*-dominated delegation. Since Zaghlul's demands were acceptable neither to the British nor to Adli,[122] he would form no part of the delegation.

Zaghlul spent the rest of the summer actively campaigning against Adli's delegation. He put his case before the British press, telling *The Times* that, if negotiations failed, 'Egypt will fight England in the same way as Ireland.'[123] Zaghlul's case was also publicised in parliament by a friendly group of Labour MPs.[124] In the middle of September, four of

---

[120] See PP 1921 (Cd. 1131) XLII. 629; and Long, *British Pro-Consuls in Egypt*, pp. 113–115.
[121] FO 407/187, No. 326, p. 273.
[122] FO 407/188, No. 209, p. 173. His substantive demands included no British appointed advisers, and no British troops east of Suez: FO 407/189, No. 26, p. 22.
[123] *The Times*, 15 September 1921, p. 7.
[124] For example, *Parl. Debs.*, 5th ser., vol. 142, col. 54 (24 May 1921); vol. 144, col. 2541 (21 July 1921); vol. 145, cols. 635ff. (28 July 1921).

these MPs arrived in Egypt on a fact-finding tour arranged by Zaghlul's supporters, who planned to hold mass meetings with them throughout Egypt. The presence of these politicians in Egypt worried both the Foreign Office and Ernest Scott, the Acting High Commissioner, since Zaghlul's campaigning threatened to cut the ground from under Adli's feet. Although there were some calls for him to be deported, Scott was reluctant to take this step: 'The one fatal policy is to deport people like Zaghlul one day and be obliged to give them a free run the next because we have not the determination or sufficient troops to follow up a drastic policy.'[125]

Matters came to a head in December, by which point Foreign Secretary Curzon's negotiations with Adli on Egypt's future had broken down. Allenby and the Foreign Office were now keen for Abdel Khalek Sarwat Pasha to become Prime Minister. However, since he was a man even more unpalatable to Zaghlul than Adli, there was concern that his appointment might lead to a revival of agitation. To smooth the path for Sarwat, Allenby banned a meeting which Zaghlul had planned for the end of December, and began to make plans for his deportation if 'he makes trouble'.[126] Zaghlul did not respond meekly. He issued a protest in the press against the prohibition, and took to the streets to welcome his agent returning from London. After two British soldiers were killed that night in Cairo, Allenby issued a martial law order prohibiting Zaghlul from any further participation in politics, and confining seven of his allies to their homes.[127] Zaghlul's response was blunt. Rejecting Allenby's 'tyrannical order', he declared that 'we are all prepared to meet what may possibly befall us with a steady heart and a calm conscience, knowing that any possible measures used against our lawful endeavours will only help the country to realise her aspirations to complete independence.'[128] In response, on 22 December Allenby ordered Zaghlul's arrest under martial law. He was rapidly moved to Suez (along with five supporters), pending deportation as soon as

---

[125] FO 407/191, No. 17, p. 21 at p. 22. Nonetheless, he was authorised to arrest and deport him if he considered it necessary: FO 407/191, No. 9, p. 4; No. 23, p. 35; No. 24, p. 35.
[126] FO 407/191, No. 47, p. 100.   [127] FO 407/191, No. 48, p. 101.
[128] FO 407/191, No. 51, p. 102.

possible. Allenby wired Curzon: 'I suggest Ceylon. This would have great effect, as it is remembered in connection with Arabi.'[129]

Although Zaghlul was arrested and removed under martial law powers, the continuing existence of martial law was a matter of some embarrassment to the authorities in their efforts to broker a constitutional settlement. It remained in place mainly because it could not be lifted until an indemnity act had been passed, which British officials thought could not be done until a constitutional settlement had been reached.[130] An indemnity bill had in fact been drafted earlier in the year by the Judicial Adviser of the Ministry, Maurice Amos;[131] but martial law was not lifted (and an indemnity act passed) until July 1923, after Britain's unilateral declaration of the ending of the protectorate in February 1922 (which in effect implemented the proposals discussed in London). In the meantime, the British flirted with issuing some kind of proclamation setting limits to the use of martial law, but abandoned the idea as legally unworkable.[132]

The British authorities had also recently tried to temper the arbitrary nature of martial law, when using a military court for the political trial of Abd al-Rahman Fahmi and the leaders of the 'Vengeance Society'.[133] On 20 July 1920, Fahmi and twenty-six others (mainly students) were put on trial in the Permanent Military Court in Cairo for seditious conspiracy and incitement to murder. Although this was a trial under martial law, the authorities were keen for it to follow correct legal procedures throughout.[134] Linton Thorp, a member of the Egyptian Native Court, was appointed Judge-Advocate; the defendants were represented by English barristers; the procedure followed that used in English criminal courts; and the proceedings were widely reported in the press, with official encouragement. The prosecution case turned largely on the evidence of accomplices, whose reliability was questionable, but on 5 October,

---

[129] FO 407/191, No. 50, p. 102.
[130] Without a settlement, the Foreign Office thought that any indemnity act would require the consent of all the powers which had capitulatory rights in Egypt: FO 407/190, No. 56, p. 231.
[131] FO 407/189, No. 202, p. 210.   [132] FO 407/189, No. 30, p. 24.
[133] See Malak Badrawi, *Political Violence in Egypt 1910–1925: Secret Societies, Plots and Assassinations* (Abingdon, Routledge, 2000), pp. 155–159.
[134] FO 407/187, No. 31, p. 21; No. 119, p. 88.

twenty-three of the accused were convicted. Seven of them, including Fahmi, were given a death sentence, which Allenby wanted to see carried out. However, they were able to invoke the provisions of the British Indemnity Act of 1920, which allowed anyone sentenced by a British military court in territory occupied during the war to have their sentences reviewed by the Judge-Advocate-General.[135] The case was sent to London for review, where a political decision was made that no penalty should exceed the maximum allowed under civilian law. This meant that all the death sentences were commuted to fifteen years' penal servitude.[136]

When it came to dealing with political dissidents against whom no legal case could be mounted, the authorities preferred expulsions to detentions under martial law. For instance, in July 1921, Prince Aziz Hassan – a supporter of Zaghlul and a 'professional anarchist', who had only recently been allowed to return to Egypt – was expelled, being given a visa only to visit France and Italy.[137] Similarly, in September, Ali Bey Kamel, vice-president of the Nationalist Party, was told that the authorities would expel him from Egypt under martial law powers if he did not leave voluntarily.[138] It is therefore notable that, when it came to Zaghlul, he was ordered to be detained without any form of trial, and not merely to be deported. From London's point of view, Zaghlul – the man with whom they had been negotiating a new constitutional dispensation for a prolonged period – needed to be removed and confined for political reasons, to prevent his interfering with the kind of settlement the British wished to impose in Egypt. The removal would require the kind of *ad hominem* legislation which had been used so commonly in West Africa, but which had not been used against that earlier nationalist leader, Urabi Pasha.

Zaghlul's Challenge to His Detention

Zaghlul was taken to Suez, and from there (on 29 December) to Aden. On 1 March 1922, he was taken to the Seychelles, to be detained under the Seychelles Ordinance No. 1 of 1922. In the meantime, on

---

[135] Indemnity Act 1920, 10 & 11 Geo. V c. 48, s. 5.   [136] FO 407/188, No. 9, p. 3.
[137] FO 407/189, No. 197, p. 207; FO 407/190, No. 2, p. 1.
[138] FO 407/190. No. 62, p. 242; No. 67, p. 244.

28 February, the government announced the termination of the protectorate and the plan to end martial law once an indemnity act had been passed. Egypt's independence was to be a qualified one, for four crucial powers were retained for British control.[139] This was not the kind of independence Zaghlul had in mind. Over the summer, Labour MPs expressed concern about his continued detention, and its effect on his health. On 8 July, Zaghlul's wife wrote to the Colonial Secretary, asking for the immediate release of her husband, enclosing medical reports which suggested that his detention there posed a serious risk to his already weak health.[140] Given these concerns about his health, a decision was taken to move him to Gibraltar. On 16 August, he was deported from the Seychelles, and two weeks later, a Political Prisoners Detention Ordinance was passed in Gibraltar.[141]

Zaghlul arrived in Gibraltar on 3 September, one day before the publication of the order. Within three weeks of his arrival, Zaghlul applied for a writ of habeas corpus to the Supreme Court of Gibraltar. Presenting his case, G. M. T. Hildyard argued that section 4 of the ordinance – which removed Zaghlul's right to the writ – was 'unconstitutional'. He contended that, under the terms of the Royal Instructions under which he acted, the Governor of Gibraltar did not have the power to suspend habeas corpus, and that his power to make laws for the 'peace, order and good governance' of the City and Garrison did not authorise the passing of a law relating to anyone outside the colony, in order to create a penal settlement on the Rock.[142] The application was dismissed by Chief Justice Daniel T. Tudor on 27 September. The Chief Justice seems to have misunderstood the facts, for he held that Zaghlul had been convicted by a court martial

---

[139] They were the security of communications within the empire (including the Suez canal); the defence of Egypt against foreign aggression; the protection of foreign interests in Egypt; and control of the Sudan. For the announcement, see *Parl. Debs.*, 5th ser., vol. 49, col. 236.

[140] Letter from Saphia Zaghlul, 8 July 1922, TS 27/172. See also *Parl. Debs.*, 5th ser., vol. 153, col. 1789 (8 May 1922); vol. 156, col. 1054 (11 July 1922).

[141] Gibraltar Order no. 9 of 1922. A copy is to be found in TS 27/172.

[142] He cited *Musgrave* v. *Pulido* (1879) 5 App. Cas. 102 (JCPC) in support of his arguments relating to the governor's limited powers. He also argued that, under the Royal Instructions, no ordinance was to be promulgated unless a draft of it had been published a month in advance, unless 'immediate promulgation' was indispensably necessary 'for the security of the City and Garrison', which could not be said to apply to a man who had not yet set foot on the Rock.

in Egypt prior to his deportation, and so could not be freed under a habeas corpus procedure. Tudor also rejected the argument that the Governor did not have the power to issue the ordinance. It was, he said, impossible to conceive 'how this enactment could have been framed' or Zaghlul detained as a political prisoner without instructions from one of the Principal Secretaries of State. It was obvious that Zaghlul's 'detention is authorised by an act of state', which the court could not look into. The judge also refused leave to appeal, not considering the matter to be 'of great, general or public importance'.[143]

While Zaghlul remained incarcerated, his plight attracted the attention of eighty-four Liberal and Labour MPs, who addressed a private letter to the Prime Minister on 9 December calling for his release (as well as the release of those still held in the Seychelles). Zaghlul's deportation had not, they argued, reduced the unrest in Egypt. Moreover, given his continued ill-health, they warned of '[t]he grave risk we are running of being accused of deliberately compassing the death of a man who commands the general respect and devotion of the mass of his countrymen'.[144] At the same time, alarming reports were circulating in Cairo about the deteriorating state of his health, which focused increasing attention on the issue of political prisoners. In this atmosphere, Allenby sought a friendly parliamentary question, to allow the government to make it clear that people were being detained not simply for their political views, but for provoking violence.[145] At this stage, however, neither Allenby nor the Foreign Office favoured releasing him.

It was in this context of continuing debate over his detention that a petition was lodged in the Privy Council for special leave to appeal against the decision of the Gibraltarian court. Zaghlul's petition raised the question of whether the crown had the power to detain him as a political prisoner without any charges being made against him.[146] The question at issue would be similar to that discussed in the Court of

---

[143] *Re Zaghlul Pasha* (1922) in (1813–1977) Gib. LR 58.
[144] The letter was co-ordinated by J. M. Kenworthy. A copy can be found in FO 141/809.
[145] Telegram from Cairo High Commission, 12 December 1922, FO 141/809. The question was duly asked and answered with Allenby's formulation: *Parl. Debs.*, 5th ser., vol. 159, col. 3353.
[146] Petition of Zaghlul Pasha, TS 27/172.

Appeal in Sekgoma's case, but with a significant difference: for in Zaghlul's case, the Governor had acted under the authority of the crown's prerogative powers, rather than under any power delegated from parliament. The case came before the judicial committee on 21 January, where W. H. Upjohn presented the argument for Zaghlul. First, he addressed Tudor CJ's holding that this was an act of state, which could not be questioned by the court. Insofar as his detention in Egypt was concerned, Upjohn – much of whose career had been spent as a Chancery lawyer – conceded that the court would have no jurisdiction, since Zaghlul was an alien detained outside the empire.[147] However, he argued that, once Zaghlul was on imperial soil, he was a 'friendly alien' entitled to the rights and liberties of a subject.[148] Upjohn did not spend much time on this point, since the judges seemed convinced that the case could not be settled by the 'act of state' arguments used by Tudor. Upjohn's second argument was that the Governor did not have the power to issue the ordinance. Since the Governor was bound by the Letters Patent appointing him to pass ordinances directed to him by the crown, Upjohn could not argue (as Hildyard had attempted) that he had exceeded the Royal Instructions. Instead, he argued that the king himself could not authorise such an ordinance, since he was bound (under Mansfield's doctrine in *Campbell v. Hall*) by the fundamental principles of the constitution.

However, the judges were sceptical about Upjohn's arguments. Haldane questioned whether the residents of conquered colonies acquired the fundamental rights of Britons as soon as they had been conquered, if the king chose not to alter an ancient local law allowing arbitrary imprisonment.[149] Sumner wondered whether it was appropriate for courts to question the decision of a Governor with the power to legislate for the peace, order and good governance of a colony that any particular provision was necessary for such purposes. The Chancery barrister Upjohn's response was that, if it was very clear that a law was not needed for such purposes – as was the case of a law

---

[147] 'In the Matter of Zaghlul Pasha: Petition for Special Leave to Appeal', TS 27/172.
[148] In support of this, he cited *Johnstone v. Pedlar* [1921] 2 AC 262, which held that the crown could not claim that the seizure of the property of a friendly alien (*alien ami*) resident in the United Kingdom was an act of state.
[149] *In the Matter of Zaghlul Pasha: Petition for Special Leave to Appeal* (First Hearing), TS 27/172, pp. 11–12.

to imprison a man of seventy without trial – then 'it is really a fraud upon the powers.'[150] This linked to Upjohn's third argument, which echoed Sir Henry de Villiers's judgment in Sigcau's case, which was that this was a *privilegium* made for one man, rather than a general law. Once again, the judges were sceptical, pointing out that this might be seen as a general law allowing the Governor to detain anyone deported from Egypt.

Upjohn's argument that it is the 'law in every civilised country of the world that a man is not to be condemned without being heard' cut little ice. Having read his Dicey, Haldane retorted that, in Belgium, freedoms all depended only on constitutional guarantees. Sumner simply observed that 'There are many kinds of civilisation, ours is not the best.'[151] The judges were not prepared to accept Upjohn's invocation of the principle of *Campbell* v. *Hall*. They wanted more specific information to show how the rights claimed for Zaghlul had become law in Gibraltar. However, the information before the highest court in the empire on what the law of Gibraltar actually was was woefully inadequate. Counsel for both sides admitted that they had not researched the matter in detail, while the judges had consulted only the main textbook on colonial law and a short article on Gibraltar. Given the lack of information, the hearing was adjourned for more research to be done.[152]

The case would return to the Privy Council on 9 March. In the meantime, officials in London and Cairo were already considering the release of Zaghlul. The Governor of Gibraltar – whose ordinance was ostensibly passed for the peace, order and good governance of his colony – was largely excluded from these discussions. The Foreign Office raised the matter at the end of January with a number of Egyptian nationalists connected with Zaghlul, who felt he could be

---

[150] *In the Matter of Zaghlul Pasha: Petition for Special Leave to Appeal* (First Hearing), TS 27/172, p. 21 (answering Lord Sumner).

[151] *In the Matter of Zaghlul Pasha: Petition for Special Leave to Appeal* (First Hearing), TS 27/172, p. 38.

[152] The brief works cited were A. W. Renton and G. G. Phillimore (eds.), *Burge's Commentaries on Colonial and Foreign Laws*, 5 vols. (London, Sweet and Maxwell and Stevens and Sons, 1908–1910), vol. 1, pp. 143–147 and a contribution by Archibald W. Fawkes (Gibraltar's Attorney General) on modes of legislation in Gibraltar in the *Journal of the Society of Comparative Legislation*, vol. 1 (1896–1897), pp. 144–146.

persuaded to give an undertaking not to return to Egypt if he were released.[153] With the prospect of an indemnity act soon being passed and a liberal constitution enacted, Allenby was keen to find a way to release Zaghlul. At the same time, he feared that, if Zaghlul were released without an undertaking not to return, there would be agitation for his return, which could be prevented only by the politically inconvenient continuation of martial law.[154] However, the authorities in Egypt calculated (correctly) that, for political reasons, Zaghlul would not want to return immediately. Allenby's plans to release Zaghlul were based on political calculations (designed to strengthen Adli's position) which were derailed as a result of bomb attacks in late February and early March, which resulted in the prolongation of martial law and the detention of six *Wafd* leaders. Officials in Cairo were discomfited by these detentions, aware that detention without trial 'leaves an open sore in public opinion here, and is calculated to provoke constant criticism at home'.[155] On the day after the Privy Council hearings resumed, Allenby was still discussing with Curzon the possibility of releasing Zaghlul on medical grounds.[156]

When the court resumed its sittings, the lawyers were much better informed about Gibraltarian law. Gibraltar was a conquered colony, ceded to Britain in the Treaty of Utrecht in 1716. It had received its first charter in 1720, empowering a Judge Advocate and two merchants to settle personal disputes in contract and tort. A second charter in 1739 reformed the judicial system, creating a Court of Civil Pleas, consisting of a Chief Judge (who had to be learned in the laws of England) and two Gibraltarians. It stipulated that the laws of England should be the measure of justice between the parties. It also created a criminal court

---

[153] Foreign Office to Allenby, 5 February 1923, FO 141/794/9.
[154] FO 407/196, No. 83, p. 121; No. 88, p. 123; Minute from Furness to Kerr (Cairo) 17 February 1923, FO 141/809/1.
[155] They thought the most palatable solution was simply to exile them, which 'worked quite well in the cases of Prince Aziz & Ali Fahmi Kamel'. In fact, the *Wafd* leaders did not remain in detention for long and were released on 15 April. Note dated 6 March 1923, and note from Furness to Kerr, 8 March 1923, FO 141/809/1; FO 407/196, No. 109, p. 157; No. 141, p. 199.
[156] Allenby to Curzon 10 March 1923, FO 141/794/9. There was also continuing pressure in parliament for his release: see *Parl. Debs.*, 5th ser., vol. 161, col. 1355 (13 March 1923).

to determine felonies and trespasses according to English law; though those suspected of treason were to be tried in England. A third charter in 1752 gave the court jurisdiction over real property and probate. A fourth charter was granted in 1817, reconstituting the Court of Civil Pleas, which was replaced by a fifth in 1830 creating a Supreme Court. This latter court was to decide cases 'according to the law in force' in the territory and all other laws enacted for the peace, order and good government of the colony. In 1867, an Order in Council was issued to clarify what law applied in Gibraltar, stating that the law of England as it then existed applied, except insofar as otherwise provided for by any Order in Council or local ordinance, made in the past or to be made in the future. A similar Order in Council was issued in 1884, which was followed by a Supreme Court Consolidation Order in 1888. A secret Order in Council – not made public until 1914 – had also been issued in 1896, which gave the Governor the power to dispense with laws during an emergency.

In the two months before the second hearing, lawyers at the Colonial Office prepared to answer the argument that the Governor's power to legislate was limited by fundamental principles of the English constitution, which had taken root in Gibraltar. Drawing on cases including *ex parte Sekgoma*, they argued that the Habeas Corpus Act did not apply to Gibraltar, either by virtue of express words or necessary intendment (as required by the Colonial Laws Validity Act).[157] Nor could the prerogative writ have any force in Gibraltar until it had been expressly introduced. Habeas corpus, they concluded, was 'merely imported by the Order in Council' of 1884 and had 'no greater force or effect there than a local ordinance on the subject'. The right to habeas corpus could accordingly be removed by a local ordinance. The Colonial Office's lawyers also addressed the argument that the Governor had gone beyond the Royal Instructions, and had passed an ordinance which was not for the peace, order and good governance of the colony. Responding to the first point, the Colonial Office's view was that this was not a matter for the courts: 'The Royal Instructions are a matter solely between the Crown and the Governor of the Colony', Sir John Risley opined, 'and if the later disobeys his Instructions he has to answer to the Secretary of State.'[158] On the second point, it was argued that the

---

[157] Letter from Sir John Risley to H. M. Greenwood, 16 January 1923: TS 27/172.
[158] Risley to Greenwood, 12 January 1923, TS 27/172.

provisions made during the First World War to allow detention without trial in Britain demonstrated that detention orders might well be made for peace, order and good government, and that, as preventative measures, they did not in themselves constitute punishment.[159] Equally, the power of the crown to make a *privilegium* for a single individual had been confirmed in Sekgoma's case.[160]

When the case returned to court, the question asked of the Privy Council was not whether Zaghlul should be freed, but whether there was a sufficiently important constitutional issue raised by his case to grant leave to appeal. In Upjohn's view, there was a serious question about the nature of prerogative powers to be determined: as he saw it, the principles of English law had been introduced into Gibraltar through the various charters, so that it was too late for them to be revoked by a prerogative Order in Council in 1884. Against this, the Attorney General, Sir Douglas Hogg, argued that, as a conquered territory, the colony was ruled only by such laws as the crown chose to impose, and that the crown retained all of its legislative powers, having specifically reserved the power to alter any of the charters it had granted. In Hogg's view, the rights of Englishmen did not migrate to colonies when they were conquered: Gibraltar had no habeas corpus in 1715, and it had never been introduced there by statute. No English statute had any force in Gibraltar save by virtue of the Order in Council of 1884, which reserved the power to change any law. Besides arguing these points of constitutional law, Hogg urged that he was 'very anxious that your Lordships ... should not give leave, for reasons that you appreciate having regard to what is going on in Egypt': it was 'a very very serious matter from the political standpoint'.[161] Given

---

[159] The reference was to Regulation 14B, issued under the Defence of the Realm Act, whose legality was confirmed by the House of Lords in R. v. *Halliday, ex p. Zadig* [1917] AC 260. See further David Foxton, 'R v *Halliday, ex parte Zadig* in Retrospect', *Law Quarterly Review*, vol. 119 (2003), pp. 455–494; A. W. Brian Simpson, *In the Highest Degree Odious: Detention without Trial in Wartime Britain* (Oxford, Oxford University Press, 1994), pp. 12–26; and Rachel Vorspan, 'Law and War: Individual Rights, Executive Authority, and Judicial Power in England during World War I', *Vanderbilt Journal of Transnational Law*, vol. 38:2 (2005), pp. 261–343.
[160] 'Note for the AG' in TS 27/172.
[161] *In the Matter of Zaghlul Pasha* (Second Hearing), TS 27/172, pp. 10, 26.

that the Colonial Office was at that moment planning Zaghlul's release, the Attorney General's comment was at best disingenuous.

During argument, the different members of the judicial committee inclined to different positions. The judge most inclined to think that there was an issue to be debated was Haldane. 'I am sorry', he interjected at one point, 'but I do think a very considerable question arises whether the Prerogative of the Crown as regards places altogether outside these Islands without a Constitution can be exercised otherwise than in accordance with the law.'[162] Haldane not only considered that prerogative powers were bound by the common law, but also thought that the decision in *ex parte Anderson* had confirmed that the writ of habeas corpus ran throughout the empire, and that it could be removed only by an Act of the Imperial Parliament.[163] By contrast, Lord Dunedin was sympathetic to Hogg's argument that, just as the Imperial Parliament had taken away many rights by the Defence of the Realm Acts, so the crown could do the same thing by ordinance in a place where no constitution had been granted or legislature established.[164] Although he had been the one judge who felt that there was a question to be discussed, it was Haldane who was delegated to hand down the decision of the court: that leave would not be granted. No reasons were given.[165]

During the discussions, Haldane had seemed to suggest a possible alternative route for Zaghlul to pursue: if the court in Gibraltar was unable to issue a writ of habeas corpus (because of the ordinance), then he could try to obtain one from the King's Bench in London. However, it proved unnecessary to pursue the legal route much further, for, notwithstanding the Attorney General's repeated comments in court about the political danger of even discussing whether Zaghlul might have a case, steps were being taken to release him. Continuing concerns about Zaghlul's health had resulted in proposals that he be allowed to recuperate in Vichy, in France.[166] A medical report on the day of the

---

[162] *In the Matter of Zaghlul Pasha* (Second Hearing), TS 27/172, p. 17.
[163] *Ex parte Anderson* (1861) 3 E & E 487. Haldane quoted the *Case of Proclamations* (1610) 12 Co Rep 74 in support of his views on the prerogative.
[164] *In the Matter of Zaghlul Pasha* (Second Hearing), TS 27/172, pp. 10–11.
[165] The decision was reported in *The Times*, 10 March 1923, p. 4 and in *Solicitor's Journal*, vol. 67 (1923), p. 382.
[166] Letter from E. M. Dowson to Scott, 11 December 1922, FO 141/809,

hearing stated that he should travel to a European watering place for the sake of his health, and Zaghlul petitioned the French government to be allowed to go there. Within two weeks of the judicial committee's decision, Allenby had formed the view that he could be released, without giving any guarantees.[167] On 4 April, Zaghlul left Gibraltar for Toulon. Rather than proceeding to Vichy, he remained at Marseilles, where he resumed his political activity. With the lifting of martial law in Egypt, Zaghlul was told in July that he could return; and he returned on 17 September, to a much smaller crowd and far less political excitement than had been the case on his return from Malta.

In Zaghlul's case, the Privy Council had simply refused to consider whether a colonial Governor had the power to pass an ordinance to hold a detainee from another part of the empire. For most of the judges on the committee, no constitutional question was raised. Indeed, the Attorney General had regarded this as a matter of routine: 'We are not doing anything new here', he told the panel: 'I have some 60 or 70 similar ordinances in Africa during the last 40 or 50 years, in which an Ordinance, very much the same as this Ordinance, has been passed and the validity of which has not been challenged.'[168] The judicial committee accepted that the crown had full legislative power in colonies without assemblies, and that this power could be delegated to the Governor. This power could be called forth, shaped and defined by the king's ministers in London, and used for the purposes of imperial rule. Within the courtroom, the judges were impressed with the notion that there was a political emergency which needed exceptional powers. Yet, at the very same time that its law officers were warning the court of the grave consequences of an adverse decision, a much more flexible political game was being played.

Zaghlul remained a highly important political figure after his return. His *Wafd* party scored a resounding victory in the January 1924 elections, which obliged the king to appoint Zaghlul Prime Minister. His continuing demands for further concessions from Britain – including his assertive claims to Sudan – led to further conflict with Allenby, leading to his resignation in November. The *Wafd* continued

---

[167] Telegrams of 22 March and 24 March 1923, FO 141/794/9.
[168] *In the Matter of Zaghlul Pasha* (Second Hearing), TS 27/172, p. 30.

to dominate at the polls, however, and Zaghlul remained president of the assembly until his death in 1927.

Conclusion

The cases discussed in this chapter gave judges in London their first chance to consider the legality of the kind of *ad hominem* legislation which had become routine in the African empire since 1880. The cases raised the question of whether the executive had the power to pass such laws, which appeared to violate the guarantees of liberty found in Magna Carta, the Star Chamber Act and the Habeas Corpus Act, either on the ground of a delegation of legislative power from parliament or through the exercise of crown prerogative. Lawyers for the detainees argued for a broad, substantive vision of the rule of law, while the crown's lawyers argued the 'formal' case, that such legislation had to be seen as valid law, since it was derived from a valid source.

The legal position articulated in these decisions hardened over time. Lord Watson's decision in Sigcau's case was read as a liberal judgment, endorsing the rule of law. This judge seemed to find it inconceivable that British legislators could pass such 'autocratic' legislation where a functioning legal system was in place; and the Law Officers commenting on his judgment five years later were convinced that prerogative powers were bound by *Campbell* v. *Hall*. Yet the Cape was allowed to pass such autocratic legislation immediately after the decision, and the Court of Appeal accepted in Sekgoma's case that *ad hominem* ordinances could be passed by officials to whom general legislative powers could be seen to have been delegated. Zaghlul's case completed the legal picture, by upholding the crown's power to legislate in this manner in conquered colonies, unfettered by *Campbell* v. *Hall*.

9

Martial Law in the Anglo-Boer War, 1899–1902

Although it had been widely used since the 1880s, detention without trial in the continent of Africa did not generate the kind of debates in the metropolis about the rule of law and the constitution which had been engendered by the use of martial law after the Morant Bay revolt.[1] This was to change at the end of the nineteenth century, when the outbreak of war in South Africa in 1899 led to the proclamation of martial law both in the Cape Colony and in Natal, which would be followed (among other things) by widescale detention without trial.[2] In contrast to Jamaica, where it was used against an insurgent black population, in the Cape martial law was used to control white British subjects, thousands of whom had joined in rebellion when the Boers invaded the borderlands. In this colony with responsible government and a liberal legal tradition, the legal and political elites were generally loath to regard martial law simply as the rule of the military commander, but sought to subject it to the rule of law in ways which

---

[1] See R. W. Kostal, *A Jurisprudence of Power: Victorian Empire and the Rule of Law* (Oxford, Oxford University Press, 2005); and Priyamvada Gopal, *Insurgent Empire: Anticolonial Resistance and British Dissent* (London, Verso, 2019), ch. 2.

[2] For histories of the war, see Thomas Pakenham, *The Boer War* (London, Weidenfeld & Nicolson, 1979); Denis Judd and Keith Surridge, *The Boer War: A History* (London, John Murray, 2002); and Bill Nasson, *The War for South Africa* (Cape Town, Tafelberg, 2010). In the following discussion, we will not consider the experience of Africans during the war and under martial law: however, for an important study, see Bill Nasson, *Abraham Esau's War: A Black South African War in the Cape, 1899–1902* (Cambridge, Cambridge University Press, 1991).

323

had been recommended by Eyre's critics on the Jamaica committee.[3] This in turn raised questions for officials in London, about how to reconcile a commitment to the rule of law with the wartime demands of the imperial military, in the context of a war which divided public opinion.[4] Furthermore, cases from this war would require the Judicial Committee of the Privy Council to be more explicit than any imperial court had hitherto been on the exact nature of martial law.

In the aftermath of the Jamaica rebellion, a Diceyan view of martial law – which subjected all actions taken under it to the scrutiny of the common law – became widely accepted. At the same time, many questions about its nature remained unsettled. One question was whether civilian courts could hold the military to account during the crisis, or whether they could exercise their jurisdiction only after it had passed.[5] Another question concerned the nature of the indemnity which would be granted to those who had violated legal rights under martial law. Did an indemnity act simply substitute 'the despotism of Parliament for the prerogative of the Crown'[6] – thereby satisfying a formalistic vision of the rule of law – or was parliament to apply the kind of tests of necessity and good faith which common law courts were expected to apply when judging particular acts, acting as a kind of court for the nation ensuring fidelity to a broader culture of the rule of law?[7]

These questions were widely debated during the Anglo-Boer war. As the example of the Cape in this era shows, the degree to which a 'substantive' view of the rule of law could shape political and legal policy depended on how committed particular actors were to its

---

[3] See Martin Chanock, *The Making of South African Legal Culture 1902–1936: Fear, Favour and Prejudice* (Cambridge, Cambridge University Press, 2001); and Albie Sachs, *Justice in South Africa* (Berkeley, University of California Press, 1973).

[4] See G. R. Searle, *A New England? Peace and War 1886–1918* (Oxford, Clarendon Press, 2004), pp. 284–291; Kenneth O. Morgan, 'The Boer War and the Media (1899–1902)', *Twentieth Century British History*, vol. 13:1 (2002), pp. 1–16.

[5] Even Dicey accepted that governments could not keep the peace in times of crisis 'without occasional use of arbitrary authority': A. V. Dicey, *Introduction to the Study of the Law of the Constitution*, 5th ed. (London, MacMillan, 1879), p. 341.

[6] Dicey, *The Law of the Constitution*, p. 342.

[7] See David Dyzenhaus, '*Schmitt v. Dicey*: Are States of Emergency inside or outside the Legal Order?', *Cardozo Law Review*, vol. 27 (2006), pp. 2005–2039; and David Dyzenhaus, 'The Puzzle of Martial Law', *University of Toronto Law Journal*, vol. 59 (2009), pp. 1–64.

culture, and how influential their voices could be. In a colony with a strong liberal political and legal tradition, and where the targets of martial law were white British subjects forming part of the political community, a broad, substantive vision of the rule of law was championed both by ministers and by members of the judiciary. They had many opportunities to explore the relationship between martial law and civilian law, given that the civilian courts remained open. At the same time, imperial military commanders and their civilian masters at the metropolis wanted their ability to defeat the enemy to remain unfettered, and often argued for a much broader vision of martial law than was espoused by the liberal politicians at the Cape. Questions about the nature of martial law would also receive the attention of metropolitan judges sitting in the Judicial Committee of the Privy Council, who had their own understanding of the legal basis of imperial rule. In this context, the language of a 'substantive' rule of law constantly interrupted imperial military efforts to assume plenary powers, though how far it would prevail remained a matter of negotiation. As shall be seen, martial law was not treated as a legal void, a state of siege in which the military's command held full sway, but rather as a space whose boundaries were defined by a process of careful negotiation between imperial, local and military authorities. Equally, when it came to legislating for indemnity, the matter was not treated simply as a formal legislative fiat, but as the product of a process in which judgments were to be made about the conduct being indemnified.

In what follows, attention will be focused on the use of martial law in the British colonies of the Cape of Good Hope and Natal. Martial law was also imposed by the British in the former republics, which were formally annexed to the crown in 1900, just as the first phase of the war was coming to an end and peace seemed likely.[8] However, the former republics continued to be treated as territories under military occupation outside the imperial constitutional system. Despite General Roberts's early proclamation that anyone found in arms would be

---

[8] Martial law was proclaimed in the new Orange River Colony on 31 May 1900, and in Transvaal on September 1, after the capture of their respective capitals, Bloemfontein on 13 March and Pretoria on 5 June.

'dealt with as rebels',[9] combatants in the former republics continued to be regarded as enemy 'Boers' and treated as prisoners of war when captured. The advice of the Law Officers was that as long as the war continued, and 'the resistance of those who were formerly subjects of the South African Republic and Orange Free State' had not in fact been suppressed, enemy belligerents could not be treated as rebels.[10] The British military response to the enemy Boer commandoes was to adopt a scorched earth policy, which entailed the resettlement of large populations in concentration camps which they were not permitted to leave without permission.[11] Over 26,000 Boer women and children and over 18,000 Africans were to die from malnutrition and disease in these camps. Although this policy was widely debated, not least because of the publicity generated by humanitarian critics such as Emily Hobhouse,[12] there was little discussion of the legalities of martial law in these areas, which remained under military administration until the end of the war, with no local civilian authority to question their powers.

The First Invasion, October 1899–October 1900

Launching a pre-emptive strike in response to British threats to their independence, the two Boer republics declared war on 11 October 1899, and sent commandoes into Natal and the Cape Colony. In the border areas which were invaded, up to 10,000 of the Dutch-speaking population supported the invasion.[13] Within four days, martial law was proclaimed in a number of border districts in Natal and the Cape, and by the middle of November, all of Natal and all the Cape districts bordering the Orange Free State and the South African

[9] Proclamation, 7 June 1900 (relating to the Orange River Colony), PP 1900 (Cd. 261) LVI. 389, enc. in No 80, p. 191.
[10] Opinion of 31 July 1901, CO 885/15, No. 95A.
[11] In June 1901, 85,410 Boers – the large majority women and children – remained in concentration camps (mainly in Transvaal and the Orange River Colony): PP 1901 (Cd. 608) X. 549. See further Aidan Forth, *Britain's Empire of Camps* (Berkeley, University of California Press, 2017), ch. 5.
[12] Figures taken from Alexander B. Downes, *Targeting Civilians in War* (Ithaca, Cornell University Press, 2008), p. 161. For Hobhouse, see Robert Eales, *The Compassionate Englishwoman: Emily Hobhouse in the Boer War* (Cape Town, UCT Press, 2015).
[13] G. H. L. Le May, *British Supremacy in South Africa 1899–1907* (Oxford, Clarendon Press, 1965), p. 43.

Republic were under martial law. After the initial invasion, the Boer troops did not seek to penetrate deeper into the Cape Colony, but besieged the towns of Kimberley, Ladysmith and Mafeking. The tide of the campaign turned with the arrival of an overwhelming amount of imperial military manpower, and by the middle of May each of the besieged towns had been relieved, Bloemfontein had been captured and Pretoria was soon to fall. With the Boers in retreat, and their republics annexed, it appeared to many that the war was largely over. Martial law was gradually withdrawn from a number of areas in the Cape between July and October, but plans for winding down martial law in all areas were arrested when a second invasion of the Cape began in December. In this phase of the war, the authorities were faced with the problem of how to deal with a large number of captured rebels, at a time when there was an expectation that the war would soon end.

It soon became apparent that the debates which had followed Governor Eyre's proclamation of martial law in 1865 had not fully clarified the legal position regarding martial law. Although the dominant view among common lawyers was that 'martial law' was nothing more than the crown's common law right to suppress insurrection, and that its justification came from necessity and not from any proclamation,[14] the Colonial Office had made it clear through Lord Carnarvon's 1867 Circular Despatch that Governors were expected to make proclamations of martial law in times of crisis and to set out procedures on how to implement it. Discussing the matter in January 1900, the High Commissioner for South Africa, Sir Alfred Milner, observed that 'the exact nature of the powers conferred by such a proclamation of Martial Law' is 'extremely difficult to decide.'[15] Considering martial law to be 'the temporary suspension of law – a purely arbitrary and singularly ill-defined condition', he regretted that the law had not made better provision for emergencies,

---

[14] Dicey, *The Law of the Constitution*, pp. 267–276; J. F. Stephen, *A History of the Criminal Law of England*, 3 vols. (London, MacMillan and Co., 1883), vol. 1, pp. 207–216; and Robert M. King, 'Martial Law I', *Cape Law Journal*, vol. 17 (1900), pp. 30–42. See also Kostal, *A Jurisprudence of Power*, pp. 455–459.

[15] CO 879/64/5, No. 126, p. 161 at p. 162. Compare the report of the Cape's Attorney General (Richard Solomon) on 25 November 1899, in PP 1900 (Cd. 420) LVI. 595, enc. 2 in No. 1, p. 2.

as had been done in Europe through legal definitions of the state of siege,[16] and thought that 'the arbitrary power of the military should be exercised in accordance with some clearly defined principles.'[17] On the vexed question of whether martial law entirely suspended the civilian courts, or whether 'the ordinary law still exercises an unimpaired ascendancy', Milner felt that a hybrid system could be used, under which ordinary crime could be left to ordinary courts, while treason would be dealt with by martial law courts, which themselves could include 'a civilian element, in the person of a magistrate or judge'.[18]

Milner was not the only one who regretted that the law had not been placed on firmer foundations. Sir John Ardagh, Director of Military Intelligence at the War Office, also thought that a 'State of Siege' should be 'legalised and regularised under the most careful safeguards and restrictions', both to protect Governors and Officers from later legal action, and to show soldiers that they had no 'legal license to hang, shoot, flog and destroy as they please'.[19] Ardagh's understanding of the current law was that a proclamation of martial law was 'exercised by the prerogative of the king' and suspended the ordinary law. It permitted 'summary methods of arrest, trial and punishment to be carried out, usually by military forces', since it reversed the normal presumption that the ordinary process of law was sufficient to maintain peace. In his view, however, martial law did not entirely oust the jurisdiction of the ordinary courts: though they would not exercise it *'flagrante bello'*, they could subsequently hold crown officers responsible for the use of unjustifiable force.[20]

Others in the military had a more extensive view of the prerogative powers of the crown, which was closer to that articulated by W. F. Finlason during the Jamaica debates. For instance, the Deputy Judge Advocate-General J. Scott argued in May 1901 that sentences imposed by martial law courts would not expire at the end of the war,

---

[16] Cecil Headlam (ed.), *The Milner Papers*, vol. 2 (London, Cassell, 1933), pp. 59–60.
[17] Milner to Roberts, 12 January 1900, CO 48/545/3845, f. 258.
[18] Milner to Chamberlain, 3 January 1900, CO 879/64/5, No. 126, p. 161 at pp. 163–164.
[19] PRO 30/40/19. At the same time, he was also concerned at political interference with the exercise of emergency powers.
[20] Memorandum and notes by Ardagh, December 1900 and 18 July 1901, PRO 30/40/19.

since (he argued) the crown had a prerogative power to resort to martial law.[21] His view seemed to be supported by no less a figure than the Lord Chancellor, Halsbury, who privately told Chamberlain that penal servitude sentences passed by a martial law court would be legally valid after the war ended.[22] This opinion raised eyebrows, not least because it was inconsistent with the view he had expressed as a Law Officer in 1878,[23] as well as being inconsistent with the rules set out in 1867. This question was referred to the Law Officers, Finlay and Carson, who reiterated the common law orthodoxy that martial law was only 'the temporary application of force by the Executive under a condition of affairs which renders necessary the abrogation of civil rights as established by law' and that, when it ended, prisoners would be entitled to their freedom, and the civil courts would have jurisdiction over them.[24]

In this context of contested understandings, the parameters and operation of martial law became the object of negotiations between various civil and military parties. Rather than seeing martial law as a state of exception where all law was silent and the executive stepped in to defend the *salus populi*, or as a state where the rules of common law necessity simply applied, they saw it as a legal order whose parameters had to be defined. Matters were complicated by the fact that the war was an imperial one, but the rebellion a colonial one. Although the military who would exercise the martial law powers were under the command of officers – Lords Roberts and Kitchener – who were responsible to the War Office in London, martial law was proclaimed at the Cape by the Governor under the seal of the colony. As the Governor of a colony with responsible government, he was expected to act on the advice of ministers who were answerable to a colonial parliament. At the same time, as an appointee of the imperial government dealing with an imperial matter, he also had to take heed

---

[21] He also argued that their proceedings had 'been conducted with such regularity that relief under a writ of *habeas corpus*, if it were applied for, would not be granted'. Opinion dated 23 May 1901, CO 885/15, No. 84A.
[22] Note by Chamberlain 28 April 1900, CO 417/305/4219, f. 180.
[23] Law Officers' Opinion, 23 July 1878, CO 879/13/5, p. 301.
[24] Opinion dated 6 July 1901, CO 885/15, No. 88. See also the Law Officers' debate with Judge Advocate-General Sir Francis Jeune over the status of martial law courts: CO 879/68/3, p. 127, enc. in No. 122; Law Officers' Opinion, 1 June 1900, CO 885/15, No. 38.

of the demands of the Colonial Office. Furthermore, the military and civilian parties had often divergent interests. The military wanted to have as free a hand as possible, to enable them to conduct the war as efficiently as possible. By contrast, the Cape ministry, which at the outbreak of the war was led by W. P. Schreiner and depended on the support of the Afrikaner Bond, had no desire for a regime which would unduly antagonise the majority Dutch-speaking white community. Sitting between these two, the Colonial Office favoured a policy which would not hamper the war effort, but which would be defensible not only at the Cape, but also before British public opinion.

Military and Civilian Trials

The kind of arrangement which Milner envisaged began to be put in place at the start of the war. An Army Order issued On 7 December 1899 set out the offences to be dealt with under martial law (including treason, sedition and aiding and abetting the enemy) and the procedure to be used.[25] The military agreed that ordinary offences should be left as far as possible to be dealt with in civilian courts, and that trials for martial law offences should 'follow the rules of military law'.[26] While Milner was happy with this arrangement, the Cape ministry insisted that high treason cases at least should be presided over by a Justice of the Supreme Court.[27] The Colonial Office was content to concede the point, considering that the presence of a judge would increase public confidence in the tribunal, and oblige the ministry both to assume responsibility for punishing the rebels and to pass an indemnity act.[28] The military reluctantly agreed, and on 3 February, Kitchener issued a Circular Memorandum stating that (save in cases of urgency), high treason cases would be heard by a mixed commission of four officers and a presiding judge.[29]

The Cape ministry nominated Justice W. H. Solomon to sit in these cases.[30] Having accepted the position, Solomon told Chief Justice Sir

[25] PP 1902 (Cd. 981) LVII. 327, pp. 21–22.
[26] CO 879/64/5, No. 132, p. 168; PP 1902 (Cd. 981), pp. 23–24.
[27] CO 879/64/5, enc. 1 in No. 383, p. 373.
[28] CO 879/63/2, No. 131, p. 207; Notes by Lambert and Cox, 28 February 1900, CO 48/545/6203, f. 435.
[29] PP 1902 (Cd. 981), pp. 26–27. For the War Office's continuing doubts, CO 879/63/2, No. 130, p. 206.
[30] CO 879/64/5, enc. in No. 436, p. 434.

Henry de Villiers that he did not 'quite like the work' he had undertaken, given the anomalous status of the court and the need for indemnity legislation to legalise anything it did. However, he felt 'it is most desirable in the interests of justice that a judge should preside at the trial': if martial law courts were bodies unknown to the ordinary law, Solomon was at least keen to make them follow civilian precedents as far as possible.[31] In the event, by the time that the War Office had agreed to Solomon's appointment at the end of March, Milner had come to the view that the question needed reconsideration.[32] In his view, the procedure set out by the military circulars was 'an odd mixture of military and civil jurisdiction, without the prompt effectiveness of the former or the unquestionable legality of the latter'. With the war by now looking as if it might soon be over, the proposal was overtaken by events, as political attention turned to creating structures to deal with the large number of rebels to be tried after the anticipated end of hostilities.[33]

Rather than being tried in mixed tribunals, rebels were tried during the first phase of the war in both civilian and military tribunals. The first to be tried – in a civil court – were thirty-six rebel prisoners captured after the engagement at Sunnyside (near Kimberley). Since it was the policy of the Boer republics to give nationality to those British subjects who joined them, Presidents Kruger and Steyn of the Boer republics sent a telegram after their capture to the Foreign Secretary requesting that they be treated as prisoners of war.[34] Faced with the threat of reprisals if this were not done – and the alternative risk of having the men acquitted by a sympathetic jury – officials considered postponing any trial until the war was over, and in the meantime removing them (along with the Boer prisoners of war) to St Helena, beyond the reach of any habeas corpus application. However, they were advised by the Law Officers that a choice had to be made between holding them as prisoners of war or putting them on trial as traitors.[35] The decision was taken to try them, since Milner thought that treating

---

[31] W. H. Solomon to H. de Villiers, 16 February 1900, de Villiers Papers, National Library of South Africa (Cape Town), MSC 7 (Box 8).
[32] CO 879/63/2, No. 133, p. 208; CO 879/63/1, No. 546, p. 176; CO 879/63/2, No. 138, p. 210.
[33] Headlam (ed.), *The Milner Papers*, vol. 2, p. 106.   [34] PP 1900 (Cd. 261), p. 5.
[35] Opinion dated 6 February 1900, CO 885/15, No. 19A.

them as prisoners of war would only encourage more to rebel.[36] The Presidents of the republics were accordingly informed that those owing allegiance to the crown would be tried, and that they would be held personally responsible for any treatment of British prisoners inconsistent with the usages of war.[37] The Sunnyside rebels were tried for treason before Buchanan J towards the end of April, and were convicted after they refused to plead, perhaps realising that since they were captured in battle, they had no real defence. The heaviest sentences – of five years' penal servitude – were imposed on three ringleaders, while twenty-two others were given three-year prison sentences.[38] In all, forty men were convicted of treason in cases tried before the Supreme Court during the course of 1900, with twenty-three more convicted for treason in trials held before circuit judges.[39]

Eighteen trials for treason or assisting the enemy were also conducted by the military, before the decision was taken in the middle of April to conduct no more martial law trials for treason.[40] The fact that such trials were being held when the civil courts were open was questioned in parliament by Sir Henry Campbell-Bannerman,[41] who drew particular attention to the cases of J. Booysens and N. A. van der Walt, who were tried by the military at Naauwpoort on 12 March.[42] The fact that such trials had taken place did not trouble officials at the Colonial Office. Sensing that this was a political attempt by the Liberal leader to drive a wedge between the civil and military authorities which should be 'nipped in the bud', assistant undersecretary of state Fred Graham minuted that

Martial law having been proclaimed, with the assent of the Civil Govt of the Colony, the civil power ceases to have any responsibility. The military can if

---

[36] CO 879/64/5, p. 210. Lambert also pointed out the risk that those mistakenly arrested might challenge their detention: note of 8 February 1900, CO 417/305/ 4219, f. 167.
[37] PP 1900 (Cd. 261), p. 6.
[38] W[estern] C[ape] A[rchives] AG 2067; and *The Times*, 24 April 1900, p. 5.
[39] The figures are taken from the printed lists in WCA AG 2117.
[40] Figures taken from PP 1902 (Cd. 981), pp. 213ff. There were also cases of breaches of regulations and arms offences. On the decision not to try more cases, see CO 879/63/2, No. 175, p. 268.
[41] *Parl. Debs.*, 4th ser., vol. 85, cols. 776 (6 July 1900), 948 (9 July 1900).
[42] They were tried by the military after the Cape premier, W. P. Schreiner, had questioned their detention without trial: see CO 879/64/5, No. 200, p. 242.

they choose hang every inhabitant without trial, they only run the risk of not being indemnified & therefore of being criminally prosecuted later on. A fortiori they can administer the criminal law of the colony.

Chamberlain's telling private reaction was, 'I know nothing of & am not responsible for the administration of martial law.' His diplomatic reply to Campbell-Bannerman confirmed the men's sentences, but added that 'military tribunals are not now taking cognisance of offences against the criminal law of the colony.'[43]

The Creation of the Special Treason Court

The number of British subjects who had joined the rebels in the frontier areas when the Boers invaded – whether as combatants or collaborators – ran into the thousands. As the rebellion faded, it became evident that it was neither possible nor desirable to try them all, either in civil or in military courts.[44] By February 1900, there was general agreement that all but the ringleaders should be allowed to return to their farms on surrendering their arms, though they would remain liable to be called to account for their actions later.[45] Meanwhile, the military was instructed to keep those regarded as ringleaders under arrest and to hold full preliminary investigations into their cases. Most of the rebels south of the Orange River took advantage of this offer: by May, over 5,000 Cape rebels had surrendered.[46]

This did not resolve the problem of what to do with the rebels. As Chamberlain realised, there were difficulties both in the use of martial law courts (whose sentences would expire) and in the use of civilian ones (whose juries might be partial and unreliable). Although he considered – as a last resort – the possibility of prolonging martial law until the longest sentence had expired, his preferred option (which

---

[43] CO 48/549/21315, f. 155; see Parl. Debs., 4th ser., vol. 85, col. 948 (9 July 1900).
[44] CO 879/63/2, No. 127, p. 180 at p. 181.
[45] PP 1902 (Cd. 981), p. 28; PP 1900 (Cd. 264), enc. 1 in No. 13 at p. 39; CO 879/64/5, No. 373, p. 362; No. 397, p. 396; No. 512, p. 555. Milner had originally wanted the rebels to enter into recognisances; but the Law Officers pointed out that such legal forms could not be used under martial law: Opinion dated 26 February 1900, CO 885/15, No. 23.
[46] H. A. Shearing, 'The Cape Rebel of the South African War, 1899–1902', University of Stellenbosch Ph.D. thesis, 2004, pp. 91–92.

he proposed to Milner on 10 March) was to create a special statutory commission to try rebel cases.[47] While the Cape ministry also favoured a statutory court to deal with charges of high treason,[48] there was less agreement between the Colonial Office and the ministry over what to do with rank and file rebels. The ministry argued that they should be given an amnesty, as had been done after the more violent Canadian rebellions of 1837–1838.[49] Chamberlain rejected the analogy, and argued that such an amnesty would be equivalent to 'offering a premium to rebellion'.[50] He wanted to see the 'political disarmament of persons who have shown that they would use the vote as they have used the rifle to destroy the Empire'.[51] A way out of the impasse was proposed by Attorney General Richard Solomon in a minute drafted on 17 May. Under his plan, rebels should be divided into two classes: those in the first class – the ringleaders – would be tried for high treason before a statutory commission with the powers of the Supreme Court. Those in the second class would be investigated by a quasi-judicial commission, and be liable to disfranchisement for a five-year period.[52]

Milner realised that passing the legislation necessary for this tribunal would not be straightforward, since politicians at the Cape did not themselves agree over how to deal with rank and file rebels. Although the Progressive party strongly supported Solomon's policy of disfranchisement, Bond members wanted a complete amnesty. The division of opinion both in the Cape cabinet and in parliament generated an impasse, which created its own problems. As Milner realised, if elections had to be called to break the deadlock, the shape

---

[47] CO 879/63/2, No. 103, p. 154; Milner agreed that a statutory commission was the best way to proceed, and passed the proposals to the ministry: CO 879/63/2, No. 149, p. 252, PP 1900 (Cd. 264), p. 11.
[48] PP 1900 (Cd. 264), enc. 2 in No. 6, p. 13; CO 879/66/2, No. 173, p. 256.
[49] PP 1902 (Cd. 264), No. 7, p. 14.
[50] CO 879/63/2, No. 182, p. 273; PP 1900 (Cd. 264), No. 4, p. 7; PP 1900 (Cd. 420), No. 5, p. 10; cf. PP 1900 (Cd. 264), No. 10, p. 33; and CO 48/546/13530, f. 309.
[51] CO 48/546/20938, f. 747. Chamberlain noted that 'The object of H.M.G. is prevention & not *punishment*', but H. W. Just reminded him that the Dutch colonists could no more be deprived of their vote for political reasons than Australians or Canadians could be. Le May, *British Supremacy in South Africa*, p. 69.
[52] PP 1900 (Cd. 264), enc. 1 in No. 13, pp. 37–38; and T. R. H. Davenport, *The Afrikaner Bond: The History of a South African Political Party* (Cape Town, Oxford University Press, 1966), p. 218.

of the next parliament might well be determined by rebel votes.[53] He considered imperial legislation to be the only way out of the dilemma, but Chamberlain was averse to this idea, both because colonists would resent the constitutional interference and because they would 'throw all the blame upon us if its proceedings did not satisfy them'. Chamberlain also worried about the difficulty of passing such a measure at Westminster, in the face of obstruction from those who opposed the war.[54]

At the same time that he sent his suggestion for a special commission to Milner, Chamberlain also sent it to the Governor of Natal, Sir Walter Hely-Hutchinson.[55] Unlike ministers at the Cape, those in Natal wanted no clemency to be shown to the relatively small number of Dutch-speaking rebels who had attacked the property of their 'English friends and neighbours'. Rather than allowing the rank and file to return home, they intended to prosecute them in the ordinary courts.[56] Hely-Hutchinson consequently told Chamberlain that his ministers considered their civil courts to be adequate, and thought that the appointment of a judicial commission would be seen as a slight on their impartiality.[57] Chamberlain, however, had other political reasons for wanting Natal to agree to his proposals: as he well understood, it would be much more difficult to pass the legislation needed for a special commission at the Cape if Natal did not also agree to it. Once this delicate matter had been explained to Natal's ministers in late April, they agreed to appoint a special commission, if the Cape undertook to do the same.[58]

Given the concern that a special court made up only of the colony's own judges might be seen as a mere device to get rid of juries, Natal's Justice A. Weir Mason suggested creating a single commission for both colonies, to be staffed by six judges taken equally from the Cape, Natal and England.[59] Although this proposal was approved by the Colonial

---

[53] CO 879/63/2, No. 175, p. 268.
[54] CO 879/63/2, No. 154, p. 256; No. 182, p. 273 at p. 274.
[55] CO 879/63/2, No. 104, p. 156; No. 155, p. 257.
[56] CO 879/63/2, enc. 8 in No. 127, p. 185.
[57] CO 879/63/2, No. 158, p. 258.
[58] CO 179/211/11603, f. 451; CO 879/63/2, No. 165, p. 264; CO 879/63/1, No. 643, p. 207.
[59] Memorandum by Justice A. Weir Mason, 20 April 1900, CO 179/211/15653.

Office,[60] there were practical problems in the way of making the necessary arrangements with the Cape government. With a large number of treason cases ready for trial, Natal wanted the legislation passed by the end of May.[61] However, the Cape was far from ready to pass its bill, given that ministers there were 'hopelessly divided'. Milner therefore pressed Natal to go ahead, to help 'make things march here'.[62] Under these circumstances, Chamberlain abandoned the idea of a joint commission,[63] and Natal ended by passing a bill it had not wanted in order to nudge the reluctant Cape legislature into passing its bill. By the time Natal's Act passed at the end of June, treason trials had already commenced in its Supreme Court, since Attorney General Bale did not feel it was fair to continue to keep prisoners in gaol waiting for the legislation to pass.[64] Under the Act, all cases of treason committed before or after its passing were to be tried by a Special Court, composed of three commissioners, all of whom had to be qualified for judicial office, and at least one of whom had to be a Judge of the Supreme Court.[65] After this Act passed, the principal clerk at the Colonial Office, H. W. Just, anticipated that between 400 and 500 treason trials would follow:[66] 'the difference will be that in Natal all or almost all rebels will be brought up for trial, whilst at the Cape it will only be a proportion of the whole number.'[67] Given the shortage of judicial personnel in Natal, the ministry asked for an English judge to be appointed. None could be spared, but eventually the Chief Justice of British Guiana, Sir William Smith, was selected.[68]

Meanwhile, in the Cape, Milner suspected ministers of 'trying to bluff me into letting off nine tenths of the rebels by threatening not to pass the act of indemnity for acts committed under martial law'. He had no intention of backing down, even if this entailed a ministerial

---

[60] CO 879/63/1, No. 756, p. 249; cf. Minute of 30 April 1900 by Fred Graham, CO 48/546/13239.
[61] CO 879/63/2, No. 226, p. 307.   [62] CO 879/63/1, No. 768, p. 254.
[63] CO 879/63/2, No. 229, p. 308. See further CO 48/546/16799.
[64] Hely-Hutchinson's Diary of events, 9 June 1900, CO 179/212/20946, f. 539; R. v. Gert, Arnold and Hendrik Boers (1900) 21 NLR 116.
[65] The Act is in PP 1902 (Cd. 981), p. 50. The power to dissolve the court was vested in the Governor, who also had the power to appoint a second Special Court.
[66] CO 179/212/20945, f. 568.   [67] Minute of 28 May 1900, CO 179/211/15649, f. 653.
[68] CO 179/213/21333, f. 19; CO 179/213/24199, f. 215.

crisis and a dissolution.[69] With Prime Minister Schreiner unable to persuade his caucus to accept the policy of disfranchisement, his ministry was replaced in the middle of June, with Sir J. Gordon Sprigg as Prime Minister and Sir James Rose-Innes as Attorney General.[70] The new ministry had enough support to pass an Indemnity and Special Tribunals Act through the Assembly. The measure was opposed in the legislative council by Sir Henry de Villiers, who argued that rebels should be tried in ordinary courts. He was answered by Rose-Innes, who insisted that the rebels would get a fairer trial before this tribunal than they would before a jury in the ordinary courts.[71] The bill finally obtained Milner's assent as Governor on 11 October.

It empowered the Governor to appoint a Special Court of three, to try all cases of high treason and 'all cases of crimes of a political character' committed before or within six months after the passing of the Act. A 'political' act was defined to be any act which in the Attorney General's opinion was 'incidental to, and forming part of, political disturbances'. The court would be made up of at least two Cape Supreme Court judges and a barrister of ten years' standing. It was to have the powers of the Supreme Court, but cases were to be heard without a jury, and indictments could be brought on the basis of preliminary investigations undertaken by the military. Only those considered to be ringleaders were to be prosecuted before the Special Court, and criteria were included for determining whether a person was a ringleader. The rank and file were to be brought before commissioners appointed by the Attorney General, with those found guilty of treason or crimes of a political character being disfranchised for five years. Those who had surrendered in response to certain proclamations, and whose names had been entered on a list by a resident magistrate, were to be presumed to have committed the offence charged, unless the contrary was proved.[72] The act also provided for a system of appeals: there was an appeal from the commissioners to the Special Court, and, where the Special Court

---

[69] Milner to Chamberlain, 28 May 1900, CO 48/546/16799, f. 601.
[70] For Milner's view of the crisis, see CO 48/546/18688, f. 735.
[71] *Cape Times*, 27 September 1900.
[72] Act No. 6 of 1900. For the act, see PP 1902 (Cd. 981), p. 58. For Milner's comments on the debates on the passage of the bill, see CO 48/547/33422, f. 315.

was not unanimous, there could be an appeal to the Supreme Court. In order to head off a proposal in the Assembly for a select committee to inquire into the administration of martial law, powers were also given to any commissioners the Governor might appoint for such an inquiry.[73]

Both Natal and the Cape also legislated for indemnity. Natal's Act indemnified the Governor and officer commanding the military and those acting under them for *bona fide* acts done under martial law. It also confirmed martial law sentences, deeming them to be sentences passed by legally constituted courts. The immunity conferred was for acts done 'before, during or after the existence of Martial Law'.[74] Such a broad and prospective immunity was out of line with precedent legislation, and contrasted with the provision in the Cape Act, where the indemnity ran only to 12 October 1900.[75] The Cape legislation also indemnified the Governor and the officer commanding the Queen's forces and those acting under them for anything done in good faith as necessary for the suppression of hostilities; but, unlike the Natal Act, it included a presumption of good faith. It also confirmed the sentences imposed by military courts, and deemed all arrests for treason to have been lawful. Furthermore, it confirmed that prisoners could be kept in legal places of confinement in the colony, or elsewhere, as the Governor directed. While the validation of martial law sentences by legislation was hardly consistent with the rule of law, it had been done previously both in the Cape and in Natal. On this occasion, it was not a matter of controversy, since only a handful of rebels had been tried for treason by martial law courts, and fewer still remained in custody. Of those convicted for treason by martial law courts in the Cape, only three had unexpired sentences by the time the act came into force in October.[76] Since their sentences were shorter than those of the

---

[73] PP 1900 (Cd. 420), No. 14; enc. 1 in No. 20, pp. 78, 88–91.
[74] Act No. 15 of 1900. For a copy of the act, see PP 1900 (Cd. 420), Appendix II, p. 118.
[75] Comparing them, permanent undersecretary Sir Montagu Ommanney noted, 'It is a pity that the Natal precedent was not followed; another Indemnity Act debate at the Cape is not a pleasant prospect.' Note 25 November 1900, CO 48/548/34209, f. 8.
[76] Albertus Bloem (sentenced to five years' penal servitude 1 January 1900, commuted to two years' imprisonment with hard labour), Nicolas van der Walt (sentenced to ten years' penal servitude 9 March 1900, commuted to one year) and Andrew Loxton (sentenced to two years' imprisonment with hard labour, 7 April 1900). PP 1902 (Cd.

Sunnyside rebels who had been tried by civil courts, they were hardly likely to demand a retrial.

Legal Challenges in the Supreme Court

In February 1900, with the British press already taking a keen interest in South African events, H. C. M. Lambert – first class clerk in the South African department at the Colonial Office – noted that '[i]t will be a difficult campaign to meet because martial law is essentially illegal.' In his view, 'the essential thing' was to 'avoid collision with the Supreme Court'.[77] It did not take long for detainees at the Cape to seek writs *de homine libero exhibendo*. A number of cases were brought to the court early in the war by rebels who had been arrested in martial law areas on suspicion of aiding the enemy, before being moved to Cape Town with other (Boer) prisoners of war, and then (when writs were issued) returned to the places where they had been arrested.[78] In these cases, the Cape Supreme Court was willing to issue writs to military officers in martial law areas – thereby asserting its jurisdiction – though without determining whether the detainees would ultimately be released.[79] No final decision was made in these initial cases, for the military released the men in question.[80]

Caution was required for, as Lambert noted, the Chief Justice of the Cape, Sir Henry de Villiers, 'is certainly not prejudiced in our favour',[81] and 'does not doubt the power of the Court to call on the military to

---

981), p. 215. In Natal, fewer than ten of those convicted by martial law courts (for a variety of offences) had unexpired sentences at this time: PP 1902 (Cd. 981), p. 190.

[77] CO 48/545/3639, f. 426.

[78] They included the cases of J. J. Michau, Hercules Du Preez, Johannes Du Preez and Hendrik Johannes Uys.

[79] *Queen v. Du Preez and others* (1900) 17 SCR 53.

[80] Du Preez and his fellow detainees were released after their cases had attracted considerable attention in England. See e.g. *Hansard* 4th ser., vol. 79, col. 921 (23 February 1900), col. 1411 (1 March 1900); vol. 83, col. 574 (18 May 1900). Michau was handed over to the civil authorities but was later released: *The Times*, 5 February 1900, p. 5; 26 March 1900, p. 5; 28 March 1900, p. 5; *Parl. Debs.*, 4th ser., vol. 83, col. 392 (17 May 1900).

[81] Note of 3 February 1900, CO 48/545/3639, f. 426. De Villiers was critical of Chamberlain's policy towards the Boer Republics before the war and had been asked by Schreiner to go to Pretoria to urge reforms which might forestall a war. See Iain R. Smith, *The Origins of the South African War 1899–1902* (London, Longman, 1996), pp. 273–274. He also kept in touch with Cape politicians who

justify the detention of Br. Subjects'.[82] Milner was even more frank in his assessment:

> Sir Henry is deeply distrusted by the English here & has often been suspected as a traitor. I think this is quite unjust. ... But he is, of course thoroughly out of sympathy with the policy of H M Government & intensely Afrikander. When he, and men like him, talk of loyalty, what they mean is acquiesence in the nominal tie of the Crown between Great Britain and a country in which, under constitutional Government Afrikanders will rule the roost.[83]

However, by the middle of 1900, de Villiers was in London on sick leave, and, in his absence, John Buchanan stepped in as Acting Chief Justice.

In May 1900, the court was asked for the first time squarely to address the nature of its jurisdiction in martial law, when Jan Fourie challenged his imprisonment by a martial law court for assisting the enemy. Taking a Diceyan position, his advocate, Henry Burton, argued that the law did not recognise 'a tribunal of officers' and that the military's right to punish rebels was limited to acts necessary for suppressing rebellion. The fact that the Sunnyside rebels, who were captured in the same area, had been handed over to the civilian authorities showed that there was no necessity for military punishment in this case. The application failed, after Buchanan held that the proclamation of martial law was *prima facie* evidence of its necessity. Quoting extensively from Chief Justice Wylde's decision in *Standen v. Godfrey*,[84] he added that 'in the existing state of war and consequent necessity for martial law, the proclamation must be taken to interrupt and suspend the function of the civil Courts in these proclaimed districts.'[85] The court again refused to interfere when an application was brought on behalf of D. P. L. Gildenhuys, who was detained after having been arrested for disloyal conduct and given a preliminary examination by a resident magistrate. Rather than

---

opposed the war. See Eric A. Walker, *Lord De Villiers and His Times: South Africa 1842–1914* (London, Constable, 1925), pp. 364–389.

[82] CO 417/286, f. 506 (note 7 March 1900).
[83] Milner to Chamberlain, 11 April 1900, in Bodleian Library, MS Milner dep. 170, f. 91.
[84] *Standen v. Godfrey* (1851) 1 Searle 61 at 63.
[85] *In re Fourie* (1900) 17 SCR 173 at 178. See also the reports in *Cape Times*, 3 May 1900 and 11 May 1900.

seeking a writ *de homine libero exhibendo*, Burton applied for the detainee to be admitted to bail, presumably with a view to having him tried or having the charges dropped. This, however, was to ask the court to recognise and control the jurisdiction of the martial law court, which it was not prepared to do.[86]

Buchanan reiterated his views on martial law in the case of J. H. N. Bekker and J. J. Naudé. They were arrested and charged with treason early in the war, but were kept in prison without a trial, since the authorities were awaiting the creation of the Special Court. When their application was made on 13 July, counsel for the crown simply stated that the applicants were detained under martial law, without answering their contention that there was no necessity for martial law in the areas where they were arrested, since the enemy had been expelled and those who had joined them had been allowed to return to their farms. When Burton argued that the crown could not simply rely on the proclamation of martial law as conclusive of its necessity, Buchanan adjourned the case, treating it as an *ex parte* application and holding that notice had to be sent to the gaoler to provide a proper return to justify the detention.[87] Three days later, he wrote to the Attorney General, Rose-Innes, pointing out that the crown's failure explicitly to reply to the allegations regarding necessity meant that there was 'no return made which would justify the court in following its previous decisions'.[88] The crown took the hint. When the case returned to court, it argued that war continued to rage over the border, and (following Finlason) that martial law existed not only to put down rebellions but to prevent their recurrence. Buchanan now took the opportunity to expand on his view that martial law might still be necessary even in areas where the courts remained open and actual fighting had ceased. In his view, the fact that the proclamation of martial law had not been withdrawn in this area (though it had been elsewhere) was strong evidence of its necessity, particularly 'when it appears that the Executive is not acting arbitrarily'. Again following *Standen* v. *Godfrey*, he said that the

---

[86] *Queen* v. *Gildenhuys* (1900) 17 SCR 267 at 269. See also the report in *Cape Times*, 19 June 1900.
[87] *Queen* v. *Bekker*, *Queen* v. *Naudé* (1900) 17 SCR 340 at 343.
[88] Buchanan to Rose-Innes, 16 July 1900, Rose-Innes Papers, National Library of South Africa (Cape Town), MSC 21, Box 3, f. 307.

process of the court was neutralised by martial law. Martial law had to be regarded as a state of affairs outside the law, with responsibility for all acts under it being taken by the authorities administering it. Any attempt by the court to intervene would lead to it justifying some acts 'which the civil law cannot tolerate'.[89]

Buchanan's was not, however, the only view of the matter on the Cape Supreme Court. In a lengthy judgment in the case of Bekker and Naudé, Solomon J outlined the rival views of Dicey and Finlason on the nature of martial law, and concluded that the latter's position was now 'practically exploded'.[90] Following the Diceyan position, he held that whether or not any acts done under martial law were justifiable depended on the particular circumstances in each case; and the determination of that question could not be reserved to the military commander. Only a statute – suspending habeas corpus – could remove the court's power. Invoking the United States Supreme Court's decision in *ex parte Milligan*,[91] he argued that martial rule could be properly applied in 'the theatre of active military operations', but he did not consider that it was applicable in the case of these men. Despite this view of the law, however, Solomon agreed in refusing the application, though in his case it was for a strategic reason: a decision to release these men from military custody now and deal with them through ordinary criminal procedures would have required the civil authorities to put all the detained rebels through those procedures. Like everyone else, Solomon was aware that a new Special Court was about to be created which would deal with the rebels in a faster and more lenient way. It was hence in the best interests both of Bekker and Naudé and of 'the country generally' that they should remain for the time being in military custody.[92]

Some members of the Natal bench also took a liberal position on martial law. When Advocate W. B. Morcom of Pietermaritzburg

---

[89] *Queen v. Bekker, Queen v. Naudé* (1900) 17 SCR 340 at 350. See also the report in *Cape Times*, 14 August 1900 and 17 August 1900.

[90] *Queen v. Bekker, Queen v. Naudé* (1900) 17 SCR 340 at 355. He may have been influenced by Robert M. King's article 'Martial Law', *Cape Law Journal*, vol. 17 (1900), pp. 30–42.

[91] *Ex parte Milligan*, 71 U.S. (4 Wall.) 2, 120–121 (1866). On this case, see Amanda Tyler, *Habeas Corpus in Time of War* (Oxford, Oxford University Press, 2017), pp. 171–174.

[92] *Queen v. Bekker, Queen v. Naudé* (1900) 17 SCR 340 at 361.

applied unsuccessfully in April for an interdict to prevent his mail being opened under martial law, Mason J expressed the view that, while the military could take any action necessary to suppress a rebellion, the subject was entitled to demand that the powers should not be used 'recklessly, needlessly, cruelly or immoderately', and to ask the courts to 'require any persons infringing his rights to justify their action'.[93] Although in Morcom's case, Chief Justice Gallwey described martial law as the rule of the General in times of emergency when civil law was set aside, by June he had come round to Mason's view. In *Umbilini and Bantomo v. General Officer Commanding*, in which a challenge was made to a martial law conviction, he cited the 1838 opinion of the English Law Officers that martial law did not supersede the ordinary tribunals,[94] and added that the 'first and most sacred duty' of the court was to administer justice, 'not to preserve the peace of the country'.[95] Alluding to Du Preez's case, he confirmed that the court had power to inquire into a case decided by a court martial, though it would not interfere if it were to be convinced that the military's actions were necessary for public safety.[96] This opinion alarmed officials in London. The assistant undersecretary of state, Bertram Cox, who considered Buchanan's view 'the more convenient for Government',[97] referred the question to the Law Officers, pointing out that, if the view stated in *Umbilini* was correct, great difficulty would be experienced in administering martial law 'unless the extreme step were taken of forcibly suspending the sittings of the Civil Courts'. The opinion he got back was that *Umbilini* was 'substantially correct': a proclamation of martial law could not prevent courts from hearing habeas corpus applications. The exercise of their jurisdiction could only be 'prevented by force, as by suspension of such tribunals'.[98]

[93] *W. R. Morcom v. Postmaster General* (1900) 21 NLR 32 at 44. Mason's decision troubled Attorney General Bale, who drafted a memorandum on the case which was sent to the Colonial Office, which passed it to the Law Officers for information. CO 179/211/13191, f. 303.
[94] William Forsyth, *Cases and Opinions on Constitutional Law* (London, Stevens and Haynes, 1869), p. 199.
[95] *Umbilini and Bantomo v. General Officer Commanding* (1900) 21 NLR 86 at 88–89.
[96] Umbilini's case was heard in July, when the court held that the conviction and sentence of the martial law court had indeed been justified: see *Umbilini and another v. General Officer Commanding* (1900) 21 NLR 169.
[97] Note dated 4 July 1900, CO 179/212/20952, f. 472.
[98] Opinion dated 17 July 1900, CO 885/15 No. 43.

The Second Invasion, October 1900–March 1902

Once the Cape Act had been passed, the authorities began to prepare for trials in the new court. Records of preliminary proceedings were handed over by the military authorities to the Law Department in Cape Town, which decided which class the offender fell into and what the exact charges would be.[99] Suspects were allowed private consultation with lawyers, and the military was instructed not to seek confessions from suspects.[100] The court, made up of Justice Solomon, Justice Lange and Mr A. F. S. Maasdorp, began its work in Cape Town at the end of October.[101] The first case it tried was not that of a rebel but of a colonial policeman charged with the murder of a Basotho farm hand. The defendant, Peter William Smith, had been part of patrol searching near Naauwpoort for farmers suspected of co-operating with the enemy. The farm hand had been sullen and unco-operative when asked to produce a bridle; and when Smith reported this to his superior officer, he was instructed to shoot him if it was not produced. This was a significant case to begin with: not only did Rose-Innes classify it as a political case within the terms of the act, but he clearly did not regard the killing as covered by the indemnity provisions. Smith was acquitted, since the court found that he had honestly believed it was his duty to obey the order given.[102]

Negotiating Martial Law

By the time the court came to deal with cases of rebels – with its first sitting at Colesberg on 5 December[103] – the second invasion had commenced. The invasion interrupted the court's proceedings, and it

---

[99] Rose-Innes to Milner, 27 June 1900, Rose-Innes Papers, National Library of South Africa (Cape Town), MSC 21, Box 11, f. 19; Memorandum by Rose-Innes, c. 15 October 1900, WCA AG 2053 (Part 2).
[100] Circular dated 14 August 1900, PP 1902 (Cd. 981), p. 39.
[101] See CO 48/548/39292, f. 226 for reports of the bail proceedings.
[102] *The Queen* v. *Smith* (1900) 17 SCR 561, *Cape Times*, 30 October 1900, 31 October 1900. The 'special treason court' dealt with a number of other similar cases, including those of J. S. Maritz and B. C. Lottering (where the defence of following orders succeeded), and of Brink and Rinke Saar and four others (where it did not), heard at Mafeking in November 1901: WCA AG 2053 (Part 2).
[103] See 'Cape Treason Trials', *Cape Law Journal*, vol. 18 (1901), pp. 164–167; and *Cape Times*, 13–15, 17 December 1900.

was not until March that it resumed its sittings at Dordrecht. The Special Court would continue to sit throughout the war, convicting 361 Class 1 rebels by August 1902, and acquitting 68.[104] However, the renewed outbreak and the accompanying extension of martial law raised the question of what was to be done with those who joined the second rebellion.[105] Although, in theory, the military could now impose such penalties as it liked, Lambert reminded his masters at the Colonial Office that the aim of martial law 'is not punishment but the suppression of rebellion' and that any martial law sentences would expire at the end of the war. At the same time, he thought it highly unsatisfactory that 'rebellion can take place twice over with so slight penalties' as those imposed under the act, and wanted all the rebels to be treated as ringleaders.[106] Attorney-General Rose-Innes, who considered 'the case of a man rebelling now to be much graver than that of the man who rebelled originally', regretted the limits on prosecution put in place by the Act, and now sought wherever possible to treat rebels as falling under the first class.[107] However, there were limits to the applicability of the Act, since it gave the court no jurisdiction over offences committed after 12 April 1901. Just before this date, Rose-Innes therefore issued a general notice on 6 April stating that any act of treason or rebellion would henceforth be tried in the ordinary courts, which would impose the usual common law penalties.[108]

The idea that this would deter rebels was not shared by the military. General Henry Settle pointed out that in districts under martial law, 'rebels well know that they are safe on hands of Dutch juries'. His view – shared by Kitchener – was that '[p]rompt punishment is necessary for serious crimes and this can only be met in present state of affairs by Military Courts.'[109] Ministers referred the matter to Rose-Innes, whose

---

[104] Ninety-one were still awaiting trial, and in sixty-two cases, the Attorney General still had to decide whether to prosecute. He had declined to do so in 127 cases: CO 48/564/40351, f. 719. Returns were regularly made of the statistics.
[105] Fifty-four rebels were captured between January and 12 April 1901: Shearing, 'The Cape Rebel', p. 147.
[106] Minute 5 February 1901, CO 48/551/4374, f. 184.
[107] Rose-Innes to C. Southey, 20 March 1901, Rose-Innes Papers, National Library of South Africa, Cape Town, MSC 21, Box 11, Letter Books, vol. 6, f. 112.
[108] PP 1902 (Cd. 903), enc. in No. 10, p. 12.
[109] Telegram 11 April 1901, Cape Archives, GH 35-83. See also Edwin Tennant's report of 13 April 1901 in CO 48/552/16435, f. 287.

view of martial law (expressed to Milner at the beginning of the year) was 'I *hate* the thing; it is abhorrent to me.' While he was prepared to accept martial law insofar as it was necessary for military operations, 'I cannot without violating my own idea of what is constitutionally right & wrong agree to its being applied where there is no disturbance & where it is not required for Military operation.'[110] However, in the memorandum drawn up for ministers on 16 April, Rose-Innes agreed that in areas where civil courts, though nominally open, were in practice unable to deal with cases of treason and rebellion, the graver cases – involving only offences directly endangering the armed forces – could be tried in military courts, provided certain conditions were laid down to ensure a fair trial. Rose-Innes also insisted that Kitchener should give notice that only offences committed thereafter would be tried by military courts, to avoid a clash with the policy of trying rebels before the special court.[111] A notice, drawn up by Richard Solomon (now legal adviser to the Transvaal administration), was accordingly issued on 22 April, stating that those who took up arms or actively assisted the enemy or committed any act which endangered the safety of the King's army or subjects after this date would be tried by courts martial.[112]

Although Kitchener initially claimed the right to try any rebel in martial law courts – considering the Cape Act to be 'a local arrangement' which had not 'in any way' abrogated military jurisdiction in proclaimed districts – he agreed by the end of August not to allow martial law trials for offences committed before 12 April.[113] For his part, Prime Minister Sprigg confirmed 'that necessary steps will be taken to ensure continuance of sentences of imprisonment passed by Courts Martial until such time as confirmation of the same has been obtained by an Act of the

---

[110] Rose-Innes to Milner, 1 January 1901, Rose-Innes Papers, National Library of South Africa (Cape Town), MSC 21 (Box 11), f. 86.
[111] PP 1902 (Cd. 903), enc 2 in No. 11, p. 13.
[112] PP 1902 (Cd. 903), enc. 6 in No. 11, p. 15.
[113] Kitchener's refusal of the Cape's request to hand over P. P. Mare and P. H. Fouche, who had surrendered at the beginning of March, but been tried by a martial law court in the middle of July, led to a dispute which was resolved by late August (letting the military sentence stand): Kitchener to Governor, 25 July 1901, CO 48/553/28939, f. 531; Legal Adviser, Pretoria to Attorney General, Cape Town, 26, 28 July, 30 August 1901, WCA AG 2091 (Part 2).

Legislature'.[114] As a result of these developments, rebels could now be dealt with in one of three ways. Those who committed offences before 12 April would be tried before the Special Court, which had given no sentences in excess of five years. Those who committed an 'aggravated form of treason' in martial law areas would be tried by courts martial, which might inflict the death penalty. For those who did not fall into either category, there could be a trial before the civil courts.[115] A political compromise thus generated a hybrid system of martial law, where the court before which a rebel was tried might be determined by the date of his offence. Instead of this martial law regime being one of sheer lawlessness or executive will, it was the product of negotiations which had to satisfy the constitutional expectations of a responsible government's ministers.

Negotiations between the civilian and military authorities over the nature of martial law can also be seen in other areas. Under the Martial Law Regulations which were issued in May 1901, magistrates were recognised as having a dual jurisdiction, with powers to deal with ordinary crimes, as well as powers to deal summarily with breaches of martial law regulations as agents of the military.[116] The Regulations also allowed officers to arrest without warrant any persons suspected of assisting the enemy, exciting disaffection or disturbing the peace. In such cases, evidence against the suspect was to be collected as expeditiously as possible, with preliminary examinations taken either before the officer administering martial law or before a magistrate, with a view to a trial. These Regulations – which 'which met with the concurrence of the Attorney-General's office'[117] – sought to map out a quasi-judicial procedure for martial law trials, and provided for co-operation between civilian and military officers. In practice, there were numerous complaints from the civilian authorities about the heavy-handed application of martial law,[118] as a result of which the arrangement was modified in

[114] Hely-Hutchinson to Chamberlain, 27 May 1901, CO 48/552/18365, f. 844.
[115] Note by Lambert, 13 April 1901, CO/48/552/16380, f. 219.
[116] PP 1902 (Cd. 981), pp. 46–49; cf. PP 1901 (Cd. 547), enc. 3 in No. 36, p. 31. See further Keith Surridge, 'Rebellion, Martial Law and British Civil–Military Relations: The War in Cape Colony 1899–1902', *Small Wars & Insurgencies*, vol. 8:2 (1997), pp. 44–45.
[117] Wynne to Hely-Hutchinson, 19 September 1901, CO 48/554/35801, f. 586.
[118] See the letters from Rose-Innes to Settle, 14 September 1901, in Rose-Innes Papers, National Library of South Africa (Cape Town), MSC 21 (Box 11), f. 171, and 14, 19, 20 December 1901 WCA AG 2091 (Part 2).

December 1901, when twelve military Administrators of Martial Law were appointed in specified areas, each of whom would use the local resident magistrates as a Deputy Administrator, to deal with minor matters (such as the regulation of food supplies).[119]

The fact that the extent and operation of martial law could be a matter of negotiation between the civilian and military authorities became particularly evident in August 1901, when the military sought to extend martial law to the Cape ports. The desire to do so was driven by intelligence reports that 'undesirables' were returning to the Cape in private ships, and that a political network existed there which aimed to foster a rebellion in the Western Cape.[120] Ministers reacted unenthusiastically to this proposal, unconvinced that there was any threat which the local police force could not deal with, and afraid that martial law would bring business to a standstill.[121] Faced with these rival pressures, Hely-Hutchinson (who had replaced Milner as Governor of the Cape in March) began to negotiate, asking Kitchener to agree to use martial law powers for specified limited purposes only, and proposing to give ministers a written undertaking that, if they were used for any other purposes, he would repeal the proclamation on their request.[122] While Kitchener was prepared to agree to 'having martial law for certain definite purposes only', ministers unanimously rejected the proposal.[123] 'We cannot work Martial Law on even terms with the Military', Rose-Innes told the Governor: 'Either they or we must be in front. I am not going to ride behind.'[124] Ministers felt that a modified martial law was an impossibility: once it was proclaimed, it would override civil law in

---

[119] Circular 'Martial Law Administration' (G. K. Cockerill), 1 December 1901, PP 1902 (Cd. 981), pp. 116–117.

[120] O 879/73/2, No. 179, p. 171; enc. 1 in No. 232, p. 210; enc. 2 in No. 263, p. 298. See also John S. Galbraith, 'British War Measures in Cape Colony, 1900–1902: A Study of Miscalculations and Mismanagement', *South African Historical Journal*, vol. 15:1 (1983), pp. 77–80; and Surridge, 'Rebellion, Martial Law and British Civil-Military Relations', pp. 50–54.

[121] In particular, Sprigg did not want the 'Supreme Court of the country and the principal public offices of the Colony within an area under the control of the Military': CO 879/73/2, enc. 4 in No. 218, p. 199.

[122] Hely-Hutchinson to Milner, 31 August 1901, CO 48/554/34826, f. 41; see also CO 879/73/2, No. 186, p. 173.

[123] CO 879/73/2, encs. 1 and 2 in No. 232, pp. 210–211; No. 196, p. 185.

[124] CO 879/73/2, No. 233, p. 213.

any case of conflict.[125] They also insisted that the responsibility for proclaiming martial law rested with them, and that they would not do so until satisfied of its necessity.[126]

At this point, civil–military relations were plunged to a new low when Kitchener sought to force the ministry's hand by threatening to impose a cordon around the Cape ports, and to divert all non-military vessels to Durban. Facing a ministerial crisis, Hely-Hutchinson protested to Chamberlain, who responded with reassurances that no action would be taken without first consulting the Cape government.[127] He realised that, without a government in the Cape, indemnity legislation would have to be passed in London, where its opponents would argue that 'ministers were driven from office in defending their constitutional rights from the lawless invasions of the military & of the Imperial Govt.'[128] Great efforts were now made to put an innocent gloss on what Chamberlain called Kitchener's 'stupid blunder', and to persuade Sprigg to consider the 'position in which Cape Colony would be placed as a member of Empire in case of request refused'.[129] As a sweetener, the army proposed setting up a Board of Administration of Martial Law in the Cape, composed of both civilian and military elements, which would investigate any complaints against martial law.[130]

The matter was finally resolved when Sprigg met Kitchener and Milner at the beginning of October in Pretoria and agreed the terms on which martial law would be extended to the Cape. Under the agreement, the military were given the right of censorship – to be exercised with as little inconvenience to the public as possible – and were authorised to impose restrictions on undesirables. Control of all works at the ports was to remain in civilian hands, though the military were empowered to appoint officers to supervise the examination of cargoes. The agreement also stipulated that there should be no martial

---

[125] CO 879/73/1, No. 761, p. 231. [126] CO 879/73/2, enc. 1 in No. 241, p. 224.
[127] CO 879/73/1, No. 747, p. 226; No. 751, p. 228; No. 780, p. 239; CO 879/73/2, No. 207, p. 189; No. 225, p. 207.
[128] Note by Lambert, 19 September 1901, CO 48/554/32906, f. 409.
[129] Note by Chamberlain, 22 September 1901, CO 48/554/33208, f. 515; CO 879/73/1, No. 774, p. 237. Sprigg retorted that 'the best means of maintaining the Empire in its supreme position is to accept the advice of those who have spent the best part of their lives in the Colony which is their home': CO 879/73/2, enc. in No. 262, p. 297.
[130] CO 879/73/1, No. 784, p. 241.

law courts for British subjects at the Cape ports. No subject was to be arrested by the military without an affidavit charging him with a crime, for which he would be tried before the Resident Magistrate by ordinary law, unless the Attorney General directed otherwise.[131] Following this agreement, on 9 October, martial law was extended to the ports, and Regulations were issued for its administration in these areas.[132] Once more, the parameters of martial law had been sketched out through a process of constitutional negotiation between the civil government, the imperial authorities and the military.

At the same time, there remained tensions between the civilian and military authorities. By September, Rose-Innes had come to the view that one effect of Kitchener's April proclamation had been 'to diffuse throughout all the ranks of those engaged in the administration of Martial Law an idea that they can go much further and be much more rigorous than they were before'. He now regretted that the government had 'consented to allow the more serious political offences to be tried by Military Courts'.[133] Sentences imposed by martial law courts were much more severe than those imposed by the treason court: by the end of the first week in September, fourteen rebels had been executed.[134] Protests were made both in Britain and at the Cape, after three rebels were hanged in their home towns, with locals being made to watch the executions.[135] In response, Lord Stanley explained that this had been simply a 'single instance', to show that the sentences imposed by martial law courts would really be carried out.[136] Further executions followed, albeit not in public.

---

[131] CO 879/71/4, enc. in No. 156, p. 211. The Resident Magistrate would also deal with breaches of martial law regulations by subjects, acting as deputy of the commandant.

[132] Hely-Hutchinson to Chamberlain, 9 October 1901, PP 1902 (Cd. 903), p. 89; PP 1902 (Cd. 981), p. 111.

[133] Rose-Innes to R. Solomon, 3 September 1901, Rose-Innes Papers, National Library of South Africa (Cape Town), MSC 21 (Box 11), f. 148.

[134] During this period, 134 rebels were sentenced by courts martial, with 90 death sentences being imposed. In forty-two of these cases, the death sentence had been commuted, while in fourteen more, the sentence awaited confirmation: CO 879/71/4, enc. in No. 125, p. 160.

[135] They were Frederick Marais, Johannes Petrus Coetzee and Cornelius Classen. Shearing, 'The Cape Rebel', pp. 153–154; and CO 879/73/2, No. 150A, p. 144. The ministry protested that the compelled involvement of civilians might implicate them in a form of procedure over which they had no control: Minute of Ministers, 19 July 1901, WCA AG 2053 (Part 1).

[136] See *Parl. Debs.*, 4th ser., vol. 99, cols. 272–273 (9 August 1901). See also Shearing, 'The Cape Rebel', pp. 155–156.

More protests followed over the heavy-handed way in which martial law was being implemented. Rose-Innes felt that commandants were taking action quite outside the printed instructions contained in the Regulations. He raised a particular concern in early September that a number of influential citizens from Paarl and Ceres were being detained by the military in civilian prisons for long periods with no investigation of their cases.[137] The matter led to a bad-tempered clash with the Chief of Staff, Colonel Arthur Wynne.[138] In Rose-Innes's view, it was 'one of the essentials of the most ordinary justice that a man should know on what ground he is detained'.[139] He also pointed out that the government would have to secure an indemnity for the military, and that to do this they would have to be 'in a position to assure the House that justice has been done in each case'.[140] Although Wynne conceded that it was wrong to commit people to prison with no charges being made, he defended the detentions, arguing that Paarl and Ceres were hotbeds of disaffection, 'ripe for active rebellion'.[141] He also considered it necessary 'to check any tendency to control the administration of martial law, not according to the discretion of responsible military officers, but according to the views of the Attorney General'.[142] In Wynne's view, commandants were solely responsible for the execution of martial law, and it was the duty of magistrates to assist them, and not 'to pry upon their actions'.[143]

Clearly resentful of being taken to task by the lawyer, Wynne responded with a lengthy memorandum explaining the difference between martial law and civil law. In times of war, he argued, the welfare of the community had to take priority over the rights of individuals. At such times, arrests had to be made on the basis of

---

[137] CO 879/73/2, No. 188, p. 174; enc. 1 in No. 233, p. 214.
[138] Wynne – who resented the fact that the Attorney General had raised the matter with Kitchener's legal adviser – accused him of acting without honour or justice: CO 879/73/2, enc. 8(L) in No. 261, p. 291 at p. 292.
[139] CO 879/73/2, enc. 6(A) in No. 261, p. 279 at p. 281. Cf. James Rose-Innes, *Autobiography*, ed. B. A. Tindall (Oxford, Oxford University Press, 1949), p. 193.
[140] CO 879/73/2, enc. 2(A) in No. 261, p. 272 at p. 263; cf. CO 879/71/4, enc. 4 in No. 46, p. 42.
[141] CO 879/73/2, enc. 8(L) in No. 261, p. 291 at p. 292; enc. 5 in No. 261, p. 277.
[142] CO 879/73/2, enc. 7 in No. 23, p. 219.
[143] CO 879/73/2, enc. 2(B) in No. 261, p. 274.

suspicion, drawing on a system of intelligence which would be exposed and undermined if any case came to court.[144] Reading over the exchanges, Fred Graham thought Wynne's memorandum to be 'excellent' and minuted that Rose-Innes had 'adopted an unreasonable position ... which would defeat the very object of martial law'. He also mused that the correspondence revealed how ministers in a self-governing colony might obstruct operations against an enemy, if they chose to stand on their legal rights.[145]

Legal Challenges

The cases which had attracted Rose-Innes's attention soon found their way into the Supreme Court. The first case was brought by D. F. Marais, a Notary Public and attorney at Paarl. Marais was arrested on 15 August by the Chief Constable, who had no warrant and did not know the cause of the arrest. Two days after his arrest, a report in the *Cape Times* alerted Rose-Innes to the matter, leading him to telegraph the magistrate at Paarl asking for full particulars of the charges. In reply, he was informed that the arrests were made on military authority and that there were no affidavits against them.[146] Two days later, Marais and four others arrested at the same time were moved to Beaufort West, 250 miles away. After nine days' incarceration in a 'badly ventilated, small, unbearably hot' prison, Marais asked to see the local commandant, but was refused.[147] Meanwhile, a firm of attorneys in Cape Town took up the case of the detainees. However, General Wynne was not prepared to allow the men to communicate with their lawyers or family, or even to answer their inquiries himself; but sharply told the Law Department at the Cape that he was 'responsible to his Military Superiors only for the action he takes under Martial Law'.[148]

Although Marais was not told of any charges against him, he was visited in prison on 27 August by an intelligence officer named Burton.

---

[144] CO 879/73/2, enc. 2 in No. 263, p. 298.
[145] Note 15 November 1901, CO 48/554/36629, f. 682.
[146] Telegram dated 17 August 1901, WCA AG 2051.
[147] D. F. Marais, Statement of Grievance (March 1902), WCA AG 3714.
[148] Major W. P. Braithwaite to Secretary to Law Dept, 27 August 1901, WCA AG 2041 (Paarl Disturbances).

After producing a flask of whisky, he showed Marais a letter which alleged that the attorney knew of stocks of ammunition hidden in the Swartberg mountains, and that, if he would locate them, he would be 'alright'. Marais flatly denied having any such knowledge: 'I now decided to petition the Court, as I feared that the strain of gaol life would prove too much for me.'[149] Notice of the petition to release him was served on Wynne on 2 September, who submitted an affidavit on the first day of the hearing, which stated that he had ascertained that there was a *prima facie* case against Marais and the other detainees, and that there were military reasons for his removal and detention. Although he was not prepared to disclose any charges, he confirmed that they would be formally charged 'as soon as possible' and would either be acquitted or be detained in custody following the verdict of a military court.[150] When his petition was brought, Marais's advocate distinguished his case from *Fourie* and *Bekker* on the ground that (unlike them) Marais had neither been charged nor convicted by the military. Although Buchanan ACJ again declined to take notice of any acts of the military,[151] he ordered a return to be made on 12 September: for while it was common knowledge that the men had been arrested under martial law, they were being detained in a civil prison by a civilian officer, who needed to answer by what authority he held the detainee. It was the conduct of the civilians, not the military, which was of concern here.

The warrants to commit Marais and the others were issued only on 8 September, two days after the first hearing. In his draft affidavit of the next day, the civilian gaoler at Beaufort West, Henry Risk, stated

> The reason I allowed these prisoners to be placed in gaol without any warrant is because in a previous case, viz that of Gert Visagie & others, the men were placed in Gaol against my wishes and by force and an armed guard placed over the Awaiting Trial yard with orders to take no orders either from the Resident Magistrate or myself.[152]

---

[149] D F Marais, Statement of Grievance (March 1902), WCA AG 3714. In fact, his petition was submitted by his lawyers, who had not been allowed to communicate with Marais.

[150] *Marais v. The General Officer Commanding the Lines of Communication and the Attorney General* [1901] 18 SCR 301 at 304 (dated in WCA AG 3714).

[151] He noted that civil courts lacked the power to enforce orders against the military: *Cape Times*, 7 September 1901 (also 2 CTR 469).

[152] WCA AG 2041 (Paarl Disturbances). On Attorney General Ward's instructions, this phrase was omitted from the submitted affidavit.

The warrant stated that the men were committed under Martial Law Regulation 14(2), for inciting others to take up arms against the king, but no substantive details of the charges were provided. When the case returned to court, it was Rose-Innes himself who opposed Marais's release on behalf of the crown, arguing that the detainees were in the custody of the civilian gaoler at the request of the military. Although he had strongly condemned this practice in his correspondence with military officials, Rose-Innes defended it in public. Buchanan ACJ rejected the application, holding as sufficient the formal return that the gaoler held Marais as an officer under the control of the military, acting on military instructions in a martial law area. He added that it had been established in previous cases that the proclamation of martial law at Beaufort West was justified by its necessity, which meant that the onus was on the applicants to establish that this necessity no longer existed. As for Adv. Currey's argument that there was no necessity for martial law at Paarl, where Marais had been arrested, Buchanan took the view that this would be relevant only if he were still being held there. Refusing to look into the charges on which Marais was being held, he also repeated his earlier view that 'while martial law was paramount the civil authority would stay its hand.'[153]

Shortly after this decision was handed down, the court heard the very similar case of Dr R. J. Reinecke. One of only two medical doctors in Ceres, he was removed by the military to Malmesbury (fifty miles away) on 28 August. One month later, his wife lodged an application for his release, pointing out that the ordinary courts exercised undisturbed jurisdiction in both towns. This time, Rose-Innes did not appear for the government, but sent his deputy, Dr Ward KC, to argue the case. Although the case looked identical to Marais's, on this occasion Buchanan ACJ ordered the detainee's release, on the ground that he was being held by civilian gaolers, rather than being in military custody. 'The gaoler, as a Civil servant of the law, has no right to hold a prisoner on the order of anybody except a duly constituted Civil officer of the Crown', he ruled, 'and as he had no warrant from any such officer, he is not entitled to keep custody of this person.'[154]

---

[153] *Marais v. The General Officer Commanding the Lines of Communication and the Attorney General* [1901] 18 SCR 301 at 309–310.

[154] *Reinecke v. Attorney-General and Others* [1901] 18 SCR 349 at 354.

Officials at the Cape and in London were both shocked and puzzled by this decision, the real grounds for which Buchanan later explained to Hely-Hutchinson. In Reinecke's case, it had not been stated in the affidavits for the crown that the detainee was being held in military custody. Although in Marais's case, Buchanan was prepared – at a stretch – to accept a verbal statement from the Attorney General that the detainee was being held in military custody, he was not prepared to accept such a statement from his deputy.[155] If Buchanan was hereby asserting the need to comply with legal formalities, officials in London were unimpressed with his alighting on a 'technical & foolish point'. 'The point of substance is that the Court interfered with the exercise of martial law which it is unwise of a Court to do', Bertram Cox minuted, 'If the soldiers had declined to permit the release the Court would have been helpless & in an undignified position.'[156] In fact, Reinecke was not released: the military authorities responded by taking over the prison in Malmesbury and appointing the civil gaoler to act in a military capacity. A circular was sent to all Resident Magistrates to inform them that all gaols were to be considered as under the orders of the commandant.[157]

'[A]ggrieved by the decision of the Supreme Court', Marais decided to appeal to the Privy Council.[158] The court which heard his application for leave to appeal on 5 November was made up of seven judges: Lord Chancellor Halsbury, Lords Macnaghten, Shand, Davey, Robertson and Lindley, and Sir Henry de Villiers. It was clear from the exchanges that the different judges on the panel did not view martial law in the same way. Lord Davey – who had a number of liberal South Africans friends including de Villiers[159] – seemed particularly

---

[155] Hely-Hutchinson to Chamberlain, 2 October 1901, CO 48/554/36639, f. 915.
[156] Minute, 22 October 1901, CO 48/554/36634, f. 838.
[157] Hely-Hutchinson to Chamberlain, 2 October 1901, CO 48/554/36634, f. 839. Reinecke was released on parole on 25 October (after a new military officer took charge at Malmesbury), pending trial by a martial law court. After a review of his case in January found there was no evidence against him, he was given permission to go to Europe (but not to return to Ceres): see his account in *The Times*, 27 March 1902, p. 6.
[158] Marais, Statement of Grievance, WCA AG 3714. Marais's decision to appeal led Chamberlain to advise Hely-Hutchinson to 'defer further action' in relation to the charges against him until its decision had been handed down: Chamberlain to Hely-Hutchinson, 16 September 1901, CO 48/554/34826, f. 303.
[159] After hosting John X. Merriman to dinner in March 1901, Davey told de Villiers that he was 'so depressed and so different from what he was when I had the pleasure of

sympathetic to Sir Richard Haldane KC's arguments for Marais, and argued that the Petition of Right forbad the use of martial law courts when the civil courts were open.[160] By contrast, Lords Halsbury and Shand inclined to the view that, in wartime, it was for the military to judge the necessity for martial law, and that, once it had been proclaimed, they could determine the area over which it applied. In Halsbury's view, '[i]f the public safety and that of the realm render it necessary to supersede the ordinary law you are not bound in every individual case to prove the necessity or even to state the charge.' Furthermore, '[t]he courts are not open when resort to them would be unsafe to the King's authority.'[161]

The petition was rejected, with three members of the court reported to be in the minority. The customary single judgment of the judicial committee was delivered by Halsbury on 18 December. The Lord Chancellor dismissed the argument that martial law courts had no jurisdiction if the civil courts were open: the fact that they were open for some purposes did not mean that war was not raging. Indeed, Halsbury stated – incorrectly – that Marais's own affidavits had made it clear that war was raging.[162] '[N]o doubt has ever existed that where war actually prevails the ordinary Courts have no jurisdiction over the action of the military authorities.'[163] The division of opinion on the bench became public in March 1902, in a debate in the House of Lords, during which Halsbury did not shy away from defending his position: 'The real English of the matter is that if you are at war there is and there can be no constitutional liberty at all.'[164] By contrast, Lord Davey insisted that it did not follow that because there was a state of war, 'persons are to be deprived of their constitutional rights . . . and the whole jurisdiction of the courts handed

meeting him at the Cape'. Davey to de Villiers, 2 April 1901, De Villiers Papers, National Library of South Africa, MSC 7 (Box 8).
[160] *Manchester Guardian*, 6 November 1901, p. 6.
[161] *Manchester Guardian*, 6 November 1901, p. 6.
[162] *D. F. Marais v. The General Officer Commanding the Lines of Communication and the Attorney General of the Cape Colony* [1902] AC 109 at 114. The petition and affidavit spoke only of Marais's arrest and removal by the military and made no explicit mention of a state of war.
[163] *D. F. Marais v. The General Officer Commanding the Lines of Communication and the Attorney General of the Colony* [1902] AC 109 at 115.
[164] *Parl. Debs.*, 5th ser., vol. 105, col. 139 (17 March 1902).

over to military tribunals set up for the purpose'.[165] He regarded Halsbury's view as unconstitutional since it seemed to recognise a prerogative power to suspend the ordinary courts, which was equivalent to the French state of siege.[166]

The decision received mixed reviews in the Cape press.[167] It was also debated by a number of jurists in the *Law Quarterly Review*. They included Frederick Pollock, who defended a Diceyan position, but felt that the judicial committee had come to the correct decision, since the effective radius of warfare was much broader in the modern age, and that 'the absence of visible disorder and the continued sitting of the courts are not conclusive evidence of a state of peace.'[168] By contrast, 'A Jurisconsult' writing in *The Speaker* lambasted 'the Liberty of the Subject according to Lord Halsbury', arguing that the court had ignored the central point that Marais – like George Gordon before him in 1865 – had been moved to a distant place where the civil courts were closed, something which violated Lord Carnarvon's rules.[169] Two months after the decision had been made, it was also discussed judicially in Ireland, in a civil suit brought by the District Commissioner of Kintampo in the Northern Territories of the Gold Coast against a senior military officer who had detained him during a time of rebellion. Addressing the jury, Chief Baron Palles said that, while he respected the Privy Council's decision, he was not prepared to accept 'that the law now is that in a country in which a state of war or rebellion exists, any act done by any officer serving in the forces of the Crown, whether it is or not one of military necessity, is not cognizable by the ordinary courts of justice'. Nor was he prepared to '[lay] down as law that if a rebellion exists in any part of a country, then the entire country is to be subjected to the license of all the officers and forces of the Crown'.[170]

---

[165] *Parl. Debs.*, 5th ser., vol. 105, col. 148 (17 March 1902).

[166] *Parl. Debs.*, 5th ser., vol. 105, col. 149 (17 March 1902). See also *Parl. Debs.*, 5th ser., vol. 106, col. 1158 (24 April 1902).

[167] See the *Cape Times*, 20 December 1900 and the press cuttings in WCA AG 3714.

[168] F. Pollock, 'What Is Martial Law?', *Law Quarterly Review*, vol. 18 (1902), pp. 152–158 at p. 157. The other articles were by H. Erle Richards, 'Martial Law', ibid., pp. 133–142 and Cyril Dodd, 'The Case of Marais', ibid. pp. 143–151.

[169] 'The Liberty of the Subject According to Lord Halsbury', *The Speaker*, 28 December 1901. See also the critical leader in *Manchester Guardian*, 19 December 1901, p. 5.

[170] *Rainsford v. Browne* (1902) 2 New Irish Jurist and Local Government Review, 179 at 186.

The decision to detain men like Marais was motivated by a desire to control potential political intrigue in the Western Cape, rather than being driven by the kind of military necessity which (as has been seen) men like Rose-Innes were prepared to accept as a justification for martial law. Colonial officials had long been suspicious of the loyalty of towns such as Paarl, whose educated inhabitants 'cherish the dreams of an African Dutch state'.[171] By the middle of 1901 there was a perception that it would take very little for local Bond politicians to rebel.[172] Indeed, in July, the military's unreliable secret agent, Capt. C. Ross, reported a claim that 'every Bond member was ready to rise'.[173] It was in this context that men like Marais – whose father had been a Bond Member of the Cape Legislature for Paarl until 1900 – came under suspicion. In upholding his detention, both the Privy Council and Pollock accepted the military's general suspicions as demonstrating the necessity for his detention, rather than Rose-Innes's more rigorous test.

Sir Henry de Villiers returned to resume his duties on the Cape bench after the judgment in *Marais* had been handed down. It soon became clear that he would take a narrow view of its meaning. He was given the first chance to express his view in April 1902, when he heard the cases of J. W. Malan and J. D. Bruyns. Both men had been detained in Calvinia on charges of treason, for offences committed before 12 April 1901. In both cases, the Attorney General had instructed the magistrates that they were to be dealt with as Class 2 rebels, who were entitled to be released. However, both men were moved by the military in November 1901 to Clanwilliam prison. They subsequently escaped from prison and were sentenced after being recaptured to six months' imprisonment with hard labour by the Resident Magistrate of Clanwilliam. In his decision, de Villiers acknowledged the Privy Council's ruling that, during wartime, the military could not be held liable for any illegal acts committed. However, he regarded the case before him as a civilian rather than a military one, for the magistrate

---

[171] Lambert note, 20 Nov 1899, CO 48/543/34343, f. 493; cf. Milner Diary of events, 16 January 1901, CO 48/551/4322, f. 146.

[172] In six border districts which rebelled, forty-eight out of seventy-three Bond officials were convicted of treason, while eight more had absconded. Hely-Hutchinson to Chamberlain, 2 June 1902, CO 48/561/25265, f. 250; PP 1902 (Cd. 903), p. 119.

[173] Report, 8 July 1901, CO 48/554/36637, f. 891.

had sentenced the men under provisions of an ordinary statute, and not under military regulations. Furthermore, de Villiers held that the decision to classify them as Class 2 rebels entitled them to be released from prison in Calvinia, so that the removal of the men to Clanwilliam without a proper warrant was unlawful. In passing, the Chief Justice criticised the use of magistrates as Deputy Administrators of Martial Law, which he saw as 'fatal to the due administration of justice'.[174]

De Villiers's decision irritated the Cape's Attorney General T. L. Graham. The Chief Justice's view on the rights of Class 2 rebels to an immediate release did not reflect the understanding which had hitherto been acted on by the Law Department, and he worried that those who had not been released might commence civil actions. He therefore wrote to all Resident Magistrates instructing them to release any remaining Class 2 rebels; and advised the military to re-arrest under martial law powers any of them they considered necessary to keep in detention. In London, Bertram Cox noted that 'the attitude of the Cape Courts shows that we must take action as to the prisoners under martial law as soon as possible by removing them or by legislation.'[175]

De Villiers had another opportunity to express his views on martial law in July, when Bailly van Reenen and Daniel van Reenen challenged their convictions for breaching martial law regulations by two magistrates, one in Durbanville and the other in Malmesbury. The men were tried for breaching a regulation which forbade people from entering or leaving the district of Malmesbury without a permit, which they had contravened by moving two mules in the early hours of the morning from one district to the other. Applying the rule in *Marais*, de Villiers held that the court could not interfere in the decision of the Durbanville court, since the Resident Magistrate there had purported to act in his capacity as Deputy Administrator of Martial Law. At the same time, he took the occasion to observe that 'it cannot be assumed that Martial law will be maintained any longer, in view of the Privy Council's decision [in *Marais*] that Martial Law can only be justified by the existence of actual hostilities.'[176]

---

[174] R. v. *Malan and Bruyns* (1902) 19 SCR 187 at 191–192.
[175] Report of T. Lynedoch Graham AG 5 May 1902, CO 48/560/21618, f. 679.
[176] *Cape Times*, 14 July 1902; cf. R. v. *Bailly van Reenen and Others* (1902) 19 SCR 332 at 334.

Turning to the decision of the Malmesbury court, he observed that the record of that case stated that it had taken place in the 'Court of the Resident Magistrate and Deputy Administrator of Martial Law'. Insofar as it purported to be the decision of a civilian court, de Villiers held that it was amenable to review; and, as its proceedings were irregular (and a sentence imposed for an offence unknown to civilian law), its proceedings were quashed.[177] As this case revealed, officials in Malmesbury had used the ordinary forms of the courts when drawing charges for breaches of martial law regulations, without deleting the words 'In the Court of the Resident Magistrate', and only sometimes adding in the initials of the Deputy Administrator of Martial Law. In response to this decision, the Administrator of Martial Law instructed them to alter the books containing the records of martial law cases, to make it appear that they had been treated only as martial law cases. The legal effect of this was considered by de Villiers in August, when a number of those sentenced at Malmesbury for breaches of martial law regulations challenged their convictions.[178] De Villiers held that these cases had to be treated in the same way as Bailly van Reenen's, since he could not sanction the alteration of the record, even if authorised by a military officer.

When Bertram Cox saw the decision in Bailly van Reenen's case, he conceded that it was 'within the law' but commented that de Villiers's 'knowledge of the Marais decision was rudimentary and ridiculous.'[179] For his part, the Cape's Attorney General thought the decision wrong, and decided to appeal to the Privy Council. The case was heard in London in December 1903. By this stage, with the war over and martial law at an end, the question was academic: but it gave the court another opportunity to clarify its view of the powers of civil courts over martial law decisions. None of the respondents was represented at the hearing, for which the Cape government secured Haldane's services.[180] Once again it was Halsbury who delivered the judgment. Overturning the

---

[177] R. v. *Bailly van Reenen and Others* (1902) 19 SCR 332; and *Cape Times*, 14 July 1902.
[178] *South African News*, 29 August 1902.
[179] Note, 8 August 1902, CO 48/563/32119, f. 98.
[180] According to Frederick Mackarness (one of the lawyers in *Marais*), 'The appeal is really a War Office one, & the War Office people were present instructing the petitioners' representatives.' Mackarness to de Villiers, 27 November 1902, De Villiers Papers, National Library of South Africa (Cape Town), MSC 7 (Box 9).

Cape court's decision, he ruled that de Villiers had gone wrong in treating the documents in question as a 'record' of a court of justice, rather than simply a memorandum of the charges. The case, he concluded, was heard by Mr C. W. Broers in his capacity of deputy administrator of martial law, and not as a magistrate, so that the Supreme Court lacked jurisdiction.[181] This was a short, simple judgment, which omitted any mention of the alteration of the documents on the orders of the military. Where both the civilian and military authorities at the Cape assumed that the civil courts retained some measure of jurisdiction, the Lord Chancellor in England held to his blunt view that, so long as the proclamation of martial law was in force, all civil jurisdiction was gone. Once more, the view from London was much less Diceyan than the view from Cape Town.

The Martial Law Board

When martial law was extended to the Cape ports in October 1901, the military agreed to the creation of a Martial Law Board to deal with complaints about the administration of martial law, to be made up of three men chosen by the General Officer Commanding Cape Colony, the Prime Minister and the Governor. H. W. Just was pleased to see the Board set up to deal with complaints, since he realised that, although martial law rendered the will of the military paramount, neither the government in Cape Town nor the Colonial Office could escape 'a very grave responsibility if there are scandals or mistakes'.[182] Chamberlain wanted the Board made up of practical legal men, but was insistent that Rose-Innes should not be on it, since he was 'peculiarly unfitted by his habit of mind for a position [...] where it is necessary to consider expediency and policy as well as his conscientious scruples'.[183] Lewis L. Michell, the general manager of the Standard Bank, was nominated as chairman by the Governor. He clearly had no intention of rocking the boat, telling Hely-Hutchinson that he saw his task as one of helping and not hindering the military authorities. Besides discouraging frivolous grievances, he noted that not too much was to be 'made

---

[181] *Attorney General for the Cape of Good Hope v. Van Reenen* [1904] AC 114 at 118–119, cf. *The Times*, 10 December 1903, p. 10.
[182] Note 21 November 1901, CO 48/555/38373, f. 15.
[183] CO 879/73/2, No. 246, p. 240.

even of substantial hardships to the individual, if clearly necessary to be inflicted in the interests of the State, which must be paramount'.[184]

The Board's work continued until July 1902, by which point it had dealt with 542 complaints in 74 meetings.[185] The largest number of complaints related to deportations, primarily those to Port Alfred. Of 141 such cases which came before the Board, it declined to intervene in 76. Thirty were 'satisfactorily adjusted' without its intervention, and only five were redressed through its recommendation, while twenty-nine were resolved by the intervention of peace. Most officials thought the work had been done well. Reporting to Hely-Hutchinson in December 1901, Michell stated that in the majority of cases 'complainants have suffered through some misconduct of their own, or were dealt with on reasonable grounds of suspicion'.[186] Looking over the first six months of its work, Sir Montagu Ommanney (who was usually sympathetic to the military) similarly observed that the report 'does not lend much support to the allegations of hardship in the administration of martial law'.[187] Others were more sceptical: as Sir Henry de Villiers told F. A. Newdigate, 'the Dutch have firmly got it into their minds that it is worse than useless.'[188]

When dealing with deportees, the Board's procedure was to ask the military to provide reasons why people had been deported, and to ask whether they might be allowed to return to their homes on bail. Military commanders did not react well to such requests. In January 1902, Major H. Shute, the Administrator responsible for Graaff-Reinet, explained to M. G. Apthorp, the secretary of the Board, that before anyone was sent to Port Alfred, their cases were investigated by a small committee of loyalists 'specially selected by me on account of their judicial capacity and unprejudiced minds' and by an intelligence officer; and full reports of the charges were sent to the commandant on the coast. In his view, it was very taxing to his over-worked subordinates

---

[184] PP 1902 (Cd. 903), No. 46, p. 116. In November 1899, Michell urged Schreiner to extend the geographical scope of martial law, to effect a moratorium on bills of exchange: 8 November 1899, CO 48/543/34334, f. 413.
[185] CO 879/77/3, enc. 1 in No. 244, p. 204.
[186] PP 1902 (Cd. 903), enc. 5 in No. 59, p. 161.
[187] Minute of 15 May 1902, CO 48/560/17300, f. 97, referring to CO 879/76/1, enc. in No. 116, p. 125; see also enc. in No. 174, p. 188.
[188] CO 879/74/1, enc. in No. 99, p. 98 at p. 104. The *South African News* (11 October 1902) described it as 'a device for evading complaint'.

to have to 'furnish full reports upon fictitious accusations'.[189] So irritated was he by the process that he suggested that complainants should be charged fees to make any application, and should be prosecuted for libel for any false complaints.

In practice, large numbers were deported simply for being suspicious characters without much in the way of investigation. For instance, the brothers J. J. and P. A. Erasmus were deported because 'they are the loudest talkers and the worst rebels in Graaff-Reinet, their shaving saloon being the meeting place of the disloyal section'. C. J. Olivier was described as a 'dangerous character' who could not be trusted, and who had been constantly warned for using seditious language and for jeering at those who joined the town guard. Many deportees were listed simply as being 'notoriously disloyal' or as 'very bitter and dangerous'. In some cases, men were deported because there was not sufficient evidence to charge them with breaching martial law regulations.[190] In other cases, deportations were made *pour décourager les autres*. The Acting Resident Magistrate at Middelburg told Shute that, while nothing could be proved against a number of deportees from his area, the effect of their detention served as a 'warning to all sympathisers with the enemy' that the least assistance given by them to the rebels 'will render them liable to be deported to Port Alfred for an indefinite period'.[191] Shute was not unsympathetic to this position, telling the Martial Law Board that 'the deportation of certain persons is not intended so much as a punishment, but as a means of keeping away from a disturbed District those who are a danger to the community at large & also as a deterrent.'[192]

The military remained reluctant to allow deportees to return home even as the war entered its later stages. The Board was powerless in the face of military opposition. Its sense of its own powerlessness can be seen in its response to a complaint from three men – J. J. Hayward of

---

[189] Shute to Secretary, Martial Law Board, 3 January 190[2], WCA AG 2091 (Part 1).
[190] H. B. Davel was 'suspected of having led Theron's Commando when French's Scouts were captured, but the evidence is not sufficiently clear to warrant an indictment'. His father was fined £500 for hiding foodstuffs for the enemy, and was deported when the military considered the fine insufficient. WCA AG 2091 (Part 1).
[191] W. Richards to H. Shute, 15 January 1902, WCA AG 2091 (Part 1).
[192] Shute to Secretary, Martial Law Board, 7 February 1902, WCA AG 2091 (Part 1).

Graaff-Reinet, J. B. Rabie of Aberdeen and G. F. Smith of Jansenville – that they had been re-arrested while on parole in Port Elizabeth and returned to Port Alfred, even though martial law had not then been in operation at Port Elizabeth. The men claimed that the military had acted illegally, since they had no power to supersede the civil jurisdiction in Port Elizabeth at that time. Hayward wanted to challenge the military's actions in court, but was unable to do so thanks to his removal to Port Alfred. After discussing the case, the Board decided not to take up the issue of the illegal action by the military: Apthorp noted that '[t]he case of Dr Reinecke who succeeded in obtaining an order from the Supreme Ct for his release from gaol but who was rearrested by the military an hour afterwards is sufficient indication that these men would gain nothing by bringing up the point now.'[193] Nor was the local commander prepared to allow Hayward to return to Graaff-Reinet when he considered all the cases at the end of January.

The Board also dealt with sixty-three cases of detention. Of these, only six were redressed through the Board's intervention.[194] Among the cases which came before the Board was that of D. F. Marais. The case was referred to them on the advice of Rose-Innes, who received a letter on 19 October 1901 from Marais's wife describing his detention as 'a cruel mockery of justice'.[195] The Board took it up with the military, but found Wynne unwilling to submit any papers to them relating to the case – or indeed to take any action in the case – pending the decision of the Privy Council.[196] The Board did not consider this to be a reason to delay their investigation: indeed, in their view, the very reason given by the Supreme Court for not intervening – that this was a matter pertaining to martial law – demonstrated that it was essentially a case for them.[197] The Board felt that Marais should be put on trial at once (for the breach of the martial law regulations), or else that they should be given reasons why

---

[193] Note dated 23 December 1901, WCA AG 2091.
[194] It declined to interfere in twenty-eight cases, while eleven were 'satisfactorily adjusted' without its intervention. CO 879/77/3, enc. 1 in No. 244, p. 204.
[195] WCA AG 3714.
[196] Wynne to Martial Law Board, 27 October 1901, WCA AG 3714.
[197] At the same time, they dropped hints to Mrs Marais that matters might be expedited if the case to the Privy Council were dropped. Secretary, Martial Law Board to Mrs E. Marais, 5 November 1901, WCA AG 3714.

this was not done.[198] After the Privy Council's decision was made, there seemed even less reason for not proceeding with the military trial of Marais and those detained with him. Attorney General Graham told Michell, 'We shall make ourselves parties to what I am sure will be grave injustice if we stand by & consent to imprisonment of these men indefinitely, without option of bail.'[199]

On 13 December, Marais and A. B. de Villiers (who had been detained with him) were told by the Administrator of Martial Law that the charge against them was that of 'using language'; and that, since they were not 'criminals', they would be sent back to Paarl the following week.[200] Four days later, de Villiers was released on bail in Beaufort West. Marais himself remained in gaol, since Wynne intended to try him in January 1902, when the standing military court reached Beaufort West.[201] However, the trial was postponed for lack of reliable evidence against him,[202] and on 18 February, he was released on bail and ordered to proceed to Port Alfred. From here, Marais continued to press his case to be allowed to return home, arguing that the abandonment of the charges against him amounted to an acquittal, so that Wynne was bound by his earlier statement to release him. In his view, 'my deportation to Port Alfred not as an undesirable in the first instance but following on a long term of imprisonment and the abandonment of a specific charge enhances the illegality of the action of the military authorities.'[203] Although the Board pressed the military on this case – asking 'whether he has not been sufficiently punished more especially as he has incurred considerable expense in connection with his application to the Privy Council'[204] – it was to no effect, for in the middle of May, Settle responded that it was not advisable to allow him back to an area as disloyal as Paarl.[205] Marais would return home (along with the other deportees) only after the coming of peace. His experience showed that there were severe limitations to the promise of legalism implied in the publication of martial law regulations, which

---

[198] Minute dated 4 November 1901, WCA AG 3714.
[199] Wynne to Martial Law Board, 23 December 1901, WCA AG 3714.
[200] Marais, Statement of Grievance, WCA AG 3714.
[201] Graham to Michell, 23 December 1901, WCA AG 3714.
[202] Settle to chair, Martial Law Board, 3 February 1902, WCA AG 3714.
[203] Marais, Statement of Grievance, WCA AG 3714.
[204] Draft letter to the General Officer Commanding, April 1902, WCA AG 3714.
[205] Settle to Ebden, 15 May 1902, WCA AG 3714.

stated both that preliminary examinations had to be held and that 'all persons who directly incite others to take up arms &c shall immediately on arrest be tried by military Court.' At the same time, his case also showed that the Board was not entirely ineffective: the persistent pressure both from the Board and from his supporters may not have enabled him to return to his home and business, but it at least induced the military to release him from custody in Beaufort West.

Ending Martial Law

After the signing of the peace of Vereeniging, the authorities had to consider how to manage the transition from martial law to peace. A policy was needed to deal both with those rebels who had been sentenced by martial law courts since April 1901[206] and with those who had not yet been tried. As part of the peace negotiations (which ensured that no legal proceedings were to be taken against burghers), the Boer General Jan Smuts secured terms which would protect the thousands of rebels who had joined his troops. The terms of this agreement were implemented in a proclamation issued on 11 June. Those rebels already in detention, as well as those who had surrendered before 10 July 1902, would be disfranchised, but would suffer no other punishment if they formally acknowledged themselves to be guilty of High Treason before a Resident Magistrate. The offer did not extend to those who held official positions in the colonial government or who had been commandants in the rebel forces, who were to be tried for treason, but were not to be sentenced to death.[207] The offer thus mirrored the bifurcated treatment of Class 1 and Class 2 rebels under the Act of 1900. By 1 July, 2,511 rebels had surrendered. As Lambert noted, the final surrender of the rebels would make the continuation of martial law difficult.[208] By the end of August, over

---

[206] In early July 1902, Settle reported that 257 prisoners had been deported to Bermuda and 75 to St Helena on penal servitude sentences, while there remained 147 martial law prisoners in colonial gaols and 153 in the military prison at Grahamstown. CO 879/75/1, enc. 1 in No. 314, p. 278.

[207] PP 1902 (Cd. 1163), enc. in No. 63, pp. 172–173. These terms did not apply to those who had committed murder or crimes against the law of civilised warfare.

[208] CO 48/562/26575, f. 183.

3,000 rebels had been convicted under the terms of the proclamation.[209] The rebels were convicted by a legal procedure, albeit an expedited one. Preliminary proceedings – in which they signed their confessions – took place before a magistrate or officer appointed to accept surrenders. Once the Attorney General had accepted the surrender, the rebel returned to court, where he was handed a document stating that he had been tried and convicted of High Treason.[210]

The Continuation of Martial Law

As the war was drawing to an end, forty-two members of the legislative assembly petitioned Milner calling for a suspension of the Cape's constitution, to avoid recalling a parliament which would include members who had been tried for treason in the war, and to avoid the turbulence which would follow contested elections on the old franchise. Milner, who had himself on various occasions urged Chamberlain to modify or suspend the constitution,[211] gave strong support to the petition. In a letter to the Governor, published (without the Colonial Office's knowledge) in the Cape press, Milner suggested that, if the constitution were not suspended, 'Martial Law may have to be maintained for a much longer time.'[212] Governor Hely-Hutchinson also told Chamberlain that, if the constitution were not suspended, martial law would have to remain in place for at least eight months.[213] Chamberlain disliked this idea and wanted the political parties at the Cape to come to a concordat. Moreover, the proposal to suspend the constitution provoked strong opposition at the Cape. Among the opponents of suspension was Sir Henry de Villiers, who was horrified by Milner's letter. Fearing that the imperial parliament might act on it, he lobbied both the Liberal Imperialist Herbert Asquith and the

---

[209] The return of 31 August 1901 in CO 879/77/3, No. 429, p. 407 gives the figure of 3,440. Shearing, 'The Cape Rebel', p. 258 states that 3,154 rebels were disfranchised under the Proclamation.
[210] Shearing, 'The Cape Rebel', pp. 259–260.
[211] See Headlam, *The Milner Papers*, vol. 2, pp. 55–61, 64–65, 182.
[212] Milner to Hely-Hutchinson, 19 May 1902, 48/561/23916, f. 176. Chamberlain was 'Dismayed and seriously embarrassed' by the letter's publication: Chamberlain Papers, University of Birmingham, JC 1/13/265.
[213] CO 879/76/1, No. 285, p. 292 at p. 295.

Canadian prime minister Wilfrid Laurier 'to assist in averting the calamity that is threatening us'.[214] In these letters, he pointed out that Milner's comments were 'peculiarly unfortunate' in light of the decision in *Marais* 'that Martial Law can only be justified by the existence of actual hostilities'.[215]

However, with 200 martial law prisoners still in detention in the Cape, and thousands of rebels surrendering, Hely-Hutchinson was convinced that martial law had to remain in place until further security legislation and an indemnity act had been passed. At the same time, he realised the danger that applications would be made to the courts to release prisoners.[216] Once it was clear that peace had been restored, they were likely to succeed. Given the political difficulty of securing the necessary legislation to validate martial law proceedings at the Cape, the Law Officers suggested imperial legislation;[217] but Chamberlain perceived difficulties in the way of getting it through parliament. Both the minister and his officials therefore contemplated moving the detainees to the former republics, out of the reach of the Cape Supreme Court, but this suggestion was opposed on political grounds by the Attorney General.[218] This left the authorities with a dilemma. 'Subject to appeal to the Privy Council, it is, in fact, at present, practically in the power of the Supreme Court to nullify the proclamations of Martial Law', Hely-Hutchinson wrote, 'even if the Government, which is responsible for the maintenance of order, does not consider it prudent as yet to rescind them.'[219]

In the middle of June, ministers at the Cape began to press for a relaxation of martial law, including allowing those who had been removed to Port Alfred to return to their homes.[220] Responding to their request, Settle said he was willing to relax unnecessary

---

[214] De Villiers to Laurier, 8 June 1902, De Villiers Papers, National Library of South Africa (Cape Town), MSC 7 (Box 8).
[215] De Villiers to Asquith 8 June 1902, De Villiers Papers, National Library of South Africa (Cape Town), MSC 7 (Box 8).
[216] CO 879/74/1, No. 157, p. 183; CO 879/77/3, No. 40, p. 16.
[217] Opinion dated 30 May 1902, CO 885/15, No. 151.
[218] Minutes, 17–18 June 1902, CO 48/561/24121.
[219] CO 879/77/3, No. 41, p. 17 at p. 18.
[220] The Cape Ministry addressed a minute to the Governor on 17 June calling for restrictions on movement to end and for the deportees to Port Alfred to be allowed to return: CO 879/77/3, enc. 1 in No. 42, p. 21. The deportees were released on a gradual basis: CO 879/77/3, enc. in No. 76.

restrictions, but did not feel that martial law could be abolished until a satisfactory system of civil policing had been established in every district.[221] By early July, when it was clear that a state of war no longer existed which would satisfy the *Marais* test, Settle – who had received a three-and-a-half-page commentary on the case from de Villiers[222] – became more conscious of the risk of a clash with the Supreme Court. He now proposed to issue orders that no further action should be taken in the Cape Colony by the Administrators under martial law and that there should be no more martial law trials, while making it clear that he was still prepared to put the machinery of martial law into action at any time at the request of ministers.[223] The proposal was that responsibility for martial law – which would remain in place until the necessary legislation was passed – would be transferred to the civilians. This was a proposal which ministers were happy to accept.[224]

By early July, military–civilian negotiations had resulted in an arrangement whereby martial law remained in place, but under civilian control. If this was regarded as a more satisfactory political arrangement, it did not remove the risk that the courts might free those who had been detained or sentenced by martial law courts. It was evident that Chief Justice de Villiers's position on the question would be crucial, and officials soon came to the view that his behaviour might be influenced by his politics. De Villiers had continued to voice his passionate opposition to the suspension of the Cape constitution. In late June, he wrote to Chamberlain to reassure him that, if the Cape parliament met, it would pass the legislation necessary for the peace of the colony. He also promised to resign his judicial office and use all his influence in favour of reconciliation if these assurances proved false.[225] Aware of these views, officials in London thought it politic for Hely-Hutchinson have a private word with the Chief Justice, to pass on Chamberlain's opinion that any conflict between the Supreme Court and the Executive over detentions 'might force the hand of H M G, and

---

[221] CO 879/77/3, enc. in No. 76, p. 42 at p. 43.   [222] Walker, *Lord De Villiers*, p. 401.
[223] CO 879/77/3, enc. 1 in No. 157, p. 115.
[224] CO 879/77/3, enc. 2 in No. 157, p. 116. The arrangement (which Kitchener disapproved of) did not apply north of the Orange River, where Lyttleton was General Officer Commanding: see CO 879/77/3, enc. 8 in No. 191, p. 151.
[225] CO 879/74/1, No. 177, p. 206.

thus prevent the settlement by "concordat".[226] Having met de Villiers, Attorney General T. L. Graham expressed his confidence that, if a habeas corpus application were brought before the court, a rule nisi would be granted at a long enough date to allow an indemnity act to be passed.[227] This removed Chamberlain's fear of a conflict between executive and judiciary, and it was soon followed by an official response turning down the petition to suspend the constitution.[228]

De Villiers did not, however, remain silent. Just at the moment when officials felt confident that the threat of a clash with the courts had been removed, he made his provocative comments in van Reenen's case. The immediate response of the Cape's Attorney-General was to recommend that any sentences passed since 31 May – the date of the peace – should be postponed indefinitely or considered for remission, to avoid the risk of a clash with the court.[229] Settle accordingly issued an order that all people held in military custody for what were civil offences – including treason – should be handed over to the civil authorities, and that those held for breaches of martial law regulations should be dealt with summarily, but 'should suffer no penalty except a severe reprimand'.[230] Officials in London agreed that the promulgation of sentences by martial law courts after the cessation of hostilities would not be defensible. At the same time, Bertram Cox was exasperated by the Chief Justice's remarks, which he felt were 'intended to have a political effect'. He pointed out that, whether or not sentences were postponed, it was now open to any martial law detainee to apply to the court for his release. In his view, the only way to avoid a clash with the Supreme Court – which would render the passing of an indemnity act politically impossible – would be to end martial law. Ommanney, however, feared that this would unleash a flood of actions against 'all officers from

---

[226] Note 20 June, CO 48/561/23916, f. 176. Though some questioned the propriety of attempting to put pressure on de Villiers on a judicial matter, Chamberlain noted 'We shall be asking advice of not putting pressure upon the CJ.' Hely-Hutchinson was uncomfortable with this, fearing it would be perceived as an indirect approach to the Bond: CO 879/74/1, No 176, p. 201.
[227] CO 879/74/1, No. 179, p 207.   [228] PP 1902 (Cd. 1162) LXIX. 425.
[229] CO 879/77/3, enc. 2 in No. 191, p. 148; CO 879/74/1, No. 190, p. 211.
[230] CO 879/77/3, enc. 4 in No. 191, p. 149.

Kitchener down', and thought it better to wait for an indemnity act and trust de Villiers not to be 'too actively mischievous'.[231]

The Martial Law Commission

One of the main issues which had to be dealt with at the end of the war was what was to be done with those convicted by martial law courts. Although they had largely followed the procedure of military courts, under the Diceyan theory, they were simply committees putting into execution the discretionary powers assumed by the military and had nothing of 'law' about them. Any sentences would therefore expire at the end of the war, which would mean either that the convicted rebels would have to be freed, or that they would have to be retried in civilian courts. Chamberlain's solution, which he put to Milner, Hely-Hutchinson and McCallum on 26 June, was to appoint a commission to examine all unexpired sentences, and report on them before they were confirmed and validated by indemnity legislation both in the Cape and in Natal.[232] A review of all outstanding sentences by a quasi-judicial body would be able to legitimise them. A particular attraction of announcing such a commission early was that it might forestall the possibility of the Cape Supreme Court hearing habeas corpus cases.[233]

Ministers at the Cape supported this proposal, but argued for a wider commission, which would include a Supreme Court judge, and which would examine expired sentences as well as unexpired ones.[234] This idea was strongly resisted by the Colonial Office and the Governor. In view of the recent acquittal of Pony De Wet by a bench of Cape judges sitting on the special treason court, Hely-Hutchinson recommended 'that the Commission should be appointed from home', and Chamberlain agreed that it had to be 'absolutely independent of local influence & feeling'.[235] It was also feared that an examination of expired sentences would put the spotlight on controversial executions. They included not only high-profile Boer

---

[231] Cox & Ommanney notes, 15 July 1901, CO 48/562/28534, f. 588.
[232] CO 879/74/1, No. 169, p. 198.
[233] See CO 879/74/1, p. 201, No. 176; No. 177, p. 206.
[234] CO 879/77/3, No. 115, p. 73; Sprigg to Chamberlain, 28 June 1901, Chamberlain Papers, JC 11/34/4.
[235] CO 879/74/1, No. 171, pp. 198, 199; CO 879/74/1, No. 194, p. 212.

commando leaders such as Gideon Scheepers,[236] but also the case of H. J. van Heerden, a farmer from Zevenfontein, who had been shot by the military authorities, apparently without any trial, on 2 March 1901.[237]

It was settled by the middle of July that a royal commission would be appointed in London, consisting of Lord Alverstone CJ, Justice Bigham and Sir John Ardagh. Legislation would be passed at the Cape to validate all martial law sentences, but granting the Governor the power to amend any sentences in light of the recommendations of the commission.[238] Once the indemnity act was passed, the martial law proclamation would be cancelled and the Peace Preservation Act 13 of 1878 proclaimed throughout the Colony.[239] The proposals were not uncontroversial. As the Bond newspaper *Ons Land* pointed out, in contrast to the position in 1900, when Rose-Innes had reviewed the sentences before parliament confirmed them, on this occasion they were to be confirmed first, and revised later.[240] At Westminster, the Irish Nationalist MP Swift Macneill criticised the appointment of English judges to a commission which dealt with 'a matter of purely domestic political concern' in a self-governing colony. He also challenged the impartiality of the members: both Alverstone (as Attorney General in Salisbury's government) and Bigham had sat on the South African Committee, appointed by the Colonial Office to investigate the Jameson Raid, and Ardagh had been director of military intelligence during the war.[241]

Once in South Africa, the commissioners worked very quickly, beginning their sittings on 26 August and presenting their report on 28 October. They looked at 794 cases in all, of which 721 were from the Cape and 14 from Natal (the rest being from the former Republics). By 10 September, the Commission was ready to recommend the immediate release of 113 prisoners, who were freed by the Governor after the passage of the Cape's Indemnity Act a few days later. The final

---

[236] His martial law trial and execution was covered in *The Times*, 21, 24, 25, 30 December 1901, 20, 21 January 1902. See Judd and Surridge, *The Boer War*, pp. 235–236.
[237] For details, see Galbraith, 'British War Measures in Cape Colony', pp. 73–75.
[238] CO 879/77/3, No. 109, p. 57.   [239] CO 879/74/2, No. 1164, p. 377.
[240] *Ons Land*, 12 August 1902.
[241] *Parl. Debs.*, 4th ser., vol. 111, cols. 1441, 1443 (28 July 1902).

report contained recommendations for the revision of sentences, in tabulated form: giving the original sentence, the recommendation of the commission, and the date of expiry. The recommendations of the commissioners were reported in the press. *The Times* noted that, in a 'large preponderance' of cases, the pattern was of a person originally sentenced to death for treason having his sentence confirmed by the military as penal servitude or life, and then reduced by the commission to two or three years.[242] The *Manchester Guardian* reported that the tendency of the commission had been to cap sentences at five years' imprisonment, though the commissioners had left some severer sentences unaltered (such as the German Max Teinart's seven-year penal servitude sentence). In all, 154 sentences were left unaltered. The commission also released men who had death sentences commuted to penal servitude for life in thirty-six cases.[243]

As a judicial body, the commissioners did not feel it was for them to recommend a general amnesty, which in any case they thought would be regarded 'as a sign of weakness, and as an adverse criticism on the action of Military Authorities'. In a memorandum drafted by Ardagh after their return to England, they praised the procedure used in the martial law courts which (in their view) had demonstrated a 'pervading spirit of impartial justice', and castigated the policy embodied in the 1900 Indemnity and Special Tribunals Act as 'disastrous', considering that the effect of its leniency was to induce a large number to join the second rebellion. They also condemned the promise held out in Proclamation 100 of 1902, and pointed out – 'in the strongest possible way' – that 'any legislative proceedings which minimise or belittle the offence of high treason are, and must be most disastrous to the well being of Governments.'[244]

Whereas the appointment of the commission was considered as essential to legitimise the martial law sentences of Cape rebels, the authorities in Natal wanted to be exempted from its operation. Governor McCallum told Chamberlain on 25 July that Natal's parliament had already confirmed all martial law sentences imposed before 10 June by its Indemnity Act, and that the government wanted

---

[242] *The Times*, 2 December 1902, p. 4.
[243] *Manchester Guardian*, 2 December 1902, p. 7.
[244] PRO 30/40/19. A printed version of the memorandum is in CO 879/90/1, No. 2, pp. 2–4.

to deal with any later cases through the prerogative of mercy.[245] In April, with the war coming to an end, Natal's Attorney General Henry Bale had expressed the view that the remaining 200 Natal rebels in the field 'should be left to be dealt with according to law'.[246] However, in light of the promises made to the Boer leaders – that rebels outside Natal would not be returned to the colony to face trial – he and his ministers decided that the best policy would be to exercise the prerogative of mercy by allowing those who surrendered for trial to return to their homes with no greater punishment than disfranchisement, and by freeing anyone serving a sentence of up to two years.[247] In response, Chamberlain indicated that, while he was happy for the Natal government to remit sentences before the commission began its work, he felt that the commission had to consider any cases where prisoners were still undergoing sentence at the time of the report. The commission's remit had been agreed with the Governor, and had been made public: it could not be altered now.[248] Natal's response was to insist that the commission should not inquire into sentences validated by the Indemnity Act, but must deal only with court martial cases since the act. It was also insisted that any action taken on the report of the commissioners would be done by the Governor acting on the advice of the ministry.[249] In the event, the commission considered only fourteen Natal cases, making no alteration of sentences in eleven cases.

Pressures for a Wider Inquiry

Many politicians at the Cape wanted to see a local commission appointed, which would have a wider remit than the Alverstone Commission. They had not forgotten Prime Minister Sprigg's promise of a general commission of inquiry into martial law in September 1900, provision for which had been made in the Indemnity and Special Tribunals Act.[250] Although Chamberlain

---

[245] CO 879/74/1, No. 203, p. 217.
[246] PP 1902 (Cd. 903), enc. in No. 12, p. 16; PP 1902 (Cd. 1096), No. 26, p. 10.
[247] CO 879/74/1, No. 188, p. 210; No. 234 and enc., pp. 231, 235.
[248] CO 879/74/1, No. 211, p. 219; No. 221, p. 226.
[249] CO 879/74/1, No. 226, p. 227, No. 233, p. 231.
[250] CO 879/74/1, No. 200, p. 216. Chamberlain opposed such a commission, seeing it as divisive: CO 879/74/1, No. 215, p. 222.

claimed that Sprigg had given him his 'personal pledge' that he would not appoint such a commission,[251] the Prime Minister changed his position when parliament met, in effect 'simply offering a bribe to the Bond' (as Ommanney saw it) in return for passing the indemnity bill.[252] In spite of stiff opposition from the Colonial Office and the Governor, Sprigg made it clear that he wanted a thorough investigation of martial law, and let London known that Justice Maasdorp had agreed to head it.[253]

In the meantime, loyalists in the Cape parliament thought they might head off the prospect of a wide-reaching local commission by extending the Alverstone Commission's remit to look into expired sentences.[254] However, Alverstone himself was opposed to this policy,[255] since he thought that the imperial government should keep control of the inquiry, and that 'under no circumstances should the conduct of the military officers or their good faith be impugned.'[256] Nor did Chamberlain have any appetite for any wider inquiry. 'I have no doubt many irregular things were done', he noted, 'but even so what is the good of raking them up unless full compensation is to be accorded to any aggrieved person?' Lambert agreed: 'I fear that a great deal of martial law [administration] will not bear investigation.' Faced with the choice of an extended Alverstone commission (the loyalist proposal) and a local investigation (Sprigg's proposal, backed by the Bond), Chamberlain preferred the latter, since London could 'wash our hands of the whole business' and let the Cape government fund any compensation claims.

[251] Minute dated 20 August 1902 in CO 48/564/34701; see also CO 879/74/1, No. 246, p. 241; No. 216, p. 222.
[252] Minute of 18 August 1902, in CO 48/564/34328, f. 16.
[253] CO 879/74/1, No. 253, p. 243.
[254] Hely-Hutchinson estimated at the end of August that there were 390 expired court martial sentences (and 7,000 expired sentences of cases before Deputy Administrators of Martial Law), alongside 700 or so unexpired martial law sentences: CO 879/74/1, No. 266, p. 250.
[255] CO 879/74/1, No. 274, p. 256. After the act had passed, the Cape assembly formally requested that the remit of Alverstone's commission be extended to take into account expired sentences, as well as unexpired sentences. However, the request was refused. While the Colonial Office could plausibly claim that the two English judges were required at home, it was clear that Alverstone himself regarded the request as 'absolutely out of the question'. Note by Lambert, 25 September 1902, CO 48/565/39911, f. 329; CO 879/74/2, No. 1399, p. 461.
[256] Alverstone to Chamberlain, 10 September 1902, CO 48/565/37743, f. 10.

In all these tortuous proceedings, London's main concern was to get an indemnity bill passed, and it was prepared 'to play Sprigg a little till this is done'.[257] At the same time, imperial officials were frightened that the Cape parliament would look closely at cases like van Heerden's before passing the indemnity act. As Hely-Hutchinson told Chamberlain, there were members of the assembly who knew the facts of the case, and although (in his view) 'Van Heerden probably deserved to be shot the proceedings of the Court Martial will not hold water'. More worryingly, the real facts did not justify the entry in the Blue Book of sentences which the Alverstone Commission was set to revise, which threatened to cast a shadow over its proceedings.[258] In the end, a promise by Sprigg to appoint a local commission of the sort anticipated in the 1900 Act – which leading Bond members saw as giving them a chance to expose the evils of military law – secured the passage of the bill without incident in the assembly.[259]

Sprigg's promise in turn generated concern among officials in London over how to deal with the recommendations of any local commission which might be appointed. One important question was whether the Governor would be bound to follow the advice of his ministers, if they instructed him to pardon those sentenced by martial law courts.[260] In October, Bertram Cox referred this question to the Law Officers, asking them whether the Governor could refuse on the grounds that imperial interests were at stake. The advice confirmed that the Governor did have the power to reject an amnesty, though officials were sensitive to the political risks of seeking to ignore the views of a ministry.[261] Officials also pondered the constitutionality of asking the Governor to refuse to appoint any local commission, and considered how its work might be frustrated, for instance by removing all relevant documents in the possession of the military out of the colony.[262]

---

[257] Note, 26 August 1902, CO 48/564/35227, f. 194; CO 879/74/1, No. 273, p. 249.
[258] CO 879/74/2, No. 1172, p. 380, referring to the entry in PP 1902 (Cd. 981), p. 125, which reported van Heerden's sentence by a court martial.
[259] CO 879/74/1, No. 287, p. 272.
[260] Graham note, 11 September 1902, CO 48/565/37710, f. 3.
[261] Law Officers' Opinion 16 October 1902, CO 48/568/43073, f. 54
[262] Chamberlain to Brodrick, 2 September 1902, CO 48/564/36016, f. 366; Hely-Hutchinson to Chamberlain, 10 September 1902, CO 48/565/37743, f. 16; CO 879/74/1, No. 306, p. 298; No. 293, p. 278; No. 295, p. 279.

The problem remained hypothetical as long as no local commission was appointed. However, in the meantime, the Cape Legislative Council began to investigate of particular cases. In August, the petition of M. J. Pretorius, a member of the assembly, was referred to a select committee. He had been detained under martial law at Middelburg – where he had been ordered to attend the execution in July 1901 of F. A. Marais – and was later sent to Port Alfred as an undesirable. He had been told by the Martial Law Board that the reason for his expulsion was that he had not handed over horses which had been commandeered (a finding he disputed); but had not been allowed to return home until 29 July 1902. When the committee proceeded to deal with his complaint, its members were told by General Settle that the officers they wished to interview had left the country, while the Martial Law Board also refused to hand over its documents.[263] The committee reported that it could find no evidence that he had used any seditious language, but that he had been subjected to indignities and restrictions on his liberty. It also concluded that the Martial Law Board had failed in its duty of protecting British subjects from 'injustice and wanton oppression'.[264]

The Board's chairman, Lewis L. Michell, lost little time in protesting about this finding, explaining to the Governor that the real charge against Pretorius had been that he was using his influence as a member of the legislature 'in the wrong direction'. He also expressed his view that his deportation to the coast had a tranquillising effect on the district of Middelburg.[265] Hely-Hutchinson was also irked by the report, since he felt it was in the interest of those wanting a general inquiry to discredit the Martial Law Board. He also considered that in its criticism of the Board, the report, drafted by Sir Henry de Villiers, had violated a principle of justice, namely that no one should be condemned unheard. In London, Bertram Cox dismissed as worthless the 'proceedings of a Bond committee taking evidence ex parte', noting that 'Pretorius seems to have been a typical Dutch Africander. He sends his sons to fight & sits & whines at home.

---

[263] CO 879/78/4, No. 28 (with encs.), p. 57.
[264] CO 879/78/4, enc. 1 in No. 118, p. 190 at p. 192.
[265] CO 879/78/4, enc. 7 in No. 118, p. 195.

Chief Justice De Villiers I believe did the same.'[266] Other cases were also investigated by select committee, without the benefit of military co-operation, revealing information which officials in London had to admit was 'certainly not favourable to military justice'.[267] Try as they might to prevent scrutiny of wartime cases, political pressure at the Cape ensured that material embarrassing to the imperial authorities came into the public domain.

The appointment of a wide-reaching local commission of inquiry was avoided, however. By the time the session of the Cape parliament ended, in the middle of November, no local commission had yet been appointed, though the promise of one was still being held out.[268] When parliament reassembled in 1903, Bond members were keen to return to the issue, but by then, Sprigg had again changed his mind, now taking the view that his promise from 1900 to appoint a commission had been superseded by events. Consequently, when in August the lawyer Henry Burton called for a Supreme Court judge to be appointed to report on the sentences imposed under martial law in any cases where fines were imposed, and to constitute a court of appeal from any decisions of the War Losses Compensation Commission, Sprigg warned that, if the motion were passed, he would resign.[269] Having taken this position, it soon became clear that the Bond would not agree to the passage of Sprigg's Supply Bill, since they were pledged to an amnesty and an inquiry into martial law. The Prime Minister consequently advised the Governor to dissolve the assembly and issue Treasury warrants, as had been done in the war, and trusting to an indemnity by a subsequent parliament. In brief, faced with Sprigg's threat to resign, and having to call on a ministry whose supporters were 'tainted with treason and rebellion', Hely-Hutchinson agreed to the dissolution.[270] When elections to the assembly were next held in 1904, a Progressive majority was returned, and the question of a commission to investigate martial law fell off the agenda.

[266] Hely-Hutchinson to Chamberlain 14 October 1902, and notes of officials: CO 48/565/45407, f. 692; see also Cox's note, 20 January 1903, in CO 48/568/51879, f. 689.
[267] Note by Lambert on the case of J. H. Schoeman, 23 October 1902, CO 48/565/45202.
[268] *Manchester Guardian*, 8 December 1902, p. 10.
[269] Davenport, *The Afrikaner Bond*, p. 246.   [270] CO 879/90/1, No. 50A, p. 49.

Conclusion

Questions about the nature of martial law, and how far it was subject to the rule of law, returned to the public agenda during the Anglo-Boer war in a way that had not been the case since the Morant Bay rebellion. This was not only because of the unprecedented scale on which martial law powers were exercised, or the numbers detained or imprisoned after martial law trials. It was also because, in this war, those who were being detained and imprisoned in this way were white subjects, with the full citizenship rights of British subjects, living in colonies with representative governments.

As R. W. Kostal has shown, the Jamaica controversy had revealed two rival conceptions of martial law, one of which (espoused by Governor Eyre's critics) saw all actions taken in emergencies as being subject to common law review, and the other of which (championed by his defenders) defended a 'jurisprudence of power' which regarded martial law as a legitimate means of defending imperial interests.[271] As has been seen in earlier chapters, as the British extended their rule in other parts of Africa, a vision endorsing the 'jurisprudence of power' was often in the ascendancy, with arbitrary actions legitimated by formal legislative fiat, issued by legislators whose authority derived ultimately from the imperial parliament in Westminster, in whose name these new subject peoples were conquered. But such an approach was not so easy to adopt where the people whose rights were violated were white subjects, as opposed to subjected black Africans. In South Africa, it became evident that the rule of law was as much a matter of culture, or state of mind, as it was of doctrine or jurisdiction.

This war raised hitherto unanswered questions about the rule of law, which often needed to be settled by negotiation by parties who took different views of it. One question concerned the status of martial law. If the military inclined to Finlason's view that the crown had a prerogative power to take all actions it considered necessary in times of emergency, and the civilians inclined to Dicey's view that all military actions were subject to judicial review, in practice both came to accept that a proclamation of martial law initiated a particular kind

---

[271] Kostal, *A Jurisprudence of Power*, p. 465.

of legal regime, whose parameters needed to be negotiated and defined. How far a culture of the rule of law could be maintained in this world depended on how influential political voices in its favour, backed by the threat not to indemnify the military, could be, in face of military demands to win the war by all means. It is notable that, in this context, the colonial courts – under Chief Justice de Villiers – became increasingly assertive in seeking to limit the military's power to detain without trial. It is equally notable that the highest imperial court, the Privy Council, in the landmark decision of *Marais* confirmed the power of the military to take action unfettered by the court during the emergency. The approach of Halsbury – who had been Eyre's lawyer – was to treat the military's powers *durante bello* as equivalent to those conferred by a continental state of siege: a formal power conferred by the state of war. His views differed entirely from the Diceyan views of de Villiers, who found himself outvoted on the same court. Their views of the rule of law might have reflected their wider political sentiments: whereas the judge from the Cape felt a deep sympathy towards the detained fellow Dutch-speakers, the conservative Lord Chancellor's views may have been more in line with those of men like Milner, for whom the Cape Dutch were at best potentially disloyal, at worst the enemy in a struggle to decide which of the two 'white races' would prevail.[272] As Halsbury had shown in 1890 in *Cox* v. *Hakes*, he was willing to give a liberal interpretation of the reach of the writ of habeas corpus when the rights of high church English clergymen were at stake; but he was not prepared to take such a liberal view when dealing with imperial enemies.[273]

Halsbury's view of martial law shielded the military only until the war ended, when an indemnity act would be needed. When it came to

---

[272] This may be said to characterise the views of the Secretary of State, Joseph Chamberlain, and the Governor of the Cape and High Commissioner Sir Alfred Milner. Milner complained to Chamberlain on 14 November 1900 of the 'superstition' held by many at home 'that you can govern a country, in which the majority of citizens are your enemies, by a system of autonomy more complete than any separatist ever proposed even for Ireland'. Bodleian Library, MS Milner dep. 170, f. 157. See also Le May, *British Supremacy in South Africa*, pp. 31–34.

[273] *Cox* v. *Hakes* (1890) 15 App. Cas. 506, where his judgment began at 514, 'For a period extending as far back as our legal history, the writ of habeas corpus has been regarded as one of the most important safeguards of the liberty of the subject.'

passing indemnity legislation, it became evident, particularly in the majority Dutch-speaking Cape, that the legislature would not be content simply with passing a formal statute to whitewash the military. Martial law sentences were confirmed, but only after a process of sentence revision, designed to assure legislators that the sentences were not unjust. In this context – where former white rebels needed to be re-integrated into a post-war political order – the same rule-of-law concerns which had animated de Villiers's judgment were once more in evidence. As shall now be seen, such concerns were far less in the ascendant when martial law returned to South Africa in 1906, with the view of suppressing a Zulu rebellion.

10

Martial Law, the Privy Council and the Zulu Rebellion of 1906

On 9 February 1906, martial law was declared in Natal. It followed the murder, on the previous day, of two white policemen near Byrnetown. The officers had come from Richmond to arrest twenty-seven African men, who had earlier defied a magistrate collecting the recently imposed poll tax. There had been rumours for several weeks about an increasingly defiant attitude among the Africans, stoking fears of an imminent rebellion. When the Richmond magistrate came to collect the tax, the crowd he met brandished their spears at him, and said, 'there will be blood today.'[1] When Sub-Inspector S. H. K. Hunt and Trooper George Armstrong came to make their arrests, the men were still armed and in no mood to co-operate. During the ensuing melee, Hunt fired a shot into the crowd, injuring one of the Africans, and prompting the attack in which both men were stabbed to death.

The murder of Hunt and Armstrong was the first act in the Zulu Rebellion of 1906, which came to be known as the Bambatha rebellion. Although it was provoked by the heavy-handed imposition of a new tax, the rebellion was fuelled by deeper resentments against a colonial government which had undermined traditional Zulu structures of authority, proletarianised much of its youth, and restricted access to land.[2] For two months, resistance took a passive

[1] Proceedings of Richmond Court Martial, CO 179/234/19935, f. 495.
[2] For different interpretations of the causes of the rebellion, see Shula Marks, *Reluctant Rebellion: The 1906–1908 Disturbances in Natal* (Oxford, Clarendon Press, 1970); John Lambert, *Betrayed Trust: Africans and the State in Colonial Natal* (Scottsville,

form, with communities defying the demands of local magistrates for the tax to be paid. Resistance turned to revolt at the beginning of April, when Bambatha kaMancinza – who had been deposed as Zondi chief in early March – abducted the man appointed to replace him, and ambushed a police column, killing three policemen. When troops were sent to quell his rebellion, he took to the forests of Nkandhla, where he was joined by the elderly Cube chief Sigananda and his son Ndabaningi. The government offered a reward for Bambatha's capture, dead or alive, and pitched battles followed, with many casualties.[3] This phase of the rebellion lasted two months, until Lt-Col. Duncan McKenzie's troops routed Bambatha at Mome Gorge on 10 June, decapitating the rebel leader, and capturing Sigananda and his followers.

Nine days later, Governor Sir Henry McCallum told his superiors in London that the back of the rebellion had been broken.[4] In fact, his confidence was premature, for on that same day, two white men were killed in an attack on a store at Thring's Post made by 400 followers of Ndhlovu, chief of the Nodunga section of the Zulu. For the next month, the unrest moved to Maphumulo, where Ndhlovu was joined by the Qwabe chief Meseni. Although Meseni assembled an impi of several thousand fighters, they were able to offer little resistance to the force of some 3,500 led by McKenzie. Ndhlovu and Meseni were captured on 12 July, with Ndhlovu being blamed for the death of Trooper Powell (killed at Thring's Post), and Meseni held responsible for the death of Oliver Veal, an official of the Public Works Department, whose dismembered body was found at his kraal.[5] By the end of July, the rebellion had been crushed and the troops

---

University of KwaZulu-Natal Press, 1995); Benedict Carton, *Blood from Your Children: The Colonial Origins of Generational Conflict in South Africa* (Charlottesville, University of Virginia Press, 2000); Jeff Guy, *The Maphumulo Uprising: War, Law and Ritual in the Zulu Rebellion* (Scottsville, University of KwaZulu-Natal Press, 2006); Jeff Guy, *Remembering the Rebellion: The Zulu Uprising of 1906* (Scottsville, University of KwaZulu-Natal Press, 2006); and Michael R. Mahoney, *The Other Zulus: The Spread of Zulu Ethnicity in Colonial South Africa* (Durham, Duke University Press, 2012), ch. 6.

[3] McCallum reported before the battle of Mome Gorge that 200 rebels had been killed in fighting up to 10 June; on 13 June, he reported that 575 rebels were killed in that battle: PP 1906 (Cd. 3027) LXXIX. 573, Nos. 51, 54, pp. 46–47.

[4] PP 1906 (Cd. 3027), No. 62, p. 50.

[5] For the trials relating to these issues, see Guy, *The Maphumulo Uprising*.

demobilised. However, martial law remained in place until the beginning of October, and would be proclaimed again between December 1907 and August 1908, during which time the colony was at peace, but when the government in Pietermaritzburg was seeking to put together a case of treason against the Zulu king Dinuzulu, who was suspected of being behind the rebellion.[6]

The use of martial law in the Zulu rebellion raised questions about its nature which had remained unsettled at the end of the Anglo-Boer War. In particular, the Privy Council's decision in the *Marais* case[7] had left open whether a civilian court could determine the necessity of martial law, and decide whether as a matter of fact a state of war or rebellion existed.[8] This question came into sharper focus in 1906, since Natal was at peace for much of the time when martial law was in place. During this time, moreover, a selective policy of prosecution in martial law courts was used by the colonial authorities for political purposes, to neutralise potentially rebellious chiefs and to control wider dissent by making swift, public examples of those who either had defied the authorities or might do so. Thanks in no small part to activist supporters of the martial law prisoners in London and Natal – especially the African lawyer Alfred Mangena[9] and Harriette Colenso[10] – the imperial and colonial authorities had to confront the question of how far such a policy was compatible with the rule of law that British jurists were so keen to champion. The answers they gave were not dictated simply by abstract legal thought, but were rather shaped by their political and cultural world-views. The fact that, in this episode, the targets of martial law were not white British subjects

---

[6] On the trial, see Marks, *Reluctant Rebellion*, ch. 11.
[7] D. F. Marais v. *The General Officer Commanding the Lines of Communication and the Attorney-General of the Colony* [1902] AC 109.
[8] See Sir Henry de Villiers CJ's comments in R. v. *Bailly van Reenen and Others* (1902) 19 Supreme Court Reports [Cape] 332.
[9] See esp. Tembeka Ngcukaitobi, *The Land Is Ours: South Africa's First Black Lawyers, and the Birth of Constitutionalism* (Cape Town, Penguin, 2018); and David Killingray, 'Significant Black South Africans in Britain before 1912: Pan-African Organisations and the Emergence of South Africa's First Black Lawyers', *South African Historical Journal*, vol. 64:3 (2012), pp. 393–417 at pp. 409–416.
[10] See esp. Jeff Guy, *The View across the River: Harriette Colenso and the Zulu Struggle against Imperialism* (Charlottesville, University Press of Virginia, 2002); and Shula Marks, 'Harriette Colenso and the Zulus, 1874–1913', *Journal of African History*, vol. 4 (1963), pp. 403–411.

whom the local colonial government wished to protect, but subject black Africans whom the colonial government wished to subdue, was crucial to the way the problem was perceived. In this context, liberal voices found a much less receptive audience than had been the case only a few years earlier during the Anglo-Boer war. Although officials at the Colonial Office were troubled by the use of martial law in 1906, their interventions were constrained by the need to respect the autonomy of a self-governing colony, many of whose officials were more interested in crushing the rebellion than in observing the rule of law. Furthermore, when it came to the matter of passing an indemnity act, Natal's wish to give a simple legislative validation to all actions done under martial law overrode any imperial desire there might have been to subject these actions to any meaningful retrospective review. Finally, when the Privy Council was asked to consider these matters, as the imperial guardian of the rule of law, it showed itself to be as executive-minded and as uninterested in the substantive common law tradition as it had been in the *Marais* case.

Martial Law before the Rebellion, February–March 1906

On 23 February, two weeks after martial law had been declared in Natal, Col. H. T. Bru-de-Wald, Commandant of the Natal Militia, gave instructions on how it was to be administered. They seemed to follow the guidelines issued by Lord Carnarvon in 1867. The ordinary civil and criminal jurisdiction of the civil courts was not to be interfered with, but cases involving sedition, arming or incitement to insurrection were to be dealt with under martial law. Minor cases were to be tried by magistrates, with more serious ones by special courts martial modelled on military courts.[11] On the same day, Natal's Minister of Justice, Thomas Watt, confirmed that martial law courts were not to be used to punish 'natives for any acts committed prior to the proclamation of Martial Law' on 9 February.[12]

In fact, there were already signs that these guidelines would not be followed to the letter. Within a week of the murder of Hunt and

---

[11] PP 1906 (Cd. 2905) LXXIX. 503, enc. 2 in No. 30, p. 24. For the Circular of 26 January 1867, see PP 1906 (Cd. 2905), Appendix 1, p. 55.
[12] CO 879/92/26, enc. 1 in No. 4, p. 4.

Armstrong, two men – Uzondwein and Njwezi – had already been tried for it and executed by a drumhead court martial.[13] Although some officials at the Colonial Office, such as Arthur Berriedale Keith, regarded the executions as 'quite needless', there were many voices, both in Natal and in Whitehall, who were prepared to defend them as being necessary 'to prevent a general rebellion'.[14] They saw the protests over the poll tax as the prelude to a general rising. Governor McCallum agreed: 'unless an example is made of those who have broken out in rebellion, the movement will be sure to spread.'[15] Uzondwein and Njwezi would not be the only men tried and executed for the Richmond murders. There would be another trial by a martial law court for this offence on the eve of Bambatha's revolt, and a further civilian trial before the lifting of martial law.

In the weeks before Bambatha's revolt, martial law powers were also used to discipline chiefs who had refused to pay the poll tax or defied the magistracy. During this time, several leaders came under particular suspicion of having encouraged their tribesmen to arm and defy the government: they included chiefs Tilonko, Miskofeli, Ngobizembe and the mixed-race chief Charlie Fynn. In dealing with these men and their followers, the authorities opted to side-step the civilian courts by resorting to martial law powers. Rather than using martial law courts as a last resort to quell a rebellion, they were used in a highly strategic way for political purposes. For instance, although the military had initially been instructed by Natal's defence minister only to assist the police in bringing the followers of chief Ngobizembe to justice (for defying a tax collecting magistrate), attitudes changed after the chief failed to comply with an order to hand them over. 'By virtue of the powers conferred upon me under Martial Law', on 10 March Col. George Leuchars imposed a heavy fine on his tribe and dispossessed it of much of its land. Having removed the women and children from the

---

[13] PP 1906 (Cd. 2905), enc. 1 in No. 25, p. 14; and James Stuart, *A History of the Zulu Rebellion, 1906: And of Dinuzulu's Arrest, Trial and Expatriation* (London, MacMillan, 1913), p. 138.
[14] Minutes by Keith and Fred Graham, CO 179/233/8435, f. 159. See also H. Cox's question in *Parl. Debs.*, 4th ser., vol. 152, col. 339 (21 February 1906), and PP 1906 (Cd. 2905), Nos. 15 and 17, p. 6. See also Graham's views in CO 179/233/8487, f. 174.
[15] PP 1906 (Cd. 2905), No. 25, p. 13; No. 27, p. 16. Cf. CO 179/234/18011, f. 367, Governor to Secretary of State (27 April 1906).

kraal, his men proceeded to shell it.[16] Although officials in London doubted the legality of this confiscation, and critical questions were raised in Westminster,[17] the action induced two other chiefs, Meseni and Swaimane, to give up their offending tribesmen 'contrary to expectations'.[18]

Other chiefs who proved more co-operative in handing over miscreants escaped with lesser fines, while their followers were tried and severely punished by martial law courts. One of these was Miskofeli, whose activities caused the white settlers in the Natal Midlands much anxiety in early 1906. After handing over the wanted offenders, he was subjected only to a fine and the division of his chiefdom.[19] His followers, by contrast, were put on trial by court martial at Ixopo, where evidence was heard that they armed on the supposition that their chief was about to be arrested, and disbanded when they discovered that this was not the case.[20] Nevertheless, seven of them were given death sentences, later commuted to imprisonment with hard labour of up to ten years. Another chief whose followers were tried by court martial, while he was merely fined, was Charlie Fynn. Fynn himself favoured paying the poll tax, but had little influence over his tribesmen, who were reported to be ready to resist the government with arms if necessary. Thirty-six of them were tried by a court martial for sedition and inciting to insurrection. Five death sentences were later commuted, with the longest remaining sentence being one of life imprisonment with hard labour.[21]

The Richmond Trial and Its Aftermath

The middle of March also saw the martial law trial of twenty more men accused of taking part in the Richmond murders of Hunt and Armstrong. They faced charges of public violence, murder and being in arms against the government in a tribunal which followed military

---

[16] *Natal Witness*, 17 March 1906; PP 1906 (Cd. 2905), No. 32, p. 25; No. 30, p. 20; CO 789/106/1, Nos. 183 and 185, pp. 65–66, and Guy, *The Maphumulo Uprising*, pp. 49–51.
[17] *Parl. Debs.*, 4th ser., vol. 154, col. 1247 (28 March 1906); vol. 153, col. 443 (7 March 1906); minutes on CO 179/233/10711, f. 373.
[18] PP 1906 (Cd. 2905), No. 57, p. 36.   [19] Marks, *Reluctant Rebellion*, p. 196.
[20] PP 1906 (Cd. 2905), Nos. 30 and 39, pp. 20, 29; and *Natal Witness*, 24 March 1906.
[21] PP 1906 (Cd. 3027), No. 6, p. 6.

court procedures. When the case began, the men's lawyer, J. F. Jackson, questioned the court's competence to try offences committed before the proclamation of martial law, but without effect.[22] Sergeant Stephens, who had been injured in the affray, gave evidence relating to the murder, as did several other policemen. Evidence was also given by Mdutshana, the brother of Mjongo, one of the leaders of the protest who had been seriously injured in the affray but was not yet fit for trial. Mdutshana identified thirteen men who were in the party which attacked Hunt, and implicated a number of the defendants. The clearest evidence was against Nkanaysi – who was also not on trial here – who had thrown a spear at Hunt after having himself been shot in the face and in the arm by the policeman. Other witnesses testified that several defendants had thrown spears or stabbed the policemen. One of the accused, Utawini, even admitted that, when they saw Nkanaysi was hurt, 'we threw our assegais'.[23] On the evidence before it, the court convicted twelve of the men of the murder and sentenced them to death.

The fact that a martial law court had imposed the death sentence would soon raise questions. Even before the trial, Governor McCallum had told his ministers that, in the present condition of the country, the murder charge should be tried by a civilian court. However, Prime Minister Charles Smythe retorted that 'the state of disaffection ... is by no means at an end' and that 'any interference with the court martial now sitting would have a disastrous effect on the natives.'[24] At the same time, McKenzie protested at the commutation of martial law death sentences imposed in the Ixopo trial, insisting that 'this golden opportunity of inflicting the most drastic punishment on all leading natives found guilty' should not be lost.[25] In response, the Governor agreed to the continuation of martial law trials, but insisted that he (rather than the commandant) would henceforth confirm or revise sentences. Having reviewed the proceedings of the Richmond case with his council, McCallum on 27 March confirmed the Richmond death sentences and the commutations of the Ixopo ones.[26]

---

[22] The transcript of the trial is in CO 179/234/19935, f. 487ff.
[23] CO 179/234/19935, f. 561.   [24] PP 1906 (Cd. 2905), No. 57 and enclosures, p. 36.
[25] CO 879/92/26, enc. 2 in No. 5, p. 9. McKenzie tendered his resignation as a result of the revisions, which the Governor refused: Governor to Secretary of State, 24 March 1906, CO 179/233/13064, f. 366 (redacted in PP 1906 (Cd. 2905), No. 67, p. 41).
[26] PP 1906 (Cd. 2905), No. 33, p. 25.

The death sentences immediately attracted attention at the Colonial Office. Keith noted that they could not be justified at common law, and 'as we must assent to an act of indemnity we must be able to do so with a clear conscience.' Even the normally hawkish Fred Graham doubted the wisdom of executing these men under martial law. A telegram was therefore sent to Natal, asking the Governor to suspend the executions until more information had been provided.[27] The telegram provoked a constitutional crisis in Pietermaritzburg. When Smythe refused to suspend an execution which had already been confirmed in council, McCallum told him he would have to cancel the warrant under prerogative powers. This prompted the resignation of the Natal government[28] and furious local protests.[29] The Governor-Generals of both Australia and New Zealand also protested against London's interference with another self-governing colony's right to decide whether to exercise the prerogative of pardon.[30] Officials in London were exasperated by Natal's reaction, which entirely overlooked the interests of the imperial authorities, on whose troops the white minority ultimately relied.[31] However, their eventual response was – in the words of Winston Churchill, the undersecretary of state – 'a complete surrender', as officials sent a telegram which explained that the Colonial Office was merely asking for information, rather than seeking to interfere in Natal's constitutional government.[32]

This episode revealed quite how muddy the legal and constitutional waters were where martial law powers were used. The Colonial Office considered that, where matters affected imperial interests, 'the Crown must reserve a certain function to the Secretary of State, and a certain independent function to the Governor.'[33] It also thought that London would ultimately have to assent to any indemnity act, either directly

---

[27] CO 179/233/10712, f. 379. The telegram (28 March 1906) is in PP 1906 (Cd. 2905), No. 35, p. 26.
[28] See PP 1906 (Cd. 2905) No. 37, p. 26. See Ronald Hyam, *Elgin and Churchill at the Colonial Office, 1905–08: The Watershed of the Empire-Commonwealth* (London, Macmillan, 1968), pp.241–242.
[29] See *Natal Witness*, 30 March 1906 and the resolutions passed at various public meetings in CO 179/234/15015, f. 92.
[30] PP 1906 (Cd. 2905), No. 40, p. 32; No. 48, p. 34.
[31] See the draft telegram in H. W. Just's hand in CO 179/233/11034, f. 398.
[32] See PP 1906 (Cd. 2905), No. 36, p. 26 and No. 38, p. 29, and drafts in CO 179/233/10712, f. 385.
[33] Draft telegram (H. W. Just) CO 179/233/11034, f. 400.

or through the imperially appointed Governor. Furthermore, as Churchill publicly pointed out, on the international plane, it would be His Majesty's Government, rather than Natal's, which would be held to account.[34] Natal's ministry, however, felt that the Governor had to act on the advice of the responsible government, with London having no part to play. The clash of interpretations on this point threatened to unravel what Just referred to as 'the delicate machinery of the British Empire'. Furthermore, if there was disagreement over whom the Governor was answerable to, there was also some uncertainty over the nature of the powers he was exercising. During the spat over whether the men were to be pardoned, officials both in London and in Pietermaritzburg treated the question as one concerning the rightful exercise of the prerogative power of pardon. Yet the men had been convicted by a martial law court, which (as officials in London later realised) was not a judicial act, but an executive act to which that prerogative could not apply.[35] But the very fact that McCallum had taken the decision to treat these as cases which had to be dealt with 'constitutionally' showed how far he was from seeing martial law as an entirely lawless zone justified only by necessity, and was treating it as a matter within his constitutional powers.

Officials in London were also at odds over the issues at stake. When, in the midst of the crisis, McCallum informed London that McKenzie's column had been demobilised and that the recalcitrant chiefs had paid their fines,[36] Keith noted that this conclusively proved that Natal was not in a position to execute the men sentenced under martial law. He expressed surprise that no one had applied to the Supreme Court to challenge the sentences, adding that the 'Marais judgment, besides being unintelligible, could not conceivably apply in a case where there has been no actual fighting between whites and blacks'. Keith felt that to execute these men under martial law would be analogous to the execution of George Gordon on Governor Eyre's orders, with the difference being that 'whereas the Jamaica revolt was a real and serious one, the Natal one so far as overt action has gone has been a trifle.'[37] However, Keith's outburst elicited a robust response from

---

[34] *Parl. Debs.*, 4th ser., vol. 155, col. 271 (2 April 1906).
[35] See minutes by Keith and Just, 10 April 1906, CO 179/234/12686, f. 167.
[36] PP 1906 (Cd. 2905), No. 41, p. 32.
[37] Minute, 31 March 1906, CO 179/233/11321, f. 511.

his colleague Bertram Cox, who thought him wrong both in law and in policy. As a matter of law, he said, the court had no jurisdiction to review martial law court judgments, for '[t]he question whether or not the circumstances of the case justify the continuance of martial law is one of policy primarily for the consideration of the Governor & his ministers.' This was to take the view that the question of whether martial law was needed or not was settled definitively by the proclamation (a view Keith continued to dispute). As a matter of policy, the line taken by Keith 'of absolutely discrediting the views & feelings of the men on the spot if put into action will lose us not only S Africa but every colony we possess'.[38] Keith was soon transferred out of the South African department of the Colonial Office.[39]

The Richmond Trial and the Privy Council

Although no steps were taken in Natal to challenge the executions, a case was brought to the Privy Council on behalf of the prisoners. It was thanks to the determination of a small group of activists, particularly African students at Lincoln's Inn, that the rebels in Natal would get their cases heard in the highest imperial court. The petitioners were represented by E. G. Jellicoe, a Liberal barrister,[40] who would later be engaged by Frank Colenso to defend Dinuzulu in his treason trial in 1907. The petition itself was organised by Alfred Mangena, an African law student at Lincoln's Inn,[41] with legal as well as financial support from Colenso. Born in Natal, Mangena had been a political campaigner in Cape Town on behalf of dock workers who had been forcibly removed to a quarantine location during the bubonic plague outbreak. These campaigns taught him the value of the press

---

[38] Minute, 2 April 1906, CO 179/233/11321, f. 512.
[39] See Hyam, *Elgin and Churchill at the Colonial Office*, p. 9 and note.
[40] Having acted as solicitor to the Treasury in South Wales, Edwin George Jellicoe emigrated for health reasons to New Zealand in 1884, where he practised as a barrister, before returning to England. Having stood for election to the New Zealand House of Representatives, he stood for the Liberal party in the 1906 election and as an independent Liberal in 1910. He was a persistent opponent of Britain's participation in the First World War, and was the author of *Playing the Game: What Mr Asquith in His Book 'The Genesis of the War' Does Not Tell Us* (London, John Long, 1924).
[41] Mangena was assisted by another African student at Lincoln's Inn (from the Gold Coast), Akilagpa Sawyerr.

and the law in advancing the cause of the oppressed Africans. He would put these skills to good use in London, where he commenced his legal studies in 1903. Having learned from the newspapers of the proclamation of martial law in Natal after the Richmond killings, he strove to bring African grievances about the poll tax in Natal to the attention of the press and politicians,[42] and to use the courts to challenge the actions of the Natal government under martial law.[43]

Jellicoe's letters informing the Colonial Office that a petition was being lodged in the Privy Council and his requests to have the executions stayed were ignored by the authorities in Natal, since ministers felt that the court would have no jurisdiction, and that this might simply be a case of 'self-advertisement'.[44] The petition for special leave to appeal from the judgment of the martial law court was consequently heard on the very day that the men were to be executed, 2 April. Presenting the case, Jellicoe argued that the judgment of the martial law court was wholly illegal. There had never been a state of war or rebellion in the colony which could justify the proclamation of martial law. He also pointed out that the event for which the men were condemned took place before martial law had been proclaimed. In addition, he quoted from McCallum's exchanges with his ministers, now published in a Blue Book, which showed that the civilian courts were open and 'capable of trying these charges'. Jellicoe also had to address the point (raised by Lord Davey) that the application had been brought directly to the Privy Council, rather than to a court in Natal. His reply was that the judicial committee had statutory jurisdiction to determine appeals from any colonial court, and that 'the prerogative of the King in Council was wide enough and strong enough to quash any illegal sentence of death in any of the Colonies.' At the very least, he argued, given the Governor's comments about the possibility of having a civilian trial, there were sufficient *prima facie* grounds to justify a further investigation.[45]

---

[42] See e.g. 'Pro-Bambata Party Formed', *Daily Mail*, 27 April 1906.
[43] Ngcukaitobi, *The Land Is Ours*, pp. 80–82; and David Killingray, 'Significant Black South Africans in Britain before 1912', pp. 409–416.
[44] Governor to Secretary of State, 20 April 1906, CO 179/234/16892, f. 270.
[45] *Mgomini, Mzinelwa and Wanda (by Their Next Friend Alfred Mangena) v. His Excellency the Governor and the Attorney General for the Colony of Natal* (1906) 22 *Times Law Reports* 413.

The application failed. In giving the judgment of the court, Lord Halsbury did not address the legal arguments made by Jellicoe. He did not consider whether martial law courts had the jurisdiction to try cases committed before its proclamation,[46] nor whether the judicial committee had its own jurisdiction to consider the matter.[47] In a one-paragraph judgment Halsbury simply noted both that the government of Natal had felt it necessary to proclaim martial law and that the colonial courts had not been applied to. He ruled that this was not an appeal from a court, 'but in substance [one] from an act of the Executive'. The court did not consider the question of whether the state of affairs in Natal justified martial law, or whether the men had been properly tried. Indeed, the Privy Council seemed in this case to close the door it had appeared to leave open in *Marais*: to judge whether there was such a state of war or rebellion as necessitated exceptional action. For as Halsbury put it, 'apart from questions as to jurisdiction, any interposition of a judicial character directed with most imperfect knowledge both of the danger that has threatened Natal, and of the facts which came before the tribunal of war, would be inconsistent with their Lordships' duties.'[48] It was an odd comment to make, given that the court was being asked for the executions to be stayed, pending a further hearing in which full arguments might be made, including arguments relating to the dangers facing Natal. At noon on the same day, the men were executed.

While Churchill privately disagreed with Natal's decision to execute the men, he publicly defended the colony's right to do it. Answering critics who questioned the right of martial law courts to deal with offences committed before its proclamation, Churchill stated that 'all martial law is illegal, and an attempt to introduce illegalities into martial law [...] is like attempting to add salt water to the sea.' He added that '[t]he only restriction on martial law is that no more force is

---

[46] Jellicoe cited Charles M. Clode, *The Administration of Justice under Martial Law*, 2nd ed., 2 vols. (London, John Murray, 1874), vol. 1, p. 189 for this proposition, which drew on debates following the proclamation in Demerara in 1823 suggesting that martial law courts had no jurisdiction to deal with offences committed before its proclamation (quoted Charles M. Clode, *The Military Forces of the Crown*, 2 vols. (London, John Murray, 1869), vol. 2, pp. 489–490).

[47] Under section 4 of the Judicial Committee Act of 1833 (3 & 4 Wm. IV c. 41), the monarch could refer any matter to the committee.

[48] *Mgomini and Others v. The Governor of Natal (Natal)* [1906] UKPC 22.

used than is necessary, and where more force is used than necessary persons may afterwards be called to account unless covered by an Act of Indemnity.'[49] Churchill's exposition of the law drew sharp comment from Frederick Pollock. In a letter to *The Times*, Pollock took issue with the implication that an act of indemnity might be required to validate acts which could never be justified by the general law. Reminding readers of the Diceyan view, he pointed out that 'the use of an Act of Indemnity is not to condone acts that were absolutely illegal, but to cover the inevitable margin of doubtful cases and honest errors of judgment.'[50] At the same time, Pollock also rejected Jellicoe's suggestion that the powers of the military under martial law derived from any proclamation, reiterating the common lawyers' view that such a proclamation was nothing more than a statement by the executive of its view that conditions were such that it was necessary to use extraordinary measures.[51] But this did not seem to be the view of the government of Natal, nor (in effect) of the Colonial Office. For by this stage – with the colony evidently at peace – martial law was being maintained in Natal for the sole reason that its parliament could not pass an indemnity act until May. Although Churchill thought that 'the mere want of an Act of Indemnity ought not in itself to justify prolongation of such a harsh & objectionable system', Fred Graham answered that it had to be maintained 'because in the interval between martial law & the Act of Indemnity the Governor & others might be indicted for murder'.[52] This seemed to indicate both that officials in London felt that a kind of 'state of siege' granting legal immunity remained in place so long as the proclamation of martial law was not withdrawn, and that they had little confidence that a justification of necessity could be pleaded.

The question of the Governor's potential liability soon became more pressing, when Mangena and Jellicoe commenced criminal proceedings in London against McCallum. Mangena was proving to be something of a thorn in the government's side, having also petitioned parliament for an inquiry into the disturbances in Natal at

---

[49] *Parl. Debs.*, 4th ser., vol. 155, col. 273 (2 April 1906). See also Hyam, *Elgin and Churchill at the Colonial Office*, pp. 242–243.
[50] *The Times*, 5 April 1906, p. 8.
[51] See also the letter of T. E. Holland in *The Times*, 5 April 1906, p. 8.
[52] Note, 7 April 1906, CO 179/233/11281, f. 307.

the end of April.[53] The prosecution was brought under two acts: one passed in 1698 to allow for the prosecution in England of Governors who committed crimes overseas, and one passed in 1802 to allow those holding public employments abroad to be tried in England.[54] Two famous governors Governors of Jamaica – Joseph Wall and E. J. Eyre – had been prosecuted under this law, the former being executed, the latter escaping trial when no true bill was found by the jury. Lawyers at the Colonial Office were keenly aware of the danger posed by this unrepealed law. In Cox's view, for the Governor of a responsible government colony which had proclaimed martial law to be prosecuted under such legislation would have disastrous effects on the empire. Since no indemnity act passed in Natal would have any effect outside the colony, he thought that the only chance for the Governor to escape trial would be if a grand jury rejected the bill, or if the Attorney General entered a *nolle prosequi*. The Attorney General confirmed Cox's view of the law, but noted that no criminal proceedings could be taken in England so long as the Governor remained in Natal.[55] McCallum was advised accordingly.

The news of Mangena's action troubled the Governor. 'The natives are watching the newspapers very closely', McCallum told the Secretary of State, Elgin, 'and did they know of the threatened proceedings my authority over them as Supreme Chief would be much weakened.' He also thought that the legislation in question, passed 'in the very early days of colonial administration', should not apply to a colony with a responsible government.[56] In the third week of May, Jellicoe and Colenso laid formal charges of homicide against McCallum in the Bow Street magistrates court, though (as officials had predicted), the proceedings ran into the ground in the absence of

---

[53] *Manchester Guardian*, 27 April 1906.
[54] 11 Wm. III c. 12, 42 Geo. III c. 85. As A. B. Keith noted, the 1861 Offences against the Person Act section 9 also gave English courts jurisdiction over murder committed anywhere. Minute, 14 April 1906, CO 179/239/12835, f. 383.
[55] Opinion of John L. Walton, 24 April 1906, CO 885/16, No. 31. W. F. Finlason had argued that a governor would be protected by an indemnity act: *Commentaries upon Martial Law* (London, Stevens and Sons, 1867), p. 268, and it had been held in *Phillips* v. *Eyre* (1869) LR 4 QB 229 that an indemnity act protected from tort liability.
[56] McCallum to Elgin, 27 April 1906, CO 879/234/18010, f. 363.

the potential defendant.[57] In the middle of these proceedings, the Colonial Office pondered whether to change the law allowing such prosecutions, but decided against it, since any such move this point would only draw attention to the government's liability.[58] Steps were taken, however, to find out more about Mangena in South Africa in order to discredit him.[59] Material about Mangena – which suggested that he was not originally from Natal and had defrauded a group of Africans in Cape Town – was sent to London in the middle of June, and published in a Blue Book. Graham commented, 'We shall probably have no further trouble from him.'[60]

Martial Law after Bambatha's Uprising, April–September 1906

Martial Law Trials of the Rebels

Any doubts that the Colonial Office had about the continuation of martial law at the time of the execution of the twelve accused of killing Hunt and Armstrong were extinguished by Bambatha's revolt. The revival of unrest saw another tranche of trials by courts martial, as well as a much larger stream of cases tried by magistrates. The Natal authorities were keen to try the rebels as quickly as possible in the locations where they had rebelled. Whereas many of the trials during the first phase had been for acts of defiance to the magistracy, and for marching with arms, many of those tried subsequently had been caught in acts of rebellion. The ambush of white policemen on the road to Keate's Drift on 4 April by followers of Bambatha, which left three dead, led to two major martial law trials at Greytown. The first case (which began on 23 June) did not result in any convictions for the murder, but twenty-one men were convicted of public violence and treason.[61] Seventeen more were charged in early August at a second

---

[57] *Manchester Guardian*, 16 May 1906, 22 May 1906.
[58] As Churchill put it, 'Leave well alone': CO 179/234/18010, f. 362.
[59] CO 879/92/26, No. 17, p. 20.
[60] Note, 21 June 1906, CO 179/235/21724, f. 350. The material was published in July in PP 1906 (Cd. 3027), No. 95, p. 95. It was reprinted in several newspapers, which were later sued by Mangena: see *Mangena* v. *Edward Lloyd Ltd* (1908) 98 LT 640; *Mangena* v. *Wright* [1909] 2 KB 958; 'Papers Relating to the Case of Mr Alfred Mangena', PP 1908 (Cd. 4403) LXXII. 819; and Ngcukaitobi, *The Land Is Ours*, pp. 93–97.
[61] PP 1906 (Cd. 3247) LXXIX. 687, No. 23, p. 17.

trial, in a court presided over by Lt-Col. Bousfield, 'one of [the] leading lawyers of Durban'.[62] They too were acquitted of the murder, but were convicted of other charges. The beginning of July also saw three of Bambatha's principal *indunas* tried at Greytown for public violence and treason, though only one was convicted. A number of trials at Nkandhla in June, July and August dealt with Sigananda and his followers. Sigananda himself surrendered on 13 June. Plans were immediately made for the trial of this chief and his sons, which took place two weeks after his capture.[63] Thirteen more of his *indunas* and headmen were tried at Nkandhla in August. Sigananda died before sentencing, but four other men tried at Nkandhla – including his son and commander in chief Ndabaningi – were given death sentences, later commuted to life imprisonment. The rebel leaders Ndhlovu and Meseni were tried by court martial in Mapumulo for high treason and murder in the middle of July, very shortly after their capture. Their trial was presided over by another Durban lawyer, Lt-Col. Wylie, who had also presided at Sigananda's trial.[64] They were also sentenced to death by the court.

All of these trials took place after the rebellion had effectively been crushed at Mome Gorge. Although the Governor thought that the rebels could be tried in civilian courts,[65] he again came under pressure both from ministers and from the military, who insisted that 'Natives cannot understand the necessity for, or wisdom of, resorting to what they consider the tedious and protracted procedure of the Civil Courts in cases of this nature.'[66] He therefore agreed to the continuation of courts martial, with the proviso that 'magnanimity should be exercised.' The death sentences imposed on the men tried at Nkandhla were commuted,[67] as were those imposed on Meseni and Ndhlovu, since McCallum was not convinced that there was sufficient evidence to connect the chiefs directly with the murders.[68]

---

[62] PP 1906 (Cd. 3247), No. 38, p. 53.
[63] CO 879/106/1, No. 494, p. 177; No. 511, p. 183; No. 560, p. 199. See also PP 1906 (Cd. 3027), enc. 3 in No. 97, p. 100.
[64] PP 1906 (Cd. 3247) No. 33, p. 34. See further Guy, *The Maphumulo Uprising*, pp. 111-128.
[65] PP 1906 (Cd. 3247), enc. 1 in No. 26, p. 18.
[66] PP 1906 (Cd. 3247), enc. 2 in No. 26, p. 19.   [67] PP 1906 (Cd. 3247), No. 57, p. 86.
[68] PP 1906 (Cd. 3247), No. 38, p. 53. At the same time, many sentences of long periods of imprisonment as well as lashings were confirmed by the Governor.

McCallum's concern that martial law trials should follow the principles of legality as closely as possible became apparent when he reviewed the case of Madamu kaMbaupanzim who had been convicted of spying on 4 May by a court martial of three officers, and sentenced to death. As soon as the trial began, his counsel objected that the court was improperly constituted, since it did not have five members, as required under military law. Having read the transcript of the two-day trial, McCallum was far from convinced of Madamu's guilt. More importantly, he considered that the court had been improperly constituted and that the conviction should be quashed, while leaving open the possibility of trying him before the civil courts.[69] Ministers protested at this, and referred the question to Natal's Attorney General, G. A. de Roquefeuil Labistour, who felt both that the evidence justified the conviction, and that there were no binding rules as to the constitution of a martial law court.[70] Officials in London sided with Labistour, Cox minuting that the Governor was confusing martial law – which was the mere will of the commander – with military law. 'I cannot say that I find anything to show that the man had not a fair trial', he noted, 'He was able to X examine & to give evidence on his own behalf & he had an advocate to defend him.'[71] Elgin consequently turned down McCallum's request for the matter to be referred to the Law Officers in London, telling him to decide the punishment on the merits of the case. The sentence was duly commuted to five years' imprisonment with hard labour.[72]

McCallum and his ministers also disagreed over whether the remaining suspects for Hunt's murder – including Mjongo – should be tried by civilian or martial law courts.[73] On this occasion, his view prevailed. Their trial began in the Supreme Court a little over a week after the end of the Nkandhla court-martial trials of Siganandha's *indunas*, with martial law still in place. The men were convicted, and McCallum congratulated himself that a civilian court had convicted these men on similar evidence to that given to the court martial.[74] Having been nursed back to health after their capture, the men were

[69] Minute by H. McCallum, 11 June 1906, CO 179/236/30631, f. 334.
[70] Minute, 19 June 1906, CO 179/236/30631, f. 339.
[71] Minute, 25 August 1906, CO 179/236/30631, f. 315.
[72] CO 879/92/26, No. 32, p. 42; PP 1906 (Cd. 3247), No. 58, p. 87.
[73] CO 179/235/18017, f. 85.   [74] PP 1906 (Cd. 3247), No. 54, p. 72.

The Zulu Rebellion of 1906

now sentenced to death.[75] Frank Colenso petitioned Elgin to spare them, but it was decided not to interfere, and they were executed on the following day.[76]

Tilonko's Trial

It was during this second, more violent phase of the rebellion that what would be the most controversial trial under martial law took place. This was the trial of Tilonko, whose followers had brandished spears in defiance of authority, in ways similar to the followers of the chiefs who had not been tried, Ngobizembe, Miskofeli and Charlie Fynn. Unlike those tried at Greytown, Nkandhla and Maphumulo, Tilonko had not been a rebel in the field. He was, however, suspected of planning the rebellion. According to McKenzie's intelligence officer, Lt-Col. Henry Lugg, Tilonko had conspired with others (including Miskofeli's *induna*, Mamba) to resist the poll tax, and it had only been 'the drastic measures' taken by the military which had prevented the whole country becoming 'ablaze with rebellion'.[77] The authorities were also suspicious about two emissaries Tilonko had apparently sent to the Zulu king Dinuzulu. With the promulgation of the poll tax, rumours had begun to circulate that Dinuzulu had ordered Africans to kill all white animals – goats, pigs and fowl – and to destroy European tools. The Natal authorities remained uncertain of Dinuzulu's role in the rebellion: although he would be tried by a civilian Special Court in Greytown for treason in the following year, they had no specific information against him in the middle of 1906.[78]

Despite their suspicions about Tilonko, the authorities did not appear to regard him as a dangerous rebel.[79] It was only after Tilonko had failed satisfactorily to explain his conduct to the Minister of Native Affairs, H. D. Winter, when summoned to Pietermaritzburg on 23 July, that the decision was taken to charge him with sedition and public violence. Even then, he was allowed to return to his tribe, and was

---

[75] PP 1906 (Cd. 3247), No. 60, p. 90.
[76] Letter from Francis Colenso to Secretary of State, 7 October 1906, CO 179/239/37069, f. 185.
[77] CO 879/92/26, enc. 1 in No. 5, p. 6.
[78] For his trial, see Marks, *Reluctant Rebellion*, chs. 10–11.
[79] PP 1906 (Cd. 3247), No. 33, p. 34.

trusted to appear for his trial.[80] The trial itself commenced on 30 July, just as the order to demobilise the active militia had been given,[81] with the Governor confident enough to tell the troops at a parade in Pietermaritzburg that 'in the moment of our success it is right that what we have done already should be allowed to sink deeply into the natives, and that we should show them as much mercy as possible.'[82] The trial was held behind closed doors, since the authorities wanted to prevent the evidence of emissaries being sent to Dinuzulu from being reported. As a result of this, Tilonko's strong supporter Harriette Colenso – described by McCallum as a woman of 'pronounced negrophile tendencies'[83] – was excluded from the courtroom. His lawyer, Eugene Renaud, opened his case by objecting that his client – who had not been captured in the field – should be tried in a civilian court.[84] The objection was summarily dismissed, but Tilonko's supporters brought it to the attention of Ramsay MacDonald, who on the following day reminded Churchill in the House of Commons of his earlier statement that 'only natives caught in the act of fighting are to be tried by court-martial.'[85] In response, the Colonial Office referred the matter to McCallum, who replied that the policy of only trying rebels caught in the field had been abandoned at the start of May.[86]

Much of the evidence at the trial focused on the fact that, in the days after Hunt's murder, Tilonko's tribesmen had armed themselves and had marched in large numbers, both in daylight and during the night. White witnesses spoke of a change in behaviour among the Africans since the previous August – 'They have been very cheeky lately'[87] – and how, around 10–11 February, men carrying spears had used much more threatening language. This had struck fear into the whites, who had gone into laager at Richmond. Numerous African witnesses gave evidence that they had been told to arm, with many stating that this was to be done to protect Tilonko, who it was feared was going to be

[80] PP 1906 (Cd. 3247), No. 37, p. 37.
[81] CO 879/106/1, No. 691, p. 243; PP 1906 (Cd. 3247), No. 39, p. 53.
[82] *Natal Witness*, 3 August 1906.
[83] Governor to Secretary of State, 10 November 1906, CO 179/237/44576, f. 288.
[84] 'Verbatim Note of Proceedings in re Tilonko', CO/179/237/44576, f. 366.
[85] *Parl. Debs.*, 4th ser., vol. 162, col. 702 (31 July 1906).
[86] PP 1906 (Cd. 3247), No. 25, p. 17.
[87] Evidence of R. W. Newbold, 'Verbatim Note of Proceedings', CO/179/237/44576, f. 450.

arrested. There was no direct evidence provided by any of the witnesses in the courtroom that Tilonko himself had given the order to arm. Rather, the orders appeared to have come from his *indunas*.

One witness, Sancubu, had, however, given a statement to Lt-Col. Lugg, which seemed to incriminate the chief. According to the statement,

TILONKO asked me if I had delivered the message which he had sent to me to tell the people to arm ... I heard that Chief DINIZULU was to send an 'UMLUNGO'[88] which would overpower the Whites and their adherents and cause their guns to belch forth water instead of fire, and to disable them that we would be able to kill them with our sticks. DINIZULU was bringing an Umlungo also an Impi to assist us against the Whites. I heard of Msutu and Mqaikana [the messengers] being sent to DINIZULU all chiefs were combined to resist the Poll-tax and fight the white man. ... A black bull was to appear from the North which would fly along and destroy everything in its road. There would have been a general rising in my opinion had the White man not been ready.[89]

At the trial, however, Sancubu denied making these allegations, and claimed only to have signed the document (which had already been prepared) when he was threatened with being tied to a pole up all day in the sun, as other witnesses had been. Renaud objected that, since the witness was discredited out of his own mouth, his statement could be of no evidentiary value. Nonetheless, the prosecutor recalled Lugg and the translator to testify that he had made the statement freely, and the statement was itself appended to the transcript of the trial, as part of the evidence against Tilonko. However inadmissible in an ordinary court, it clearly played a key role in Tilonko's conviction. Evidence was also given by the two emissaries to Dinuzulu, Msutu and Mqaikane. Mqaikane, the tribe's witness who dealt with Dinuzulu, denied claims made by Msutu (his cook and helper, who had run away after two days) that they had been sent to ask for assistance to fight. In any event, the evidence was clear that Dinuzulu favoured their paying the tax, and that by the time they returned home, there was no talk of fighting.

Tilonko's defence appeared in many ways similar to the arguments which had exonerated Miskofeli and Charlie Fynn in the eyes of the authorities. He claimed that he himself favoured payment of the tax,

---

[88] This is probably a mis-transcription of the Zulu word 'umlingo', meaning 'magic' rather than 'umlungu', meaning a 'white person'.
[89] 'Verbatim Note of Proceedings', CO/179/237/44576, ff. 616–617.

though the tribe was against it. Since the tax was not legally due before the end of May, he had done no wrong in failing to pay when the magistrate came to collect it in February. He denied instructing the tribe to arm, claiming that he had little control over the *indunas*, and he said that he had gone into hiding from fear of being arrested. Although, in the case of Charlie Fynn, the authorities appeared to accept that tribesmen could arm without being ordered by their chief, and that they might do so in order to protect their chief, such arguments were rejected in Tilonko's case. Although the accusation that Tilonko had ordered his men to arm rested largely on conjecture and hearsay evidence rather than the kind of concrete proof which would satisfy a civilian court, he was convicted by the court, and sentenced on 17 August to ten years' imprisonment with hard labour, together with a fine of cattle. Confirming the prison sentence, McCallum commented that the Attorney General had informed him that the 'greatest possible care' had been exercised in the trial 'and that no civil tribunal could have done better'.[90] In fact, his trial would prove to be much more controversial than the Governor assumed, for it raised a host of questions about the nature of martial law, which would continue to be debated in legal and political circles for some months to come. These questions were further complicated by the manner in which Natal passed its Indemnity Act.

Natal's Indemnity Act, the Privy Council and the Rule of Law

The Indemnity Act 1906

If great political care had been taken in the Cape to ensure that sentences imposed under martial law on white rebels had been just and proportionate, the same cannot be said of Natal's approach when dealing with black rebels in 1906. For Natal's parliament passed the measure before many of the trials had even begun, requesting the Governor to withhold his assent until such a moment when those trials had ended and martial law could be lifted. As officials in London perceived, this was to treat martial law as if it were a continental-style state of siege.

---

[90] PP 1906 (Cd. 3247), No. 38, p. 53.

The Indemnity Bill which came to Natal's parliament in June 1906 contained no provision for the revision of sentences. It was also radically innovative in one crucial respect. Section 9 of the bill provided for 'future measures for suppression of disturbances and punishment of offenders', giving the Governor the power to punish any rebel by court martial (including by death) during the continuance of the rebellion.[91] It abandoned any idea that the legislature should review sentences before confirming them. Opponents of the measure in the Natal Assembly spoke of it as giving the government a blank cheque.[92] Officials at the Colonial Office were also unimpressed.[93] In R. V. Vernon's view, the clause 'empowers the Governor to set up practically a "state of siege"' and went against the 'recognised principles' on which indemnity acts were passed.[94] H. C. M. Lambert noted that the clause had been borrowed from legislation passed after the Union 'for the suppression of rebellion in Ireland',[95] and noted that other colonies (such as Jamaica in 1845)[96] had passed similar legislation to establish a state of siege: 'But there is no modern precedent for such legislation, which is in effect the suspension of the constitution or at least of the fundamental rights of the subjects which depend for their enforcement on the Courts.'[97] This was not simply an abstract question for the Colonial Office: for Ramsay MacDonald had tabled

---

[91] A copy of the act is in PP 1906 (Cd. 3247), enc. 1 in No. 63, p. 92.
[92] *Times of Natal*, 28 June 1906.
[93] Cox assumed that the 'future indemnity' clause had been motivated by Mangena's proceedings in Bow Street, which R. V. Vernon thought reflected a 'remarkable confusion of thought' on the part of Natal's Minister of Justice. CO 179/235/26687, f. 493.
[94] Minute dated 13 July 1906, CO 179/238/25217, f. 249.
[95] An Act for the Suppression of Rebellion in Ireland, 43 Geo. III c. 117. This re-enacted earlier Irish legislation which had spoken of 'His Majesty's undoubted prerogative in executing Martial Law', which some commentators took as proving the right of the crown to proclaim martial law. See Clode, *Military Forces of the Crown*, vol. II, pp. 170–174.
[96] Jamaica's 9. Vic. c. 35 (An Act to consolidate and amend the Militia Laws), sections 96–97 gave the Governor power to proclaim martial law on the advice of a council of war, and (section 111) allowed those sued for acts done during martial law to plead the general issue and give evidence of the 'special matter'. In February 1866, the Law Officers (Roundell Palmer and R. P. Collier) advised that, under this act, the Governor could not be prosecuted for proclaiming martial law without necessity, and military officers were not liable for exceeding the necessity of the case, provided they acted *bona fide*: CO 885/3/17, p. 33.
[97] Minute dated 14 July 1906, CO 179/238/25217, f. 246.

a question on the matter in the Commons, and officials were aware of English eyes watching the government's reaction.

Once again, there were imperial complications. Characteristically overlooking His Majesty's African subjects, the permanent undersecretary of state Sir Montagu Ommanney noted that, 'If this particular community of British subjects likes to forego its fundamental rights in order that its officials & the officers & men of its local forces shall not be exposed to vexatious actions under the ordinary law, I can't see why we should interfere.' But Cox was more concerned by imperial interests. In his view, the bill gave the Governor dictatorial powers to act without any restraint even by his ministers. For him, the question was not whether the colony wanted it or not, but whether an imperial officer should be given such powers, in effect shifting the responsibility for the use of such brute force 'from ministerial shoulders onto HMGovt'.[98] After the bill had passed through Natal's assembly and Legislative Council, Elgin sent a telegram to the Governor, pointing out the undesirability of prospective legislation, since the prospect of needing to pass an indemnity measure provided 'a useful check on the operation of martial law', and asking ministers to consider following the Boer war precedents.[99]

McCallum's ministers held firm. Attorney General Labistour was of the view that Natal was perfectly within its rights to pass such a measure, adding that the Governor would be expected to use his powers in a 'constitutional' way, on the advice of his ministers. Natal clearly regarded this as a local matter.[100] Furthermore, given that ministers still wanted martial law in place – to allow the trials of the remaining rebel leaders – McCallum pointed out that, if this bill were not passed, it would have to be prolonged until Natal's parliament met again in nine months' time.[101] Although Cox protested that this meant that life and property were 'to be endangered to suit the convenience of legislators', officials in London began to concede the argument,

---

[98] Minutes, 14–16 July 1906, CO 179/238/25217, ff. 246–248.
[99] CO 879/106/1, No. 636, p. 225.
[100] McCallum did not consider that the bill fell within the classes of reserved legislation listed in the Royal Instructions of 1893: PP 1906 (Cd. 3247), No. 29, p. 28; No. 34, p. 36. On the Instructions, see A. B. Keith, *Responsible Government in the Dominions*, 3 vols. (Oxford, Clarendon Press, 1912), vol. 2, p. 1014.
[101] CO 879/106/1, No. 695, p. 245.

admitting both that the colony had the power to pass such legislation – on the Jamaica precedent – and that the Governor would be expected to act on ministerial advice. To avoid 'throw[ing] down the gauntlet to Natal', officials suggested asking Natal to end martial law 'at an early date'.[102] McCallum took the view that it was unnecessary to insist on the amendment of the measure, since the disturbances were practically over by early August, and martial law would soon be ended.[103] In the event, he delayed assenting to the measure until martial law was ended on 1 October.

Tilonko's Challenges and the Privy Council

In the meantime, Alfred Mangena submitted a petition to the King in Council, which recited that the Governor had 'grievously and illegally oppressed divers loyal and dutiful subjects' by imposing martial law, and which requested the King to refer the matter to a committee of the Privy Council, to investigate and advise disallowance of the indemnity bill.[104] This unorthodox petition provoked much discussion in Whitehall. Although officials thought that it was a political matter which did not concern the judicial committee, they were aware that, under section 4 of the Privy Council Act of 1833, there was a power to refer such questions to that committee. They concluded that the best way to proceed was to pass it on *pro forma* to the Council Office with an explanatory note, setting out that Lord Elgin proposed advising the king not to disallow the measure. As the legal assistant J. S. Risley pointed out to his colleagues, where the recommendation was against a petition, 'the matter never comes before the Council at all but the petition is "squelched" in the Council Office.'[105]

Having failed in this attempt, Tilonko's supporters entered a supplementary petition, invoking the Natal Constitution Act 1893 which empowered the crown by Order in Council to disallow legislation which had been assented to by the Governor.[106] Once more officials sought to put bureaucratic obstacles in the way. In the face of the

---

[102] Note by Ommanney, 2 August 1906, CO 179/236/28242, f. 372.
[103] PP 1906 (Cd. 3247), No. 28, p. 28.
[104] The petition is in CO 179/238/33117, ff. 29–48.
[105] Minute dated 24 September 1906, CO 179/238/33117, f. 23.
[106] 'The Humble Petition of Tilonko', CO 179/239/38431, f. 262.

Colonial Office's insistence that the question of disallowance was one for Elgin to advise on – and its further insistence that he would not advise disallowance – Tilonko's lawyers countered that the Secretary of State was thereby usurping the Privy Council's power.[107] With continued pressure from Tilonko's solicitors, as well as from friendly MPs, the Colonial Office felt constrained to follow constitutional procedure to the letter, with Elgin formally submitting Tilonko's petitions to the king and advising against disallowance.[108]

This was not the only legal strategy deployed to secure his freedom. At the end of August, Tilonko petitioned the Supreme Court of Natal for his release.[109] During the argument, the two differing views of the nature of martial law were put forward. Drawing both on *Marais* and on *Mgomini*, Attorney General Labistour argued that the court had no jurisdiction while martial law was in force. A declaration of martial law, like a declaration of war, was in his view conclusive for the court. Renaud, however, insisted that the court had the right to consider whether a state of war existed and to determine whether Tilonko was being legally confined. Although Labistour insisted on precedents which showed 'that your Lordships will not interfere with the decision of the Executive or the Governor for the simple reason that you have not the power to carry it into effect',[110] the judges were not wholly convinced. 'Suppose that one could conceive of an absolutely misguided Executive as to declare Martial Law in a time of peace', Justice Dove-Wilson asked, 'would the civil court be debarred from saying that Martial Law was illegally declared?'[111] In the end the court was divided, with the majority taking the more liberal position that a mere declaration of martial law did not oust the jurisdiction of the court. However, they decided to give the Attorney General more time to provide evidence of the necessity for martial law. If this was a significant assertion by the court of its authority, it was to serve

---

[107] See letters from Helder, Roberts, Walton & Giles Solicitors to Churchill, 26 November and 7 December 1906 in CO 179/239/43630, f. 279; CO 179/239/45156, f. 284.

[108] This was to avoid any possibility of the secretary of state being sued in tort for failure to present the petition: see *Irwin* v. *Grey* (1862) 3 F. & F. 635.

[109] *In re Tilonko* (1906) 27 Natal Law Reports 567; a full transcript is in CO 179/237/44376, ff. 310–361.

[110] *In re Tilonko*, CO 179/237/44376, f. 336.

[111] *In re Tilonko*, CO 179/237/44376, f. 333.

little purpose, for, having waited for the decision which enunciated the principles he wished to see established, Renaud dropped the proceedings, in light of Labistour's comments to the court that an act of indemnity had been assented to, though not yet published.

In fact, Labistour's remarks had been misleading. The fact that Elgin had approved the Governor's assenting to the measure did not mean that the crown's assent had been formally given: indeed, the requisite assent would not be given for another month. This meant that Tilonko's incarceration had not yet been rendered lawful by statute. When the papers were sent to London, together with a new petition from Tilonko for the crown to exercise its prerogative of mercy, concerns were raised at the Colonial Office about Labistour's misstatement. 'I do not think we can ignore the point raised in this minute', Vernon noted, 'though Tilonko's friends have failed to take it.' While his colleagues agreed that the judges were right to assert their jurisdiction,[112] they felt that it had made no difference to Tilonko. In Lambert's view, 'even if the Court had ordered the release the Govt could have proceeded further against T under martial law & their acts would have been validated if not the original proceedings.' In Cox's view, the military would simply have ignored the order and later been justified by the indemnity. These observations – which were hardly an endorsement of the rule of law – overlooked the fact that what was at stake was not just Tilonko's incarceration, but his ten-year sentence. Given the controversy caused by London's earlier attempts to intercede to spare the Richmond convicts, there was little appetite to interfere now. This was all the more so since McCallum had made it clear he expected no sympathy for Tilonko, who 'appears to forget that rebellion is one of the worst crimes of which a native can be guilty'.[113]

While still pursuing his petition to disallow the Indemnity Act, on 17 October, Tilonko's supporters petitioned the Privy Council in its judicial capacity, for special leave to appeal from the decision of the

---

[112] CO 179/237/44376, f. 281. As Lambert explained, 'otherwise a proclamation of Martial Law in February if not withdrawn would remain ipso facto a bar to judicial proceedings in August or indeed indefinitely, a theory which may indeed be recognised in the continental "state of siege", but which our Courts have never accepted.'

[113] Under Zulu law, he added, rebels and their entire families were 'exterminated' and their homesteads laid waste. Governor to Secretary of State, 10 November 1906, CO 179/237/44576, f. 288.

martial law court. The case was argued on 2 November, when Jellicoe argued that Tilonko had never taken up arms against the Government, that Natal had not been in a state of war, that the civil courts were open, and that his trial before the martial law court was therefore without jurisdiction. In contrast to the proceedings in *Mgomini and Others* v. *The Governor of Natal*, on this occasion the judges in the judicial committee did not doubt their jurisdiction to hear a case brought directly before them from a Natal martial law court. Furthermore, Lord Halsbury took the opportunity briefly to address questions of law which he had left aside in the earlier case. Martial law was not 'law' at all, he declared, but 'the right to administer force against force in actual war'. Echoing the comments of Pollock on the earlier case, he noted that its existence did not depend on a proclamation, but on the factual 'question whether there is war or not'. Halsbury now conceded that there might 'be a question of doubt' about whether such a state of war existed, which 'might have required consideration' by the court – a view of the law which might have given the Richmond prisoners a reprieve had he turned his mind to it in April. However, in this case, Halsbury concluded, there was nothing for the court to discuss, since Natal's parliament had already passed an Indemnity Act which provided that the sentences of martial law courts should be deemed valid. 'The only thing for persons who are subject to such an Act of Parliament to do is to obey.'[114]

This was not the end of Tilonko's appeals against his sentence. In April 1907, habeas corpus proceedings were brought once more in Pietermaritzburg to secure his liberation. Although the application was dismissed after Labistour put in a document certifying that Tilonko's sentence came within the Indemnity Act,[115] the case provided another opportunity to seek special leave to appeal to the Privy Council. On this occasion, Jellicoe came prepared with arguments to dislodge the Indemnity Act. They rested on the fact that Natal's parliament had been

---

[114] *Tilonko* v. *Attorney General of the Colony of Natal* [1907] AC 93 at 95. In *Responsible Government* (vol. 1, p. 272), A. B. Keith stated that the principles relating to martial law were 'admirably laid down' in this judgment; but in a later work, he read the case as extending the principle of *Marais* – that courts could not interfere with the actions of the military in time of war – to times of rebellion: *An Introduction to British Constitutional Law* (Oxford, Clarendon Press, 1931), p. 73.
[115] *In re Tilonko* (1907) 28 Natal Law Reports 190.

dissolved on 15 August, a month and a half before the Governor had assented to the bill. In order for the legislation to be valid, Jellicoe argued, it had to be passed by the concurrence of the whole legislature, which was not possible if the Assembly and Legislative Council had been dissolved before the Act had been passed. He added that to suggest that assent to legislation could be withheld after the dissolution for any indefinite period 'in order to validate subsequent illegal transactions or to destroy rights which vested after the dissolution of Parliament was a libel upon the Sovereign and the Constitution'.[116] For good measure, he added an argument that the act, which prejudiced the royal prerogative – by denying the prerogative writ of habeas corpus – was repugnant to the law of England and against common right and reason.

Similar arguments had already been made in a petition submitted on Tilonko's behalf to the House of Commons. In this petition, Tilonko had complained that Natal's *ex post facto* Indemnity Act had legalised the unlawful proceedings of an illegal tribunal, and that it was repugnant to Magna Carta.[117] Having read the petition, Churchill could not see how Tilonko's treatment could be defended if it were raised in the Commons, adding 'It is a hateful business.' His officials were less troubled, however, Cox noting that *ex post facto* legislation was essential where martial law was proclaimed and that its passage proved the necessity for it. Lambert commented, 'Tilonko's legal learning is so extensive and so amazingly incorrect that I think he must have derived it from Mr Jellicoe.'[118] Nor did the arguments cut much ice with the Judicial Committee of the Privy Council. In a judgment even briefer than its earlier one, the court, through the voice of the new Lord Chancellor, Loreburn, said the matter was settled by Natal's Indemnity Act, whose policy or expediency the court had no power to consider.[119] The way was thus paved for Tilonko, and the other martial law convicts, to serve out their sentences. But before this could be done, there were further legal problems to encounter.

---

[116] *Tilonko v. Attorney General of Natal* (1907) 23 TLR 668 at 669. See also *The Times*, 6 July 1907, p. 11.
[117] The petition dated 1 March 1907 is in CO 179/243/12449, f. 546. *Parl. Debs.*, 4th ser., vol. 161, col. 1452 (25 March 1907).
[118] Minutes 11 April 1907, CO 179/243/12449, f. 545.
[119] *Tilonko v. Attorney General of the Colony of Natal* [1907] AC 461.

Tilonko's Deportation

Removing the Ringleaders

As early as May 1906, Natal's ministers were clear that the ringleaders tried by martial law courts should be removed from the colony.[120] They were to include not only the rebel leaders tried at Greytown, Nkandhla and Maphumulo, but also Tilonko. The initial plan was to deport them to the Seychelles, which McCallum felt would have 'far-reaching effects as a deterrent'.[121] Although London's response was unenthusiastic, with officials seeing numerous legal obstacles to this attempt to export martial law,[122] ministers continued to explore the possibilities of deportation. Towards the end of August, they received offers to take the leaders both from St Helena and from the Cape. Neither was accepted: for St Helena, which had no accommodation for convicts, could take only political prisoners, a status Natal's government was determined to deny these men; while the Cape's offer to put the men to work at East London Harbour initially seemed too expensive.[123]

The question of what to do with the ringleaders became more pressing in January, after the government – having found no solution to the problem of what to do with the large numbers of rank and file rebels still in prison – released 178 elderly rebels in a way which revived concerns about the prospect of renewed rebellion. For, rather than being sent to distant places, as had been intended, they were inadvertently allowed to return to their homes, where rumours began to proliferate that the king wanted to free all rebels and compensate them. Fearing renewed unrest, Natal's government resolved to stop the releases, and to remove the ringleaders from proximity to those they might influence. For Natal, the matter of deporting these dangerous chiefs was now a matter of priority. The idea of taking up the Cape's offer was finally abandoned, since 'they would still be in touch with

---

[120] Only twenty-five of the 4,192 rebels sentenced to periods of imprisonment by December 1906 were so removed: the large majority were sentenced by magistrates to lesser periods of imprisonment: CO 879/106/1, No. 1099, p. 409.
[121] CO 879/92/26, No. 6, p. 11. [122] CO 879/92/26, No. 14, p. 17.
[123] CO 879/92/26, No. 49, p. 57.

native community' there.[124] Instead, McCallum secured the agreement of the Governor of Mauritius.[125]

The government of Natal wanted the men to be removed under the Colonial Prisoners Removal Act of 1884, which could now be done, given that their martial law sentences had been legalised by the Indemnity Act. However, ministers in London were uncomfortable with the proposal that the chiefs should be removed as ordinary criminals. Churchill wanted their sentences to be revised, and for them to be treated as political exiles rather than convicts, who could be allowed home when the unrest ceased.[126] Without such conditions, he did not feel that the policy could be justified in the House of Commons.

On Elgin's prompting, McCallum raised Tilonko's case with his Minister of Justice, impressing on him the fact that he 'did not actually fight us'. However, Natal's ministers refused to budge: not only was he 'recognized as one of the principal leaders in rebel movement in Natal' but he had 'maintained to the last his attitude of defiance after arrest, and enlisted on his side, for the purposes of appeal to the Privy Council, that small but active section of English-speaking persons who regard rebellious and dangerous characters as useful instruments for the furtherance of political animosities'.[127] Officials in London also remained uncomfortable about using the Colonial Prisoners Removal Act: for, although its wording specified that it was to be used where 'the removal of the prisoner is expedient for his safe custody or for more efficiently carrying his sentence into effect',[128] Natal's intention was to use it (as Cox pointed out) 'to alarm and impress other natives who may be contemplating rebellion'.[129] Natal's insistence on a tough policy caused major discomfort in Whitehall. 'Unless I can prove that our action has diminished & substantially diminished the total sum of human pain', Churchill minuted, 'there will be grave inconvenience.'[130]

---

[124] Governor to Secretary of State, 17 February 1907, CO 179/240/4452, f. 138.
[125] Sir C. Boyle (Governor of Mauritius) to Elgin, 17 January 1907, CO 167/778/6017. The general correspondence relating to the removal is in PP 1907 (Cd. 3563) LVII. 381.
[126] Minute, 16 January 1907, CO 179/240/1738, f. 28.   [127] CAB 37/87/20.
[128] 47 & 48 Vic. c. 31, s. 2(d).   [129] CO 167/778/2786.
[130] Minute, 21 January 1907, CO 179/243/2605, f. 183.

In the event, the plan to deport them to Mauritius collapsed due to the outbreak of beri-beri on the island. Natal's ministers, ever anxious that the continued presence of the rebels in Natal might encourage revolt, urged that the men be sent to Mauritius, and kept in temporary buildings, fenced-off from other prisoners, as had been done with Boer prisoners of war, where they might be quarantined from the outbreak. But they were undone by their own insistence that the men be treated simply as removed prisoners: Cox determined 'to ram this point into the wooly ministerial heads in Natal' that '[i]f they deport them as convicts as convicts they must be treated.'[131] As ever, the colonial government seemed to have a rather more cavalier approach to legality than officials in Whitehall, whose own views of the matter were shaped by the political pressures they needed to respond to.

With deportation to Mauritius out of the question, the Natal government turned once more to St Helena, whose Governor agreed to take the twenty-five rebel leaders.[132] By then, some officials in London were sympathetic to Natal's view. Given recent reports on Dinuzulu's activities, Lambert noted, 'The whole situation is dangerous and the moral is I think that we should do what we can to help Natal by taking the 25 ringleaders at St Helena as soon as possible.'[133] The legal procedure to remove them began at the end of April, with the Colonial Office ensuring that all the legal formalities were punctiliously followed. Winston Churchill protested, minuting that 'This is highly irregular; if not actually illegal. I cannot concur in any degree in this indefensible transaction: nor will I defend it.'[134] On 1 June, the rebel leaders left Natal by the steamship *Inyati*.[135] Although Elgin was informed that Natal's Prime Minister, F. R. Moor, had given instructions (when departing on leave) that Tilonko should not be deported, he was one of the prisoners on the ship.[136] The Acting Prime Minister informed McCallum that the rest of the Cabinet felt

---

[131] Minutes, 5–6 March 1907, CO 179/240/8241, ff. 251, 258. London had developed its own plans to ameliorate the conditions for the prisoners on Mauritius, which would require local legislation there: CO 167/778/2786.
[132] PP 1907 (Cd. 3563), No. 19, p. 8.
[133] Minute, 21 March 1907, CO 179/240/9666, f. 201. Lambert referred to the despatch printed in PP 1908 (Cd. 3888) LXXII. 47, No. 14, p. 20.
[134] See CO 879/106/6, No. 250, p. 90; minute of 25 April 1907, CO 179/240/14392, f. 457.
[135] PP 1907 (Cd. 3563), No. 26, p. 14.   [136] CO 879/106/6, No. 293, p. 103.

the suggestion was 'quite impracticable' and took no action. Colonial Officials were sympathetic to these views, but Churchill saw it as 'Another piece of Natal blackguardism & bad faith'.[137] Of the twenty-five deported chiefs, seventeen had been tried by courts martial which had been set up after the Natal Assembly had passed the Indemnity Bill.

Tilonko's Final Challenges

Tilonko's deportation did not end his supporters' efforts to secure his liberty before the Privy Council. After the failure of the attempt to appeal the decision of Natal's Supreme Court to refuse him habeas corpus, Jellicoe and Colenso returned to the King's Bench in October, seeking judicial review of the decision to remove him under the Colonial Prisoners Removal Act. On this occasion, Jellicoe raised the same argument which had worried officials in Whitehall – that the legislation allowed removal only for 'safer custody' or for carrying out the sentence 'more efficiently'. He argued that material in the African Blue Book showed that the removal was designed to put an end to the rumour that the Home Government was about to order the release of all prisoners. The motion was refused by Lord Alverstone CJ, who disagreed with this interpretation of the facts. Deportation was necessary, he held, to prevent disorder; and the Secretary of State had acted within his powers.[138] Jellicoe's first application was made before he had obtained a copy of the deportation order from the Colonial Office; but, having received a copy, he tried again. Besides challenging the order on technical grounds, he rehearsed the broader arguments he had made before the Privy Council: that Tilonko had not been legally imprisoned and that the Indemnity Act was invalid. Even if the Act itself could be said to be valid, he argued, it could not validate a sentence passed on 17 August, since the parliament which passed it had been dissolved in 15 August 1906. On this occasion, Justices Darling and A. T. Lawrence rejected the application. The technical objection – that the date of conviction had been wrongly entered – was dismissed as not affecting the validity of the order. On the substantive

---

[137] Governor to Secretary of State, 2 June 1907, and minute by Churchill, 4 June 1907, CO 179/241/19778, ff. 248–249.
[138] *Ex p. Tilonko*, The Times, 14 October 1907, p. 4.

questions, the King's Bench Division judges held that the Indemnity Act had been validly passed and that it had been prospective as well as retrospective.[139] In the court's view, Elgin had ample evidence for making the order; indeed, in view of the advice of the Colonial Government, he could not have done otherwise. The court did not look closely at the purpose of the 1884 Act which had so troubled officials, let alone the broader constitutional questions raised by Jellicoe.

Tilonko's legal team continued to press their point. In January 1908, an unsuccessful attempt was made to sue Justice Beaumont and Governor McCallum in the Natal Supreme Court, the former for violating the Star Chamber Act of 1641 (when refusing habeas corpus), and the latter for Tilonko's wrongful imprisonment.[140] In May, Jellicoe applied once more to the Privy Council to appeal from this judgment. The Privy Council judges considered this as simply another attempt to raise the question about the correctness of the Natal court's decision to refuse habeas corpus, on which they had already pronounced in July 1907. When Jellicoe sought to argue that the court had not previously considered his arguments about the validity of the Indemnity Act, Lord Macnaghten dismissed the attempted argument as hopeless. He explained that the court could only consider whether the Act had passed, and not pronounce on its wisdom.[141] Once more, the Privy Council declined to consider Jellicoe's substantive arguments, taking a narrow view of legality: a statute was a statute, whatever it did to a subject's rights.

The argument that Natal's Indemnity Act was invalid because of the nature of its passing might have merited more consideration. It was trite law that the Royal Assent had to be given in England while parliament was sitting. Nor was it self-evident that Natal's 1893 Constitution Act – which provided for the crown to legislate with the advice and consent of the Legislative Council and Assembly – set a different rule. For although the Governor was then instructed not to assent to certain measures unless he had previously been given instructions on them, or unless a suspending clause was included in

---

[139] Notes from solicitors Sutton, Ommanney & Rendall, 26 November 1907, CO 179/243/37445, f. 522.
[140] *The Times*, 27 January 1908, p. 5.
[141] *Tilonko v. Attorney General of Natal*, in *The Times*, 28 May 1908, p. 3.

the measure, the Act did not specifically provide for him to assent after a parliament had been dissolved. Given that different colonies with responsible government had varying provisions for the crown to reserve bills for approval (or disallowance) in London, the question of the possible invalidity of Natal's statute might have offered the chance for complex constitutional debate. Significantly, however, the Privy Council opted to have no debate on the matter at all.

Jellicoe and Colenso continued to try to keep Tilonko's case in the public eye. In June 1908, a petition was presented to parliament, asking for an inquiry into his imprisonment.[142] At the end of the year, Jellicoe sent a petition from Tilonko and Colenso to the Lord Chancellor, asking for the case to be investigated by the 'magnum concilium' or High Court of Parliament. Having failed in all other avenues, this was an attempt to invoke a medieval form of petitioning. This one last attempt to find a legal venue to consider Tilonko's case again raised legal conundrums for officials to ponder. The application left the permanent secretary, Sir Muir McKenzie, somewhat nonplussed as to how to proceed.[143] Having asked both the clerk to the Crown in Chancery and the clerk to the Commons for their observations, H. W. Just referred the matter to the Law Officers, who confirmed that the petitions were 'wholly irregular in form and no action can be taken upon them'.[144]

Tilonko returned to South Africa in 1910, along with the other prisoners who had been sent to St Helena. Their return followed the release of Dinuzulu, who had been sentenced to four years' imprisonment after his 1908 conviction on some of the lesser charges of which he had been accused in the special court set up to try him. After he had been released by Louis Botha, the first Prime Minister of the new Union of South Africa, an order was given also to allow the St Helena exiles to return to Natal, though not to their own homes.

Conclusion

In many ways, the authorities both in London and in Pietermaritzburg found themselves in uncharted waters in 1906. Martial law remained

---

[142] *The Times*, 16 June 1906, p. 5. [143] *Manchester Guardian*, 1 January 1909, p. 3.
[144] Opinion of 8 February 1909, CO 885/16, No. 109.

a grey area, with few clear rules to guide officials. Towards the end of May 1906, McCallum wrote to Elgin that nothing definite had ever been laid down to guide the Governor dealing with martial law in a colony with responsible government. While the 1867 instructions to crown colonies guidelines were useful as a general guide, 'I have had to depend on the exercise of common sense in the absence of precedents.'[145] At the height of the crisis over the proposed pardons for the Richmond convicts, he had told Elgin that the previous seven weeks had been 'a time to me of very grave anxiety' since there were no precedents to guide a Governor 'in the case of a responsible Government with a huge black population practically in rebellion'.[146] By the time he came to leave Natal, in April 1907, McCallum took the opportunity to suggest to the Colonial Office that the government should draw up general instructions to guide Governors in future cases. Officials were keen to let it lie. Vernon noted that 'there is a danger of the issue of instructions obscuring the most important of all facts about martial law, viz. that it is in its very nature illegal.' Cox added that there would be political dangers in laying down instructions for martial law: 'It wd be said that we were endeavouring to create a despotic system to be brought into force at the will of every Governor.' Indeed, in his view, the very difficulty of its administration was a deterrent to its use.[147] This was, perhaps, wishful thinking. On 7 December 1907, on the unanimous advice of his ministers, McCallum once again proclaimed martial law, even though in his view it was (in the absence of any armed resistance to the ordinary processes of law) 'premature'.[148] On this occasion, martial law served the government's purpose of preventing Jellicoe – who had gone to Natal to defend Dinuzulu – from getting access to witnesses or visiting Zululand.[149]

Whitehall and Pietermaritzburg clearly had different conceptions of the rule of law. At the Colonial Office, officials were constantly

---

[145] Governor to Secretary of State, 25 May 1906, CO 179/235/21572, f. 102.
[146] Governor to Secretary of State, CO 879/92/26, No. 9, p. 12.
[147] Governor to Secretary of State and officials' notes, 12 April 1907, CO 179/240/16116, f. 399.
[148] Governor to Secretary of State, 3 December 1907, PP 1908 (Cd. 3888), No. 74, p. 174.
[149] Marks, *Reluctant Rebellion*, p. 263.

worried about the legality of the steps which were being taken. Despite some disagreements among officials, they generally took a Diceyan view of the ambit of martial law, according to which acts done under martial law would ultimately have to be justifiable either in the courts (which retained a supervisory power, at least to determine whether the necessity for martial law existed) or before the political court of parliament. In part, their fidelity to this culture of the rule of law was prompted by the ever-present watchfulness of members of parliament and the press, who were able to monitor every step as a result both of modern communications and of the governmental openness dictated by the Blue Books. From the perspective of Pietermaritzburg, things looked very different: both ministers and the settler population were driven by the need to suppress African unrest and reimpose imperial rule. Natal's ministers and ministry felt the need to make examples of men like Tilonko. In response, officials at the Colonial Office, mindful of the need to respect the rights of responsible governments, tended to give way, and try to make their excuses at Westminster.

This left the defence of the rule of law to the courts, and in particular, the highest imperial court, the Judicial Committee of the Privy Council. However, this court did not see fit to intervene in the cases of these obscure Africans to uphold the vision of the rule of law found in chapter 29 of Magna Carta. Although in Tilonko's first case, Lord Halsbury accepted the Diceyan principle that courts could examine the necessity for martial law, he never applied the principle: it was simply overlooked in Mgomini's case, where the Privy Council simply deferred to the judgment of executive, while in Tilonko's case, it was held to have been rendered irrelevant by the Indemnity Act which had passed.

Although English jurists continued to pride themselves on having a constitution which subjected all to the rule of law, the effect of litigation and legislation of 1906 was to recognise that English law – and imperial law – did in practice provide for a state of siege. Once the executive had proclaimed martial law, the courts would not (according to Halsbury's approach in *Mgomini*) look behind it; once an Indemnity Act had been passed, the court would do nothing (according to *Tilonko*) but obey. In between the two, it was now legally open for governments to follow Natal's path of keeping a proclamation of martial law in force until its work had been done, and ratifying all acts under it by pre-ordered indemnities. Fidelity to the rule of law would depend on political pressure rather than the protection of the Judicial Committee of the Privy Council; but, in the world of imperial politics, the rights of Africans did not have a high political priority.

11

Conclusion

As the British empire expanded in Africa, many political leaders found themselves detained and deported from their homelands, deprived of their liberty without that due process of law which Britons had long regarded as the hallmark of their constitutional culture. They were detained under legal regimes of 'exception', under the cover of martial law or by virtue of *ad hominem* ordinances tailored to authorise the detention or deportation of named individuals by simple legislative fiat. The use of such detentions raises questions about the role of law in imperial expansion, about how far common law perceptions of the rule of law were applied in the empire, and about what the African experience can tell us about English ideas about the rule of law in the era in which Dicey wrote his celebratory *Law of the Constitution*.

Why did an imperial power committed to bringing the rule of law to its wider empire resort to detention without trial so frequently? As has been seen, detention was not a policy dictated from the centre. It was generally driven by the demands of officials on the ground, and many officials at the Colonial Office remained uncomfortable with the incarceration of political prisoners by ordinance.[1] There were a number of reasons why the authorities resorted to 'exceptional' forms of incarceration. In several cases – including Cetshwayo's and Prempeh's – the detainee was a ruler whose kingdom had been

---

[1] As R. H. Meade observed in 1887, 'We dislike this special kind of legislation unless absolutely necessary': minute dated 14 September, CO 96/182/1829.

conquered. In such cases, there was no offence for which they could be legally held, and with the end of hostilities, they should have been released. However, since their continued presence in their homelands was politically untenable for the imperial authorities, they found a precedent for exiling such rulers in the example of Napoleon, whose removal to St Helena had been validated by statute. Napoleon's continued detention as a prisoner of war was justified in the eyes of the British government by the fact that he had been put in their custody under a convention agreed by the allied powers after his defeat.[2] By contrast, in Africa, where rulers were removed after imperial wars of aggression, the colonial authorities were largely unconcerned with finding international law justifications for the ruler's continued detention; but they did need to insure themselves against possible habeas corpus applications brought by friends of the detainee.

In other cases, the detainee was not a vanquished potentate, but a political troublemaker, whom the authorities wished to silence. In such cases, there might be no offence with which the activist could be charged, or there might be a concern that any trial would end in an acquittal, either for want of evidence or from jury sympathy. These activists could be detained as political prisoners under ordinances designed either to curtail their present activities or to forestall the danger of any future ones. Examples of this can be found in a number of detentions on the Gold Coast of activists, such as Yaw Awua, who threatened to unsettle British policy towards Asante. It can also be seen in the exile of Zubayr, who was removed from Egypt for the sake of British military convenience. In such cases, detention ordinances – which might be passed in a single day by a legislative body dominated by the Governor – had the look of a cynical form of 'lawfare', being exercises of naked executive power in the guise of legislation. In other cases, however, the authorities were concerned

---

[2] *British and Foreign State Papers 1815–1816* (London, James Ridgway and Sons, 1838), p. 200. For the government's quest for legal justifications for his treatment as a prisoner of war, see R. A. Melikan, 'Caging the Emperor: The Legal Basis for Detaining Napoleon Bonaparte', *Tijdschrift voor Rechtsgeschiedenis*, vol. 67 (1999), pp. 349–362; and Renaud Morieux, *The Society of Prisoners: Anglo-French Wars and Incarceration in the Eighteenth Century* (Oxford, Oxford University Press, 2019), pp. 358–368.

Conclusion

with dealing with someone who had committed some kind of wrong, which the ordinary forms of law were powerless to deal with, as in Sierra Leone, where detention ordinances were used for peacekeeping purposes, occasionally even when it was felt that the ordinary criminal law might be too severe.

Jurisdictional Ambiguities

The decision to detain a political prisoner, rather than attempting a trial, often reflected jurisdictional uncertainties, when the colonial authorities were unsure whether they had the jurisdiction to proceed to trial. It was self-evident that rulers like Prempeh, whose kingdom lay beyond both the colony and the 'protectorate' of the Gold Coast, and over whose land the British had not purported to exercise an extraterritorial jurisdiction, could not be tried before British courts, though (as has been seen), the colonial authorities were keen to charge his prime minister, John Owusu Ansa, in a colonial court for an offence committed within its jurisdiction. There could also be uncertainty over how to deal with 'external' agitators who had settled within areas under British control. When the authorities in the Gold Coast considered how to deal with the intrigues of Asafu Agyei and King Tackie, they felt unable to put the former on trial – since he was an outsider who had taken refuge in the British protected area – but contemplated a trial for Tackie, who was thought to be under British jurisdiction in Accra.

The fact that *ad hominem* ordinances were most frequently used in West Africa to detain political prisoners may reflect the particular jurisdictional ambiguities in this region, where areas annexed as colonies shaded into 'protected' areas, which then bordered onto areas under wholly independent rulers. Although the British had exercised extraterritorial jurisdiction in West Africa under various Orders in Council issued under the Foreign Jurisdiction Acts, doubts remained over how far it extended. According to the understanding which prevailed in the years before the Berlin Conference, the extraterritorial jurisdiction given by the Orders in Council of 1872 and 1885 was limited in scope, being primarily intended to give jurisdiction over British subjects. When such instruments purported to grant jurisdiction over 'persons properly enjoying Her Majesty's protection', this phrase was taken to connote only those attached to British consular offices, rather than being read broadly to cover all Africans considered to be somehow under British protection. Although the Orders in Council also granted jurisdiction over Africans where their chiefs had by treaty agreed to it, these treaties were not generally worded in such a way as to confer such general jurisdiction. For instance, even Consul Edward Hewett did not think that he had the jurisdiction to deal with Jaja, even though the standard form treaty which he took to the Niger delta in 1884 conferred exclusive jurisdiction on British consular officials over 'foreign subjects enjoying British protection'.[3] In this context of 'protection', Jaja was treated like Abdullah of Perak – a ruler who could not be tried, but who should be investigated by a quasi-legal inquiry, whose findings could be used to justify a Napoleonic-style ordinance.

By the 1890s, a different view of protectorates was emerging. In July 1890, Sir Robert Herbert observed that 'the notion that the consent of minor chiefs is necessary as an antecedent to the establishment of a British protectorate over their territories has become out of date through the political development of the last two or three years.'[4] In this decade, the jurisdiction conferred via the Africa Orders in Council over those 'enjoying Her Majesty's Protection' could be read much more broadly. In contrast to Hewett, Sir Claude MacDonald was confident in his jurisdiction to try Nana Olomu in his consular court for offences defined by the British. The fact that the basis of this jurisdiction was still not entirely secure, for all MacDonald's confidence, is evident not only from the flaws in the process – with officials in London puzzling over how the charges and sentences matched up – but also from the fact that Nana was eventually exiled under an *ad hominem* ordinance, rather than through ordinary legal processes. Where doubts remained that the colonial authorities lacked jurisdiction, an ordinance had to be used. This can also be seen in Sierra Leone, whose officials – under the watchful eye of the Colonial Office – were much more cautious in asserting their jurisdiction against 'rebels' than the Foreign Office's consular

[3] Article III of the treaty, as found in FO 403/31, enc. in No. 88, p. 58.
[4] CO 417/43/13242, quoted in W. Ross Johnston, *Sovereignty and Protection: A Study of British Jurisdictional Imperialism in the Late Nineteenth Century* (Durham, Duke University Press, 1973), p. 231.

officials in the Niger Coast Protectorate. In Sierra Leone, Bai Bureh's projected trial was derailed by the Law Officers' advice that an African living in the protectorate could not be regarded as a subject liable to the law of treason, even if he could be tried for a lesser offence. In his case, legal punctiliousness lay behind the decision to detain by ordinance: it was the fear of officials at the Colonial Office that the English lawyer sent to preside over the rebel trials might raise difficult legal questions which led them to refer the matter to the Law Officers in the first place. By the early twentieth century, when British jurisdiction in these areas had become more clearly defined, the use of such ordinances fell away, for political crime could be dealt with by other forms of legislation.

Alongside their use to authorise detentions in places where the British were unsure of their jurisdiction, *ad hominem* laws were also used to validate the outcome of flawed processes. One example of this was the case of Ovonramwen: having captured Benin City, Ralph Moor purported to apply an African customary law which he had no authority to exercise, and then proceeded to exile the Oba by simple pronouncement. In this case, it would take more than a decade for the authorities to validate his deportation by ordinance. Nor was it only in these frontier areas that such questions might arise. As Langalibalele's case shows, even in areas with settled legal systems, such as Natal, the detention of a political opponent might need validation by legislation to overcome jurisdictional errors which had been made by an over-zealous local official. In this colony, jurisdictional ambiguity arose from the system of legal pluralism formally introduced in 1849, when an ordinance re-established a jurisdiction of African customary law, while at the same time giving the Lieutenant Governor effective control over 'native law'.[5] If this legislation was intended to recognise the need for African customary law to be the law applicable between Zulus – something which well suited Theophilus Shepstone's policy of 'indirect rule' – it proved highly problematic when applied to cases of political crime against the colonial authorities. It was not simply that Governor Pine's decision to try Langalibalele under 'native law' went against the established practice of using the ordinary courts to deal with serious crimes. It also demonstrated how incoherent his view of law was. Pine's aim was to convict Langalibalele of offences against the

[5] Ordinance No. 12 of 1845, modified by Ordinance No. 3 of 1849.

state which he conceived of in terms derived from an English law which did not apply in Natal. Aware that the evidence available would not be sufficient for a conviction under English law, he framed the charges under 'native' law to give him the scope to convict. As with Nana and Ovonramwen, there were deep flaws in the jurisdiction which was purportedly exercised over Langalibalele, which needed to be regularised by legislative fiat.

'Reason of State' and the 'Rule of Law'

In the 1880s, the Colonial Office made it clear that legal cover, in the form of an ordinance, had to be given, if political prisoners were detained without trial. Officials did not take the view that detentions could be justified as acts of state, which would be beyond the jurisdiction of any court to consider. It was long settled that the crown could not, by virtue of its prerogative powers, detain any subject within its dominions for reasons of state: any such prisoner could be released on obtaining a writ of habeas corpus. The writ was also available to those who were not subjects, who had been unlawfully detained in the crown's dominions.[6] This protection extended not only to natural born subjects, but also to 'alien amis', foreigners who were considered to owe a temporary 'local allegiance' to the crown and who consequently enjoyed the protection of its laws.[7] This meant that there was little scope to invoke the notion of acts of state when it came to the detention of British subjects or of aliens within British territory.

By contrast, it was also well settled that 'alien enemies' were 'not entitled to any of the privileges of Englishmen'[8] and could be held as prisoners of war or dealt with under martial law. While courts were willing to examine whether any detainee might properly be classed as a prisoner of war,[9] the category was often a very fluid one,[10] and the

---

[6] See e.g. *The Case of the Hottentot Venus* (1810) 13 East 195.
[7] See *Calvin's Case* (1608) 7 Co. Rep. 1a, and the discussion in Hannah Weiss Muller, *Subjects and Sovereign: Bonds of Belonging in the Eighteenth-Century British Empire* (Oxford, Oxford University Press, 2017), ch. 1.
[8] *The Case of the Three Spanish Sailors* (1779) 2 W. Bl. 1324.
[9] Paul D. Halliday, *Habeas Corpus: from England to Empire* (Cambridge, Mass., Harvard University Press), pp. 168–174.
[10] Morieux, *The Society of Prisoners*, ch. 1.

case law suggested that the judiciary did not consider that it was limited to active combatants captured in the field.[11] The crown's power to detain such enemies derived from its prerogative power to make war and peace. International lawyers saw the detention of such prisoners as a continuation of hostilities, and expected warring nations to make agreements for the exchange of prisoners of war when hostilities ceased.[12] This raised the possibility that vanquished African chiefs, with whom no treaty of peace had been made, might be considered simply as continuing prisoners of war. It also raised the possibility that 'bands of marauders' – who were not considered to merit the status of prisoners of war but had long been considered as *hostis humani generis*[13] – might also be held under acts of state exercised under prerogative power. On a few occasions, officials did suggest that detainees might be held as prisoners of war. In Sierra Leone, many of those captured in the Yoni wars were initially held as such. Similarly, after the end of the Anglo-Zulu war, both the Cape's Attorney General, Thomas Upington,[14] and the Law Officers in London felt that the defeated king Cetshwayo could be held at the Cape as a prisoner of war. The Cape authorities also thought that the Griqua rebels of 1878 could be detained as such prisoners. However, in none of these cases were the detainees held as prisoners of war for long: in the case of the Yoni prisoners and Cetshwayo, legislation was passed to validate their detention, while in the case of the Griqua prisoners, their designation as such was successfully challenged in the Cape Supreme Court, when it was shown that these rebels had been treated by the colonial authorities as subjects. Although there might have been enough legal ambiguity about the status of prisoners of war or 'bands of marauders' to tempt colonial authorities to classify non-subjects as such, it is notable that officials did not seek to hold them as such without additional legal cover. They seem instead to have inclined to

---

[11] See *R. v. Schiever* (1750) 2 Burr. 765.
[12] Emer de Vattel, *The Law of Nations*, ed. Bela Kapossy and Richard Whatmore (Indianapolis, Liberty Fund, 2008 [1797]) Bk. III, ch. 8, § 154, p. 365; Henry Wheaton, *Elements of International Law*, 4th ed., ed. J. B. Atlay (London, Stevens and Sons, 1904), § 344, p. 478.
[13] Robert Phillimore, *Commentaries upon International Law* (London, William G. Benning & Co, 1857), vol. III, p. 145.
[14] CO 879/16/5, enc. 13 in No. 116, p. 281.

the view that those who were not the subjects of an enemy state with which Britain was at war should not be held as prisoners of war.

By the middle of the nineteenth century, it was also well established that people who owed no allegiance to the crown, whose rights had been infringed by acts authorised by the British government, could find no redress in English courts, since they were acts of state, which fell within the crown's prerogative to deal with foreign states and their subjects.[15] While the case law (on invasions of property rights) suggested that the courts might consider whether the act in question 'bore the character of political acts of state',[16] once that was established, they would take no further cognizance of them. In light of this doctrine, the detention of 'alien' political prisoners by the crown outside its own dominions might have been justified as an act of state, without any further legal cover. Nevertheless, it is striking how infrequently colonial officials invoked the act of state doctrine. It was generally invoked only to justify action taken in moving detainees from one colony to another, through areas over which the crown had no jurisdiction, as in the transportation of Abdullah to the Seychelles and of Jaja to St Vincent. Indeed, in Jaja's case, the Foreign Office went so far as formally to ratify Col. Harry Johnston's actions in moving Jaja from Opobo to Accra, in order to remove any risk that the officer might be sued for infringing his rights, since the ratification made this an act of state.[17]

Officials at the Colonial Office and Foreign Office do not seem to have thought they had the power to hold detainees in Africa simply for reasons of state. Instead, they consistently sought to provide a legal justification, in the form of an ordinance. Detainees were to be held by law. One reason for this may have been a purely practical one. The

---

[15] See J. F. Stephen, *A History of the Criminal Law of England*, 3 vols. (London, MacMillan and Co., 1883), vol. II, pp. 61–62, 65. See further Amanda Perreau-Saussine, 'British Acts of State in English Courts', *British Yearbook of International Law*, vol. 78:1 (2007), pp. 176–254. There was much case authority, often arising from India, which showed that, where property rights had been infringed by crown, the matter was not justiciable: e.g. *Secretary of State for India* v. *Kamachee Boye Sahaba* (1859) 13 Moore 22.

[16] *Musgrave* v. *Pulido* (1879) 5 App. Cas. 102 at 113.

[17] For this doctrine, see *Buron* v. *Denman* (1848) 2 Ex. 166, discussed in C. Mitchell and L. Turano, 'Burón v Denman (1848)', in C. Mitchell and P. Mitchell (eds.), *Landmark Cases in the Law of Tort* (Oxford, Hart, 2010), pp. 33–68.

colonial authorities sought to detain all their prisoners in gaols within British dominions, whether in Freetown, Gibraltar, St Vincent or the Seychelles, and, once in these places, detainees would obtain the rights enjoyed by all those with local allegiance. Viewed this way, ordinances were consequently a form of insurance against legal challenges. At the same time, it may be noted that, at a time when protectorates were not considered as being 'dominions' of the crown – and where 'reason of state' arguments might have run – ordinances continued to be passed to authorise the detention of political prisoners in such areas, such as Sekgoma Letsholathibe. Furthermore, as has been seen, ordinances were also passed to regularise proceedings which were thought to be legally flawed. Rather than accepting such proceedings as a *pis aller*, officials insisted on complying with proper legal forms. Whatever steps were taken had to be taken in a properly legal domain.

Officials' punctilious insistence on the forms of legalism often made no practical difference to the detainee: as Ovonramwen found, an ordinance simply dotted the 'i's and crossed the 't's. In some ways, this was little more than a bureaucratic following of forms, to ensure the formal validity of steps taken. Viewed in this way, the formalistic rule of law this represented did nothing for the liberties of the detainees, and was a world away from the common law ideology championed by the likes of Dicey. At the same time, however, the insistence by the metropolitan authorities on the forms of law being followed was not wholly insignificant: London, which had the power to disallow colonial legislation, could better monitor what was happening at the frontiers of empire if Governors and their law officers had to give reasoned justifications for their ordinances. This raises the question of how committed officials were to the rule of law. As has been seen, the concept of the 'rule of law' is an ambiguous one. According to one point of view, all that it requires is formal validation – whether direct or indirect – by a sovereign lawmaker. According to another, it connotes a commitment to a set of substantive principles long associated with the English common law, including the demand that no one be imprisoned without being tried in a court for a previously defined offence.[18] The

---

[18] For discussions of these aspects of the rule of law, see Joseph Raz, 'The Rule of Law and Its Virtue', in his *The Authority of Law* (Oxford, Clarendon Press, 1979), ch. 11; Lon L. Fuller, *The Morality of Law*, 2nd ed. (New Haven, Yale University Press, 1969), pp. 46–91; Friedrich A. Hayek, *The Road to Serfdom* (New York, Routledge,

formal version is undemanding but empowering: provided the correct procedures are followed, the most draconian legislation can be imposed for the benefit of those in power. The substantive version is more demanding, and there may be degrees to how far actual practices are able to live up to its demands. Nor is the rule of law in this sense self-executing: fidelity to its principles requires a commitment to its practice.

Looking at their domestic constitution, mid-Victorian jurists like Dicey were confident that the two versions of the rule of law were not in tension: the sovereign lawmaker was a parliament which could be trusted to speak in the name of a people whose constitutional culture was suffused with a commitment to the values of the common law. In the empire, however, the tension between those two visions became much more visible. The discomfort which officials at the Colonial Office and their political masters often showed towards 'exceptional' detention ordinances indicates that the common law principles they valued at home continued to nag their consciences; but how far it exerted an influence on their actions depended on how strong the counterweights were. When faced with the pressing demands of officials on the ground for tough action against political adversaries, as in West Africa, officials in London were generally prepared to put aside any qualms they had, and allow the formal rule of law to be used for imperial 'lawfare'. Elsewhere, however, the pressures exerted by public opinion, and groups such as the Anti-Slavery Society, might incline officials to insist more on the need for the due process of law to be observed. The strikingly contrasting approaches taken to Urabi Pasha and Al-Zubayr Rahma Mansur in Egypt may be explained in part by the very different reactions of British public opinion to these figures and the policy which lay behind their detention. Public and political opinion at the periphery might also need to be taken into account. In Natal, the pressure exerted by Bishop Colenso's campaign on behalf of Langalibalele may not have resulted in that chief's release, given the strong opposition of Natal's political elite; but, in the longer term, it was to exert an important influence on the

---

2008), pp. 112–124; David Dyzenhaus, *The Constitution of Law: Legality in a Time of Emergency* (Cambridge, Cambridge University Press, 2006), p. 2; and T. R. S. Allan, *Law, Liberty, and Justice: The Legal Foundations of British Constitutionalism* (Oxford, Oxford University Press, 1993), p. 22.

decision that Dinuzulu could not simply be exiled by legislation, but had to be tried.

In an era in which London often deferred to the demands of the men on the ground, the approach taken to political detention was also importantly shaped by the character of the local legal culture. In this respect, the practice of the Cape Colony stands in sharp contrast to that of the West African colonies. At the Cape, there was not only a powerful Supreme Court, whose judges were learned in both Roman-Dutch law and common law, but also a liberal political system which recognised that Her Majesty's African subjects had the same legal rights as her European ones. In contrast to West Africa, where the colonial authorities resorted to *ad hominem* laws to hold perceived enemies through exceptional means, at the Cape detainees were treated in court by judges like Sir Henry de Villiers as British subjects who should no more be deprived of their rights than any Englishman in the colony. In areas where the political prisoner was regarded as a member of the political community, he was much more likely to be treated in a way which respected a substantive vision of the rule of law than in areas where he was seen as a Schmittian 'enemy'.[19]

Whereas in the frontier areas of West Africa, jurisdictional uncertainty led to a raft of ordinances authorising individual incarcerations, detention without trial was little used on the Cape frontier. There were of course men on the ground who were prepared to take draconian measures to deal with those standing in their way, as Sir Henry Pottinger and Sir Harry Smith did when holding Sandile without any apparent legal authority. However, for the most part, those who were not subjects were dealt with as prisoners of war, being released at the end of the conflict, whereas those who were subjects were treated as rebels. These rebels were still subjected to 'exceptional measures', for the 'Hottentots' of Kat River who rebelled in 1850 and the Ngqika who joined the war of Ngcayecibi in 1877 were tried and sentenced by martial law courts, rather than civilian ones. However, as the debates over the use of martial law in these episodes demonstrated, the Law Officers both in the colony and in the metropolis were aware of the legal problems it raised. With the

---

[19] See Carl Schmitt, *The Concept of the Political*, trans. G. Schwab (Chicago, University of Chicago Press, 2007), pp. 26ff.

debates over Jamaica in mind, officials in 1878 strove to find a formula which would satisfy the demands of the rule of law. On numerous occasions throughout the century, from Chief Justice Sir John Wylde's advice in 1835 to Sir Henry de Villiers's ruling on the detention of Sigcau sixty years later, legal voices could be heard in the Cape reminding officials of the need to follow due process. The fact that this liberal regime did not extend beyond the Cape's borders can be seen from the fact that, after its conquest, British Kaffraria was governed under a permanent system of martial law; but even here, the desire of imperial officials to impose draconian penalties could be subject to some restraint, as when the liberal Attorney General William Porter's damning report on Mhala's trial in a special court resulted in a lighter sentence than had originally been intended.

The Cape's experience suggests that the extent to which a substantive vision of the rule of law was followed owed a good deal to how far local officials were committed to it. In turn, this might depend on how far they regarded those who challenged their authority as being part of their political community, and how far they regarded them as Schmittian enemies. During the Anglo-Boer war, politicians and lawyers at the Cape saw the Dutch-speaking rebels who joined the Boer forces as members of their political community, who ought to be afforded the protection of a substantive rule of law. In contrast to the experience of West Africa, where it was often the local officials who pressed for draconian measures, and officials in London who wished to restrain them, during the Anglo-Boer war, the demand for draconian measures generally came from the imperial authorities, who were apt to regard the Dutch speakers as enemies.[20] Here, it was the local political elites who called for restraint and for a commitment to the rule of law. This was not simply a matter of local legal consciences being more faithful to the English common law tradition than the English: the liberalism of men like Sir James Rose-Innes and Sir Henry de Villiers had its roots in a political culture which had developed at the Cape since the 1820s.

---

[20] For example, Milner wrote to Chamberlain on 16 July 1901, 'By all means let the greatest care be taken to make the trials correct, as military trials, & serious. Let every allowance be made for mitigating circumstances. But, where there are none, when a British subject has simply of his own deliberate choice gone out to join the invaders & to assist them in robbing his fellow citizens & burning their houses, why not shoot him?' Chamberlain Papers, University of Birmingham, JC 13/1/160.

Conclusion

The Cape colonists had long manifested a desire to defend their own rights when faced with imperial demands: the British project in 1849 to transport convicts to the Cape was met with a defiant response which not only scuppered the penal project but also paved the way for the creation of representative government in 1853.[21] During the Anglo-Boer war, the language of the rule of law was for a number of liberals a means to defend local rights against imperial invasions, whether in the form of the detention of respectable Dutch-speaking citizens or in projects to suspend the Cape constitution.[22]

The Anglo-Boer war consequently generated debates about the nature of martial law of a kind which had not been seen since the Jamaica controversy. Rather than being accepted simply as the rule of the military commander which had to be followed during the course of the war, the scope of martial law became a subject of negotiation between the imperial military and civilian authorities and the local political and legal establishments. If the courts came to accept that they could not interfere with military detentions during wartime, they asserted their right to hold the military to account after the war had ended. Nor was the legislative indemnity given to the military granted by simple fiat: instead, the legislation was itself the product of political negotiation which ensured that the sentences of those still incarcerated would be reviewed. This approach contrasted strongly with that taken in Natal after the Zulu rebellion of 1906. Here, the targets of martial law were not regarded as part of the same political community, but as dangerous enemies of the white settlers, enemies who needed to be controlled. Where care had been taken at the Cape to subject martial law to some form of legal supervision, in Natal, both the legal and the political authorities were content to give the Governor *carte blanche* to

---

[21] Timothy Keegan, *Colonial South Africa and the Origins of the Racial Order* (London, Leicester University Press, 1996), pp. 225–233; and Philip Harling, 'The Trouble with Convicts: From Transportation to Penal Servitude, 1840–67', *Journal of British Studies*, vol. 53 (2014), pp. 90–93.

[22] The limits of this political liberalism can be seen from the use of martial law and statutory emergency powers in South Africa after 1910: see Keith Shear, 'Legal Liberalism, Statutory Despotism and State Power in Early Twentieth-Century South Africa', *Journal of Imperial and Commonwealth History*, vol. 38:4 (2010), pp. 523–548; and Jonathan Hyslop, 'Martial Law and Military Power in the Construction of the South African State: Jan Smuts and the "Solid Guarantee of Force" 1899–1924', *Journal of Historical Sociology*, vol. 22:2 (2009), pp. 234–268.

deal with these enemies. Here, the most formal legal cover was thought to suffice, in the form of an indemnity act which the local legislature was prepared to make prospective. In a colony where the targets of martial law were regarded as outsiders in the political community, the constitutional culture which in other contexts led officials to recognise the importance of following the principles of the common law when dealing with all subjects had little purchase.

The Role of the Courts

Although the writ of habeas corpus reached throughout the British empire, there were few legal challenges made to detention without trial, and fewer still which were considered by members of the English judiciary. This was in part for practical reasons, most obviously the difficulty detainees might have in acquiring legal assistance and funding legal challenges. Occasionally, as in the case of Bo Amponsam, such attempts were themselves frustrated when the authorities rapidly passed detention ordinances. Nevertheless, questions remained regarding the validity of such ordinances, and the power of local lawmakers to issue them. Such ordinances also raised important questions about the constitution of the empire: how far 'fundamental' common law principles applied beyond British shores, and how far either the Westminster parliament or the crown through its prerogative could authorise local officials to detain without trial. They were also pertinent to domestic law: for the kind of powers delegated to colonial officials might be delegated to domestic ones as well. The few cases which did come before imperial judges were therefore very significant.

When cases eventually came to London, detainees found English judges less committed to a substantive vision of the rule of law than they might have hoped. As Sekgoma's case showed, the judges were prepared to uphold detention ordinances by tracing the slenderest pedigree to an authorising statue which would confer validity on them, and by rejecting arguments based on the idea that delegated powers had to be read within a broader framework of fundamental principles found in Magna Carta or cases such as *Campbell* v. *Hall*. The decision in *ex parte Sekgoma* exhibited a pro-executive approach to delegated legislation which would be echoed in the English cases brought during the First World War, when challenges were made to regulations issued under the broad provisions of the Defence of the Realm Acts, which conferred a general power on the executive to issue regulations for the defence of the realm.[23] In the best known challenge, R. v. *Halliday, ex p. Zadig*, the House of Lords upheld Regulation 14B, which allowed the executive to detain persons of 'hostile origins or associations'.[24] The executive-minded approach taken by judges in cases like Zadig's rested on the assumption that in a time of war parliament had intended to confer draconian powers and that it was for parliament to control them. This approach was subsequently criticised by jurists who saw it as abandoning the principles of the rule of law: yet it was much more plausible for these judges to interpret the broadly drafted statute of a wartime parliament as conferring such powers than it had been for Sekgoma's judges to find such an intention in the Foreign Jurisdiction Act. In the First World War cases, the majority of judges accepted that wartime exigencies demanded an executive-minded interpretation of the law, since 'a war could not be carried on according to the principles of Magna Charta'.[25] They regarded such emergency powers as necessary to defend the state itself.[26] By contrast, in Sekgoma's case, the executive-minded reading came from the judges' perception that draconian powers were needed to control parts of an empire 'peopled by lawless and warlike savages, who outnumber the European inhabitants by more than one hundred to one'.[27]

---

[23] Defence of the Realm (Consolidation Act) 1914, 5 Geo. V c. 8, s. 1.
[24] R. v. *Halliday, ex p. Zadig* [1917] AC 260. Lord Shaw of Dunfermline dissented, opining (at p. 277) that parliament, in passing the Defence of the Realms Acts, had never sanctioned 'such a violent exercise of arbitrary power'.
[25] *Ronnfeldt v. Phillips and Others* (1918) 35, Times Law Reports 36 at 37. Frederick Pollock's response to Shaw's judgment echoed Halsbury's parliamentary defence of *Marais*. '[m]y private opinion is that there is no liberty of the subject in time of war within the realm.' Mark De Wolfe Howe (ed.), *The Pollock–Holmes Letters: Correspondence of Sir Frederick Pollock and Mr Justice Holmes 1874–1932*, 2 vols. (Cambridge, Cambridge University Press, 1942), vol. 2, p. 245.
[26] For a study of judicial activism in the war, see Rachel Vorspan, 'Law and War: Individual Rights, Executive Authority, and Judicial Power in England during World War I', *Vanderbilt Journal of Transnational Law*, vol. 38 (2005), pp. 261–343.
[27] *R v. Crewe, ex parte Sekgome* [1910] 2 KB 576 at 627 (Kennedy LJ).

Rather than using a substantive vision of the rule of law to protect the liberties of detainees, judges in cases like Sekgoma's went so far as to indicate that the detention of political prisoners in protectorates might even be justified as acts of state, without needing further legal authority. The suggestion that Sekgoma's detention was an act of state was made – almost as an afterthought – in the last paragraph of Secretary of State Crewe's affidavit in answer to the application.[28] This might have given the judges an opportunity to look closely at the doctrine, and its relationship to the writ of habeas corpus. In the event, the judgments did not clearly explain the application of this doctrine, but rather used it as a fall-back justification for refusing the application. Vaughan Williams LJ and Kennedy LJ appeared to accept that the detention of an individual outside the crown's dominions could be properly denominated a political act of state, which the detainee – like any foreigner whose property rights had been infringed by an act of state – could remedy only via diplomatic means. They did not regard the writ of habeas corpus as a tool to test whether the crown's officers were acting lawfully, wherever they were situated.[29] Instead, they thought that the writ was available only to those whose right to the court's protection derived from their allegiance to the crown.

The court did consider whether Africans living in protectorates over which the British had taken effective control could claim the writ's protection, by virtue of owing some kind of allegiance to the crown. This raised questions about the status of protectorates. Mid-century case law suggested that the subjects of 'protected states' – such as the Ionian islands, which were recognised as an 'independent state' under the protection of the British crown in the Treaty of Paris in 1815 – were

---

[28] CO 879/103/3, Appendix B, pp. 248–249.
[29] According to Paul D. Halliday and G. Edward White, 'the critical concern of habeas jurisprudence as it evolved in early modern England and expanded into eighteenth-century imperial contexts was to emphasize the franchisal authority of the sovereign's officials, not the territory in which a prisoner was being held or the nationality status of the prisoner', 'The Suspension Clause: English Text, Imperial Contexts, and American Implications', *Virginia Law Review*, vol. 94 (2008), p. 700. However, Vaughan Williams LJ's judgment held that the writ could be used in Bechuanaland by British subjects, but that, in respect of non-subjects, the act of state defence could be raised. *R. v. Crewe, ex parte Sekgome* [1910] 2 KB 576 at 604–606.

not British subjects.[30] However, by the end of the nineteenth century, the line between colonies and protectorates was often a very blurred one, with the imperial power in fact exercising the full powers of a sovereign in these areas. In such places, there was no other state to which inhabitants could look for diplomatic protection if their rights had been infringed by imperial 'acts of state', which might have suggested that the latter doctrine could not apply. However, in Sekgoma's case, the judges held to the view that protectorates were outside the crown's dominions, so that the act of state doctrine could be applied. According to Kennedy LJ, what distinguished a protectorate from annexed territories was that only the latter entailed territorial sovereignty, 'that absolute ownership which was signified by the word "dominium" in Roman law'.[31] Given that, by 1910, the crown had long claimed the right to take ownership of 'waste' lands in African protectorates,[32] this was not a convincing distinction.

The judgments in Sekgoma's case were not particularly consistent, with the judges appearing to strive for arguments which would justify his continued detention. However, their loose dicta on acts of state were taken up by the Court of Appeal for Eastern Africa in 1913, in the case brought by the Maasai against the colonial government for a violation of their land rights. Dismissing their case, Chief Justice Morris Carter held that the British East Africa Protectorate was 'technically a foreign country', where each inhabitant was 'technically a foreigner in relation to the protecting State'.[33] This meant that agreements between the Maasai and the British relating to land were treaties which were not justiciable in the court. Although he acknowledged that the remedies of diplomacy and war which were available 'to a foreigner, the subject of an independent state' were not

---

[30] *In re Ionian Ships* (1855) 2 Spinks Ecc. and Adm. 212 at 226. It was held that to regard them as such 'would set the whole treaty [of Paris] at nought; it would be to make a mockery of the most stringent stipulations contained in that treaty'.
[31] *R. v. Crewe, ex parte Sekgome* [1910] 2 KB 576 at 620.
[32] Law Officers' opinion, 13 December 1899, FO 403/283, No. 101, p. 113.
[33] *Ol le Njogo and Others v. the Attorney General and Others* (1913) 5 East Africa Law Reports 70 at 89. On the case, see Lotte Hughes, *Moving the Maasai: A Colonial Misadventure* (Basingstoke, Palgrave Macmillan, 2006), pp. 89–104; and Aman W. Kabourou, 'The Maasai Land Case of 1912: A Reappraisal', *Transafrican Journal of History*, vol. 17 (1988), pp. 1–20.

available for 'a native of the Protectorate', Carter justified it by quoting Lord Justice Vaughan Williams's comment that 'the Protectorate is over a country in which a few dominant civilised men have to control a great multitude of the semi-barbarous.'[34] The decision in *Sekgoma* had clearly sharpened a legal tool which could be used against African claimants; though the threat it posed to detainees was drawn in 1960, when the Court of Appeal confirmed that an African held in a protectorate was able to challenge his detention using the writ of habeas corpus.[35]

Rather than seeking to rein in imperial administrators by insisting on the need for due process and the rule of law associated with the common law tradition, judges in London were prepared to find formal powers to detain, both in statute law (in Sekgoma's case) and in prerogative powers (in Zaghlul's). In this way, they appeared to be less sensitive to the demands of that tradition than some colonial judges, as well as some officials in the Colonial Office. Their decisions on martial law also consistently upheld the demands of the executive, with their deference to the executive perhaps most chillingly seen in Lord Halsbury's refusal to consider the application of those sentenced to death at Richmond in *Mgomini* v. *The Governor of Natal*.[36] The legacy of the two main South African cases – *Marais*[37] and *Tilonko*[38] – for the rule of law was ambiguous. On the one hand, they confirmed that, during a time of war or rebellion, the civilian courts would not have any power to review the actions of the military, settling a question which had remained open since the Jamaica controversy in a way favourable to the crown. On the other, the decisions confirmed that the courts had to be satisfied as a matter of fact that a state of war existed.[39] These decisions confirmed that the

---

[34] *Ol le Njogo and Others* v. *the Attorney General and Others* (1913) 5 East Africa Law Reports 70 at 97. The protected African's 'only remedy is an appeal to the consideration of the Government'.
[35] *Ex parte Mwenya* [1960] 1 QB 241.
[36] *Mgomini and Others* v. *The Governor of Natal (Natal)* [1906] UKPC 22.
[37] D. F. *Marais* v. *The General Officer Commanding the Lines of Communication* [1902] AC 109.
[38] *Tilonko* v. *Attorney-General of the Colony of Natal* [1907] AC 93.
[39] After martial law had been proclaimed in Ireland in 1920, the Irish courts did assert their jurisdiction to determine 'whether a state of war exists which justifies the application of martial law': Molony CJ in *R. (Garde and Others)* v. *Strickland* [1921] 2 IR 317 at 329, quoted in Colm Campbell, *Emergency Law in Ireland*,

crown did not have a prerogative power to proclaim martial law, and thereby protect the military from any lawsuits which might be brought after peace had been restored. Martial law was not an executive matter, but was subject to post-conflict review, whether by the courts or the legislature. How far the rule of law would be protected in future martial law episodes would depend on how far the courts would go in testing whether a state of war or rebellion existed, and how closely legislatures would examine military conduct during the crisis prior to passing indemnity acts.

The decision in *Marais* also narrowed the common law doctrine in another significant way. In debating the ambit of martial law, common lawyers after the Jamaica controversy had laid stress on the question of whether martial law powers were necessary to restore order. However, after *Marais*, the focus of the courts' attention shifted away from the question of necessity to that of whether a state of war or rebellion existed. The consequences of this can be seen in the approach taken in Ireland after 1920, when martial law was proclaimed in four counties, even though a statutory regime giving power to military courts had already been created by the Restoration of Order in Ireland Act.[40] In *R. v. Allen*, Molony CJ followed *Marais* in holding that whether or not a state of war existed was a matter of fact, which did not depend on whether the civilian courts were open. Once the court had been satisfied that a state of war existed – as it had here – it had no jurisdiction to question any acts done by the military. In Molony's view, the fact of the state of war determined the necessity for martial law: and so he did not consider the necessity of using martial law courts to impose death sentences in an area where statutory military courts had been given non-capital jurisdiction over the same offences.[41] Faced with this approach, lawyers defending the Irish rebels began to argue that martial law was a prerogative power, which had been abrogated

---

1918–1925 (Oxford, Clarendon Press, 1994), p. 138. In *R. (O'Brien) v. Military Government of North Dublin Union Military Internment Camp* [1924] 1 IR 32 at 42, he found that a state of war did not exist in Dublin to justify the use of martial law powers.

[40] This readopted the provisions of the wartime Defence of the Realm Acts. For a detailed examination, see Campbell, *Emergency Law in Ireland*; and David Foxton, *Revolutionary Lawyers: Sinn Fein and Crown Courts in Ireland and Britain, 1916–1923* (Dublin, Four Courts Press, 2008).

[41] *R. v. Allen* [1921] 2 IR 241 at 271.

by the statutory regime created by the Restoration of Order in Ireland Act. Although Molony CJ rejected this argument,[42] it persuaded the Irish Master of the Rolls, O'Connor, in *Egan* v. *Macready*.[43] His decision to order the military to order the release of John Egan, who had been sentenced to death by a martial law court, generated exactly the kind of clash between courts and military which the Cape's Acting Chief Justice, Buchanan, had in mind in Marais's case, when he asked 'suppose the military refuse to carry it out, who is going to enforce it?'[44] The fact that the British political authorities forced Macready to comply – after he had declared his intention to ignore the court's order – showed that Buchanan's fear was not a strong reason for the courts to abstain from intervening.[45] However, O'Connor's prerogative view of martial law did not flourish.[46]

In the event, this newly developed theory of martial law was not much called on, for, just as Britain's parliament created a statutory regime of emergency powers during the war through its Defence of the Realm Act, so the King-in-Council provided for emergency regimes to be put in place in the empire. In 1916, the British Protectorates (Defence) Order in Council gave Governors in African protectorates the power to make regulations for public security and defence, which included detention without trial and courts martial trials.[47] Further orders in council conferring emergency powers followed,[48] including the 1931 Palestine (Defence) Order in Council (which became 'a model for dealing with later insurrections' after its use during the Arab Revolt of 1936)[49] and the 1939 Emergency Powers (Colonial Defence) Order in Council. Powers given by such instruments were extensively used in

[42] *R. (Romayne and Mulcahy)* v. *Strickland and Another* [1921] 2 IR 333.
[43] *Egan* v. *Macready* [1921] 1 IR 265.   [44] *Cape Times*, 7 September 1901.
[45] See Foxton, *Revolutionary Lawyers*, pp. 285–293.
[46] O'Connor himself rowed back from it in *R. (Childers)* v. *Adjutant General of the Provisional Forces* [1923] 1 IR 5.
[47] British Protectorates (Defence) Order in Council, issued 30 March 1916. As has been seen, a secret Order in Council had been made on 26 October 1896, which gave the Governor of Gibraltar emergency powers, but it was not made public until 1914.
[48] They included the Defence (Certain British Possessions) Order in Council 1928 and the Malta (Governor's Emergency Powers) Order in Council 1928.
[49] See Simpson, *Human Rights and the End of Empire*, p. 86. For these regulations, see Matthew Hughes, *Britain's Pacification of Palestine: The British Army, the Colonial State, and the Arab Revolt, 1936–1939* (Cambridge, Cambridge University Press, 2019), ch. 2.

the post-war empire to restrict movement, censor the press, and arrest and detain without warrant. In some colonies, such powers were used to resettle populations and to demarcate zones in which the security forces could use lethal force against suspected insurgents.[50] Although the military did not consider that a statutory scheme precluded the use of martial law, it was soon found that more powers could be enumerated in legislative schemes, which would need no post-emergency indemnity to evade scrutiny. As a number of important recent histories have shown, in the dirty wars of decolonisation, in which legislative instruments had granted extensive rule-by-law powers to violate the very kinds of rights which British foreign policy makers wanted to see enshrined in international human rights instruments, the techniques of counter-insurgency used often involved mass detention, torture and extra-judicial killings, often deliberately and carefully hidden from judicial scrutiny.[51] This was a world away from the constitutionalist rule of law which Dicey had espoused just as the 'scramble for Africa' began.

[50] See David French, *The British Way in Counter-Insurgency, 1945–1967* (Oxford, Oxford University Press, 2011), pp. 76–82.
[51] Besides French, *The British Way in Counter-Insurgency*, see David Anderson, *Histories of the Hanged: Britain's Dirty War in Kenya and the End of Empire* (London, Weidenfeld & Nicolson, 2005); Caroline Elkins, *Britain's Gulag: The Brutal End of Empire in Kenya* (London, Jonathan Cape, 2005); Fabian Klose, *Human Rights in the Shadow of Colonial Violence: The Wars of Independence in Kenya and Algeria* (Philadelphia, University of Pennsylvania Press, 2013); and Brian Drohan, *Brutality in an Age of Human Rights: Activism and Counterinsurgency at the End of the British Empire* (Ithaca, Cornell University Press, 2017).

Index

Abdullah, Sultan of Perak, 22–25, 37, 159, 173, 176, 188, 213, 224, 236, 247, 257, 422, 426
Abinger, James Scarlett, Lord, 6
Aborigines Protection Society, 25, 92, 117, 120, 192, 196, 234
act of state, 157, 188, 212, 239, 292–293, 297, 298, 303–304, 314, 315, 426, 434–435
Ad hominem legislation, 20–22, 24–25, 30, 33, 35–36, 82, 91, 122, 124, 159, 171–197, 199, 213, 235, 278, 283, 288, 306, 322, 419, 421
  Bechuanaland
    Sekgoma (1891), 291
  Cape of Good Hope
    Cetshwayo (1880), 99
    Langalibalele (1874), 94
    Langalibalele (1875), 96
    Sigcau (1895), 282
  Gambia
    Bocarry Governor and George Bapoo (1889), 182
    Yoni Political Prisoners (1887), 179
  Gilbralar
    Zaghlul (1922), 313
  Gold Coast
    Asafu Agyei and King Tackie (1881), 172
    Ashanti Political Prisoners (Kwaku Foku and Kwame Boatin) (1896), 253
    Ashanti Political Prisoners (Yaa Asantewaa and others) (1901), 257
    Bo Amponsam (1888), 191
    Bo Amponsam (1890), 191
    Denkera Political Prisoners (1887), 190
    Denkera Political Prisoners (1890), 192
    Doombuyah and Beah Jack (1882), 175
    Geraldo de Lima (1885), 187
    Katanu Political Prisoners (1883), 186
    Kumasi Political Prisoners (1896), 248
    Nana Olomu (1896), 224
    Opobo Political Prisoners (1887), 210
    Srahah Political Prisoners (1890), 192
    Taviefe Political Prisoners (1888), 193
    Yaw Awua (1884), 188
    Yaw Awua (1888), 189
    Yaw Awua (1890), 190
  Mauritius
    Abdullah of Perak (1877), 24, 173
  Seychelles
    Zaghlul (1922), 312

Index

Sierra Leone
  Alimamy Lahai and others (1899), 272
  Bai Bureh (1898), 271
  Bangang (1890), 185
  Bey Yormah and others (1883), 178
  Bocarry Governor and George Bapoo (1888), 182
  Buyah Sammah (1882), 177
  Doombuyah and Beah Jack (1881), 175
  Koliama (1887), 179
  Kondor (1890), 181
  Lahsurru (1882), 177
  Makaia and Gpabor (1889), 181
  Momodou Canoobah and others (1888), 182
  Mormoh Darwah (1891), 184
  Pa Mahung (1890), 181, 185
  Political prisoners (Gbanna Lewis, Bimba Kelli and Nyagwa) (1899), 273
  Political Prisoners (Prempeh and others) (1896), 253
  Santiggy Karay (1891), 185
  Yoni Political Prisoners (1886), 179
  Yoni Political Prisoners (1888), 180
Southern Nigeria
  Ovonramwen (1911), 234
United Kingdom
  Napoleon Bonaparte (1816), 21
Adli Yakan Pasha, 309-310, 317
Adye, Sir John, 149, 152
Africa Order in Council (1893), 220-221, 223, 224, 230, 276
Afrikaner Bond, 330, 334, 358, 372, 375-376
Aggery, King John, 167-169, 170
Ahmad, Mohammed. *See Mahdi, the (Mohammed Ahmad)*
Allenby, Edmund, Viscount, 308, 310-312, 314, 317, 321-322
Alverstone, Richard Webster, Viscount, 269, 297, 298, 372, 374, 376, 413
Amos, Sir Maurice, 311
Anderson, John, 4
Anglo-Boer War (1899-1902), 323-366
  civilian trials of rebels, 332
  martial law extended to Cape ports (1901), 348-350
  Sunnyside rebels, 331-332, 339, 340
Anglo-Zulu war (1879), 80, 81, 98

Annesley, George, 216, 226
Ansa, John Owusu, the elder, 188-189
Ansa, John Owusu, the younger, 241, 248-252, 258, 421
Anti-Slavery Society, 4, 92, 144, 152, 428
Apthorp, M. G., 364
Ardagh, Sir John, 328, 372
Asafu Agyei, 171-173, 421
Asante, 36, 162, 171-172, 188-192, 238-258, 277-278, 420
  war of 1873-1874, 163-165, 169

Bahadur Shah II, Mughal emperor, 17, 70
Bai Bureh, 224, 238-239, 260-264, 266, 269-272, 273-277, 423
  arrest of, 263
Bai Forki, 275
Baker, Valentine (Baker Pasha), 144
Bale, Sir Henry, 336, 374
Bambatha kaMancinza, 383, 386, 396
Bannerman, Edward, 210, 280
Barbados, 10, 212
Baring, Sir Evelyn. *See Cromer, Evelyn Baring, Earl of*
Barkly, Sir Henry, 50
Beah Jack, 174, 175
Beaumont, William Henry, 414
Bechuanaland, 289-304
  protectorate declared (1885), 289
Beecroft, John, 200, 214
Bekker, J. H. N., 341-342, 353
Bella Kwabla (Bella Kwabina), 192-193
Benin, kingdom, 225-235
Berlin Conference (1884-1885), 198, 199, 203, 204, 207, 213, 224, 421
Bigham, John. *See Mersey, John Bigham, Viscount*
Bimba Kelli, 273, 275
Birch, J. W. W., 22, 23, 247
Blackall, Sir Samuel, 167, 168
Blackstone, Sir William, 57, 284
Blunt, Wilfrid Scawen, 132
Blyth, Capt Matthew, 50-52, 74-77
Bo Amponsam, king of Adanse, 190-192, 194, 432
Boatin, Kwame, 244, 250, 252-254
Bokari Bamp, 260
Bollontoh, Sharkah, 174-175
Bombolie, Bocary, 170-171
Bond. *See Afrikaner Bond*
Bonner, G. A., 267-269

Borelli, Octave, 133
Botha, Andries, 63
Bowles, Thomas Gibson, 92
Bramston, Sir John, 114, 247, 249
British Kaffraria, 44, 58–61, 70, 78, 430
Broadley, A. Meyrick, 132, 133–135, 138
Brownlee, Charles, 78
Bru-de-Wald, Col. H. T., 385
Buchanan, Sir Ebenezer John, 332, 340, 343, 353–355, 438
Bulwer, Sir Henry, 101, 104
Bundoo, Alimamy Lahai, 170
Burgess, George, 115, 121
Burton, Henry, 340–341, 378
Burton, Richard, 225
Bury, William Coutts Keppel, Viscount, 150
Byles, Sir William, 234

Cairns, Hugh McCalmont, Lord, 95
Cally Mahdoo, 165–166, 170
Campbell v. *Hall* (1774), 300–301, 316, 322, 432
Campbell-Bannerman, Sir Henry, 332–333
Canada, 1837 rebellions, 5, 10, 11
Canning, Charles John, Earl, 19, 70
Cape of Good Hope, 3
  constitution, debate over suspension, 367, 369
  frontier wars
    eighth, 44–46
    ninth, 47–49
    seventh, 42–43
    sixth, 41–42
  Martial Law Board (1901-1902), 349, 361–366, 377
  political system, 33
  special treason court (1900-1902), 333–338, 344–347
Cardew, Sir Frederick, 258–269, 271, 274, 275
Carnarvon, Henry Herbert, Earl of, 2, 13, 73, 81, 92–95, 122, 167–169, 176, 327, 357, 385
Carter, Sir Gilbert, 219
Cathcart, Sir George, 45–46, 65
Caulker, George, 173
Caulker, Richard Canraybah, 182–183
Caulker, Thomas Neale, 183
Caulker, Thomas S., 166, 170

Caulker, William T. G., 173–174, 182–184
Cetshwayo, 80–82, 84, 97–106, 121–123, 133, 159, 280, 283, 419
  law authorising detention of, 99–100
Ceylon, 125, 138–139, 141, 311
  martial law in, 10, 62
  Urabi's exile in, 138–139
Chalmers, Sir David, 263, 267, 271–274
Chamberlain, Joseph, 242–246, 250, 251–256, 261–262, 265, 268, 269–271, 274–277, 287, 292, 329, 333–336, 349, 361, 367–370, 371, 373–376
Churchill, Lord Randolph, 140–141
Churchill, Winston, 389–390, 393, 400, 409, 411–413
Clarke, Sir Marshal, 118
Cockburn, Sir Alexander, 12, 14, 66, 69
Colenso, Frank, 391, 395, 399, 413, 415
Colenso, Harriette, 108, 113, 114, 115, 116, 118, 120, 123, 280, 384, 400
Colenso, John William, 82, 89–94, 100, 108, 123, 280, 428
Colonial Laws Validity Act (1865), 301–302, 318
Colonial Prisoners Removal Act (1869), 91, 93–94
Colonial Prisoners Removal Act (1884), 117, 224, 411, 413
Comaroff, Jean, 17
Comaroff, John, 17
Connor, Sir Henry, 91, 109
Cox, Hugh Bertram, 266, 299, 304, 343, 355, 359–360, 370, 376, 377
Crewe, Robert Crewe-Milnes, Marquess of, 294, 296–298, 434
Cromer, Evelyn Baring, Earl of, 142, 145–148, 149, 153–154, 155, 156
Curzon, George Nathaniel, Marquess, 310, 311, 317

Dalrymple, J. S., 192, 197
Darfur, 143–145
Darling, Charles, Baron, 298, 413
Davey, Horace, Baron, 356, 392
Davidson, William Edward, 212
Davitt, Michael, 254
de homine libero exhibendo, writ. *See habeas corpus*
de Lima, Geraldo, 186–188

Index

de Villiers, Sir Henry (Lord de Villiers), 74, 76–78, 281, 284–285, 288, 305, 316, 331, 337, 339, 355, 358–361, 362, 367, 368–371, 377, 380, 429–431
De Worms, Baron Henry, 118, 197
Defence of the Realm Acts (1914), 320, 433, 438
Denman, Thomas, Lord, 6
Derby, Edward Henry Stanley, Earl of, 178
Dicey, A. V., 1, 4, 7, 8, 9, 13, 14, 15, 18, 25, 158, 279, 316, 342, 379, 419, 427, 428
　Diceyan views, 324, 340, 342, 357, 361, 371, 380, 394, 417
Dilke, Sir Charles, 9, 134–136
Dingane, king, 85
Dinuzulu, 82, 104–121, 123, 280, 384, 391, 399, 400, 401, 412, 415, 416, 429
　trial of (1889), 114–118
Doombuyah, 171, 175
Dove-Wilson, John, 406
Dreyer, Thomas, 62
Dufferin, Frederick Hamilton-Temple-Blackwood, Marquess of, 135–138
Dunedin, Andrew Murray, Viscount, 320
D'Urban, Sir Benjamin, 41–42, 55–58, 71
Durnford, Major Anthony, 85

East Africa, 26–33
Egerton, Edwin, 153
Egerton, Sir Walter, 234
Egypt, 34–35, 124–142, 152–156, 280, 306–322, 420, 428
　Alexandria riots (June 1882), 128
　British invasion (1882), 128–130
　declared protectorate, 307
　Wolff mission to, 153, 154, 156
Elgin, Victor Bruce, Earl of, 292–293, 293, 395, 398, 404, 407, 412–414, 416
Escombe, Harry, 88, 110, 114, 117–120
Eyre, Edward John, Governor, 10, 11–13, 19, 324, 327, 379, 380, 390, 395

Fahmi, Abd al-Rahman, 311–312
Fairfield, Edward, 68, 92, 113–114, 117, 191, 269

Fanti, people, 161–162
Farwell, Sir George, 302–303, 305
Fergusson, Sir James, 209
Finlason, William Francis, 12, 328, 341, 342, 379
Finlay, Robert, Viscount, 269, 329
Fitzgerald, John David, Baron, 150–151
Foku, Kwaku, 244, 248, 250, 252–254
Foreign Jurisdiction Act (1843), 162–163, 167
Foreign Jurisdiction Act (1890), 258, 270, 277, 289, 297–304, 433
Freeling, Sanford, 171
Frere, Sir (Henry) Bartle Edward, 47–49, 65–68, 72, 81, 99
Fugitive Offenders Act (1881), 109, 110, 219
Fumo Omari, Sultan of Witu, 26
Fynn, Charlie, 387, 399, 401

Gaekwar of Baroda, 23
Gallwey, Capt. H. L., 216, 226
Gallwey, Sir Michael, 112, 343
Gambetta, Léon, 126
Gambia, 159, 161, 163, 179, 181–182, 184, 274
Gcaleka, people, 45–49, 51, 71
Geary, William, 248, 250
Gessi, Romolo, 144
Gibraltar, 35, 125, 143, 148–152, 153–155, 157, 313–321, 427
　Order in Council (1884), 318, 319
Giffard, Hardinge. *See* Halsbury, Hardinge Giffard, first Earl of
Gildenhuys, D.P.L., 340
Gladstone, Herbert, 305
Gladstone, William Ewart, 101, 127, 130–131, 135–136, 141, 148
Glenelg, Charles Grant, Baron, 41, 54
Gold Coast, 20, 174, 175
　British colonial expansion in, 159–165
　detention of political prisoners, 167–173, 185–195
　Yaa Asantewaa revolt, 190, 256–257
Gordon, Col. Charles George, 142–148
Gordon, George, 12
Gorst, Sir John, 150
Graham, Frederick, 332, 352, 389, 394, 396
Graham, T. L., 359, 365, 370

Granville, Granville George Leveson-
    Gower, Earl, 145–146, 150
Grey, Henry George, Earl, 43, 58,
    61–63, 95
Grey, Sir George, 46, 49, 60–61, 70, 75
Griffith, Sir William Brandford, 186–189,
    191, 193–194, 215, 240–241
Griqualand East, 49–50, 84, 282
    rebellion, 50–52, 73
    case of Willem Kok and Nathanial
        Bailie, 73–78
Guy, Jeff, 120

habeas corpus, 1, 4–7, 18, 21, 25, 39, 72,
    98, 104, 118, 149, 158, 190, 192,
    195, 234, 236, 265, 285, 294, 331,
    339, 342, 343, 370, 371, 380, 420,
    424, 432, 434, 436
  applications
    Anderson, John, 4–5
    Bekker, J. H. N. and J. J. Naudé,
        341–342
    Canadian prisoners (Leonard
        Watson), 5–7
    Fourie, Jan, 340
    Kok, Willem and Nathanial Bailie,
        73–78
    Marais, D. F., 352–354, 355–357
    Reinecke, R. J., 354–355
    Sekgoma Letsholathibe, 296–305
    Tilonko, 406–407, 408–409
    Zaghlul Pasha, 313–322
  Habeas Corpus Act (1679), 18, 288,
        318, 322
  Habeas Corpus Act (1862), 297, 302
  Star Chamber Act (1641), 301, 414
  suspension, 7–8, 18, 288, 343
Hailsham, Douglas Hogg, Viscount,
    319, 321
Haldane, Richard Burdon, Viscount,
    315–316, 320, 356, 360
Hale, Sir Matthew, 57
Halsbury, Hardinge Giffard, first Earl of,
    35, 69, 111, 115–116, 299, 302,
    329, 355–357, 360, 380, 393, 408,
    417–418, 436
Hamilton, Sir Edward, 127
Harcourt, Lewis Vernon, Viscount, 234
Harding, Arthur, consul-general and
    commissioner, 26–30
Hare, John, Lieutenant-Governor, 42

Harley, Col. R. W., 169
Havelock, Sir Arthur, 105–106, 108,
    109–111, 116, 118, 174–175,
    177–178
Hely-Hutchinson, Sir Walter, 119, 335,
    348–349, 355, 361–362, 367–371,
    376, 377
Hemming, Sir Augustus William Lawson,
    170, 172, 182, 184, 189, 192, 243
Herbert, Sir Robert, 422
Hewett, Edward, 201–203, 204–208,
    215, 225, 235, 422
Hicks Beach, Sir Michael, 67, 69, 98
Hicks, Col. William, 139, 142
Hilal-bin-Amr, 27
Hildyard, G.M.T., 313, 315
Hill, Sir Clement, 234
Hintsa, 71–72
Hlubi, people, 80, 82–86
Hobhouse, Emily, 326
Hodgson, Sir Frederick Mitchell, 240,
    241, 250, 253, 255–256
Hogg, Sir Douglas. See Hailsham,
    Douglas Hogg, Viscount
Holker, Sir John, 69
Holland. See Knutsford, Henry Thurston
    Holland, Viscount
Hopwood, Charles, 174–178, 183
Humphrey, Rev. William, 262–263,
    264, 273
Hunt, Sub-Inspector S. H. K., 382, 385,
    387–388
Hunt-Grubbe, Admiral Sir Walter,
    210–212

Indemnity and Special Tribunals Act
    (Cape of Good Hope, 1900), 337,
    373, 374
indemnity, legislation for, 12, 62, 79, 349,
    368, 370–376, 385, 394–395, 432
  Cape of Good Hope (1836), 54
  Cape of Good Hope (1847), 54
  Cape of Good Hope (1878), 67–69
  Cape of Good Hope (1880), 99
  Cape of Good Hope (1900),
        336–338, 373
  Cape of Good Hope (1902), 370–372
  Egypt (1923), 311
  Jamaica (1865), 301
  Natal (1900), 338–339
  Natal (1902), 373

Index

Natal (1906), 402–409, 411, 413–414, 417
United Kingdom (1920), 312
India, 3, 20, 138
  emergency powers in, 18–20, 23, 29
  laws applied in East Africa, 26–27
  'Mutiny' of 1857, 17, 19, 66, 70
  princely states, 299
  Viceroy, 138
Ireland, 7, 9, 141, 195, 357, 403, 437–438
Ismail, Khedive, 126, 143

Jaja, king of Opobo, 204–214, 217, 221, 224, 225, 235–236, 422, 426
Jamaica, 395, 403
  Morant Bay rebellion (1865), 10, 11–13, 66, 69, 92, 122, 167, 168, 301, 323, 324, 328, 379, 390, 430, 431, 436, 437
James, Sir Henry (Baron James of Hereford), 150
James, W. H., 77
Jellicoe, E. G., 391–395, 408–409, 413–415, 416
Jervois, Sir William Francis Drummond, 22–25
Johnston, Sir Henry (Harry), 206–213, 225, 426
jurisdiction, 27, 30, 32, 39, 57, 90, 133, 157, 166, 167, 188, 193, 214, 250–251, 293
  ambiguities, 72, 177, 195, 421–424, 429
  disputes over, 167, 215, 219
  extraterritorial, 26, 32, 36, 59, 62, 75, 160–161, 163, 201, 202, 224, 304, 421
  imperial, 4, 26, 36, 76, 160, 162, 177, 179, 182, 187, 258, 270, 277, 289, 297, 299–305
Just, H. W., 336, 361, 390, 415

Kabarega, king of Bunyoro, 31–33
Kakari, Kofi, Asantehene, 188–189
Kat River Settlement, 40
  rebellion, 45, 50, 429
  trials, 62–65
Katanu, 186
Keith, Arthur Berriedale, 386, 389, 390

Kennedy, Sir William Rann, 303, 434–435
Khalid bin Barghash of Zanzibar, 28
Khartoum, siege of (1885), 142, 147
Kimberley, John Wodehouse, Earl of, 95, 96, 100–104, 169–176
Kitchener, Horatio, Earl, 291, 329, 330, 345, 348–350, 371
Knutsford, Henry Thurston Holland, Viscount, 112, 114, 116–117, 168, 179, 184
Kobina Edjen, 169–170
Kok, Adam, 49–50, 74, 76, 84
Kok, Adam 'Muis', 50–51, 76
Kok, Willem, 74, 285
Kostal, R. W., 16, 379
Kwaku Dua III. *See Prempeh, Asantehene*

Labistour, G. A. de Roquefeuil, 109, 398, 404, 406–407, 408
Lagos, 159, 163, 172, 175, 180, 186
Lambert, H. C. M., 296, 304, 339, 345, 366, 375, 403, 407, 409, 412
Langalibalele, 80–100, 104, 108, 109, 111, 112, 113, 117, 121–123, 159, 176, 233, 280, 283, 423–424, 428
  law authorising detention, 93–95
  trial in 'native court', 89
Lange, Sir John, 344
Laurier, Sir Wilfrid, 368
Law Officers' opinions, 36, 277, 288, 298, 326
  on Bai Bureh's case (1898), 224, 269–270, 272, 275, 276, 423
  on Cetshwayo's case (1879), 98
  on Cetshwayo's case (1882), 101
  on Dinuzulu's case (1889), 110
  on Jaja's case (1888), 212
  on Langalibalele's case (1874), 94
  on martial law in Lower Canada (1838), 11, 343
  on martial law in the Anglo-Boer war, 329, 331, 343, 368, 376
  on martial law in the Eastern Cape (1878), 68, 69, 329
  on Tilonko's case (1909), 415
  on Zubayr's case (1885), 151
Lawrence, Alfred Tristram (Baron Trevethin), 413
Lawson, T.G., 166, 170, 173

Lewis, Gbanna, Bai Sherbro of Yoni, 260, 273, 274, 275
Lofft, Capel, 21
Longden, Sir James, 138–139
Loreburn, Robert Threshie Reid, Earl, 409
Lugard, Frederick John Dealtry, 30
Lush, Sir Montague, 300–303, 305

Maasdorp, Sir A. F. S., 344, 375
MacDonald, Ramsay, 400, 403
MacDonald, Sir Claude, 203, 213, 216, 219–223, 226–227, 422
Macfarlane, John, 84
Mackintosh, Sir James, 11
Macnaghten, Edward, Baron, 355, 414
Macneill, John Gordon Swift, 372
Magna Carta, 1, 7, 25, 122, 279, 288, 299, 322, 409, 417
Mahdi, the (Mohammed Ahmad), 125, 139, 142, 144, 145–150, 152
Mahdist revolt, 125, 142–148
Maitland, Sir Peregrine, 42–43, 55–56, 61
Makhanda (Nxele), 70
Malcolm, William R., 68, 93
Malet, Sir Edward, 127, 128, 135, 140
Mangena, Alfred, 384, 391, 394–396, 405
Mansfield, William Murray, Earl of, 300–301, 302, 315
Maqoma, 40, 43, 46–47, 60, 71, 78
Marais, D. F., 352–358, 364–366
martial law, 5, 9–14, 20, 29, 35, 77
    Circular Despatch (1867), 13, 67, 327, 357, 385
    in Anglo-Boer war, 13, 323–381
        Alverstone Commission, 372–376
        at Cape ports (1901), 348–350
        civil–military relations, 330–331, 345–352
        legal challenges, 339–343, 352–357, 358–361
        Martial Law Board, 361–366
        special treason court, 333–338, 346–347
    in Barbados, 10
    in British Kaffraria, 58–60
    in Cephalonia, 10
    in Ceylon, 10
    in Demerara, 10
    in Eastern Cape, 38, 39–49, 52–70, 79
    in Egypt, 308, 311, 312–313
    in India, 18–19
    in Jamaica, 10
    in Karene, Sierra Leone, 262
    in Natal (1873), 85–86
    in Natal (1906), 382–405
    in New Zealand, 10
    in Upper and Lower Canada, 10
    legal challenges to detentions, 339, 340–342, 352–357, 359–361, 406–409
    legal views of, 10–14, 58, 64, 66–69, 327–329
    D. F. Marais's case (1901), 354, 355–357
    R. v. Allen (1921), 437
    R. v. Halliday, ex p. Zadig (1917), 433
    Standen v. Godfrey (1851), 54, 340
    Tilonko v. AG of Natal (1907), 407–408
    trials
        J. Booysens and N. A. van der Walt (1900), 332
        Kat River Rebels (1851), 62–65
        Ninth Frontier War (1877), 68
        Richmond murders (1906), 391–393
        Tilonko (1906), 399–402
        Zulu rebels (1906), 396–399
Martial Law Board (1901-1902). See *Cape of Good Hope*
Mason, A. Weir, 335, 343
Matabeleland, High Court of, 299
Mathiba, 290–292, 293, 296, 306
Matroos, Hermanus, 45, 63
Mauritius, 24, 411, 412
Maxwell, Sir William, 242–258
McCallum, Sir Henry Edward, 371, 373, 383, 386, 388–390, 392, 394–396, 397–398, 400, 402, 404–405, 407, 410–411, 412, 414–416
McKenzie, Sir Duncan, 383, 388, 390, 399
McKenzie, Sir Muir, 415
Meade, Sir Robert Henry, 181, 185, 190, 194, 252
Mende, people, 179, 181, 260
    revolt 1898, 263–266
Menzies, William, 56
Mercer, W. H., 268, 274
Mersey, John Bigham, Viscount, 372

Index

Merriman, John Xavier, 91, 287
Meseni kaMusi, 383, 387, 397
Mfengu, people, 47, 49
Mhala, 47, 60–61, 78, 430
Mhlangazo, 51
Michell, Lewis L., 361, 365, 377
Mill, John Stuart, 2
Miller, Brother and Co., 206, 209, 212
Milner, Alfred, Viscount, 287, 308, 309, 327–328, 330–340, 348, 349, 367–368, 371, 380
   Milner–Zaghlul Agreement, 309
Miskofeli, 386–387, 399, 401
Mjongo, 388, 398
Mlanjeni, 44, 70
Molony, Sir Thomas Francis, 437–438
Molteno, Sir John Charles, 48, 66–67
Moor, Sir Frederick Robert, 412
Moor, Sir Ralph, 216–219, 221–224, 226–235, 237, 423
Morcom, W.B., 342
Moshoeshoe, king, 74, 84
Moshoeshoe, Nehemiah, 74
Mpondo, people, 49–51, 281. See also Pondoland, Sigcau
Mqikela, 51–52
Muis, Adam. See Kok, Adam 'Muis'
Musgrave, William, 62
Mwanga, king of Buganda, 30–33

Nana Olomu, 214–225, 226, 228, 231–233, 235–237, 276, 422
Napier, Mark, 132
Napoleon Bonaparte, 21, 133
Natal, 34, 80–99, 101–112, 114–123, 326
   Alverstone Commission, 373
   Constitution Act 1893, 405
   debates over special treason court (1900), 335 336
   Indemnity Act (1900), 338–339
   litigation over martial law, 342–343
Nathan, Sir Matthew, 272, 274–275
Naudé, J. J., 341–342
Ndabuko, 105, 108, 112–115
Ndhlovu kaThimuni, 383, 397
New Zealand, 10, 265, 266, 389
Ngobizembe, 386, 399
Ngqika ka Mlawu, chief, 41, 70
Ngqika, people (Gaika), 40–49, 65, 71–73, 429

Niger Coast Protectorate
   establishment of, 224
Njwezi, 386
Norman, J. P., 18
Nyagwa, chief of Panguma, 272–273, 274–276

O'Connor, Charles, 438
Oba of Benin. See Ovonramwen, Oba of Benin
Oil Rivers Protectorate
   establishment of, 216
Ommanney, Sir Montagu, 362, 370, 375, 404
Osborn, Melmoth, 106–107, 112, 118
Ovonramwen, Oba of Benin, 225–237, 423, 427

Palles, Christopher, 357
Panzera, Col. F. W., 292–294, 297–298, 305
Pauncefote, Sir Julian (Baron Pauncefote), 129, 138
Pennington, A. R., 234
Phato, 43, 47, 60, 78
Phillips, James R., 227–229, 232
Pine, Sir Benjamin, 84–94, 95, 109, 122, 233, 235, 423
Pine, Sir Richard, 167
Pinkett, Francis, 174, 178
Pollock, Sir Frederick, 357–358, 394, 408
Pondoland, 49, 51
   Pondoland Annexation Act (1894), 283, 286, 305
Porter, William, 53, 59–62, 64, 430
Pottinger, Sir Henry, 43, 56, 58, 61, 72, 429
Prempeh, Asantehene, 189, 238–258, 277, 419, 421
   ordinance authorising detention (1896), 248
Pretorius, Andries, 62
Pretorius, M.J., 377
Privy Council, 405 406
   Judicial Committee, 35, 60, 82, 123, 223, 269, 279, 281, 293, 297, 302, 324, 325, 358, 368, 385
   Bailly van Reenen's case, 360
   D. F. Marais's case, 355–357, 359, 364, 380, 384
   Dinuzulu's case, 110–111, 115–116, 121

Richmond appeal, 391–393
  Sigcau's case, 285–288
  Staples's case, 299
  Tilonko's case, 407–409, 411, 414, 417
  Zaghlul's case, 314–322
protection
  treaties of, 199, 201
    Hewett's standard form, 202, 208, 235, 422
    Itsekiri chiefs, 217
    Jaja of Opobo, 205–211
    Katanu (1879), 186
    Mwanga (1890-93), 30
    Nana Olomu, 215, 221, 224
    offered to Prempeh, 240
    Ovonramwen, 226, 233
protectorate, 200, 201, 203, 277, 293
  Bechuanaland, 289–290, 297
  East Africa Protectorate, 26, 29
  Egypt, 124, 307–309, 311, 313
  Gold Coast, 160–165, 168, 172, 188, 192–193, 243, 421
  legal conception of, 36, 198–199, 213–214, 224, 269–271, 290, 297, 304, 422, 427, 434–436
  Oil Rivers, 203, 216, 219–220, 224
    Niger Coast Protectorate, 224, 236
  Protectorates (Defence) Order in Council (1916), 438
  Sierra Leone, 258–260, 269
  Uganda, 26, 30–33
  Witu, 26
  Zanzibar, 27
Putini, people, 83, 85

Queen Adelaide Province, 41, 56–58

Rassool, Abdul, 151–152, 154
Reckless, George, 242
Redmond, William, 212
Reinecke, R. J., 354–355, 364
Renaud, Eugene, 400, 401, 406
Restoration of Order in Ireland Act (1920), 437
Ribblesdale, Thomas Lister, Lord, 150–151, 157
Riley, Charles, 295–296, 298, 305
Ripon, George Frederick Samuel, Marquess, 118, 120, 241
Risley, Sir John, 318

Robben Island, 70, 71, 78, 91, 94–95
Roberts, Frederick, Earl, 325, 329
Robinson, Sir Hercules (Baron Rosmead), 101, 282
Robinson, Sir John, 119
Roebuck, John Arthur, 6
Rosebery, Archibald Philip Primrose, Earl of, 150, 207, 208
Rose-Innes, Sir James, 337, 341, 344–346, 348, 350–352, 354, 358, 361, 372, 430
Roth, Felix N., 229
Roupell, E. P. S., 230
Rowe, Sir Samuel, 173–174, 179–180
Rowlatt, Sir Sidney, 301, 302
Royal Niger Company, 203, 215
rule of law, 1–5, 8–9, 16–17, 33–37, 39, 79, 92, 95, 105, 121–123, 141–142, 158, 195, 279–280, 284, 286, 306, 322, 323–325, 379–380, 384–385, 416–418, 419–421, 427–439

Salisbury, Robert Cecil, Marquess of, 32, 153, 154, 156, 207, 208, 210, 212, 234, 372
Sami, Col. Suleiman, 128, 136–137, 140
Sandile, 41, 42–46, 49, 61, 72–73, 78, 429
Sarhili, 45–48, 72–73
Sarwat, Abdel Khalek Pasha, 310
Schmitt, Carl, 15–16, 25, 430
Schreiner, W. P., 330, 337
Sebele, chief of Bakwena, 291
Sekgoma Letsholathibe, 280, 289–298, 303–306, 315, 318, 322, 427, 432–436
Sekhukhune, 98–99, 109
Selborne, Roundell Palmer, first Earl of, 131, 133, 140
Selborne, William Waldegrave Palmer, second Earl of, 271, 291–294, 295–296, 298, 305
Settle, Sir Henry, 345, 365, 368, 370, 377
Seychelles, 22, 24, 25, 30, 32, 116, 139, 239, 255–257, 291, 292, 294, 312, 314, 410, 426
Seymour, Sir Beauchamp, 128–129
Seyolo, 45–46, 49, 65
Shaka, king, 83, 106

Index

Shand, Alexander, Baron, 355
Sharpe, Capt. W. S., 260–262, 271
Shaw, Flora (Lady Lugard), 152, 157
Shepstone, Henrique, 108
Shepstone, John, 83, 102
Shepstone, Sir Theophilus, 80–82, 83–85, 86, 90, 93, 106, 423
Shingana, 107, 114, 115
Sierra Leone, 159–163, 165–167, 170–171, 172–175, 176–185, 194, 199, 224, 236, 238–239, 246, 253, 255, 258–278, 421, 422, 425
   detention of political prisoners, 165–167, 170–171, 173–175, 176–185
   Hut Tax war, 238, 258–269, 271, 278
   protectorate proclaimed, 258
   Yoni wars, 179–181, 425
Sigananda, 383, 397–398
Sigcau, 280, 281–289, 292, 297, 301, 304–305, 316, 322, 430
Smith, Sir Henry George Wakelyn (Harry), 41, 43–46, 52, 55, 57, 62–65, 70–73
Smith, Sir William, 336
Smuts, Gen. Jan, 366
Smythe, Charles, 388–389
Solomon, Richard, 334, 346
Solomon, Saul, 74, 91
Solomon, Sir William Henry, 330, 342, 344
Somhlolo, 114
Somkhele, 107, 114
South African Republic, 99, 108, 119, 289, 326
special treason court. *See Cape of Good Hope*
Sprigg, Sir (John) Gordon, 49, 73, 287, 337, 346, 349, 374, 375, 376, 378
St. Helena, 21, 82, 91, 96, 116, 117, 118, 119, 120, 122, 136, 188, 189, 208, 211, 331, 410, 412, 415, 420
Stephen, Sir James, 58
Stockenstrom, Andries (1844-1880), 65–68, 73, 75–76
Stockenström, Sir Andries (1792–1864), 40, 57
Sudan, 35, 142–148
Suleiman, son of Zubayr, 143
Sumner, John Andrew Hamilton, Viscount, 315
Sutherst, Thomas, 244, 250

Tackie Tawiah I, King, 173, 421
Temne, people
   revolt 1898, 260–263, 266
Tewfik, Khedive, 126–133, 135–138, 140, 142, 147, 157
Tilonko, 386, 399–402, 405–415, 417, 436
treaties, 160, 165, 166, 170, 199, 201, 202, 203, 208, 240, 244, 309
   Anglo-Dutch (1872), 163
   Asante (1817), 162
   Batlapin and Barolong (1884), 289
   Hewett's treaties of protection, 202, 204, 215, 217, 225, 235. *See also* Jaja (1884), Nana Olomu (1884), Ovonramwen (1892)
   Jaja (1873), 204, 206–208
   Jaja (1884), 205, 206–209, 213, 236
   Katanu treaty of protection (1879), 186
   Mpondo (1844), 49, 281
   Mwanga (1890-1893), 30, 32
   Nana Olomu (1884), 215, 220–221, 224, 236
   Ngqika (1819), 39
   Ovonramwen (1892), 226, 233
   peace of Vereeniging (1902), 366
   Royal Niger Company's, 202, 203
   treaty of Fomena (1874), 163, 241
   treaty of Pangkor (1874), 22
   treaty of Paris (1815), 434
   treaty of Utrecht (1716), 317
   Webster–Ashburton (1842), 5
   Xhosa (1835), 41, 56
   Xhosa (1836–1837), 41, 58
   Xhosa (1844), 42, 43
Tudor, Daniel T., 313–315

Uganda, 26, 29–33
Uithaalder, Willem, 45
Upington, Sir Thomas, 67–69, 73, 75, 97, 425
Upjohn, W. H., 315–316, 319
Urabi, Ahmed (Urabi Pasha), 35, 124–143, 148, 149–150, 152, 157, 176, 280, 312, 428
   exile in Ceylon, 138–139
   political activities of, 125–130
   trial of, 132–138
Ussher, H. T., 172
Uzondwein, 386

Vangang, 173, 174
Vattel, Emer de, 97
Vaughan Williams, Sir Roland, 303, 434, 436
Vernon, R. V., 403, 407, 416
Vroom, Hendrick, 252, 255

Watson, William, Lord, 286–287, 288, 301, 304–305, 322
Watt, Sir Thomas, 385
Webster, Richard. *See Alverstone, Richard Webster, Viscount*
Wellington, Arthur Wellesley, Duke of, 10, 54
West Africa Settlements Act (1871), 161
Westlake, John, 92
Williams, Sir Ralph, 290
Wilson, H. F., 265–266
Wilson, Sir Charles, 132, 134, 136–137
Wilson, Woodrow, 307
Wingate, Sir Reginald, 307
Wingfield, Edward, 175, 184, 271, 274–276
Wolff, Sir Henry Drummond, 153–154, 155–156

Wolseley, Sir Garnet (Viscount Wolseley), 95–96, 98, 102, 129, 130, 147, 149, 152–154, 156, 171
Wragg, Walter, 112, 113
Wylde, Sir John, 53, 57, 340, 430
Wynne, Col. Arthur, 351–353, 364–365

Xhosa, people, 38–48, 60–61, 71–73
  cattle killing 1856-1857, 46

Yaa Asantewaa, 190, 240, 257, 278
Yaw Awua, 188–191, 194, 420
Yaw Twereboanna, 245, 256
Yoni, people, 179–181

Zaghlul, Saad Pasha, 280, 288, 306–311, 312–317, 319–322, 436
  deportation to Gibraltar, 312
  deportation to Malta, 308
Zanzibar, 26–30
Zibhebhu, 103–107, 112, 114, 123
Zubayr Rahma Mansur, al-, 35, 124–125, 142–158, 159, 210, 420, 428
Zululand, 83, 84, 99, 102–106, 111–123
Zululand Annexation Act, 121

Printed in the United States
by Baker & Taylor Publisher Services